Actors' Television Credits

Supplement II:
1977-1981

JAMES ROBERT PARISH
and
VINCENT TERRACE

The Scarecrow Press, Inc.
Metuchen, N.J., & London
1982

Also published by Scarecrow Press, Inc.:

Actors' Television Credits: 1950-1972 (1973)
Actors' Television Credits: Supplement I (1978)

Library of Congress Cataloging in Publication Data

Parish, James Robert.
    Actors' television credits. Supplement II,
1977-1981.

    1. Television personalities--United States.
2. Actors--United States. 3. Television programs--
United States. I. Terrace, Vincent, 1948-   .
II. Title.
PN1992.4.A2P32   1982   791.45'028'0922   82-5961
ISBN 0-8108-1559-1   AACR2

DEDICATED TO:

All the performers who have been, are, and will be
a part of television history.

CONTENTS

v

FOREWORD

Once again, the enthusiastic response to both Actors' Television Credits 1950-1972 and the first supplement (covering the period from 1973 to 1976) has indicated the great need to document performers' credits on United States television and has made this second supplement (1977 to 1981) possible.

As with past editions of this series, the main source of information has been the New York Metropolitan area edition of TV Guide. We are also grateful to the readers who have supplied many of the additions and corrections appearing in this volume.

Every attempt has been made to compile Supplement II as accurately as possible, but certain problems arise in documenting television: series are premiered or cancelled at the flicker of a rating point; and performers who are sometimes not listed in TV Guide nor on the main body of a program's credit crawl, suddenly emerge as superstars. We have tried to correct this last problem by turning to sources other than TV Guide. Thus, in many instances, some performers, particularly new entries, will have credits that do not appear in TV Guide.

When utilizing this supplement, or the previous two volumes, it is suggested that the reader take advantage of the following supplemental materials:

TV Guide (New York City market edition).

The BIB (Broadcast Information Bureau--TV Series Source Book) (New York City; semi-annual updates).

The Complete Encyclopedia of Television Programs, 1947-1979 (A.S. Barnes, 1980).

The Complete Prime Time Directory to Network TV Programs (Ballantine, 1981).

The Emmy Awards: A Pictorial History (Crown, 1971).

How Sweet It Was (Shorecrest, 1966).

Movies Made for Television (Arlington House, 1980).

A Pictorial History of Television (Chilton/Bonanza, 1959).

Television Drama Series Programming: A Comprehensive
Chronicle, 1947-1959 (Scarecrow Press, 1980).

Television Drama Series Programming: A Comprehensive
Chronicle, 1959-1975 (Scarecrow Press, 1978).

Television 1970-1980 (A.S. Barnes 1981).

Please keep in mind when using this volume that our aim has
been three-fold: 1) to update performers' entries for the years 1977
through 1981; 2) to amplify (e.g., with full episode titles wherever
possible), correct (e.g. erroneous telecast dates, improper series
and or episode title tags) and delete (e.g., repeat episodes, non-
verified credits) data from the first two volumes; and 3) to add new
performers' entries, giving listings for their television work from
January 1, 1977, through December 31, 1981 (or earlier, depending
on the performer).

For future supplements to this work, the authors would be
grateful for data concerning corrections, additions, and amplifica-
tions of published entries.

James Robert Parish   Vincent Terrace
12053 Emelita Street #3   1830 Delancey Place
North Hollywood, CA 91607   Bronx, New York 10462

March 3, 1982

ACKNOWLEDGMENTS

Patricia Anders

Louis Arbex

Steve Eberly

Films in Review

Larry Gianakos

Alex Gildzen

Barry Gillam

David Glagovsky

Doug McClelland

Alvin H. Marill

Jeb H. Perry

Robert Reed

David P. Strauss

Laura Stuart

Charles K. Stumpf

D. D. Woodruff

KEY

A&C[1]   Additions & Corrections to materials found in
                      in the base volume and Supplement I

ABC   American Broadcasting Company, Inc.

CBS   Columbia Broadcasting System, Inc.

ep   episode

ep hos   episode host/hostess

ms   mini series

nar   narrator

NBC   National Broadcasting Company, Inc.

NN   non-network

PBS   Public Broadcasting Service

pt   pilot

sp   special

sr   series regular

sr ret   series regular returning for another season

SUPP.   Supplement: covering the years 1977-1981

tf   telefeature

vo   voice only

*   new subject entry in this volume

AREAS NOT COVERED IN THIS VOLUME[2]

Cable Programs   Reality Programs
Documentaries   Showtime
Game Shows   Sports Shows
Home Box Office   Talk Shows
Live Special Events   Theatrical Motion Pictures
News Shows   Variety Shows
Quiz Shows

---

1. Shows listed under A&C have been a) amplified, with full episode titles, or b) corrected, with an underscore indicating the now
corrected segment of information, or c) deleted, when repeated episodes or non-verified credits appeared in the base volume.
   2. Repeats of any type of any show are NOT tabulated.

ACKER, SHARON
  A&C:
  The Wild Wild West ep The Night of the Sedgewick Curse
    10. 18. 68 CBS
  SUPP. :
  The Streets of San Francisco ep 5. 12. 77 ABC
  The Hostage Heart tf 9. 9. 77 CBS
  This Is the Life ep 4. 2. 78 NN
  Operation: Runaway ep 5. 18. 78 NBC
  Quincy, M. E. ep The Last Six Hours 9. 21. 78 NBC
  The Love Boat ep 10. 21. 78 ABC
  The Rockford Files ep 2. 10. 79 NBC
  Quincy, M. E. ep 3. 1. 79 NBC
  Police Story ep A Cry for Justice 5. 23. 79 NBC
  Stone ep 1. 14. 80 ABC
  Battles: The Murder That Wouldn't Die tf 3. 9. 80 NBC
  The Incredible Hulk ep Deep Shock 12. 12. 80 CBS
  Quincy, M. E. ep Memories of Allison 10. 28. 81 NBC
  Simon and Simon ep Details at Eleven 11. 24. 81 CBS

ACKERMAN, LESLIE*
  Barnaby Jones ep Fatal Witness 11. 14. 75 CBS
  Roxy Page pt 9. 6. 76 NBC
  The Streets of San Francisco ep 12. 2. 76 ABC
  The City tf 1. 12. 77 NBC
  Quincy, M. E. ep Main Man 11. 11. 77 NBC
  The Hallmark Hall of Fame ep The Last Hurrah sp 11. 16. 77
    NBC
  CHiPs ep 1. 19. 78 NBC
  Project UFO ep 12. 7. 78 NBC
  Insight ep 1. 28. 79 NN
  Women at West Point tf 2. 27. 79 CBS
  Once a Daughter sp 5. 9. 79 PBS
  Young Love, First Love tf 11. 20. 79 CBS
  Skag sr 1. 6. 80 NBC
  The Incredible Hulk ep 2. 6. 81 CBS
  Trapper John, M. D. ep Is There a Doctor in the Big House?
    11. 29. 81 CBS

ACTMAN, JANE*
  Room 222 ep The Laughing Majority 9. 30. 70 ABC
  The Partridge Family ep My Son the Feminist 12. 10. 70 ABC

Room 222   ep   10. 22. 71 ABC
Hawaii Five-O   ep   R&R&R 3. 7. 72 CBS
The Paul Lynde Show   sr   9. 13. 72 ABC
Room 222   ep   11. 17. 72 ABC
The Chadwick Family   tf   4. 17. 74 ABC
Mannix   ep   9. 29. 74 CBS
Planet of the Apes   ep   11. 1. 74 CBS
Medical Center   ep   Tainted Lady 11. 11. 74 CBS
Marcus Welby, M. D.   ep   11. 12. 74 ABC
The Rookies   ep   Deadly Image 2. 24. 75 ABC
The Invisible Man   ep   10. 6. 75 NBC
Barnaby Jones   ep   The Price of Terror 10. 10. 75 CBS
Joe Forrester   ep   11. 4. 75 NBC
Three for the Road   ep   11. 30. 75 CBS
Hunter   ep   4. 8. 77 CBS
The Cabot Connection   pt   5. 10. 77 CBS
Classics Illustrated   ep   Last of the Mohicans   tf   11. 23. 77 NBC
Black Beauty   ms   1. 31-2. 4. 78 NBC
The New Adventures of Wonder Woman   ep   The Man Who
    Wouldn't Tell 3. 31. 78 CBS
Your Place Or Mine   pt   5. 27. 78 CBS
The New Adventures of Wonder Woman   ep   The Girl with a
    Gift for Disaster 3. 17. 79 CBS

ADAMS, DON
    SUPP. :
    The Love Boat   ep   1. 14. 78 ABC
    Fantasy Island   ep   10. 27. 79 ABC
    Murder Can Hurt You   tf nar   5. 21. 80 ABC

ADAMS, EDIE
    A&C:
    Police Story   ep   The Return of Joe Forrester 5. 6. 75 NBC
    Harry O   ep   1. 22. 76 ABC
    The Blue Knight   ep   3. 3. 76 CBS
    SUPP. :
    Rosetti and Ryan   ep   10. 20. 77 NBC
    Police Woman   ep   1. 4. 78 NBC
    Superdome   tf   1. 9. 78 ABC
    The Love Boat   ep   9. 16. 78 ABC
    The Eddie Capra Mysteries   ep   11. 3. 78 NBC
    Mrs. Columbo   ep   2. 26. 79 NBC
    Fast Friends   tf   3. 19. 79 NBC
    The Seekers   ms   12. 3. 79, 12. 4. 79 NN
    A Man Called Sloane   ep   12. 8. 79 NBC
    Make Me an Offer   tf   1. 11. 80 ABC
    Portrait of an Escort   tf   10. 8. 80 CBS
    Vega$ ep   Sourdough Suite 1. 7. 81 ABC
    Fantasy Island   ep   3. 1. 81 ABC

ADAMS, JULIE
    A&C:
    The Lux Video Theatre   ep   Design for November 6. 13. 57 NBC

Yancy Derringer   ep   Return to New Orleans 10. 2. 58 CBS
The Man and the Challenge   ep   Experiments in Terror 10. 10. 59
    NBC
Wrangler   ep   The Affair with Browning's Woman 8. 25. 60 NBC
The Outlaws   ep   Return to New March 6. 22. 61 NBC
Hollywood Television Theatre   ep   Six Characters in Search of
    an Author 10. 17. 76 PBS
SUPP. :
McMillan   ep   1. 2. 77 NBC
This Is the Life   ep   Man in the Middle 5. 25. 77 NN
Quincy, M. E.   ep   11. 11. 77 NBC
Police Woman   ep   2. 22. 78 NBC
The Incredible Hulk   ep   5. 12. 78 CBS
Greatest Heroes of the Bible   ep   The Story of Moses and the
    Ten Commandments 11. 21. 78 NBC
Quincy, M. E.   ep   1. 10. 80 NBC
Trapper John, M. D.   ep   3. 30. 80 CBS
Vega$ ep   1. 21. 81 ABC
Too Close for Comfort   ep   2. 3. 81 ABC
Code Red   tf   9. 20. 81 ABC
Code Red   sr   11. 1. 81 ABC

ADAMS, MAUD*
Kojak   ep   Kojak's Days 2. 1. 77, 2. 8. 77 CBS
Hawaii Five-O   ep   12. 8. 77 CBS
Big Bob Johnson and His Fantastic Speed Circus   tf   6. 27. 78
    NBC
Switch   ep   9. 3. 78 CBS
Starsky and Hutch   ep   No Deposit, No Return 12. 12. 78 ABC
The Hostage Tower   tf   5. 13. 80 CBS
Playing for Time   tf   9. 30. 80 CBS

AHN, PHILIP
A&C:
Hong Kong   ep   The Dragon Cup 12. 14. 60 ABC
Follow the Sun   ep   Cry Fraud 9. 24. 61 ABC
SUPP. :
Police Woman   ep   3. 22. 77 NBC
M*A*S*H   ep   11. 8. 77 CBS
Switch   ep   1. 9. 78 CBS

AIDMAN, CHARLES*
Alcoa Premiere   ep   Epilogue 2. 24. 59 ABC
The Twilight Zone   ep   And When the Sky Was Opened 12. 11. 59
    CBS
Bonanza   ep   The Rival 4. 15. 61 NBC
The FBI   ep   The Tunnel 4. 21. 68 ABC
Mission: Impossible   ep   Heir Apparent 9. 29. 68 CBS
The Sound of Anger   tf   12. 10. 68 NBC
The Outcasts   ep   12. 23. 68 ABC
Gunsmoke   ep   The Money Store 12. 30. 68 CBS
Gunsmoke   ep   8. 25. 69 CBS
The Name of the Game   ep   The Broken Puzzle 3. 12. 71 NBC

The Bold Ones: The Lawyers   ep   11.28.71 NBC
The Man and the City   ep   1.5.72 ABC
Mannix   ep   Moving Target 1.19.72 CBS
Ghost Story   ep   10.27.72 NBC
The Rookies   ep   The Rabbits on the Runway 12.25.72 ABC
Emergency   ep   1.24.73 NBC
Wide World of Mystery   ep   The Picture of Dorian Gray 4.23.73
    ABC
Deliver Us from Evil   tf   9.11.73 ABC
Hec Ramsey   ep   Scar Tissue 3.10.74 NBC
Hec Ramsey   ep   Only Birds and Fools 4.7.74 NBC
The Night Stalker   ep   The Zombie 9.20.74 ABC
Barnaby Jones   ep   The Challenge 9.24.74 CBS
The Red Badge of Courage   tf   12.3.74 NBC
Nakia   ep   12.7.74 ABC
Kung Fu   ep   4.26.75 ABC
The Barbary Coast   ep   5.4.75 ABC
The Streets of San Francisco   ep   12.18.75 ABC
The Rookies   ep   12.25.75 ABC
The Blue Knight   ep   12.31.75 CBS
Cannon   ep   3.3.76 CBS
S.W.A.T.   ep   3.13.76 ABC
Spencer's Pilots   ep   10.8.76 CBS
Amelia Earhart   tf   10.25.76 NBC
The Six Million Dollar Man   ep   Fires of Hell 1.30.77 ABC
Little House on the Prairie   ep   3.21.77 NBC
The Rockford Files   ep   11.25.77 NBC
Kojak   ep   Justice for All 1.7.78 CBS
Police Woman   ep   3.8.78 NBC
Quincy, M.E.   ep   2.1.79 NBC
Quincy, M.E.   ep   Nowhere to Run 10.4.79 NBC
Quincy, M.E.   ep   11.8.79 NBC
Lou Grant   ep   Andrew (part 2) 12.10.79 CBS
Skag   ep   1.17.80 NBC
The Long Days of Summer   tf nar   5.23.80 ABC
Alcatraz: The Whole Shocking Story   tf   11.5.80, 11.6.80 NBC
Quincy, M.E.   ep   The Hope of Elkwood 12.3.80 NBC
Quincy, M.E.   ep   D.U.I. 12.2.81 NBC

AKINS, CLAUDE*
The Tales of Wells Fargo   ep   The Most Dangerous Man Alive
    11.10.58 NBC
Bonanza   ep   Desert Justice 2.20.60 NBC
The Twilight Zone   ep   Monsters Due on Maple Street 3.4.60
    CBS
Bonanza   ep   The Mill 10.1.60 NBC
Bonanza   ep   Sam Hill 6.3.61 NBC
The Twilight Zone   ep   The Little People 3.20.62 CBS
Bonanza   ep   The Deserter 10.21.62 NBC
The Untouchables   ep   The Spoiler 3.26.63 ABC
Kraft Suspense Theatre   ep   Operation Grief 10.8.64 NBC
Branded   ep   The Vindicator 1.31.65 NBC
Daniel Boone   ep   The Place of 1000 Spirits 2.4.65 NBC

Laredo   sr   9. 16. 65 NBC
The Big Valley   ep   The Brawlers 12. 15. 65 ABC
The Man from U. N. C. L. E.   ep   The Very Important Zombie
    Affair 12. 31. 65 NBC
Laredo   sr ret   9. 16. 66 NBC
Lock, Stock and Barrel   tf   9. 24. 71 NBC
River of Mystery   tf   10. 1. 71 NBC
McMillan and Wife   ep   The Face of Murder 1. 5. 72 NBC
The Night Stalker   tf   1. 11. 72 ABC
Longstreet   ep   1. 20. 72 ABC
Gunsmoke   ep   The Predators 1. 31. 72 CBS
Mission: Impossible   ep   2. 16. 73 CBS
The Norliss Tapes   tf   2. 21. 73 NBC
Medical Center   ep   9. 17. 73 CBS
The Rookies   ep   Margin for Error 9. 17. 73 ABC
Cannon   ep   10. 3. 73 CBS
Police Story   ep   The Ten Year Honeymoon 10. 23. 73 NBC
Marcus Welby, M. D.   ep   12. 11. 73 ABC
The Death Squad   tf   1. 8. 74 ABC
The Streets of San Francisco   ep   2. 7. 74 ABC
McCloud   ep   2. 24. 74 NBC
Mannix   ep   3. 3. 74 CBS
In Tandem   tf   5. 8. 74 NBC
Medical Story   tf   9. 4. 75 NBC
Movin' On   sr   9. 9. 75 NBC
The Hallmark Hall of Fame   ep   Eric   sp   11. 10. 75 NBC
Police Story   ep   2. 13. 76 NBC
Kiss Me, Kill Me   tf   5. 8. 76 ABC
Yesterday's Child   tf   2. 3. 77 NBC
The Rhinemann Exchange   ms   3. 10. 77, 3. 17. 77, 3. 24. 77 NBC
Nashville 99   sr   4. 1. 77 CBS
Killer on Board   tf   10. 10. 77 NBC
Tarantulas: The Deadly Cargo   tf   12. 28. 77 CBS
Police Story   ep   The Broken Badge 3. 19. 78 NBC
Little Mo   tf   9. 5. 78 NBC
B. J. and the Bear   tf   10. 4. 78 NBC
Murder in Music City (a. k. a. The Music City Murders) 1. 16. 79
    NBC
B. J. and the Bear   sr   2. 10. 79 NBC
Ebony, Ivory and Jade   tf   8. 3. 79 CBS
The Misadventures of Sheriff Lobo   sr   9. 18. 79 NBC
Concrete Cowboys   tf   10. 17. 79 CBS
Lobo   sr   12. 30. 80 NBC
Fantasy Island   ep   The Lagoon 11. 28. 81 ABC
Darkroom   ep   Uncle George 12. 4. 81 ABC

ALBERT, EDDIE
    A&C:
    Lights' Out   ep   Friday the 19th 11. 19. 51
    Philco Television Playhouse   ep   The Bachelor Party 10. 11. 53
        NBC
    The Alcoa Hour   ep   No License to Kill 2. 3. 57 NBC
    The Alcoa Hour   ep   No License to Kill (restaged) 9. 1. 57 NBC

Laramie   ep   Glory Road 9. 22. 59 NBC
Riverboat   ep   The Unwilling 10. 11. 59 NBC
SUPP. :
Switch   sr ret   9. 23. 77 CBS
Evening in Byzantium   ms   8. 14. 78,   8. 15. 78 NN
The Word   ms   11. 12-11. 15. 78 CBS
Trouble in High Timber Country   tf   6. 27. 80 ABC
Beulah Land   ms   10. 7. 80,   10. 8. 80,   10. 9. 80 NBC
Living in Paradise   pt   2. 1. 81 NBC
Peter and Paul   tf   4. 12. 81,   4. 14. 81 CBS
The Fall Guy   ep   10. 28. 81 ABC
Goliath Awaits   ms   11. 17. 81,   11. 18. 81   NN

ALBERT, EDWARD
A&C:
Orson Welles' Great Mysteries   ep   A Terribly Strange Bed
   9. 12. 73   NN
The Killer Bees   tf   2. 26. 74 CBS
SUPP. :
Black Beauty   ms   1. 31. 78,   2. 1. 78,   2. 2. 78,   2. 3. 78,   2. 4. 78
   NBC
The Legend of the Black Hand   ms ep   8. 17. 78 ABC
The Love Boat   ep   1. 25. 78 ABC
The Millionaire   tf   12. 19. 78 CBS
Silent Victory: The Kitty O'Neil Story   tf   2. 24. 79 CBS
The Last Convertible   ms   9. 24. 79,   9. 25. 79,   9. 26. 79 NBC
Walking Tall   ep   1. 31. 81 NBC

ALBERTSON, JACK*
The Thin Man   sr   9. 20. 57 NBC
The Twilight Zone   ep   The Shelter   9. 29. 61 CBS
Ensign O'Toole   sr   9. 23. 62 NBC
The Twilight Zone   ep   I Dream of Genie 3. 21. 63 CBS
The Defenders   ep   The Objector 2. 11. 65 CBS
Bonanza   ep   A Girl Named George 1. 14. 68 NBC
Ironside   ep   Side Pocket 12. 5. 68 NBC
Land of the Giants   ep   3. 16. 69 ABC
The Big Valley   ep   The Battle of Mineral Springs 3. 24. 69 ABC
The Virginian   ep   3. 26. 69 NBC
The Monk   tf   10. 21. 69 ABC
A Clear and Present Danger   tf   3. 21. 70 NBC
Daniel Boone   ep   Run for the Money 2. 19. 70 NBC
The Name of the Game   ep   The Showdown 3. 19. 71 NBC
Dr. Simon Locke   sr   9. 13. 71   NN
Once upon a Dead Man   tf   9. 17. 71 NBC
Congratulations, It's a Boy   tf   9. 21. 71 ABC
Lock, Stock and Barrel   tf   9. 24. 71 NBC
Alias Smith and Jones   ep   9. 30. 71 ABC
The Man and The City   ep   12. 29. 71 ABC
Gunsmoke   ep   One for the Road 1. 24. 72 CBS
The Bold Ones: The Doctors   ep   A Nation of Human Pincush-
   ions 10. 3. 72 NBC
Bonanza   ep   The Sound of Loneliness 12. 5. 72 NBC

The Streets of San Francisco ep The Hunters 1. 25. 73 ABC
Hollywood Television Theatre ep Montserrat 11. 11. 73 PBS
Gunsmoke ep 3. 11. 74 CBS
Chico and the Man sr 9. 13. 74 NBC
Chico and the Man sr ret 9. 12. 75 NBC
The Oath pt 8. 26. 76 ABC
Chico and the Man sr ret 10. 1. 76 NBC
Chico and the Man sr ret 9. 16. 77 NBC
The Comedy Company tf 7. 21. 78 CBS
Grandpa Goes to Washington sr 9. 7. 78 NBC
Insight ep 4. 1. 79 NN
Marriage Is Alive and Well tf 1. 25. 80 NBC
Charlie's Angels ep From Street Models to Hawaiian Angels
    11. 30. 80 ABC
Charlie and the Great Balloon Race tf 7. 12. 81 NBC

ALBRIGHT, LOLA
    SUPP. :
    Delta County, U. S. A. tf 5. 20. 77 ABC
    Terraces tf 6. 27. 77 NBC
    Switch ep 1. 16. 78 CBS
    The Incredible Hulk ep The First 3. 6. 81 CBS

ALDA, ALAN
    SUPP. :
    M*A*S*H sr ret 9. 20. 77 CBS
    Kill Me If You Can tf 9. 25. 77 NBC
    M*A*S*H sr ret 9. 18. 78 CBS
    M*A*S*H sr ret 9. 17. 79 CBS
    M*A*S*H sr ret 11. 17. 80 CBS
    M*A*S*H sr ret 10. 26. 81 CBS

ALDA, ROBERT
    A&C:
    Lux Video Theatre ep Force of Circumstance 7. 2. 53 CBS
    Robert Montgomery Presents ep Fear Street 4. 15. 57 NBC
    Rhoda ep 9. 30. 74 CBS
    M*A*S*H ep 1. 21. 75 CBS
    SUPP. :
    Quincy, M. E. ep 1. 2. 77 NBC
    The Nancy Drew Mysteries ep Mystery of the Fallen Angels
        4. 17. 77 ABC
    The Feather and Father Gang ep 5. 28. 77 ABC
    Police Story ep River of Promises 1. 14. 78 NBC
    Perfect Gentlemen tf 3. 14. 78 CBS
    The Incredible Hulk ep 3. 31. 78 CBS
    The Amazing Spider-Man ep 4. 5. 78 CBS
    The Rock Rainbow pt 7. 15. 78 ABC
    The New Adventures of Wonder Woman ep Formicida 11. 3. 78
        CBS
    Sword of Justice ep 10. 19. 78 NBC
    The Rockford Files ep 11. 10. 78 NBC
    Greatest Heroes of the Bible ep The Story of Moses and the
        Ten Commandments 11. 21. 78 NBC

Grandpa Goes to Washington   ep   12. 5. 78 NBC
Supertrain   sr   2. 7. 79 NBC
Supertrain   sr ret   4. 7. 79 NBC
Ten Speed and Brown Shoe   ep   3. 30. 80 ABC
The Facts of Life   ep   8. 22. 80 NBC
Quincy, M. E.   ep   Jury Duty 1. 28. 81 NBC
Code Red   tf   9. 20. 81 ABC

ALDEN, NORMAN*
Mr. Lucky   ep   3. 26. 60 CBS
The Cara Williams Show   ep   11. 25. 64 CBS
Batman   ep   The Joker Trumps an Ace 4. 6. 66 ABC
Rango   sr   1. 13. 67 ABC
Gunsmoke   ep   The Night Riders 2. 24. 69 CBS
The Psychiatrist: God Bless the Children   tf   2. 14. 70 NBC
My Three Sons   ep   9. 26. 70 CBS
This Is the Life   ep   12. 11. 71   NN
The Trackers   tf   12. 14. 71 ABC
Mission: Impossible   ep   2. 12. 72 CBS
The Mod Squad   ep   2. 22. 72 ABC
Medical Center   ep   A Game for One Player 12. 13. 72 CBS
The Rookies   ep   1. 8. 73 ABC
Kung Fu   ep   The Praying Mantis Kills 3. 8. 73 ABC
Murdock's Gang   tf   3. 20. 73 CBS
Super Friends   sr vo   9. 8. 73 ABC
Griff   ep   The Framing of Billy the Kid 9. 29. 73 ABC
Cannon   ep   Night Flight to Murder 10. 17. 73 CBS
Owen Marshall, Counselor at Law   ep   The Prowler 12. 12. 73
   ABC
Cry Panic   tf   2. 6. 74 ABC
The FBI   ep   2. 24. 74 ABC
Bachelor's 4   ep   Jerry   pt   5. 16. 74 CBS
Devlin   sr vo   9. 7. 74 ABC
Terror on the 40th Floor   tf   9. 17. 74 NBC
Planet of the Apes   ep   9. 27. 74 CBS
Mannix   ep   9. 29. 74 CBS
Marcus Welby, M. D.   ep   10. 29. 74 ABC
Owen Marshall, Counselor at Law   ep   11. 30. 72 ABC
The Manhunter   ep   12. 18. 74 CBS
Barnaby Jones   ep   12. 31. 74 CBS
Cannon   ep   2. 12. 75 CBS
The Rookies   ep   3. 3. 75 ABC
The Streets of San Francisco   ep   3. 13. 75 ABC
Fay   sr   9. 4. 75 NBC
Kojak   ep   11. 16. 75 CBS
Mary Hartman, Mary Hartman   sr   1. 6. 76   NN
Bronk   ep   The Vigilante 3. 26. 76 CBS
The Krofft Super Show   ep   Electra Woman and Dyna Girl   sr
   9. 11. 76 ABC
Most Wanted   ep   2. 19. 77 ABC
The New Super Friends Hour   sr vo   9. 19. 77 ABC
Quincy, M. E.   ep   9. 23. 77 NBC
Young Dan'l Boone   ep   10. 10. 77 CBS

Switch   ep   1. 27. 78 CBS
Ring of Passion   tf   2. 4. 78 NBC
Eight Is Enough   ep   3. 22. 78 ABC
The Plant Family   pt   9. 2. 78 CBS
Challenge of the Super Friends   sr vo   9. 9. 78 ABC
The Godzilla Power Hour   sr vo   9. 9. 78 NBC
The Rockford Files   ep   9. 22. 78 NBC
Starsky and Hutch   ep   11. 14. 78 ABC
California Fever   ep   10. 23. 79 CBS
Charlie's Angels   ep   Dancin' Angels 2. 6. 80 ABC
The Love Boat   ep   Honeymoon Pressure 3. 29. 80 ABC
Flamingo Road   tf   5. 12. 80 NBC
Charlie's Angels   ep   Taxi Angels 2. 7. 81 ABC
Enos   ep   4. 8. 81 CBS
Nero Wolfe   ep   4. 17. 81 NBC
Code Red   ep   Dark Fire 11. 15. 81

ALETTER, FRANK*

Bringing up Buddy   sr   10. 10. 60 CBS
The Cara Williams Show   sr   9. 23. 64 CBS
The Fugitive   ep   Trial by Fire 10. 5. 65 ABC
It's About Time   sr   9. 11. 66 ABC
The FBI   ep   Act of Violence 1. 21. 68 ABC
The Banana Splits Adventure Hour   ep   Danger Island   sr
   9. 7. 68 NBC
The Doris Day Show   ep   2. 11. 69 CBS
Nancy   sr   9. 17. 70 NBC
The Name of the Game   ep   The War Merchants 10. 30. 70 NBC
Love, American Style   ep   10. 22. 71 ABC
Cannon   ep   Girl in the Electric Coffin 10. 26. 71 CBS
Funny Face   ep   12. 11. 71 CBS
Ironside   ep   1. 6. 72 NBC
The FBI   ep   A Second Chance 1. 9. 72 ABC
The Don Rickles Show   sr   1. 14. 72 CBS
The Bold Ones: The Lawyers   ep   1. 30. 72 NBC
Emergency   ep   2. 12. 72 NBC
Banyon   ep   9. 15. 72 NBC
Maude   ep   10. 24. 72 CBS
Jigsaw   ep   2. 24. 73 ABC
Ironside   ep   Forests of the Night 9. 27. 73 NBC
M*A*S*H   ep   10. 6. 73 CBS
Marcus Welby, M. D.   ep   A Question of Fault 10. 16. 73 ABC
Planet of the Apes   ep   12. 6. 74 CBS
Sierra   ep   12. 12. 74 NBC
Planet of the Apes   ep   12. 20. 74 CBS
Marcus Welby, M. D.   ep   1. 7. 75, 1. 14. 75 ABC
The Six Million Dollar Man   ep   1. 10. 75 ABC
The Night Stalker   ep   1. 31. 75 ABC
Kojak   ep   9. 21. 75 CBS
Marcus Welby, M. D.   ep   9. 30. 75 ABC
The Invisible Man   ep   11. 24. 75 NBC
Petrocelli   ep   1. 21. 76 NBC
Switch   ep   1. 27. 76 CBS

Rich Man, Poor Man ms ep **2.9.76** ABC
Police Woman ep **11.9.76** NBC
The Quest ep **11.17.76, 11.24.76** NBC
Blansky's Beauties ep **5.21.77** ABC
All in the Family ep **1.8.78** CBS
Project UFO ep **3.12.78** NBC
Police Woman ep **3.30.78**
Columbo ep How to Dial a Murder **4.15.78** NBC
Operation Petticoat ep **5.6.78** ABC
Quincy, M.E. ep **12.7.78** NBC
David Cassidy--Man Undercover ep **12.21.78** NBC
The Love Boat ep **11.24.79** ABC
Lou Grant ep **3.9.81** CBS
The Star Maker tf **5.11.81, 5.12.81** NBC
Three's Company ep **10.27.81** ABC
Quincy, M.E. ep Memories of Allison **10.28.81** NBC

ALEXANDER, JANE
  SUPP.:
  A Circle of Children tf **3.10.77** CBS
  Eleanor and Franklin: The White House Years tf **3.13.77** ABC
  A Question of Love tf **11.26.78** ABC
  Lovey: A Circle of Children, Part II tf **12.13.78** CBS
  Playing for Time tf **9.30.80** CBS

ALLEN, SIAN BARBARA
  A&C:
  The Waltons ep The Love Story **1.18.73**
  Love, American Style ep **2.23.73** ABC
  Columbo ep Lovely but Lethal **9.23.73** NBC
  The Waltons ep The Thanksgiving Story **11.16.73** CBS
  Kojak ep **3.20.74** CBS
  Captains and the Kings ms **9.30.76, 10.7.76, 10.14.76,**
      11.4.76, 11.11.76 NBC
  SUPP.:
  Kingston Confidential ep **7.13.77** NBC
  Hawaii Five-O ep **12.29.77** CBS
  Baretta ep **3.9.78** ABC
  W.E.B. ep **9.21.78** NBC
  Sword of Justice ep Dead Birds Don't Sing **10.7.78** NBC
  The Incredible Hulk ep **5.11.79** CBS
  Makeup tf **12.18.81**

ALLEN, STEVE
  SUPP.:
  The Love Boat ep **11.19.77** ABC
  The Hallmark Hall of Fame ep Have I Got a Christmas for
      You ep **12.16.77** NBC
  The Steve Allen Comedy Hour sr **10.18.80** NBC

ALLYSON, JUNE
  SUPP.:
  Switch ep **2.20.77** CBS

Curse of the Black Widow tf 9.16.77 ABC
Three on a Date tf 2.17.78 ABC
Vega$ tf 4.25.78 ABC
The Love Boat ep Her Own Two Feet 11.17.78 ABC
The Incredible Hulk ep 10.5.79 CBS

ALVARADO, TRINI*
    The ABC Afterschool Special ep A Movie Star's Daughter sp
        10.10.79 ABC
    The ABC Afterschool Special ep Star Struck sp 10.14.81
        ABC

AMECHE, DON
    A&C:
    Julia ep 11.25.69 NBC
    SUPP.:
    The Love Boat ep 10.13.79 ABC
    Quincy, M.E. ep The Trick of Death 9.28.80 NBC
    Fantasy Island ep 12.6.80 ABC

AMES, LEON
    A&C:
    delete: Twilight Theatre ep Ace of Spades 8.10.53 ABC
    Stars over Hollywood ep Ace of Spades 8.10.51 NBC
    Lux Video Theatre ep It Happened on Fifth Avenue 1.3.57 NBC
    SUPP.:
    Emergency ep 4.2.77 NBC
    The Best Place to Be tf 5.28.79 NBC

AMOS, JOHN
    A&C:
    Future Cop tf 5.1.76 ABC
    SUPP.:
    Roots ep 1.25.77, 1.26.77, 1.27.77 ABC
    Future Cop sr 3.5.77 ABC
    The Cops and Robin tf 3.28.78 NBC
    Willa tf 3.17.79 CBS
    Alcatraz: The Whole Shocking Story tf 11.5.80, 11.6.80 NBC
    Here's Boomer ep 11.8.81 NBC

AMSTERDAM, MOREY
    SUPP.:
    Mixed Nuts pt 5.12.77 ABC
    The Love Boat ep Crash Diet Crush 5.13.78 ABC
    Vega$ ep 9.20.78 ABC
    Sooner or Later tf 3.25.79 NBC
    Project UFO ep 7.5.79 NBC

ANDERSON, BARBARA
    SUPP.:
    The New, Original Wonder Woman ep Last of the $2 Bills
        1.8.77 CBS
    SST--Death Flight tf 2.25.77 ABC

Insight ep 1.15.78 NN
Doctors' Private Lives tf 3.20.78 ABC
The Love Boat ep Ship of Ghouls 10.28.78 ABC
Hawaii Five-O ep 1.18.79 CBS

ANDERSON, JOHN
A&C:
Scalplock tf 4.10.66 ABC
The FBI ep The Loner 11.19.72 ABC
Set This Town on Fire tf 1.8.73 NBC
Hec Ramsey ep 2.18.73 NBC
Call to Danger tf 2.27.73 CBS
Heat Wave tf 1.26.74 ABC
Smile Jenny, You're Dead tf 2.3.74 ABC
The Manhunter tf 2.26.74 CBS
Log of the Black Pearl tf 1.4.75 NBC
Barnaby Jones ep 4.1.75 CBS
Dead Man on the Run tf 4.2.75 CBS
Death Among Friends tf 5.20.75 NBC
The Dark Side of Innocence tf 5.20.76 NBC
Bridger tf 9.10.76 NBC
Once an Eagle ms 12.2.76, 12.9.76, 12.16.76, 12.23.76,
    12.30.76, 1.6.77, 1.13.77 NBC
SUPP.:
Tail Gunner Joe tf 2.6.77 NBC
Tales of the Unexpected ep The Force of Evil 3.13.77 NBC
Peter Lundy and the Medicine Hat Stallion tf 11.6.77 NBC
The Hallmark Hall of Fame ep The Last Hurrah sp 11.16.77
    NBC
Lou Grant ep 12.6.77 CBS
Donner Pass: The Road to Survival tf 10.24.78 CBS
The Incredible Hulk ep 12.15.78 CBS
The Deerslayer tf 12.18.78 NBC
The Incredible Hulk ep 1.16.79 CBS
The World of Disney ep Shadow of Fear 1.28.79 NBC
Backstairs at the White House ms ep 2.12.79 NBC
Project UFO ep 7.5.79 NBC
The Misadventures of Sheriff Lobo ep 1.8.80 NBC
Ten Speed and Brown Shoe ep 6.6.80 ABC
The ABC Weekend Special ep Mayday! Mayday! 1.24.81 ABC
The Greatest American Hero ep 11.4.81 ABC

ANDERSON, LONI*
Barnaby Jones ep A Little Glory, A Little Death 4.29.73 CBS
Harry O ep Lester II 9.25.75 ABC
Phyllis ep 10.27.75 CBS
Barnaby Jones ep Sins of Thy Father 10.21.76 CBS
The McLean Stevenson Show ep 12.22.76 NBC
Winner Take All pt 4.1.77 CBS
The Magnificent Magnet of Santa Mesa tf 6.19.77 NBC
Three on a Date tf 2.17.78 ABC
The Incredible Hulk ep 3.24.78 CBS
WKRP in Cincinnati sr 9.18.78 CBS

Whodunit?   ep   5. 17. 79 NBC
WKRP in Cincinnati   sr ret   9. 17. 79 CBS
The Love Boat   ep   1. 19. 80 ABC
The Fantastic Funnies   hos sp   5. 15. 80 CBS
The Jayne Mansfield Story   tf   10. 29. 80 CBS
WKRP in Cincinnati   sr ret   11. 1. 80 CBS
The Love Boat   ep   Sis and the City Slicker   11. 22. 80 ABC
Fantasy Island   ep   11. 22. 80 ABC
WKRP in Cincinnati   sr ret   10. 7. 81 CBS
Sizzle   tf   11. 29. 81 ABC

ANDERSON, MELISSA SUE*
Little House on the Prairie   tf   3. 30. 74 NBC
Little House on the Prairie   sr   9. 11. 74 NBC
Little House on the Prairie   sr ret   9. 10. 75 NBC
Little House on the Prairie   sr ret   9. 22. 76 NBC
The Loneliest Runner   tf   12. 20. 76 NBC
The ABC Afterschool Special   ep   Very Good Friends   sp
    4. 6. 77 ABC
Little House on the Prairie   sr ret   9. 12. 77 NBC
James at 15   tf   9. 15. 77 NBC
Little House on the Prairie   sr ret   9. 11. 78 NBC
The Love Boat   ep   11. 11. 78 ABC
The Survival of Dana   tf   5. 29. 79 CBS
Little House on the Prairie   sr ret   9. 17. 79 NBC
CHiPs   ep   CHiPs Goes Roller Disco   9. 22. 79 NBC
The ABC Afterschool Special   ep   Which Mother Is Mine?   sp
    9. 26. 79 ABC
The Love Boat   ep   Chubs   11. 11. 79 ABC
Fantasy Island   ep   1. 19. 80 ABC
Special Treat   ep   Treasure Island   hos sp   4. 29. 80 NBC
Little House on the Prairie   sr ret   9. 22. 80 NBC
The Love Boat   ep   Matchmaker, Matchmaker Times Two
    11. 29. 80 ABC
Midnight Offerings   tf   2. 27. 81 ABC
Little House on the Prairie   ep   10. 5. 81 NBC
Advice to the Lovelorn   tf   11. 30. 81 NBC

ANDERSON, RICHARD*
Bus Stop   sr   10. 1. 61 ABC
The Eleventh Hour   ep   Who Chopped Down the Cherry Tree
    1. 29. 64 NBC
The Man from U. N. C. L. E.   ep   The Quadripartite Affair
    10. 6. 64 NBC
The Fugitive   ep   The Iron Maiden   12. 15. 64 ABC
Slattery's People   ep   Does Nero Still at Ringside Sit?   2. 5. 65
    CBS
The Fugitive   ep   Runner in the Dark   3. 30. 65 ABC
Perry Mason   sr   9. 65 CBS
The Fugitive   ep   Three Cheers for Little Boy Blue   10. 19. 65
    ABC
The Green Hornet   ep   Bad Bet on 459-Silent   2. 3. 67 ABC
Ironside   ep   Eat, Drink and Be Buried   10. 5. 67 NBC

The Big Valley   ep   The Disappearance 11. 6. 67 ABC
Bonanza   ep   Showdown at Tahoe 11. 19. 67 NBC
The Wild Wild West   ep   The Night of the Headless Woman
   1. 5. 68 CBS
The Big Valley   ep   Fall of a Hero 2. 5. 68 ABC
The FBI   ep   The Mercenary 4. 28. 68 ABC
The Big Valley   ep   The Long Ride 11. 25. 68 ABC
Mannix   ep   Fear I Have to Fall 12. 21. 68 CBS
My Friend Tony   ep   Let George Do It 1. 26. 69 NBC
Judd, for the Defense   ep   Between the Dark and the Daylight
   2. 7. 69 ABC
The Big Valley   ep   Alias Nellie Handly 2. 24. 69 ABC
Daniel Boone   ep   For Want of a Hero 3. 6. 69 NBC
The FBI   ep   The Challengers 11. 2. 69 ABC
Along Came a Spider   tf   2. 3. 70 ABC
Dan August   sr   9. 23. 70 ABC
Cade's County   ep   9. 21. 71 CBS
O'Hara: U. S. Treasury   ep   9. 24. 71 CBS
Owen Marshall, Counselor at Law   ep   11. 18. 71 ABC
Cannon   ep   11. 30. 71 CBS
Ironside   ep   License to Kill 12. 2. 71 NBC
Columbo   ep   Lady in Waiting 12. 15. 71 NBC
Dead Men Tell No Tales   tf   12. 17. 71 ABC
The Astronaut   tf   1. 8. 72 NBC
Longstreet   ep   Sad Songs and Other Conversations 2. 10. 72 ABC
The Longest Night   tf   9. 12. 72 ABC
Say Goodbye, Maggie Cole   tf   9. 27. 72 ABC
The FBI   ep   The Franklin Papers 10. 8. 72 ABC
The Bold Ones: The Doctors   ep   A Quality of Fear 11. 14. 72
   NBC
Ironside   ep   Cold, Hard Cash 12. 14. 72 NBC
Hawaii Five-O   ep   The Child Stealers 1. 2. 73 CBS
The Night Strangler   tf   1. 16. 73 ABC
The Streets of San Francisco   ep   2. 8. 73 ABC
Jigsaw   ep   3. 3. 73 ABC
The Six Million Dollar Man   tf   3. 24. 73 ABC
Partners in Crime   tf   3. 24. 73 NBC
Jarrett   tf   8. 11. 73 NBC
The FBI   ep   The Big Job 9. 16. 73 ABC
The New Adventures of Perry Mason   ep   The Case of the Tell-
   tale Drunk 10. 14. 73 CBS
The Six Million Dollar Man   sr   10. 20. 73 ABC
Cannon   ep   The Perfect Alibi 10. 31. 73 CBS
Barnaby Jones   ep   Fatal Flight 12. 9. 73 CBS
Owen Marshall, Counselor at Law   ep   A Killer with a Badge
   2. 9. 74 ABC
The Six Million Dollar Man   sr ret   9. 18. 74 ABC
Gunsmoke   ep   9. 23. 74 CBS
Ironside   ep   1. 16. 75 NBC
The Six Million Dollar Man   sr ret   9. 14. 75 ABC
The Bionic Woman   sr   1. 14. 76 ABC
The Six Million Dollar Man   sr ret   9. 19. 76 ABC
The Bionic Woman   sr ret   9. 22. 76 ABC

The Bionic Woman   sr ret   9. 10. 77 NBC
The Six Million Dollar Man   sr ret   9. 11. 77 ABC
Pearl   ms   11. 16. 78,   11. 17. 78,   11. 19. 78 ABC
The Immigrants   ms   11. 20. 78,   11. 21. 78 NN
The Love Boat   ep   Aftermath 2. 1. 79 ABC
Murder by Natural Causes   tf   2. 17. 79 CBS
The French-Atlantic Affair   ms   11. 15. 79,   11. 16. 79,   11. 18. 79
    ABC
Condominium   ms   11. 20. 80,   11. 24. 80   NN
Lobo   ep   The Dirtiest Girls in Town 12. 30. 80 NBC
Charlie's Angels   ep   Waikiki Angels 1. 4. 81 ABC
Nero Wolfe   ep   3. 20. 81 NBC
Dark Room   ep   Closed Circuit 11. 27. 81 ABC
Fantasy Island   ep   Night of the Tormented Soul 12. 5. 81 ABC

ANDES, KEITH
    A& C:
    Caribe   ep   4. 14. 75 ABC
    SUPP. :
    The Ultimate Imposter   tf   5. 12. 79 CBS
    Buck Rogers in the 25th Century   ep   3. 20. 80 NBC
    Blinded by the Light   tf   12. 16. 80 CBS

ANDREWS, DANA
    SUPP. :
    The Hallmark Hall of Fame   ep   The Last Hurrah   sp   11. 16. 77
        NBC
    The American Girls   ep   The Cancelled Czech 9. 23. 78 CBS
    The Hardy Boys   ep   10. 15. 78 ABC
    Ike   ms   5. 3. 79,   5. 4. 79,   5. 6. 79 ABC

ANSARA, MICHAEL
    A& C:
    Police Story   ep   Requiem for an Informer 10. 9. 73 NBC
    Shoot-out in a One-Dog Town   tf   1. 9. 74 ABC
    Police Surgeon   ep   8. 8. 74 NN
    SUPP. :
    Centennial   ms ep   Only the Banks Live Forever 10. 1. 78 NBC
    Vega$ ep   5. 9. 79 ABC
    Buck Rogers in the 25th Century   ep   Flight of the War Witch
        11. 29. 79 NBC
    Fantasy Island   ep   1. 12. 80 ABC
    Buck Rogers in the 25th Century   ep   1. 24. 80 NBC
    Buck Rogers in the 25th Century   ep   4. 3. 80 NBC
    Fantasy Island   ep   My Fair Pharaoh 5. 10. 80 ABC
    CHiPs   ep   Poachers 10. 19. 80 NBC
    Greatest Heroes of the Bible   ep   The Story of Esther 7. 26. 81
        NBC

ARDEN, EVE
    A& C:
    The Girl with Something Extra   ep   1. 18. 74 NBC

SUPP.:
A Guide for the Married Woman tf 10.13.78 ABC
Flying High ep 10.20.78 CBS
Vega$ ep 10.31.79 ABC
The Love Boat ep Kinfolk 1.19.80 ABC
Hart to Hart ep 3.18.80 ABC
The Dream Merchants ms 5.12.80, 5.19.80 NN
Nuts and Bolts pt 8.24.81 ABC

ARNAZ, DESI
SUPP.:
Alice ep 2.26.78 CBS

ARNAZ, DESI, JR.
SUPP.:
Flight to Holocaust tf 3.27.77 NBC
The Courage and the Passion tf 5.27.78 NBC
Black Market Baby tf 10.7.77 ABC
The Love Boat ep 1.21.78 ABC
To Kill a Cop tf 4.10.78, 4.11.78 NBC
Fantasy Island ep 10.14.78 ABC
How to Pick Up Girls tf 11.3.78 ABC
Crisis in Mid-Air tf 2.13.79 CBS
The Great American Traffic Jam tf 10.2.80 NBC
The Night the Bridge Fell Down tf 10.21.80 NBC
Wacked Out pt 9.26.81 NBC
Advice to the Lovelorn tf 11.30.81 NBC

ARNAZ, LUCIE
SUPP.:
Fantasy Island ep 4.29.78 ABC
The Mating Season tf 12.30.80 CBS

ARNESS, JAMES
SUPP.:
How the West Was Won ms 2.6.77-2.14.77 ABC
How the West Was Won sr 1.12.78 ABC
How the West Was Won sr ret 1.15.79 ABC
McClain's Law sr 11.20.81 NBC

ARQUETTE, ROSANNA*
Having Babies II tf 10.28.77 ABC
The Dark Secret of Harvest Home tf 1.23.78, 1.24.78 NBC
What Really Happened to the Class of '65? ep Mr.
    Potential 2.23.78 NBC
The ABC Afterschool Special ep Mom and Dad Can't Hear Me
    sp 4.5.78 ABC
Zuma Beach tf 9.22.78 NBC
Shirley sr 10.26.79 NBC
Here's Boomer ep Looking Good 11.1.81 NBC
A Long Way Home tf 12.6.81 ABC

ASNER, ED*
Route 66 ep Shoulder the Sky, My Lad 3.2.62 CBS

The Defenders   ep   The Cruel Hook 11. 2. 63 CBS
The Outer Limits   ep   It Crawled Out of the Woodwork 12. 9. 63
   ABC
Slattery's People   sr   9. 21. 64 CBS
The Defenders   ep   Hero of the People 10. 8. 64 CBS
The Reporter   ep   Vote for Murder 12. 18. 64 CBS
The Fugitive   ep   Masquerade 3. 23. 65 ABC
The Fugitive   ep   Three Cheers for Little Boy Blue 10. 19. 65
   ABC
The FBI   ep   The Tormentors 4. 10. 66 ABC
The Rat Patrol   ep   The Life Against Death Raid 9. 19. 66 ABC
Gunsmoke   ep   Whispering Tree 11. 12. 66 CBS
The Doomsday Flight   tf   12. 13. 66 NBC
The Fugitive   ep   Run the Man Down 1. 3. 67 ABC
Ironside   ep   The 14th Runner 12. 28. 67 NBC
The FBI   ep   The Dynasty 1. 7. 68 ABC
The Wild Wild West   ep   The Night of the Amnesiac 2. 9. 68
   CBS
Here Come the Brides   ep   12. 11. 68 ABC
Mission: Impossible   ep   The Mind of Stefan Miklos 1. 12. 69
   CBS
The FBI   ep   2. 16. 69 ABC
Ironside   ep   Not with a Whimper but a Bang 4. 10. 69 NBC
The Name of the Game   ep   The Perfect Image 11. 7. 69 NBC
CBS Playhouse   ep   Sadbird   sp   12. 1. 69 CBS
Daughter of the Mind   tf   12. 9. 69 ABC
The House on Greenapple Road   tf   1. 11. 70 ABC
The Mary Tyler Moore Show   sr   9. 19. 70 CBS
The Old Man Who Cried Wolf   tf   10. 13. 70 ABC
The Mary Tyler Moore Show   sr ret   9. 18. 71 CBS
The Mod Squad   ep   The Color of Laughter 10. 12. 71 ABC
The Last Child   tf   10. 5. 71 ABC
They Call It Murder   tf   12. 17. 71 NBC
The Mary Tyler Moore Show   sr ret   9. 16. 72 CBS
Haunts of the Very Rich   tf   9. 20. 72 ABC
The Mod Squad   ep   The Connection 12. 14. 72 ABC
The Police Story   tf   3. 20. 73 NBC
The Mary Tyler Moore Show   sr ret   9. 15. 73 CBS
The Girl Most Likely To...   tf   11. 6. 73 ABC
The Mary Tyler Moore Show   sr ret   9. 14. 74 CBS
Rhoda   ep   Rhoda's Wedding 10. 28. 74 CBS
Twigs   sp   3. 6. 75 CBS
The Imposter   tf   3. 18. 75 NBC
The Mary Tyler Moore Show   sr ret   9. 13. 75 CBS
Death Scream   tf   9. 26. 75 ABC
Hey, I'm Alive   tf   11. 7. 75 ABC
Hawaii Five-O   ep   12. 11. 75 CBS
Rich Man, Poor Man   ms ep   2. 2. 76, 2. 9. 76 ABC
The Mary Tyler Moore Show   sr ret   9. 25. 76 CBS
Police Story   ep   11. 9. 76 NBC
Roots   ep   1. 23. 77, 1. 24. 77 ABC
The Life and Assassination of the Kingfish   tf   3. 21. 77 NBC
Lou Grant   sr   9. 20. 77 CBS
The Gathering   tf   12. 4. 77 ABC

Lou Grant   sr ret   9. 18. 78 CBS
Great Performances   ep   The Good Doctor 10. 5. 78 PBS
Insight   ep   12. 23. 78 NN
Lou Grant   sr ret   9. 17. 79 CBS
The Family Man   tf   12. 19. 79 CBS
Lou Grant   sr ret   9. 22. 80 CBS
Lights!   Action!   Africa!   nar sp   7. 1. 81 CBS
Greatest Heroes of the Bible   ep   Abraham's Sacrifice 8. 15. 81
    NBC
Lou Grant   sr ret   11. 2. 81 CBS
A Small Killing   tf   11. 24. 81 CBS

ASTAIRE, FRED
    SUPP. :
    A Family Upside Down   tf   4. 9. 78 NBC
    Battlestar Galactica   ep   1. 28. 79 ABC
    The Man in the Santa Claus Suit   tf   12. 23. 79 NBC

ASTIN, JOHN
    SUPP. :
    Operation Petticoat   tf   9. 4. 77 ABC
    Operation Petticoat   sr   9. 17. 77 ABC
    Halloween with the Addams Family   sp   10. 30. 77 NBC
    The Love Boat   ep   9. 16. 78 ABC
    Fantasy Island   ep   9. 30. 78 ABC
    Insight   ep   11. 19. 78, 7. 15. 79 NN

ASTIN, PATTY DUKE (previously listed as Patty Duke)
    SUPP. :
    Fire   tf   5. 8. 77 NBC
    Rosetti and Ryan: Men Who Love Women   tf   5. 19. 77 NBC
    Curse of the Black Widow   tf   9. 16. 77 ABC
    Killer on Board   tf   10. 10. 77 NBC
    The Love Boat   ep   Take My Granddaughter, Please 10. 29. 77
        ABC
    The Story Teller   tf   12. 5. 77 NBC
    Rosetti and Ryan   ep   2. 5. 78 NBC
    The Love Boat   ep   Memories of You 2. 13. 78 ABC
    Having Babies III   tf   3. 3. 78 ABC
    A Family Upside Down   tf   4. 9. 78 NBC
    Insight   ep   12. 17. 78 NN
    Before and After   tf   1. 5. 79 ABC
    Women in White   sr   2. 8. 79 ABC
    Hanging by a Thread   tf   5. 8. 79, 5. 9. 79 NBC
    Insight   ep   7. 15. 79 NN
    The Miracle Worker   tf   10. 14. 79 NBC
    The Women's Room   tf   9. 14. 80 ABC
    Mom, the Wolfman and Me   tf   10. 20. 80 NN
    The Baby Sitter   tf   11. 28. 80 ABC
    Girl on the Edge of Town   sp   4. 21. 81 NN
    The Violation of Sarah McDavid   tf   5. 19. 81 CBS
    ABC Theatre for Young Americans   ep   Please Don't Hit Me,
        Mom 9. 20. 81 ABC

AUBERJONOIS, RENE*
    Once upon a Dead Man tf 9.17.71 NBC
    The Birdman tf 9.18.71 NBC
    Night Gallery ep Camera Obscura 12.8.71 NBC
    Shirts/Skins tf 10.9.73 ABC
    Conflicts ep Incident at Vichy 12.6.73 PBS
    Benjamin Franklin: The Ambassador sp 11.21.74 CBS
    The Rookies ep 2.9.75 ABC
    Harry O ep 9.11.75 ABC
    Ellery Queen ep 10.23.75 NBC
    The Bob Newhart Show ep 10.25.75 CBS
    Panache tf 5.15.76 ABC
    Delvecchio ep 9.26.76 CBS
    Baa Baa Black Sheep (a.k.a. The Black Sheep Squadron) ep
      9.28.76 NBC
    Charlie's Angels ep The Seance 12.15.76 ABC
    The Rhinemann Exchange ms 3.10.77, 3.17.77, 3.24.77 NBC
    The Bionic Woman ep 3.16.77 ABC
    The TV TV Show pt 4.30.77 NBC
    Rosetti and Ryan ep 10.20.77
    The Man from Atlantis ep 11.22.77 NBC
    The Dark Secret of Harvest Home tf 1.23.78, 1.24.78 NBC
    Richie Brockelman, Private Eye ep 3.31.78 NBC
    Starsky and Hutch ep 11.14.78 ABC
    The Rockford Files ep 1.5.79 NBC
    The New Adventures of Wonder Woman ep Spaced Out 1.26.79
      CBS
    Mrs. Columbo ep 2.26.79 NBC
    Family ep 3.15.79 ABC
    The Wild Wild West Revisited tf 5.9.79 CBS
    Hart to Hart ep 11.13.79 ABC
    Charlie's Angels ep Angels on Skates 11.21.79 ABC
    Kate Loves a Mystery ep 12.6.79 NBC
    Beyond Westworld ep 3.19.80 CBS
    Ten Speed and Brown Shoe ep 6.13.80 ABC
    More Wild Wild West tf 10.7.80, 10.8.80 CBS
    Scalpels pt 10.26.80 NBC
    Benson sr 10.31.80 ABC
    Benson sr ret 11.6.81 ABC

AUMONT, JEAN PIERRE
    SUPP. :
    The Love Boat ep 10.20.79 ABC
    The French-Atlantic Affair ms 11.15.79, 11.16.79, 11.18.79
      ABC
    Beggarman, Thief tf 11.26.79, 11.27.79 NBC
    The Love Boat ep Reunion 4.5.80 ABC
    The Memory of Eva Ryker tf 5.7.80 CBS
    A Time for Miracles tf 12.21.80 ABC

AVALON, FRANKIE
    SUPP. :
    The Love Boat ep 2.13.78 ABC

Police Story   ep   9. 17. 78 NBC
Fantasy Island   ep   2. 9. 80 ABC

AYRES, LEW
  SUPP. :
  The Bionic Woman   ep   Doomsday Is Tomorrow 1. 26. 77, 2. 7. 77
      ABC
  The Fantastic Journey   ep   6. 16. 77 NBC
  The New Adventures of Wonder Woman   ep   The Man Who
      Could Move the World 9. 30. 77 CBS
  Battlestar Galactica   ep   Saga of a Star World 9. 17. 78 ABC
  Greatest Heroes of the Bible   ep   The Story of Noah 11. 19, 20. 78
      NBC
  Flying High   ep   11. 24. 78 CBS
  Suddenly Love   tf   12. 4. 78 NBC
  Fantasy Island   ep   3. 17. 79 ABC
  Letters from Frank   tf   11. 22. 79 CBS
  The Love Boat   ep   The Frugal Pair 1. 3. 81 ABC
  Magnum, P. I.   ep   The Curse of the King Kamehameha Club
      2. 19. 81 CBS
  Of Mice and Men   tf   11. 29. 81 NBC

AZZARA, CANDACE*
  Calucci's Department   sr   9. 14. 73 CBS
  Rhoda   ep   12. 9. 74 CBS
  Wives   pt   3. 21. 75 CBS
  Fay   ep   10. 9. 75 NBC
  The Cop and the Kid   ep   3. 4. 76 NBC
  The Love Boat II   tf   1. 21. 77 ABC
  Eddie and Herbert   pt   5. 30. 77 CBS
  Kojak   ep   Caper on a Quiet Street 11. 6. 77 CBS
  The Incredible Hulk   ep   5. 31. 78 CBS
  Soap   sr   9. 27. 79 ABC
  House Calls   ep   12. 17. 79, 12. 31. 79 CBS
  Ten Speed and Brown Shoe   ep   5. 30. 80 ABC
  CHiPs   ep   12. 14. 80 NBC
  Trapper John, M. D.   ep   12. 21. 80 CBS
  The Grady Nutt Show   pt   7. 24. 81 NBC

-B-

BABCOCK, BARBARA*
  The Munsters   ep   Bats of a Feather 2. 4. 65 CBS
  The Green Hornet   ep   Programmed for Death 9. 23. 66 ABC
  Star Trek   ep   A Taste of Armageddon 2. 23. 67 NBC
  Mission: Impossible   ep   The Cardinal 11. 17. 68 CBS
  Star Trek   ep   Plato's Step Children 11. 22. 68 NBC
  Mannix   ep   11. 23. 68 CBS
  Hogan's Heroes   ep   3. 22. 69, 9. 27. 70 CBS

The Last Child   tf   10.5.71 ABC
The FBI   ep   The Test 2.20.72 ABC
The Sixth Sense   ep   Coffin, Coffin in the Sky 9.23.72 ABC
Banyon   ep   11.10.72 NBC
Cannon   ep   12.6.72, 1.10.73 CBS
Mannix   ep   2.25.73 CBS
Mannix   ep   The Deadly Madonna 12.2.73 CBS
Medical Center   ep   Nightmare 12.3.73 CBS
The Streets of San Francisco   ep   12.4.75 ABC
Starsky and Hutch   ep   1.28.76 ABC
Jigsaw John   ep   5.31.76 NBC
McMillan   ep   Affair of the Heart 3.20.77 NBC
Quincy, M.E.   ep   A Good Smack in the Mouth 4.15.77 NBC
Rafferty   ep   9.19.77 CBS
The Rockford Files   ep   Irving the Explainer 11.18.77 NBC
Christmas Miracle in Caulfield County, U.S.A.   tf   12.26.77
   NBC
Dallas   sr   11.19.78 CBS
Paris   ep   9.29.79 CBS
Operating Room   pt   10.4.79 NBC
Flo   ep   2.21.81 CBS
Hill Street Blues   ep   Politics as Usual 3.25.81 NBC
Dallas   sr ret   10.9.81
Hill Street Blues   ep   Dressed to Kill 10.29.81 NBC
Taxi   ep   11.12.81 ABC
McClain's Law   ep   A Time of Change 12.4.81 NBC

BACALL, LAUREN
   SUPP.:
   Perfect Gentlemen   tf   3.14.78 CBS
   The Rockford Files   ep   10.12.79 NBC

BACH, CATHERINE*
   Matt Helm   tf   5.7.75 ABC
   Murder in Peyton Place   tf   10.3.77 NBC
   The Dukes of Hazzard   sr   1.26.79 CBS
   The Love Boat   ep   5.3.80 ABC
   The Dukes of Hazzard   sr ret   10.25.80 CBS
   Enos   ep   One Daisy for Summer 1.21.81 CBS
   The Dukes of Hazzard   sr ret   10.6.81 CBS

BACKUS, JIM
   A&C:
   Cain's Hundred   ep   Five for One 12.5.61 NBC
   Gunsmoke   ep   2.10.75 CBS
   SUPP.:
   The ABC Afterschool Special   ep   The Amazing Cosmic Aware-
      ness of Duffy Moon   sp   3.23.77 ABC
   Ark II   ep   5.28.77 CBS
   What's New, Mr. Magoo?   sr vo   9.10.77 CBS
   Charlie's Angels   ep   Angels on Ice 9.21.77 ABC
   CHiPs   ep   9.22.77 NBC
   The Hallmark Hall of Fame   ep   Have I Got a Christmas for
      You   sp   12.16.77 NBC

The Love Boat   ep   The Inspector 2.11.78 ABC
Rescue from Gilligan's Island   tf   10.14.78 NBC
Gift of the Magi   tf   12.21.78 NBC
Sweepstakes   ep   2.16.79 NBC
The Castaways on Gilligan's Island   tf   5.3.79 NBC
Fantasy Island   ep   5.17.80 ABC
The Harlem Globetrotters on Gilligan's Island   tf   5.15.81 NBC

BADDELEY, HERMIONE
  SUPP.:
The Love Boat   ep   10.8.77 ABC
Flying High   ep   11.3.78 CBS
Charlie's Angels   ep   11.15.78 ABC
Sweepstakes   ep   3.9.79 NBC
The New Adventures of Wonder Woman   ep   Stolen Faces
    3.10.79 CBS
Trapper John, M.D.   ep   Second Sight 4.5.81 CBS
Aloha Paradise   ep   4.15.81 ABC

BAIN, BARBARA
  SUPP.:
The Harlem Globetrotters on Gilligan's Island   tf   5.15.81 NBC

BAIN, CONRAD*
Maude   sr   9.12.72 CBS
Maude   sr ret   9.15.73 CBS
Maude   sr ret   9.30.74 CBS
Maude   sr ret   9.8.75
Maude   sr ret   9.20.76
Maude   sr ret   9.12.77 CBS
Grandpa Goes to Washington   ep   10.3.78 NBC
Diff'rent Strokes   sr   11.3.78 NBC
The Love Boat   ep   11.11.78 ABC
The Facts of Life   ep   8.24.79 NBC
Diff'rent Strokes   sr ret   9.21.79 NBC
The Love Boat   ep   Locked Away 11.11.79 ABC
Diff'rent Strokes   sr ret   11.12.80 NBC
CHiPs   ep   12.7.80 NBC
Diff'rent Strokes   sr ret   10.29.81 NBC
The Child Bride of Short Creek   tf   12.7.81 NBC

BAIO, SCOTT*
Blansky's Beauties   sr   2.12.77 NBC
The Love Boat   ep   Graham and Kelly 10.8.77 ABC
Legs   pt   5.19.78 NBC
Happy Days   sr   9.12.78 ABC
Who's Watching the Kids?   sr   9.22.78 NBC
Fantasy Island   ep   5.13.79 ABC
Happy Days   sr ret   9.11.79 ABC
The Boy Who Drank Too Much   tf   2.6.80 CBS
Happy Days   sr ret   11.11.80 ABC
The ABC Afterschool Special   ep   Stoned   sp   11.12.80 ABC
The ABC Afterschool Special   ep   Run, Don't Walk   sp   3.4.81
    ABC

Happy Days   sr ret   10. 6. 81 ABC
Senior Trip   tf   12. 30. 81 CBS

BAKER, DIANE
   A& C:
   delete: Medical Center   ep   12. 23. 74 (repeat of 9. 30. 74)
   Insight   ep   1. 26. 75 NN
   Columbo   ep   5. 2. 76 NBC
   SUPP. :
   The Love Boat   ep   Pacific Princess Overtures 5. 20. 77 ABC
   Barnaby Jones   ep   9. 29. 77 CBS
   Police Story   ep   11. 9. 77 NBC
   Kojak   ep   12. 4. 77 CBS
   Fantasy Island   ep   5. 6. 78 ABC
   The ABC Afterschool Special   ep   One of a Kind   sp   1. 9. 80
     ABC
   Fugitive Family   tf   10. 1. 80 CBS
   Fantasy Island   ep   12. 20. 80 ABC
   Trapper John, M. D.   ep   The Albatross 5. 20. 81 CBS
   Fantasy Island   ep   10. 31. 81 ABC

BAKER, JOE DON
   SUPP. :
   To Kill a Cop   tf   4. 10. 78, 4. 11. 78 NBC
   Eischied   sr   9. 21. 79 NBC
   Power   tf   1. 14. 80, 1. 15. 80 NBC

BALIN, INA
   A& C:
   Mannix   ep   A Matter of the Heart 1. 6. 74, 1. 13. 74 CBS
   SUPP. :
   Danger in Paradise   tf   5. 12. 77 NBC
   Quincy, M. E.   ep   9. 16. 77 NBC
   The Immigrants   ms   11. 20. 78, 11. 21. 78 NN
   Magnum, P. I.   ep   10. 15. 81

BALL, LUCILLE
   SUPP. :
   The Lucille Ball Comedy Special   sp   11. 21. 77 CBS
   Lucy Moves to NBC   sp/pt   2. 8. 80 NBC

BALLARD, KAYE
   A& C:
   Kraft Theatre   ep   The Gentle Grafters 4. 25. 56 NBC
   SUPP. :
   Alice   ep   2. 5. 77 CBS
   The Love Boat   ep   5. 20. 78 ABC
   Li'l Abner in Dogpatch Today   sp   11. 9. 78 NBC
   Fantasy Island   ep   9. 7. 79 ABC
   The Love Boat   ep   The Gift 12. 15. 79 ABC
   Trapper John, M. D.   ep   3. 23. 80 CBS
   The Dream Merchants   ms   5. 12. 80, 5. 19. 80 NN
   The Love Boat   ep   That Old Gang of Mine 4. 11. 81 ABC
   Irene   pt   8. 19. 81 NBC

Here's Boomer   ep   10. 25. 81 NBC
Trapper John, M. D.   ep   Cooperative Care 11. 15. 81 CBS

BALSAM, MARTIN
   A&C:
   Goodyear Playhouse   ep   Stardust II 11. 11. 56 NBC
   SUPP:
   Raid on Entebbe   tf   1. 9. 77 NBC
   Contract on Cherry Street   tf   11. 19. 77 NBC
   The Story Teller   tf   12. 5. 77 NBC
   Siege   tf   4. 26. 78 CBS
   Rainbow   tf   11. 6. 78 NBC
   The Millionaire   tf   12. 19. 78 CBS
   The Seeding of Sarah Burns   tf   4. 7. 79 CBS
   The House on Garibaldi Street   tf   5. 28. 79 ABC
   Archie Bunker's Place   sr   9. 23. 79 CBS
   The Hallmark Hall of Fame   ep   Aunt Mary   sp   12. 5. 79 CBS
   The Love Tapes   tf   5. 9. 80 ABC
   Archie Bunker's Place   sr ret   11. 2. 80 CBS
   The People vs. Jean Harris   tf   5. 7. 81, 5. 8. 81 NBC

BALSAM, TALIA*
   Alexander: The Other Side of Dawn   tf   5. 16. 77 NBC
   Happy Days   ep   9. 13. 77, 9. 20. 77 ABC
   Rosetti and Ryan   ep   10. 20. 77 NBC
   The Initiation of Sarah   tf   2. 6. 78 ABC
   Stickin' Together   tf   4. 14. 78 ABC
   Fast Lane Blues   pt   12. 25. 78 ABC
   The Survival of Dana   tf   5. 29. 79 CBS
   The Runaways   tf   6. 5. 79 NBC
   Ohms   tf   1. 2. 80 CBS
   When the Whistle Blows   ep   4. 25. 80, 6. 14. 80 ABC
   Taxi   ep   12. 3. 80 ABC
   Kent State   tf   2. 8. 81 NBC
   Crazy Times   tf   4. 10. 81 ABC

BANCROFT, ANNE
   SUPP. :
   Jesus of Nazareth   ms   4. 3. 77, 4. 10. 77 NBC

BARASH, OLIVIA*
   Code R   ep   3. 4. 77 CBS
   Daughters   pt   7. 20. 77 NBC
   The Incredible Hulk   tf   11. 4. 77 CBS
   The World of Disney   ep   Child of Glass 5. 14. 78 NBC
   The ABC Weekend Special   ep   The Contest Kid and the Big
      Prize 9. 16. 78 ABC
   In the Beginning   sr   9. 20. 78 CBS
   Charlie's Angels   ep   Mother Angel 10. 15. 78 ABC
   Out of the Blue   sr   9. 9. 79 ABC
   The ABC Weekend Special   ep   Zack and the Magic Factory
      1. 10. 81 ABC
   Little House on the Prairie   ep   Sylvia 2. 9. 81, 2. 16. 81 NBC

Aloha Paradise   ep   3. 25. 81 ABC
Park Place   ep   4. 16. 81 CBS
Ron Howard's Through the Magic Pyramid   tf   12. 6. 81,   12. 13. 81
   NBC

BARBEAU, ADRIENNE
   SUPP. :
   Red Alert   tf   5. 18. 77 CBS
   Quincy, M. E.   ep   5. 27. 77 NBC
   Maude   sr ret   9. 12. 77 CBS
   The Hallmark Hall of Fame   ep   Have I Got a Christmas for
      You   sp   12. 16. 77 NBC
   Return to Fantasy Island   tf   1. 20. 78 ABC
   The Love Boat   ep   1. 21. 78 ABC
   Crash   tf   10. 29. 78 ABC
   The Fighting Nightingales   pt   11. 6. 78 CBS
   A Question of Love   tf   11. 26. 78 ABC
   Someone Is Watching Me!   11. 29. 78 NBC
   Sweepstakes   ep   2. 23. 79 NBC
   The Darker Side of Terror   tf   4. 3. 79 CBS
   Fantasy Island   ep   Class of '69 11. 24. 79 ABC
   Top of the Hill   ms   2. 6. 80,   2. 7. 80 NN
   Valentine Magic on Love Island   tf   2. 15. 80 NBC
   Tourist   pt   7. 17. 80 NN
   Charlie and the Great Balloon Race   tf   7. 12. 81 NBC

BARNES, JOANNA
   A&C:
   Acapulco   ep   3. 20. 61 NBC
   The Investigators   ep   In a Mirror, Darkly 11. 16. 61 CBS
   Follow the Sun   ep   The Primitive Clay 12. 3. 61 ABC
   Alcoa Premiere   ep   Mr. Easy 2. 13. 62 ABC
   Sam Benedict   ep   Tears for a Nobody Doll 10. 13. 62 NBC
   The Eleventh Hour   ep   My Name Is Judith, I'm Lost, You See
      1. 16. 62 NBC
   Alcoa Premiere   ep   The Glass Palace 1. 17. 63 ABC
   Empire   ep   3. 12. 63 ABC
   Dr. Kildare   ep   Make Way for Tomorrow 2. 18. 65 NBC
   Marcus Welby, M. D.   ep   The Working Heart 2. 13. 73 ABC
   The New Adventures of Perry Mason   ep   9. 30. 73 CBS
   McCloud   ep   The Solid Gold Swingers 12. 2. 73 NBC
   Marcus Welby, M. D.   ep   Death Is Only a Side Effect 12. 18. 73
      ABC
   SUPP. :
   The Betty White Show   ep   12. 19. 77 CBS
   Fantasy Island   ep   10. 7. 78 ABC
   Charlie's Angels   ep   Angels on Skates 11. 21. 79 ABC
   When the Whistle Blows   ep   3. 28. 80 ABC

BARNES, PRISCILLA*
   The Rockford Files   ep   The Mayor's Committee from Deer
      Lick Falls 11. 25. 77 NBC
   Starsky and Hutch   ep   3. 1. 78 ABC

Kojak   ep   3. 11. 78 CBS
The American Girls   sr   9. 23. 78 CBS
The Time Machine   tf   11. 5. 78 NBC
Vacation in Hell   tf   5. 21. 79 ABC
Vega$ ep   11. 26. 80 ABC
Scruples   tf   5. 22. 81 ABC
Three's Company   sr   10. 6. 81 ABC

BARRIE, BARBARA
    A&C:
Naked City   ep   To Walk Like a Lion 2. 28. 62 ABC
Route 66   ep   Even Stones Have Eyes 3. 30. 62 CBS
Naked City   ep   And by the Sweat of Thy Brow 10. 10. 62 ABC
The Twilight Zone   ep   Miniature 2. 21. 63 CBS
Alcoa Premiere   ep   The Dark Labyrinth 3. 21. 63 ABC
Ben Casey   ep   Lullaby for Billy Digman 5. 6. 63 ABC
The Nurses   ep   The Love of a Smart Operator 6. 25. 64 CBS
The Defenders   ep   The Seven Hundred-Year-Old Gang 9. 24. 64,
    10. 1. 64 CBS
Ben Casey   ep   A Rambling Discourse on Egyptian Water Clocks
    2. 1. 65 ABC
    SUPP. :
79 Park Avenue   ms   10. 16. 77, 10. 17. 77, 10. 18. 77 NBC
G. E. Theatre   ep   Tell Me My Name   sp   12. 20. 77 CBS
The World of Disney   ep   Child of Glass 5. 14. 78 NBC
Summer of My German Soldier   tf   10. 30. 78 NBC
Visions   ep   Blackout   11. 13. 78 PBS
Barney Miller   ep   12. 14. 78 ABC
Roots--The Next Generations   ms   2. 18-23. 79, 2. 25. 79 ABC
Backstairs at the White House   ms ep   2. 19. 79 NBC
Lou Grant   ep   12. 3. 79, 12. 10. 79 CBS
To Race the Wind   tf   3. 12. 80 CBS
Breaking Away   sr   11. 29. 80 ABC
The Harlem Globetrotters on Gilligan's Island   tf   5. 15. 81 NBC
Private Benjamin   ep   Bye Bye Benjamin 11. 30. 81 CBS
The Children Nobody Wanted   tf   12. 5. 81 CBS

BARRY, GENE
    SUPP. :
Ransom for Alice   tf   6. 2. 77 NBC
Aspen   ms   11. 5. 77, 11. 6. 77, 11. 7. 77 NBC
Charlie's Angels   ep   Angels in the Wings 11. 23. 77 ABC
Fantasy Island   ep   3. 11. 78 ABC
The Love Boat   ep   10. 14. 78 ABC
Greatest Heroes of the Bible   ep   The Story of Abraham 5. 22. 79
    NBC
A Cry for Love   tf   10. 20. 80 NBC
Fantasy Island   ep   1. 3. 81 ABC
Charlie's Angels   ep   Hula Angels 1. 11. 81 ABC
The Love Boat   ep   Vicki the Gambler 4. 11. 81 ABC
Aloha Paradise   ep   4. 29. 81 ABC
The Girl, the Gold Watch and Dynamite   pt   5. 21. 81 NN
The Adventures of Nellie Bly   tf   6. 11. 81 NBC

Greatest Heroes of the Bible   ep   Abraham's Sacrifice 8. 15. 81
    NBC
Fantasy Island   ep   Lillian Russell 11. 28. 81 ABC

BASEHART, RICHARD
    A&C:
    Marcus Welby, M. D.   ep   11. 26. 74 ABC
    SUPP. :
    Stonestreet: Who Killed the Centerfold Model?   tf   1. 16. 77 NBC
    How the West Was Won   ep   2. 19. 78 ABC
    Once Upon a Classic   ep   A Connecticut Yankee in King Arthur's
        Court 5. 23. 78 PBS
    Critical List   tf   9. 11. 78, 9. 12. 78 NBC
    W. E. B.   sr   9. 13. 78 NBC
    Greatest Heroes of the Bible   ep   The Story of the Tower of
        Babel 5. 15. 79 NBC
    The Rebels   ms ep   5. 21. 79 NN
    Marilyn: The Untold Story   tf   9. 28. 80 ABC
    Tales of the Unexpected   ep   The Turn of the Tide 3. 14. 81 NN
    Vega$ ep   3. 25. 81 ABC
    Mysterious Powers of Man   sp hos   10. 11. 81 ABC
    The Love Boat   ep   11. 7. 81 ABC

BASELEON, MICHAEL*
    Route 66   ep   Cries of Persons Close to One 1. 31. 64 CBS
    NET Playhouse   ep   Ten Blocks on the Camino Road 10. 10. 69
        NN
    The Mod Squad   ep   Search and Destroy 10. 27. 70 ABC
    Ironside   ep   The Professionals 9. 28. 71 NBC
    The Mod Squad   ep   The Color of Laughter 10. 12. 71 ABC
    Nichols   ep   The Dirty Half Dozen Run Amuck 10. 28. 71 NBC
    Sarge   ep   11. 16. 71 NBC
    Night Gallery   ep   The Dark Boy 11. 24. 71 NBC
    The FBI   ep   11. 28. 71 ABC
    Cade's County   ep   1. 16. 72 CBS
    Man on a String   tf   2. 18. 72 CBS
    The Sixth Sense   ep   11. 11. 72 ABC
    The Bold Ones: The Doctors   ep   A Quality of Fear 11. 14. 72
        NBC
    The Bold Ones: The Lawyers   ep   12. 12. 72 NBC
    Jigsaw   ep   3. 3. 73 ABC
    The FBI   ep   Sweet Evil 3. 4. 73 ABC
    Toma   ep   3. 21. 73 ABC
    The Rookies   ep   Cauldron 9. 10. 73 ABC
    Chase   ep   The Wooden Horse Caper 9. 11. 73 NBC
    Ironside   ep   Murder by One 9. 20. 73 NBC
    Police Story   ep   The Ten Year Honeymoon 10. 23. 73 NBC
    Toma   ep   Still Water 492 2. 8. 74 ABC
    Lucas Tanner   tf   5. 8. 74 NBC
    Cannon   ep   9. 25. 74 CBS
    Lucas Tanner   ep   10. 23. 74 NBC
    Harry O   ep   Second Sight 11. 7. 74 ABC
    Manhunter   ep   1. 1. 75 CBS

Movin' On   ep   2. 6. 75 NBC
Petrocelli   ep   3. 27. 75 NBC
Last Hours Before Morning   tf   4. 19. 75 NBC
Police Story   ep   11. 28. 75 NBC
Baretta   ep   They Don't Make 'em Like They Used To 10. 20. 76
   ABC
The Streets of San Francisco   ep   11. 18. 76 ABC
Baretta   ep   3. 23. 77 ABC
Barnaby Jones   ep   5. 12. 77 CBS
Cover Girls   tf   5. 18. 77 NBC
Barnaby Jones   ep   10. 13. 77 CBS
Kojak   ep   No License to Kill 2. 11. 78 CBS
Police Story   ep   Day of Terror, Night of Fear 3. 4. 78 NBC
Starsky and Hutch   ep   Deckwatch 5. 17. 78 ABC
The Users   tf   10. 1. 78 ABC
CHiPs   ep   2. 17. 79 NBC
The Duke   ep   4. 5. 79 NBC
Detective School   ep   8. 21. 79 ABC
Eischied   ep   12. 30. 79 NBC
Barnaby Jones   ep   1. 31. 80 CBS
CHiPs   ep   2. 2. 80 NBC
Flamingo Road   ep   3. 9. 81, 4. 2. 81 NBC
Return of the Rebels   tf   10. 17. 81 CBS

BASINGER, KIM*
Charlie's Angels   ep   Angels in Chains 10. 20. 76 ABC
McMillan   ep   Dark Sunrise 1. 2. 77 NBC
Dog and Cat   sr   3. 5. 77 ABC
Dog and Cat   tf   7. 22. 77 ABC
Ghost on Flight 401   tf   2. 19. 78 NBC
Katie: Portrait of a Centerfold   tf   10. 23. 78 NBC
Vega$ ep   11. 1. 78 ABC
From Here to Eternity   ms   2. 14. 79, 2. 21. 79, 2. 28. 79 NBC
From Here to Eternity   sr   3. 10. 80 NBC
From Here to Eternity   sr ret   8. 3. 80 NBC
Killjoy   tf   10. 22. 81 CBS

BAXTER, MEREDITH   see   BIRNEY, MEREDITH BAXTER

BEATTY, NED*
Footsteps   tf   10. 3. 72 CBS
The Waltons   ep   3. 1. 73 CBS
The Execution of Private Slovik   tf   3. 13. 74 NBC
The Rockford Files   ep   Profit and Loss 12. 20. 74, 12. 27. 74
   NBC
Gunsmoke   ep   1. 13. 75 CBS
Attack on Terror: The FBI vs. the Ku Klux Klan   tf   2. 20. 75,
   2. 21. 75 CBS
Lucas Tanner   ep   4. 3. 75 NBC
Petrocelli   ep   9. 10. 75 NBC
The Deadly Tower   tf   10. 18. 75 NBC
The Rookies   ep   Shadow of a Man 4. 20. 76 ABC
Hawaii Five-O   ep   10. 14. 76 CBS

The Rockford Files   ep   Return to the 38th Parallel 12.10.76
    NBC
Visions   ep   The Gardener's Son 1.6.77 PBS
Tales of the Unexpected   ep   2.2.77 NBC
Tail Gunner Joe   tf   2.6.77 NBC
Delvecchio   ep   2.20.77 CBS
Nashville 99   ep   4.1.77 CBS
Lucan   tf   5.22.77 ABC
Szysznyk   sr   8.1.77 CBS
Visions   ep   Alambrista!   The Illegal 10.16.77 PBS
Szysznyk   sr ret   12.7.77 CBS
A Question of Love   tf   11.26.78 ABC
Friendly Fire   tf   4.22.79 ABC
All God's Children   tf   2.28.80 ABC
Guyana Tragedy: The Story of Jim Jones   tf   4.15.80 CBS
The Violation of Sarah McDavid   tf   5.19.81 CBS
Splendor in the Grass   tf   10.26.81 NBC
NBC Live Theatre   ep   All the Way Home   sp   12.21.81 NBC

BEDELIA, BONNIE
    SUPP.:
    Walking Through the Fire   tf   5.15.79 CBS
    Salem's Lot   tf   11.17.79, 11.24.79 CBS
    Tourist   pt   7.17.80 NN
    Fighting Back   tf   12.7.80 ABC

BELFORD, CHRISTINE*
    Vanished   tf   3.8.71, 3.9.71 NBC
    Owen Marshall, Counselor at Law   ep   10.14.71 ABC
    Marcus Welby, M.D.   ep   Basic Moment 1.4.72 ABC
    Banacek: Detour to Nowhere   tf   3.20.72 NBC
    Cool Million   tf   10.16.72 NBC
    Alias Smith and Jones   ep   Bushwack 10.21.72 ABC
    Owen Marshall, Counselor at Law   ep   11.16.72 ABC
    Mannix   ep   12.17.72 CBS
    Cannon   ep   2.14.73 CBS
    Jigsaw   ep   3.3.73 ABC
    Barnaby Jones   ep   3.18.73 CBS
    The Six Million Dollar Man   ep   Survival of the Fittest 1.25.74
        ABC
    Marcus Welby, M.D.   ep   9.24.74 ABC
    Manhunter   ep   12.18.74 ABC
    Kate McShane   tf   4.11.75 CBS
    Medical Story   ep   Us Against the World 12.4.75 NBC
    Harry O   ep   Legacy 12.11.75 ABC
    The New, Original Wonder Woman   ep   Wonder Woman Meets
        Baroness Von Gunther 4.21.76 ABC
    The Million Dollar Rip-off   tf   9.22.76 NBC
    Barnaby Jones   ep   10.7.76 CBS
    Most Wanted   ep   1.15.77 ABC
    Tales of the Unexpected   ep   2.16.77 NBC
    Susan and Sam   pt   7.13.77 NBC
    Quincy, M.E.   ep   Holding Pattern 11.4.77 NBC

To Kill a Cop   tf   4. 10. 78,   4. 11. 78 NBC
Colorado C. I.   pt   5. 26. 78 CBS
The White Shadow   ep   12. 4. 78 CBS
The Incredible Hulk   ep   12. 15. 78,   1. 17. 79 CBS
The Paper Chase   ep   1. 19. 79 CBS
Barnaby Jones   ep   2. 8. 79 CBS
Dear Detective   ep   4. 11. 79 CBS
High Midnight   tf   11. 27. 79 CBS
Hart to Hart   ep   12. 4. 79 ABC
Desperate Voyage   tf   11. 29. 80 CBS
CHiPs   ep   Wheels of Justice 12. 21. 80 NBC
The Incredible Hulk   ep   2. 13. 81 CBS
Nero Wolfe   ep   4. 10. 81 NBC
The Greatest American Hero   ep   The Beast in the Black
   12. 9. 81 ABC
Insight   ep   Missing Person's Bureau 12. 21. 81 NN

BEL GEDDES, BARBARA
   SUPP. :
   Dallas   sr   4. 2. 78 CBS
   Dallas   sr ret   9. 23. 78 CBS
   Dallas   sr ret   9. 21. 79 CBS
   Dallas   sr ret   11. 7. 80 CBS
   Dallas   sr ret   10. 9. 81 CBS

BELLAMY, RALPH
   A&C:
   Our American Heritage   ep   Divided We Stand 10. 18. 59 NBC
   Adventures of the Queen   tf   2. 14. 75 CBS
   Return to Earth   tf   5. 14. 76 ABC
   SUPP. :
   Hunter   sr   2. 18. 77 CBS
   Charlie Cobb: Nice Night for a Hanging   tf   6. 9. 77 NBC
   Westside Medical   ep   8. 11. 77,   8. 18. 77 ABC
   Julie Farr, M. D.   ep   4. 11. 78 ABC
   Testimony of Two Men   ms   5. 1. 78,   5. 2. 78,   5. 3. 78 NN
   Wheels   ms   5. 7. 78,   5. 8. 78,   5. 9. 78,   5. 14. 78,   5. 15. 78 NBC
   The Clone Master   tf   9. 14. 78 NBC
   The Millionaire   tf   12. 19. 78 CBS
   The Billion Dollar Threat   tf   4. 15. 79 ABC
   Power   tf   1. 14. 80,   1. 15. 80 NBC
   The Memory of Eva Ryker   tf   5. 7. 80 CBS
   Fantasy Island   ep   5. 17. 80 ABC
   Condominium   ms   11. 20. 80,   11. 24. 80 NN
   The Love Boat   ep   Split Personality 2. 14. 81 ABC
   Walking Tall   ep   2. 14. 81 NBC
   Aloha Paradise   ep   3. 25. 81 ABC

BELLER, KATHLEEN*
   Baretta   ep   The Copelli Oath 3. 7. 75 ABC
   Crime Club   tf   4. 3. 75 CBS
   Hawaii Five-O   ep   11. 21. 75 CBS
   At Ease   pt   9. 7. 76 CBS

Visions ep The Great Cherub Knitwear Strike 11. 25. 76 PBS
The Six Million Dollar Man ep To Catch the Eagle 3. 6. 77
  ABC
Most Wanted ep 3. 21. 77 ABC
Something for Joey tf 4. 6. 77 CBS
Barnaby Jones ep Runaway to Terror 5. 19. 77 CBS
Having Babies III tf 3. 3. 78 ABC
What Really Happened to the Class of '65? ep Class Misfit
  3. 9. 78 NBC
Are You in the House Alone? tf 9. 20. 78 CBS
Mother and Daughter: The Loving War tf 1. 25. 80 ABC
American Short Story ep Rappaccini's Daughter 2. 25. 80 PBS
No Place to Hide tf 3. 4. 81 CBS
The Manions of America ms ep 10. 1. 81, 10. 2. 81 ABC

BELLWOOD, PAMELA*
Ironside ep Once More for Joey 1. 17. 74 NBC
Wide World of Mystery ep The Book of Murder 3. 19. 74 ABC
Rhoda ep 11. 11. 74 CBS
Mannix ep 1. 12. 75 CBS
Police Story ep 2. 11. 75 NBC
Matt Helm ep 10. 11. 75 ABC
Baretta ep 11. 12. 75 ABC
Serpico ep 1. 14. 77 NBC
The Hallmark Hall of Fame ep Emily, Emily sp 2. 7. 77
  NBC
Visions ep The War Widow 2. 10. 77 PBS
Westside Medical ep 3. 24. 77 ABC
Deadman's Curve tf 2. 3. 78 CBS
Switch ep 8. 13. 78 CBS
W. E. B. sr 9. 13. 78 NBC
Hagen ep 3. 1. 80, 3. 22. 80 CBS
Dynasty sr 1. 12. 81 ABC
Dynasty sr ret 11. 4. 81 ABC

BENJAMIN, RICHARD
  SUPP. :
  Quark pt 5. 7. 77 NBC
  Quark sr 2. 24. 78 NBC
  The Hallmark Hall of Fame ep Fame sp 11. 30. 78 NBC

BENNETT, JOAN
  SUPP. :
  Suddenly Love tf 12. 4. 78 NBC
  This House Possessed tf 2. 6. 81 ABC

BENTON, BARBI*
  The Great American Beauty Contest tf 2. 13. 73 ABC
  Third Girl from the Left tf 10. 16. 73 ABC
  McCloud ep 9. 21. 75 NBC
  Sugar Time sr 8. 13. 77 ABC
  Fantasy Island ep 4. 15. 78 ABC
  Sugar Time sr ret 4. 17. 78 ABC

Murder at the Mardi Gras tf 5.10.78 NBC
The Love Boat ep Parlez Vous 9.16.78 ABC
Fantasy Island ep 11.18.78, 10.5.79 ABC
Vega$ ep 10.31.79 ABC
The Love Boat ep Not Now, I'm Dying 11.24.79 ABC
Fantasy Island ep 1.26.80 ABC
When the Whistle Blows ep Miss Hardhat U.S.A. 6.7.80 ABC
Fantasy Island ep 11.22.80 ABC
Charlie's Angels ep 12.14.80 ABC
Fantasy Island ep 1.31.81 ABC
The Love Boat ep 2.21.81 ABC
CHiPs ep Ponch's Angels 2.28.81 NBC
Lobo ep The Cowboy Connection 3.31.81 NBC
Fantasy Island ep Ziegfeld Girls 10.17.81 ABC

BERGEN, POLLY
   SUPP.:
   79 Park Avenue ms 10.16.77, 10.17.77, 10.18.77 NBC
   Telethon tf 11.6.77 ABC
   The Love Boat ep 11.19.77 ABC
   How to Pick Up Girls tf 11.3.78 ABC
   Li'l Abner in Dogpatch Today sp 11.9.78 NBC
   The Million Dollar Face tf 3.12.81 NBC

BERGMAN, INGRID*
   Childhood sr hos 2.16.77 PBS

BERLE, MILTON
   SUPP.:
   Sheila pt 8.29.77 CBS
   The Love Boat ep Gotcha 10.15.77 ABC
   The Hallmark Hall of Fame ep Have I Got a Christmas for
      You sp 12.16.77 NBC
   The Love Boat ep The Harder They Fall 12.8.79 ABC
   CHiPs ep 12.7.80 NBC
   The Love Boat ep Zeke and Zack 12.5.81 ABC

BERLINGER, WARREN
   SUPP.:
   Charlie's Angels ep Dirty Business 2.2.77 ABC
   Alice ep 2.12.77 CBS
   Operation Petticoat sr 9.18.78 ABC
   CHiPs ep 9.23.78 NBC
   The Love Boat ep 3.3.79 ABC
   The Misadventures of Sheriff Lobo ep 10.16.79 NBC
   Charlie's Angels ep One of Our Angels Is Missing 1.16.80
      ABC
   The Dukes of Hazzard ep 1.18.80 CBS
   CHiPs ep 1.26.80 NBC
   Alice ep 11.9.80 CBS
   Happy Days ep 1.27.81 ABC
   Concrete Cowboys ep 3.14.81 CBS
   Crash Island pt 4.11.81 NBC

Quick and Quiet   pt   8. 18. 81 CBS
CHiPs   ep   Suicide Stunt 10. 4. 81 NBC
Trapper John, M. D.   ep   Hate Is Enough 10. 25. 81 CBS
Strike Force   ep   11. 13. 81 ABC
Today's FBI   ep   Fugitive 11. 29. 81 ABC

BERNARDI, HERSCHEL
    SUPP. :
    Seventh Avenue   ms   2. 10. 77, 2. 17. 77, 2. 24. 77 NBC
    Hollywood Television Theatre   ep   Actor 2. 21. 78 PBS
    Sweepstakes   ep   2. 23. 79 NBC

BERRY, KEN
    A& C:
    Over and Out   pt   8. 11. 76 NBC
    SUPP. :
    The Life and Times of Grizzly Adams   ep   2. 23. 77 NBC
    The Love Boat II   tf   1. 21. 77 ABC
    The ABC Short Story Special   ep   Valentine's Second Chance
        1. 29. 77 ABC
    Apple Pie   ep   9. 30. 78 ABC
    Fantasy Island   ep   10. 21. 78 ABC
    Fantasy Island   ep   3. 3. 79 ABC
    The Love Boat   ep   Second String Mom 5. 12. 79 ABC
    Featherstone's Nest   pt   8. 1. 79 CBS
    Little House on the Prairie   ep   10. 15. 79 NBC
    Fantasy Island   ep   12. 22. 79, 11. 29. 80 ABC
    Aloha Paradise   ep   3. 11. 81 ABC
    Fantasy Island   ep   5. 9. 81 ABC

BERTINELLI, VALERIE*
    One Day at a Time   sr   12. 16. 75 CBS
    One Day at a Time   sr ret   9. 28. 76 CBS
    One Day at a Time   sr ret   9. 20. 77 CBS
    The CBS Festival of Lively Arts   ep   The Secret of Charles
        Dickens   sp   4. 16. 78 CBS
    The Hardy Boys   ep   5. 7. 78 ABC
    One Day at a Time   sr ret   9. 18. 78 CBS
    One Day at a Time   sr ret   9. 25. 79 CBS
    Young Love, First Love   tf   11. 20. 79 CBS
    One Day at a Time   sr ret   11. 9. 80 CBS
    The Promise of Love   tf   11. 11. 80 CBS
    One Day at a Time   sr ret   10. 11. 81 CBS
    The Princess and the Cabbie   tf   11. 3. 81 CBS

BESSELL, TED
    SUPP. :
    Breaking Up Is Hard to Do   tf   9. 5. 79, 9. 7. 79 ABC
    Goodtime Harry   sr   7. 26. 80 NBC
    The Acorn People   tf   3. 2. 81 NBC

BETHUNE, ZINA
    SUPP. :
    CHiPs   ep   10. 22. 77 NBC

The Hardy Boys/Nancy Drew Mysteries   ep   Arson and Old
    Lace 4. 1. 78 ABC
The Next Step Beyond   ep   7. 10. 79 NN
The ABC Afterschool Special   ep   The Gymnast 10. 29. 80 ABC

BETTGER, LYLE
   A& C:
   Hawaii Five-O   ep   9. 12. 75 CBS
   SUPP. :
   Hawaii Five-O   ep   12. 22. 77,   3. 23. 78,   12. 14. 78,   12. 25. 79,
    4. 5. 80 CBS
   M Station: Hawaii   tf   6. 10. 80 CBS

BETZ, CARL
   A& C:
   Insight   ep   10. 21. 73 NN
   The Daughters of Joshua Cabe Return   tf   1. 28. 75 ABC
   Jigsaw John   ep   4. 19. 76 NBC
   SUPP. :
   Most Wanted   ep   2. 5. 77 ABC
   Quincy, M. E.   ep   3. 11. 77 NBC
   The Hardy Boys/Nancy Drew Mysteries   ep   A Haunting We
    Will Go 4. 3. 77 ABC
   Kingston Confidential   ep   7. 13. 77 NBC

BIERI, RAMON
   A& C:
   The Doctors and the Nurses   ep   The Politician 3. 16. 65 CBS
   Search   ep   1. 31. 73 NBC
   Cannon   ep   2. 14. 73 CBS
   Kung Fu   ep   The Salamander 12. 6. 73 ABC
   Manhunter   ep   10. 23. 74 CBS
   The Gun   tf   11. 13. 74 ABC
   The Rockford Files   ep   12. 6. 74 NBC
   SUPP. :
   Tales of the Unexpected   ep   The Final Chapter 2. 2. 77 NBC
   The Rhinemann Exchange   ms   3. 10. 77,   3. 17. 77,   3. 24. 77 NBC
   The San Pedro Bums   tf   5. 13. 77 ABC
   Panic in Needle Park   tf   6. 23. 77 NBC
   A Love Affair: The Eleanor and Lou Gehrig Story   tf   1. 15. 78
    NBC
   Quincy, M. E.   ep   Gone but Not Forgotten 2. 17. 78 NBC
   Charlie's Angels   ep   Circus of Terror 3. 29. 78 ABC
   Wheels   ms   5. 7. 78,   5. 8. 78,   5. 9. 78,   5. 14. 78,   5. 15. 78 NBC
   True Grit: A Further Adventure   tf   5. 19. 78 ABC
   Switch   ep   6. 25. 78 CBS
   The Eddie Capra Mysteries   ep   Who Killed Lloyd Wesley Jor-
    dan? 9. 29. 78 NBC
   The Amazing Spider-Man   ep   11. 25. 78 CBS
   How the West Was Won   ep   3. 5. 79 ABC
   Charlie's Angels   ep   Rosemary for Remembrance 5. 2. 79 ABC
   Joe's World   sr   1. 2. 80 NBC
   CHiPs   ep   2. 2. 80 NBC
   Joe's World   sr ret   5. 10. 80 NBC

A Christmas Without Snow   tf   12. 9. 80 CBS
A Matter of Wife and Death   tf   1. 13. 81 CBS
Nero Wolfe   ep   1. 30. 81 NBC
Palmerstown   ep   3. 10. 81 CBS
Bret Maverick   sr   12. 1. 81 NBC

BIKEL, THEODORE
   A&C:
   Directions   ep   The Fifth Cup 4. 18. 76 NN
   Victory at Entebbe   tf   12. 13. 76 ABC
   SUPP.:
   Charlie's Angels   ep   Angels on a String 1. 19. 77 ABC
   Columbo   ep   5. 22. 77 NBC
   The San Pedro Beach Bums   ep   10. 10. 77 ABC
   Police Woman   ep   2. 15. 78 NBC
   Loose Change   ms   2. 26. 78, 2. 27. 78, 2. 28. 78 NBC
   The Amazing Spider-Man   ep   4. 19. 78 CBS
   Fantasy Island   ep   5. 6. 78 ABC
   Testimony of Two Men   ms   5. 1. 78, 5. 2. 78, 5. 3. 78 NN
   Stingiest Man in Town   sp vo   12. 23. 78 NBC
   Higher Than Heaven   sp   9. 23. 79 NN
   Return of the King   tf vo   5. 11. 80 ABC

BILL, TONY
   SUPP.:
   Washington: Behind Closed Doors   ms   9. 6. 77, 9. 7. 77, 9. 8. 77,
      9. 9. 77, 9. 10. 77, 9. 11. 77 ABC
   What Really Happened to the Class of 65?   sr hos   12. 8. 77 NBC
   The Initiation of Sarah   tf   2. 6. 78 ABC
   With This Ring   tf   5. 5. 78 ABC
   Are You in the House Alone?   tf   9. 20. 78 CBS

BIRNEY, DAVID
   A&C:
   Playhouse New York   ep   The Last GIs 5. 24. 72 NN
   Hawaii Five-O   ep   9. 12. 75 CBS
   The Adams Chronicles   ep   3. 2. 76 PBS
   SUPP.:
   Tales of the Unexpected   ep   2. 23. 77 NBC
   Hawaii Five-O   ep   2. 9. 78 CBS
   Testimony of Two Men   ms   5. 1. 78, 5. 2. 78, 5. 3. 78 NN
   Fantasy Island   ep   9. 16. 78 ABC
   Greatest Heroes of the Bible   ep   The Story of Daniel in the
      Lion's Den 11. 22. 78 NBC
   Someone Is Watching Me!   tf   11. 29. 78 NBC
   Family   ep   1. 25. 79 ABC
   High Midnight   tf   11. 27. 79 CBS
   Ohms   tf   1. 2. 80 CBS
   Mom, the Wolfman and Me   tf   10. 20. 80 NN
   The CBS Afternoon Playhouse   ep   I Think I'm Having a Baby
      sp   3. 3. 81 CBS
   The Five of Me   tf   5. 12. 81 CBS
   Jacqueline Susann's Valley of the Dolls 1981   tf   10. 19. 81, 10. 20. 81
      CBS

BIRNEY, MEREDITH BAXTER (previously listed as Meredith Baxter)
SUPP. :
The Love Boat   ep   Centerfold 9. 24. 77 ABC
What Really Happened to the Class of '65?   ep   1. 5. 78 NBC
Family   sr ret   9. 21. 78 ABC
Little Women   tf   10. 2. 78,   10. 3. 78 NBC
The Family Man   tf   12. 19. 79 CBS
Beulah Land   ms   10. 7. 80,   10. 8. 80,   10. 9. 80 NBC
The Two Lives of Carol Litner   tf   10. 14. 81 CBS

BISHOP, JOEY
A& C:
Chico and the Man   ep   2. 25. 76 NBC
SUPP. :
Sorority '62   pt   1. 78 NN
Trapper John, M. D.   ep   The Pagoda Curse 1. 25. 81 CBS

BIXBY, BILL
A& C:
The Twilight Zone   ep   Thirty Fathom Grave 1. 10. 63 CBS
Insight   ep   3. 5. 74,   3. 12. 74 NN
Rich Man, Poor Man   ep   2. 2. 76,   2. 9. 76,   2. 16. 76,   3. 1. 76 ABC
Insight   ep   6. 29. 74 NN
SUPP. :
Fantasy Island   ep   1. 14. 77 ABC
The Natural Look   pt   7. 6. 77 NBC
Tales of the Unexpected   ep   8. 24. 77 NBC
Black Market Baby   tf   10. 7. 77 ABC
The Love Boat   ep   Message for Maureen 10. 15. 77 ABC
The Incredible Hulk   tf   11. 4. 77 CBS
The Incredible Hulk   sp ep   Death in the Family 11. 28. 77 CBS
The Oregon Trail   ep   11. 30. 77 NBC
The Incredible Hulk   sr   3. 10. 78 CBS
The Incredible Hulk   sr ret   9. 22. 78 CBS
The Incredible Hulk   sr ret   9. 21. 79 CBS
The Incredible Hulk   sr ret   11. 7. 80 CBS

BLACK, KAREN
SUPP. :
The Strange Possession of Mrs. Oliver   tf   2. 28. 77 NBC
Power   tf   1. 14. 80,   1. 15. 80 NBC
Where the Ladies Go   tf   3. 14. 80 ABC
Police Story   ep   Confessions of a Lady Cop 4. 28. 80 NBC

BLAINE, VIVIAN
SUPP. :
Fantasy Island   ep   9. 23. 78 ABC
Katie: Portrait of a Centerfold   tf   10. 23. 78 NBC
The Cracker Factory   tf   3. 16. 79 ABC
Fast Friends   tf   3. 19. 79 NBC
Sooner or Later   tf   3. 25. 79 NBC

BLAIR, JANET
    SUPP. :
    Switch   ep   12. 12. 77 CBS
    Fantasy Island   ep   1. 26. 80 ABC

BLAKE, AMANDA
    A&C:
    Schlitz Playhouse of Stars   ep   Crossroads 8. 1. 52 CBS
    Cavalcade of America   ep   Breakfast at Nancy's 10. 13. 53 ABC
    SUPP. :
    The Quest   ep   10. 27. 76 NBC
    The Love Boat   ep   9. 22. 79 ABC

BLAKE, ROBERT
    SUPP. :
    Baretta   sr ret   9. 28. 77 ABC
    Joe Dancer   tf   1. 29. 81 NBC
    Joe Dancer: The Monkey Mission   tf   3. 23. 81 NBC
    Of Mice and Men   tf   11. 29. 81 NBC

BLAKELY, SUSAN
    SUPP. :
    Secrets   tf   2. 20. 77 ABC
    Make Me an Offer   tf   1. 11. 80 ABC
    A Cry for Love   tf   10. 20. 80 NBC
    The Oklahoma City Dolls   tf   1. 23. 81 ABC
    The Bunker   tf   1. 27. 81

BLAKLEY, RONEE*
    Vega$ ep   1. 26. 78
    Desperate Women   tf   10. 25. 78 NBC
    Visions   ep   Ladies in Waiting 1. 8. 79 PBS
    Runaways   tf   6. 26. 79 NBC
    The Love Boat   ep   The Gift 12. 15. 79 ABC
    Beyond Westworld   ep   3. 19. 80 CBS
    The Oklahoma City Dolls   tf   1. 23. 81 ABC

BLANCHARD, SUSAN*
    How to Succeed in Business Without Really Trying   pt   6. 27. 75
        ABC
    Police Woman   ep   12. 23. 75 NBC
    Mr. T & Tina   sr   9. 25. 76 ABC
    The Magnificent Magnet of Santa Mesa   tf   6. 19. 77 NBC
    Police Woman   ep   1. 11. 78 NBC
    The President's Mistress   tf   2. 10. 78 CBS
    The Love Boat   ep   Until the Last Goodbye 2. 11. 78 ABC
    The New Maverick   tf   9. 3. 78 ABC
    Young Maverick   sr   11. 28. 79 CBS
    Saint Peter   pt   3. 8. 81 NBC
    She's in the Army Now   pt   5. 22. 81 ABC

BLONDELL, JOAN
    SUPP. :
    Rosetti and Ryan   ep   10. 13. 77 NBC

Battered   tf 9. 26. 78 NBC
The Love Boat   ep   Ship of Ghouls 10. 28. 78 ABC
Sweepstakes   ep   2. 2. 79 NBC
Fantasy Island   ep   5. 12. 79 ABC
The Rebels   ms   5. 14. 79, 5. 21. 79 NN

BLOOM, CLAIRE
SUPP. :
The CBS Children's Library: Misunderstood Monsters   ep
    Beauty and the Beast   sp vo 4. 7. 81 CBS

BLYTH, ANN
SUPP. :
Quincy, M. E.   ep   The Trick of Death 9. 28. 78 NBC

BOCHNER, LLOYD*
Hong Kong   sr   10. 28. 60 ABC
The Twilight Zone   ep   To Serve Man 3. 26. 62 CBS
The Richard Boone Show   sr   9. 24. 63 NBC
The Man from U. N. C. L. E.   ep   The See-Paris-and-Die Affair
    3. 1. 65 NBC
Kraft Suspense Theatre   ep   The Trains of Silence 6. 10. 65 NBC
The Wild Wild West   ep   The Night of the Puppeteer 2. 25. 66
    CBS
Daniel Boone   ep   The Trap 3. 17. 66 NBC
The Green Hornet   ep   The Silent Gun 9. 9. 66 ABC
Bonanza   ep   The Prince 4. 2. 67 NBC
The Man from U. N. C. L. E.   ep   The Summit-Five Affair
    9. 11. 67 NBC
The Big Valley   ep   Time After Midnight 10. 2. 67 ABC
Strangers on the Run   tf   10. 31. 67 NBC
Daniel Boone   ep   The Secret Code 12. 14. 67 NBC
Daniel Boone   ep   The Imposter 1. 18. 68 NBC
The Name of the Game   ep   Ordeal 11. 22. 68 NBC
Judd, for the Defense   ep   Transplant 12. 27. 68 ABC
Mannix   ep   The Girl Who Came In with the Tide 2. 1. 69 CBS
Mission: Impossible   ep   The Glass Cage 2. 2. 69 CBS
It Takes a Thief   ep   2. 18. 69 ABC
Bewitched   ep   2. 20. 69 ABC
The Outsider   ep   All the Social Graces 4. 12. 69 NBC
Daniel Boone   ep   The Landlords 3. 5. 70 NBC
Crowhaven Farm   tf   11. 24. 70 ABC
The D. A.   ep   10. 15. 71 NBC
The Bold Ones: The Doctors   ep   Moment of Crisis 1. 2. 72
    NBC
Emergency   ep   9. 16. 72 NBC
Mission: Impossible   ep   The Deal 9. 30. 72 CBS
Hec Ramsey   ep   The Green Feather 11. 17. 72 NBC
Ironside   ep   Shadow Soldiers 12. 21. 72 NBC
McCloud   ep   The Park Avenue Rustlers 12. 24. 72 NBC
Mannix   ep   2. 25. 73 CBS
Columbo   ep   The Most Dangerous Match 3. 4. 73 NBC
Barnaby Jones   ep   3. 18. 73 CBS

The Magician   ep   Man on Fire 11. 20. 73 NBC
The Six Million Dollar Man   ep   Day of the Robot 2. 8. 74 ABC
Gunsmoke   ep   The Iron Blood of Courage 2. 18. 74 CBS
Cannon   ep   Triangle of Terror 3. 13. 74 CBS
Chopper One   ep   3. 14. 74 ABC
Police Story   ep   3. 19. 74 NBC
Medical Center   ep   Tainted Lady 11. 11. 74 CBS
The Rookies   ep   S. W. A. T.   2. 17. 75 ABC
Adams of Eagle Lake   ep   The Treasure Chest Murder 2. 26. 75
    ABC
Hawaii Five-O   ep   9. 12. 75 CBS
The Barbary Coast   ep   9. 22. 75 ABC
Barnaby Jones   ep   10. 17. 75 CBS
Ellery Queen   ep   10. 23. 75 NBC
Switch   ep   11. 11. 75 CBS
Bronk   ep   2. 1. 76 CBS
McCloud   ep   3. 21. 76 NBC
Richie Brockelman, Private Eye   pt   10. 27. 76 NBC
Mystery of the Week   ep   The Nurse Killer 11. 11. 76 ABC
The Bionic Woman   ep   Biofeedback 1. 12. 77 ABC
McMillan   ep   Philip's Game 1. 23. 77 ABC
The Six Million Dollar Man   ep   Carnival of Spies 2. 13. 77 ABC
The Feather and Father Gang   ep   3. 27. 77 ABC
Terraces   tf   6. 27. 77 NBC
The Six Million Dollar Man   ep   Deadly Countdown 9. 25. 77,
    10. 2. 77 ABC
The San Pedro Beach Bums   ep   12. 19. 77 ABC
The Hardy Boys/Nancy Drew Mysteries   ep   1. 22. 78 ABC
Vega$ ep   10. 25. 78 ABC
The Immigrants   ms   11. 20. 78, 11. 27. 78 NN
Greatest Heroes of the Bible   ep   The Story of Moses and the
    Ten Commandments 11. 21. 78 NBC
Charlie's Angels   ep   12. 6. 78 ABC
Fantasy Island   ep   12. 16. 78 ABC
The Best Place to Be   tf   5. 27. 79 NBC
Mary and Joseph: A Story of Faith   tf   12. 9. 79 NBC
Charlie's Angels   ep   Angel Hunt 12. 5. 79 ABC
Hawaii Five-O   ep   1. 1. 80 CBS
Trapper John, M. D.   ep   2. 3. 80 CBS
Vega$ ep   2. 27. 80 ABC
Hart to Hart   ep   5. 6. 80 ABC
Dynasty   sr   1. 12. 81 ABC
Fantasy Island   ep   Cyrano 10. 24. 81 ABC
Darkroom   ep   Daisies 12. 25. 81 ABC

BOLGER, RAY
   SUPP. :
   The Love Boat   ep   11. 10. 77 ABC
   Three on a Date   tf   2. 17. 78 ABC
   Fantasy Island   ep   The Over-the-Hill Caper 4. 15. 78 ABC
   The Love Boat   ep   My Sister Irene 1. 13. 79 ABC
   Little House on the Prairie   ep   1. 22. 79 NBC
   Aloha Paradise   ep   4. 1. 81 ABC
   Most Joyful Mystery   sp   12. 24. 81 NN

BOLOGNA, JOSEPH
    A&C:
    Woman of the Year   tf   7. 28. 76 CBS
    SUPP. :
    Torn Between Two Lovers   tf   5. 2. 79 CBS

BONADUCE, DANNY
    A&C:
    Partridge Family: 2200 AD   sr vo   9. 7. 74 CBS
    Police Story   ep   11. 21. 75 NBC
    SUPP. :
    Honest Al's A-Ok Used Car and Trailer Rental Tigers   pt   1. 78
      NN
    Eight Is Enough   ep   1. 11. 78 ABC
    The CBS Afternoon Playhouse   ep   Joey and Redhawk 12. 4-8. 78
      CBS
    CHiPs   ep   9. 30. 78 NBC
    California Fever   ep   12. 4. 79 CBS
    CHiPs   ep   Karate 3. 8. 81 NBC

BONO, SONNY
    SUPP. :
    Fantasy Island   ep   9. 23. 78 ABC
    The Love Boat   ep   Oh, My Aching Brother 9. 30. 78 ABC
    Murder in Music City   tf   1. 16. 79 NBC
    The Love Boat   ep   The Sounds of Silence 3. 17. 79 ABC
    Fantasy Island   ep   11. 10. 79 ABC
    The Love Boat   ep   The Gift 12. 15. 79 ABC
    Top of the Hill   ms   2. 6. 80, 2. 7. 80 NN
    CHiPs   ep   Go Cart Terror 9. 21. 80 NBC
    Fantasy Island   ep   12. 6. 80 ABC
    Charlie's Angels   ep   Angels of the Deep 12. 7. 80 ABC
    Fantasy Island   ep   Slam Dunk 10. 10. 81 ABC

BOOKE, SORRELL*
    Brenner   ep   The Buff 7. 25. 59 CBS
    T. H. E. Cat   ep   9. 16. 66 ABC
    Preview Tonight   ep   Great Bible Adventures: Seven Rich
      Years ... And Seven Lean   pt   9. 11. 66 ABC
    The Borgia Stick   tf   2. 25. 67 NBC
    Mission: Impossible   ep   Shock 3. 25. 67 CBS
    Ironside   ep   9. 19. 68 NBC
    The Wild Wild West   ep   The Night of the Egyptian Queen
      11. 15. 68 CBS
    Owen Marshall, Counselor at Law   ep   9. 12. 71 ABC
    Cannon   ep   Death Chain 9. 21. 71 CBS
    Owen Marshall, Counselor at Law   ep   2. 10. 72 ABC
    M*A*S*H   ep   Requiem for a Lightweight 10. 1. 72 CBS
    Temperatures Rising   ep   10. 17. 72 ABC
    Gunsmoke   ep   11. 6. 72 CBS
    Alias Smith and Jones   ep   The Strange Fate of Conrad Meyer
      Zulick 12. 2. 72 ABC
    All in the Family   ep   3. 31. 73 CBS

The New Adventures of Perry Mason   ep   The Horoscope Homi-
   cide 9. 23. 73 CBS
The New Dick Van Dyke Show   ep   10. 1. 73 CBS
Kung Fu   ep   1. 17. 74 ABC
The New Dick Van Dyke Show   ep   2. 25. 74 CBS
Columbo   ep   Swan Song 3. 3. 74 NBC
Dr. Max   tf   4. 4. 74 CBS
The Last Angry Man   tf   4. 16. 74 ABC
Manhunter   ep   11. 6. 74 CBS
Police Story   ep   1. 7. 75 NBC
Archer   ep   The Arsonist 2. 6. 75 NBC
Adventures of the Queen   tf   2. 14. 75 CBS
The Night Stalker   ep   2. 14. 75 ABC
On the Rocks   ep   9. 11. 75 ABC
All in the Family   ep   9. 22. 75 CBS
Joe and Sons   ep   10. 21. 75 CBS
The Streets of San Francisco   ep   10. 23. 75 ABC
All in the Family   ep   11. 10. 75 CBS
On the Rocks   ep   11. 27. 75 ABC
Harry O   ep   The Mysterious Case of Lester and Dr. Fong
   3. 18. 76 ABC
Manhunter   ep   4. 3. 76 CBS
Brenda Starr   tf   5. 8. 76 ABC
Zero Intelligence   pt   9. 10. 76 ABC
Baa Baa Black Sheep (a. k. a. The Black Sheep Squadron)   ep
   2. 22. 77 NBC
The Amazing Howard Hughes   tf   4. 13. 77, 4. 14. 77 CBS
Columbo   ep   5. 22. 77 NBC
The Greatest Thing That Almost Happened   tf   10. 26. 77 CBS
All in the Family   ep   10. 30. 77 CBS
Little House on the Prairie   ep   1. 23. 78 NBC
Last Chance   pt   4. 21. 78 NBC
The Rockford Files   ep   The Jersey Bounce 10. 6. 78 NBC
What's Happening! !   ep   10. 12. 78 ABC
The Dukes of Hazzard   sr   1. 26. 79 CBS
The Dukes of Hazzard   sr ret   9. 21. 79 CBS
The Dukes of Hazzard   sr ret   11. 5. 80
The Dukes of Hazzard   sr ret   10. 6. 81

BOONE, DEBBY*
   Gift of the Magi   tf   12. 21. 78 NBC

BOONE, RICHARD
   SUPP. :
   The Last Dinosaur   tf   2. 11. 77 ABC

BORGNINE, ERNEST
   A& C:
   Future Cop   tf   5. 1. 76 ABC
   SUPP. :
   Future Cop   sr   3. 5. 77 ABC
   Jesus of Nazareth   ms   4. 3. 77, 4. 10. 77 NBC
   Fire   tf   5. 8. 77 NBC

The Ghost on Flight 401 tf 2.19.78 NBC
The Cops and Robin tf 3.28.78 NBC
The Hallmark Hall of Fame ep All Quiet on the Western
  Front ep 11.14.79 CBS

BOSLEY, TOM*
Code Name Jericho ep Dutch and Go 9.15.66 CBS
Bonanza ep The Last Vote 10.20.68 NBC
Get Smart ep 12.7.68 NBC
The Mod Squad ep 3.11.69 ABC
Marcus Welby, M.D. tf 3.26.69 ABC
The Debbie Reynolds Show sr 9.16.69 NBC
Bonanza ep A Lawman's Lot Is Not a Happy One 10.5.69 NBC
Night Gallery tf 11.8.69 NBC
The Name of the Game ep A Love to Remember 9.25.70 NBC
Night Gallery ep Make Me Laugh 1.6.71 NBC
The Name of the Game ep Seek and Destroy 2.5.71 NBC
A Step Out of Line tf 2.26.71 CBS
Vanished tf 3.8.71, 3.9.71 NBC
Funny Face sr 9.18.71 CBS
Mission: Impossible ep 9.18.71 CBS
Congratulations, It's a Boy! tf 9.21.71 ABC
Love, American Style ep Love and the Artful Dodger 10.1.71
  ABC
Mr. and Mrs. Bo Jo Jones tf 11.16.71 ABC
Me and the Chimp ep 3.23.72 CBS
The Sandy Duncan Show sr 9.1.72 CBS
The Streets of San Francisco tf 9.16.72 ABC
No Place to Run tf 9.19.72 ABC
Banyon ep 9.29.72 NBC
The Sixth Sense ep 12.23.72 ABC
Temperatures Rising ep 1.9.73 ABC
Medical Center ep 1.10.73 CBS
The Paul Lynde Show ep 1.24.73 ABC
Maude ep 1.30.73 CBS
Chase ep Gang War 9.18.73 NBC
Love, American Style ep Love and the Comedienne 9.21.73
  ABC
Tenafly ep Joyride to Nowhere 10.10.73 NBC
The Streets of San Francisco ep Going Home 10.11.73 ABC
McMillan and Wife ep Free Fall to Terror 11.11.73 NBC
Miracle on 34th Street tf 12.14.73 CBS
Happy Days sr 1.15.74 ABC
The Girl Who Came Gift-Wrapped tf 1.29.74 CBS
Death Cruise tf 10.30.74 ABC
Who Is the Black Dahlia? tf 3.1.75 NBC
The Last Survivors tf 3.3.75 NBC
The Night Stalker ep 3.28.75 ABC
Happy Days sr ret 9.9.75 ABC
The Night That Panicked America tf 10.31.75 ABC
That's Hollywood sr nar 9.10.76 NN
The Love Boat tf 9.18.76 ABC
Happy Days sr ret 9.21.76 ABC

The Streets of San Francisco   ep   10.21.76 ABC
Black Market Baby   tf   10.7.77 ABC
Happy Days   sr ret   9.20.77 ABC
Testimony of Two Men   ms   5.1.78, 5.2.78, 5.3.78 NN
With This Ring   tf   5.5.78 ABC
The Bastard/Kent Family Chronicles   ms   5.22.78, 5.23.78 NN
Happy Days   sr ret   9.14.78 ABC
The Stingiest Man in Town   sp vo   12.23.78 NBC
The Triangle Factory Fire   tf   1.30.79 NBC
The Castaways on Gilligan's Island   tf   5.3.79 NBC
Return of the Mod Squad   tf   5.18.79 ABC
The Rebels   ms   5.14.79, 5.21.79 NN
Happy Days   sr ret   9.11.79 ABC
Here's Boomer   ep   6.13.80 NBC
For the Love of It   tf   9.26.80 ABC
Happy Days   sr ret   11.11.80 ABC
Happy Days   sr ret   10.6.81 ABC
Tales of the Unexpected   ep   I Like It Here in Wilmington
    11.14.81 NN

BOTTOMS, JOSEPH*
    Owen Marshall, Counselor at Law   ep   A Piece of God   12.14.72
        ABC
    Trouble Comes to Town   tf   1.10.73 ABC
    Holocaust   ms   4.16-19.78 NBC
    The Hallmark Hall of Fame   ep   Return Engagement   sp   11.17.78
        NBC
    The Intruder Within   tf   2.20.81 ABC

BOTTOMS, TIMOTHY
    SUPP. :
    A Shining Season   tf   12.26.79 CBS
    Escape   tf   2.20.80 CBS
    East of Eden   ms   2.8.81, 2.9.81, 2.11.81 ABC

BOXLEITNER, BRUCE*
    The Mary Tyler Moore Show   ep   I Gave at the Office   12.8.73
        CBS
    The Chadwick Family   tf   4.17.74 ABC
    A Cry for Help   tf   2.12.75 ABC
    Gunsmoke   ep   3.31.75 CBS
    Hawaii Five-O   ep   2.18.75 CBS
    Police Woman   ep   Paradise Mall 2.26.75 NBC
    Baretta   ep   1.7.76 ABC
    The Macahans   tf   1.19.76 ABC
    Hawaii Five-O   ep   2.12.76 CBS
    Kiss Me, Kill Me   tf   5.28.76 ABC
    How the West Was Won   ms   2.6.77, 2.7.77, 2.13.77 ABC
    Murder at the World Series   tf   3.20.77 ABC
    How the West Was Won   sr   1.12.78 ABC
    Happily Ever After   tf   9.5.78 CBS
    How the West Was Won   sr ret   1.15.79 ABC
    The Last Convertible   ms   9.24.79, 9.25.79, 9.26.79 NBC

Wild Times   ms   1. 24. 80, 1. 31. 80 NN
Fly Away Home   tf   9. 18. 81 ABC

BOYD, STEPHEN
   SUPP. :
   Hunter   ep   3. 18. 77 CBS
   Hawaii Five-O   ep   9. 15. 77 CBS

BOYLE, PETER
   SUPP. :
   Tail Gunner Joe   tf   2. 6. 77 NBC
   From Here to Eternity   ms   2. 14. 79, 2. 21. 79, 2. 28. 79 NBC

BRADBURY, LANE*
   The Fugitive   ep   Wings of an Angel 9. 14. 65 ABC
   Gunsmoke   ep   10. 14. 68 CBS
   The FBI   ep   11. 10. 68 CBS
   Judd, for the Defense   ep   Between the Dark and the Daylight
      2. 7. 69 ABC
   Dial Hot Line   tf   3. 8. 70 ABC
   The Mod Squad   ep   See the Eagle Dying 9. 29. 70 ABC
   The Partridge Family   ep   Love At First Sight 10. 30. 70 ABC
   Maybe I'll Come Home in the Spring   tf   2. 16. 71 ABC
   Owen Marshall, Counselor at Law ep Run, Carol, Run 1. 20. 72
      ABC
   McCloud   ep   Give My Regards to Broadway 2. 23. 72 NBC
   Mannix   ep   3. 1. 72 CBS
   Hollywood Television Theatre   ep   Another Part of the Forest
      10. 2. 72 PBS
   The FBI   ep   The Loner 11. 19. 72 ABC
   Banyon   ep   11. 24. 72 NBC
   Alias Smith and Jones   ep   11. 25. 72 ABC
   The Bold Ones: The Lawyers   ep   End Theme 12. 12. 72 NBC
   Kung Fu   ep   An Eye for an Eye 1. 25. 73 ABC
   The Streets of San Francisco   ep   2. 21. 74 ABC
   McMillan and Wife   ep   Greed 2. 15. 76 NBC
   The Rockford Files   ep   Where's Houston 2. 20. 76 NBC
   Serpico: The Deadly Game   tf   4. 24. 76 NBC
   Visions   ep   Monkey in the Middle 12. 16. 76 PBS
   Westside Medical   ep   8. 11. 77, 8. 18. 77 ABC
   Just a Little Inconvenience   tf   10. 2. 77 NBC
   A Real American Hero   tf   12. 9. 78 CBS
   Boston and Kilbride   pt   3. 3. 79 CBS
   Breaking Up Is Hard to Do   tf   9. 5. 79, 9. 7. 79 ABC
   The Waltons   ep   10. 4. 79 CBS
   Walking Tall   ep   2. 14. 81 NBC
   Strike Force   ep   The Predator 12. 4. 81 ABC

BRADY, SCOTT
   A&C:
   Police Story   ep   Requiem for an Informer 10. 9. 73 NBC
   Police Story   ep   Cop in the Middle 1. 29. 74 NBC
   Police Story   ep   11. 9. 74, 1. 7. 75, 2. 6. 76 NBC

The Kansas City Massacre   tf   9. 19. 75 ABC
The Rockford Files   ep   9. 26. 75,   10. 3. 75 NBC
Police Story   ep   9. 30. 75 NBC
Law and Order   tf   6. 6. 76 ABC
All in the Family   ep   3. 8. 76,   9. 22. 76,   9. 29. 76 CBS
SUPP. :
Welcome Back, Kotter   ep   1. 6. 77 ABC
The Rockford Files   ep   1. 21. 77,   1. 28. 77 NBC
Police Story   ep   Pressure Point 9. 27. 77 NBC
Baretta   ep   11. 30. 77 ABC
Supertrain   ep   2. 28. 79 NBC
When Everyday Was the Fourth of July   tf   3. 12. 78 NBC
To Kill a Cop   tf   4. 10. 78,   4. 11. 78 NBC
Suddenly Love   tf   12. 4. 78 NBC
The Rockford Files   ep   12. 8. 78 NBC
Wheels   ms   5. 7. 78,   5. 8. 78,   5. 9. 78,   5. 14. 78,   5. 15. 78 NBC
Eischied   ep   11. 9. 79 NBC
Charlie's Angels   ep   Taxi Angels 2. 7. 81 ABC
Riker   ep   4. 11. 81 CBS
McClain's Law   ep   11. 20. 81 NBC

BRAEDEN, ERIC* (a. k. a. Hans Gudegast)
Combat   ep   The Hostage 1. 28. 64 ABC
Kraft Suspense Theatre   ep   The Safe House 5. 20. 65 NBC
Run for Your Life   ep   The Cold, Cold War of Paul Bryan
   9. 13. 65 NBC
The Man from U. N. C. L. E.   ep   The Discotheque Affair 10. 15. 65
   NBC
The Virginian   ep   No Drums, No Trumpets 4. 6. 66 NBC
The Rat Patrol   sr   9. 12. 66 ABC
Mission: Impossible   ep   The Short Tail Spy 12. 17. 66 CBS
The Rat Patrol   sr ret   9. 11. 67 ABC
Mission: Impossible   ep   Echo of Yesterday 12. 10. 67 CBS
Honeymoon with a Stranger   tf   12. 23. 69 ABC
The Mask of Sheba   tf   3. 9. 70 NBC
Hawaii Five-O   ep   The Second Bullet 9. 30. 70 CBS
O'Hara, United States Treasury   ep   9. 17. 71 CBS
Bearcats!   ep   9. 23. 71 CBS
Bearcats!   ep   Dos Gringos 9. 30. 71 CBS
Mannix   ep   Woman in the Shadows 10. 13. 71 CBS
Gunsmoke   ep   The Bullet 11. 29. 71,   12. 6. 71,   12. 13. 71 CBS
Marcus Welby, M. D.   ep   10. 3. 72 ABC
The Judge and Jake Wyler   tf   12. 2. 72 NBC
McCloud   ep   The Million Dollar Round Up 2. 4. 73 NBC
Hawaii Five-O   ep   The Diamond that Nobody Stole 3. 6. 73 CBS
Barnaby Jones   ep   Perchance to Kill 3. 11. 73 CBS
Intertect   pt   3. 11. 73 ABC
Owen Marshall, Counselor at Law   ep   N Is for Nightmare
   10. 17. 73 ABC
The Six Million Dollar Man   ep   Wine, Women and Song 10. 20. 73
   ABC
Death Race   tf   11. 10. 73 ABC
Banacek   ep   Vanishing Chalice 1. 15. 74 NBC

The Rookies   ep   The Assassin 1. 29. 74 ABC
The Magician   ep   The Illusion of Black Gold 2. 11. 74 NBC
Gunsmoke   ep   The Iron Blood of Courage 2. 18. 74 CBS
The FBI   ep   3. 10. 74 ABC
Marcus Welby, M. D.   ep   10. 22. 74 ABC
The Night Stalker   ep   11. 1. 74 ABC
Get Christie Love!   ep   11. 20. 74 ABC
Barnaby Jones   ep   Jeopardy for Two 4. 1. 75 CBS
The Barbary Coast   ep   9. 15. 75 ABC
Death Scream   tf   9. 26. 75 ABC
The New, Original Wonder Woman   tf   11. 7. 75 ABC
Bronk   ep   1. 18. 76 CBS
Cannon   ep   2. 4. 76 CBS
The Mary Tyler Moore Show   ep   The Critic 1. 8. 77 CBS
Kojak   ep   When You Hear the Beep Drop Dead 1. 18. 77
   CBS
Most Wanted   ep   2. 5. 77 ABC
Code Name: Diamond Head   tf   5. 3. 77 NBC
Switch   ep   9. 23. 77 CBS
Switch   ep   12. 26. 77 CBS
The Six Million Dollar Man   ep   1. 1. 78 ABC
How the West Was Won   ep   4. 30. 78 ABC
Project UFO   ep   4. 30. 78 NBC
How the West Was Won   ep   5. 14. 78 ABC
Happily Ever After   tf   9. 5. 78 CBS
The Eddie Capra Mysteries   ep   Who Killed Lloyd Wesley Jor-
   dan?   9. 29. 78 NBC
The New Adventures of Wonder Woman   ep   Skateboard Whiz
   11. 24. 78 CBS
CHiPs   ep   1. 13. 79 NBC
A Man Called Sloane   ep   11. 17. 79 NBC
The Aliens Are Coming   tf   3. 2. 80 NBC
Hagen   ep   3. 15. 80 CBS
Charlie's Angels   ep   6. 3. 81 ABC

BRAND, NEVILLE
   A&C:
   The Quest   tf   5. 13. 76 NBC
   SUPP. :
   Fire   tf   5. 8. 77 NBC
   Captains Courageous   tf   12. 4. 77 ABC
   The Man from Atlantis   ep   5. 2. 78 NBC
   The Eddie Capra Mysteries   ep   12. 22. 78 NBC
   Quincy, M. E.   ep   2. 15. 79 NBC
   Fantasy Island   ep   3. 1. 80 ABC

BRANDON, MICHAEL
   SUPP. :
   Red Alert   tf   5. 18. 77 CBS
   The Comedy Company   tf   7. 21. 78 ABC
   A Vacation in Hell   tf   5. 21. 79 ABC
   A Perfect Match   tf   10. 5. 80 CBS

BRAZZI, ROSSANO
  SUPP. :
  Hawaii Five-O   ep   9. 22. 77 CBS
  Charlie's Angels   ep   2. 7. 79 ABC
  Fantasy Island   ep   11. 21. 81 ABC

BRENNAN, EILEEN*
  McMillan and Wife   ep   The Night of the Wizard 9. 24. 72 NBC
  Playmates   tf   10. 3. 72 ABC
  Jigsaw   ep   3. 3. 73 ABC
  The Blue Knight   ms   11. 13. 73, 11. 14. 73, 11. 15. 73, 11. 16. 73,
    11. 19. 73 NBC
  My Father's Home   tf   6. 1. 75 ABC
  The Night That Panicked America   tf   10. 31. 75 ABC
  Barnaby Jones   ep   11. 28. 75 CBS
  Kojak   ep   A House of Prayer, a Den of Thieves 12. 14. 75 CBS
  The Death of Richie   tf   1. 10. 77 NBC
  All That Glitters   sr   1977 NN
  Black Beauty   ms   1. 31. 78, 2. 1. 78, 2. 2. 78, 2. 3. 78, 2. 4. 78
    NBC
  Visions   ep   Fans of the Kosko Show 10. 23. 78 PBS
  13 Queens Blvd.   sr   3. 20. 79 ABC
  A New Kind of Family   sr   9. 16. 79 ABC
  When She Was Bad   tf   11. 25. 79 ABC
  My Old Man   tf   12. 7. 79 CBS
  Taxi   ep   1. 14. 81 ABC
  When the Circus Came to Town   tf   1. 20. 81 CBS
  Taxi   ep   2. 5. 81 ABC
  Private Benjamin   sr   4. 6. 81 CBS
  Private Benjamin   sr ret   10. 12. 81 CBS
  Incident at Crestridge   tf   12. 29. 81 CBS

BRENNER, DORI*
  Kojak   ep   The Only Way Out 5. 8. 74 CBS
  The Oath   pt   8. 26. 76 ABC
  Delvecchio   ep   11. 7. 76 CBS
  I Want to Keep My Baby   tf   11. 19. 76 CBS
  All Together Now   tf   2. 5. 77 ABC
  Seventh Avenue   ms   2. 10. 77, 2. 17. 77, 2. 24. 77 NBC
  Sheila   pt   8. 29. 77 CBS
  The Love Boat   ep   1. 7. 78 ABC
  Sparrow   pt   1. 12. 78 CBS
  What Really Happened to the Class of '65?   ep   3. 2. 78 NBC
  Friends   pt   8. 19. 78 CBS
  Julie Farr, M. D.   ep   6. 19. 79 ABC
  Sex and the Single Parent   tf   9. 19. 79 CBS
  Brothers   pt   7. 30. 80 CBS
  Trapper John, M. D.   ep   Finders Keepers 3. 8. 81 CBS
  Aloha Paradise   ep   4. 15. 81 ABC

BRIDGES, BEAU
  SUPP. :
  The Four Fathers   tf   1. 1. 78 NBC

The President's Mistress   tf   2. 10. 78 CBS
The Hallmark Hall of Fame   ep   Stubby Pringle's Christmas
    sp   12. 17. 78 NBC
The Child Stealer   tf   3. 9. 79 ABC
United States   sr   3. 11. 80 NBC
Mom, I Want to Come Home Now   sp   2. 5. 81 NN

BRIDGES, LLOYD
    A&C:
    Police Story   ep   11. 19. 74 NBC (delete: The Return of Joe
        Forrester)
    Police Story   ep   The Return of Joe Forrester 5. 6. 75 NBC
    SUPP. :
    Roots   ms ep   1. 29. 77, 1. 30. 77 ABC
    Tales of the Unexpected   ep   The Force of Evil 3. 13. 77 NBC
    Telethon   tf   11. 6. 77 ABC
    How the West Was Won   ep   1. 12. 78 ABC
    The Great Wallendos   tf   2. 2. 78 NBC
    How the West Was Won   ep   2. 19. 78, 2. 26. 78, 3. 5. 78 ABC
    The Critical List   tf   9. 11. 78, 9. 12. 78 NBC
    World War II: G. L. Diary   sr nar   9. 26. 78 NN
    Battlestar Galactica   ep   11. 26. 78 ABC
    Disaster on the Coastliner   tf   10. 28. 79 ABC
    Moviola: This Year's Blonde   tf   5. 18. 80 NBC
    East of Eden   ms   2. 8. 81, 2. 9. 81, 2. 11. 81 ABC
    The Love Boat   ep   11. 21. 81 ABC

BRISEBOIS, DANIELLE*
    All in the Family   sr   9. 24. 78 CBS
    Archie Bunker's Place   sr   9. 23. 79 CBS
    Mom, the Wolfman and Me   tf   10. 20. 80 NN
    Archie Bunker's Place   sr ret   11. 2. 80 CBS
    Archie Bunker's Place   sr ret   10. 4. 81 CBS

BRITTANY, MORGAN*
    The Amazing Howard Hughes   tf   4. 13. 77, 4. 14. 77 CBS
    Delta County, U. S. A.   tf   5. 20. 77 ABC
    The Initiation of Sarah   tf   2. 6. 78 ABC
    California Fever   ep   10. 16. 79 CBS
    Buck Rogers in the 25th Century   ep   1. 10. 80 NBC
    The Dream Merchants   ms   5. 12. 80, 5. 19. 80 NN
    Moviola: The Scarlett O'Hara War   tf   5. 19. 80 NBC
    Fantasy Island   ep   1. 3. 81 ABC
    The Love Boat   ep   5. 2. 81 ABC
    Dallas   ep   10. 30. 81, 11. 6. 81 CBS

BROLIN, JAMES
    A&C:
    Bus Stop   ep   The Resurrection of Annie Ahearn 10. 15. 61 ABC
    The Virginian   ep   Crime Wave at Buffalo Springs 1. 29. 69 NBC
    SUPP. :
    Steel Cowboy   tf   12. 6. 78 NBC

BRONSON, CHARLES
    SUPP. :
    Raid on Entebbe   tf   1. 9. 77 NBC

BROWNE, ROSCOE LEE
    SUPP. :
    Maude   ep   10. 3. 77 CBS
    King   ms   2. 12. 78, 2. 13. 78, 2. 14. 78 NBC
    Dr. Scorpion   tf   2. 24. 78 ABC
    Maude   ep   3. 11. 78 CBS
    Miss Winslow and Son   sr   3. 28. 79 CBS
    Soap   sr   9. 13. 79 ABC
    Hart to Hart   ep   3. 11. 80 ABC
    Soap   sr ret   10. 29. 80 ABC

BUCHHOLZ, HORST
    SUPP. :
    Raid on Entebbe   tf   1. 9. 77 NBC
    Dead of Night   ep   No Such Thing As a Vampire   tf   3. 29. 77
      NBC
    Logan's Run   ep   9. 30. 77 CBS
    How the West Was Won   ep   1. 12. 78 ABC
    Return to Fantasy Island   tf   1. 20. 78 ABC
    How the West Was Won   ep   2. 19. 78 ABC
    The Return of Captain Nemo   ep   3. 22. 78 CBS
    Charlie's Angels   ep   Angel Come Home   9. 20. 78 ABC
    The French-Atlantic Affair   ms   11. 15. 79, 11. 16. 79, 11. 18. 79
      ABC
    Berlin Tunnel   tf   3. 25. 81 CBS

BUJOLD, GENEVIEVE
    SUPP. :
    Mistress of Paradise   tf   10. 4. 81 ABC

BULIFANT, JOYCE
    A&C:
    Wide Country   ep   A Guy for Clementine 9. 27. 62 NBC
    Alcoa Premiere   ep   Mr. Lucifer 11. 1. 62 ABC
    Empire   ep   2. 12. 63 NBC
    The Virginian   ep   Roar from the Mountain 1. 8. 64 NBC
    Bonanza   ep   Return Engagement 3. 1. 70 NBC
    Insight   ep   11. 11. 73 NN
    Love, American Style   ep   Love and the Awkward Age 12. 7. 73
      ABC
    The Michele Lee Show   pt   4. 5. 74 CBS
    The Mary Tyler Moore Show   ep   1. 31. 76 CBS
    Police Story   ep   11. 30. 76 NBC
    SUPP. :
    Little Women   tf   10. 2. 78, 10. 3. 78 NBC
    Turnabout   ep   2. 9. 79 NBC
    Hanging by a Thread   tf   5. 8. 79, 5. 9. 79 NBC
    The Misadventures of Sheriff Lobo   ep   10. 16. 79 NBC

Flo   sr   3. 24. 80 CBS
Flo   sr ret   10. 27. 80 CBS

BUONO, VICTOR
  A&C:
  Ellery Queen   ep   2. 29. 76 NBC
  The Practice   ep   5. 7. 76 NBC
  Brenda Starr   tf   5. 8. 76 ABC
  SUPP. :
  The Man from Atlantis   tf   3. 4. 77 NBC
  The Hardy Boys/Nancy Drew Mysteries   ep   A Haunting We
    Will Go 4. 3. 77 ABC
  The Man from Atlantis   sr   9. 22. 77 NBC
  The Rita Moreno Show   pt   5. 2. 78 CBS
  Flying High   ep   North by Northeast 10. 13. 78 CBS
  Backstairs at the White House   ms ep   1. 29. 79 NBC
  Supertrain   ep   2. 28. 79 NBC
  Return of the Mod Squad   tf   5. 18. 79 ABC
  Better Late Than Never   tf   10. 17. 79 NBC
  Murder Can Hurt You!   tf   5. 21. 80 ABC
  More Wild Wild West   tf   10. 7. 80, 19. 8. 80 CBS
  Vega$ ep   11. 12. 80 ABC
  Fantasy Island   ep   11. 29. 80 ABC
  Taxi   ep   12. 17. 80 ABC
  Vega$ ep   4. 15. 81, 4. 22. 81 ABC
  Taxi   ep   6. 4. 81 ABC
  Judgement Day   pt   12. 6. 81 NBC

BURGHOFF, GARY
  A&C:
  Ellery Queen   ep   4. 4. 76 NBC
  SUPP. :
  The Love Boat   ep   11. 26. 77 ABC
  Fantasy Island   ep   3. 25. 78 ABC
  The New Adventures of Wonder Woman   ep   The Man Who
    Wouldn't Tell 3. 31. 78 CBS
  M*A*S*H   sr ret   9. 18. 78 CBS
  Sweepstakes   ep   3. 2. 79 NBC
  M*A*S*H   sr ret   9. 17. 79 CBS
  The Man in the Santa Claus Suit   tf   12. 23. 79 NBC
  Casino   tf   8. 1. 80 ABC
  Tales of the Unexpected   ep   The Best Policy 10. 25. 80 NN
  Fantasy Island   ep   11. 22. 80 ABC
  The Love Boat   ep   Lost and Found 5. 9. 81 ABC

BURKE, PAUL
  SUPP. :
  Little Ladies of the Night   tf   1. 16. 77 ABC
  The Love Boat   ep   Until the Last Goodbye 2. 11. 78 ABC
  Wild and Wooly   tf   2. 20. 78 ABC
  Fantasy Island   ep   Lady of the Evening 2. 25. 78 ABC
  The Love Boat   ep   3. 10. 79 ABC
  The Beach Patrol   tf   4. 30. 79 ABC

Hawaii Five-O   ep   3. 29. 80 CBS
Trapper John, M. D.   ep   3. 30. 80 CBS
The Littlest Hobo   ep   1. 10. 81 NN
The Love Boat   ep   1. 24. 81 ABC
Fantasy Island   ep   3. 7. 81 ABC
Vega$ ep   4. 15. 81 ABC
Killing At Hell's Gate   tf   10. 31. 81 CBS
Advice to the Lovelorn   tf   11. 30. 81 NBC

BURNETT, CAROL
    A& C:
    The Paul Winchell Show   sr   12. 55 NBC
    No Place Like Home   tf   11. 24. 60 NBC
    The Jack Benny Show   ep   Tarzan and Jane 1962 CBS
    The Jack Benny Show   ep   Riverboat Gambler 1963 CBS
    Calamity Jane   sp   11. 12. 63 CBS
    The Lucy Show   ep   Librarian-Roommate Performs in Palm
        Springs 10. 31. 66, 11. 7. 66 CBS
    The Lucy Show   ep   Stewardess School Musical Salute to Aviation
        1. 27. 69, 2. 3. 69 CBS
    Here's Lucy   ep   High School Show 1969 CBS
    Here's Lucy   ep   Beauty Contest 3. 20. 70 CBS
    Here's Lucy   ep   Unemployment Follies 2. 8. 71 CBS
    Drink, Drank, Drunk   sp   10. 21. 74 NN
    SUPP. :
    The Grass Is Always Greener Over the Septic Tank   tf   10. 25. 78
        CBS
    Insight   ep   This Side of Eden 12. 23. 78 NN
    Friendly Fire   tf   4. 22. 79 ABC
    The Tenth Month   tf   9. 16. 79 CBS

BURNS, GEORGE
    A& C:
    Here's Lucy   ep   11. 23. 70 CBS
    Ellery Queen   ep   11. 13. 75 NBC
    SUPP. :
    Alice   ep   1. 1. 78 CBS
    The Comedy Company   tf   7. 21. 78 CBS

BURNS, MICHAEL
    A& C:
    The Wrangler   ep   The Affair with Browning's Woman 8. 25. 60
        NBC
    Kraft Mystery Theatre   ep   Shadow of a Man 6. 19. 63 NBC
    Virginian   ep   Long Journey Home 12. 14. 66 NBC
    Virginian   ep   Seth 3. 20. 68 NBC
    Insight   ep   9. 2. 73, 12. 29. 73 NN
    SUPP. :
    The Magnificent Magnet of Santa Mesa   tf   6. 19. 77 NBC
    The Tony Randall Show   ep   9. 24. 77 CBS
    The Bionic Woman   ep   Fembots in Las Vegas 9. 24. 77, 10. 1. 77
        NBC
    Police Woman   ep   12. 28. 77 NBC

BURR, RAYMOND
    A&C:
    Stars Over Hollywood   ep   Prison Doctor 3.14.51 NBC
    Stars Over Hollywood   ep   Pearls from Paris 4.4.51 NBC
    delete: Mr. Lucky at 7   ep   Pearls from Paris 11.10.52 ABC
    Lux Video Theatre   ep   Shall Not Perish 2.11.54 CBS
    SUPP.:
    Kingston Confidential   sr   3.23.77 NBC
    79 Park Avenue   ms   10.16.77, 10.17.77, 10.18.77 NBC
    The Bastard/Kent Family Chronicles   ms nar   5.22.78, 5.23.78
      NN
    Centennial   ms ep   Only the Banks Live Forever 10.1.78 NBC
    Centennial   ms ep   The Yellow Apron 10.8.78 NBC
    The Jordan Chance   tf   12.12.78 CBS
    The Love Boat   ep   Class Reunion 2.3.79 ABC
    Love's Savage Fury   tf   5.20.79 ABC
    Eischied   ep   Only the Pretty Girls Die 9.21.79, 9.28.79 NBC
    The Misadventures of Sheriff Lobo   ep   10.23.79 NBC
    Disaster on the Coastliner   tf   10.28.79 ABC
    The 13th Day: The Story of Esther   pt nar   11.18.79 ABC
    The Curse of King Tut's Tomb   tf   5.8.80, 5.9.80 NBC
    The Night the City Screamed   tf   12.14.80 ABC
    Peter and Paul   tf   4.12.81, 4.14.81 CBS

BURSTYN, ELLEN
    SUPP.:
    The People vs. Jean Harris   tf   5.7.81, 5.8.81 NBC

BURTON, LeVAR*
    Roots   ms ep   1.23.77, 1.24.77 ABC
    Billy: Portrait of a Street Kid   tf   9.12.77 NBC
    American Short Story   ep   Almos' a Man 8.11.78 PBS
    One in a Million: The Ron Le Flore Story   tf   9.26.78 CBS
    Battered   tf   9.26.78 NBC
    Dummy   tf   5.27.79 CBS
    Guyana Tragedy: The Story of Jim Jones   tf   4.15.80 CBS
    The Acorn People   tf   3.2.81 NBC
    Grambling's White Tiger   tf   10.4.81 NBC

BUSEY, GARY*
    Bonanza   ep   The Hidden Enemy 11.28.72 NBC
    Blood Sport   tf   12.5.73 ABC
    The Execution of Private Slovik   tf   3.13.74 NBC
    The Texas Wheelers   sr   9.13.74 ABC
    The Law   tf   10.22.74 NBC
    Gunsmoke   ep   3.10.75 CBS
    The Texas Wheelers   sr ret   6.26.75 ABC

BUTTONS, RED
    SUPP.:
    The Sunshine Boys   pt   6.9.77 NBC
    Telethon   tf   11.6.77 ABC
    Vega$ ep   4.25.78 ABC

The Users tf 10.1.78 ABC
The Love Boat ep 10.14.78 ABC
Fantasy Island ep 11.11.78 ABC
Vega$ ep 12.20.78 ABC
Fantasy Island ep 5.6.79 ABC
The Love Boat ep The Gift 12.15.79 ABC
Power tf 1.14.80, 1.15.80 NBC
The Dream Merchants ms 5.12.80, 5.19.80 NN
Aloha Paradise ep 4.29.81 ABC
Side Show tf 6.5.81 NBC

BUZZI, RUTH
    SUPP.:
    The Love Boat ep The Dummies 12.16.78 ABC
    CHiPs ep Chips Goes Roller Disco 9.22.79 NBC

BYNER, JOHN
    SUPP.:
    McNamara's Band pt 5.11.77, 12.5.77 ABC
    Three on a Date tf 2.17.78 ABC
    Soap sr 9.13.79 ABC

BYRNES, EDD*
    77 Sunset Strip sr 10.10.58 ABC
    77 Sunset Strip sr ret 9.18.59 ABC
    77 Sunset Strip sr ret 9.16.60 ABC
    77 Sunset Strip sr ret 9.22.61 ABC
    77 Sunset Strip sr ret 9.12.62 ABC
    The Kraft Suspense Theatre ep The Jack Is High 11.19.64
        NBC
    The Silent Gun tf 12.16.69 ABC
    Adam-12 ep 9.13.72 NBC
    Alias Smith and Jones ep 11.4.72 ABC
    Faraday and Company ep A Wheelbarrow Full of Trouble
        10.24.73 NBC
    Marcus Welby, M.D. ep 1.15.74 ABC
    Mobile Two ep 9.25.75 ABC
    Police Story ep 11.21.75 NBC
    Police Woman ep 2.3.76 NBC
    Mystery of the Week ep Where the Action Is 8.10.77 ABC
    Telethon tf 11.6.77 ABC
    The Hardy Boys/Nancy Drew Mysteries ep 2.26.78 ABC
    Vega$ tf 4.25.78 ABC
    Fantasy Island ep 5.20.78 ABC
    Sword of Justice ep 10.19.78 NBC
    The Hardy Boys ep 11.19.78, 11.26.78 ABC
    Sweepstakes sr 1.26.79 NBC
    B.J. and the Bear ep 4.28.79 NBC
    California Fever ep 12.11.79 CBS
    CHiPs ep 2.2.80 NBC
    Fantasy Island ep 3.1.80 ABC
    House Calls ep 12.1.80 CBS
    B.J. and the Bear ep 3.29.80 NBC

Charlie's Angels   ep   Waikiki Angels 1. 4. 81 ABC
Twirl   tf   10. 25. 81 NBC

-C-

CAESAR, SID
    A&C:
    Good Heavens   ep   6. 19. 76 ABC
    SUPP. :
    Flight to Holocaust   tf 3. 27. 77 NBC
    Curse of the Black Widow   tf   9. 16. 77 ABC
    W. E. B.   ep   10. 5. 78 NBC
    The Love Boat   ep   The Dummies 12. 16. 78 ABC
    Lobo   ep   2. 24. 81 NBC

CAGNEY, JAMES
    SUPP. :
    James Cagney: That Yankee Doodle Dandy   sp   12. 1. 81 NN

CALHOUN, RORY
    SUPP. :
    Starsky and Hutch   ep   3. 19. 77 ABC
    Flight to Holocaust   tf   3. 27. 77 NBC
    Fantasy Island   ep   9. 23. 78 ABC
    Hawaii Five-O   ep   11. 16. 78 CBS
    Flatbed Annie and Sweetiepie: Lady Truckers tf 2. 10. 79 CBS
    Harris and Company   ep   3. 15. 79 NBC
    Pottsville   pt   8. 6. 80 CBS
    Lobo   ep   The Cowboy Connection 3. 31. 81 NBC

CALLAN, MICHAEL
    A&C:
    Medical Story   ep   10. 9. 75 NBC
    S. W. A. T.   ep   12. 13. 75 ABC
    SUPP. :
    Quincy, M. E.   ep   2. 25. 77 NBC
    Delvecchio   ep   3. 6. 77 CBS
    Fantasy Island   ep   3. 11. 78 ABC
    The Love Boat   ep   I'll Never Fall in Love Again 5. 13. 78 ABC
    Donner Pass: The Road to Survival   tf   10. 24. 78 CBS
    Vega$ ep   11. 15. 78 ABC
    Mark Twain's America   sp   1. 11. 79 NBC
    Fantasy Island   ep   2. 10. 79 ABC
    Blind Ambition   ms   5. 20-23. 79 CBS
    This Is the Life   ep   8. 12. 79 NN
    Fantasy Island   ep   11. 17. 79 ABC
    Charlie's Angels   ep   Chorus Line Angels 2. 21. 81 ABC

CALLAS, CHARLIE
SUPP. :
Switch sr ret 9. 23. 77 CBS
The Love Boat ep Cyrano de Bricker 3. 17. 79 ABC

CAMERON, JOANNA
SUPP. :
McMillan ep 4. 24. 77 NBC
Switch ep 6. 25. 78 CBS
The Amazing Spider-Man ep 4. 12. 78 CBS

CAMPANELLA, JOSEPH
A& C:
Kraft Theatre ep No Warning 1. 16. 57 NBC
Robert Montgomery Presents ep Fear Street 4. 15. 57 NBC
The Nurses ep The Fly Shadow 10. 11. 62 CBS
The Nurses ep Credo 1. 9. 64 CBS
The Nurses ep The Bystanders 5. 28. 64 CBS
The Virginian ep Ride the Misadventure 11. 6. 68 NBC
SUPP. :
The Cliffwood Avenue Kids ep 10. 12. 77 NN
One Day at a Time ep 10. 18. 77 CBS
Hollywood Television Theatre ep The Ascent of Mt. Fuji
    1. 7. 78 PBS
Return to Fantasy Island tf 1. 20. 78 ABC
Ring of Passion tf 2. 4. 78 NBC
What Really Happened to the Class of '65? ep Class Misfit
    3. 9. 78 NBC
One Day at a Time ep 9. 18. 78, 9. 25. 78 CBS
Greatest Heroes of the Bible ep The Story of Moses in Egypt
    11. 20. 78 NBC
Vega$ ep 12. 6. 78 ABC
This Is the Life ep 9. 16. 79 NN
Quincy, M. E. ep 3. 20. 80 NBC
Vega$ ep 5. 7. 80 ABC
Quincy, M. E. ep 2. 25. 81 NBC

CANNON, DYAN
SUPP. :
Lady of the House tf 11. 14. 78 CBS

CANNON, J. D. *
East Side/West Side ep One Drink at a Time 1. 27. 64 CBS
The Defenders ep A Man Against Himself 9. 19. 64 CBS
The Fugitive ep Middle of a Heatwave 9. 21. 65 ABC
The Wild Wild West ep The Night of the Deadly Bed 9. 24. 65
    CBS
The Fugitive ep The Judgement 8. 22. 67, 8. 29. 67 ABC
The FBI ep 10. 13. 68 ABC
The Mod Squad ep A Design of Guns 2. 25. 69 ABC
U. M. C. tf 4. 17. 69 CBS
The D. A. : Murder One tf 12. 8. 69 NBC
McCloud sr 9. 16. 70 NBC

The Name of the Game   ep   A Love to Remember 9. 25. 70 NBC
Alias Smith and Jones   sr   1. 21. 71 ABC
Sam Hill: Who Killed the Mysterious Mr. Foster?   tf   2. 1. 71
   NBC
Cannon   tf   3. 26. 71 CBS
McCloud   sr ret   9. 22. 71 NBC
McCloud   sr ret   10. 1. 72 NBC
Lady Luck   pt   2. 12. 73 NBC
McCloud   sr ret   10. 14. 73 NBC
McCloud   sr ret   9. 22. 74 NBC
McCloud   sr ret   9. 21. 75 NBC
McCloud   sr ret   10. 4. 76 NBC
The Hardy Boys/Nancy Drew Mysteries   ep   10. 2. 77, 10. 9. 77
   ABC
Testimony of Two Men   ms   5. 1. 78, 5. 2. 78, 5. 3. 78 NN
Killing Stone   tf   5. 2. 78 NBC
Ike   ms   5. 3. 79, 5. 4. 79, 5. 6. 79 ABC
Walking Through the Fire   tf   5. 15. 79 CBS
Top of the Hill   ms   2. 6. 80, 2. 7. 80 NN
Pleasure Palace   tf   10. 22. 80 CBS
My Kidnapper, My Love   tf   12. 8. 80 NBC

CANOVA, DIANA*
Happy Days   ep   4. 2. 74 ABC
The Love Boat II   tf   1. 21. 77 ABC
Soap   sr   9. 13. 77 ABC
The Love Boat   ep   Taking Sides 2. 18. 78 ABC
With This Ring   tf   5. 5. 78 ABC
Soap   sr ret   9. 14. 78 ABC
Fantasy Island   ep   9. 23. 78 ABC
Soap   sr ret   9. 13. 79 ABC
The Death of Ocean View Park   tf   10. 19. 79 ABC
Fantasy Island   ep   10. 27. 79 ABC
Barney Miller   ep   11. 1. 79 ABC
Soap   sr ret   10. 29. 80 ABC
I'm a Big Girl Now   sr   10. 31. 80 ABC

CANOVA, JUDY
   SUPP. :
   The Love Boat   ep   11. 26. 77 ABC

CAREY, MACDONALD
   A&C:
   Studio One   ep   The Dusty Godmother 3. 13. 50 CBS
   Lux Video Theatre   ep   The Bachelor of Granby Oaks 1. 21. 54
      CBS
   Kraft Mystery Theatre   ep   The Image Merchants 6. 26. 63 NBC
   SUPP. :
   Roots   ms   1. 23-30. 77 ABC
   Switch   ep   8. 20. 78 CBS
   Stranger in Our House   tf   10. 31. 78 NBC
   The Hardy Boys   ep   11. 5. 78 ABC
   The Rebels   ms   5. 14. 79, 5. 21. 79 NN

Buck Rogers in the 25th Century   ep   Planet of the Slave Girls
    9.27.79 NBC
Fantasy Island   ep   12.15.79 ABC
The Girl, the Gold Watch and Everything   pt   6.13.80 NN
Top of the Hill   ms ep   2.6.80 NN

CAREY, MICHELE*
    Amos Burke, Secret Agent   ep   Balance of Terror 9.15.65 ABC
    The Wild Wild West   ep   The Night of the Feathered Fury
        1.13.67 CBS
    The Wild Wild West   ep   The Night of the Winged Terror
        1.17.69, 1.24.69 CBS
    The Name of the Game   ep   Blind Man's Bluff 10.3.69 NBC
    Gunsmoke   ep   1.17.72 CBS
    Savage   tf   3.31.73 NBC
    The Norliss Tapes   tf   2.21.73 NBC
    The Six Million Dollar Man   ep   Wine, Women and War 10.20.73
        ABC
    Adam's Rib   ep   Murder 11.9.73 ABC
    Dirty Sally   ep   1.11.74, 3.1.74 CBS
    Where's Momma   pt   5.15.74 NBC
    Delta County, U.S.A.   tf   5.20.77 ABC
    The Man from Atlantis   ep   12.13.77 NBC
    Starsky and Hutch   ep   2.15.78 ABC
    Legend of the Golden Gun   tf   4.10.79 NBC
    A Man Called Sloane   sr vo   9.22.79 NBC
    Undercover with the KKK   tf   10.23.79 NBC
    Death Ray 2000   tf vo   3.5.81 NBC

CARLIN, LYNN*
    Silent Night, Lonely Night   tf   12.16.69 NBC
    A Step Out of Line   tf   2.26.71 CBS
    Mr. and Mrs. Bo Jo Jones   tf   11.16.71 ABC
    The Bold Ones: The Doctors   ep   The Glass Cage 12.5.71 NBC
    Cannon   ep   The Nowhere Man 12.14.71 CBS
    Gunsmoke   ep   11.6.72 CBS
    Love, American Style   ep   11.24.72 ABC
    Ironside   ep   Confessions 9.13.73 NBC
    Hawaii Five-O   ep   The Finishing Touch 11.20.73 CBS
    The Morning After   tf   2.13.74 ABC
    The Last Angry Man   tf   4.16.74 ABC
    Terror on the 40th Floor   tf   9.17.74 NBC
    Petrocelli   ep   10.2.74 NBC
    Mannix   ep   10.27.74 CBS
    Lucas Tanner   ep   11.20.74 NBC
    Paper Moon   ep   11.28.74 ABC
    American Heritage   ep   Honorable Sam Houston   sp   1.22.75
        ABC
    The Waltons   ep   The Reunion 10.2.75 CBS
    The Lives of Jenny Dolan   tf   10.27.75 NBC
    City of Angels   ep   3.2.76 NBC
    Dawn: Portrait of a Teenage Runaway   tf   9.27.76 ABC
    Serpico   ep   11.19.76 NBC

The Waltons   ep   3. 10. 77 CBS
Bravo Two   pt   3. 25. 77 CBS
The Waltons   ep   9. 15. 77 CBS
James at 15   tf   9. 15. 77 NBC
James at 15   sr   10. 27. 77 NBC
The Bionic Woman   ep   The Martians Are Coming, the Mar-
    tians Are Coming 1. 28. 78 NBC
James at 16   sr   2. 9. 78 NBC
Insight   ep   11. 12. 78 NN
Not Until Today   pt   6. 27. 79 NBC
Charlie's Angels   ep   Caged Angel 10. 1. 79 ABC
The Incredible Hulk   ep   10. 5. 79 CBS
Barnaby Jones   ep   Design for Madness 10. 18. 79 CBS
Kate Loves a Mystery   ep   11. 1. 79 NBC
Chicken   sp   3. 18. 80 NN
Ten Speed and Brown Shoe   ep   4. 27. 80 ABC
Insight   ep   6. 29. 80 NN
Lou Grant   ep   9. 29. 80 CBS
Girl on the Edge of Town   sp   4. 30. 81 NN
Strike Force   ep   11. 13. 81 ABC
Darkroom   ep   Catnip 12. 25. 81 ABC

CARNEY, ART
    A&C:
    The DuPont Show of the Week   ep   The Trumpet of Gerald Q.
        West 6. 9. 63 NBC
    SUPP. :
    Lanigan's Rabbi   sr   1. 30. 77 NBC
    The Honeymooners Christmas Special   sp   11. 28. 77 ABC
    You Can't Take It with You   sp   5. 16. 79 CBS
    Letters from Frank   tf   11. 22. 79 CBS
    The Honeymooners' Valentine Special   sp   2. 13. 78 ABC
    The Honeymooners' Christmas   sp   12. 10. 78 ABC
    Alice   ep   12. 9. 79 CBS
    Alcatraz: The Whole Shocking Story   tf   11. 5. 80 NBC
    Fighting Back   tf   12. 7. 80 CBS
    Bitter Harvest   tf   5. 18. 81 NBC
    The Leprechaun's Christmas Gold   sp vo/nar   12. 23. 81 ABC

CARR, DARLEEN*
    Mayberry, R. F. D.   ep   12. 30. 68 CBS
    Family Affair   ep   10. 9. 69 CBS
    The Smith Family   sr   1. 20. 71 ABC
    The Smith Family   sr ret   9. 21. 71 ABC
    The FBI   ep   Till Death Do Us Part 10. 22. 72 ABC
    Medical Center   ep   Doctor and Mr. Harper 10. 25. 72 CBS
    All My Darling Daughters   tf   11. 22. 72 ABC
    Alias Smith and Jones   ep   12. 9. 72 ABC
    Barnaby Jones   ep   To Catch a Dead Man 2. 4. 73 CBS
    The Horror at 37,000 Feet   tf   2. 13. 73 CBS
    Marcus Welby, M. D.   ep   The Tortoise Dance 3. 6. 73 ABC
    The Streets of San Francisco   ep   3. 8. 73 ABC
    Runaway!   tf   9. 29. 73 ABC

The Streets of San Francisco ep   Harem 10. 25. 73 ABC
My Darling Daughters' Anniversary   tf   11. 7. 73 ABC
The Streets of San Francisco ep   Commitment 1. 3. 74 ABC
The Rookies   ep   The Late Mr. Brent 1. 28. 74 ABC
Chopper One   ep   4. 4. 74 ABC
Chopper One   ep   4. 11. 74 ABC
The Chadwick Family   tf   4. 17. 74 ABC
The Rookies   ep   The Assassin 12. 9. 74 ABC
Barnaby Jones   ep   12. 31. 74 CBS
The Waltons   ep   The Beguiled 1. 16. 75 CBS
The Streets of San Francisco   ep   1. 23. 75 ABC
Medical Center   ep   3. 3. 75 CBS
S. W. A. T.   ep   3. 17. 75 ABC
Caribe   ep   3. 24. 75 ABC
The Streets of San Francisco   ep   10. 2. 75, 10. 16. 75 ABC
Medical Center   ep   12. 1. 75 CBS
The Streets of San Francisco   ep   12. 4. 75 ABC
Jigsaw John   ep   3. 8. 76 NBC
Law of the Land   tf   4. 29. 76 NBC
Once an Eagle   ms   12. 2, 9, 16, 23, 30. 76, 1. 6, 13. 77 NBC
The Man from Atlantis   ep   The Disappearance 6. 20. 77 NBC
Young Joe, the Forgotten Kennedy   tf   9. 18. 77 ABC
The Oregon Trail   sr   9. 21. 77 NBC
The Man from Atlantis   ep   1. 22. 78 NBC
Mystery of the Week   ep   Sleepwalker 3. 1. 78 ABC
Fantasy Island   ep   3. 25. 78 ABC
The Paper Chase   ep   A Day in the Life 9. 19. 78 CBS
The Hardy Boys   ep   10. 22. 78 ABC
Flying High   ep   12. 8. 78 CBS
Miss Winslow and Son   sr   3. 28. 79 CBS
Eischied   ep   11. 23. 79, 11. 30. 79 NBC
The White Shadow   ep   1. 15. 80 CBS
Vega$ ep   3. 12. 80 ABC
Hagen   ep   4. 5. 80 CBS
Charlie's Angels   ep   6. 3. 81 ABC
Bret Maverick   sr   12. 1. 81 NBC
Simon and Simon   ep   The Least Dangerous Game 12. 29. 81 CBS

CARRADINE, DAVID
   SUPP. :
   Mr. Horn   tf   2. 3. 79, 2. 5. 79 CBS
   High Noon, Part II: The Return of Will Kane   tf   11. 15. 80
      CBS
   Today's FBI   ep   Hostage 11. 1. 81 ABC

CARRADINE, JOHN
   A& C:
   Sure As Fate   ep   Macbeth 1. 9. 51 CBS
   Faith Baldwin Theatre   ep   Barry and the Beautiful Doll 6. 30. 51
      ABC
   The Web   ep   Golden Secret 11. 14. 51 CBS
   Lights Out   ep   The Lonely Albatross 6. 30. 52 NBC
   Death at Love House   tf   9. 3. 76 ABC

SUPP. :
Tail Gunner Joe   tf   2. 6. 77 NBC
Christmas Miracle in Caulfield, U.S.A.   tf   12. 26. 77 NBC
Starsky and Hutch   ep   1. 7. 78 ABC
Vega$ ep   9. 27. 78 ABC
Greatest Heroes of the Bible   ep   Solomon and Bathsheba
   11. 21. 78, 11. 22. 78 NBC
The New Adventures of Wonder Woman   ep   Gault's Brain
   12. 29. 78 CBS
B. J. and the Bear   ep   3. 10. 79 NBC
The Seekers   ms   12. 3. 79, 12. 4. 79 NN
The CBS Library: Misunderstood Monsters   ep   The Reluctant
   Dragon   nar   4. 7. 81 CBS
Goliath Awaits   ms   11. 17. 81, 11. 23. 81 NN

CARRADINE, KEITH*
A Rumor of War   tf   9. 24. 80, 9. 25. 80 CBS

CARROLL, DIAHANN
SUPP. :
The Love Boat   ep   10. 22. 77 ABC
Roots: The Next Generations   ms ep   2. 23. 79 ABC
I Know Why the Caged Bird Sings   tf   4. 28. 79 CBS

CARTER, LYNDA
SUPP. :
The New Adventures of Wonder Woman   sr ret   9. 16. 77 CBS
The New Adventures of Wonder Woman   sr ret   9. 22. 78 CBS
The Last Song   tf   10. 23. 80 CBS
Born to Be Sold   tf   11. 2. 81 NBC

CARTER, NELL*
Cindy   tf   3. 24. 78 ABC
Lobo   sr   12. 30. 80 NBC
Gimme a Break   sr   10. 29. 81 NBC

CASEY, BERNIE*
Brian's Song   tf   11. 30. 71 ABC
Cade's County   ep   Slay Ride 1. 30. 72, 2. 6. 72 CBS
Longstreet   ep   2. 17. 72 ABC
Gargoyles   tf   11. 21. 72 CBS
The Snoop Sisters   ep   Fear Is a Free Throw 1. 29. 74 NBC
Panic on the 5:22   tf   11. 20. 74 ABC
Police Story   ep   12. 19. 75 NBC
Joe Forrester   ep   2. 2. 76 NBC
Police Story   ep   3. 22. 77 NBC
Mary Jane Harper Cried Last Night   tf   10. 5. 77 CBS
It Happened at Lakewood Manor   tf   12. 2. 77 ABC
Ring of Passion   tf   2. 4. 78 NBC
Love Is Not Enough   tf   6. 12. 78 NBC
Roots: The Next Generations   ms ep   2. 21. 79 ABC
Harris and Company   sr   3. 15. 79 NBC
The Martian Chronicles   ms ep   1. 27. 80 NBC
The Sophisticated Gents   tf   9. 29. 81, 9. 30. 81, 10. 1. 81 NBC

CASH, JOHNNY
    A&C:
    The Rebel   ep   The Death of Gray 1. 3. 60 ABC
    SUPP. :
    Thaddeus Rose and Eddie   tf   2. 24. 78 CBS
    The Pride of Jesse Hallan   tf   3. 3. 81 CBS

CASSAVETTES, JOHN
    A&C:
    Danger   ep   Lonesome Road 6. 8. 54 CBS
    Danger   ep   No Passport for Death 1. 8. 55 NBC
    Armstrong Circle Theatre   ep   Buckskin 4. 5. 55 NBC
    Danger   ep   Wire Tap 3. 15. 55 CBS
    SUPP. :
    Flesh and Blood   tf   10. 14. 79, 10. 16. 79 CBS

CASSIDY, DAVID
    SUPP. :
    Police Story   ep   A Chance to Live 5. 28. 78 NBC
    David Cassidy--Man Undercover   sr   11. 2. 78 NBC
    David Cassidy--Man Undercover   sr ret   7. 5. 79 NBC
    Fantasy Island   ep   1. 12. 80 ABC
    Gauguin the Savage   tf   4. 29. 80 CBS
    The Love Boat   ep   11. 8. 80 ABC
    The Night the City Screamed   tf   12. 14. 80 ABC

CASSIDY, JACK
    SUPP. :
    Benny and Barney: Las Vegas Undercover   tf   1. 19. 77 NBC
    The Feather and Father Gang   ep   7. 2. 77 ABC

CASSIDY, JOANNA*
    Rollergirls   sr   4. 24. 78 NBC
    Taxi   ep   10. 24. 78 ABC
    Starsky and Hutch   ep   The Avenger 10. 31. 78 ABC
    Kaz   ep   3. 7. 79 CBS
    240-Robert   sr   8. 28. 79 ABC
    The Love Boat   ep   10. 13. 79 ABC
    She's Dressed to Kill   tf   12. 10. 79 NBC
    Trapper John, M. D.   ep   2. 3. 80 CBS
    Dallas   ep   12. 5. 80, 12. 12. 80 CBS
    Charlie's Angels   ep   Hula Angels 1. 11. 81 ABC
    Enos   ep   Head Hunter 2. 11. 81 CBS
    Hart to Hart   ep   Slow Boat to Murder 2. 17. 81 ABC
    Flo   ep   Footsie 4. 4. 81 CBS
    Trapper John, M. D.   ep   COD 10. 11. 81 CBS

CASSIDY, SHAUN*
    The Hardy Boys/Nancy Drew Mysteries   sr   9. 11. 77 ABC
    The Hardy Boys   sr   10. 1. 78 ABC
    Like Normal People   tf   4. 13. 79 ABC
    Breaking Away   sr   11. 29. 80 ABC

CATTRALL, KIM*
   Good Against Evil   tf   5.22.77 NBC
   Quincy, M.E.   ep   Let Me Light the Way 5.27.77 NBC
   Logan's Run   ep   10.31.77 CBS
   Switch   ep   12.5.77 CBS
   What Really Happened to the Class of '65?   ep   The Girl Nobody
      Knew 12.29.77 NBC
   The Hardy Boys/Nancy Drew Mysteries   ep   2.12.78 ABC
   Columbo   ep   How to Dial a Murder 4.15.78 NBC
   The Bastard/Kent Family Chronicles   ms   5.22.78, 5.23.78 NN
   Starsky and Hutch   ep   9.26.78 ABC
   The Paper Chase   ep   10.31.78 CBS
   Family   ep   11.9.78 ABC
   The Incredible Hulk   ep   4.6.79 CBS
   How the West Was Won   ep   4.23.79 ABC
   Vega$ ep   5.9.79 ABC
   The Night Rider   pt   5.11.79 ABC
   The Rebels   ms   5.14.79, 5.21.79 NN
   Charlie's Angels   ep   Angels at the Altar 10.3.79 ABC
   Trapper John, M.D.   ep   11.4.79 CBS
   Scruples   ms   2.25.80, 2.26.80, 2.28.80 CBS
   The Gossip Columnist   pt   3.21.80 NN
   Hagen   ep   4.17.80 CBS

CHAKIRIS, GEORGE
   A&C:
   Medical Center   ep   11.8.72 CBS
   Police Surgeon   ep   A Bullet for the General 1.4.74 NN
   SUPP.:
   Return to Fantasy Island   tf   1.20.78 ABC
   The New Adventures of Wonder Woman   ep   Death in Disguise
      2.10.78 CBS

CHAMBERLAIN, RICHARD
   SUPP.:
   The Man in the Iron Mask   tf   1.17.77 NBC
   Centennial   ms ep   Only the Banks Live Forever 10.1.78 NBC
   Centennial   ms ep   The Yellow Apron 10.8.78 NBC
   Centennial   ms ep   The Wagon and the Elephant 10.29.78 NBC
   Centennial   ms ep   For as Long as the Water Flows 11.4.78
      NBC
   Great Performances   ep   The Good Doctor 11.1.78 PBS
   Shogun   ms   9.15-20.80 NBC

CHANNING, CAROL*
   The Love Boat   ep   Aunt Sylvia 10.17.81 ABC

CHANNING, STOCKARD
   SUPP.:
   Lucan   tf   5.22.77 ABC
   Silent Victory: The Kitty O'Neil Story 2.24.79 CBS
   Stockard Channing in Just Friends   sr   3.4.79 CBS
   The Stockard Channing Show   sr   3.24.80 CBS

CHARISSE, CYD
    SUPP. :
    Hawaii Five-O   ep   11. 16. 78 CBS
    Fantasy Island   ep   11. 25. 78 ABC
    The Love Boat   ep   5. 5. 79 ABC
    Portrait of an Escort   tf   10. 8. 80 CBS

CHARO
    A& C:
    Charo and the Sergeant   pt   8. 24. 76 ABC
    SUPP. :
    The Love Boat   ep   The Acapulco Connection 10. 15. 77 ABC
    Chico and the Man   ep   1. 27. 78 NBC
    Flying High   ep   12. 1. 78 CBS
    The Love Boat   ep   5. 5. 78 ABC
    The Love Boat   ep   April the Ninny 1. 17. 81 ABC
    The Love Boat   ep   Return of the Ninny 2. 14. 81 ABC
    Fantasy Island   ep   La Liberadora 11. 7. 81 ABC

CHILES, LINDEN*
    The Twilight Zone   ep   Four O'Clock 4. 6. 62 CBS
    The Munsters   ep   Munster Masquerade 9. 24. 64 CBS
    The Kraft Suspense Theatre   ep   Operation Grief 10. 8. 64 NBC
    The Man from U. N. C. L. E.   ep   The Yellow Scarf Affair
        1. 25. 65 NBC
    Perry Mason   ep   The Case of the Telltale Tap 2. 4. 65 CBS
    Convoy   sr   9. 17. 65 NBC
    The FBI   ep   The Contaminator 12. 4. 66 ABC
    The Green Hornet   ep   May the Best Man Lose 12. 23. 66 ABC
    The Fugitive   ep   The Breaking of the Habit 1. 31. 67 ABC
    The FBI   ep   The Predators 4. 7. 68 ABC
    Land of the Giants   ep   11. 10. 68 ABC
    Judd, for the Defense   ep   Thou Shalt Not Suffer a Witch to
        Live 12. 13. 68 ABC
    Lancer   ep   2. 11. 69 CBS
    Ironside   ep   Moonlighting Means Money 2. 26. 69 NBC
    The FBI   ep   Target of Interest 9. 14. 69 ABC
    The FBI   ep   Judas Goat 1. 23. 72 ABC
    Hawaii Five-O   ep   10. 24. 72 CBS
    Owen Marshall, Counselor at Law   ep   11. 16. 72 ABC
    Cannon   ep   11. 29. 72 CBS
    Banacek   ep   The Two Million Clams of Cap'n Jack 2. 7. 73 NBC
    Banacek   ep   No Stone Unturned 10. 3. 73 NBC
    Cannon   ep   Murder by Proxy 10. 10. 73 CBS
    Banacek   ep   The Three Million Dollar Piracy 11. 21. 73 NBC
    The Streets of San Francisco   ep   Winter Kill 12. 13. 73 ABC
    Hitchhike   tf   2. 23. 74 ABC
    Barnaby Jones   ep   3. 10. 74 CBS
    The Rockford Files   ep   The Dark and Bloody Ground 9. 20. 74
        NBC
    Insight   ep   9. 22. 74 NN
    Sierra   ep   10. 31. 74 NBC
    Panic on the 5:22   tf   11. 20. 74 ABC

Death Be Not Proud   tf   **2. 4. 75** ABC
Adventures of the Queen   tf   **2. 14. 75** CBS
Who Is the Black Dahlia?   tf   **3. 1. 75** NBC
Harry O   ep   Shades **10. 2. 75** ABC
Cannon   ep   **12. 10. 75** CBS
The Streets of San Francisco   ep   **1. 15. 76** ABC
Switch   ep   **1. 27. 76** CBS
Barnaby Jones   ep   **2. 5. 76** CBS
Helter Skelter   tf   **4. 1. 76, 4. 2. 76** CBS
Freeman   pt   **6. 19. 76** ABC
The Six Million Dollar Man   ep   **10. 24. 76** ABC
The Bionic Woman   ep   Jaime's Shield **12. 15. 76** ABC
The Six Million Dollar Man   ep   **12. 15. 76, 12. 22. 76** ABC
The Tony Randall Show   ep   **2. 10. 77** ABC
The Streets of San Francisco   ep   **4. 28. 77** ABC
Quincy, M. E.   ep   **5. 6. 77** NBC
Barnaby Jones   ep   **5. 19. 77** CBS
Washington Behind Closed Doors   ms   **9. 6-11. 77** ABC
James at 15   tf   **9. 15. 77** NBC
Logan's Run   ep   **9. 23. 77** CBS
James at 15   sr   **10. 27. 77** NBC
James at 16   sr   **2. 9. 78** NBC
Charlie's Angels   ep   Haunted Angels **10. 25. 78** ABC
Dallas   ep   **3. 9. 79** CBS
Act of Violence   tf   **11. 10. 79** CBS
Barnaby Jones   ep   The Final Victim **3. 6. 80** CBS
CHiPs   ep   **10. 5. 80** NBC
Scared Straight: Another Story   tf   **11. 6. 80** CBS
Enos   ep   **1. 21. 81** CBS
Buck Rogers in the 25th Century   ep   **2. 5. 81** NBC
Flo   ep   **2. 22. 81** CBS
Nero Wolfe   ep   **3. 6. 81** NBC
Red Flag: The Ultimate Game   tf   **10. 3. 81** CBS
Quincy, M. E.   ep   Slow Boat to Madness **11. 11. 81, 11. 18. 81**
   NBC

CIOFFI, CHARLES*
Cannon   ep   Call Unicorn **1. 28. 71** CBS
Medical Center   ep   The Pawn **12. 1. 71** CBS
Mongo's Back in Town   tf   **12. 10. 71** CBS
See the Man Run   tf   **12. 11. 71** ABC
Bonanza   ep   **2. 13. 72** NBC
The Bold Ones: The Doctors   ep   The Velvet Trap **12. 19. 72**
   NBC
Madigan   ep   **2. 28. 73** NBC
Wheeler and Murdoch   pt   **5. 9. 73** ABC
The FBI   ep   **1. 6. 74** ABC
Faraday and Company   ep   **1. 9. 74** NBC
Nicky's World   tf   **4. 19. 74** CBS
Hawaii Five-O   ep   **10. 15. 74** CBS
Cannon   ep   **3. 19. 75** CBS
Kate McShane   tf   **4. 11. 75** CBS
Hawaii Five-O   ep   **9. 19. 75** CBS

Matt Helm   ep   11.1.75 ABC
The Streets of San Francisco   ep   12.11.75 ABC
Medical Center   ep   12.29.75 CBS
Return to Earth   tf   5.14.76 ABC
Tail Gunner Joe   tf   2.6.77 NBC
Dog and Cat   tf   7.22.77 ABC
Kojak   ep   The Queen of Hearts Is Wild 10.2.77 CBS
Just a Little Inconvenience   tf   10.2.77 NBC
The New Adventures of Wonder Woman   ep   The Bermuda
    Triangle Crisis 10.7.77 CBS
The Six Million Dollar Man   ep   Just a Matter of Time 1.8.78
    ABC
Hawaii Five-O   ep   2.16.78 CBS
The Bionic Woman   ep   Long Live the King 3.25.78 NBC
Little House on the Prairie   ep   3.5.79 NBC
Hawaii Five-O   ep   3.22.79 CBS
Nero Wolfe   ep   2.20.81 NBC
Flamingo Road   ep   4.2.81 NBC
McClain's Law   ep   Let the Victim's Beware 12.11.81 NBC

CLARK, DANE
    A&C:
    Ford Theatre Hour   ep   Strange Harbor 10.13.50 CBS
    Somerset Maugham Theatre   ep   Partners 1.31.51 CBS
    Danger   ep   Nightmare 3.20.51 CBS
    Sure as Fate   ep   The Guinea Pigs 4.3.51 CBS
    Lights Out   ep   The Witness 4.16.51 NBC
    Danger   ep   The Actor 3.16.54 CBS
    Armstrong Circle Theatre   ep   No Room to Breathe 2.8.55
        NBC
    SUPP.:
    Hawaii Five-O   ep   3.3.77 CBS
    The Hardy Boys/Nancy Drew Mysteries   ep   5.1.77 ABC
    Police Woman   ep   11.1.77 NBC
    Switch   ep   12.26.77 CBS
    Police Story   ep   A Chance to Live 5.28.78 NBC
    Vega$ ep   9.20.78 ABC
    The Hardy Boys   ep   10.29.78 ABC
    Salvage 1   ep   2.5.79 ABC
    Fantasy Island   ep   11.24.79, 11.22.80 ABC

CLARK, SUSAN
    SUPP.:
    Jimmy B. and Andre   tf   3.19.80 CBS
    The Choice   tf   2.10.81 CBS

CLAYTON, JAN
    A&C:
    Medical Story   ep   1.8.76 NBC
    SUPP.:
    Sam   ep   4.18.78 CBS
    The Dukes of Hazzard   ep   1.9.81 CBS
    The Love Boat   ep   The Floating Bridge Game 12.12.81 ABC

CLINGER, DEBRA*
　　The Hardy Boys/Nancy Drew Mysteries   ep   1.8.78 ABC
　　Operation Runaway   ep   5.11.78 NBC
　　The American Girls   sr   9.23.78 CBS
　　Barnaby Jones   ep   10.27.77 CBS
　　Jack Frost   sp vo   12.13.79 NBC
　　Willow B: Women in Prison   pt   6.29.80 ABC
　　The Love Boat   ep   5.2.81 ABC

COBB, JULIE
　　SUPP.:
　　CHiPs   ep   3.2.78 NBC
　　Fantasy Island   ep   4.1.78 ABC
　　The Incredible Hulk   ep   11.24.78 CBS
　　Ladies' Man   ep   2.14.81 CBS
　　Riker   ep   3.21.81 CBS

COBB, LEE J.
　　Legend of the Black Hand   ms   8.17.78 ABC

COBURN, JAMES
　　A&C:
　　Bourbon Street Beat   ep   Target of Hate 3.7.60 ABC
　　Tate   ep   6.8.60 NBC
　　Combat   ep   Masquerade 10.1.63 ABC
　　SUPP.:
　　The Dain Curse   ms   5.22.78, 5.23.78   5.24.78 CBS
　　Escape   pt nar   3.7.81 NN
　　Jacqueline Susann's Valley of the Dolls 1981   tf   10.19.81,
　　　　10.20.81 CBS
　　Darkroom   sr hos   11.27.81 ABC

COCA, IMOGENE
　　SUPP.:
　　Getting There   pt   2.12.80 CBS
　　Trapper John, M.D.   ep   3.23.80 CBS
　　The Return of the Beverly Hillbillies   tf   10.6.81 CBS

COCO, JAMES
　　SUPP.:
　　The Love Boat   ep   Who's Who? 9.23.78 ABC
　　The Eddie Capra Mysteries   ep   12.22.78 NBC
　　Trapper John, M.D.   ep   9.30.79 CBS
　　The French-Atlantic Affair   ms   11.15.79, 11.16.79, 11.18.79
　　　　ABC
　　The Diary of Anne Frank   tf   11.17.80 NBC

COLE, DENNIS
　　A&C:
　　Love, American Style   ep   Love and the Hidden Meaning
　　　　11.30.73 ABC
　　Medical Center   ep   9.8.75, 9.15.75 CBS
　　The Quest   ep   9.22.76 NBC

SUPP. :
Charlie's Angels   ep   2. 23. 77 ABC
The Feather and Father Gang   ep   6. 4. 77 ABC
Police Story   ep   Pressure Point 9. 27. 77 NBC
The Love Boat   ep   10. 1. 77 ABC
Charlie's Angels   ep   Unidentified Flying Angels 11. 2. 77 ABC
Police Woman   ep   2. 22. 78 NBC
Fantasy Island   ep   3. 18. 78 ABC
The Eddie Capra Mysteries   ep   Who Killed Lloyd Wesley Jordan? 9. 29. 78 NBC
Flying High   ep   12. 22. 78 CBS
Charlie's Angels   ep   2. 7. 79 ABC
The Love Boat   ep   2. 24. 79 ABC
Fantasy Island   ep   3. 17. 79 ABC
Big Shamus, Little Shamus   ep   10. 13. 79 CBS
Fantasy Island   ep   10. 20. 79 ABC
A Man Called Sloane   ep   12. 22. 79 NBC
Vega$ ep   1. 23. 80 ABC
Fantasy Island   ep   3. 8. 80 ABC
The Young and the Restless   sr   Fall 1980 CBS
The Love Boat   ep   10. 25. 80 ABC
Fantasy Island   ep   11. 8. 80 ABC
Fantasy Island   ep   1. 31. 81 ABC
Fantasy Island   ep   11. 14. 81 ABC

COLE, MICHAEL
   SUPP. :
   The Eddie Capra Mysteries   ep   1. 5. 79 NBC
   The Love Boat   ep   Class Reunion 2. 3. 79 ABC
   Return of the Mod Squad   tf   5. 18. 79 ABC
   CHiPs   ep   Chips Goes Roller Disco 9. 22. 79 NBC
   The New Adventures of Wonder Woman   ep   The Man Who Wouldn't Tell 3. 31. 78 CBS
   Evening in Byzantium   ms   8. 14. 78, 8. 15. 78 NN
   Fantasy Island   ep   1. 3. 81 ABC
   Vega$ ep   No Way to Treat a Victim 3. 4. 81 ABC
   CHiPs   ep   5. 3. 81 NBC

COLE, OLIVIA*
   Roots   ms ep   1. 28. 77, 1. 29. 77, 1. 30. 77 ABC
   Family   ep   5. 2. 78 ABC
   Backstairs At the White House   ms   1. 29. 79, 2. 5. 79, 2. 12. 79, 2. 19. 79 NBC
   The Lazarus Syndrome   ep   9. 11. 79 ABC
   American Short Story   ep   The Sky Is Gray 4. 22. 80 PBS
   Children of Divorce   tf   11. 24. 80 NBC
   Fly Away Home   tf   9. 18. 81 ABC
   Mistress of Paradise   tf   10. 4. 81 ABC

COLEMAN, DABNEY*
   The Kraft Suspense Theatre   ep   The Threatening Eye 3. 12. 64 NBC
   The Invaders   ep   The Saucer 9. 12. 67 ABC

Bonanza ep Queen High 12. 1. 68 NBC
The Mod Squad ep The Guru 12. 31. 68 ABC
Bonanza ep A Darker Shadow 11. 23. 69 NBC
Brotherhood of the Bell tf 9. 17. 70 CBS
The FBI ep The Game of Terror 11. 7. 71 ABC
Owen Marshall, Counselor at Law ep Who Saw Him Die?
 11. 2. 72 ABC
Banyon ep 11. 17. 72 NBC
Room 222 ep 1. 12. 73 ABC
Ironside ep The Caller 1. 25. 73 NBC
Search ep 3. 28. 73 NBC
Barnaby Jones ep Blind Terror 9. 16. 73 CBS
Dying Room Only tf 9. 18. 73 CBS
Egan pt 9. 18. 73 ABC
Griff ep All the Lonely People 10. 13. 73 ABC
The President's Plane Is Missing tf 10. 23. 73 ABC
Cannon ep Dead Lady's Tears 11. 7. 73 CBS
McMillan and Wife ep Cross and Double Cross 2. 17. 74 NBC
Kojak ep Therapy in Dynamite 4. 10. 74 CBS
Bad Ronald tf 10. 23. 74 ABC
The Streets of San Francisco ep 10. 24. 74 ABC
Sons and Daughters ep 10. 30. 74 CBS
Manhunter ep 12. 11. 74 CBS
Attack on Terror: The FBI Vs. the Ku Klux Klan tf 2. 20. 75,
 2. 21. 75 CBS
Medical Center ep 3. 10. 75 CBS
Caribe ep 4. 28. 75 ABC
Returning Home tf 4. 29. 75 ABC
Mary Hartman, Mary Hartman sr 1. 6. 76 NN
The Mary Tyler Moore Show ep The Seminar 1. 10. 76 CBS
Cannon ep 1. 14. 76 CBS
Switch ep 2. 10. 76 CBS
Police Story ep 2. 20. 76 NBC
Bert D'Angelo, Superstar ep 3. 13. 76 ABC
Kiss Me, Kill Me tf 5. 8. 76 ABC
Mary Hartman, Mary Hartman sr ret 10. 4. 76 NN
The Streets of San Francisco ep 10. 28. 76 ABC
Police Story ep 11. 9. 76 NBC
Quincy, M. E. ep A Good Smack in the Mouth 4. 15. 77 NBC
Quincy, M. E. ep A Dead Man's Truth 9. 30. 77 NBC
Barnaby Jones ep 1. 26. 78 CBS
Maneaters Are Loose! tf 5. 3. 78 CBS
Apple Pie sr 9. 23. 78 ABC
More Than Friends tf 10. 20. 78 ABC
The Love Boat ep The Last Hundred Bucks 12. 9. 78 ABC
Diff'rent Strokes ep 9. 21. 79 NBC
Barnaby Jones ep Indoctrination in Evil 11. 1. 79 CBS
When She Was Bad tf 11. 25. 79 ABC
Callie and Son tf 10. 13. 81 CBS

COLEMAN, GARY*
 America 2-Night, Good Times and The Jeffersons (various
  episodes, none of which are credited in TV Guide, 1977-
  1978)

Diff'rent Strokes   sr   11. 3. 78 NBC
Diff'rent Strokes   sr ret   9. 21. 79 NBC
The Facts of Life   ep   8. 24. 79 NBC
The Kid from Left Field   tf   9. 30. 79 NBC
Buck Rogers in the 25th Century   ep   11. 22. 79 NBC
Scout's Honor   tf   9. 30. 80 NBC
Diff'rent Strokes   sr ret   11. 12. 80 NBC
The Facts of Life   ep   11. 19. 80 NBC
Diff'rent Strokes   sr ret   10. 29. 81 NBC

COLLINS, GARY*
The Wackiest Ship in the Army   sr   9. 19. 65 NBC
Iron Horse   sr   9. 12. 66 ABC
The Virginian   ep   3. 12. 69 NBC
Quarantined   tf   2. 24. 70 ABC
Owen Marshall, Counselor at Law   ep   11. 11. 71 ABC
Getting Away from It All   tf   1. 18. 72 ABC
The Sixth Sense   sr   1. 15. 72 ABC
McCloud   ep   Fifth Man in a String Quartet 2. 2. 72 NBC
Police Story   ep   Country Boy 2. 19. 74 NBC
Houston, We've Got a Problem   tf   3. 2. 74 NBC
Born Free   sr   9. 9. 74 NBC
The Bionic Woman   ep   4. 14. 76 ABC
The Quest   ep   11. 17. 76, 11. 24. 76 NBC
Most Wanted   ep   1. 8. 77 ABC
Roots   ms   1. 23-30. 77 ABC
Fantastic Journey 2. 3. 77,   2. 10. 77 NBC
Tales of the Unexpected   ep   8. 17. 77 NBC
Mystery of the Week   ep   Double Kill 8. 17. 77 ABC
The Night They Took Miss Beautiful   tf   10. 24. 77 NBC
Mystery of the Week   ep   Dial a Deadly Number 3. 22. 78 ABC
Police Woman   ep   3. 23. 78 NBC
The Love Boat   ep   Pacific Princess Overtures 5. 20. 78 ABC
The World of Disney   ep   The Young Runaways 5. 28. 78 NBC
This Is the Life   ep   6. 25. 78 NN
Alice   ep   10. 15. 78 CBS
Charlie's Angels   ep   11. 15. 78 ABC
Insight   ep   12. 3. 78 NN
Alice   ep   12. 10. 78 CBS
The Kid from Left Field   tf   9. 30. 79 NBC
Fantasy Island   ep   11. 24. 79 ABC
Charlie's Angels   ep   Angels on Campus 11. 28. 79 ABC
Vega$ ep   1. 2. 80 ABC
Disney's Wonderful World   ep   The Secret of Lost Valley
    4. 27. 80 NBC
Daredevils   sp ho   11. 2. 80 NBC
Jacqueline Susann's Valley of the Dolls 1981   tf   10. 19. 81,
    10. 20. 81 CBS

COLLINS, JOAN
A& C:
Space: 1999   ep   11. 11. 75 NN
SUPP. :
Fantastic Journey   ep   4. 7. 77 NBC

Future Cop   ep   4. 30. 77 ABC
Starsky and Hutch   ep   9. 17. 77 ABC
Fantasy Island   ep   My Fair Pharaoh 5. 10. 80 ABC
Tales of the Unexpected   ep   Neck 5. 31. 80 NN
Dynasty   sr   11. 4. 81 ABC

COMER, ANJANETTE
   A&C:
   The Young Lawyers   ep   10. 28. 69 ABC
   Baretta   ep   11. 10. 76 ABC
   SUPP. :
   Dead of Night   tf ep   No Such Thing As a Vampire 3. 29. 77
      NBC

CONN, DIDI*
   Genesis II   tf   3. 23. 73 ABC
   Happy Days   ep   4. 29. 75 ABC
   The Practice   sr   1. 30. 76 NBC
   The Practice   sr ret   10. 13. 76 NBC
   Handle with Care   pt   5. 9. 77 CBS
   Three on a Date   tf   2. 17. 78 ABC
   Murder at the Mardi Gras   tf   5. 10. 78 NBC
   Sweepstakes   ep   3. 30. 79 NBC
   Semi Tough   ep   6. 6. 80 ABC
   Fonz and the Happy Days Gang   sr vo   11. 8. 80 ABC
   Benson   sr   11. 27. 81 ABC

CONNELLY, CHRISTOPHER*
   Peyton Place   sr   9. 15. 64 ABC
   The Mod Squad   ep   Peace Now--Arly Blau! 4. 8. 69 ABC
   In Name Only   tf   11. 25. 69 ABC
   Incident in San Francisco   tf   2. 28. 71 CBS
   The Man and the City   ep   I Should Have Let Him Die 9. 21. 71
      ABC
   Cannon   ep   Blood on the Vine 1. 18. 72 CBS
   Night Gallery   ep   Spectre in Tap-Shoes 10. 29. 72 NBC
   Owen Marshall, Counselor at Law   ep   2. 7. 73 ABC
   Ironside   ep   2. 15. 73 NBC
   Circle of Fear   ep   2. 23. 73 NBC
   Gunsmoke   ep   10. 22. 73 CBS
   Griff   ep   Her Name Was Nancy 12. 8. 73 ABC
   The Brian Keith Show   ep   Here Comes the What? 1. 11. 74 NBC
   Barnaby Jones   ep   The Deadly Jinx 1. 13. 74 CBS
   Marcus Welby, M. D.   ep   Fear of Silence 1. 29. 74 ABC
   Cannon   ep   The Hit Man 9. 18. 74 CBS
   Police Story   ep   11. 19. 74 NBC
   Ironside   ep   12. 12. 74 NBC
   The Last Day   tf   2. 15. 75 NBC
   Medical Story   ep   11. 13. 75 NBC
   Police Story   ep   12. 19. 75 NBC
   The Quest   ep   9. 22. 76 NBC
   Petrocelli   ep   12. 8. 76 NBC
   Police Story   ep   12. 14. 76, 12. 21. 76 NBC
   Hawaii Five-O   ep   2. 24. 77 CBS

Quincy, M. E.   ep   5.13.77 NBC
Charlie Cobb, Nice Night for a Hanging   tf   6.9.77 NBC
Murder in Peyton Place   tf   10.3.77 NBC
The Hardy Boys/Nancy Drew Mysteries   ep   11.20.77 ABC
The Incredible Rocky Mountain Race   tf   12.17.77 NBC
Fantasy Island   ep   3.18.78 ABC
Police Story   ep   No Margin for Error 4.30.78 NBC
Crash   tf   10.29.78 ABC
B.J. and the Bear   ep   4.28.79 NBC
Salvage I   ep   5.14.79 ABC
Stunt 7   tf   5.30.79 CBS
Fantasy Island   ep   9.21.79 ABC
Trapper John, M.D.   ep   11.4.79 CBS
The Love Boat   ep   11.17.79 ABC
The Martian Chronicles   ms ep   1.29.80 CBS
Beyond Westworld   ep   3.12.80 CBS
CHiPs   ep   New Guy in Town 3.15.81 NBC
B.J. and the Bear   ep   S.T.U.N.T.S.   3.31.81 NBC
Fantasy Island   ep   5.2.81 ABC
Return of the Rebels   tf   10.17.81 CBS
Skyward Christmas   pt   12.3.81 NBC

CONNORS, CHUCK
   A&C:
   Police Story   ep   11.16.76 NBC
   SUPP.:
   Roots   ms ep   1.27.77, 1.28.77 ABC
   The Night They Took Miss Beautiful   tf   10.24.77 NBC
   Standing Tall   tf   1.21.78 NBC
   Stone   ep   1.28.80 ABC
   Walking Tall   ep   1.31.81 NBC
   The Great Mysteries of Hollywood   pt hos   3.7.81 NN

CONNORS, MIKE
   A&C:
   Redigo   ep   Shadow of the Cougar 11.26.63 NBC
   SUPP.:
   Police Story   ep   11.9.77 NBC
   Long Journey Back   tf   12.15.78 ABC
   The Death of Ocean View Park   tf   10.19.79 ABC
   High Midnight   tf   11.27.79 CBS
   Casino   tf   8.1.80 ABC
   Night Kill   tf   12.18.80 NBC
   The Love Boat   ep   5.2.81 ABC
   Today's FBI   sr   10.25.81 ABC

CONRAD, MICHAEL
   A&C:
   Wagon Train   ep   The Sarah Cummings Story 12.2.63 ABC
   The Twilight Zone   ep   Black Leather Jackets 1.31.64 CBS
   Rawhide   ep   Prairie Fire 3.19.65 CBS
   Search   ep   1.24.73 NBC

Emergency ep 9.29.73 NBC
The Bob Newhart Show ep 9.29.73 CBS
Mannix ep 11.4.73 CBS
The FBI ep 12.30.73 ABC
The Bob Newhart Show ep 3.2.74 CBS
Starsky and Hutch ep 12.18.76 ABC
SUPP.:
The Six Million Dollar Man ep The Infiltrators 2.6.77 ABC
Little House on the Prairie ep 11.7.77 NBC
How the West Was Won ep 4.16.78 ABC
How the West Was Won ep 5.14.78 ABC
Charlie's Angels ep Angels in Vegas 9.13.78 ABC
The Waltons ep 9.21.78 CBS
The World of Disney ep Donovan's Kid 1.14.79, 1.21.79 NBC
Vega$ ep 1.17.79 ABC
CHiPs ep 2.17.79 NBC
Police Story ep A Cry for Justice 5.23.79 NBC
Julie Farr, M.D. ep 6.26.79 ABC
Paris ep 10.27.79 CBS
Hill Street Blues sr 1.15.81 NBC
The Incredible Hulk ep 4.3.81 CBS
Hill Street Blues sr ret 10.29.81 NBC
Fire on the Mountain tf 11.23.81 NBC

CONRAD, ROBERT
A&C:
77 Sunset Strip ep Who Killed Cock Robin 2.5.60 ABC
SUPP.:
Baa Baa Black Sheep (a.k.a. The Black Sheep Squadron) sr
    ret 12.14.77 NBC
Centennial ms ep Only the Banks Live Forever 10.1.78 NBC
Centennial ms ep The Yellow Apron 10.8.78 NBC
The Duke sr 4.5.79 NBC
The Wild Wild West Revisited tf 5.9.79 CBS
A Man Called Sloane sr 9.22.79 NBC
Daredevils sp hos 11.21.80 NBC
Coach of the Year tf 12.21.80 NBC
More Wild Wild West tf 10.7.81, 10.8.81 CBS

CONRAD, WILLIAM
A&C:
The Man and the Challenge ep Invisible Force 10.17.59 NBC
Target: The Corruptors ep Yankee Dollar 5.11.62 ABC
Gunsmoke ep Women for Sale nar 9.10.73, 9.17.73 CBS
Wild Wild World of Animals sr nar 9.11.73 NN
SUPP.:
The City tf nar 1.12.77 NBC
Tales of the Unexpected sr nar 2.2.77 NBC
How the West Was Won ms nar 2.6.77, 2.7.77, 2.13.77 ABC
Night Cries tf 1.29.78 NBC
How the West Was Won sr nar 2.12.78 ABC
Keefer tf 3.16.78 ABC
How the West Was Won sr ret nar 1.15.79 ABC
Battles: The Murder That Wouldn't Die tf 3.9.80 NBC

The Return of Frank Cannon   tf   11.1.80 CBS
Return of the King   tf vo   5.11.80 ABC
Turnover Smith   tf   6.8.80 ABC
Nero Wolfe   sr   1.16.81 NBC
The Fall Guy   sr vo   11.4.81 ABC

CONSTANTINE, MICHAEL*
   The Twilight Zone   ep   I Am the Night--Color Me Black
      3.27.64 CBS
   The Outer Limits   ep   Counterweight 12.26.64 ABC
   Death Valley Days   ep   Paid in Full 2.12.65 NN
   Hey, Landlord!   sr   9.11.66 NBC
   12 O'Clock High   ep   9.16.66 ABC
   The Good Guys   ep   2.26.69 CBS
   Room 222   sr   9.17.69 ABC
   Room 222   sr ret   9.23.70 ABC
   Room 222   sr ret   9.17.71 ABC
   The Mary Tyler Moore Show   ep   9.25.71 CBS
   The Impatient Heart   tf   10.8.71 NBC
   Suddenly Single   tf   10.19.71 ABC
   Room 222   sr ret   9.15.72 ABC
   Deadly Harvest   tf   9.26.72 CBS
   Say Goodbye, Maggie Cole   tf   9.27.72 ABC
   Love, American Style   ep   10.13.72 ABC
   The Bold Ones: The Doctors   ep   A Terminal Career 12.26.72
      NBC
   Room 222   sr ret   9.14.73 ABC
   Big Rose   tf   3.26.74 CBS
   Kojak   ep   9.15.74 CBS
   Death Cruise   tf   10.30.74 ABC
   Manhunter   ep   1.22.75 CBS
   The Secret Night Caller   tf   2.18.75 NBC
   Police Woman   ep   9.19.75 NBC
   The Night That Panicked America   tf   10.31.75 ABC
   Ellery Queen   ep   1.25.76 NBC
   Police Woman   ep   1.27.76 NBC
   Conspiracy of Terror   tf   4.10.76 NBC
   Twin Detectives   tf   5.1.76 ABC
   Wanted: The Sundance Woman 10.1.76 ABC
   Sirota's Court   sr   12.1.76 NBC
   Daughters   pt   7.20.77 NBC
   Billy: Portrait of a Street Kid   tf   9.12.77 NBC
   79 Park Avenue   ms   10.16.77, 10.17.77, 10.18.77 NBC
   Summer of My German Soldier   tf   10.30.78 NBC
   The Pirate   tf   11.21.78, 11.22.78 CBS
   Crisis in Mid-Air   tf   2.13.79 CBS
   Roots: The Next Generations   ms ep   2.25.79 ABC
   The Love Tapes   tf   5.9.80 ABC
   Quincy, M.E.   ep   Gentle into That Good Night 12.16.81 NBC
   Lou Grant   ep   Marathon 1.19.81 CBS
   Vega$ ep   1.28.81 ABC
   Evita Perone   tf   2.23.81, 2.24.81 NBC
   Trapper John, M.D.   ep   Brain Child 5.17.81 CBS
   Palmerstown   ep   The Suitor 6.2.81 CBS

CONVERSE, FRANK
 A&C:
 Circle of Fear   ep   1. 19. 73 NBC
 Movin' On (a. k. a. In Tandem)   tf   8. 16. 74 NBC
 SUPP. :
 Quincy, M. E.   ep   2. 4. 77 NBC
 Kingston Confidential   ep   6. 1. 77 NBC
 Killer on Board   tf   10. 10. 77 NBC
 Cruise into Terror   tf   2. 3. 78 ABC
 The Love Boat   ep   2. 4. 78 ABC
 The Bionic Woman   ep   2. 18. 78 NBC
 The Black Sheep Squadron   ep   3. 15. 78 NBC
 Sergeant Matlovich vs. the U. S. Air Force   tf   8. 21. 78 NBC
 The American Girls   ep   9. 30. 78 CBS
 David Cassidy--Man Undercover   ep   Death in Cell Block D
     11. 16. 78 NBC
 Steeltown   pt   5. 19. 79 CBS
 The ABC Afterschool Special   ep   A Movie Star's Daughter
     10. 10. 79 ABC
 Marilyn: The Untold Story   tf   9. 28. 80 ABC
 Tales of the Unexpected   ep   11. 1. 80 NN
 Momma the Detective   pt   1. 9. 81 NBC
 Great Performances   ep   Guests of the Nation 2. 9. 81 PBS
 Gabe and Walker   pt   7. 20. 81 ABC
 The Miracle of Kathy Miller   tf   10. 5. 81 CBS
 The CBS Children's Mystery Theatre   ep   Mystery at Fire
     Island 11. 27. 81 CBS
 Fantasy Island   ep   Romance Times Three 12. 5. 81 ABC

CONVY, BERT
 SUPP. :
 The Love Boat II   tf   1. 21. 77 ABC
 SST--Death Flight   tf   2. 25. 77 ABC
 Thou Shalt Not Commit Adultery   tf   11. 1. 78 NBC
 Fantasy Island   ep   11. 18. 78 ABC
 The Love Boat   ep   12. 2. 78 ABC
 The Dallas Cowboys Cheerleaders   tf   1. 14. 79 ABC
 Charlie's Angels   ep   Love Boat Angels 9. 12. 79 ABC
 The Man in the Santa Claus Suit   tf   12. 23. 79 NBC
 Aloha Paradise   ep   3. 4. 81 ABC
 Jacqueline Susann's Valley of the Dolls 1981   tf   10. 19. 81,
     10. 20. 81 CBS

COOGAN, JACKIE
 A&C:
 Hawaiian Eye   ep   Dangerous Eden 11. 4. 59 ABC
 SUPP. :
 Halloween with the Addams Family   sp   10. 30. 77 NBC
 Sweepstakes   ep   3. 9. 79 NBC

COOK, ELISHA
 A&C:
 The Islanders   ep   The Twenty-Six Paper 1. 8. 61 ABC

Laramie   ep   The Tumble Weed Wagon 5. 9. 61 NBC
The Deputy   ep   Brand of Honesty 6. 10. 61 NBC
77 Sunset Strip   ep   The Inverness Capes Caper 10. 13. 61 ABC
The Dick Powell Theatre   ep   Borderline 11. 27. 62 NBC
Rawhide   ep   Piney 10. 9. 64 CBS
SUPP. :
Dead of Night   tf ep   No Such Thing As a Vampire 3. 29. 77 NBC
The Bionic Woman   ep   5. 4. 77 ABC
Quincy, M. E.   ep   12. 2. 77 NBC
Lucan   ep   11. 20. 78 ABC
Salem's Lot   tf   11. 17. 79, 11. 24. 79 CBS
Magnum, P. I.   ep   12. 24. 81 CBS

COOPER, JACKIE
   A&C:
   Starlight Theatre   ep   The Fascinating Mr. Hogan 6. 14. 51 CBS
   The Clock   ep   Dream Beach 8. 3. 51 NBC
   Robert Montgomery Presents   ep   Private Purkey's Private
      Place 9. 7. 53 NBC
   Robert Montgomery Presents   ep   Really The Blues 12. 7. 53
      NBC
   SUPP. :
   Police Story   ep   2. 1. 77 NBC
   Operation Petticoat   tf   9. 4. 77 ABC
   The Rockford Files   ep   2. 24. 78 NBC

CORBETT, GLENN
   SUPP. :
   The Rockford Files   ep   1. 12. 79 NBC
   Barnaby Jones   ep   2. 22. 79 CBS
   Stunts Unlimited   tf   1. 4. 80 ABC

CORBETT, GRETCHEN*
   Marcus Welby, M. D.   ep   Fear of Silence 1. 29. 74 ABC
   The Rockford Files   sr   9. 13. 74 NBC
   Sierra   ep   11. 14. 74 NBC
   Hawaii Five-O   ep   Study in Rage 2. 11. 75 CBS
   The Barbary Coast   ep   11. 14. 75 ABC
   Matt Helm   ep   12. 13. 75 ABC
   Farewell to Manzanar   tf   3. 11. 76 NBC
   The Savage Bees   tf   11. 22. 76 CBS
   The New, Original Wonder Woman   ep   Wonder Woman vs.
      Gargantua 12. 18. 76 ABC
   Kingston Confidential   ep   6. 22. 77 NBC
   Family   ep   9. 13. 77, 9. 20. 77 ABC
   W. E. B.   ep   10. 5. 78 NBC
   Secrets of Three Hungry Wives   tf   10. 9. 78 NBC
   Lucan   ep   12. 4. 78 ABC
   Mandrake   tf   1. 24. 79 NBC
   She's Dressed to Kill   tf   12. 10. 79 NBC
   Magnum, P. I.   ep   The Curse of the King Kamehameha Club
      2. 19. 81 CBS
   Lobo   ep   3. 24. 81 NBC
   One Day at a Time   ep   12. 20. 81 CBS

CORD, ALEX
    A&C:
    Insight ep 11.11.73 NN
    SUPP. :
    Fire tf 5.8.77 NBC
    The Hallmark Hall of Fame ep Have I Got a Christmas for
        You 12.16.77 NBC
    W. E. B. sr 9.13.78 NBC
    The Love Boat ep 11.17.79 ABC
    Beggarman, Thief tf 11.26.79, 11.27.79 NBC
    The Love Boat ep Doc's Dismissal 1.3.81 ABC
    Fantasy Island ep 4.11.81 ABC
    Fantasy Island ep La Liberadora 11.7.81 ABC
    Goliath Awaits ms 11.17.81, 11.23.81 NN

CORNELL, LYDIA*
    Too Close for Comfort sr 10.28.80 ABC
    Too Close for Comfort sr ret 11.11.81 ABC

COSBY, BILL
    SUPP. :
    Fat Albert and the Cosby Kids sr ret 9.77 CBS
    Top Secret tf 6.4.78 NBC
    Fat Albert and the Cosby Kids sr ret 9.78 CBS
    Like You, Like Me sp hos 8.25.79 NN
    The New Fat Albert Show sr 9.79 CBS
    The New Fat Albert Show sr ret 9.80 CBS
    The New Fat Albert Show sr ret 9.81 CBS

COTTEN, JOSEPH
    A&C:
    G. E. Theatre ep The Enemies 10.14.56 CBS
    SUPP. :
    Aspen ms 11.5.77, 11.6.77, 11.7.77 NBC
    Return to Fantasy Island tf 1.20.78 ABC
    The Hardy Boys/Nancy Drew Mysteries ep Arson and Old
        Lace 4.1.78 ABC
    Legend of the Black Hand ms ep 8.17.78 ABC
    Fantasy Island ep 11.3.79 ABC
    Tales of the Unexpected ep 5.24.80 NN
    Casino tf 8.1.80 ABC
    The Love Boat ep Aunt Hilly 3.14.81 ABC

COX, RONNY
    SUPP. :
    Tales of the Unexpected ep Devil Pack 2.16.77 NBC
    Corey: For the People tf 6.12.77 NBC
    The Girl Called Hatter Fox tf 10.12.77 CBS
    Transplant tf 4.17.79 CBS
    When Hell Was in Session tf 10.8.79 NBC
    The Courage of Kavik tf 1.20.80 NBC
    The Last Resort ep 1.28.80 CBS
    Fugitive Family tf 10.1.80 CBS

The Last Song   tf   10. 23. 80 CBS
First Time, Second Time   pt   10. 25. 80 CBS
Alcatraz: The Whole Shocking Story   tf   11. 5. 80,   11. 6. 80 NBC
Fallen Angel   tf   2. 24. 81 CBS
Darkroom   ep   The Siege of 31 August 12. 11. 81 ABC

CRABBE, BUSTER
   SUPP. :
   Buck Rogers in the 25th Century   ep   Planet of the Slave Girls
      9. 27. 79 NBC
   B. J. and the Bear   ep   S. T. U. N. T.   3. 31. 81 NBC

CRANE, BOB
   SUPP. :
   The Hardy Boys/Nancy Drew Mysteries   ep   A Haunting We
      Will Go 4. 3. 77 ABC
   The Love Boat   ep   1. 7. 78 ABC

CRAWFORD, BRODERICK
   A&C:
   Danger   ep   Borrowed Furs 6. 9. 53 CBS
   Lux Video Theatre   ep   Return of Sock Renard 10. 29. 53 CBS
   Kraft Mystery Theatre   ep   Shadow of a Man 6. 19. 63 NBC
   SUPP. :
   Flying High   ep   North by Northeast 10. 13. 78 CBS
   Fantasy Island   ep   Lillian Russell 11. 28. 81 ABC

CRENNA, RICHARD
   SUPP. :
   The War Between the Tates   tf   6. 13. 77 NBC
   Centennial   ms ep   Only the Banks Live Forever 10. 1. 78 NBC
   Devil Dog: The Hound of Hell   tf   10. 31. 78 CBS
   First You Cry   tf   11. 8. 78 CBS
   Fire in the Sky   tf   11. 26. 78 NBC
   Joshua's World   pt   8. 21. 80 CBS
   Fugitive Family   tf   10. 1. 80 CBS
   Look at Us   sr hos   9. 19. 81 NN
   The Ordeal of Bill Carney   tf   12. 23. 81 CBS

CRISTAL, LINDA
   SUPP. :
   When the West Was Fun   sp   6. 5. 79 ABC
   Barnaby Jones   ep   Homecoming for a Dead Man 11. 8. 79 CBS
   Condominium   ms   11. 20. 80,   11. 24. 80 NN
   The Love Boat   ep   The Duel 3. 14. 81 ABC
   Fantasy Island   ep   5. 23. 81 ABC

CRONYN, HUME
   A&C:
   Pulitzer Prize Playhouse   ep   The Poni Story 12. 8. 50 ABC
   SUPP. :
   The Many Faces of Love   sp   3. 7. 79 PBS

CROSBY, CATHY LEE
 A&C:
 Wonder Woman tf 3.12.74 ABC
 SUPP.:
 Keefer tf 3.16.78 ABC
 Coach tf 3.6.79 CBS
 The Three Wives of David Wheeler pt 8.1.79 NBC
 Hawaii Five-O ep 12.18.79 CBS
 Roughnecks ms 7.15.80, 7.16.80 NN

CROSBY, MARY (a.k.a. Mary Frances Crosby)*
 With This Ring tf 5.5.78 ABC
 A Guide for the Married Woman tf 10.13.78 ABC
 Starsky and Hutch ep 10.24.78 ABC
 CHiPs ep 1.20.79 NBC
 Brothers and Sisters sr 1.21.79 NBC
 Dallas sr 10.19.79 CBS
 Midnight Lace tf 2.9.81 NBC
 Golden Gate tf 9.25.81 ABC

CROWLEY, PATRICIA (a.k.a. Pat Crowley)
 A&C:
 Maverick ep A Tale of Three Cities 10.18.59 ABC
 The Virginian ep The Hell Wind 2.14.68 NBC
 Police Story ep The Return of Joe Forrester 5.6.75 NBC
 SUPP.:
 Family ep 1.18.77 ABC
 Tales of the Unexpected ep Force of Evil 3.13.77 NBC
 The Feather and Father Gang ep 6.18.77 ABC
 Return to Fantasy Island tf 1.20.78 ABC
 The Love Boat ep 2.4.78 ABC
 A Family Upside Down tf 4.9.78 NBC
 The Eddie Capra Mysteries ep 12.8.78 NBC
 The Millionaire tf 12.19.78 CBS
 The Rockford Files ep 1.19.79 NBC
 Charlie's Angels ep Angels in Waiting 3.21.79 ABC
 The World of Disney ep Skytrap 5.23.79 NBC
 Hawaii Five-O ep 4.5.80 CBS
 Police Story ep Confessions of a Lady Cop 4.28.80 NBC
 Charlie's Angels ep Hula Angels 1.11.81 ABC
 The Love Boat ep Jealousy 1.17.81 ABC

CULP, ROBERT
 A&C:
 The Rifleman ep The Hero 2.2.60 ABC
 Americans ep The Guerrillas 3.20.61 NBC
 Cain's Hundred ep The Swinger 4.3.62 NBC
 The Rifleman ep Waste 10.1.62, 10.8.62 ABC
 The Virginian ep The Black Stallion 9.30.64 NBC
 From Sea to Shining Sea (Part 2) ep Land of the Free sp
  12.19.74 NN
 SUPP.:
 Spectre tf 5.21.77 NBC
 Last of the Good Guys tf 3.7.78 CBS

Greatest Heroes of the Bible   ep   The Story of Joshua 11. 20. 78
   NBC
Women in White   tf   2. 8. 79 ABC
Roots: The Next Generations   ms ep   2. 22. 79 ABC
Mrs. Columbo   ep   2. 26. 79 NBC
Police Story   ep   A Cry for Justice 5. 23. 79 NBC
Hot Rod   tf   5. 25. 79 ABC
A Man Called Sloane   ep   The Seduction Squad 9. 22. 79 NBC
The Dream Merchants   ms   5. 12. 80, 5. 19. 80 NN
The Love Boat   ep   11. 8. 80 ABC
The Night the City Screamed   tf   12. 14. 80 ABC
The Greatest American Hero   sr   3. 18. 81 ABC
Killjoy   tf   10. 22. 81 CBS
The Greatest American Hero   sr ret   10. 28. 81 ABC

CUMMINGS, BOB (a. k. a. Robert Cummings)
   A& C:
   Somerset Maugham Theatre   ep   Theatre 4. 16. 51 CBS
   SUPP. :
   The ABC Afterschool Special   ep   It Isn't Easy Being a Teen-
      age Millionaire 3. 8. 78 ABC
   The Love Boat   ep   Third Wheel 5. 12. 79 ABC

CUMMINGS, QUINN*
   Big Eddie   sr   8. 23. 75 CBS
   Jeremiah of Jacob's Neck   pt   8. 13. 76 CBS
   The Six Million Dollar Man   ep   A Bionic Christmas 12. 12. 76
      ABC
   Night Terror   tf   2. 7. 77 NBC
   Visions   ep   The Dancing Bear 10. 23. 77 PBS
   Intimate Strangers   tf   11. 11. 77 ABC
   Family   sr   9. 21. 78 ABC
   Loser Take All   sp   4. 18. 79 NN
   Family   sr ret   12. 24. 79 ABC
   Family   sr ret   6. 4. 80 ABC
   The Babysitter   tf   11. 28. 80 ABC
   Darkroom   ep   The Bogey Man Will Get You 12. 4. 81 ABC

CURTIS, JAMIE LEE*
   The Nancy Drew Mysteries   ep   Mystery of the Fallen Angels
      4. 17. 77 ABC
   Operation Petticoat   tf   9. 4. 77 ABC
   Operation Petticoat   sr   9. 17. 77 ABC
   The Love Boat   ep   11. 11. 78 ABC
   Charlie's Angels   ep   Winning Is for Losers 10. 18. 78 ABC
   Buck Rogers in the 25th Century   ep   11. 1. 79 NBC
   The Love Boat   ep   Locked Away   11. 11. 79 ABC
   She's in the Army Now   tf   5. 20. 81 ABC
   Death of a Centerfold: The Dorothy Stratton Story   tf   11. 1. 81
      NBC

CURTIS, TONY
   SUPP. :
   Vega$ tf   4. 25. 78 ABC

Vega$ sr 9. 20. 78 ABC
The Users tf 10. 1. 78 ABC
Moviola: The Scarlett O'Hara War tf 5. 19. 80 NBC
The Million Dollar Face tf 3. 12. 81 NBC

-D-

DAHL, ARLENE
    SUPP. :
    The Love Boat ep 3. 10. 79 ABC
    The Love Boat ep Return of the Captain's Brother 12. 6. 80
        ABC
    Fantasy Island ep 2. 28. 81 ABC
    One Life to Live sr 12. 81 ABC

DAILEY, DAN
    SUPP. :
    Testimony of Two Men ms 5. 1. 78, 5. 2. 78, 5. 3. 78 NN

DALY, JAMES
    A&C:
    The Clock ep The Joke 10. 6. 50 NBC
    Danger ep The Double Deal 7. 1. 52 CBS
    Armstrong Circle Theatre ep Return the Favor 8. 12. 52 NBC
    Robert Montgomery Presents ep Keane vs. Keane 10. 20. 52
        NBC
    Combat ep Encounter 1. 31. 67 ABC
    The Virginian ep Silver Image 9. 25. 68 NBC
    SUPP. :
    Roots: The Next Generations ms ep 2. 20. 79 ABC

DALY, TYNE*
    Mission: Impossible ep Nerves 12. 4. 70 CBS
    In Search of America tf 3. 23. 71 ABC
    Longstreet ep One in the Reality Column 9. 30. 71 ABC
    A Howling in the Woods tf 11. 5. 71 NBC
    McMillan and Wife ep 11. 10. 71 NBC
    Hollywood Television Theatre ep Young Marrieds at Play
        12. 9. 71 PBS
    Medical Center ep The Choice 2. 9. 72 CBS
    Heat of Anger tf 3. 3. 72 CBS
    The Mod Squad ep 10. 26. 72 ABC
    The Rookies ep A Farewell Tree from Marly 3. 5. 73 ABC
    Young Dr. Kildare ep 3. 9. 73 NN
    The Man Who Could Talk to Kids tf 10. 17. 73 ABC
    Hawkins ep A Life for a Life 11. 13. 73 CBS
    Medical Center ep Deadly Game 12. 10. 73 CBS
    The Streets of San Francisco ep Commitment 1. 3. 74 ABC
    Doc Elliot ep The Touch of God 1. 23. 74 ABC

The Rookies   ep   Primelock 3. 4. 74 ABC
Barnaby Jones   ep   A Gathering of Thieves 9. 10. 74 CBS
Wide World of Mystery   ep   The Haunting of Penthouse D
     10. 16. 74 ABC
The Rookies   ep   Cliffy 3. 3. 75 ABC
Medical Center   ep   12. 8. 75 CBS
The Entertainer   tf   3. 10. 76 NBC
Visions   ep   The Dancing Bear 10. 23. 77 PBS
Intimate Strangers   tf   11. 11. 77 ABC
Greatest Heroes of the Bible   ep   Solomon and Bathsheba
     11. 21. 78, 11. 22. 78 NBC
Better Late Than Never   tf   10. 17. 79 NBC
Shirley   ep   12. 14. 79 NBC
The Women's Room   tf   9. 14. 80 ABC
Quincy, M. E.   ep   11. 26. 80 NBC
A Matter of Life and Death   tf   1. 13. 81 CBS
Lou Grant   ep   Violence 4. 6. 81 CBS
Cagney and Lacey   tf   10. 8. 81 CBS
Quincy, M. E.   ep   Gentle into That Good Night 12. 16. 81 NBC

DAMON, CATHRYN*
   The Bionic Woman   ep   Deadly Ringer 2. 2. 77, 2. 9. 77 ABC
   Soap   sr   9. 13. 77 ABC
   Rafferty   ep   11. 28. 77 CBS
   Soap   sr ret   9. 14. 78 ABC
   The Love Boat   ep   The Man Who Loved Women 9. 30. 78 ABC
   Soap   sr ret   9. 13. 79 ABC
   Friendships, Secrets and Lies   tf   12. 3. 79 NBC
   Getting There   pt   2. 12. 80 CBS
   Soap   sr ret   10. 20. 80 ABC
   Midnight Offerings   tf   2. 27. 81 ABC

DANA, BILL*
   The Bill Dana Show   sr   9. 22. 63 NBC
   The Man From U. N. C. L. E.   ep   The Matterhorn Affair 3. 3. 67
     NBC
   The Snoop Sisters   ep   12. 18. 72 NBC
   Rosetti and Ryan: Men Who Love Women   tf   5. 19. 77 NBC
   Rosetti and Ryan   ep   10. 20. 77 NBC
   Windows, Doors and Keyholes   sp   5. 16. 78 NBC
   A Guide for the Married Woman   tf   10. 13. 78 ABC
   Flying High   ep   12. 29. 78 CBS
   Sweepstakes   ep   2. 2. 79 NBC
   Too Close for Comfort   ep   11. 24. 81 ABC

DANA, LEORA
   A&C:
   Masterpiece Playhouse   ep   Uncle Vanya 9. 30. 50 NBC
   The Web   ep   A Name for Death 7. 25. 54 CBS
   Armstrong Circle Theatre   ep   Flare-Up 11. 16. 54 NBC
   Armstrong Circle Theatre   ep   Sudden Disaster 2. 22. 55 NBC
   U. S. Steel Hour   ep   Sauce for the Goose 10. 10. 56 CBS
   The Asphalt Jungle   ep   Scott Machine 6. 25. 61 ABC
   The Adams Chronicles   ep   2. 17. 76, 2. 24. 76 PBS

SUPP. :
Seventh Avenue   ms   2. 10. 77,   2. 17. 77,   2. 24. 77 NBC
Nurse   tf   4. 9. 80 CBS

DANIELS, WILLIAM
A& C:
Robert Montgomery Presents   ep   Three Men from Tomorrow
    1. 2. 56 NBC
The Nurses   ep   Field of Battle 5. 30. 63 CBS
Medical Story   ep   11. 13. 75 CBS
The Bob Newhart Show   ep   11. 29. 75 CBS
SUPP. :
Instant Family   pt   7. 28. 77 NBC
Killer On Board   tf   10. 10. 77 NBC
The Incredible Hulk   sp ep   Death in the Family 11. 28. 77 CBS
The Hallmark Hall of Fame   ep   The Court Martial of George
    Armstrong Custer 12. 1. 77 NBC
Family   ep   5. 16. 78 ABC
The Bastard/ Kent Family Chronicles   ms   5. 22. 78, 5. 23. 78
    NN
Big Bob Johnson and His Fantastic Speed Circus   tf   6. 27. 78
    NBC
Sergeant Matlovich vs. the U. S. Air Force   tf   8. 21. 78 NBC
Grandpa Goes to Washington   ep 9. 7. 78 NBC
The Rebels   ms   5. 14. 79, 5. 21. 79 NN
Blind Ambition   ms   5. 20. 79, 5. 21. 79, 5. 22. 79, 5. 23. 79 CBS
BAD Cats   ep   1. 18. 80 ABC
The Misadventures of Sheriff Lobo   ep   2. 19. 80 NBC
City in Fear   tf   3. 30. 80 ABC
Galactica 1980   ep   4. 20. 80 ABC
Freebie and the Bean   sr   12. 6. 80 CBS
The Million Dollar Face   tf   3. 12. 81 NBC
Trapper John, M. D.   ep   Second Sight 4. 5. 81 CBS
The Wonderful World of Philip Malley   pt   5. 18. 81 CBS
Nuts and Bolts   pt   8. 24. 81 ABC
Private Benjamin   ep   Bye Bye Benjamin 11. 30. 81 CBS

DANNER, BLYTHE
A& C:
Theatre in America   ep   Eccentricities of a Nightmare 6. 16. 76
    PBS
SUPP. :
The Hallmark Hall of Fame   ep   The Court Martial of George
    Armstrong Custer 12. 1. 77 NBC
A Love Affair: The Eleanor and Lou Gehrig Story 1. 15. 78 NBC
Are You in the House Alone?   tf   9. 20. 78 CBS
You Can't Take It with You   sp   5. 16. 79 CBS

DANZIGER, MAIA*
The Garden Party   sp   10. 17. 74 PBS
The ABC Afterschool Special   ep   The Late Great Me: The
    Story of a Teenage Alcoholic   ep   11. 14. 79 ABC

DARBY, KIM
  A&C:
  Dr. Kildare   ep   A Nickel's Worth of Prayer 4. 16. 64 NBC
  Don't Be Afraid of the Dark   tf   10. 10. 73 ABC
  Rich Man, Poor Man   ms ep   **2. 2. 76**, **2. 23. 76**, **3. 1. 76**, **3. 8. 76**
    ABC
  SUPP. :
  Family   ep   1. 10. 78 ABC
  The Love Boat   ep   Class Reunion 2. 3. 79 ABC
  Flatbed Annie and Sweetiepie: Lady Truckers   tf   2. 10. 79 CBS
  The Last Convertible   ms   9. 24. 79, 9. 25. 79, 9. 26. 79 NBC
  Enola Gay   tf   11. 23. 80 NBC

DARDEN, SEVERN*
  Daniel Boone   ep   11. 25. 68 NBC
  The Movie Murderer   tf   2. 2. 70 NBC
  The Man and the City   ep   I Should Have Let Him Die 9. 29. 71
    ABC
  Getting Together   ep   12. 4. 71 ABC
  Bonanza   ep   The Rattlesnake Brigade 12. 5. 71 NBC
  Cannon   ep   9. 13. 72 CBS
  Playmates   tf   10. 3. 72 ABC
  Banyon   ep   10. 6. 72 NBC
  The Man Who Died Twice   tf   4. 13. 73 ABC
  Skyway to Death   tf   1. 19. 74 ABC
  The Night Stalker   ep   12. 6. 74 ABC
  Baretta   ep   1. 31. 75 ABC
  Harry O   ep   10. 16. 75 ABC
  The Barbary Coast 10. 31. 75 ABC
  The New, Original Wonder Woman   tf   11. 7. 75 ABC
  The Six Million Dollar Man   ep   Bigfoot 1. 28. 76, 2. 4. 76 ABC
  Jigsaw John   ep   3. 8. 76 NBC
  City of Angels   ep   3. 16. 76 NBC
  The Six Million Dollar Man   ep   The Return of Big Foot 9. 19. 76,
    9. 26. 76 ABC
  Captains and the Kings   ms   9. 30. 76, 10. 7. 76, 10. 14. 76,
    10. 28. 76, 11. 4. 76, 11. 11. 76 NBC
  The Quest   ep   10. 27. 76 NBC
  The Disappearance of Aimee   tf   11. 17. 76 NBC
  Victory at Entebbe   tf   12. 13. 76 ABC
  Visions   ep   Prison Game 1. 13. 77 PBS
  Starsky and Hutch   ep   2. 22. 78 ABC
  Flying High   ep   10. 6. 78 CBS
  Salvage I   ep   3. 5. 79 ABC
  Rendezvous Hotel   tf   7. 11. 79 CBS
  CBS Library: Once Upon a Midnight Dreary   ep   The House
    with a Clock in Its Walls 10. 21. 79 CBS
  Orphan Train   tf   12. 22. 79 CBS
  Evita Peron   tf   2. 23. 81, 2. 24. 81 NBC
  Home Room   pt   8. 10. 81 ABC
  The Fall Guy   ep   The Human Torch 12. 9. 81 ABC

DARREN, JAMES
    SUPP. :
    Baa Baa Black Sheep   ep   1.4.77 NBC
    The Feather and Father Gang   ep   5.28.77 ABC
    Police Story   ep   11.9.77 NBC
    Fantasy Island   ep   3.7.78 ABC
    Charlie's Angels   ep   Circus of Terror 3.29.78 ABC
    Hawaii Five-O   ep   12.28.78, 1.4.79 CBS
    Fantasy Island   ep   12.1.79 ABC
    Vega$ ep   2.27.80 ABC
    Turnover Smith   tf   6.8.80 ABC
    The Love Boat   ep   Computerman 1.31.81 ABC
    Scruples   tf   5.22.81 ABC
    Portrait of a Legend   sr hos   8.1.81 NN

DARROW, HENRY*
    The Wild Wild West   ep   The Night of the Tottering Tontine
        1.6.67 CBS
    The High Chaparral   sr   9.10.67 NBC
    The High Chaparral   sr ret   9.20.68 NBC
    The High Chaparral   sr ret   9.19.69 NBC
    The High Chaparral   sr ret   9.18.70 NBC
    Primus   ep   9.15.71 NN
    Hawaii Five-O   ep   9.21.71 CBS
    Primus   ep   10.6.71 NN
    Hernandez, Houston P.D.   pt   1.16.73 NBC
    The FBI   ep   11.26.72 ABC
    Brock's Last Case   tf   3.5.73 CBS
    Kung Fu   ep   The Brujo 10.25.73 ABC
    Chase   ep   Vacation for a President 2.6.74 NBC
    Hitchhike!   tf   2.23.74 CBS
    Night Games   tf   3.16.74 NBC
    Aloha Means Goodbye   tf   10.11.74 NBC
    The Invisible Man   tf   5.6.75 NBC
    McMillan and Wife   ep   10.26.75 NBC
    Hawaii Five-O   ep   1.8.76 CBS
    The Streets of San Francisco   tf   3.11.76 ABC
    Sara   ep   3.22.76 CBS
    Baretta   ep   9.22.76 ABC
    The New, Original Wonder Woman   ep   The Bushwackers
        1.29.77 ABC
    Kingston Confidential   ep   7.6.77 NBC
    Hawaii Five-O   ep   9.29.77 CBS
    Halloween with the Addams Family   sp   10.30.77 NBC
    The New Adventures of Wonder Woman   ep   I Do, I Do 11.11.77
        CBS
    The Bionic Woman   ep   2.18.78 NBC
    A Man Called Sloane   ep   9.29.79 NBC
    The Waltons   ep   10.18.79 CBS
    Attica   tf   3.2.80 ABC
    Quincy, M.E.   ep   2.11.81 NBC
    B.J. and the Bear   ep   7 Lady Captives 3.24.81 NBC
    The Tarzan/Lone Ranger/Zorro Adventure Hour   vo   (Zorro
        segment) 9.12.81 CBS

The Incredible Hulk   ep   11. 6. 81 CBS
Simon and Simon   ep   Love, Christie 12. 1. 81 CBS

DA SILVA, HOWARD
   A&C:
   The Nurses   ep   Disaster Call 12. 5. 63 CBS
   The Doctors and the Nurses   ep   Act of Violence 2. 23. 65 CBS
   SUPP. :
   Power   tf   1. 14. 80,   1. 15. 80 NBC
   Great Performances   ep   Verna: USO Girl 1. 25. 78 PBS

DAVID, THAYER
   A&C:
   Dark Shadows   sr   6. 27. 66 ABC
   The Wild Wild West   ep   The Night of the Spanish Curse 1. 3. 69
      CBS
   The Invisible Man   ep   9. 29. 75 NBC
   Petrocelli   ep   2. 4. 76 NBC
   Francis Gary Powers: The True Story of the U-2 Spy Incident
      9. 29. 76 NBC
   Charlie's Angels   ep   10. 27. 76 ABC
   Hawaii Five-O   ep   12. 2. 76 CBS
   SUPP. :
   Roots   ms   1. 23-30. 77 ABC
   The Amazing Howard Hughes   tf   4. 13. 77,   4. 14. 77 CBS
   Washington: Behind Closed Doors   ms   9. 6. -11. 77 ABC
   The Hardy Boys/Nancy Drew Mysteries   ep   11. 6. 77 ABC
   Nero Wolfe   pt   12. 18. 79 ABC

DAVIDSON, JOHN
   SUPP. :
   Roger and Harry   tf   5. 2. 77 ABC

DAVIS, BETTE
   A&C:
   The 20th Century-Fox Hour   ep   Crack-Up 2. 8. 56 CBS
   SUPP. :
   The Dark Secret of Harvest Home   tf   1. 23. 78,   1. 24. 78 NBC
   Strangers: The Story of a Mother and Daughter   tf   5. 13. 79
      CBS
   White Mama   tf   3. 5. 80 CBS
   Skyward   tf   11. 20. 80 NBC
   Family Reunion   tf   10. 11. 81,   10. 12. 81 NBC

DAVIS, CLIFTON
   SUPP. :
   Little Ladies of the Night   tf   1. 16. 77 ABC
   Police Story   ep   1. 25. 77 NBC
   Superdome   tf   1. 9. 78 ABC
   Cindy   tf   3. 24. 78 ABC
   The Love Boat   ep   4. 19. 80 ABC
   The Night the City Screamed   tf   12. 14. 80 ABC

DAVIS, JIM*
    Stories of the Century   sr   1956 NN
    Rescue 8   sr   11.9.58 NN
    Hondo   ep   9.15.67 ABC
    The Virginian   ep   The Heritage 4.16.69 NBC
    Gunsmoke   ep   10.7.68, 11.25.68 CBS
    Vanished   tf   3.8.71, 3.9.71 NBC
    The FBI   ep   Dynasty of Hate 10.10.71 ABC
    The Trackers   tf   12.14.71 ABC
    Night Gallery   ep   The Waiting Room 1.26.72 NBC
    Amanda Fallon   pt   3.5.72 NBC
    The FBI   ep   Desperate Runner 9.17.72 ABC
    Jigsaw   ep   9.21.72 ABC
    The World of Disney   ep   High Flying Spy 10.22.72 NBC
    Kung Fu   ep   The Soul Is the Warrior 2.8.73 ABC
    Gunsmoke   ep   2.19.73 CBS
    Cannon   ep   2.28.73 CBS
    The Streets of San Francisco   ep   Shattered Image 3.22.73 ABC
    Deliver Us from Evil   tf   9.11.73 ABC
    Kung Fu   ep   The Well 9.27.73 ABC
    Gunsmoke   ep   The Town Tamers 1.28.74 CBS
    The Cowboys   sr   2.6.74 ABC
    The Streets of San Francisco   ep   2.21.74 ABC
    Satan's Triangle   tf   1.14.75 ABC
    Caribe   ep   3.17.75 ABC
    Law of the Land   tf   4.29.76 NBC
    The Quest   ep   11.10.76 NBC
    Hunter   ep   3.11.77 CBS
    Just a Little Inconvenience   tf   10.2.77 NBC
    Project UFO   ep   Mass Sighting 2.26.78 NBC
    The World of Disney   ep   Trail of Danger 3.12.78, 3.19.78
      NBC
    Dallas   sr   4.2.78 CBS
    Killing Stone   tf   5.2.78 NBC
    Dallas   sr ret   9.23.78 CBS
    Dallas   sr ret   9.21.79 CBS
    Dallas   sr ret   11.7.80 CBS
    Don't Look Back   tf   5.31.81 ABC

DAVIS, OSSIE
    SUPP.:
    Billy: Portrait of a Street Kid   tf   9.12.77 NBC
    King   ms   2.12.78, 2.13.78, 2.14.78 NBC
    Roots: The Next Generations   ms ep   2.20.79 ABC
    Freedom Road   tf   10.29.79, 10.30.79 NBC
    All God's Children   tf   4.22.80 ABC
    Don't Look Back   tf   5.31.81 ABC

DAVIS, PATTI*
    Death Valley Days   sr   various episodes 1964-1967 NN
    Here's Boomer   ep   Boomer and Miss 21st Century 12.7.80 NBC
    Nero Wolfe   ep   Gambit 4.3.81 NBC
    Vega$ ep   Love Affair 4.4.81 ABC
    For Ladies Only   tf   11.9.81 NBC

DAVIS, PHYLLIS ELIZABETH (a. k. a. Phyllis Davis)*
    Love, American Style   sr   (Blackout segment regular) 9. 22. 69
      ABC
    Love, American Style   sr ret   9. 70 ABC
    Love, American Style   sr ret   9. 71 ABC
    Love, American Style   sr ret   9. 72 ABC
    Love, American Style   sr ret   9. 14. 73 ABC
    Wives   pt   3. 21. 75 CBS
    The Odd Couple   ep   Moonlighter 1. 4. 74 ABC
    The Boys   pt   5. 16. 74 CBS
    Vega$ tf   4. 25. 78 ABC
    Vega$ sr   9. 20. 78 ABC
    Fantasy Island   ep   2. 17. 79 ABC
    Vega$ sr ret   9. 19. 79 ABC
    Fantasy Island   ep   3. 1. 80 ABC
    Vega$ sr ret   11. 5. 80 ABC
    Fantasy Island   ep   11. 15. 80, 3. 21. 81 ABC
    Fantasy Island   ep   Lillian Russell 11. 28. 81 ABC
    Sizzle   tf   11. 29. 81 ABC

DAVIS, SAMMY, JR.
    A& C:
    G. E. Theatre   ep   The Patsy 2. 21. 60 CBS
    The Rifleman   ep   Two Ounces of Tin 2. 19. 62 ABC
    SUPP. :
    Charlie's Angels   ep   The Sammy Davis, Jr. Kidnap Caper
      12. 7. 77 ABC
    One Life to Live   several ep   8. 79 ABC

DAWBER, PAM*
    Sister Terri   pt   5. 27. 78 ABC
    Mork and Mindy   sr   9. 14. 78 ABC
    Mork and Mindy   sr ret   9. 16. 79 ABC
    The Girl, the Gold Watch and Everything   pt   6. 13. 80 NN
    Mork and Mindy   sr ret   11. 13. 80 ABC
    Mork and Mindy   sr ret   10. 8. 81 ABC

DAY, DENNIS
    SUPP. :
    The Stingiest Man in Town   sp vo   12. 23. 78 NBC

DAY, LARAINE
    A& C:
    Playhouse 90   ep   Rendezvous in Black 10. 25. 56 CBS
    Moment of Fear   ep   Cage of Air 9. 9. 60 NBC
    SUPP. :
    Return to Fantasy Island   tf   1. 20. 78 ABC
    Fantasy Island   ep   11. 3. 79 ABC
    Lou Grant   ep   12. 17. 79 CBS

DEAN, JIMMY
    SUPP. :
    The City   tf   1. 12. 77 NBC
    Vega$ ep   10. 18. 78 ABC

DE BENNING, BURR
   A&C:
   The Virginian   ep   11. 13. 68 NBC
   Medical Story   ep   10. 9. 75 CBS
   SUPP. :
   The Man from Atlantis   tf   5. 7. 77 NBC
   Most Wanted   ep   8. 20. 77 ABC
   The New Adventures of Wonder Woman   ep Knockout 10. 14. 77
      CBS
   Little House on the Prairie   ep   10. 31. 77 NBC
   The Return of Captain Nemo   sr   3. 8. 78 CBS
   Hawaii Five-O   ep   11. 30. 78 CBS
   CHiPs   ep   12. 16. 78 NBC
   Quincy, M. E.   ep   2. 7. 79 NBC
   Barnaby Jones   ep   Man on Fire 9. 20. 79 CBS
   Hart to Hart   ep   11. 6. 79 ABC
   Trapper John, M. D.   ep   1. 6. 80 CBS
   The Return of Frank Cannon   tf   11. 1. 80 CBS
   B. J. and the Bear   ep   2. 10. 81 NBC
   Lobo   ep   3. 3. 81 NBC
   Nero Wolfe   ep   3. 6. 81 NBC
   Code Red   tf   9. 20. 81 ABC
   McClain's Law   ep   Portrait of a Playmate 12. 18. 81 NBC

DE CAMP, ROSEMARY
   A&C:
   The 87th Precinct   ep   Killer's Choice 3. 5. 62 NBC
   Medical Story   ep   10. 16. 76 NBC
   Police Story   ep   12. 12. 75 NBC
   SUPP. :
   The Love Boat   ep   1. 7. 78 ABC
   The Time Machine   tf   11. 5. 78 NBC
   Mark Twain's America   sp   1. 11. 79 NBC
   The Misadventures of Sheriff Lobo   ep   1. 5. 80 NBC
   Buck Rogers in the 25th Century   ep   1. 29. 81 NBC
   B. J. and the Bear   ep   Adults Only 3. 10. 81 NBC

DE CARLO, YVONNE
   A&C:
   The Girl on the Late, Late Show   tf   4. 1. 74 NBC
   SUPP. :
   Fantasy Island   ep   12. 1. 79 ABC
   The Munsters' Revenge   tf   2. 27. 81 NBC

DEE, RUBY
   SUPP. :
   Roots: The Next Generations   ms ep   2. 20. 79, 2. 23. 79 ABC
   I Know Why the Caged Bird Sings   tf   4. 28. 79 CBS

DEE, SANDRA
   A&C:
   The Manhunter   tf   4. 3. 76 CBS
   SUPP. :
   The Rockford Files   ep   1. 14. 77 NBC

Police Woman   ep   1. 4. 78 NBC
Fantasy Island   ep   1. 14. 79 ABC

DE FORE, DON
  A&C:
  Mobile One   ep   12. 15. 75 ABC
  Marcus Welby, M. D.   ep   12. 16. 75 ABC
  SUPP. :
  The Love Boat   ep   1. 7. 78 ABC
  Black Beauty   ms   1. 31. 78, 2. 1. 78, 2. 2. 78, 2. 3. 78, 2. 4. 78
    NBC
  Fantasy Island   ep   10. 7. 78 ABC
  Vega$ ep   12. 20. 78 ABC

DE HAVEN, GLORIA
  A&C:
  U. S. Steel Hour   ep   Who Is This Woman? 3. 7. 62 CBS
  The Rifleman   ep   Eddie's Daughter 11. 3. 59 ABC
  SUPP. :
  The Cabot Connection   pt   5. 10. 77 CBS
  Sharon: Portrait of a Mistress   tf   10. 31. 77 NBC
  Evening in Byzantium   ms   8. 14. 78, 8. 15. 78 NN
  Fantasy Island   ep   10. 14. 78 ABC
  The Eddie Capra Mysteries   ep   12. 8. 78 NBC
  Delta House   sr   2. 3. 79 ABC
  The Misadventures of Sheriff Lobo   ep   10. 9. 79 NBC
  Lucy Moves to NBC   ep   The Music Mart   pt   2. 8. 80 NBC
  B. J. and the Bear   ep   3. 22. 80 NBC
  Darkroom   ep   The Bogeyman Will Get You 12. 4. 81 ABC

DE HAVILLAND, OLIVIA
  SUPP. :
  Roots: The Next Generations   ms ep   2. 18. 79, 2. 19. 79 ABC
  The Love Boat   ep   Aunt Hilly 3. 14. 81 ABC

DELL, GABRIEL (a. k. a. Gabe Dell)
  SUPP. :
  Serpico   ep   1. 7. 77 NBC
  A Year at the Top   sr   8. 5. 77 CBS
  Visions   ep   Blessings 10. 30. 78 PBS
  Challenge of the Superheroes   sp   1. 18. 79 NBC

DENNEHY, BRIAN*
  Serpico   ep   1. 7. 77 NBC
  Johnny We Hardly Knew Ye   tf   1. 27. 77 NBC
  Lanigan's Rabbi   ep   1. 30. 77 NBC
  Handle with Care   pt   5. 9. 77 CBS
  Lucan   ep   9. 12. 77 ABC
  The Fitzpatricks   ep   10. 4. 77 CBS
  Lou Grant   ep   10. 18. 77 CBS
  It Happened at Lakewood Manor   tf   12. 2. 77 ABC
  Ruby and Oswald   tf   2. 8. 78 CBS
  A Death in Canaan 3. 1. 78 CBS
  A Real American Hero   tf   12. 9. 78 CBS

Silent Victory: The Kitty O'Neil Story   tf   2. 24. 79 CBS
The Jericho Mile   tf   3. 18. 79 ABC
Dummy   tf   5. 27. 79 CBS
Big Shamus, Little Shamus   sr   9. 29. 79 CBS
Pearl   ms   11. 16. 78, 11. 17. 78, 11. 19. 78 ABC
The Seduction of Miss Leona   tf   8. 26. 80 CBS
A Rumor of War   tf   9. 24. 80, 9. 25. 80 CBS
Knots Landing   ep   12. 11. 80 CBS
Dynasty   sr   3. 9. 81 ABC
Great Performances   ep   Three Stories By Irwin Shaw; segment:
   The Monument 6. 1. 81 PBS
Fly Away Home   tf   9. 18. 81 ABC
Dynasty   sr ret   11. 4. 81 ABC
Skokie   tf   11. 17. 81 CBS
Darkroom   ep   Make Up 12. 18. 81 ABC

DENNING, RICHARD
   SUPP. :
   Hawaii Five-O   ep   2. 17. 77, 11. 17. 77, 1. 5. 78, 3. 30. 78,
      10. 19. 78, 1. 18. 79 CBS
   The Asphalt Cowboy   pt   12. 7. 80 NBC

DENNIS, SANDY
   SUPP. :
   Police Story   ep   Day of Terror, Night of Fear 3. 4. 78 NBC
   Perfect Gentlemen   tf   3. 14. 78 CBS
   Trouble with Mother   sp   3. 30. 79 NN
   Wilson's Reward   sp   6. 29. 80 NN

DENVER, BOB
   SUPP. :
   Whatever Happened to Dobie Gillis?   pt   5. 10. 77 CBS
   Rescue from Gilligan's Island   tf   10. 14. 78, 10. 21. 79 NBC
   The Love Boat   ep   Class Reunion 2. 3. 79 ABC
   The Castaways on Gilligan's Island   tf   5. 3. 79 NBC
   Fantasy Island   ep   5. 17. 80 ABC
   The Harlem Globetrotters on Gilligan's Island   tf   5. 15. 81 NBC

DEVANE, WILLIAM
   SUPP. :
   Red Alert   tf   5. 18. 77 CBS
   Black Beauty   ms   1. 31. 78, 2. 1. 78, 2. 2. 78, 2. 3. 78, 2. 4. 78
      NBC
   From Here to Eternity   ms   2. 14. 79, 2. 21. 79, 2. 28. 79 NBC
   From Here to Eternity   sr   3. 10. 80 NBC
   From Here to Eternity   sr ret   8. 3. 80 NBC
   Red Flag: The Ultimate Game   tf   10. 3. 81 CBS
   The Other Victim   tf   11. 4. 81 CBS

DEWHURST, COLLEEN
   SUPP. :
   Silent Victory: The Kitty O'Neil Story   tf   2. 24. 79 CBS
   Studs Lonigan   ms   3. 7. 79, 3. 14. 79, 3. 21. 79 NBC

And Baby Makes Six   tf   10. 22. 79 NBC
Mary and Joseph: A Story of Faith   tf   12. 9. 79 NBC
Escape   tf   2. 20. 80 CBS
Guyana Tragedy: The Story of Jim Jones   tf   4. 15. 80 CBS
Baby Comes Home   tf   10. 16. 80 CBS
A Few Days in Weasel Creek   tf   10. 21. 81 CBS

DeWITT, JOYCE*
   Risko   pt   5. 9. 76 CBS
   Three's Company   sr   3. 15. 77 ABC
   Three's Company   sr ret   9. 13. 77 ABC
   With This Ring   tf   5. 5. 78 ABC
   Three's Company   sr ret   9. 12. 78 ABC
   Super Train   ep   4. 7. 79 NBC
   Three's Company   sr ret   9. 11. 79 ABC
   The Ropers   ep   9. 15. 79 ABC
   The Love Boat   ep   10. 6. 79 ABC
   The B. B. Beagle Show   pt   1. 14. 80 NN
   Three's Company   sr ret   10. 28. 80 ABC
   Three's Company   sr ret   10. 6. 81 ABC

DEY, SUSAN
   A&C:
   Partridge Family: 2200 A. D.   sr vo   9. 7. 74 CBS
   SUPP. :
   Barnaby Jones   ep   Testament of Power 1. 20. 77 CBS
   Loves Me, Loves Me Not   sr   3. 20. 77 CBS
   Mary Jane Harper Cried Last Night   tf   10. 5. 77 CBS
   Little Women   tf   10. 2. 78, 10. 3. 78 NBC
   The Comeback Kid   tf   4. 11. 80 ABC

DE YOUNG, CLIFF
   SUPP. :
   The 3,000 Mile Chase   tf   6. 16. 77 NBC
   Sunshine Christmas   tf   12. 12. 77 NBC
   What Really Happened to the Class of '65?   ep   1. 19. 78 NBC
   King   ms   2. 12. 78, 2. 13. 78, 2. 14. 78 NBC
   Centennial   ms ep   The Massacre 11. 11. 78 NBC
   Centennial   ms ep   The Longhorns 12. 3. 78 NBC
   Centennial   ms ep   The Shepherds 12. 10. 78 NBC
   Centennial   ms ep   The Storm 1. 14. 79 NBC
   The Seeding of Sarah Burns   tf   4. 7. 79 CBS
   Hunter's Moon   pt   12. 1. 79 CBS
   Family   ep   2. 4. 80 ABC
   Fun and Games   tf   5. 26. 80 ABC
   Scared Straight: Another Story   tf   11. 6. 80 CBS

DHIEGH, KHIGH
   A&C:
   Kung Fu   ep   11. 15. 74, 11. 22. 74 ABC
   SUPP. :
   Fantasy Island   ep   2. 24. 79 ABC
   Hawaii Five-O   ep   4. 5. 80 CBS

DICKINSON, ANGIE
  SUPP. :
  A Sensitive, Passionate Man   tf   6. 6. 77 NBC
  Police Woman   sr ret   10. 25. 77 NBC
  Overboard   tf   9. 25. 78 NBC
  Pearl   ms   11. 16. 78, 11. 17. 78, 11. 19. 78 ABC
  The Suicide's Wife   tf   11. 7. 79 CBS
  Dial "M" for Murder   tf   4. 9. 81 NBC

DIETRICH, DENA
  A& C:
  Fay   ep   9. 11. 75 NBC
  Emergency   ep   10. 19. 74 NBC
  SUPP. :
  Getting Married   tf   5. 17. 78 CBS
  The Love Boat   ep   The Last Hundred Bucks 12. 9. 78 ABC
  But Mother!   pt   6. 27. 79 NBC
  Gossip   pt   7. 10. 79 NBC

DILLER, PHYLLIS
  SUPP. :
  CHiPs   ep   3. 9. 78 NBC
  The Love Boat   ep   10. 6. 79, 3. 1. 80 ABC

DILLMAN, BRADFORD
  A& C:
  Street Killing   tf   9. 12. 76 CBS
  SUPP. :
  The Hostage Heart   tf   9. 9. 77 CBS
  Insight   ep   1. 1. 78 NN
  Barnaby Jones   ep   1. 26. 78 CBS
  Sword of Justice   ep   10. 28. 78 NBC
  Jennifer: A Woman's Story   tf   3. 5. 79 NBC
  Before and After   tf   10. 5. 79 ABC
  The Incredible Hulk   ep   12. 7. 79 CBS
  The Memory of Eva Ryker   tf   5. 7. 80 CBS
  Fantasy Island   ep   11. 8. 80 ABC
  Charlie's Angels   ep   Angels of the Deep 12. 7. 80 ABC

DIXON, DONNA*
  Bosom Buddies   sr   11. 27. 80 ABC
  Bosom Buddies   sr ret   10. 8. 81 ABC
  The Love Boat   ep   The Expedition 10. 10. 81 ABC
  Mickey Spillane's Margin for Murder   tf   10. 15. 81 CBS

DOBSON, KEVIN*
  The Mod Squad   ep   Feet of Clay 12. 14. 71 ABC
  Kojak   sr   10. 24. 73 CBS
  Kojak   sr ret   9. 15. 74 CBS
  Kojak   sr ret   9. 14. 75 CBS
  Kojak   sr ret   9. 22. 76 CBS
  Stranded   pt   5. 26. 76 CBS

Kojak   sr ret   10. 2. 77 CBS
The Immigrants   ms   11. 20. 78, 11. 21. 78 NN
Greatest Heroes of the Bible   ep   The Story of Solomon and
    Bathsheba 11. 21. 78, 11. 22. 78 NBC
Transplant   tf   4. 17. 79 CBS
Orphan Train   tf   12. 22. 79 CBS
Hardhat and Legs   tf   2. 9. 80 CBS
Mark, I Love You   tf   12. 10. 80 CBS
Mickey Spillane's Margin for Murder   tf   10. 15. 81 CBS
Shannon   sr   11. 11. 81 CBS

DONAHUE, ELINOR
    A& C:
    Goodyear Theatre   ep   Marked Down for Connie 4. 25. 60 NBC
    SUPP. :
    Police Story   ep   3. 8. 77 NBC
    The Feather and Father Gang   ep   3. 21. 77 ABC
    The Father Knows Best Reunion   sp   5. 15. 77 NBC
    Mulligan's Stew   tf   6. 20. 77 NBC
    Mulligan's Stew   sr   10. 25. 77 NBC
    Father Knows Best: Home for Christmas   sp   12. 18. 77 NBC
    Doctor's Private Lives   tf   3. 20. 78 ABC
    Police Story   ep   No Margin for Error 4. 30. 78 NBC
    Please Stand By   sr   9. 8. 78 NN
    Diff'rent Strokes   ep   1. 19. 79 NBC
    The Love Boat   ep   3. 3. 79 ABC
    Sweepstakes   ep   3. 9. 79 NBC
    Diff'rent Strokes   ep   6. 22. 79 NBC
    The Grady Nutt Show   pt   7. 24. 81 NBC
    Fantasy Island   ep   Night of the Tormented Soul 12. 5. 81 ABC
    The Love Boat   ep   He's My Brother 12. 5. 81 ABC

DONAHUE, TROY
    SUPP. :
    The Hardy Boys/Nancy Drew Mysteries   ep   2. 26. 78 ABC
    CHiPs   ep   9. 16. 78 NBC
    Vega$ ep   9. 27. 78 ABC
    Fantasy Island   ep   11. 18. 78 ABC
    The Eddie Capra Mysteries   ep   12. 15. 78 NBC
    The Love Boat   ep   Matchmaker, Matchmaker Times Two
        11. 29. 80 ABC
    Fantasy Island   ep   3. 21. 81 ABC

DONNELL, JEFF
    A& C:
    The June Allyson Show   ep   A Thief or Two 12. 1. 60 CBS
    SUPP. :
    The Bob Newhart Show   ep   1. 7. 78 CBS

DOUGLAS, KIRK
    SUPP. :
    I'd Rather Be Dead   sp nar-hos   5. 14. 79 NN

DOUGLAS, MELVYN
SUPP. :
The ABC Weekend Special   ep   Portrait of Grandpa Doc 11. 5. 77
ABC
Intimate Strangers   tf   11. 11. 77 ABC
Gift to Last   sp   12. 26. 79 NN (taped in 1976)

DOYLE, DAVID*
The Patty Duke Show   sr   9. 18. 63 ABC
The Patty Duke Show   sr ret   9. 64 ABC
The Patty Duke Show   sr ret   9. 15. 65 ABC
Funny Face   ep   11. 6. 71 CBS
Cade's County   ep   11. 28. 71 CBS
The Doris Day Show   ep   12. 27. 71 CBS
The New Dick Van Dyke Show   ep   1. 11. 72, 2. 12. 72 CBS
Hawaii Five-O   ep   Follow the White Brick Road 2. 1. 72 CBS
The New Dick Van Dyke Show   ep   3. 4. 72 CBS
Singles   pt   3. 17. 72 CBS
Bridget Loves Bernie   sr   9. 16. 72 CBS
Of Thee I Sing   sp   10. 24. 72 CBS
Banacek   ep   1. 10. 73 NBC
Ozzie's Girls   ep   Silver Threads Among the Swingers 9. 30. 73
NN
Incident on a Dark Street   tf   1. 13. 73 NBC
The New Dick Van Dyke Show   ep   2. 25. 73 CBS
The Police Story   tf   3. 20. 73 NBC
Adam's Rib   ep   Danish Pastry 9. 28. 73 ABC
Love, American Style   ep   Love and the Heavy Set 9. 28. 73 ABC
Money to Burn   tf   10. 27. 73 ABC
Love Story   ep   Mirabelle's Summer 11. 7. 73 NBC
Blood Sport   tf   12. 5. 73 ABC
Miracle on 34th Street   tf   12. 14. 73 CBS
Ozzie's Girls   ep   I'm Harriet, Don't Fly Me 1. 20. 74 NN
All in the Family   ep   1. 26. 74 CBS
Petrocelli   ep   9. 18. 74 NBC
The Stranger Within   tf   10. 1. 74 ABC
Police Story   ep   10. 8. 74 NBC
Police Story   ep   10. 29. 74 NBC
The Night Stalker   ep   11. 8. 74 ABC
Kojak   ep   11. 24. 74 CBS
Karen   ep   4. 17. 75 ABC
The First Thirty Six Hours of Dr. Durant   tf   5. 13. 75 ABC
Ellery Queen   ep   9. 11. 75 NBC
Charlie's Angels   tf   3. 21. 76 ABC
Charlie's Angels   sr   9. 22. 76 ABC
Charlie's Angels   sr   9. 22. 76 ABC
Charlie's Angels   sr ret   9. 14. 77 ABC
The ABC Short Story Special   ep   Homer and the Wacky Dough-
nut Machine 4. 30. 77 ABC
Black Market Baby   tf   10. 7. 77 ABC
Wild and Wooly   tf   2. 20. 78 ABC
Fantasy Island   ep   5. 6. 78 ABC
Charlie's Angels   sr ret   9. 13. 78 ABC

The Love Boat ep The Man Who Loved Women 9. 30. 78 ABC
Fantasy Island ep 9. 7. 79 ABC
Charlie's Angels sr ret 9. 12. 79 ABC
Fantasy Island ep 11. 15. 80 ABC
Charlie's Angels sr ret 11. 30. 80 ABC
Charlie's Angels sr ret 6. 3. 81 ABC
Hart to Hart ep 11. 3. 81 ABC

DUFF, HOWARD
  A&C:
  Insight ep 2. 10. 74 NN
  Police Story ep 12. 19. 75 NBC
  SUPP. :
  The Rockford Files ep 1. 7. 77 NBC
  In the Glitter Palace tf 2. 27. 77 NBC
  Police Story ep 3. 22. 77 NBC
  Switch ep 1. 16. 78 CBS
  The Hardy Boys/Nancy Drew Mysteries ep A Haunting We
    Will Go 2. 12. 78 ABC
  Fantasy Island ep 2. 18. 78 ABC
  Ski Lift to Death tf 3. 3. 78 CBS
  Sweepstakes ep 2. 9. 79 NBC
  Lou Grant ep 12. 17. 79 CBS
  Young Maverick ep 12. 26. 79 CBS
  Valentine Magic on Love Island tf 2. 15. 80 NBC
  Charlie's Angels ep Harrigan's Angel 2. 20. 80 ABC
  Flamingo Road tf 5. 12. 80 NBC
  The Dream Merchants ms 5. 12. 80, 5. 19. 80 NN
  Flamingo Road sr 1. 6. 81 NBC
  East of Eden ms 2. 8. 81, 2. 9. 81, 2. 11. 81 ABC
  Flamingo Road sr ret 11. 3. 81 NBC

DUFFY, PATRICK*
  The Stranger Who Looks Like Me tf 3. 6. 74 ABC
  The Man from Atlantis tf 3. 4. 77 NBC
  The Man from Atlantis sp ep 5. 7. 77 NBC
  The Man from Atlantis sp ep 5. 17. 77 NBC
  The Man from Atlantis sp ep The Disappearances 6. 20. 77
    NBC
  The Man from Atlantis sr 9. 22. 77 NBC
  Dallas sr 4. 2. 78 CBS
  Dallas sr ret 9. 21. 79 CBS
  Knots Landing ep 12. 27. 79 CBS
  Dallas sr ret 11. 7. 80 CBS
  Enola Gay tf 11. 23. 80 NBC
  Knots Landing ep 2. 19. 81 CBS
  Dallas sr ret 10. 9. 81 CBS
  The Love Boat ep The Three R's 10. 10. 81 ABC

DUGGAN, ANDREW*
  Bourbon Street Beat sr 10. 5. 59 ABC
  Room for One More sr 1. 27. 62 ABC
  The Defenders ep The Captive 10. 12. 63 CBS

The Eleventh Hour   ep   Four Feet in the Morning 11. 23. 63 NBC
Kraft Suspense Theatre   ep   Leviathin Five 10. 30. 64 NBC
The Alfred Hitchcock Hour   ep   The McGregor Affair 11. 23. 64
   NBC
A Walk in the Night   pt   7. 15. 68 CBS
Lancer   sr   9. 24. 68 CBS
Ironside   ep   The Riddle in Room Six 2. 25. 71 NBC
Cannon   ep   Fool's Gold 10. 19. 71 CBS
Hollywood Television Theatre   ep   Neighbors 11. 18. 71 PBS
Mannix   ep   The Man Outside 11. 24. 71 CBS
McMillan and Wife   ep   Death Is a Seven-Point Favorite 12. 8. 71
   NBC
The Streets of San Francisco   ep   9. 16. 72 ABC
Ghost Story   ep   Half a Death 11. 3. 72 NBC
Owen Marshall, Counselor at Law   ep   9. 21. 72 ABC
Cannon   ep   12. 13. 72 CBS
McMillan and Wife   ep   12. 13. 72 NBC
Kung Fu   ep   2. 1. 73 ABC
Banacek   ep   The Two Million Clams of Cap'n Jack 2. 7. 73 NBC
Owen Marshall, Counselor at Law   ep   Sweet Harvest 10. 3. 73
   ABC
Medical Center   ep   10. 8. 73 CBS
Faraday and Company   ep   A Wheelbarrow Full of Trouble
   10. 24. 73 NBC
Medical Center   ep   Strangers in Two Worlds 10. 29. 73 CBS
The New Adventures of Perry Mason   ep   The Case of the
   Jailed Justice 12. 2. 73 CBS
Hawaii Five-O   ep   Death with Father 1. 22. 74 CBS
Cannon   ep   1. 30. 74 CBS
The Last Angry Man   tf   4. 16. 74 ABC
The Streets of San Francisco   ep   9. 26. 74 ABC
Manhunter   ep   11. 13. 74 CBS
The Missiles of October   tf   12. 18. 74 ABC
Attack on Terror: The FBI vs. the Ku Klux Klan   tf   2. 20. 75,
   2. 21. 75 CBS
Lucas Tanner   ep   4. 9. 75 NBC
The Barbary Coast   ep   9. 29. 75 ABC
Cannon   ep   2. 4. 76 CBS
Jigsaw John   ep   2. 9. 76 NBC
McMillan and Wife   ep   3. 7. 76 NBC
Tail Gunner Joe   tf   2. 6. 77 NBC
The Deadliest Season   tf   3. 16. 77 CBS
Pine Canyon Is Burning   tf   5. 18. 77 NBC
Mystery of the Week   ep   Violence in Blue 6. 1. 77 ABC
Switch   ep   10. 14. 77, 11. 4. 77 CBS
The Hunted Lady   tf   11. 28. 77 NBC
The Bionic Woman   ep   On the Run 5. 13. 78 NBC
Down Home   pt   8. 16. 78 CBS
Overboard   tf   9. 25. 78 NBC
Hawaii Five-O   ep   9. 28. 78 CBS
The Eddie Capra Mysteries   ep   10. 20. 78 NBC
The Time Machine   tf   11. 5. 78 NBC
The New Adventures of Wonder Woman   ep   The Starships Are
   Coming 2. 2. 79 CBS

Backstairs at the White House   ms ep   **2. 12. 79**, **2. 19. 79** NBC
Lou Grant   ep   **4. 2. 79** CBS
Insight   ep   **4. 8. 79** NN
Vega$ ep   **9. 19. 79** ABC
CHiPs   ep   **10. 20. 79** NBC
Hawaii Five-O   ep   **11. 29. 79** CBS
Hagen   ep   **4. 24. 80** CBS
The Long Days of Summer   tf   **5. 23. 80** ABC
M Station: Hawaii   tf   **6. 10. 80** CBS
Jake's Way   pt   **6. 28. 80** CBS
Momma the Detective   pt   **1. 9. 81** NBC
CHiPs   ep   Ponch's Angels **2. 28. 81**, **3. 1. 81** NBC
Greatest Heroes of the Bible   ep   Abraham's Sacrifice **8. 15. 81**
    NBC

DUKE, PATTY see PATTY DUKE ASTIN

DULLEA, KEIR
    A&C:
    The New Breed   ep   Prime Target **10. 10. 61** ABC
    Checkmate   ep   A Very Rough Sketch **1. 24. 62** CBS
    SUPP. :
    Legend of the Golden Gun   tf   **4. 10. 79** NBC
    Brave New World   tf   **3. 7. 80** NBC
    The Hostage Tower   tf   **5. 13. 80** CBS
    No Place to Hide   tf   **3. 4. 81** CBS

DUNAWAY, FAYE
    SUPP. :
    Evita Peron   tf   **2. 23. 81**, **2. 24. 81** NBC

DUNCAN, SANDY
    SUPP. :
    Roots   ms ep   **1. 27. 77** ABC
    The Love Boat   ep   **11. 19. 77** ABC

DUNNE, DOMINIQUE*
    Diary of a Teenage Hitchhiker   tf   **9. 21. 79** ABC
    Family   ep   **1. 21. 80** ABC
    Valentine Magic on Love Island   tf   **2. 15. 80** NBC
    Lou Grant   ep   **11. 24. 80** CBS
    Breaking Away   sr   **12. 6. 80** ABC
    Unit 4   pt   **9. 29. 81** CBS
    The Day the Loving Stopped   tf   **10. 16. 81** ABC

DUNNOCK, MILDRED
    A&C:
    Great Ghost Tales   ep   The Monkey's Paw **7. 20. 61** NBC
    Murder or Mercy   tf   **4. 10. 74** ABC
    SUPP. :
    The Best Place to Be   tf   **5. 27. 79** NBC
    And Baby Makes Six   tf   **10. 22. 79** NBC
    Project Peacock   ep   The Big Stuffed Dog   sp   **2. 8. 81** NBC
    The Patricia Neal Story   tf   **12. 8. 81** CBS

DURNING, CHARLES*
   Madigan   ep   10. 4. 72 NBC
   Connection   tf   2. 27. 73 ABC
   All in the Family   ep   3. 17. 73 CBS
   Rx for the Defense   pt   4. 15. 73 ABC
   The Trial of Chaplain Jim   tf   2. 11. 75 ABC
   Queen of the Stardust Ballroom   tf   2. 13. 75 CBS
   Switch   tf   3. 10. 75 CBS
   Cannon   ep   9. 17. 75 CBS
   Baretta   ep   10. 29. 75 ABC
   Hawaii Five-O   ep   11. 7. 75 CBS
   The Cop and the Kid   sr   12. 4. 75 NBC
   The Hallmark Hall of Fame   ep   The Rivalry   sp   12. 12. 75
      NBC
   Captains and the Kings   ms   9. 30. 76, 10. 7. 76, 10. 14. 76,
      10. 28. 76, 11. 4. 76, 11. 11. 76 NBC
   Visions   ep   The Dancing Bear 10. 23. 77 PBS
   Special Olympics   tf   2. 22. 78 CBS
   Studs Lonigan   ms   3. 7. 79, 3. 14. 79, 3. 21. 79 NBC
   Attica   tf   3. 2. 80 ABC
   A Perfect Match   tf   10. 5. 80 CBS
   Crisis at Central High   tf   2. 4. 81 CBS
   The Hallmark Hall of Fame   ep   Casey Stengel   sp   5. 6. 81 PBS
   The Best Little Girl in the World   tf   5. 11. 81 ABC
   Great Performances: Three Stories by Irwin Shaw   ep   The
      Monument 6. 1. 81 PBS
   Dark Night of the Scarecrow   tf   10. 24. 81 CBS

DUSSAULT, NANCY*
   The New Dick Van Dyke Show   sr   9. 18. 71 CBS
   Love, American Style   ep   10. 8. 71 ABC
   CBS Triple Play: The Nancy Dussault Show   pt   5. 8. 73 CBS
   Love, American Style   ep   Love and the Fractured Fibula
      10. 12. 73 ABC
   Barney Miller   ep   2. 20. 75 ABC
   Flying High   ep   11. 17. 78 CBS
   Sweepstakes   ep   3. 2. 79 NBC
   Too Close for Comfort   sr   11. 11. 80 ABC
   Too Close for Comfort   sr ret   10. 13. 81 ABC
   The Love Boat   ep   The Lady from Laramie 11. 14. 81 ABC

DUVALL, ROBERT
   A&C:
   Route 66   ep   The Newborn 5. 5. 61 CBS
   Great Ghost Tales   ep   William Wilson 7. 6. 61 NBC
   Route 66   ep   Birdcage on My Foot 10. 13. 61 CBS
   SUPP. :
   Ike   ms   5. 3. 79, 5. 4. 79, 5. 6. 79 ABC

DUVALL, SHELLEY*
   Love, American Style   ep   Love and Mr. and Ms. 3. 2. 73 ABC
   Baretta   ep   3. 24. 76 ABC
   American Short Story   ep   Bernice Bobs Her Hair 4. 5. 77 PBS

DZUNDZA, GEORGE*
    Movin' On   ep   9.16.75 NBC
    Starsky and Hutch   ep   10.1.75 ABC
    The Waltons   ep   11.20.75 CBS
    Joe Forrester   ep   12.9.75 NBC
    Bert D'Angelo, Superstar   ep   2.21.76 ABC
    The Streets of San Francisco   ep   6.2.77 ABC
    Starsky and Hutch   ep   9.28.77 ABC
    The Defection of Simas Kudirka   tf   1.23.78 CBS
    Salem's Lot   tf   11.17.79, 11.24.79 CBS
    Young Maverick   ep   12.26.79 CBS
    Skokie   tf   11.17.81 CBS
    Open All Night   sr   11.28.81 ABC
    A Long Way Home   tf   12.6.81 ABC

-E-

EBSEN, BONNIE*
    Barnaby Jones   ep   Venus--as in Flytrap 1.6.74 CBS
    Marcus Welby, M.D.   ep   1.15.74 ABC
    Barnaby Jones   ep   12.31.74, 12.4.75 CBS
    The Kallikaks   sr   8.3.77 NBC
    The Hardy Boys/Nancy Drew Mysteries   ep   The Creatures
        Who Came on Sunday 10.30.77 ABC
    Barnaby Jones   ep   The Coronado Triangle 3.2.78 CBS
    Barnaby Jones   ep   Target for a Wedding 4.12.79 CBS
    The Paradise Connection   tf   9.15.79 CBS
    Barnaby Jones   ep   2.7.80 CBS
    The Fall Guy   ep   The Human Torch 12.9.81 ABC

EBSEN, BUDDY
    SUPP.:
    Barnaby Jones   sr ret   9.15.77 CBS
    Leave Yesterday Behind   tf   5.14.78 ABC
    The Bastard/Kent Family Chronicles   ms   5.22.78, 5.23.78 NN
    The Critical List   tf   9.11.78, 9.12.78 NBC
    Barnaby Jones   sr ret   9.21.78 CBS
    The Paradise Connection   tf   9.15.79 CBS
    Barnaby Jones   sr ret   9.20.79 CBS
    The Return of the Beverly Hillbillies   tf   10.6.81 CBS
    Fire on the Mountain   tf   11.23.81 NBC

EDELMAN, HERB*
    The Good Guys   sr   9.25.68 CBS
    The Good Guys   sr ret   9.26.69 CBS
    In Name Only   tf   11.25.69 ABC
    The Feminist and the Fuzz   tf   1.26.71 ABC
    The Neon Ceiling   tf   2.8.71 NBC

Bewitched   ep   2. 25. 71 ABC
Banyon   tf   3. 15. 71 NBC
Once upon a Dead Man   tf   9. 17. 71 NBC
Love, American Style   ep   1. 21. 72 ABC
Banacek   ep   9. 27. 72 NBC
Of Thee I Sing   sp   10. 24. 72 CBS
Love, American Style   ep   11. 10. 72 ABC
The Bold Ones: The Doctors   ep   A Quality of Fear 11. 14. 72
    NBC
Ironside   ep   9. 20. 73 NBC
The New Dick Van Dyke Show   ep   9. 24. 73 CBS
The Partridge Family   ep   The Strike Out King 10. 6. 73 ABC
Police Story   ep   The Ho Chi Minh Trail 11. 6. 73 NBC
The Streets of San Francisco   ep   The 24-Karat Plague 11. 8. 73
    ABC
Kosta and His Family   pt   12. 31. 73 NBC
Cannon   ep   Photo Finish 1. 2. 74 CBS
Maude   ep   1. 25. 74 CBS
Hawkins   ep   Murder on the 13th Floor 2. 5. 74 CBS
The Boys   pt   5. 16. 74 CBS
The Strange and Deadly Occurrence   tf   9. 22. 74 NBC
Happy Days   ep   1. 21. 75 ABC
The Streets of San Francisco   ep   3. 20. 75 ABC
Crossfire   tf   3. 24. 75 NBC
Medical Center   ep   12. 8. 75 CBS
Cannon   ep   12. 31. 75 CBS
Jigsaw John   ep   2. 9. 76 NBC
Ellery Queen   ep   3. 21. 76 NBC
Big John, Little John   sr   9. 11. 76 NBC
Smash-Up on Interstate 5   tf   12. 3. 76 ABC
Lanigan's Rabbi   ep   4. 24. 77 NBC
Tales of the Unexpected   ep   8. 17. 77 NBC
Rafferty   ep   9. 5. 77 CBS
The San Pedro Beach Bums   ep   9. 19. 77 ABC
Welcome Back, Kotter   ep   10. 20. 77 ABC
The Hallmark Hall of Fame   ep   Have I Got a Christmas for
    You   sp   12. 16. 77 NBC
Honest Al's A-OK Used Car and Trailer Rental Tigers   pt
    1. 78 NN
Kojak   ep   The Captain's Brother's Wife 2. 4. 78 CBS
Special Olympics   tf   2. 22. 78 CBS
CHiPs   ep   3. 2. 78 NBC
Mystery of the Week   ep   Distant Early Warning 4. 26. 78 ABC
The Comedy Company   tf   7. 21. 78 CBS
Charlie's Angels   ep   Angels in Vegas 9. 13. 78 ABC
Frankie and Annette: The Second Time Around   pt   11. 18. 78
    NBC
Marathon   tf   1. 30. 80 CBS
Ladies' Man   sr   10. 27. 80 CBS
A Cry for Help   tf   10. 20. 80 NBC
Strike Force   sr   11. 13. 81 ABC
The Love Boat   ep   He's My Brother 12. 5. 81 ABC

EDEN, BARBARA
    A&C:
    Target: The Corruptors   ep   Babes in Wall Street 3.9.62 ABC
    SUPP.:
    Stonestreet: Who Killed the Centerfold Model?   tf   1.16.77
        NBC
    The Girls in the Office   tf   2.2.79 ABC
    Men Who Rate a 10   sp hos   10.7.80 NBC
    Condominium   ms   11.20.80, 11.24.80 NN
    Harper Valley, PTA   sr   1.16.81 NBC
    Return of the Rebels   tf   10.17.81 CBS
    Harper Valley   sr   (revised) 10.29.81 NBC
    It's Only Human   pt   11.13.81 NBC

EDWARDS, VINCE
    SUPP.:
    Cover Girls   tf   5.18.77 NBC
    The Courage and the Passion   tf   5.27.78 NBC
    Police Story   ep   A Chance to Live 5.28.78 NBC
    Greatest Heroes of the Bible   ep   The Story of the Tower of
        Babel 5.15.79 NBC

EGGAR, SAMANTHA
    SUPP.:
    Columbo   ep   5.22.77 NBC
    Starsky and Hutch   ep   9.17.77 ABC
    Ziegfeld: The Man and His Women   tf   5.21.78 NBC
    Hawaii Five-O   ep   10.5.78 CBS
    Fantasy Island   ep   11.11.78 ABC
    The Love Boat   ep   3.3.79 ABC
    Fantasy Island   ep   11.3.79 ABC
    Hagen   ep   3.15.80 CBS
    The Love Boat   ep   Touchdown 2.14.81 ABC
    Aloha Paradise   ep   3.11.81 ABC

EILBACHER, CYNTHIA (a.k.a. Cindy Eilbacher)*
    My Mother, the Car   sr   9.14.65 NBC
    It Takes a Thief   ep   4.1.69 ABC
    Crowhaven Farm   tf   1.24.70 ABC
    A Clear and Present Danger   tf   3.21.70 NBC
    The Bold Ones: The Senator   sr   9.13.70 NBC
    Owen Marshall: Counselor at Law   ep   A Lonely Stretch of
        Beach 9.23.71 ABC
    Alias Smith and Jones   ep   The Posse That Wouldn't Quit
        10.14.71 ABC
    Adam-12   ep   9.27.72 NBC
    The Waltons   ep   The Hunt 10.5.72 CBS
    The Great Man's Whiskers   tf   2.13.73 NBC
    The Waltons   ep   The Braggart 11.1.73 CBS
    Happy Days   ep   The Lemon 1.22.74 ABC
    The Fess Parker Show   pt   3.28.74 CBS
    Planet of the Apes   ep   9.27.74 CBS
    The Waltons   ep   The Ring 10.17.74 CBS

Bad Ronald   tf   10. 23. 74 ABC
The ABC Afterschool Special   ep   Blind Sunday   sp   10. 27. 76
    ABC
The Waltons   ep   11. 11. 76 CBS
The Death of Richie   tf   1. 10. 77 NBC
Code R   ep   3. 4. 77 CBS
Tales of the Unexpected   ep   The Face of Evil 3. 13. 77 NBC
The Young and the Restless   sr   4. 77 CBS
Donner Pass: The Road to Survival   tf   10. 24. 78 CBS
The Immigrants   ms   11. 20. 78, 11. 27. 78 NN
A Fire in the Sky   tf   11. 26. 78 NBC
The New Adventures of Wonder Woman   ep   Skateboard Whiz
    11. 24. 78 CBS
Last Cry for Help   tf   1. 19. 79 ABC
Shirley   sr   10. 26. 79 NBC

EILBACHER, LISA*
In Name Only   tf   11. 25. 69 ABC
Alias Smith and Jones   ep   The Posse That Wouldn't Quit
    10. 14. 71 ABC
Bonanza   ep   First Love 12. 26. 72 NBC
Gunsmoke   ep   2. 12. 73 CBS
Owen Marshall: Counselor at Law   ep   The Pool House 9. 26. 73
    ABC
Doc Elliot   ep   A Time to Grow 3. 6. 74 ABC
Apple's Way   ep   10. 13. 74 CBS
Bad Ronald   tf   10. 23. 74 ABC
Movin' On   ep   1. 16. 75 NBC
Gunsmoke   ep   3. 31. 75 CBS
Caribe   ep   4. 21. 75 ABC
The Hardy Boys Mysteries   sr   1. 30. 77 ABC
Spider-Man   tf   9. 14. 77 CBS
The Man from Atlantis   ep   12. 6. 77 NBC
Hawaii Five-O   ep   3. 2. 78 CBS
The Ordeal of Patty Hearst   tf   3. 4. 79 ABC
Wheels   ms   5. 7. 78, 5. 8. 78, 5. 9. 78, 5. 14. 78, 5. 15. 78 NBC
Love for Rent   tf   11. 11. 79 ABC
To Rose the Wind   tf   3. 12. 80 CBS
This House Possessed   tf   2. 6. 81 ABC

EISENMANN, IKE*
Gunsmoke   ep $11 10. 30. 72 CBS
Gunsmoke   ep   1. 22. 73 CBS
Dirty Sally   ep   1. 18. 74 CBS
Gunsmoke   ep   The Town Tamers 1. 28. 74 CBS
The World of Disney   ep   The Sky's the Limit 1. 26. 75 NBC
The World of Disney   ep   The Secret of the Pond 10. 12. 75 NBC
Doctors' Hospital   ep   11. 5. 75 NBC
The ABC Afterschool Special   ep   My Dad Lives in a Downtown
    Hotel 11. 28. 73 ABC
Little House on the Prairie   ep   3. 17. 76 NBC
Banjo Hackett   tf   5. 3. 76 NBC
Police Woman   ep   3. 22. 77 NBC

The ABC Afterschool Special   ep   The Amazing Awareness of
     Duffy Moon 3. 23. 77 ABC
The ABC Weekend Special   ep   The Winged Colt 9. 10. 77, 9. 17. 77,
     9. 24. 77 ABC
Little House on the Prairie   ep   10. 30. 78 NBC
Black Beauty   ms   1. 31. 78, 2. 2. 78, 2. 3. 78, 2. 4. 78 NBC
Eight Is Enough   ep   2. 15. 78 ABC
The Bastard/Kent Family Chronicles   ms   5. 22. 78, 5. 23. 78 NN
Devil Dog: The Hound of Hell   tf   10. 31. 78 CBS
CHiPs   ep   12. 9. 78 NBC
Terror out of the Sky   tf   12. 26. 78 CBS
Starting Fresh   pt   6. 27. 79 NBC
The World of Disney   ep   Shadow of Fear 1. 28. 79 NBC
The New Adventures of Wonder Woman   ep   Phantom of the
     Roller Coaster 9. 4. 79, 9. 11. 79 CBS
Fantasy Island   ep   12. 15. 79 ABC
Enos   ep   The Guts and Green Strike Again 1. 26. 80 CBS
Fitz and Bones   ep   Difficult Lesson 11. 14. 81 NBC
Strike Force   ep   Magic Man 12. 11. 81 ABC

EKLAND, BRITT
     SUPP. :
     McCloud   ep   1. 23. 77 NBC
     The Great Wallendos   tf   2. 2. 78 NBC
     Ring of Passion   tf   2. 4. 78 NBC
     Battlestar Galactica   ep   The Gun on the Ice Planet 10. 22. 79,
          10. 29. 79 ABC
     Fantasy Island   ep   2. 2. 80 ABC
     The Love Boat   ep   4. 5. 80 ABC
     The Hostage Tower   tf   5. 13. 80 CBS
     Jacqueline Susann's Valley of the Dolls 1981   tf   10. 19. 81,
          10. 20. 81 CBS
     Fantasy Island   ep   3. 21. 81 ABC
     The Love Boat   ep   Accident Prone 9. 14. 81 ABC

ELAM, JACK*
     Mr. Lucky   ep   The Big Squeeze 3. 12. 60 CBS
     The Twilight Zone   ep   Will the Real Martian Please Stand Up?
          5. 26. 61 CBS
     Daniel Boone   ep   The Sound of Fear 2. 11. 65 NBC
     The Legend of Jesse James   ep   Three Men from Now 9. 13. 65
          ABC
     Gunsmoke   ep   4. 2. 66 CBS
     The Wild Wild West   ep   The Night of Montezuma's Hoardes
          10. 27. 67 CBS
     Walt Disney's World   ep   Ride a Northbound Horse 3. 16. 69
          NBC
     The Outcasts   ep   The Glory Wagon 2. 3. 69 ABC
     The Over-the-Hill Gang   tf   10. 7. 69 ABC
     Cat Ballou   pt   9. 5. 71 NBC
     Gunsmoke   ep   P. S. Murry Christmas 12. 27. 71 CBS
     Alias Smith and Jones   ep   3. 2. 72 ABC
     Gunsmoke   ep   9. 11. 72, 9. 18. 72 CBS

The Daughters of Joshua Cabe   tf   9. 13. 72 ABC
The Red Pony   tf   3. 18. 73 NBC
Kung Fu   ep   The Squaw Man 11. 1. 73 ABC
Shoot-Out in a One-Dog Town   tf   1. 9. 74 CBS
The Brian Keith Show   ep   3. 8. 74 NBC
Sidekicks   tf   3. 21. 74 CBS
The Texas Wheelers   sr   9. 13. 74 ABC
Huckleberry Finn   tf   3. 25. 75 ABC
The New Daughters of Joshua Cabe   tf   5. 29. 76 ABC
Phyllis   ep   10. 11. 76 CBS
How the West Was Won   ep   2. 7. 77, 2. 14. 77 ABC
The ABC Weekend Special   ep   The Ransom of Red Chief
      10. 22. 77 ABC
Black Beauty   ms   1. 31. 78, 2. 2. 78, 2. 3. 78, 2. 4. 78 NBC
Lacy and the Mississippi Queen   tf   5. 17. 78 NBC
Eight Is Enough   ep   11. 29. 78 ABC
Fantasy Island   ep   12. 16. 78 ABC
Sweepstakes   ep   2. 16. 79 NBC
The Sacketts   tf   5. 16. 79 CBS
Struck by Lightning   sr   9. 19. 79 CBS
The ABC Weekend Special   ep   The Revenge of Red Chief
      12. 15. 79 ABC
Eight is Enough   ep   2. 13. 80 ABC
Mark Twain's America   ep   Young Will Rogers   sp   8. 18. 80 NBC
The Girl, the Gold Watch and Dynamite   pt   5. 21. 81 NN
Here's Boomer   ep   Boomer and the Musket Cove Treasure
      10. 4. 81 NBC
Fantasy Island   ep   Kid Corey Rides Again 10. 17. 81 ABC
Father Murphy   ep   By the Bear That Bit Me 12. 1. 81, 12. 8. 81
      NBC
Skyward Christmas   pt   12. 3. 81 NBC

ELCAR, DANA*

Dark Shadows   sr   Spring 1966 ABC
The Borgia Stick   tf   2. 25. 67 NBC
The Sound of Anger   tf   12. 10. 68 NBC
The Outsider   tf   11. 13. 68 NBC
Mannix   ep   Fear I Have to Fall 12. 21. 68 CBS
Deadlock   tf   2. 22. 69 NBC
The Whole World Is Watching   tf   3. 11. 69 NBC
Ironside   ep   Eye of the Hurricane 10. 9. 69 NBC
The D.A. :   Murder One   tf   12. 8. 69 NBC
Mission: Impossible   ep   Flip Side 9. 20. 70 CBS
San Francisco International   tf   9. 29. 70 NBC
Gunsmoke   ep   Snow Train 10. 26. 70 CBS
Sarge: The Badge or the Cross   tf   2. 22. 71 NBC
The Bold Ones: The Lawyers   ep   The Invasion of Kevin Ire-
      land 9. 26. 71 NBC
Longstreet   ep   The Shape of Nightmares 10. 21. 71 ABC
Love, American Style   ep   10. 22. 71 ABC
Ironside   ep   Joss Sticks and Wedding Bells 10. 26. 71 NBC
The FBI   ep   11. 28. 71 ABC
The Bravos   tf   1. 9. 72 NBC
Fireball Forward   tf   3. 5. 72 ABC

Cannon   ep   3. 7. 72 CBS
Marcus Welby, M. D.   ep   We'll Walk out of Here Together
    9. 26. 72 ABC
Cannon   ep   10. 25. 72 CBS
Bonanza   ep   The 26th Grave 10. 31. 72 CBS
Marcus Welby, M. D.   ep   Don and Denise 10. 31. 72 ABC
Owen Marshall, Counselor at Law   ep   Who Saw Him Die?
    11. 2. 72 ABC
The Delphi Bureau   ep   The Top-Secret Secret Project 12. 14. 72
    ABC
Alias Smith and Jones   ep   1. 13. 73 ABC
Hernandez: Houston P. D.   pt   1. 16. 73 NBC
The Partridge Family   ep   1. 19. 73 ABC
Kung Fu   ep   2. 15. 73 ABC
Hawkins on Murder   tf   3. 13. 73 CBS
Dying Room Only   tf   9. 18. 73 CBS
The Waltons   ep   The Prize 10. 25. 73 CBS
Columbo   ep   Any Old Port in a Storm 10. 7. 73 NBC
The FBI   ep   Fatal Reunion 11. 4. 73 ABC
Heat Wave   tf   1. 26. 74 ABC
Chase   ep   Hot Beef 2. 13. 74 NBC
Senior Year   tf   3. 22. 74 CBS
Kung Fu   ep   4. 18. 74 ABC
Petrocelli   ep   10. 2. 74 NBC
Manhunter   ep   10. 23. 74 CBS
Panic on the 5:22   tf   11. 20. 74 ABC
Love Nest   pt   3. 14. 75 CBS
The Rockford Files   ep   10. 17. 75 NBC
Cannon   ep   12. 10. 75 CBS
Law of the Land   tf   4. 29. 76 NBC
The Gemini Man   ep   5. 10. 76 NBC
Baa Baa Black Sheep (a. k. a. The Black Sheep Squadron)   sr
    12. 4. 77 NBC
Family   ep   1. 24. 78
What Really Happened to the Class of '65?   ep   3. 2. 78 NBC
The Incredible Hulk   ep   12. 1. 78 CBS
Greatest Heroes of the Bible   ep   The Story of the Tower of
    Babel 5. 15. 79 NBC
One Day at a Time   ep   12. 2. 79 CBS
B. J. and the Bear   ep   12. 15. 79 NBC
Death Penalty   tf   1. 22. 80 NBC
Eight Is Enough   ep   4. 2. 80 ABC
Galactica 1980   ep   4. 27. 80 ABC
Mark, I Love You   tf   12. 10. 80 CBS
Foul Play   ep   2. 16. 81 ABC
Wendy Hooper--U. S. Army   pt   8. 14. 81 NBC
Flamingo Road   ep   The Arrangement 11. 3. 81 NBC
Benson   ep   11. 6. 81 ABC
Falcon Crest   ep   The Tangled Vines 12. 18. 81 CBS

ELY, RON
    SUPP. :
    The New Adventures of Wonder Woman   ep   The Deadly Sting
        10. 6. 78 CBS

Fantasy Island   ep   10. 27. 79 ABC
Fantasy Island   ep   My Fair Pharaoh 5. 10. 80 ABC
The Love Boat   ep   Swag and Mag 12. 6. 80 ABC
The Seal   pt   11. 27. 81 NBC

ENGEL, GEORGIA*
The Mary Tyler Moore Show   sr   12. 16. 72 CBS
The Mary Tyler Moore Show   sr ret   9. 15. 73 CBS
The Mary Tyler Moore Show   sr ret   9. 14. 74 CBS
Rhoda   ep   Rhoda's Wedding 10. 28. 74 CBS
The Mary Tyler Moore Show   sr ret   9. 13. 75 CBS
The Mary Tyler Moore Show   sr ret   9. 25. 76 CBS
The Love Boat III (a. k. a. The New Love Boat) tf   5. 5. 77 ABC
The Betty White Show   sr   9. 12. 77 CBS
A Love Affair: The Eleanor and Lou Gehrig Story   tf   1. 15. 78
    NBC
The Love Boat   ep   Going by the Book 2. 18. 78 ABC
Fantasy Island   ep   9. 16. 78, 12. 8. 79 ABC
Mork and Mindy   ep   12. 16. 79, 12. 23. 79 ABC
The Goodtime Girls   sr   1. 22. 80 ABC
The Day the Women Got Even   tf   12. 4. 80 NBC
The Love Boat   ep   Seal of Approval 1. 10. 81 ABC
The CBS Library: Misunderstood Monsters   ep   Creole   vo
    4. 7. 81 CBS
Fantasy Island   ep   Romance Times Three 12. 5. 81 ABC

ERICKSON, LEIF
A&C:
The Virginian   ep   Blaze of Glory 12. 29. 65 NBC
SUPP. :
Fantastic Journey   ep   2. 3. 77 NBC
Project UFO   ep   3. 19. 78 NBC
The Rockford Files   ep   Trouble in Paradise Cove 9. 28. 79 NBC
Hunter's Moon   pt   12. 1. 79 CBS
Wild Times   ms   1. 24. 80, 1. 31. 80 NN

ERICSON, DEVON*
The Waltons   ep   The First Day 9. 19. 74 CBS
Manhunter   ep   12. 11. 74 CBS
The Dream Makers   tf   1. 7. 75 NBC
The Runaway Barge   tf   3. 24. 75 NBC
Barnaby Jones   ep   Bond of Fear 4. 15. 75 CBS
Movin' On   ep   1. 6. 76 NBC
Eleanor and Franklin   tf   1. 11. 76, 1. 12. 76 ABC
Stranded   pt   5. 26. 76 CBS
Barnaby Jones   ep   11. 18. 76 CBS
Police Story   ep   1. 25. 77 NBC
Most Wanted   ep   2. 12. 77 ABC
The Streets of San Francisco   ep   3. 3. 77 ABC
Westside Medical   ep   3. 31. 77 ABC
Young Dan'l Boone   sr   9. 12. 77 CBS
The Awakening Land   ms   2. 19. 78, 2. 20. 78, 2. 21. 78 NBC
Testimony of Two Men   ms   5. 1. 78, 5. 2. 78, 5. 3. 78 NN

The Busters   pt   5. 22. 78 CBS
Ishi: The Last of His Tribe   tf   12. 20. 78 NBC
Studs Lonigan   ms ep   3. 14. 79 NBC
Can You Hear the Laughter?   The Story of Freddie Prinze
    tf   9. 11. 79 CBS
This Is the Life   ep   9. 16. 79 NN
Barnaby Jones   ep   9. 27. 79 CBS
The Chisholms   sr   1. 19. 80 CBS
Family   ep   3. 3. 80 ABC
When the Whistle Blows   ep   3. 28. 80 ABC
Baby Comes Home   tf   10. 16. 80 CBS
CHiPs   ep   Wheels of Justice 12. 21. 80 NBC
Quincy, M. E.   ep   To Kill in Plain Sight 3. 4. 81 NBC
Buck Rogers in the 25th Century   ep   4. 16. 81 NBC
Magnum, P. I.   ep   11. 12. 81 CBS

ERICSON, JOHN
    A&C:
    Kraft Mystery Theatre   ep   The Home of Rue Riviera 8. 30. 61
        NBC
    Route 66   ep   1800 Days to Justice 1. 26. 62 CBS
    Assignment: Vienna   ep   Annalisa 12. 7. 72 ABC
    The FBI   ep   2. 1. 73 ABC
    Tenafly   tf   2. 12. 73 NBC
    Escape   ep   4. 1. 73 NBC
    The World of Disney   ep   Hog Wild 1. 20. 74, 1. 27. 74 NBC
    Police Story   ep   1. 29. 74 NBC
    Hawkins   ep   Confidential for Murder 3. 5. 74 CBS
    Murder: Impossible   tf   3. 26. 74 ABC
    Doc Elliot   ep   3. 27. 74 ABC
    Police Story   ep   3. 27. 74 NBC
    Barbary Coast   ep   2. 18. 75 ABC
    S. W. A. T.   ep   11. 15. 75 ABC
    SUPP. :
    Police Woman   ep   11. 8. 77 NBC
    The Hardy Boys/Nancy Drew Mysteries   ep   12. 18. 77 ABC
    CHiPs   ep   11. 4. 78 NBC
    Hunter's Moon   pt   12. 1. 79 CBS

ESTRADA, ERIK*
    Hawaii Five-O   ep   2. 27. 73 CBS
    Owen Marshall, Counselor at Law   ep   Once a Lion 9. 19. 73
        ABC
    Kojak   ep   1. 5. 75 CBS
    Mannix   ep   1. 12. 75 CBS
    The Night Stalker   ep   2. 14. 75 ABC
    The Six Million Dollar Man   ep   10. 19. 75 ABC
    Joe Forrester   ep   11. 25. 75 NBC
    Police Woman   ep   12. 2. 75 NBC
    Medical Center   ep   12. 15. 75 CBS
    Barnaby Jones   ep   2. 5. 76 CBS
    The Quest   ep   12. 1. 76, 12. 8. 76 NBC
    Delvecchio   ep   1. 30. 77 CBS

Fire   tf   5. 8. 77 NBC
CHiPs   sr   9. 15. 77 NBC
CHiPs   sr ret   9. 16. 78 NBC
The Love Boat   ep   10. 14. 78 ABC
CHiPs   sr ret   9. 22. 79 NBC
CHiPs   sr ret   9. 21. 80 NBC
Women Who Rate a 10   sp hos   2. 15. 81 NBC
CHiPs   sr ret   10. 4. 81 NBC
Mitchell and Woods   pt   12. 18. 81 NBC

EVANS, LINDA*
    Bachelor Father   ep   1957 CBS (under her real name, Linda
        Evanstad)
    The Adventures of Ozzie and Harriet 1960 ABC
    My Favorite Martian   ep   5. 16. 65 CBS
    The Big Valley   sr   9. 15. 65 ABC
    The Big Valley   sr ret   9. 12. 66 ABC
    The Big Valley   sr ret   9. 11. 67 ABC
    The Big Valley   sr ret   9. 23. 68 ABC
    Female Artillery   tf   1. 17. 73 ABC
    McCloud   ep   Butch Cassidy Rides Again 10. 14. 73 NBC
    Banacek   ep   Rocket to Oblivion 2. 12. 74 NBC
    Mannix   ep   3. 31. 74 CBS
    Nakia   ep   4. 17. 74 ABC
    Harry O   ep   Guardian at the Gates 9. 26. 74 ABC
    McMillan and Wife   ep   Night Train to L.A. 1. 19. 75 NBC
    The Rockford Files   ep   Claire 1. 31. 75 NBC
    The Big Ripoff   tf   3. 11. 75 NBC
    The Rockford Files   ep   The Farnsworth Stratagem 9. 19. 75 NBC
    Hunter   sr   2. 18. 77 CBS
    Nowhere to Run   tf   1. 16. 78 NBC
    Standing Tall   tf   1. 21. 78 NBC
    The Love Boat   ep   2. 13. 78 ABC
    Dynasty   sr   1. 12. 81 ABC
    Dynasty   sr ret   11. 4. 81 ABC
    The Love Boat   ep   11. 21. 81 ABC
    The Fall Guy   ep   Colt's Angels 12. 2. 81 ABC

EVANS, MAURICE
    SUPP. :
    Fantasy Island   ep   9. 30. 78 ABC
    The Girl, the Gold Watch and Everything   pt   6. 13. 80 NN

EVERETT, CHAD
    A&C:
    Hawaiian Eye   ep   The Reluctant Visit 11. 15. 61 ABC
    Surfside Six   ep   Neutral Corner 6. 11. 62 ABC
    SUPP. :
    In the Glitter Palace   tf   2. 27. 77 NBC
    Police Story   ep   Day of Terror, Night of Fear 3. 4. 78 NBC
    Centennial   ms ep   Only the Banks Live Forever 10. 1. 78 NBC
    Centennial   ms ep   The Wagon and the Elephant 10. 29. 78 NBC
    Centennial   ms ep   For As Long As the Water Flows 11. 4. 78 NBC

Centennial ms ep The Massacre 11. 11. 78 NBC
The French-Atlantic Affair ms 11. 15. 79, 11. 16. 79, 11. 18. 79
   ABC
Hagen sr 3. 1. 80 CBS
The Intruder Within tf 2. 20. 81 ABC
Mistress of Paradise tf 10. 4. 81 ABC

EVERS, JASON
   A&C:
   Wrangler sr 8. 4. 60 NBC
   Hong Kong ep Suitable for Framing 1. 4. 61 ABC
   Bonanza ep The Duke 3. 11. 61 NBC
   The Rebel ep Miz Rundy 4. 2. 61 ABC
   Laramie ep The Debt 4. 18. 61 NBC
   Surfside Six ep Count Seven 9. 18. 61 ABC
   Adventures in Paradise ep Please Believe Me 2. 4. 62 ABC
   Alcoa Premiere ep Of This Time, of That Place 3. 6. 62 ABC
   The Defenders ep The Bigamist 11. 3. 62 CBS
   The Virginian ep An Echo of Thunder 10. 5. 66 NBC
   Mobile One ep 12. 15. 75 ABC
   McMillan and Wife ep 12. 5. 76 NBC
   Barnaby Jones ep 12. 16. 76 CBS
   SUPP. :
   Most Wanted ep 3. 7. 77 ABC
   The Bionic Woman ep Rodeo 10. 15. 77 NBC
   Happy Days ep 9. 12. 78 ABC
   CHiPs ep 12. 2. 78 NBC
   Hawaii Five-O ep 11. 1. 79 CBS
   Fantasy Island ep 2. 21. 81 ABC
   Golden Gate tf 9. 25. 81 ABC

EVIGAN, GREG*
   The Six Million Dollar Man ep 11. 7. 76 ABC
   All That Glitters sr 1977 NN
   A Year at the Top sr 8. 5. 77 CBS
   Operation: Runaway ep 5. 11. 78 NBC
   B. J. and the Bear tf 10. 4. 78 NBC
   One Day at a Time ep 12. 4. 78 CBS
   B. J. and the Bear sr 2. 10. 79 NBC
   Barnaby Jones ep Target for a Wedding 4. 12. 79 CBS
   B. J. and the Bear sr ret 9. 29. 79 NBC
   The Misadventures of Sheriff Lobo ep 11. 6. 79 NBC
   B. J. and the Bear sr ret 1. 13. 81 NBC

EWELL, TOM
   SUPP. :
   Baretta sr ret 9. 28. 77 ABC
   Fantasy Island ep The Over-the-Hill Caper 4. 15. 78 ABC
   Return of the Mod Squad tf 5. 18. 79 ABC
   Best of the West sr 9. 10. 81 ABC

-F-

FABARES, SHELLEY
  SUPP. :
  Forever Fernwood   sr   9.77 NN
  Fantasy Island   ep   10.14.78 ABC
  Vega$ ep   9.27.78 ABC
  One Day at a Time   ep   2.13.78 CBS
  The Incredible Hulk   ep   12.1.78 CBS
  Fantasy Island   1.13.79 ABC
  The World of Disney   ep   Donovan's Kid 1.14.79, 1.21.79 NBC
  One Day at a Time   ep   2.7.79 CBS
  Highcliffe Manor   sr   4.12.79 NBC
  Hello, Larry   ep   10.12.79, 10.19.79, 10.26.79 NBC
  Fantasy Island   ep   11.10.79 ABC
  Friendships, Secrets and Lies   tf   12.3.79 NBC
  The Love Boat   ep   4.19.80 ABC
  The Great American Traffic Jam   tf   10.2.80 NBC
  One Day at a Time   ep   11.16.80 CBS
  Fantasy Island   ep   1.24.81 ABC
  One Day at a Time   sr   10.11.81 CBS
  Mork and Mindy   ep   The Wedding 10.15.81 ABC

FABRAY, NANETTE
  A&C:
  Laramie   ep   Glory Road 9.22.59 NBC
  SUPP. :
  The Love Boat   ep   1.14.78 ABC
  One Day at a Time   ep   4.8.79 CBS
  The Love Boat   ep   Grandmother's Day 5.12.79 ABC
  Faculty Lounge   pt   5.13.79 NBC
  One Day at a Time   ep   10.21.79 CBS
  The Man in the Santa Claus Suit   tf   12.23.79 NBC
  One Day at a Time   ep   12.30.79, 1.27.80, 2.10.80 CBS
  One Day at a Time   ep   The Merry Widow 12.14.80 CBS
  One Day at a Time   ep   2.1.81 CBS
  Aloha Paradise   ep   3.4.81 ABC
  The Love Boat   ep   The Floating Bridge Game 12.12.81 ABC

FAIRBANKS, DOUGLAS, JR.
  SUPP. :
  The Love Boat   ep   11.10.79 ABC
  The Hostage Tower   tf   5.13.80 CBS
  The Love Boat   ep   Aunt Sylvia 10.17.81 ABC

FAIRCHILD, MORGAN*
  Kojak   ep   Hair-Trigger Away 11.7.76 CBS
  Rafferty   ep   9.19.77 CBS
  Switch   ep   9.30.77 CBS
  Rosetti and Ryan   ep   10.13.77 NBC
  79 Park Avenue   ms   10.16.77, 10.17.77, 10.18.77 NBC
  Happy Days   ep   11.22.77 ABC

The Initiation of Sarah   tf   **2. 6. 78** ABC
Police Woman   ep   **2. 22. 78** NBC
Escapade   pt   5. 19. 78 CBS
Barnaby Jones   ep   A Dangerous Affair 9. 28. 78 CBS
Dallas   ep   10. 7. 78 CBS
Mork and Mindy   ep   10. 12. 78, 12. 14. 78 ABC
Sweepstakes   ep   2. 9. 79 NBC
Time Express   ep   5. 3. 79 CBS
Concrete Cowboys   tf   10. 17. 79 CBS
A Man Called Sloane   ep   10. 27. 79 NBC
Young Maverick   ep   1. 9. 80 CBS
The Memory of Eva Ryker   tf   5. 7. 80 CBS
Flamingo Road   tf   5. 12. 80 NBC
The Dream Merchants   ms   5. 12. 80, 5. 19. 80 NN
Flamingo Road   sr   1. 6. 81 NBC
The Girl, The Gold Watch and Dynamite   pt   5. 21. 81 NN
Flamingo Road   sr ret   11. 3. 81 NBC
The Love Boat   ep   **11. 21. 81** ABC

FALK, PETER
  A& C:
  The Aquanauts   ep   The Double Adventure 3. 29. 61 CBS
  Naked City   ep   A Very Cautious Boy 4. **26.** 61 ABC
  SUPP. :
  Columbo   sp ep   **5. 22. 77**, 11. 21. 77 NBC
  Columbo   sp ep   Make Me a Perfect Murder **2. 25. 78** NBC
  Columbo   sp ep   How to Dial a Murder 4. 15. 78 NBC
  Columbo   sp ep   The Conspirators 5. 13. 78 NBC

FARENTINO, JAMES
  SUPP. :
  The Hallmark Hall of Fame   ep   Emily, Emily   sp   **2. 7. 77** NBC
  Jesus of Nazareth   ms   4. 3. 77, 4. 10. 77 NBC
  The Possessed   tf   5. 1. 77 NBC
  Police Story   ep   No Margin for Error 4. 30. 78 NBC
  Silent Victory: The Kitty O'Neil Story 2. 24. 79 CBS
  Evita Peron   tf   **2. 23. 81**, 2. 24. 81 NBC
  Dynasty   sr   11. 25. 81 ABC

FARGAS, ANTONIO
  A& C:
  Adventuring with the Chopper   pt   8. 7. 76 NBC
  SUPP. :
  The Love Boat   ep   Cabin Fever 5. 20. 78 ABC
  Nurse   tf   4. 9. 80 CBS
  Charlie's Angels   ep   Angels of the Deep 12. 7. 80 ABC
  Nurse   ep   Long Days Journey into Morning 4. 30. 81 CBS

FARR, JAMIE
  A& C:
  The Rebel   ep   3. 26. 61 ABC
  SUPP. :
  M*A*S*H   sr ret   9. 20. 77 CBS

The Love Boat   ep   Parlez Vous **2. 13. 78** ABC
M*A*S*H   sr ret   **9. 18. 78** CBS
Amateur Night at the Dixie Bar and Grill   tf   **1. 8. 79** NBC
Supertrain   ep   **4. 7. 79** NBC
M*A*S*H   sr ret   **9. 17. 79** CBS
Murder Can Hurt You!   tf   **5. 21. 80** ABC
M*A*S*H   sr ret   **11. 17. 80** CBS
Return of the Rebels   tf   **10. 17. 81** CBS
M*A*S*H   sr ret   **10. 26. 81** CBS
The Fall Guy   ep   The Japanese Connection **12. 16. 81** ABC

FARRELL, MIKE
A& C:
Lassie   ep   **2. 26. 67** CBS
Jigsaw   ep   **6. 16. 73** ABC
SUPP. :
M*A*S*H   sr ret   **9. 20. 77** CBS
M*A*S*H   sr ret   **9. 18. 78** CBS
Battered   tf   **9. 26. 78** NBC
M*A*S*H   sr ret   **9. 17. 79** CBS
Sex and the Single Parent   tf   **9. 19. 79** CBS
Letters from Frank   tf   **11. 22. 79** CBS
Father Damien: The Leper Priest   tf   **10. 27. 80** NBC
M*A*S*H   sr ret   **11. 17. 80** CBS
M*A*S*H   sr ret   **10. 26. 81** CBS

FARRELL, SHARON
A& C:
Empire   ep   Stopover on the Way to the Moon **1. 6. 63** NBC
Police Story   ep   Requiem for an Informer **10. 9. 73** NBC
Insight   ep   **1. 26. 75** NN
SUPP. :
Switch   ep   **2. 6. 77** CBS
Hawaii Five-O   ep   **2. 17. 77** CBS
The Man from Atlantis   **6. 6. 78** NBC
Hawaii Five-O   ep   **12. 14. 78** CBS
Hawaii Five-O   sr   **10. 4. 79** CBS
Last Ride of the Dalton Gang   tf   **11. 20. 79** NBC
Kate Loves a Mystery   ep   **11. 29. 79** NBC
BAD Cats   ep   **2. 8. 80** ABC
Enos   ep   Blue Flu **12. 10. 80** CBS

FAWCETT, FARRAH (previously listed as Farrah Fawcett-Majors)
A& C:
The Partridge Family   ep   **10. 2. 70** ABC
Harry O   ep   Double Jeopardy **2. 13. 75** ABC
Harry O   ep   Lester **2. 20. 75** ABC
Harry O   ep   Elegy for a Cop **2. 27. 75** ABC
Harry O   ep   Lester II **9. 25. 75** ABC
Harry O   ep   Tender Killing Care **10. 30. 75** ABC
Harry O   ep   Past Imperfect **1. 22. 76** ABC
Harry O   ep   Forbidden City **2. 26. 76** ABC

SUPP. :
Charlie's Angels   ep   Angel Come Home 9. 20. 78 ABC
Charlie's Angels   ep   Mother Angel 11. 15. 78 ABC
Charlie's Angels   ep   Angel in a Box 2. 14. 79 ABC
Charlie's Angels   ep   Fallen Angel 10. 24. 79 ABC
Charlie's Angels   ep   The Prince and the Angel 11. 14. 79 ABC
Charlie's Angels   ep   An Angel's Trail 2. 27. 80 ABC
Murder in Texas   tf   5. 3. 81, 5. 4. 81 NBC
The Fall Guy   ep   11. 4. 81 ABC

FAYE, ALICE
   SUPP. :
   The Love Boat   ep   Celebration 3. 29. 80 ABC

FELDON, BARBARA
   A&C:
   Griff   ep   Death by Prescription 10. 6. 73 ABC
   What Are Best Friends For?   tf   12. 18. 73 ABC
   SUPP. :
   The Natural Look   pt   7. 6. 77 NBC
   The Four of Us   pt   7. 18. 77 ABC
   Sooner or Later   tf   3. 25. 79 NBC
   Vacation in Hell   tf   5. 21. 79 ABC
   Before and After   tf   10. 5. 79 ABC
   Children of Divorce   tf   11. 24. 80 NBC
   Real Life Stories   pt   4. 13. 81 CBS

FELDSHUH, TOVAH*
   Scream, Pretty Peggy   tf   11. 24. 73 ABC
   Gibbsville   ep   12. 9. 76 NBC
   Serpico   ep   12. 10. 76 NBC
   The Amazing Howard Hughes   tf   4. 13. 77, 4. 14. 77 CBS
   The World of Darkness   pt   4. 17. 77 CBS
   Barnaby Jones   ep   3. 3. 77 CBS
   The Love Boat   ep   10. 1. 77 ABC
   Holocaust   ms   4. 16. 78, 4. 17. 78, 4. 18. 78, 4. 19. 78 NBC
   Once upon a Classic   ep   A Connecticut Yankee in King Arthur's
      Court 5. 23. 78 PBS
   Terror out of the Sky   tf   12. 26. 78 CBS
   The Triangle Factory Fire   tf   1. 30. 79 NBC
   Beggarman, Thief   tf   11. 26. 79, 11. 27. 79 NBC
   The Women's Room   tf   9. 14. 80 ABC

FELL, NORMAN*
   The Man from U. N. C. L. E.   ep   The Moonglow Affair 2. 25. 66
      NBC
   The FBI   ep   2. 23. 69 ABC
   Dan August   sr   9. 23. 70 ABC
   The Partridge Family   ep   10. 8. 71 ABC
   O'Hara, U. S. Treasury   ep   Operation: Smokescreen 3. 10. 72
      CBS
   The Heist   tf   11. 29. 72 ABC

McCloud   ep   The Park Avenue Rustlers 12. 24. 72 NBC
Marcus Welby, M. D.   ep   2. 6. 73 ABC
Going Places   pt   3. 19. 73 NBC
Needles and Pins   sr   9. 21. 73 NBC
Griff   ep   Hammerlock 12. 15. 73 ABC
Police Story   ep   11. 19. 74 NBC
Death Stalk   tf   1. 21. 75 NBC
Rhoda   ep   2. 3. 75 CBS
Lucas Tanner   ep   2. 26. 75 NBC
Cannon   ep   12. 1. 75 CBS
Starsky and Hutch   ep   12. 17. 75 ABC
Risko   pt   5. 9. 76 CBS
Executive Suite   sr   9. 20. 76 CBS
The Streets of San Francisco   ep   The Thrill Killers 9. 30. 76,
    10. 7. 76 ABC
Richie Brockelman: The Missing 24 Hours   tf   10. 27. 76 NBC
Three's Company   sr   3. 15. 77 ABC
Three's Company   sr ret   9. 13. 77 ABC
Charlie's Angels   ep   Angels in Paradise 9. 14. 77 ABC
Three's Company   sr ret   9. 12. 78 ABC
The Love Boat   ep   Julie's Dilemma 9. 23. 78 ABC
Roots: The Next Generations   ms ep   2. 25. 79 ABC
The Ropers   sr   3. 13. 79 ABC
The Ropers   sr ret   9. 15. 79 ABC
Getting There   pt   2. 12. 80 CBS
Moviola: This Year's Blonde   tf   5. 18. 80 NBC
For the Love of It   tf   9. 26. 80 ABC

FERRER, JOSE
    SUPP. :
    The Rhinemann Exchange   ms   3. 10. 77, 3. 17. 77, 3. 24. 77 NBC
    Exo-Man   tf   6. 18. 77 NBC
    The Return of Captain Nemo   sr   3. 8. 78 CBS
    The Hallmark Hall of Fame   ep   Fame   sp   11. 30. 78 NBC
    The French-Atlantic Affair   ms   11. 15. 79, 11. 16. 79, 11. 18. 79
        ABC
    Battles: The Murder That Wouldn't Die   tf   3. 9. 80 NBC
    Tales of the Unexpected   ep   4. 12. 80 NN
    The Hallmark Hall of Fame   ep   Gideon's Trumpet   sp   4. 30. 80
        CBS
    The Dream Merchants   ms   5. 12. 80, 5. 19. 80 NBC
    Magnum, P. I.   ep   2. 12. 81 CBS
    Evita Peron   tf   2. 23. 81, 2. 24. 81 NBC
    Peter and Paul   tf   4. 12. 81, 4. 14. 81 CBS
    The Love Boat   ep   The Mongala 10. 10. 81 ABC

FERRER, MEL
    SUPP. :
    Hawaii Five-O   ep   1. 6. 77 CBS
    Baretta   ep   2. 23. 77 ABC
    Hawaii Five-O   ep   3. 17. 77 CBS
    Lanigan's Rabbi   ep   4. 24. 77 NBC
    The New Adventures of Wonder Woman   ep   Anschluss '77 9. 23. 77
        CBS

Logan's Run   ep   10. 14. 77 CBS
Sharon: Portrait of a Mistress   tf   10. 31. 77 NBC
How the West Was Won   ep   1. 12. 78 ABC
Black Beauty   ms   1. 31. 78, 2. 1. 78, 2. 2. 78, 2. 3. 78, 2. 4. 78
   NBC
How the West Was Won   ep   2. 19. 78 ABC
Legend of the Black Hand   ms ep   8. 23. 78 ABC
Dallas   ep   12. 21. 79, 1. 18. 80 CBS
Top of the Hill   ms   2. 6. 80, 2. 7. 80 NN
The Memory of Eva Ryker   tf   5. 7. 80 CBS
Fugitive Family   tf   10. 1. 80 CBS
Pleasure Palace   tf   10. 22. 80 CBS
Behind the Screen   sr   10. 9. 81 CBS
Falcon Crest   ep   In His Father's House 12. 4. 81 CBS

FIELD, SALLY
   SUPP. :
   NBC Live Theatre   ep   All the Way Home   sp   12. 21. 81 NBC

FISHER, GAIL
   SUPP. :
   Fantasy Island   ep   9. 7. 79 ABC

FITZGERALD, GERALDINE
   A& C:
   Naked City   ep   The Man Who Kills Ants Is Coming 3. 7. 62
      ABC
   Theatre in America   ep   Beyond the Horizon 1. 14. 76 PBS
   SUPP. :
   Yesterday's Child   tf   2. 3. 77 NBC
   The Quinns   tf   7. 1. 77 ABC
   Theatre in America   ep   Tartuffe 5. 31. 78 PBS
   Lou Grant   ep   11. 6. 78 CBS
   Great Performances   ep   Ah, Wilderness 1. 24. 79 PBS

FLANAGAN, FIONNUALA*
   Bonanza   ep   Heritage of Anger 9. 19. 72 NBC
   Mannix   ep   10. 1. 72 CBS
   Gunsmoke   ep   10. 9. 72 CBS
   Wide World of Mystery   ep   The Picture of Dorian Gray
      4. 23. 73, 4. 24. 73 ABC
   The New Adventures of Perry Mason   ep   The Case of the
      Horoscope Homicide 9. 16. 73 CBS
   Marcus Welby, M. D.   ep   A Joyful Song 9. 18. 73 ABC
   The Rookies   ep   Trial by Doubt 1. 7. 74 ABC
   Shaft   ep   The Murder Machine 2. 19. 74 CBS
   Hec Ramsey   ep   Only Birds and Fools 4. 7. 74 NBC
   The Godchild   tf   11. 26. 74 ABC
   The Legend of Lizzie Borden   tf   2. 10. 75 ABC
   The Streets of San Francisco   ep   1. 22. 76 ABC
   Rich Man, Poor Man   ms   2. 1-23. 76, 3. 1-15. 76 ABC
   Medical Center   ep   2. 2. 76 CBS
   Marcus Welby, M. D.   ep   2. 24. 76 ABC
   Kojak   ep   A Summer Madness 10. 3. 76 CBS

The Bionic Woman   ep   Road to Nashville 10. 20. 76 ABC
Nightmare in Badham County   tf   11. 5. 76 ABC
Serpico   ep   12. 31. 76 ABC
The Bionic Woman   ep   1. 5. 77 ABC
Mary White   tf   11. 18. 77 ABC
How the West Was Won   sr   1. 12. 78 ABC
Three By Four   ep   In the Region of Ice   sp   10. 13. 78 PBS
Young Love, First Love   tf   11. 20. 79 CBS
Palmerstown   ep   Roadhouse 5. 5. 81 CBS
Trapper John, M. D.   ep   Is There a Doctor in the Big House?
    11. 29. 81 CBS

FLEMING, RHONDA
    A&C:
    Needles and Pins   ep   It Was a Very Good Line 10. 5. 73 NBC
    SUPP. :
    The Love Boat   ep   11. 25. 78 ABC
    Love for Rent   tf   11. 11. 79 ABC

FOCH, NINA
    SUPP. :
    McMillan   ep   1. 23. 77 NBC
    The World of Disney   ep   Child of Glass 5. 14. 78 NBC
    Ebony, Ivory and Jade   tf   8. 3. 79 CBS
    Lou Grant   ep   12. 17. 79 CBS
    Pottsville   pt   8. 6. 80 CBS

FONDA, HENRY
    A&C:
    The Alpha Caper   tf   10. 6. 73 ABC
    SUPP. :
    Home to Stay   tf   5. 2. 78 CBS
    Roots: The Next Generations   ms ep   2. 18. 79, 2. 19. 79,
        2. 20. 79 ABC
    Family   ep   11. 20. 79 ABC
    American Short Story   sr hos   2. 4. 80 PBS
    NBC Live Theatre   ep   The Oldest Living Graduate   sp   4. 7. 80
        NBC
    Gideon's Trumpet   tf   4. 30. 80 CBS
    Summer Solstice   sp   12. 30. 81 ABC

FONDA, PETER
    SUPP. :
    The Hostage Tower   tf   5. 13. 80 CBS

FONTANE, CHAR*
    Banyon   ep   10. 13. 72 NBC
    Love, American Style   ep   10. 20. 72 ABC
    Joe and Valerie   sr   4. 24. 78 NBC
    Pearl   ms   11. 16. 78, 11. 17. 78, 11. 19. 78 ABC
    Joe and Valerie   sr ret   1. 5. 79 NBC
    Supertrain   ep   2. 7. 79 NBC
    Sweepstakes   ep   3. 16. 79 NBC

Barnaby Jones   ep   Echo of a Distant Battle 11. 11. 79 CBS
The Love Boat   ep   12. 1. 79 ABC
The Night the Bridge Fell Down   tf   10. 21. 80 NBC
Nero Wolfe   ep   1. 30. 81 NBC

FONTAINE, JOAN
   SUPP. :
   The Users   tf   10. 1. 78 ABC
   Aloha Paradise   ep   3. 25. 81 ABC
   The Love Boat   ep   11. 7. 81 ABC

FORD, GLENN
   SUPP. :
   The 3,000 Mile Chase   tf   6. 16. 77 NBC
   The Last of the Mohicans   tf   11. 23. 77 NBC
   When Havoc Struck   sr nar   1. 11. 78 NN
   Police Story   ep   No Margin for Error 4. 30. 78 NBC
   Evening in Byzantium   ms   8. 14. 78, 8. 15. 78 NN
   The Sacketts   tf   5. 15. 79, 5. 16. 79 NBC
   When the West Was Fun   sp hos   6. 5. 79 ABC
   Beggarman, Thief   tf   11. 26. 79, 11. 27. 79 NBC
   The Gift   tf   12. 15. 79 CBS

FORREST, STEVE
   A&C:
   Target: The Corruptors   ep   Quicksand 12. 29. 61 ABC
   Gunsmoke   ep   The Widowmaker 10. 8. 73 CBS
   Insight   ep   4. 6. 75 NN
   SUPP. :
   Maneaters Are Loose!   tf   5. 3. 78 CBS
   Fantasy Island   ep   10. 21. 78 ABC
   The Deerslayer   tf   12. 18. 78 NBC
   Captain America   tf   1. 19. 79 CBS
   Roughnecks   ms   7. 15. 80, 7. 16. 80 NN
   A Rumor of War   tf   9. 24. 80, 9. 25. 80 CBS
   Condominium   ms   11. 20. 80, 11. 24. 80 NN
   The Manions of America   ms   9. 30. 81, 10. 1. 81, 10. 2. 81 ABC

FORSLUND, CONSTANCE*
   The Legend of Valentino   tf   11. 23. 75 ABC
   Big Bob Johnson and His Fantastic Speed Circus   tf   6. 27. 78
      NBC
   Pleasure Cove   tf   1. 3. 79 NBC
   Dear Detective   ep   3. 28. 79 CBS
   Taxi   ep   10. 30. 79 ABC
   A Shining Season   tf   12. 26. 79 CBS
   Moviola: This Year's Blonde   tf   5. 18. 80 NBC
   Enos   ep   12. 17. 80 CBS
   Trapper John, M. D.   ep   The Pagoda Curse 1. 25. 81 CBS
   The Harlem Globetrotters on Gilligan's Island   tf   5. 15. 81 NBC
   Trapper John, M. D.   ep   The Ego Experience 11. 8. 81 CBS
   CHiPs   ep   Fast Money   12. 6. 81 NBC

FORSTER, ROBERT
   A&C:
   Gibbsville   ep   12. 16. 76 NBC
   SUPP. :
   The City   tf   1. 12. 77 NBC
   Police Story   ep   3. 8. 77 NBC
   Police Story   ep   Pressure Point 9. 27. 77 NBC
   Standing Tall   tf   1. 21. 78 NBC
   The Darker Side of Terror   tf   4. 3. 79 CBS
   Goliath Awaits   ms   11. 17. 81, 11. 23. 81 NN

FORSYTH, ROSEMARY
   A&C:
   Route 66   ep   I Wouldn't Start from Here 11. 15. 63 CBS
   Barnaby Jones   ep   10. 31. 75 CBS
   SUPP. :
   Vega$ ep   9. 26. 79 ABC
   CHiPs   ep   12. 15. 79 NBC
   The Incredible Hulk   ep   12. 5. 80 CBS
   Fantasy Island   ep   2. 21. 81 ABC
   WKRP in Cincinnati   ep   Bomb Threat 10. 7. 81 CBS

FORSYTHE, JOHN
   A&C:
   Insight   ep   8. 18. 74 NN
   SUPP. :
   Tail Gunner Joe   tf   2. 6. 77 NBC
   The Hallmark Hall of Fame   ep   Emily, Emily 2. 7. 77 NBC
   Charlie's Angels   sr ret vo   9. 14. 77 ABC
   Cruise into Terror   tf   2. 3. 78 ABC
   The Feather and Father Gang   ep   3. 14. 78 ABC
   With This Ring   tf   5. 5. 78 ABC
   Charlie's Angels   sr ret vo   9. 13. 78 ABC
   The Users   tf   10. 1. 78 ABC
   Charlie's Angels   sr ret vo   9. 12. 79 ABC
   Charlie's Angels   sr ret vo   11. 30. 80 ABC
   A Time for Miracles   tf   12. 21. 80 ABC
   Dynasty   sr   1. 12. 81 ABC
   Charlie's Angels   sr ret vo   6. 3. 81 ABC
   Dynasty   sr ret   11. 4. 81 ABC
   Sizzle   tf   11. 29. 81 ABC

FOSTER, JODIE
   SUPP. :
   The ABC Afterschool Special   ep   Rookie of the Year   sp
      10. 8. 77 ABC

FOSTER, MEG*
   The Death of Me Yet   tf   10. 27. 71 ABC
   The Mod Squad   ep   Death of a Nobody 12. 7. 71 ABC
   The FBI   ep   A Second Chance 1. 9. 72 ABC
   Medical Center   ep   3. 1. 72 CBS
   The Sixth Sense   ep   12. 16. 72 ABC

Mannix   ep   12. 24. 72 CBS
Hawaii Five-O   ep   The Child Stealers 1. 2. 73 CBS
Circle of Fear   ep   Spare Parts 2. 23. 73 NBC
Cannon   ep   Come Watch Me Die 10. 24. 73 CBS
Sunshine   tf   11. 9. 73 NBC
Medical Center   ep   Web of Intrigue 1. 7. 74 CBS
Barnaby Jones   ep   Gold Record for Murder 2. 10. 74 CBS
Barnaby Jones   ep   10. 29. 74 CBS
The Six Million Dollar Man   ep   Straight on 'Til Morning
    11. 8. 74 ABC
Things in Their Season   tf   11. 27. 74 CBS
Baretta   ep   Ragtime Billy Peaches 2. 28. 75 ABC
Sunshine   sr   3. 6. 75 NBC
Promise Him Anything...   tf   5. 14. 75 ABC
The Streets of San Francisco   ep   10. 30. 75 ABC
Bronk   ep   11. 2. 75 CBS
Three for the Road   ep   11. 16. 75 CBS
Baretta   ep   Count the Days I'm Gone 11. 26. 75 ABC
James Dean   tf   2. 19. 76 NBC
Hawaii Five-O   ep   12. 2. 76 CBS
Washington: Behind Closed Doors   ms   9. 6-11. 77 ABC
Police Story   ep   Pressure Point 9. 27. 77 NBC
Sunshine Christmas   tf   12. 12. 77 NBC
The Scarlet Letter   sr   4. 2. 79 PBS
Guyana Tragedy: The Story of Jim Jones   tf   4. 15. 80 CBS
The Legend of Sleepy Hollow   tf   10. 31. 80 NBC

FOXWORTH, ROBERT
    A& C:
    Love Story   ep   All My Tomorrows 10. 10. 73 NBC
    SUPP. :
    Tales of the Unexpected   ep   2. 9. 77 NBC
    Susan and Sam   pt   7. 13. 77 NBC
    It Happened at Lakewood Manor   tf   12. 2. 77 ABC
    Death Moon   tf   5. 31. 78 CBS
    Insight   ep   6. 11. 78 NN
    The Memory of Eva Ryker   tf   5. 7. 80 CBS
    Act of Love   tf   9. 24. 80 NBC
    Peter and Paul   tf   4. 12. 81, 4. 14. 81 CBS
    Falcon Crest   sr   12. 4. 81 CBS

FOXX, REDD
    SUPP. :
    My Buddy   pt   7. 3. 79 NBC
    Sanford   sr   3. 15. 80 NBC
    Sanford   sr ret   5. 29. 81 NBC

FRANCIOSA, TONY (a. k. a. Anthony Franciosa)
    SUPP. :
    Curse of the Black Widow   tf   9. 16. 77 ABC
    Aspen   ms   11. 5. 77, 11. 6. 77, 11. 7. 77 NBC
    Wheels   ms   5. 7. 78, 5. 8. 78, 5. 9. 78, 5. 14. 78, 5. 15. 78 NBC
    Side Show   tf   6. 5. 81 NBC

FRANCIS, ANNE
  A&C:
  The New Breed   ep   Lady Killer 12. 12. 61 ABC
  Cannon   ep   Murder by Proxy 10. 10. 73
  Insight   ep   10. 28. 73 NN
  S. W. A. T.   ep   12. 13. 75 ABC
  Bert D'Angelo/Superstar   ep   6. 26. 76 ABC
  SUPP. :
  Baa Baa Black Sheep   ep   1. 11. 77, 1. 18. 77 NBC
  Great Performances   ep   Abide with Me 12. 7. 77 PBS
  What Really Happened to the Class of '65?   ep   1. 19. 78 NBC
  Police Woman   ep   2. 22. 78 NBC
  Hawaii Five-O   ep   3. 16. 78 CBS
  The World of Disney   ep   The Young Runaways   tf   5. 28. 78
    NBC
  Insight   ep   6. 18. 78 NN
  Little Mo   tf   9. 5. 78 NBC
  Flying High   ep   9. 29. 78 CBS
  Fantasy Island   ep   10. 7. 78 ABC
  Charlie's Angels   ep   Pom Pom Angels 11. 1. 78 ABC
  The Eddie Capra Mysteries   ep   11. 3. 78 NBC
  Greatest Heroes of the Bible   ep   The Story of Moses in Egypt
    11. 20. 78 NBC
  Quincy, M. E.   ep   2. 22. 79 NBC
  The Rebels   ms ep   5. 21. 79 NN
  Beggerman, Thief   tf   11. 26. 79, 11. 27. 79 NBC
  Fantasy Island   ep   2. 9. 80 ABC
  Detour to Terror   tf   2. 22. 80 NBC
  Charlie's Angels   ep   Angels of the Deep 12. 7. 80 ABC
  Trapper John, M. D.   ep   12. 7. 80 CBS
  Dallas   sr   1. 16. 81 CBS
  Trapper John, M. D.   ep   Slim Chance 4. 12. 81 CBS
  Fantasy Island   ep   5. 16. 81 ABC
  Dallas   sr ret   10. 9. 81 CBS

FRANCIS, IVOR
  A&C:
  Room 222   ep   5. 18. 73 ABC
  Room 222   ep   Cry Uncle 1. 11. 74 ABC
  McCoy   ep   1. 25. 76 NBC
  SUPP. :
  Spider-Man   tf   9. 14. 77 CBS
  Little House on the Prairie   ep   12. 5. 77 NBC
  Snavely   pt   6. 24. 78 ABC
  Lou Grant   ep   3. 5. 79 CBS
  This Is the Life 9. 7. 80 NN
  The Home Front   pt   10. 9. 80
  Lou Grant   ep   10. 27. 80 CBS
  240-Robert   ep   Hostages 3. 21. 81 ABC
  Quincy, M. E.   ep   Memories of Allison 10. 28. 81 NBC

FRANCISCUS, JAMES
  A&C:
  The Twilight Zone   ep   Judgement Night 12. 4. 59 CBS

Americans   ep   The Invaders 3. 27. 61 NBC
Combat   ep   Decision 11. 15. 66 ABC
SUPP. :
Hunter   sr   2. 18. 77 CBS
Secrets of Three Hungry Wives   tf   10. 9. 78 NBC
The Pirate   tf   11. 21. 78, 11. 22. 78 CBS
Night Kill   tf   12. 18. 80 NBC
Jacqueline Bouvier Kennedy   tf   10. 14. 81 ABC

FRANKLIN, BONNIE
   A& C:
   The Munsters   ep   4. 14. 66 CBS
   SUPP. :
   One Day at a Time   sr ret   9. 20. 77 CBS
   The Love Boat   ep   The Captain and the Lady 9. 24. 77 ABC
   One Day at a Time   sr ret   9. 18. 78 CBS
   A Guide for the Married Woman   tf   10. 13. 78 ABC
   The Mary Tyler Moore Hour   ep   3. 18. 79 CBS
   Breaking Up Is Hard to Do   tf   9. 5. 79, 9. 7. 79 ABC
   One Day at a Time   sr ret   9. 25. 79 CBS
   One Day at a Time   sr ret   11. 9. 80 CBS
   One Day at a Time   sr ret   10. 11. 81 CBS

FRANKLIN, PAMELA
   A& C:
   Mystery of the Week   ep   Won't Write Home, Mom--I'm Dead
      3. 3. 75 ABC
   SUPP. :
   Police Story   ep   1. 18. 77 NBC
   Westside Medical   ep   6. 30. 77 ABC
   The Love Boat   ep   12. 3. 77 ABC
   Police Woman   ep   3. 1. 78 NBC
   Lucan   ep   3. 13. 78 ABC
   Fantasy Island   ep   4. 29. 78 ABC
   Project UFO   ep   6. 4. 78 NBC
   Fantasy Island   ep   11. 4. 78 ABC
   The Hardy Boys   ep   11. 19. 78, 11. 26. 78 ABC
   Julie Farr, M. D.   ep   6. 26. 79 ABC
   Fantasy Island   ep   9. 21. 79 ABC
   Barnaby Jones   ep   1. 31. 80 CBS
   Trapper John, M. D.   ep   12. 7. 80 CBS
   Fantasy Island   ep   2. 7. 81 ABC
   Aloha Paradise   ep   3. 11. 81 ABC
   Slim Chance   tf   4. 12. 81 NBC
   Vega$ ep   4. 15. 81 ABC

FRANZ, ARTHUR
   A& C:
   The New Adventures of Perry Mason   ep   10. 7. 73 CBS
   Manhunter   ep   11. 20. 74 CBS
   Medical Story   ep   1. 8. 76 NBC
   The Quest   ep   12. 22. 76 NBC
   SUPP. :
   The Hallmark Hall of Fame   ep   The Last Hurrah sp 11. 16. 77 NBC

FREEMAN, DEENA*
    In Trouble   pt   8. 24. 81 ABC
    ABC Theatre for Young Americans   ep   Please Don't Hit Me,
        Mom 9. 20. 81 ABC
    Too Close for Comfort   sr   10. 27. 81 ABC

FULLER, ROBERT
    SUPP. :
    Donner Pass: The Road to Survival   tf   10. 24. 78 CBS
    Disaster on the Coastliner   tf   10. 28. 79 ABC
    Jake's Way   pt   6. 28. 80 CBS

FUNICELLO, ANNETTE*
    The Mickey Mouse Club   sr   10. 3. 55 ABC
    The Mickey Mouse Club   ep   (serial) Adventures in Dairyland
        1955 Season ABC
    The Mickey Mouse Club   ep   (serial) Annette 1955-56 Season
        ABC
    The Mickey Mouse Club   ep   (serial) The Further Adventures
        of Spin and Marty 1957-58 Season ABC
    The Mickey Mouse Club   ep   (serial) The New Adventures of
        Spin and Marty 1957-58 Season ABC
    Zorro   sr   9. 19. 57 ABC
    The Danny Thomas Show 1958 Season CBS
    Wagon Train   ep   The Sam Pulaski Story 11. 4. 63 NBC
    Love, American Style   ep   Love and the Tuba 12. 3. 71 ABC
    The Love Boat   ep   I'll Never Fall in Love Again 5. 13. 78 ABC
    Frankie and Annette: The Second Time Around   pt   11. 18. 78 NBC
    Fantasy Island   ep   3. 3. 79, 3. 8. 80 ABC
    Disney's Wonderful World   ep   The Mouseketeer's Reunion   sp
        hos 11. 23. 80 NBC
    Fantasy Island   ep   The Unkillable 4. 11. 81 ABC

-G-

GABOR, EVA
    A& C:
    Ellery Queen   ep   12. 18. 75 NBC
    SUPP. :
    The Love Boat   ep   12. 3. 77 ABC
    Fantasy Island   ep   12. 16. 78, 1. 3. 81 ABC

GABOR, ZSA ZSA
    SUPP. :
    Supertrain   ep   4. 14. 79 NBC
    The Love Boat   ep   Return of the Captain's Brother 12. 6. 80
        ABC
    The Facts of Life   ep   2. 25. 81 NBC
    As the World Turns   several ep   11. 81 CBS

GAIL, MAX (a. k. a. Maxwell Gail)
  SUPP. :
  Barney Miller   sr ret   9. 15. 77 ABC
  Barney Miller   sr ret   9. 14. 78 ABC
  Like Mom, Like Me   tf   10. 22. 78 CBS
  Desperate Women   tf   10. 25. 78 NBC
  Barney Miller   sr ret   9. 13. 79 ABC
  Eleventh Victim   tf   11. 6. 79 CBS
  Pearl   ms   11. 16. 78,   11. 17. 78,   11. 19. 78 ABC
  Tales of the Unexpected   ep   2. 9. 80 NN
  The Aliens Are Coming   tf   3. 2. 80 NBC
  Fun and Games   tf   5. 26. 80 ABC
  Barney Miller   sr ret   10. 30. 80 ABC
  Barney Miller   sr ret   10. 29. 81 ABC

GALLOWAY, DON
  A& C:
  The Alfred Hitchcock Hour   ep   Death and the Joyful Women
    4. 12. 63 NBC
  SUPP. :
  Cover Girls   tf   5. 18. 77 NBC
  Police Woman   ep   1. 11. 78 NBC
  Ski Lift to Death   tf   3. 3. 78 CBS
  Charlie's Angels   ep   12. 6. 78 ABC
  Hizzoner   sr   5. 10. 79 NBC
  Hart to Hart   ep   10. 30. 79 ABC
  Condominium   ms   11. 20. 80,   11. 24. 80 NN
  CHiPs   ep   12. 7. 80 NBC
  Fantasy Island   ep   1. 24. 81,   4. 11. 81 ABC

GARAS, KAZ
  A& C:
  Manhunter   ep   1. 29. 75 CBS
  Insight   ep   9. 11. 75 NN
  SUPP. :
  Police Story   ep   1. 11. 77 NBC
  The Streets of San Francisco   ep   6. 2. 77 ABC
  Murder in Peyton Place   tf   10. 3. 77 NBC
  CHiPs   ep   11. 25. 78 NBC
  The New Adventures of Wonder Woman   ep   Going Going Gone
    1. 12. 79 CBS
  Starsky and Hutch   ep   2. 6. 79 ABC
  This Is the Life   ep   2. 11. 79 NN
  Hawaii Five-O   ep   12. 4. 79 CBS

GARLAND, BEVERLY
  A& C:
  The Man from Blackhawk   ep   Logan's Policy 10. 9. 59 ABC
  The Twilight Zone   ep   The Four of Us Are Dying 1. 1. 60 CBS
  Insight   ep   7. 30. 67,   8. 7. 67 NN
  Owen Marshall, Counselor at Law   ep   Sometimes Tough Is
    Good   1. 17. 73 ABC

Insight   ep   9. 22. 74,   4. 6. 75   NN
SUPP. :
The Six Million Dollar Man   ep   1. 9. 77 ABC
The Nancy Drew Mysteries   ep   Mystery of the Fallen Angels
   4. 17. 77 ABC
The Tony Randall Show   ep   12. 24. 77 CBS
Insight   ep   2. 25. 79 NN
How The West Was Won   ep   4. 23. 79 ABC
Charlie's Angels   ep   Cruising Angels 12. 12. 79 ABC
Trapper John, M. D.   ep   Girl Under Glass 11. 23. 80 CBS
Enos   ep   Blue Flu 12. 10. 80 CBS
Greatest Heroes of the Bible   ep   Abraham's Sacrifice 8. 15. 81
   NBC
Judgement Day   pt   12. 6. 81 NBC

GARNER, JAMES
   SUPP. :
   The Rockford Files   sr ret   9. 16. 77 NBC
   The New Maverick   tf   9. 3. 78 ABC
   The Rockford Files   sr ret   9. 22. 78 NBC
   The Rockford Files   sr ret   9. 28. 79 NBC
   Young Maverick   ep   11. 28. 79 CBS
   The Presidents: 80 Years on Camera   sr hos-nar   5. 8. 80 NN
   Bret Maverick   sr   12. 1. 81 NBC

GARNER, PEGGY ANN
   A&C:
   Our American Heritage   ep   The Practical Dreamer 11. 22. 59 NBC
   SUPP. :
   Betrayal   tf   11. 13. 78 NBC

GARR, TERI
   A&C:
   The New Dick Van Dyke Show   ep   11. 19. 73 CBS
   Maude   ep   10. 20. 75 CBS
   SUPP. :
   The Franken Project   tf   1. 13. 80 NBC

GARRETT, LEIF*
   Cade's County   ep   11. 28. 71 CBS
   Cannon   ep   12. 7. 71 CBS
   Gunsmoke   ep   11. 20. 72 CBS
   Circle of Fear   ep   Doorway to Death 1. 26. 73 NBC
   Doc Elliot   ep   A Man of Importance 11. 3. 73 ABC
   The Odd Couple   ep   9. 26. 74 ABC
   Strange Homecoming   tf   10. 29. 74 NBC
   The Last Survivors   tf   3. 3. 75 NBC
   The Odd Couple   ep   3. 7. 75 ABC
   Flood   tf   11. 24. 76 NBC
   Peter Lundy and the Medicine Hat Stallion   tf   11. 6. 77 NBC
   The New Adventures of Wonder Woman   ep   My Teenage Idol Is
      Missing   tf   9. 22. 78 CBS
   Family   ep   9. 28. 78,   11. 2. 78 ABC

CHiPs   ep   Chips Goes Roller Disco 9. 22. 79 NBC
House Calls   ep   3. 17. 80 CBS

GARSON, GREER
   SUPP. :
   Little Women   tf   10. 2. 78, 10. 3. 78 NBC

GAUTIER, DICK
   A& C:
   The Eleventh Hour   ep   I Feel Like a Rutabaga 4. 24. 63 NBC
   Love American Style   ep   10. 2. 73 ABC
   SUPP. :
   Benny and Barney: Las Vegas Undercover   tf   1. 19. 77 NBC
   Switch   ep   2. 27. 77 CBS
   The Hardy Boys/Nancy Drew Mysteries   ep   4. 10. 77 ABC
   Sex and the Married Woman   tf   9. 13. 77 NBC
   Mulligan's Stew   ep   11. 8. 77 NBC
   The Man from Atlantis   ep   4. 25. 78 NBC
   The Love Boat   ep   5. 6. 78 ABC
   The Eddie Capra Mysteries   ep   11. 10. 78 NBC
   Flying High   ep   12. 29. 78 CBS
   Sweepstakes   ep   3. 9. 79 NBC
   Eischied   ep   11. 9. 79 NBC
   The Love Boat   ep   Doc's "Ex" Change 12. 15. 79 ABC
   Charlie's Angels   ep   Homes Sweet Homes 1. 23. 80 ABC
   Marathon   tf   1. 30. 80 CBS
   Fantasy Island   ep   12. 6. 80 ABC
   Happy Days   ep   2. 3. 81 ABC
   Too Close for Comfort   ep   2. 10. 81 ABC
   Trapper John, M. D.   ep   Who's The Lucky Father? 2. 15. 81 CBS

GAVIN, JOHN
   A& C:
   Mannix   ep   3. 11. 73 CBS
   SUPP. :
   The Love Boat   ep   12. 10. 77 ABC
   Fantasy Island   ep   2. 18. 78 ABC
   Doctors' Private Lives   tf   3. 20. 78 ABC
   Flying High   ep   North By Northeast 10. 13. 78 CBS
   The New Adventures of Heidi   tf   12. 13. 78 NBC
   Doctors' Private Lives   sr   4. 5. 79 ABC
   Sophia Loren: Her Own Story   tf   10. 26. 80 NBC
   Hart to Hart   ep   11. 11. 80 ABC
   Fantasy Island   ep   2. 14. 81 ABC

GAYNOR, JANET
   SUPP. :
   The Love Boat   ep   The Frugal Pair 1. 3. 81 ABC

GAZZARA, BEN
   SUPP. :
   The Death of Richie   tf   1. 10. 77 NBC
   The Trial of Lee Harvey Oswald   tf   9. 30. 77, 10. 1. 77 ABC

GEER, WILL
  SUPP. :
  The Waltons   sr ret   9. 15. 77 CBS
  The Love Boat   ep   The Old Man and the Runaway 12. 24. 77
     ABC
  The Waltons   sr ret   9. 21. 78 CBS
  A Woman Called Moses   tf   12. 11. 78,   12. 12. 78 NBC

GEESON, JUDY
  SUPP. :
  Star Maidens   sr   10. 1. 77 NN
  Return of the Saint   ep   3. 14. 80 CBS

GEORGE, CHRISTOPHER*
  The Rat Patrol   sr   9. 12. 66 ABC
  The Rat Patrol   sr ret   9. 11. 67 ABC
  The Immortal   tf   9. 30. 69 ABC
  The Immortal   sr   9. 24. 70 ABC
  The House on Greenapple Road   tf   1. 11. 70 ABC
  Escape   tf   4. 6. 71 ABC
  Man on a String   tf   2. 18. 72 CBS
  The Heist   tf   11. 29. 72 ABC
  Love, American Style   ep   Love and the Burglar 2. 16. 73 ABC
  Police Story   ep   Cop in the Middle 1. 29. 74 NBC
  Owen Marshall, Counselor at Law   ep   The Break-In 3. 2. 74
     ABC
  Mission: Impossible   ep   12. 4. 74 CBS
  McCloud   ep   Sharks 2. 23. 75 NBC
  The Last Survivors   tf   3. 3. 75 NBC
  S. W. A. T.   ep   4. 28. 75, 9. 13. 75 ABC
  Mayday at 40,000 Feet   tf   11. 12. 76 CBS
  Cruise into Terror   tf   2. 3. 78 ABC
  Fantasy Island   ep   2. 25. 78 ABC
  The Love Boat   ep   5. 13. 78 ABC
  Fantasy Island   ep   10. 7. 78 ABC
  Vega$ ep   12. 20. 78 ABC
  The Love Boat   ep   Class Reunion 2. 3. 79 ABC
  Charlie's Angels   ep   2. 7. 79 ABC
  The Misadventures of Sheriff Lobo 9. 18. 79 NBC
  The Love Boat   ep   10. 27. 79 ABC
  Fantasy Island   ep   11. 22. 80 ABC

GEORGE, LYNDA DAY (a. k. a. Lynda Day)
  A& C:
  Route 66   ep   A Long Way from St. Louis 12. 6. 63 CBS
  Bonanza   ep   The Stronghold 5. 26. 68 NBC
  Twin Detectives   tf   5. 1. 76 ABC
  SUPP. :
  Roots   ms ep   1. 24. 77, 1. 25. 77, 1. 26. 77 ABC
  Murder at the World Series   tf   3. 20. 77 ABC
  Switch   ep   3. 27. 77 CBS
  It Happened at Lakewood Manor   tf   12. 2. 77 ABC
  Cruise into Terror   tf   2. 3. 78 ABC

The Love Boat   ep   A Selfless Love   2. 25. 78 ABC
Return of Captain Nemo   ep   3. 15. 78, 3. 22. 78 CBS
Fantasy Island   ep   4. 1. 78 ABC
Fantasy Island   ep   9. 16. 78 ABC
Vega$ ep   12. 20. 78 ABC
The Love Boat   ep   10. 27. 79 ABC
Casino   tf   8. 1. 80 ABC
The Littlest Hobo   ep   10. 11. 80 NN
Fantasy Island   ep   11. 29. 80 ABC
Quick & Quiet   pt   8. 18. 81 CBS
Fantasy Island   ep   10. 31. 81 ABC

GERARD, GIL*
Baretta   ep   11. 10. 76 ABC
Ransom for Alice   tf   6. 2. 77 NBC
Hawaii Five-O   ep   10. 27. 77 CBS
Killing Stone   tf   5. 2. 78 NBC
Buck Rogers in the 25th Century   pt   9. 20. 79 NBC
Buck Rogers in the 25th Century   sr   9. 27. 79 NBC
CHiPs   ep   12. 7. 80 NBC
Buck Rogers in the 25th Century   sr ret   1. 15. 81 NBC

GERRITSEN, LISA
SUPP. :
It Can't Happen to Me   sp   11. 24. 78 NN

GHOSTLY, ALICE
SUPP. :
One Day at a Time   ep   11. 22. 77 CBS
CHiPs   ep   1. 12. 78 NBC

GIBSON, HENRY
A& C:
Love, American Style   ep   Love and the Spendthrift 12. 7. 73 ABC
The Bureau   pt   7. 26. 76 NBC
SUPP. :
Escape from Bogen County   tf   10. 7. 77 CBS
The Night They Took Miss Beautiful   tf   10. 24. 77 NBC
The New Adventures of Wonder Woman   ep   Screaming Javelin
    1. 20. 78 CBS
Fantasy Island   ep   2. 4. 78 ABC
Amateur Night at the Dixie Bar and Grill   tf   1. 8. 79 NBC
Sweepstakes   ep   3. 9. 79 NBC
The Halloween That Almost Wasn't   sp   10. 28. 79 ABC
The Dukes of Hazzard   ep   2. 8. 80, 9. 19. 80 CBS
For the Love of It   tf   9. 26. 80 ABC

GIFTOS, ELAINE
A& C:
Love, American Style   ep   1. 5. 73 ABC
SUPP. :
Stonestreet: Who Killed the Centerfold Model?   tf 1. 16. 77 NBC
Hawaii Five-O   ep   10. 13. 77 CBS
The Six Million Dollar Man   ep   2. 20. 78, 2. 27. 78 ABC

Wild About Harry   pt   5. 26. 78 NBC
Breaking Up Is Hard to Do   tf   9. 5. 79, 9. 7. 79 ABC
Quincy, M. E.   ep   10. 18. 79 NBC
Hawaii Five-O   ep   3. 8. 80 CBS
Three's Company   ep   11. 18. 80 NBC
Number 96   sr   12. 10. 80 NBC
Fisherman's Wharf   pt   2. 1. 81 NBC
Ron Howard's Through the Magic Pyramid   tf   12. 6. 81, 12. 13. 81
    NBC

GILBERT, MELISSA*
Emergency   ep   12. 2. 72 NBC
Little House on the Prairie   tf   3. 30. 74 NBC
Little House on the Prairie   sr   9. 11. 74 NBC
Little House on the Prairie   sr ret   9. 10. 75 NBC
Little House on the Prairie   sr ret   9. 22. 76 NBC
Circus, Lions, Tigers and Melissas Too   hos sp   5. 21. 77 NBC
Little House on the Prairie   sr ret   9. 12. 77 NBC
Christmas Miracle in Caulfield, U. S. A.   tf   12. 26. 77 NBC
Little House on the Prairie   sr ret   9. 11. 78 NBC
The Love Boat   ep   Rocky 9. 23. 78 ABC
Little House on the Prairie   sr ret   9. 17. 79 NBC
The Miracle Worker   tf   10. 14. 79 NBC
Little House on the Prairie   sr ret   9. 22. 80 NBC
The Diary of Anne Frank   tf   11. 17. 80 NBC
Little House on the Prairie   sr ret   10. 5. 81 NBC
Splendor in the Grass   tf   10. 26. 81 NBC

GILFORD, JACK
A&C:
Once Upon a Mattress   sp   6. 3. 64 CBS
Hotel 90   sp   3. 26. 73 CBS
All in the Family   ep   1. 26. 76 CBS
SUPP. :
Seventh Avenue   ms ep   2. 10. 77 NBC
The Andros Targets   ep   5. 16. 77 CBS
Apple Pie   sr   9. 23. 78 ABC
Lou Grant   ep   2. 26. 79 CBS
Trapper John, M. D.   9. 23. 79 CBS
The Littlest Hobo   ep   11. 1. 80 NN
Goldie and the Boxer Go to Hollywood   tf   2. 19. 81 NBC
The Love Boat   ep   That Old Gang of Mine 4. 11. 81 ABC
Heaven on Earth (a. k. a. Heaven Sent)   pt   4. 12. 81 NBC
Taxi   ep   11. 21. 81 ABC
Alice   ep   Mel's Christmas Carol 12. 20. 81 CBS

GING, JACK L.
A&C:
Man and the Challenge   ep   The Windowless Room 1. 30. 60 NBC
Dr. Kildare   ep   Four Feet in the Morning 11. 27. 63 NBC
Search   ep   2. 7. 73 NBC
The Fabulous Dr. Fable   pt   6. 17. 73 ABC
Lassie   ep   5. 5. 74 NN
Cannon   ep   11. 19. 75 CBS

SUPP. :
Barnaby Jones   ep   1. 6. 77 CBS
The Waltons   ep   2. 10. 77 CBS
What Really Happened to the Class of '65?   ep   Mr. Potential
    2. 23. 78 NBC
Keefer   tf   3. 16. 78 ABC
The Hardy Boys/Nancy Drew Mysteries   ep   5. 7. 78 ABC
Starsky and Hutch   ep   9. 19. 78 ABC
Barnaby Jones   ep   10. 11. 79 CBS
The Misadventures of Sheriff Lobo   ep   1. 8. 80 NBC
Hart to Hart   ep   11. 18. 80 ABC
Hart to Hart   ep   3. 17. 81 ABC
The Greatest American Hero   ep   My Heroes Have Always Been
    Cowboys 4. 29. 81 ABC
Quincy, M. E.   ep   Dead Stop 12. 23. 81 NBC

GINGGOLD, HERMIONE
    SUPP. :
    Trapper John, M. D.   ep   Mother's Day 12. 6. 81 CBS

GISH, LILLIAN
    A&C:
    The Defenders   ep   Stowaway 6. 13. 64 CBS
    Twin Detectives   tf   5. 1. 76 ABC
    SUPP. :
    Sparrow   pt   8. 11. 78 CBS
    The Love Boat   ep   Isaac's Teacher 1. 10. 81 ABC
    Thin Ice   tf   2. 17. 81 CBS

GLASER, PAUL MICHAEL
    SUPP. :
    Starsky and Hutch   sr ret   9. 17. 77 ABC
    Starsky and Hutch   sr ret   9. 12. 78 ABC

GLEASON, JACKIE
    SUPP. :
    The Honeymooners' Christmas Special   sp   11. 28. 77 ABC
    The Honeymooners' Valentine Special   sp   2. 13. 78 ABC
    The Honeymooners' Christmas Special   sp   12. 10. 78 ABC

GLESS, SHARON*
    McCloud   ep   10. 1. 72 NBC
    All My Daughters   tf   11. 22. 72 ABC
    Cool Million   ep   12. 6. 72 NBC
    Marcus Welby, M. D.   ep   Dinner of Herbs 12. 19. 72 ABC
    Faraday and Company   sr   9. 26. 73 NBC
    Owen Marshall, Counselor at Law   ep   Sweet Harvest 10. 3. 73
        ABC
    Ironside   ep   House of Terror 10. 25. 73 NBC
    My Darling Daughters' Anniversary   tf   11. 6. 73 ABC
    Marcus Welby, M. D.   sr   11. 6. 73 ABC
    Toma   ep   The Frame 11. 15. 73 ABC
    The Bob Newhart Show   ep   1. 12. 74 CBS

Clinic on 18th Street   pt   3. 13. 74 NBC
Wide World of Mystery   A Little Bit Like Murder 4. 2. 74 ABC
The Rockford Files   ep   This Case Is Closed 10. 18. 74 NBC
Sierra   ep   11. 7. 74 NBC
Switch   tf   3. 10. 75 CBS
Switch   sr   9. 9. 75 CBS
Emergency   ep   9. 27. 75 NBC
Lucas Tanner   ep   12. 2. 75 NBC
Switch   sr ret   9. 21. 76 CBS
The Rockford Files   ep   The Fourth Man 9. 24. 76 NBC
Kojak   ep   Law Dance 10. 10. 76 CBS
Richie Brockelman: The Missing 24 Hours   tf   10. 27. 76 NBC
Switch   sr ret   9. 23. 77 CBS
The Islander   tf   9. 16. 78 CBS
Crash   tf   10. 29. 78 ABC
The Immigrants   ms   11. 20. 78, 11. 21. 78 NN
Turnabout   sr   1. 26. 79 NBC
Centennial   ep   The Scream of Eagels 2. 4. 79 NBC
The Last Convertible   ms   9. 24. 79, 9. 25. 79, 9. 26. 79 NBC
Hardhat and Legs   tf   2. 9. 80 CBS
Moviola: The Scarlett O'Hara War   tf   5. 19. 80 NBC
Revenge of the Stepford Wives   tf   10. 12. 80 NBC
The Miracle of Kathy Miller   tf   10. 5. 81 CBS
Tales of the Unexpected   ep   Youth from Vienna 10. 10. 81 NN

GOBEL, GEORGE
   SUPP. :
   Benny and Barney: Las Vegas Undercover 1. 19. 77 NBC
   Lanigan's Rabbi   ep   3. 20. 77 NBC
   Flying High   ep   10. 6. 78 CBS
   A Guide for the Married Woman   tf   10. 13. 78 ABC
   Faculty Lounge   pt   5. 31. 79 NBC
   Harper Valley PTA   sr   1. 16. 81 NBC
   The Love Boat   ep   The Trigamist 1. 17. 81 ABC
   Harper Valley   sr   (revised) 10. 29. 81 NBC

GODFREY, ARTHUR
   SUPP. :
   Flying High   ep   12. 29. 78 CBS
   Flatbed Annie and Sweetiepie: Lady Truckers   tf   2. 10. 79
      CBS
   The Love Boat   ep   3. 3. 79 ABC

GOLONKA, ARLENE
   A& C:
   The Nurses   ep   A Kind of Loving 4. 2. 64 CBS
   Young Dr. Kildare   ep   1. 1. 73 NN
   M*A*S*H   ep   1. 28. 73 CBS
   Bert D'Angelo/Superstar   ep   6. 12. 76 ABC
   Jeremiah of Jacobs Neck   pt   8. 13. 76 CBS
   Mary Hartman, Mary Hartman   ep   1. 22. 75 NN
   SUPP. :
   Most Wanted   ep   2. 19. 77 ABC

Insight   ep   9. 10. 78 NN
One Day at a Time   ep   10. 2. 78 CBS
Taxi   ep   10. 24. 78 ABC
Joe and Valerie   sr   1. 5. 79 NBC
Sweepstakes   ep   2. 9. 79 NBC
The Love Boat   ep   9. 29. 79 ABC
Fantasy Island   ep   10. 5. 79 ABC
The Secrets of Midland Heights   ep   12. 13. 80, 1. 10. 81 CBS
Trapper John, M. D.   ep   Who's The Lucky Father? 2. 15. 81
     CBS

GOODMAN, DODY (previously listed as Dodie Goodman)
     SUPP. :
     Forever Fernwood   sr   9. 77 NN
     The Love Boat   ep   Who's Who? 9. 23. 78 ABC
     CHiPs   ep   Chips Goes Roller Disco 9. 22. 79 NBC

GORDON, RUTH
     SUPP. :
     The Prince of Central Park   tf   6. 17. 77 CBS
     The Love Boat   ep   Take My Granddaughter, Please 10. 29. 77
          ABC
     Columbo   ep   11. 21. 77 NBC
     Perfect Gentlemen   tf   3. 14. 78 CBS

GORSHIN, FRANK
     SUPP. :
     Charlie's Angels   ep   Angels at Sea 3. 23. 77 ABC
     The New Adventures of Wonder Woman   ep   The Deadly Toys
          12. 30. 77 CBS
     Greatest Heroes of the Bible   ep   The Story of Moses in Egypt
          11. 20. 78 NBC
     The Challenge of the Superheroes   sp   1. 18. 79 NBC
     Death Car on the Freeway   tf   9. 25. 79 CBS
     Buck Rogers in the 25th Century   ep   10. 11. 79, 10. 18. 79 NBC
     Goliath Awaits   ms   11. 17. 81, 11. 23. 81 NN

GOSSETT, LOU (a. k. a. Louis Gossett and Lou[is] Gossett, Jr.)
     A& C:
     The Nurses   ep   The Prisoner 11. 8. 62 CBS
     Lucas Tanner   ep   1. 8. 75 NBC
     Petrocelli   ep   1. 22. 75 NBC
     Police Story   ep   1. 30. 76 NBC
     The Jeffersons   ep   5. 15. 76 CBS
     SUPP. :
     Little Ladies of the Night   tf   1. 16. 77 ABC
     Roots   ms ep   1. 24. 77 ABC
     Visions   ep   Freeman 10. 9. 77 PBS
     To Kill a Cop   tf   4. 10. 78, 4. 11. 78 NBC
     The Critical List   tf   9. 11. 78, 9. 12. 78 NBC
     Backstairs at the White House   ms ep   1. 29. 79 NBC
     This Man Stands Alone   tf   5. 30. 79 NBC
     The Lazarus Syndrome   sr   9. 4. 79 ABC

Palmerstown   ep   Future City 4. 7. 81 CBS
Don't Look Back   tf   5. 31. 81 ABC

GOULET, ROBERT
   SUPP. :
   Police Story   ep   4. 5. 77 NBC
   The Love Boat   ep   11. 4. 78 ABC
   Flying High   ep   12. 15. 78 CBS
   Fantasy Island   ep   1. 19. 80 ABC
   The Dream Merchants   ms   5. 12. 80, 5. 19. 80 NN
   Alice   ep   11. 16. 80 CBS

GRANDY, FRED*
   Love, American Style   ep   Love and the See-Through Mind 9. 28. 73
      ABC
   Maude   ep   10. 30. 73 CBS
   The Girl Most Likely To...   tf   11. 6. 73 ABC
   Phyllis   ep   10. 20. 75 CBS
   Doc   ep   1. 31. 76 CBS
   The Monster Squad   sr   9. 11. 76 NBC
   The Love Boat II   tf   1. 21. 77 ABC
   Quincy, M. E.   ep   2. 11. 77 NBC
   The New Love Boat (a. k. a. The Love Boat III)   tf 5. 5. 77 ABC
   Duffy   pt   5. 6. 77 CBS
   The Love Boat   sr   9. 24. 77 ABC
   The Love Boat   sr ret   9. 16. 78 ABC
   Fantasy Island   ep   11. 18. 78, 5. 5. 79 ABC
   Blind Ambition   ms ep   5. 21. 79 CBS
   The Love Boat   sr ret   9. 15. 79 ABC
   Fantasy Island   ep   Class of '69 12. 24. 79 ABC
   The Love Boat   sr ret   10. 25. 80 ABC
   The Love Boat   sr ret   10. 10. 81 ABC

GRANGER, FARLEY
   SUPP. :
   Black Beauty   ms   1. 31. 78, 2. 1. 78, 2. 2. 78, 2. 3. 78, 2. 4. 78
      NBC
   The Love Boat   ep   Matchmaker, Matchmaker Times Two
      11. 29. 80 ABC

GRANT, LEE
   A&C:
   Great Ghost Tales   ep   Lucy 7. 13. 61 NBC
   SUPP. :
   The Spell   tf   2. 20. 77 NBC
   Great Performances   ep   The Good Doctor 11. 8. 78 PBS
   Backstairs At the White House   ms ep   2. 5. 79 NBC
   You Can't Go Home Again   tf   4. 25. 79 CBS
   For Ladies Only   tf   11. 9. 81 NBC
   The Million Dollar Face   tf   3. 12. 81 NBC

GRAVES, PETER
   SUPP. :
   SST--Death Flight   tf   2. 25. 77 ABC

The Love Boat   ep   The Minister and the Stripper 11. 17. 78
    ABC
Fantasy Island   ep   11. 25. 78 ABC
Gift of the Maji   tf   12. 21. 78 NBC
The Rebels   ms   5. 14. 79,   5. 21. 79 NN
Fantasy Island   ep   9. 7. 79 ABC
Death Car on the Freeway   tf   9. 25. 79 CBS
Buck Rogers in the 25th Century   ep   10. 25. 79 NBC
The Love Boat   ep   11. 1. 80 ABC
300 Miles for Stephanie   tf   1. 12. 81 NBC
Simon and Simon   ep   Details at Eleven 11. 24. 81 CBS

GRAY, ERIN*
    Evening in Byzantium   ms   8. 14. 78,   8. 15. 78 NN
    The Rockford Files   ep   With the French Heel Back, Can the
        Nehru Jacket Be Far Behind? 1. 5. 79 NBC
    The Ultimate Imposter   tf   5. 12. 79
    Buck Rogers in the 25th Century   pt   9. 20. 79 NBC
    Buck Rogers in the 25th Century   sr   9. 27. 79 NBC
    Fantasy Island   ep   11. 8. 80 ABC
    Vega$ ep   Black Cat Killer 11. 12. 80 ABC
    Coach of the Year   tf   12. 21. 80 NBC
    Buck Rogers in the 25th Century   sr ret   1. 15. 81 NBC
    Magnum, P. I.   ep   4. 9. 81 CBS
    The Fall Guy   ep   License to Kill 11. 18. 81 ABC

GRAY, LINDA*
    The Big Ripoff   tf   3. 11. 75 NBC
    McCloud   ep   12. 26. 76 NBC
    All That Glitters   sr   1977 NN
    Switch   ep   1. 30. 77 CBS
    Murder in Peyton Place   tf   10. 3. 77 NBC
    Big Hawaii   ep   10. 12. 77 NBC
    Dallas   sr   4. 2. 78 CBS
    Dallas   sr ret   9. 23. 78 CBS
    The Grass Is Always Greener over the Septic Tank   tf   10. 25. 78
        CBS
    Dallas   sr ret   9. 21. 79 CBS
    The Two Worlds of Jennie Logan   tf   10. 31. 79 CBS
    Haywire   tf   5. 14. 80 CBS
    Dallas   sr ret   11. 7. 80 CBS
    The Wild and the Free   tf   11. 26. 80 CBS
    Women Who Rate a 10   sp hos   2. 15. 81 NBC
    Dallas   sr ret   10. 9. 81 CBS
    The Body Human: The Loving Process--Men   sp hos   11. 10. 81
        CBS

GREENE, LORNE
    SUPP. :
    Roots   ms ep   1. 24. 77,   1. 25. 77 ABC
    SST--Death Flight   tf   2. 25. 77 ABC
    The Hardy Boys/Nancy Drew Mysteries   ep   9. 11. 77,   9. 18. 77
        ABC
    The Trial of Lee Harvey Oswald   tf   9. 30. 77,   10. 7. 77 ABC

The Bastard/Kent Family Chronicles   ms   5. 22. 78, 5. 23. 78 NN
Battlestar Galactica   sr   9. 15. 78 ABC
The Love Boat   ep   9. 15. 79 ABC
Galactica 1980   sr   1. 27. 80 ABC
Vega$ ep   11. 5. 80 ABC
A Time for Miracles   tf   12. 21. 80 ABC
Aloha Paradise   ep   2. 25. 81 ABC
Code Red   tf   9. 20. 81 ABC
Cod Red   sr   11. 1. 81 ABC

GREGORY, JAMES*

Police Story   ep   Detective Sergeant, Martin Stevens 4. 4. 52
   CBS
Studio One   ep   The Hero 7. 26. 54 CBS
Studio One   ep   The Deserter 11. 29. 54 CBS
Studio One   ep   The Staring Match 6. 17. 57 CBS
Studio One   ep   Presence of the Enemy 2. 10. 58 CBS
The Lawless Years   sr   4. 16. 59 NBC
The Lawless Years   sr ret   10. 59 NBC
The Twilight Zone   ep   Where Is Everybody? 10. 2. 59 CBS
The Twilight Zone   ep   The Passerby 10. 1. 61 CBS
The Lieutenant   ep   A Very Private Affair 10. 12. 63 NBC
The Rogues   ep   The Day They Gave Diamonds Away 9. 20. 64
   NBC
Kraft Suspense Theatre   ep   One Tiger to a Hill 12. 3. 64 NBC
Bonanza   ep   A Man to Admire 12. 6. 64 NBC
Hogan's Heroes   ep   9. 16. 66 CBS
The Big Valley   ep   Pursuit 10. 10. 66 ABC
Star Trek   ep   Dagger of the Mind 11. 3. 66 NBC
Bonanza   ep   Second Chance 9. 17. 67 NBC
The Big Valley   ep   Ambush 9. 18. 67 ABC
Ironside   ep   Message from Beyond 9. 21. 67 NBC
Daniel Boone   ep   The Value of a King 11. 9. 67 NBC
The Big Valley   ep   The Challenge 3. 18. 68 ABC
Call to Danger   pt   7. 1. 68 CBS
The Outcasts   ep   10. 7. 68 ABC
The Mod Squad   ep   12. 3. 68 ABC
Ironside   ep   1. 30. 69 NBC
Bonanza   ep   Company of Forgotten Men 2. 2. 69 NBC
The Virginian   ep   The Price of Love 2. 12. 69 NBC
The Outsider   ep   A Lot of Muscle 3. 26. 69 NBC
The Big Valley   ep   The Other Face of Justice 3. 21. 69 ABC
The Name of the Game   ep   Man of the People 3. 6. 70 NBC
The Name of the Game   ep   So Long, Baby, and Amen 9. 18. 70
   NBC
Cade's County   ep   10. 10. 71 CBS
Mission: Impossible   ep   The Bride 1. 1. 72 CBS
Columbo   ep   Short Fuse 1. 19. 72 NBC
Night Gallery   ep   Stop Killing Me 2. 9. 72 NBC
Ironside   ep   Programmed for Panic 9. 28. 72 NBC
All in the Family   ep   10. 21. 72 CBS
Search   ep   10. 25. 72 NBC
Jigsaw   ep   11. 2. 72 ABC

Escape   ep   4. 1. 73 NBC
Love, American Style   ep   9. 14. 73 ABC
The Streets of San Francisco   ep   For the Love of God 9. 27. 73
    ABC
Ironside   ep   The Hidden Man 11. 29. 73 NBC
Miracle on 34th Street   tf   12. 14. 73 CBS
McCloud   ep   Cowboy in Paradise 1. 20. 74 NBC
The Partridge Family   ep   Danny Drops Out 1. 26. 74 ABC
Police Story   ep   3. 12. 74 NBC
The FBI   ep   4. 7. 74 ABC
The Night Stalker   ep   9. 27. 74 ABC
M*A*S*H   ep   Iron Guts Kelly 10. 1. 74 CBS
The Abduction of St. Anne   tf   1. 21. 75 ABC
Emergency   ep   1. 25. 75 NBC
Barney Miller   sr   9. 11. 75 ABC
McCoy   ep   Bless the Big Fish 10. 5. 75 NBC
Cannon   ep   10. 15. 75 CBS
Police Story   ep   10. 28. 75 NBC
Barney Miller   sr ret   9. 23. 76 ABC
Francis Gary Powers: The True Story of the U-2 Spy Incident
    tf   9. 29. 76 NBC
All's Fair   ep   5. 30. 77 CBS
Stop the Presses   pt   7. 15. 77 CBS
Barney Miller   sr ret   9. 15. 77 ABC
Quincy, M. E.   ep   Death Casts a Vote 10. 21. 77 NBC
The Bastard/Kent Family Chronicles   ms   5. 22. 78, 5. 23. 78 NN
Barney Miller   sr ret   9. 14. 78 ABC
Flying High   ep   10. 6. 78 CBS
Detective School   sr   7. 31. 79 ABC
Detective School   sr ret   9. 15. 79 ABC
Barney Miller   sr ret   10. 4. 79 ABC
The Love Boat   ep   3. 15. 80 ABC
The Comeback Kid   tf   4. 11. 80 ABC
The Great American Traffic Jam   tf   10. 2. 80 NBC
Barney Miller   sr ret   10. 30. 80 ABC
Goldie and the Boxer Go to Hollywood   tf   2. 19. 81 NBC
Aloha Paradise   ep   3. 4. 81 ABC
Barney Miller   sr ret   10. 29. 81 ABC

GRIER, ROSEY (a. k. a. Roosevelt Grier)
    SUPP. :
    Chips   ep   10. 13. 77 NBC
    Quincy, M. E.   ep   12. 23. 77 NBC
    Quincy, M. E.   ep   1. 6. 78 NBC
    To Kill a Cop   tf   4. 10. 78, 4. 11. 78 NBC
    Flying High   ep   10. 6. 78 CBS
    Roots: The Next Generations   ms ep   2. 21. 79 ABC
    Sweepstakes   ep   3. 30. 79 NBC
    The Love Boat   ep   12. 1. 79 ABC
    The Seekers   ms   12. 3. 79, 12. 4. 79 NN
    The White Shadow   ep   10. 30. 80 CBS
    The Concrete Cowboys   ep   2. 28. 81 CBS
    Aloha Paradise   ep   4. 29. 81 ABC
    The Sophisticated Gents   tf   9. 29. 81, 9. 30. 81, 10. 1. 81 NBC

GRIFFITH, ANDY
  A&C:
  The Doris Day Show ep 1. 8. 73 CBS
  Adams of Eagle Lake pt 8. 30. 75 ABC
  SUPP. :
  The Girl in the Empty Grave tf 9. 20. 77 NBC
  Washington: Behind Closed Doors ms 9. 6-11. 77 ABC
  Deadly Game tf 12. 3. 77 NBC
  Hollywood Television Theatre ep Six Characters in Search of
    an Author 1. 12. 78 PBS
  Salvage 1 tf 1. 20. 79 ABC
  Salvage 1 sr 1. 29. 79 ABC
  Centennial ms ep The Scream of Eagles 2. 4. 79 NBC
  From Here to Eternity ms 2. 14. 79, 2. 21. 79, 2. 28. 79 NBC
  Roots: The Next Generations ms ep 2. 23. 79 ABC
  Salvage 1 sr ret 11. 4. 79 ABC
  Murder in Texas tf 5. 3. 81, 5. 4. 81 NBC
  Best of the West ep 10. 8. 81 ABC

GRIMES, TAMMY
  SUPP. :
  Theatre in America ep Tartuffle 5. 31. 78 PBS
  The Love Boat ep 1. 27. 79 ABC
  You Can't Go Home Again tf 4. 25. 79 CBS

GRIZZARD, GEORGE
  A&C:
  Attack on Terror: The FBI Vs. the Ku Klux Klan tf 2. 21. 75
    CBS
  SUPP. :
  Hawaii Five-O ep 2. 16. 78 CBS
  Night Rider tf 5. 11. 79 ABC
  Attica tf 3. 2. 80 ABC
  NBC Live Theatre ep The Oldest Living Graduate sp 4. 7. 80
    NBC

GRODIN, CHARLES*
  Accidential Family ep 9. 15. 67 NBC
  Judd, for the Defense ep An Elephant in a Cigar Box 2. 28. 69
    ABC
  Just You and Me tf 5. 22. 78 NBC
  The Grass Is Always Greener over the Septic Tank tf 10. 25. 78
    CBS
  Laverne and Shirley ep Friendly Persuasion 12. 15. 81 ABC

GROH, DAVID*
  Rhoda sr 9. 9. 74 CBS
  Rhoda sr ret 9. 8. 75 CBS
  Police Story ep 10. 21. 75, 11. 7. 75, 1. 23. 76 NBC
  Smash-Up on Interstate 5 tf 12. 3. 76 ABC
  Victory at Entebbe tf 12. 13. 76 ABC
  Police Story ep 2. 15. 77, 4. 5. 77 NBC
  The Love Boat ep 10. 22. 77 ABC

Another Day   sr   4. 8. 78 CBS
Murder at the Mardi Gras   tf   5. 10. 78 NBC
The Child Stealer   tf   3. 9. 79 ABC
Buck Rogers in the 25th Century   ep   Planet of the Slave Girls
   9. 27. 79 NBC
Power   tf   1. 4. 80, 1. 15. 80 NBC
The Dream Merchants   ms   5. 12. 80, 5. 19. 80 NN
Tourist   pt   7. 17. 80 NN
Fantasy Island   ep   2. 28. 81 ABC
Fantasy Island   ep   Romance Times Three 12. 5. 81 ABC

GUARDINO, HARRY
   A&C:
   The Overland Trail   ep   Daughter of the Sioux 3. 20. 60 NBC
   Target: The Corruptors   ep   Babes in Wall Street 3. 9. 62 ABC
   Police Story   ep   The Wyatt Earp Syndrome 3. 5. 74 NBC
   SUPP. :
   Future Cop   tf   3. 25. 77 ABC
   Contract on Cherry Street   tf   11. 19. 77 NBC
   The New Adventures of Wonder Woman   ep   The Girl from
      Ilandia 4. 7. 78 CBS
   Police Story   ep   No Margin for Error 4. 30. 78 NBC
   Evening in Byzantium   ms   8. 14. 78, 8. 15. 78 NN
   Pleasure Cove   tf   1. 3. 79 NBC
   Bender   pt   9. 12. 79 CBS
   Hawaii Five-O   ep   10. 4. 79 CBS
   Barnaby Jones   ep   The Final Victim 3. 6. 80 CBS
   The Sophisticated Gents   tf   9. 29. 81, 9. 30. 81, 10. 1. 81 NBC

GUILLAUME, ROBERT*
   Soap   sr   9. 13. 77 ABC
   Soap   sr ret   9. 14. 78 ABC
   Benson   sr   9. 13. 79 ABC
   The Love Boat   ep   The Affair 1. 19. 80 ABC
   Benson   sr ret   10. 31. 80 ABC
   The Love Boat   ep   Two Grapes on the Vine 10. 17. 81 ABC
   Benson   sr ret   11. 6. 81 ABC

GULAGER, CLU
   A&C:
   The Deputy   ep   Shadow of the Noose 10. 3. 59 NBC
   Laramie   ep   Fugitive Road 10. 6. 59 NBC
   The Untouchables   ep   The Vincent "Mad Dog" Coll Story
      11. 19. 59 ABC
   Line-Up   ep   Seven Sinners 1. 2. 60 CBS
   The Rebel   ep   Paint a Horse with Scarlet 5. 15. 60 ABC
   Whispering Smith   ep   The Devil's Share 5. 2. 61 NBC
   The Defenders   ep   Death Across the Counter 9. 30. 61 CBS
   The Virginian   ep   Run Quiet 11. 13. 63 NBC
   Dr. Kildare   ep   Tyger, Tyger 1. 16. 64, 1. 23. 64 NBC
   Khan!   ep   2. 7. 75 CBS
   Insight   ep   8. 22. 76 NN
   Once and Eagle   ms   12. 2. 76, 12. 30. 76 NBC

SUPP. :
Dog and Cat   ep   4. 23. 77 ABC
Charlie Cobb: Nice Night for a Hanging   tf   6. 9. 77 NBC
Black Beauty   ms   1. 31. 78, 2. 1. 78, 2. 2. 78, 2. 3. 78, 2. 4. 78
   NBC
King   ms   2. 12. 78, 2. 13. 78, 2. 14. 78 NBC
Stickin' Together   tf   4. 14. 78 ABC
A Question of Love   tf   11. 26. 78 ABC
Willa   tf   3. 17. 79 CBS
This Man Stands Alone   tf   5. 30. 79 NBC
The MacKenzies of Paradise Cove   sr   3. 27. 79 ABC
Skyward   tf   11. 20. 80 NBC

GUNN, MOSES*
Carter's Army   tf   1. 12. 70 ABC
Hawaii Five-O   ep   Nine, Ten, You're Dead 11. 30. 71 CBS
McCloud   ep   A Little Plot at Tranquil Valley 1. 12. 72 NBC
Haunts of the Very Rich   tf   9. 20. 72 ABC
ABC Theatre   ep   If You Give a Dance You Gotta Pay the Band
   sp   12. 19. 72 ABC
The Cowboys   sr   2. 6. 74 ABC
The Jeffersons   ep   2. 22. 75 CBS
The World of Disney   ep   The Secret of the Pond 10. 12. 75 NBC
Movin' On   ep   10. 13. 75 NBC
Law of the Land   tf   4. 29. 76 NBC
Roots   ms ep   1. 25. 77 ABC
Switch   ep   4. 3. 77 CBS
Quincy, M. E.   ep   9. 23. 77 NBC
Little House on the Prairie   ep   11. 21. 77 NBC
Vega$ ep   11. 22. 78 ABC
Little House on the Prairie   ep   11. 27. 78, 2. 19. 79 NBC
Salvage 1   ep   4. 2. 79 ABC
The Contender   sr   4. 3. 80 CBS
Little House on the Prairie   ep   1. 26. 81 NBC
Father Murphy   sr   11. 3. 81 NBC

GWYNNE, FRED
SUPP. :
Captains Courageous   tf   12. 4. 77 ABC
Sanctuary of Fear   tf   4. 23. 79 NBC
How, What and Witch   sp   10. 27. 79 NN
American Short Story   ep   The Man That Corrupted Hadleyburg
   3. 17. 80 PBS
The Munsters' Revenge   tf   2. 27. 81 NBC

-H-

HACK, SHELLEY*
Charlie's Angels   sr   9. 12. 79 ABC

Death Car on the Freeway tf 9. 25. 79 CBS
The Love Boat ep 3. 15. 80 ABC

HACKETT, BUDDY
   SUPP. :
   Quincy, M. E. ep 2. 4. 77 NBC
   Bud and Lou tf 11. 15. 78 NBC
   The Love Boat ep 9. 29. 79 ABC
   Jack Frost sp vo 12. 13. 79 NBC
   The Love Boat ep Phantom Bride 11. 14. 81 ABC

HACKETT, JOAN
   A& C:
   Dr. Kildare ep The Witch Doctor 3. 8. 62 NBC
   SUPP. :
   Stonestreet: Who Killed the Centerfold Model? tf 1. 16. 77
      NBC
   Dead of Night tf ep Bobby 3. 29. 77 NBC
   The Possessed tf 5. 1. 77 NBC
   Another Day sr 4. 8. 78 CBS
   Great Performances ep Mourning Becomes Electra 12. 6. 78
      PBS
   Pleasure Cove tf 1. 3. 79 NBC
   Sweepstakes ep 2. 9. 79 NBC
   The Love Boat ep 9. 22. 79 ABC
   Trapper John, M. D. ep 11. 4. 79 CBS
   Tales of the Unexpected ep Scrimshaw 10. 4. 80 NN

HADDOCK, JULIE ANNE*
   Mulligan's Stew tf 6. 20. 77 NBC
   Mulligan's Stew sr 10. 25. 77 NBC
   The New Adventures of Wonder Woman ep The Girl from
      Ilandia 4. 7. 78 CBS
   Little House on the Prairie ep 10. 2. 78 NBC
   The Facts of Life sr 8. 24. 79 NBC
   The Facts of Life sr ret 3. 12. 80 NBC
   The Facts of Life sr ret 10. 28. 81 NBC
   Gimme a Break ep Julie's Rejection 12. 1. 81 NBC

HAGEN, JEAN
   SUPP. :
   Alexander: The Other Side of Dawn tf 5. 16. 77 NBC

HAGGERTY, DAN*
   The Life and Times of Grizzly Adams sr 2. 9. 77 NBC
   Desperate Women tf 10. 25. 78 NBC
   The Life and Times of Grizzly Adams sp ep Once upon a
      Starry Night 12. 19. 78 NBC
   Terror out of the Sky tf 12. 26. 78 CBS
   CHiPs ep Chips Goes Roller Disco 9. 22. 79 NBC
   Condominium ms 11. 20. 80, 11. 24. 80 NN
   Charlie's Angels ep Waikiki Angels 1. 4. 81 ABC

HAGMAN, LARRY
A&C:
DuPont Show of the Week ep The Silver Burro 11. 3. 63 NBC
The Alpha Caper tf 10. 6. 73 ABC
SUPP. :
The Rhinemann Exchange ms 3. 10. 77, 3. 17. 77, 3. 24. 77 NBC
McMillan ep 3. 20. 77 NBC
Intimate Strangers tf 11. 11. 77 ABC
The Rockford Files ep 12. 9. 77 NBC
What Really Happened to the Class of '65? ep The Girl No-
    body Knew 12. 29. 77 NBC
The President's Mistress tf 2. 10. 78 CBS
Last of the Good Guys tf 3. 7. 78 CBS
Dallas sr 4. 2. 78 CBS
Dallas sr ret 9. 23. 78 CBS
Police Story ep A Cry for Justice 5. 23. 79 NBC
Dallas sr ret 9. 21. 79 CBS
Knots Landing ep 1. 3. 80 CBS
Dallas sr ret 11. 7. 80 CBS
Knots Landing ep 3. 26. 81 CBS
Dallas sr ret 10. 9. 81 CBS

HAID, CHARLES*
Cannon ep Dead Lady's Tears 11. 7. 73 CBS
Gunsmoke ep Like Old Times 1. 21. 74 CBS
The Execution of Private Slovik tf 3. 13. 74 NBC
Remember When tf 3. 23. 74 CBS
Harry O ep The Admiral's Lady 9. 19. 74 ABC
Things in Their Season tf 11. 27. 74 CBS
Movin' On ep 1. 2. 75 NBC
Kate McShane tf 4. 11. 75 CBS
Kung Fu ep 4. 26. 75 ABC
Kate McShane sr 9. 10. 75 CBS
Foster and Laurie tf 11. 13. 75 CBS
Switch ep 1. 6. 76 CBS
Police Woman ep 3. 2. 76 NBC
Delvecchio sr 9. 9. 76 CBS
A Death in Canaan tf 3. 1. 78 CBS
The Bastard/Kent Family Chronicles ms 5. 22. 78, 5. 23. 78
    NN
Death Moon tf 5. 31. 78 CBS
Grandpa Goes to Washington ep 9. 19. 78, 12. 5. 78 NBC
Sweepstakes ep 2. 23. 79 NBC
The New Adventures of Wonder Woman ep The Girl with a
    Gift for Disaster 3. 17. 79 CBS
Scalpels pt 10. 26. 80 NBC
Hill Street Blues sr 1. 15. 81 NBC
B. J. and the Bear ep 3. 22. 81 NBC
Twirl tf 10. 25. 81 NBC
Hill Street Blues sr ret 10. 29. 81 NBC

HAMEL, VERONICA*
The Bob Newhart Show ep 2. 28. 76 CBS

Switch   ep   3. 23. 76 CBS
City of Angels   ep   4. 20. 76 NBC
Starsky and Hutch   ep   11. 20. 76 NBC
Family   ep   10. 4. 77 ABC
79 Park Avenue   ms   10. 16. 77, 10. 17. 77, 10. 18. 77 NBC
Starsky and Hutch   ep   2. 22. 78 ABC
The Eddie Capra Mysteries   ep   11. 10. 78 NBC
Dallas   ep   2. 23. 79 CBS
Doctors' Private Lives   ep   4. 12. 79 ABC
The Gathering Part II   tf   12. 17. 79 NBC
Eischied   ep   1. 20. 80 NBC
Hill Street Blues   sr   1. 15. 81 NBC
Jacqueline Susann's Valley of the Dolls 1981   tf   10. 19. 81,
     10. 20. 81 CBS
Hill Street Blues   sr ret   10. 29. 81 NBC

HAMILL, MARK*
Owen Marshall, Counselor at Law   ep   Smiles from Yesterday
     2. 17. 72 ABC
Owen Marshall, Counselor at Law   ep   1. 31. 73 ABC
Room 222   ep   I've Got the Hammer 9. 14. 73 ABC
Owen Marshall, Counselor at Law   ep   The Pool House 9. 26. 73
     ABC
The Magician   ep   Lightning on a Dry Day 10. 30. 73 NBC
The Texas Wheelers   sr   9. 13. 74 ABC
Petrocelli   ep   2. 26. 75 NBC
The Streets of San Francisco   ep   9. 11. 75 ABC
Bronk   ep   11. 9. 75 CBS
The Hallmark Hall of Fame   ep   Eric   sp   11. 10. 75 NBC
Mallory: Circumstantial Evidence   tf   2. 8. 76 NBC
One Day at a Time   ep   11. 30. 76 CBS
The City   tf   1. 12. 77 NBC
SPFX: The Empire Strikes Back   sp hos   9. 22. 80 CBS

HAMILTON, GEORGE
SUPP. :
McCloud   ep   1. 16. 77 NBC
Roots   ms ep   1. 28. 77 ABC
The Strange Possession of Mrs. Oliver   tf   2. 28. 77 NBC
The Sword of Justice   ep   7. 11. 79 NBC
The Eddie Capra Mysteries   ep   Who Killed Charles Pendragon?
     9. 8. 78 NBC
The Users   tf   10. 1. 78 ABC
Death Car on the Freeway   tf   9. 25. 79 CBS
The Seekers   ms   12. 3. 79, 12. 4. 79 NN
The Great Cash Giveaway Getaway   tf   4. 21. 80 NBC

HAMILTON, MARGARET
SUPP. :
Letters from Frank   tf   11. 22. 79 CBS
Lou Grant   ep   12. 17. 79 CBS
Nurse   ep   4. 23. 81 CBS

HANLEY, BRIDGET
    SUPP. :
    How the West Was Won   ep   2. 14. 77 ABC
    CHiPs   ep   2. 9. 78 NBC
    Breaking Up Is Hard to Do   tf   9. 5. 79, 9. 7. 79 ABC
    Reward   tf   5. 23. 80 ABC
    Harper Valley PTA   sr   1. 16. 81 NBC
    Harper Valley   sr   (revised) 10. 29. 81 NBC

HARDIN, TY
    A&C:
    Sugarfoot   ep   The Trail of the Canary Kid 9. 15. 59 ABC
    From Sea to Shining Sea   sp ep   The Unwanted 4. 16. 75 NN
    SUPP. :
    Fire   tf   5. 8. 77 NBC
    David Cassidy--Man Undercover   ep   11. 9. 78 NBC
    The Love Boat   ep   First Voyage, Last Voyage 1. 17. 81 ABC

HARMON, MARK*
    Ozzie's Girls   ep   Sorry, Right Number 1. 6. 74 NN
    Adam-12   ep   4. 1. 75 NBC
    The Hardy Boys/Nancy Drew Mysteries   ep   5. 2. 77 ABC
    Sam   pt   5. 24. 77 CBS
    Sam   sr   3. 14. 78 CBS
    Getting Married   tf   5. 17. 78 CBS
    Little Mo   tf   9. 5. 78 NBC
    Centennial   ep   For As Long As the Water Flows 11. 4. 78 NBC
    Centennial   ep   The Massacre 11. 11. 78 NBC
    240-Robert   sr   8. 28. 79 ABC
    The Love Boat   ep   9. 15. 79 ABC
    Flamingo Road   tf   5. 12. 80 NBC
    The Dream Merchants   ms   5. 12. 80, 5. 19. 80 NN
    Flamingo Road   sr   1. 6. 81 NBC
    Flamingo Road   sr ret   11. 3. 81 NBC
    Goliath Awaits   ms   11. 17. 81, 11. 23. 81 NN

HARPER, VALERIE
    A&C:
    The Mary Tyler Moore Show   ep   11. 22. 75 CBS
    SUPP. :
    Night Terror   tf   2. 7. 77 NBC
    Rhoda   sr ret   10. 2. 77 CBS
    Rhoda   sr ret   9. 23. 78 CBS
    Fun and Games   tf   5. 26. 80 ABC
    The Shadow Box   tf   12. 28. 80 ABC
    The Day the Loving Stopped   tf   10. 16. 81 ABC

HARRINGTON, PAT*
    The Danny Thomas Show   sr   1960 CBS
    The Man from U. N. C. L. E.   ep   The Bow-Wow Affair 2. 15. 65
      NBC
    The Munsters   ep   Mummy Munster 4. 29. 65 CBS

The Man from U. N. C. L. E.   ep   The Come with Me to the
    Casbah Affair 11. 11. 66 NBC
The Man from U. N. C. L. E.   ep   The Hula Doll Affair 2. 17. 67
    NBC
The Outsider   ep   11. 13. 68 NBC
The Outsider   ep   4. 2. 69 NBC
Mr. Deeds Goes to Town   sr   9. 26. 69 ABC
The Partridge Family   ep   11. 6. 70 ABC
Owen Marshall, Counselor at Law   ep   Legacy of Fear 9. 16. 71
    ABC
The Bold Ones: The Lawyers   ep   The Invasion of Kevin Ire-
    land 9. 26. 71 NBC
Love, American Style   ep   11. 12. 71 ABC
Nanny and the Professor   ep   12. 6. 71 ABC
The Courtship of Eddie's Father   ep   2. 2. 72 ABC
Owen Marshall, Counselor at Law   ep   Murder in the Abstract
    3. 2. 72 ABC
Wednesday Night Out   pt   4. 24. 72 NBC
Owen Marshall, Counselor at Law   ep   9. 21. 72, 10. 12. 72 ABC
Owen Marshall, Counselor at Law   ep   A Piece of God 12. 14. 72
    ABC
Temperature's Rising   ep   12. 19. 72 ABC
Owen Marshall, Counselor at Law   ep   2. 7. 73 ABC
Owen Marshall, Counselor at Law   ep   Some People in the
    Park 2. 21. 73 ABC
Savage   tf   3. 31. 73 NBC
Owen Marshall, Counselor at Law   ep   The Pool House 9. 26. 73
    ABC
The Rookies   ep   Cry Wolf 10. 15. 73 ABC
Owen Marshall, Counselor at Law   ep   N Is for Nightmare
    10. 17. 73 ABC
Owen Marshall, Counselor at Law   ep   The Camerons Are a
    Special Clan 10. 24. 73 ABC
Owen Marshall, Counselor at Law   ep   Poor Children of Eve
    10. 31. 73 ABC
The Partridge Family   ep   The Diplomat 11. 3. 73 ABC
The New Adventures of Perry Mason   ep   The Case of the
    Furious Father 11. 11. 73 CBS
The Affair   tf   11. 20. 73 ABC
Faraday and Company   ep   Fire and Ice 12. 12. 73 NBC
Owen Marshall, Counselor at Law   ep   Etude for a Kidnapper
    1. 2. 74 ABC
Chase   ep   1. 23. 74 NBC
Owen Marshall, Counselor at Law   ep   The Attacker 1. 26. 74
    ABC
Owen Marshall, Counselor at Law   ep   A Killer with a Badge
    2. 9. 74 ABC
The New Dick Van Dyke Show   ep   2. 18. 74 CBS
Columbo   ep   9. 15. 74 NBC
McMillan and Wife   ep   Guilt by Association 12. 8. 74 NBC
Let's Switch   tf   1. 7. 75 ABC
The Night Stalker   ep   1. 17. 75 ABC

Police Story   ep   **2. 4. 75** ABC
Fay   ep   **9. 25. 75** NBC
McMillan and Wife   ep   Deadly Inheritance 9. 28. 75 NBC
Ellery Queen   ep   **10. 9. 75** NBC
The Invisible Man   ep   **10. 20. 75** NBC
The Invisible Man   ep   **11. 3. 75** NBC
One Day at a Time   sr   **12. 16. 75** CBS
One Day at a Time   sr ret   **9. 28. 76** CBS
The New Love Boat (a. k. a. Love Boat III)   tf   **5. 5. 77** ABC
One Day at a Time   sr ret   **9. 20. 77** CBS
The Critical List   tf   **9. 11. 78, 9. 12. 78** NBC
One Day at a Time   sr ret   **9. 18. 78** CBS
The Love Boat   ep   **12. 2. 78** ABC
The Last Convertible   ms ep   **9. 25. 79** NBC
The Love Boat   ep   **11. 8. 80** ABC
One Day at a Time   sr ret   **11. 9. 80** CBS
One Day at a Time   sr ret   **10. 11. 81** CBS

HARRIS, JO ANN*
Gunsmoke   ep   **10. 6. 69** CBS
Cat Ballou   pt   **9. 6. 71** NBC
Medical Center   ep   **2. 16. 72** CBS
The World of Disney   ep   Michael O'Hara the Fourth **4. 2. 72**
   NBC
The Mod Squad   ep   **9. 28. 72** ABC
The Streets of San Francisco   ep   **10. 7. 72** ABC
The Bold Ones: The Doctors   ep   A Very Strange Triangle
   10. 31. 72 NBC
Banyon   ep   **12. 1. 72** NBC
The FBI   ep   Sweet Evil **3. 4. 73** ABC
The Streets of San Francisco   ep   The Victims **11. 29. 73** ABC
The FBI   ep   Ransom **12. 30. 73** ABC
Nakia   ep   **10. 5. 74** ABC
Barnaby Jones   ep   Odd Man Loses **10. 8. 74** CBS
Hawaii Five-O   ep   **2. 18. 75** CBS
Manhunter   ep   **2. 26. 75** CBS
Kate McShane   ep   **11. 5. 75** CBS
Movin' On   ep   **11. 11. 75** NBC
Barnaby Jones   ep   **12. 1. 75** CBS
Rich Man, Poor Man   ms ep   **3. 8. 76, 3. 15. 76** ABC
Most Wanted   tf   **3. 21. 76** ABC
Most Wanted   sr   **10. 16. 76** ABC
The Love Boat   ep   **11. 19. 77** ABC
Cruise into Terror   tf   **2. 3. 78** ABC
Fantasy Island   ep   **3. 11. 78** ABC
Barnaby Jones   ep   Death of a Friendship **11. 9. 78** CBS
B. J. and the Bear   ep   **2. 10. 79** NBC
Vega$ ep   **2. 28. 79** ABC
The Wild Wild West Revisited   tf   **5. 9. 79** CBS
Detective School   sr   **7. 31. 79** ABC
B. J. and the Bear   ep   **12. 1. 79** NBC
A Man Called Sloane   ep   **12. 22. 79** NBC
M Station: Hawaii   tf   **6. 10. 80** CBS
The American Dream   ep   **5. 6. 81** ABC

HARRIS, JULIE
  A&C:
  delete: Salty sr 9.11.74 NN
  Hollywood Television Theatre ep The Last of Mrs. Lincoln
    9.16.76 PBS
  SUPP.:
  The Hallmark Hall of Fame ep Stubby Pringle's Christmas
    sp 12.17.78 NBC
  Backstairs at the White House ms ep 1.29.79 NBC
  Roald Dahl's Tales of the Unexpected ep Mrs. Bixby and the
    Colonel's Coat 10.20.79 NN
  The Gift tf 12.15.79 CBS
  Knots Landing sr 12.3.81 CBS

HARRIS, PHIL
  SUPP.:
  Fantasy Island ep 12.2.78 ABC
  The Love Boat ep 1.26.80 ABC

HARRIS, ROSEMARY
  SUPP.:
  The Chisholms ms 3.29.79, 4.5.79, 4.12.79 4.19.79 CBS
  The Chisholms sr 1.19.80 CBS

HARRISON, GREGORY*
  Triology of Terror tf 3.4.75 ABC
  Barnaby Jones ep 10.7.76 CBS
  Logan's Run sr 9.16.77 CBS
  The Gathering tf 12.4.77 ABC
  Centennial ms ep The Massacre 11.11.78 NBC
  Centennial ms ep The Longhorns 12.3.78 NBC
  Centennial ms ep The Shepherds 12.10.78 NBC
  Centennial ms ep The Storm 1.14.79 NBC
  The Best Place to Be tf 5.27.79 NBC
  Trapper John, M.D. sr 9.23.79 CBS
  The Women's Room tf 9.14.80 ABC
  Trapper John, M.D. sr ret 11.23.80 CBS
  Trapper John, M.D. sr ret 10.4.81 CBS
  For Ladies Only tf 11.9.81 NBC

HARRISON, JENILEE*
  Three's Company sr 12.16.80 ABC
  Three's Company sr ret 10.6.81 ABC
  The Love Boat ep The Three R's 10.10.81 ABC
  Fantasy Island ep Slam Dunk 10.10.81 ABC

HARRISON, NOEL
  SUPP.:
  Hart to Hart ep Murder in Paradise 1.13.81 ABC

HARTLEY, MARIETTE*
  The Twilight Zone ep The Long Morrow 1.10.64 CBS
  The Virginian ep The Drifter 1.29.64 NBC
  Bonanza ep Right Is the Fourth R 3.7.65 NBC

Peyton Place sr 1965 ABC
The Hero sr 9.8.66 NBC
Bonanza ep The Survivors 11.10.68 NBC
Daniel Boone ep The Valley of the Sun 11.28.68 NBC
Star Trek ep All Our Yesterdays 3.14.69 NBC
Daniel Boone ep An Angel Cried 1.8.70 NBC
Bonanza ep Is There Any Man Here? 2.8.70 NBC
The FBI ep The Impersonator 11.22.70 ABC
Love, American Style ep Love and the Fighting Couple 1971 ABC
Cade's County ep The Armageddon Contract 11.7.71 CBS
Bonanza ep 11.28.71 NBC
Earth II tf 11.28.71 ABC
Mannix ep Death in Fifth Gear 3.8.72 CBS
The Sixth Sense ep 3.18.72 ABC
Gunsmoke ep 10.2.72 CBS
Sandcastles tf 10.17.72 CBS
The Delphi Bureau ep 11.16.72 ABC
Ghost Story ep 11.24.72 NBC
The Bold Ones: The Doctors ep A Purge of Madness 12.5.72
    NBC
The World of Disney ep The Mystery in Dracula's Castle
    1.7.73 NBC
The FBI ep Double Play 2.4.73 ABC
Genesis II tf 3.23.73 ABC
The Bob Newhart Show ep 10.20.73 CBS
The Streets of San Francisco ep Shield of Honor 11.15.73 ABC
Emergency ep Zero 11.24.73 NBC
Owen Marshall, Counselor at Law ep Snatches of a Crazy
    Song 12.5.73 ABC
Columbo ep Publish or Perish 1.13.74 NBC
Gunsmoke ep The Iron Blood of Courage 2.18.74 CBS
Paul Sand in Friends and Lovers ep 10.26.74 CBS
The Streets of San Francisco ep 11.7.74 ABC
Barnaby Jones ep Mystery Cycle 11.12.74 CBS
McCloud ep Lady on the Run 1.26.75 NBC
Little House on the Prairie ep For My Lady 3.10.76 NBC
The Killer Who Wouldn't Die tf 4.4.76 ABC
Most Wanted ep 10.30.76 ABC
Mystery of the Week ep Tight as a Drum 1.5.77 ABC
Police Woman ep 1.18.77 NBC
Delvecchio ep 1.23.77 CBS
The African Queen pt 3.18.77 CBS
Kingston Confidential ep 3.23.77 NBC
The Hallmark Hall of Fame ep The Last Hurrah sp 11.16.77
    NBC
Columbo ep 11.21.77 NBC
Logan's Run ep 12.26.77, 1.2.78 CBS
Calloway's Climb sp 8.28.78 NN
The Incredible Hulk ep 9.22.78 CBS
M*A*S*H ep Inga 1.8.79 CBS
The Second Time Around pt 7.24.79 ABC
Stone pt 8.26.79 ABC
The Rockford Files ep Trouble in Paradise Cove 9.28.79 NBC
The Halloween That Almost Wasn't sp 10.28.79 ABC

The Love Tapes   tf   5. 9. 80 ABC
The Secret War of Jackie's Girls   tf   11. 29. 80 NBC
No Place to Hide   tf   3. 4. 81 CBS
Rainy Day   sp   6. 10. 81 PBS

HARTMAN, LISA*
    Police Woman   ep   1. 11. 77 NBC
    Tabitha   pt   5. 7. 77 ABC
    Tabitha   sr   9. 10. 77 ABC
    Tabitha   sp ep   11. 12. 77,   11. 19. 77 ABC
    Tabitha   sr ret   11. 26. 77 ABC
    Fantasy Island   ep   2. 11. 78 ABC
    The Love Boat   ep   Class Reunion 2. 3. 79 ABC
    Fantasy Island   ep   2. 17. 79 ABC
    The Love Boat   ep   9. 15. 79 ABC
    Fantasy Island   ep   9. 21. 79 ABC
    Vega$ ep   11. 14. 79 ABC
    Fantasy Island   ep   2. 9. 80 ABC
    Valentine Magic on Love Island   tf   2. 15. 80 NBC
    Where the Ladies Go   tf   3. 14. 80 ABC
    The Great American Traffic Jam   tf   10. 2. 80 NBC
    The Love Boat   ep   The Loan Arranger 1. 17. 81 ABC
    Fantasy Island   ep   2. 21. 81 ABC
    Aloha Paradise   ep   3. 4. 81 ABC
    Jacqueline Susann's Valley of the Dolls 1981   tf   10. 19. 81,
        10. 20. 81 CBS

HASKELL, PETER
    A&C:
    Dr. Kildare   ep   Please Let My Baby Live 1. 28. 65 NBC
    Ben Casey   ep   A Rambling Discourse on Egyptian Water Clocks
        2. 1. 65 ABC
    Ben Casey   ep   26 Ways to Spell Heartbreak 2. 28. 66 ABC
    Barnaby Jones   ep   5. 6. 73 CBS
    Police Surgeon   ep   10. 12. 74 NN
    Insight   ep   8. 4. 75 NN
    SUPP. :
    The Bionic Woman   ep   Biofeedback 1. 12. 77 ABC
    The Night They Took Miss Beautiful   tf   10. 24. 77 NBC
    Charlie's Angels   ep   Angel in Love 10. 26. 77 ABC
    Superdome   tf   1. 9. 78 ABC
    Fantasy Island   ep   3. 11. 78 ABC
    This Is the Life   ep   7. 2. 78 NN
    The Jordan Chance   tf   12. 12. 78 CBS
    The World of Disney   ep   Shadow of Fear 1. 28. 79 NBC
    The Cracker Factory   tf   3. 16. 79 ABC
    The Duke   ep   4. 5. 79 NBC
    B. J. and the Bear   ep   11. 10. 79 NBC
    Vega$ ep   11. 21. 79 ABC
    Shirley   ep   12. 28. 79 NBC
    Barnaby Jones   ep   2. 14. 80 CBS
    Vega$ ep   Ladies in Blue (pt)   3. 19. 80 ABC
    B. J. and the Bear   ep   The Eyes of Texas (pt) 5. 24. 80 NBC
    The Love Boat   ep   2. 21. 81 ABC

Hart to Hart   ep   Getting Aweigh with Murder 4. 14. 81 ABC
Vega$ ep   4. 22. 81 ABC
Code Red   ep   The Land of Make Believe 11. 29. 81 ABC

HASSO, SIGNE
   A&C:
   Route 66   ep   A Feat of Strength 5. 18. 62 CBS
   This Is the Life   ep   12. 1. 74 NN
   SUPP. :
   Winner Take All   pt   4. 1. 77 CBS
   Starsky and Hutch   ep   1. 25. 78 ABC
   Evita Peron   tf   2. 23. 81, 2. 24. 81 NBC
   Magnum, P. I.   ep   12. 17. 81 CBS

HATFIELD, HURD
   SUPP. :
   The Word   ms   11. 12. 78, 11. 13. 78, 11. 14. 78   11. 15. 78 CBS
   You Can't Go Home Again   tf   4. 25. 79 CBS

HAVOC, JUNE
   SUPP. :
   The Paper Chase   ep   3. 20. 79 CBS

HAYES, HELEN
   SUPP. :
   A Family Upside Down   tf   4. 9. 78 NBC
   The Love Boat   ep   5. 3. 80 ABC

HAYNES, LLOYD
   SUPP. :
   79 Park Avenue   ms   10. 16. 77, 10. 17. 77, 10. 18. 77 NBC
   Dynasty   sr   4. 13. 81 ABC
   Born to Be Sold   tf   11. 2. 81 NBC

HAYS, ROBERT*
   The Young Pioneers   tf   3. 1. 76 ABC
   The Blue Knight   ep   10. 20. 76 CBS
   Most Wanted   ep   11. 27. 76 ABC
   The Young Pioneers Christmas   tf   12. 17. 76 ABC
   The New, Original Wonder Woman   ep   Wonder Woman in Holly-
      wood 2. 16. 77 ABC
   Delta County U. S. A.   tf   5. 20. 77 ABC
   The Initiation of Sarah   tf   2. 6. 78 ABC
   The Young Pioneers   sr   4. 2. 78 ABC
   Almost Heaven   pt   12. 28. 78 ABC
   Angie   sr   2. 8. 79 ABC
   Angie   sr ret   9. 11. 79 ABC
   The Girl, the Gold Watch and Everything   pt   6. 13. 80 NN
   Mark Twain's America   ep   Young Will Rogers 8. 18. 80 NBC

HEATHERTON, JOEY
   SUPP. :
   Laverne and Shirley   ep   Night at the Awards 1. 24. 81 ABC

HECKART, EILEEN
  A&C:
Naked City ep Hold for Gloria Christmas 9.19.62 ABC
The Mary Tyler Moore Show ep 2.7.76 CBS
Rhoda ep 2.23.76 CBS
Switch ep 11.9.76 CBS
The Mary Tyler Moore Show ep 11.20.76 CBS
Alice ep 12.11.76, 12.18.76 CBS
  SUPP.:
Sunshine Christmas tf 12.12.77 NBC
Suddenly Love tf 12.4.78 NBC
Flying High ep 9.29.78 CBS
Little House on the Prairie ep 1.22.79 NBC
Backstairs at the White House ms ep 2.12.79, 2.19.79 NBC
Out of the Blue sr 9.9.79 ABC
Great Performances ep The Sorrows of Gin 10.24.79 PBS
White Mama tf 3.5.80 CBS
Lou Grant ep 10.27.80 CBS
Joe Dancer tf 1.29.81 NBC
Trapper John, M.D. ep Mother's Day 12.6.81 CBS

HEDISON, DAVID
  A&C:
Hollywood Television Theatre ep For the Use of the Hall
    1.2.75 PBS
Bronk ep 12.14.75 CBS
The Art of Crime tf 12.3.75 NBC
  SUPP.:
Murder in Peyton Place tf 10.3.77 NBC
The Love Boat ep 11.10.77 ABC
Project UFO ep 5.20.78 NBC
Colorado C.I. pt 5.26.78 CBS
The New Adventures of Wonder Woman ep The Queen and the
    Thief 10.28.78 CBS
Charlie's Angels ep 12.20.78 ABC
The Love Boat ep 2.17.79 ABC
Benson ep 9.13.79 ABC
Charlie's Angels ep 1.31.81 ABC
Fantasy Island ep 2.7.81 ABC
The Love Boat ep 2.21.81 ABC
Fantasy Island ep 5.16.81 ABC
Greatest Heroes of the Bible ep Daniel and King Nebuchadnez-
    zar 7.26.81 NBC
Fantasy Island ep Show Me a Hero 10.10.81 ABC

HELMOND, KATHERINE*
  Gunsmoke ep 10.2.72 CBS
  The FBI ep 12.10.72 ABC
  ABC's Matinee Today ep The Other Woman 12.4.73 ABC
  Mannix ep 2.24.74 CBS
  The Snoop Sisters ep A Black Day for Bluebeard 3.19.74 NBC
  Dr. Max tf 4.4.74 CBS
  Larry tf 4.23.74 CBS

Mannix ep 10.6.74 CBS
The Rookies ep The Old Neighborhood 11.25.74 ABC
The Legend of Lizzie Borden tf 2.10.75 ABC
The Family Nobody Wanted tf 2.19.75 ABC
Cage Without a Key tf 3.14.75 CBS
The First 36 Hours of Dr. Durant tf 5.13.75 ABC
Barnaby Jones ep The Orchid Killer 10.3.75 CBS
The Six Million Dollar Man ep 11.23.75 ABC
The Blue Knight ep 1.14.76 CBS
Harry O ep Portrait of a Murderer 10.9.75 ABC
James Dean tf 2.19.76 NBC
Joe Forrester ep 3.22.76 NBC
People Like Us pt 4.19.76 NBC
Wanted: The Sundance Woman tf 10.1.76 ABC
Visions ep Liza's Pioneer Diary 11.18.76 PBS
Spencer's Pilots ep 11.19.76 CBS
Little Ladies of the Night tf 1.16.77 ABC
The Bionic Woman ep Deadly Ringer 2.2.77, 2.9.77 ABC
Soap sr 9.13.77 ABC
Getting Married tf 5.17.78 CBS
Soap sr ret 9.14.78 ABC
Pearl ms 11.16.78, 11.17.78, 11.19.78 ABC
Sweepstakes ep 1.26.79 NBC
Soap sr ret 9.13.79 ABC
Diary of a Teenage Hitchhiker tf 9.21.79 ABC
Benson ep 11.8.79 ABC
Scout's Honor tf 9.30.80
Soap sr ret 10.29.80 ABC
The Love Boat ep The Professor's Wife 10.10.81 ABC

HENDERSON, FLORENCE
SUPP.:
The Love Boat ep 12.10.77 ABC
The Love Boat ep The Remake 2.2.80 ABC
The Love Boat ep The Successor 1.10.81 ABC
The Brady Girls Get Married sr 2.6.81 NBC
The Brady Brides sr 3.6.81 NBC
The Brady Girls Get Married tf 10.27.81 NBC
Hart to Hart ep 11.3.81 ABC

HENDLER, LAURI*
The ABC Afterschool Special ep It Isn't Easy Being a Teen-
age Millionaire sp 3.8.78 ABC
The ABC Weekend Special ep Little Lulu 11.4.78 ABC
Three's Company ep The Crush 11.21.78 ABC
The Child Stealer tf 3.9.79 ABC
A New Kind of Family sr 9.16.79 ABC
Magnum, P.I. ep 12.25.80 CBS
Why Us? pt 8.21.81 NBC
Gimme a Break sr 10.29.81 NBC

HENNER, MARILU*
Off Campus pt 6.8.77 CBS
The Paper Chase ep 9.9.78 CBS

Taxi   sr   9. 12. 78 ABC
Taxi   sr ret   9. 11. 79 ABC
Taxi   sr ret   11. 19. 80 ABC
Taxi   sr ret   10. 8. 81 ABC
Dream House   tf   11. 28. 81 CBS

HENSLEY, PAMELA*
Kojak   ep   Death Is Not a Passing Grade 1. 30. 74 CBS
Toma   ep   3. 8. 74 ABC
McMillan and Wife   ep   Downshift to Danger 9. 29. 74 NBC
Ironside   ep   Trial of Terror 10. 3. 74 NBC
The Law   tf   10. 22. 74 NBC
Lucas Tanner   ep   10. 2. 74 NBC
The Rockford Files   ep   Say Goodbye to Jennifer 2. 7. 75 NBC
Marcus Welby, M. D.   ep   2. 18. 75 ABC
Death Among Friends   tf   5. 20. 75 NBC
Marcus Welby, M. D.   sr   9. 9. 75 ABC
Kingston: The Power Play   tf   9. 15. 76 NBC
The Six Million Dollar Man   ep   1. 2. 77 ABC
Kingston Confidential   sr   3. 23. 77 NBC
The Six Million Dollar Man   ep   9. 11. 77, 9. 18. 77 ABC
Switch   ep   10. 21. 77 CBS
The Rebels   ms   5. 14. 79, 5. 21. 79 NN
Buck Rogers in the 25th Century   pt   9. 20. 79 NBC
Buck Rogers in the 25th Century   ep   11. 29. 79, 4. 3. 80 NBC
Condominium   ms   10. 20. 80, 10. 24. 80 NN
Buck Rogers in the 25th Century   ep   12. 4. 80 NBC
240-Robert   sr   3. 7. 81 ABC

HEPBURN, KATHARINE
SUPP. :
The Corn Is Green   tf   1. 29. 79 CBS

HERSHEY, BARBARA
A& C:
Kung Fu   ep   11. 15. 74, 11. 22. 74 ABC
SUPP. :
In the Glitter Palace   tf   2. 27. 77 NBC
Just a Little Inconvenience   tf   10. 2. 77 NBC
Sunshine Christmas   tf   12. 12. 77 NBC
Switch   ep   8. 6. 78 CBS
A Man Called Intrepid   ms   5. 20. 79, 5. 21. 79, 5. 22. 79 NBC
From Here to Eternity   sr   3. 10. 80 NBC
Angel on My Shoulder   tf   5. 11. 80 ABC
From Here to Eternity   sr ret   8. 3. 80 NBC

HERVEY, IRENE
SUPP. :
Roots: The Next Generations   ms ep   2. 18. 79 ABC

HESSEMAN, HOWARD*
The Bob Newhart Show   ep   1. 19. 74 CBS
Firehouse   ep   The Hottest Place in Town 1. 31. 74 ABC

Rhoda   ep   9.23.74 CBS
The Bob Newhart Show   ep   2.22.75 CBS
The Blue Knight   tf   5.9.75 CBS
Switch   ep   9.21.76 CBS
Mary Hartman, Mary Hartman   sr   10.4.76 NN
Laverne and Shirley   ep   12.21.76 ABC
The Amazing Howard Hughes   tf   4.13.77, 4.14.77 CBS
The TV TV Show   pt   4.30.77 NBC
Blansky's Beauties   ep   6.27.77 ABC
Tarantulas: The Deadly Cargo   tf   12.28.77 CBS
The Ghost on Flight 401   tf   2.19.78 NBC
Soap   ep   3.14.78 ABC
The Comedy Company   tf   7.21.78 CBS
WKRP in Cincinnati   sr   9.18.78 CBS
More Than Friends   tf   10.20.78 ABC
You Can't Take It with You   sp   5.16.79 CBS
WKRP in Cincinnati   sr ret   9.17.79 CBS
The Great American Traffic Jam   tf   10.2.80 NBC
WKRP in Cincinnati   sr ret   11.1.80 CBS
Skyward   tf   11.20.80 NBC
Women Who Rate a 10   sp hos   2.15.81 NBC
WKRP in Cincinnati   sr ret   10.7.81 CBS

HICKMAN, DWAYNE
    SUPP.:
    Whatever Happened to Dobie Gillis?   pt   5.10.77 CBS
    Don't Push, I'll Charge When I'm Ready   tf   12.18.77 NBC

HICKS, CATHERINE*
    Sparrow   pt   8.11.78 CBS
    The Bad News Bears   sr   3.24.79 CBS
    The Bad News Bears   sr ret   9.15.79 CBS
    Love for Rent   tf   11.11.79 ABC
    To Race the Wind   tf   3.12.80 CBS
    The Bad News Bears   sr ret   6.7.80 CBS
    Marilyn: The Untold Story   tf   9.28.80 ABC
    Jacqueline Susann's Valley of the Dolls 1981   tf   10.19.81,
        10.20.81 CBS

HIGGINS, JOEL*
    Cat Ballou   pt   9.5.71 NBC
    Salvage 1   tf   1.20.79 ABC
    Salvage 1   sr   1.29.79 ABC
    Salvage 1   sr ret   11.4.79 ABC
    Best of the West   sr   9.10.81 ABC
    Killing at Hell's Gate   tf   10.31.81 CBS

HILL, ARTHUR
    A&C:
    Great Ghost Tales   ep   Who's The Finest One of All? 9.21.61
        NBC
    The Nurses   ep   Night Shift 9.27.62 CBS

SUPP. :
G. E. Theatre ep Tell Me My Name sp 12. 20. 77 CBS
Little House on the Prairie ep 4. 18. 77 NBC
Hagen sr 3. 1. 80 CBS
The Ordeal of Dr. Mudd tf 3. 25. 80 CBS
Revenge of the Stepford Wives tf 10. 12. 80 NBC
The Return of Frank Cannon tf 11. 1. 80 CBS
Angel Dusted tf 2. 16. 81 NBC

HILL, DANA*
    The Paul Williams Show pt 6. 27. 79 NBC
    Featherstone's Nest pt 8. 1. 79 CBS
    The French-Atlantic Affair ms ep 11. 16. 79 ABC
    The $5. 20 an Hour Dream tf 1. 26. 80 CBS
    The ABC Afterschool Special ep What Are Best Friends For?
        sp 3. 19. 80 ABC
    Family ep 6. 18. 80 ABC
    Fallen Angel tf 2. 24. 81 CBS
    The Two of Us sr 4. 6. 81 CBS
    The Two of Us sr ret 10. 12. 81 CBS

HILL, STEVEN
    A& C:
    The Line-Up ep The Strange Return of Army Armitage
        10. 7. 59 CBS
    SUPP. :
    The Andros Targets ep 2. 7. 77, 2. 21. 77 CBS

HILLERMAN, JOHN*
    Sweet, Sweet Rachel tf 10. 2. 71 ABC
    Mannix ep 12. 1. 72 CBS
    The Great Man's Whiskers tf 2. 13. 73 NBC
    Kojak ep The Only Way Out 5. 18. 74 CBS
    The Law tf 10. 22. 74 NBC
    Mannix ep 4. 6. 75 CBS
    The Invasion of Johnson County tf 7. 31. 76 NBC
    Hawaii Five-O ep 10. 21. 76 CBS
    Serpico ep 12. 10. 76 NBC
    The New, Original Wonder Woman ep Wonder Woman vs.
        Gargantua 12. 18. 76 ABC
    Delvecchio ep 2. 13. 77 CBS
    The Betty White Show sr 9. 12. 77 CBS
    Relentless tf 9. 14. 77 CBS
    Kill Me If You Can tf 9. 25. 77 NBC
    Hawaii Five-O ep 4. 27. 78 CBS
    One Day at a Time sr 9. 18. 78 CBS
    Flying High ep 9. 29. 78 CBS
    A Guide for the Married Man tf 10. 13. 78 ABC
    Little House on the Prairie ep 10. 30. 78 NBC
    Betrayal tf 11. 13. 78 NBC
    Institute for Revenge tf vo 1. 22. 79 NBC
    Flying High ep 1. 23. 79 CBS
    Beane's of Boston pt 5. 30. 79 CBS

Gossip   pt   7. 10. 79 NBC
The Love Boat   ep   11. 10. 79 ABC
Young Maverick   ep   1. 9. 80 CBS
Marathon   tf   1. 30. 80 CBS
Battles: The Murder That Wouldn't Die   tf   3. 9. 80 NBC
One Day at a Time   ep   3. 23. 80 CBS
Ten Speed and Brown Shoe   ep   6. 27. 80 ABC
Lou Grant   ep   10. 27. 80 CBS
One Day at a Time   ep   11. 16. 80 CBS
Magnum, P. I.   sr   12. 11. 80 CBS
Magnum, P. I.   sr ret   10. 8. 81 CBS

HINGLE, PAT
    SUPP. :
    Hawaii Five-O   ep   3. 17. 77 CBS
    Kingston Confidential   ep   3. 30. 77 NBC
    Nashville 99   ep   4. 8. 77 CBS
    Escape from Bogen County   tf   10. 7. 77 CBS
    Sunshine Christmas   tf   12. 12. 77 NBC
    Elvis   tf   2. 11. 79 ABC
    Barnaby Jones   ep   3. 15. 79, 3. 22. 79 CBS
    Stone   pt   8. 26. 79 ABC
    Vega$ ep   10. 24. 79 ABC
    Disaster on the Coastliner   tf   10. 28. 79 ABC
    Stone   sr   1. 14. 80 ABC
    Wild Times   ms   1. 24. 80, 1. 31. 80 NN
    M*A*S*H   ep   3. 24. 80 CBS
    Walking Tall   ep   2. 14. 81 NBC
    The Private History of a Campaign That Failed   tf   4. 6. 81 PBS
    Trapper John, M. D.   ep   King of the Road 5. 3. 81 CBS
    Of Mice and Men   tf   11. 29. 81 NBC

HIRSCH, JUDD
    A& C:
    The Keegans   tf   5. 3. 76 CBS
    A& C:
    Taxi   sr   9. 12. 78 ABC
    Sooner or Later   tf   3. 25. 79 NBC
    Taxi   sr ret   9. 11. 79 ABC
    The Halloween That Almost Wasn't   sp   10. 28. 79 ABC
    Marriage Is Alive and Well   tf   1. 25. 80 NBC
    Taxi   sr ret   11. 19. 80 ABC
    Taxi   sr ret   10. 8. 81 ABC

HOLBROOK, HAL
    SUPP. :
    The Awakening Land   ms   2. 19. 78, 2. 20. 78, 2. 21. 78 NBC
    Murder by Natural Causes   tf   2. 17. 79 CBS
    Legend of the Golden Gun   tf   4. 10. 79 NBC
    When Hell Was in Session   tf   10. 8. 79 NBC
    The Minnesota Strip   tf   5. 5. 80 ABC
    Omnibus   sp hos   6. 15. 80 ABC
    Omnibus II   sp hos   12. 28. 80 ABC

The Killing of Randy Webster tf 3. 11. 81 CBS
Omnibus III sp hos 7. 19. 81 ABC

HOLLIDAY, POLLY*
　　Alice sr 9. 29. 76 CBS
　　American Short Story ep Bernice Bobs Her Hair 4. 5. 77 PBS
　　Alice sr ret 10. 2. 77 CBS
　　Alice sr ret 9. 24. 78 CBS
　　You Can't Take It with You sp 5. 16. 79 CBS
　　Alice sr ret 9. 23. 79 CBS
　　Flo sr 3. 24. 80 CBS
　　Flo sr ret 10. 27. 80 CBS
　　NBC Live Theatre ep All the Way Home sp 12. 21. 81 NBC

HOLLIMAN, EARL
　　A& C:
　　Checkmate ep The Bold and the Tough 5. 16. 62 CBS
　　SUPP. :
　　Alexander: The Other Side of Dawn tf 5. 16. 77 NBC
　　Police Woman sr ret 10. 25. 77 NBC
　　The Solitary Man tf 10. 9. 79 CBS
　　Where the Ladies Go tf 3. 14. 80 ABC

HOLM CELESTE
　　A& C:
　　Insight ep 5. 25. 75 NN
　　SUPP. :
　　The Love Boat II tf 1. 21. 77 ABC
　　The New Adventures of Wonder Woman ep I Do, I Do 11. 11. 77
　　　　CBS
　　Lucan ep 3. 13. 78 ABC
　　Fantasy Island ep 9. 30. 78 ABC
　　Backstairs at the White House ms ep 2. 5. 79 NBC
　　The Love Boat ep 2. 17. 79 ABC
　　Trapper John, M. D. ep 10. 28. 79 CBS
　　Fantasy Island ep The Winetasters 12. 22. 79 ABC
　　Midnight Lace tf 2. 9. 81 NBC
　　Archie Bunker's Place ep 11. 29. 81, 12. 6. 81 CBS

HOPKINS, ANTHONY
　　SUPP. :
　　Mayflower: The Pilgrims' Adventure tf 11. 21. 79 CBS
　　The Bunker tf 1. 27. 81 CBS
　　Peter and Paul tf 4. 12. 81, 4. 14. 81 CBS

HOPKINS, BO
　　A& C:
　　The Guns of Will Sonnett ep 11. 29. 68 ABC
　　Cat Ballou pt 9. 5. 71 NBC
　　Doc Elliot pt 3. 5. 73 ABC
　　Hawaii Five-O ep One Big Happy Family 10. 2. 73 CBS
　　The Runaway Barge tf 3. 24. 75 NBC
　　The Rookies ep 3. 31. 75 ABC

SUPP. :
Woman on the Run   pt   9. 7. 77 CBS
Aspen   ms   11. 5. 77, 11. 6. 77, 11. 7. 77 NBC
Thaddeus Rose and Eddie   tf   2. 24. 78 CBS
Having Babies   tf   3. 21. 78 ABC
Crisis in Sun Valley   tf   3. 29. 78 NBC
The Busters   pt   5. 28. 78 CBS
Supertrain   ep   3. 14. 79 NBC
Charlie's Angels   ep   Love Boat Angels 9. 12. 79 ABC
Last Ride of the Dalton Gang   tf   11. 20. 79 NBC
Beggarman, Thief   tf   11. 26. 79, 11. 27. 79 NBC
The Plutonium Incident   tf   3. 11. 80 CBS
Casino   tf   8. 1. 80 ABC
Rodeo Girl   tf   9. 17. 80 CBS
Dynasty   sr   1. 12. 81 ABC

HOUSEMAN, JOHN*
Six Million Dollar Man   ep   Kill Oscar (part 2) 10. 31. 76 ABC
Bionic Woman   ep   Kill Oscar 10. 27. 76, 11. 3. 76 (parts 1 & 2) ABC
Washington: Behind Closed Doors   ms   9. 6-11. 77 ABC
American Short Story   ep   The Displaced Person 10. 14. 77 PBS
Aspen   ms   11. 5. 77, 11. 7. 77 NBC
Hollywood Television Theatre   ep   Six Characters in Search of
   an Author 1. 12. 78 PBS
The Paper Chase   sr   9. 9. 78 CBS
The French-Atlantic Affair   ms   11. 15. 79, 11. 16. 79, 11. 18. 79 ABC
The Hallmark Hall of Fame   ep   Gideon's Trumpet   sp   4. 30. 80
   CBS
The Associates   ep   3. 27. 80 ABC
Tales of the Unexpected   sr hos   9. 80 NN
The Baby Sitter   tf   11. 28. 80 ABC
A Christmas Without Snow   tf   12. 9. 80 CBS
Tales of the Unexpected   sr ret hos   10. 81 NN

HOWARD, KEN
SUPP. :
The Hallmark Hall of Fame   ep   The Court Martial of George
   Armstrong Custer   sp   12. 1. 77 NBC
Superdome   tf   1. 9. 78 ABC
The Critical List   tf   9. 11. 78, 9. 12. 78 NBC
The White Shadow   sr   11. 27. 78 CBS
The White Shadow   sr ret   9. 17. 79 CBS
The White Shadow   sr ret   10. 16. 80 CBS
Father Damien: The Leper Priest   tf   10. 27. 80 NBC
The Body Human: Facts for Boys   sp hos   11. 5. 80 CBS

HOWARD, RON (previously listed as Ronny Howard)
A&C:
The June Allyson Show   ep   Child Lost 11. 16. 59 CBS
Love, American Style   ep   Love and the Happy Days 2. 25. 72 ABC
Laverne and Shirley   ep   10. 26. 76 ABC
SUPP. :
American Short Story   ep   I'm a Fool 4. 5. 77 PBS

Happy Days   sr ret   9. 13. 77 ABC
Happy Days   sr ret   9. 12. 78 ABC
Happy Days   sr ret   9. 11. 79 ABC
Act of Love   tf   9. 24. 80 NBC
Fonz and the Happy Days Gang   sr vo   11. 8. 80 ABC
Bitter Harvest   tf   5. 18. 81 NBC
Fire on the Mountain   tf   11. 23. 81 NBC
Insight   ep   Needle's Eye 11. 26. 81 NN

HOWARD, SUSAN
   SUPP. :
   Most Wanted   ep   4. 4. 77 ABC
   Killer on Board   tf   10. 10. 77 NBC
   Barnaby Jones   ep   10. 13. 77 CBS
   Superdome   tf   1. 9. 78 ABC
   The Busters   pt   5. 28. 78 CBS
   Dallas   sr   3. 16. 79 CBS
   Julie Farr, M. D.   ep   6. 12. 79 ABC
   Vega$ ep   12. 12. 79 ABC
   The Love Boat   ep   The Baby Alarm 11. 29. 80 ABC
   Dallas   sr ret   10. 9. 81 CBS

HOWARD, TREVOR
   SUPP. :
   Legend of the Black Hand   ms ep   8. 24. 78 ABC
   Great Performances   ep   Staying On 5. 11. 81 PBS

HOWLAND, BETH*
   The Mary Tyler Moore Show   ep   Have I Got a Guy for You
      11. 18. 72 CBS
   Love American Style   ep   Love and the Cover 12. 28. 73 ABC
   CBS Triple Play   ep   The Ted Bessell Show   pt   5. 8. 73 CBS
   The Mary Tyler Moore Show   ep   Mary Richards Falls in Love
      11. 22. 75 CBS
   Alice   sr   9. 29. 76 CBS
   Eight Is Enough   ep   9. 14. 77 ABC
   Alice   sr ret   10. 2. 77 CBS
   Alice   sr ret   9. 24. 78 CBS
   The Love Boat   ep   Second String Mom 5. 12. 79 ABC
   You Can't Take It with You   sp   5. 16. 79 CBS
   Alice   sr ret   9. 23. 79 CBS
   Alice   sr ret   11. 2. 80 CBS
   Alice   sr ret   10. 4. 81 CBS
   The Love Boat   ep   11. 21. 81 CBS

HUBLEY, SEASON*
   Bobby Jo and the Big Apple Good Time Band   pt   3. 31. 72 CBS
   The Partridge Family   ep   The Princess and the Partridge
      9. 29. 72 ABC
   She Lives   tf   9. 12. 73 ABC
   The Healers   tf   5. 22. 74 NBC
   The Rookies   ep   Time to Mourn 11. 4. 75 ABC
   Good Heavens   ep   3. 22. 76 ABC

Family   ep   3. 23. 76 ABC
Starsky and Hutch   ep   2. 12. 77 ABC
SST--Death Flight   tf   2. 25. 77 ABC
Kojak   ep   3. 15. 77 CBS
Westside Medical   ep   3. 15. 77 ABC
Family   ep   3. 22. 77 ABC
Visions   ep   All I Could See from Where I Stood 11. 20. 77 PBS
Loose Change   ms   2. 26. 78, 2. 27. 78, 2. 28. 78 NBC
Mrs. R's Daughter   tf   9. 19. 79 NBC
Elvis   tf   2. 11. 79 ABC

HUDDLESTON, DAVID*
Sarge: The Badge or the Cross   tf   2. 22. 71 NBC
The Priest Killer   tf   9. 14. 71 NBC
McMillan and Wife   ep   Murder by the Barrel 9. 29. 71 NBC
Bonanza   ep   Bushwacked 10. 3. 71 NBC
Partners   ep   10. 16. 71 NBC
Suddenly Single   tf   10. 19. 71 ABC
Brian's Song   tf   11. 30. 71 ABC
The Homecoming   tf   12. 19. 71 CBS
Longstreet   ep   12. 30. 71 ABC
Medical Center   ep   The Choice 2. 9. 72 CBS
Temperatures Rising   ep   9. 26. 72 ABC
The Rookies   ep   The Bear That Didn't Get Up 10. 23. 72 ABC
The Sixth Sense   ep   10. 28. 72 ABC
The Waltons   ep   The Writer 11. 30. 72 CBS
Bonanza   ep   The Hidden Enemy 11. 28. 72 NBC
Tenafly   tf   2. 21. 73 NBC
Brock's Last Case   tf   3. 5. 73 NBC
Hawkins on Murder   tf   3. 13. 73 CBS
Gunsmoke   ep   The Widow Maker 10. 8. 73 CBS
Tenafly   sr   10. 10. 73 NBC
The New Adventures of Perry Mason   ep   The Case of the
    Deadly Deeds 10. 21. 73 CBS
Kung Fu   ep   The Salamander 12. 6. 73 ABC
The New Dick Van Dyke Show   ep   12. 31. 73 CBS
Heatwave   tf   1. 26. 74 ABC
Ironside   ep   Come Eleven, Come Twelve 3. 7. 74 NBC
The Snoop Sisters   ep   A Black Day for Bluebeard 3. 19. 74 NBC
The Gun and the Pulpit   tf   4. 3. 74 ABC
Dirty Sally   ep   4. 19. 74 CBS
Petrocelli   sr   9. 18. 74 NBC
Paper Moon   ep   9. 26. 74 ABC
Nakia   ep   10. 5. 74 ABC
The Mary Tyler Moore Show   ep   11. 16. 74 CBS
Gunsmoke   ep   11. 18. 74 CBS
The Rookies   ep   Test of Courage 12. 2. 74 ABC
Kung Fu   ep   1. 25. 75 ABC
Emergency   ep   3. 1. 75 NBC
Karen   ep   4. 10. 75 ABC
Police Woman   ep   The Purge 11. 25. 75 NBC
The Rockford Files   ep   The Reincarnation of Angie 12. 5. 75
    NBC

The Oregon Trail   tf   1. 10. 76 NBC
Bronk   ep   1. 25. 76 CBS
Hawaii Five-O   ep   2. 26. 76 CBS
Shark Kill   tf   5. 20. 76 CBS
Spencer's Pilots   ep   11. 19. 76 CBS
The Practice   ep   12. 29. 76 NBC
Once an Eagle   ms   12. 2. 76, 12. 9. 76, 12. 16. 76, 12. 23. 76,
   12. 30. 76, 1. 6. 77, 1. 13. 77 NBC
Barnaby Jones   ep   1. 27. 77 CBS
How the West Was Won   ep   2. 7. 77 ABC
Tales of the Unexpected   ep   2. 23. 77 NBC
The Waltons   ep   3. 17. 77 CBS
Winner Take All   pt   4. 1. 77 CBS
The Kallikaks   sr   8. 3. 77 NBC
The Young Pioneers   ep   4. 2. 78 ABC
Kate Bliss and the Ticker Tape Kid   tf   5. 26. 78 ABC
Kaz   ep   2. 28. 79 CBS
Hizzoner   sr   5. 17. 79 NBC
The Oklahoma City Dolls   tf   1. 23. 81 ABC
Family Reunion   tf   10. 11. 81, 10. 12. 81 NBC

HUDSON, ROCK
   SUPP. :
   Wheels   ms   5. 7. 78, 5. 8. 78, 5. 9. 78, 5. 14. 78, 5. 15. 78 NBC
   The Martian Chronicles   ms   1. 27. 80, 1. 28. 80, 1. 29. 80 NBC
   The Star Maker   tf   5. 11. 81, 5. 12. 81 NBC

HUGHES, BARNARD
   A&C:
   Love Story   ep   All My Tomorrows 10. 10. 73 NBC
   The Bob Newhart Show   ep   12. 25. 76 CBS
   SUPP. :
   Hawaii Five-O   2. 17. 77 CBS
   Ransom for Alice   tf   6. 2. 77 NBC
   Kill Me If You Can   tf   9. 25. 77 NBC
   Lou Grant   ep   11. 15. 77 CBS
   G. E. Theatre   ep   Tell Me My Name   sp   12. 20. 77 CBS
   The Bob Newhart Show   ep   1. 14. 78 CBS
   The World Beyond   pt   1. 27. 78 CBS
   See How She Runs   tf   2. 1. 78 CBS
   Sanctuary of Fear   tf   4. 23. 79 NBC
   Homeward Bound   tf   11. 19. 80 CBS
   Mr. Merlin   sr   10. 7. 81 CBS
   Most Joyful Mystery   sp   12. 24. 81 NN

HUNNICUTT, GAYLE
   A&C:
   Fall of Eagles   sp   12. 26. 76 NN
   SUPP. :
   The Million Dollar Face   tf   3. 12. 81 NBC

HUNT, HELEN*
   Pioneer Woman   tf   9. 19. 73 ABC

All Together Now   tf   2.5.76 ABC
Swiss Family Robinson   sr   9.14.75 ABC
Death Scream   tf   9.26.75 ABC
Family   ep   10.19.76 ABC
The Mary Tyler Moore Show   ep   2.19.77 CBS
The Spell   tf   2.20.77 NBC
The Fitzpatricks   sr   9.5.77 CBS
The Bionic Woman   ep   Sanctuary Earth 2.11.78 NBC
Transplant   tf   4.17.79 CBS
Family   ep   12.8.80 ABC
Angel Dusted   tf   2.16.81 NBC
The Miracle of Kathy Miller   tf   10.5.81 CBS
Darkroom   ep   The Bogeyman Will Get You 12.4.81 ABC
Child Bride of Short Creek   tf   12.7.81 NBC
The Two of Us   ep   12.28.81 CBS

HUNTER, KIM
   A&C:
   The Line-Up   ep   The Strange Return of Army Armitage 10.7.59
      CBS
   This Is the Life   ep   10.12.75 NN
   SUPP.:
   The Oregon Trail   ep   9.28.77 NBC
   Project UFO   ep   Sighting 4017: The Devilish Lights Incident
      9.28.78 NBC
   The Hallmark Hall of Fame   ep   Stubby Pringle's Christmas
      sp   12.17.78 NBC
   Insight   ep   1.21.79 NBC
   Backstairs at the White House   ms ep   1.29.79 NBC
   The Rockford Files   ep   3.3.79 NBC
   The Edge of Night   sr   6.27.79 ABC
   The Golden Gate Murders   tf   10.3.79 CBS
   Skokie   tf   11.17.81 CBS

HUNTER, TAB
   SUPP.:
   Forever Fernwood   sr   9.77 NN
   Police Woman   ep   1.4.78 NBC
   Hawaii Five-O   ep   10.5.78 CBS
   Katie: Portrait of a Centerfold   tf   10.23.78 NBC
   The Love Boat   ep   Take My Granddaughter, Please 10.29.77
      ABC
   Sweepstakes   ep   3.9.79 NBC
   The Kid from Left Field   tf   9.30.79 NBC
   Charlie's Angels   ep   Nips and Tucks 3.5.80 ABC
   Strike Force   ep   Night Nurse 12.18.81 ABC

HUTTON, JIM
   A&C:
   Don't Be Afraid of the Dark   tf   10.10.73 ABC
   SUPP.:
   Flying High   tf   8.28.78 CBS
   Sweepstakes   ep   3.9.79 NBC

The World of Disney   ep   Skytrap 5. 13. 79 NBC
Butterflies   pt   8. 1. 79 NBC

HUTTON, LAUREN
 SUPP. :
 The Rhinemann Exchange   ms   3. 10. 77,   3. 17. 77,   3. 24. 77 NBC
 Someone Is Watching Me   tf   11. 29. 78 NBC

HUTTON, TIMOTHY*
 Friendly Fire   tf   4. 22. 79 ABC
 The Best Place to Be   tf   5. 27. 79 NBC
 And Baby Makes Six   tf   10. 22. 79 NBC
 Young Love, First Love   tf   11. 20. 79 CBS
 NBC Live Theatre   ep   The Oldest Living Graduate   sp   4. 7. 80
  NBC
 Disney's Wonderful World   ep   Sultan and the Rock Star 4. 20. 80
  NBC
 Father Figure   tf   10. 26. 80 CBS
 A Long Way Home   tf   12. 6. 81 ABC

HYDE-WHITE, WILFRID
 A& C:
 Columbo   ep   5. 2. 76 NBC
 SUPP. :
 Battlestar Galactica   ep   Saga of a Star World 9. 17. 78 ABC
 Vega$ ep   5. 2. 79 ABC
 The Associates   sr   9. 23. 79 ABC
 Laverne and Shirley   ep   2. 11. 80 ABC
 The Associates   sr ret   3. 27. 80 ABC
 Scout's Honor   tf   9. 30. 80 NBC
 Father Damien: The Leper Priest   tf   10. 27. 80 NBC
 Buck Rogers in the 25th Century   sr   1. 15. 81 NBC

HYLAND, DIANA
 A& C:
 Naked City   ep   Stop the Parade!   A Baby Is Crying 3. 20. 63
  ABC
 SUPP. :
 Eight Is Enough   sr   3. 15. 77 ABC

HYLANDS, SCOTT
 A& C:
 Police Woman   ep   12. 16. 75 NBC
 Medical Center   ep   3. 15. 76 CBS
 SUPP. :
 Most Wanted   ep   3. 21. 77 ABC
 The Black Sheep Squadron   ep   12. 14. 77 NBC
 With This Ring   tf   5. 5. 78 ABC
 The Winds of Kitty Hawk   tf   12. 17. 78 NBC
 Jennifer: A Woman's Story   tf   3. 5. 79 NBC

INGELS, MARTY
    A&C:
Dan Raven ep Amateur Night 12.9.60 NBC
Dan Raven ep The Satchel Man 12.30.60 NBC
The Detectives ep Tobey's Place 9.29.61 NBC
The Rookies ep Down Home Boy 11.19.73 ABC
    SUPP.:
CHiPs ep 11.24.77 NBC
The Love Boat ep Oh, My Aching Brother 9.30.78 ABC
Family ep 5.10.79 ABC

IRELAND, JILL
    SUPP.:
The Girl, the Gold Watch and Everything pt 6.13.80 NN

IRELAND, JOHN
    SUPP.:
Quincy, M.E. ep 5.27.77 NBC
Little House on the Prairie ep 9.25.78 NBC
The Millionaire tf 12.19.78 CBS
Sweepstakes ep 3.9.79 NBC
Quincy, M.E. ep 11.29.79 NBC
Hawaii Five-O ep 12.11.79 CBS
The Courage of Kovik tf 1.20.80 NBC
Hagen ep 3.29.80 CBS
Tourist pt 7.17.80 NN
Marilyn: The Untold Story tf 9.28.80 ABC
Hart to Hart ep 2.24.81 ABC
Quincy, M.E. ep To Kill in Plain Sight 3.4.81 NBC
Magnum, P.I. ep 4.2.81 CBS

IRVING, AMY*
The Rookies ep 9.16.75 ABC
Police Woman ep 12.9.75 NBC
Happy Days ep 12.16.75 ABC
James Dean tf 2.19.76 NBC
James A. Michener's Dynasty tf 3.13.76 NBC
Panache tf 5.15.76 ABC
Once an Eagle ms 12.2.76, 1.13.77 NBC
American Short Story ep I'm a Fool 4.5.77 PBS

IVES, BURL
    A&C:
Little House on the Prairie ep 12.20.76 NBC
    SUPP.:
Roots ms 1.23-30.77 ABC
The Bermuda Depths tf 1.27.78 ABC
The New Adventures of Heidi tf 12.13.78 NBC

-J-

JACKSON, ANNE
    SUPP.:
    The Family Man   tf   12.19.79 CBS
    A Private Battle   tf   10.7.80 CBS
    Blinded by the Light   tf   12.16.80 CBS

JACKSON, KATE
    SUPP.:
    Charlie's Angels   sr ret   9.14.77 ABC
    James at 15   tf   9.15.77 NBC
    The San Pedro Beach Bums   ep   9.19.77 ABC
    Charlie's Angels   sr ret   9.13.78 ABC
    Topper   tf   11.9.79 ABC
    Inmates: A Love Story   tf   2.13.81 ABC
    Thin Ice   tf   2.17.81 CBS

JACKSON, SHERRY
    A&C:
    Hawaiian Eye   ep   A Scent of Whales 3.7.62 ABC
    SUPP.:
    The Streets of San Francisco   ep   1.6.77 ABC
    Enigma   pt   5.27.77 CBS
    Barnaby Jones   ep   1.26.78 CBS
    The Incredible Hulk   ep   5.19.78 CBS
    Greatest Heroes of the Bible   ep   The Story of Daniel in the
        Lion's Den 11.22.78 NBC
    Brenda Starr, Reporter   pt   1.79 NN
    Fantasy Island   ep   1.22.79 ABC
    Alice   ep   1.6.80 CBS
    Charlie's Angels   ep   Homes Sweet Homes 1.23.80 ABC
    CHiPs   ep   2.16.80 NBC
    Casino   tf   8.1.80 ABC

JACOBI, LOU
    SUPP.:
    Better Late Than Never   tf   10.17.79 NBC
    Saint Peter   pt   3.8.81 NBC
    Enos   ep   3.11.81 CBS

JAECKEL, RICHARD
    A&C:
    Tightrope   ep   The Cracking Point 10.6.59 CBS
    The Rebel   ep   Run, Killer, Run 10.30.60 ABC
    Combat   ep   Gideon's Army 12.31.63 ABC
    Ellery Queen   ep   12.18.75 NBC
    SUPP.:
    Big Hawaii   ep   11.16.77, 11.30.77 NBC
    The Oregon Trail   ep   11.30.77 NBC
    Go West Young Girl   tf   4.27.78 ABC

Centennial   ms ep   The Wagon and the Elephant 10. 29. 78 NBC
Champions: A Love Story   tf   1. 13. 79 CBS
Salvage 1   tf   1. 20. 79 ABC
Salvage 1   sr 1. 29. 79 ABC
Lou Grant   ep   11. 12. 79 CBS
The $5. 20 an Hour Dream   tf   1. 26. 80 CBS
Reward   tf   5. 23. 80 ABC
Charlie's Angels   ep   Island Angels 12. 14. 80 ABC
Hot W. A. C. S.   pt   6. 1. 81 ABC
Little House on the Prairie   ep   Sylvia 2. 9. 81,   2. 16. 81 NBC

JAFFE, SAM
   A&C:
   Bonanza   ep   The Emperor Norton 2. 27. 66 NBC
   SUPP. :
   Kojak   ep   Tears for All Those Who Loved Her 11. 20. 77 CBS
   Flying High   ep   9. 29. 78 CBS
   Buck Rogers in the 25th Century   ep   4. 3. 80 NBC
   The Hallmark Hall of Fame   ep   Gideon's Trumpet   sp   4. 30. 80
      CBS
   Foul Play   ep   2. 2. 81 ABC

JAGGER, DEAN
   SUPP. :
   Hunter   ep   4. 22. 77 CBS
   The Waltons   ep   3. 22. 79 CBS
   This Is the Life   ep   12. 16. 79 NN
   The Hallmark Hall of Fame   ep   Gideon's Trumpet   sp   4. 30. 80
      CBS

JAMES, SHEILA
   SUPP. :
   Whatever Happened to Dobie Gillis?   pt   5. 10. 77 CBS

JANIS, CONRAD
   A&C:
   Cannon   ep   12. 18. 74 CBS
   Manhunter   ep   3. 5. 75 CBS
   Baretta   ep   3. 14. 75 ABC
   The Invisible Man   ep   9. 18. 75 NBC
   The Waltons   ep   9. 23. 75 CBS
   Medical Story   ep   10. 23. 75 NBC
   Police Story   ep   11. 30. 76 NBC
   SUPP. :
   Quark   pt   5. 7. 77 NBC
   Quark   sr   2. 24. 78 NBC
   Mork and Mindy   sr   9. 14. 78 ABC
   Mork and Mindy   sr ret   9. 16. 79 ABC
   Mork and Mindy   sr ret   11. 13. 80 ABC
   Mork and Mindy   sr ret   10. 8. 81 ABC

JANSSEN, DAVID
   A&C:
   Naked City   ep   A Wednesday Night Story 11. 1. 61 ABC

Thriller   ep   The Storm 1. 22. 62 NBC
SUPP. :
A Sensitive, Passionate Man   tf   6. 6. 77 NBC
Police Story   ep   Pressure Point 9. 27. 77 NBC
Superdome   tf   1. 9. 78 ABC
Nowhere to Run   tf   1. 16. 78 NBC
The Word   ms   11. 12. 78, 11. 13. 78, 11. 14. 78, 11. 15. 78 CBS
Centennial   ms ep   The Scream of Eagles 2. 4. 79 NBC
S. O. S. Titanic   tf   9. 23. 79 ABC
The Golden Gate Murders   tf   10. 3. 79 CBS
High Ice   tf   1. 7. 80 NBC
City in Fear   tf   3. 30. 80 ABC

JARRETT, RENNE*
Nancy   sr   9. 17. 70 NBC
In Search of America   tf   3. 23. 71 ABC
Cat Creature   tf   2. 11. 73 CBS
Love, American Style   ep   Love and the Secret Spouse 10. 19. 73
     ABC
ABC's Matinee Today   ep   I Never Said Goodbye 12. 3. 73 ABC
The Family Kovack   tf   4. 5. 74 CBS
The Streets of San Francisco   ep   10. 10. 74 ABC
Barnaby Jones   ep   Death on Deposit 12. 3. 74 CBS
The First 36 Hours of Dr. Durant   tf   5. 13. 75 ABC
Barnaby Jones   ep   A Taste for Murder 12. 4. 75 CBS
Joe Forrester   ep   1. 13. 76 NBC
The New Daughters of Joshua Cabe   tf   5. 29. 76 ABC
Barnaby Jones   ep   A Simple Case of Terror 2. 3. 77 CBS
Most Wanted   ep   2. 26. 77 ABC
Quincy, M. E.   ep   3. 11. 77 NBC
Barnaby Jones   ep   3. 15. 79 CBS
When Hell Was in Session   tf   10. 8. 79 NBC
The Misadventures of Sheriff Lobo   ep   11. 6. 79 NBC
Archie Bunker's Place   ep   Archie Alone 11. 2. 80 CBS
Disney's Wonderful World   ep   Ghosts of Buxley Hall 12. 28. 80 NBC

JEFFREYS, ANNE
A& C:
Police Story   ep   1. 30. 76 NBC
SUPP. :
Vega$ ep   3. 7. 79 ABC
Buck Rogers in the 25th Century   ep   11. 8. 79 NBC

JENS, SALOME
A& C:
Great Ghost Tales   ep   Who's The Fairest One of All? 9. 21. 61
     NBC
The Untouchables   ep   Arsenal 6. 28. 62 ABC
All's Fair   ep   9. 20. 76 CBS
SUPP. :
Mary Hartman, Mary Hartman   sr   1. 6. 76 NN
Mary Hartman, Mary Hartman   sr ret   10. 4. 76 NN
Barnaby Jones   ep   The Reincarnation 11. 17. 77 CBS
Hart to Hart   ep   Harts and Flowers 10. 6. 81 ABC

JILLIAN, ANN*
  The Twilight Zone   ep   Mute 1. 31. 63 CBS
  Hazel   ep   9. 13. 65 CBS
  Kojak   ep   Die Before They Wake 2. 6. 74 CBS
  It's a Living   sr   10. 30. 80 ABC
  Fantasy Island   ep   Delphine 1. 9. 81 ABC
  Fantasy Island   ep   4. 11. 81 ABC
  It's a Living   sr ret   7. 21. 81 ABC
  Making a Living   sr   10. 24. 81 ABC

JOHNSON, ARTE*
  Many Happy Returns   ep   11. 23. 64 CBS
  Love, American Style   ep   Love and the Living Doll 10. 6. 69
    ABC
  Arnold's Closet Review   pt   8. 30. 71 NBC
  Night Gallery   ep   The Flipside of Satan 9. 29. 71 NBC
  Love, American Style   ep   1. 28. 72 ABC
  The Partridge Family   ep   2. 4. 72 ABC
  Call Holme   pt   4. 24. 72 NBC
  The Houndcats   sr vo   9. 9. 72 NBC
  The Partridge Family   ep   1. 12. 73 ABC
  Here's Lucy   ep   1. 2. 74 CBS
  Family Theatre   ep   Married Is Better   sp   1. 9. 74 NBC
  Twice in a Lifetime   tf   3. 16. 74 NBC
  Get Christie Love!   ep   2. 5. 75 ABC
  The Rookies   ep   2. 17. 75 ABC
  Jigsaw John   ep   2. 16. 76 NBC
  Bunco   pt   1. 13. 77 NBC
  The Love Boat   ep   The Painters 12. 24. 77 ABC
  Fantasy Island   ep   9. 16. 78 ABC
  Bud and Lou   tf   11. 15. 78 NBC
  The Sacketts   tf   5. 15. 79, 5. 16. 79 NBC
  Faculty Lounge   pt   5. 31. 79 NBC
  Fantasy Island   ep   12. 15. 79 ABC
  If Things Were Different   tf   1. 16. 80 CBS
  Detour to Terror   tf   2. 22. 80 NBC
  The Love Tapes   tf   5. 9. 80 ABC
  Fantasy Island   ep   10. 25. 80 ABC
  Condominium   ms   11. 20. 80, 11. 24. 80 NN
  A Snow White Christmas   sp vo   12. 19. 80 CBS
  CBS Library: Misunderstood Monsters   ep   Creole   sp vo
    4. 7. 81 CBS
  Fantasy Island   ep   Kid Corey Rides Again 10. 17. 81 ABC

JOHNSON, BEN
  SUPP. :
  Wild Times   ms   1. 24. 80, 1. 31. 80 NN

JOHNSON, VAN
  SUPP. :
  Quincy, M. E.   ep   2. 4. 77 NBC
  Superdome   tf   1. 9. 78 ABC
  Black Beauty   ms   1. 31. 78, 2. 2. 78, 2. 3. 78, 2. 4. 78 NBC
  Getting Married   tf   5. 17. 78 CBS

The Love Boat   ep   Her Own Two Feet 11. 17. 78 ABC
Aloha Paradise   ep   2. 25. 81 ABC

JONES, CAROLYN
  SUPP. :
  Little Ladies of the Night   tf   1. 16. 77 ABC
  Roots   ms ep   1. 27. 77 ABC
  The New, Original Wonder Woman   ep   Wonder Woman in
    Hollywood 2. 16. 77 ABC
  Quincy, M. E.   ep   5. 13. 77 NBC
  Halloween with the Addams Family   sp   10. 30. 77 NBC
  The French-Altantic Affair   ms   3. 15. 79, 3. 16. 79, 3. 18. 79
    ABC
  The Love Boat   ep   10. 27. 79 ABC
  Fantasy Island   ep   11. 10. 79 ABC
  The Dream Merchants   ms   5. 12. 80, 5. 19. 80 NN
  Fantasy Island   ep   11. 29. 80, 2. 7. 81 ABC
  Quincy, M. E.   ep   1. 14. 81 NBC
  Midnight Lace   tf   2. 9. 81 NBC

JONES, DEAN
  A& C:
  Ben Casey   ep   A Fire in the Sacred Fruit Tree 11. 20. 63 ABC
  Good Heavens   ep   6. 26. 76 ABC
  SUPP. :
  When Everyday Was the 4th of July   tf   3. 12. 78 NBC
  The Long Days of Summer   tf   5. 23. 80 ABC
  Aloha Paradise   ep   2. 25. 81 ABC
  I Love Her Anyway   pt   8. 3. 81 ABC

JONES, HENRY
  A& C:
  Alcoa Premiere   ep   Of This Time, of That Place 3. 6. 62 ABC
  The Outlaws   ep   Ride the Man Down 3. 8. 62 NBC
  Kung Fu   ep   10. 19. 74 ABC
  SUPP. :
  Tail Gunner Joe   tf   2. 6. 77 NBC
  Barney Miller   ep   10. 19. 78 ABC
  Quincy, M. E.   ep   A Test for Living 10. 19. 78 NBC
  Project UFO   ep   11. 2. 78 NBC
  Lucan   ep   11. 20. 78 ABC
  Salvage 1   ep   1. 29. 79 ABC
  Turnabout   ep   2. 2. 79 NBC
  Mrs. Columbo   sr   2. 26. 79 NBC
  This Is the Life   ep   10. 7. 79 NN
  Kate Loves a Mystery   sr   10. 18. 79 NBC
  Here's Boomer   ep   5. 2. 80 NBC
  Fantasy Island   ep   11. 22. 80 ABC
  B. J. and the Bear   ep   Adults Only 3. 10. 81 NBC
  California Gold Rush   tf   7. 30. 81 NBC
  Quincy, M. E.   ep   The Golden Hour 11. 4. 81 NBC
  CHiPs   ep   Diamond in the Rough 11. 22. 81 NBC

JONES, JAMES EARL
    SUPP. :
    Jesus of Nazareth   ms   4. 3. 77, 4. 10. 77 NBC
    The Greatest Thing That Almost Happened   tf   10. 26. 77 CBS
    Roots: The Next Generations   ms ep   2. 25. 79 ABC
    Paris   sr   9. 29. 79 CBS
    Guyana Tragedy: The Story of Jim Jones   tf   4. 15. 80 CBS
    The Golden Moment: An Olympic Love Story   tf   5. 25. 80,
       5. 26. 80 NBC
    Summershow 1980   sr hos   7. 7. 80 NN
    CBS Library: Misunderstood Monsters   ep   Beauty and the
       Beast   nar   4. 7. 81 CBS

JONES, SHIRLEY
    SUPP. :
    McMillan   ep   1. 23. 77 NBC
    Yesterday's Child   tf   2. 3. 77 NBC
    Evening in Byzantium   ms   8. 14. 78, 8. 15. 78 NN
    Who'll Save Our Children?   tf   12. 16. 78 CBS
    Last Cry for Help   tf   1. 19. 79 ABC
    Shirley   sr   10. 26. 79 NBC
    The Children of An Lac   tf   10. 9. 80 CBS
    Inmates: A Love Story   tf   2. 13. 81 ABC

JORY, VICTOR
    A& C:
    The New Breed   ep   Cross the Little Line 1. 9. 62 ABC
    Hawaiian Eye   ep   They'll Be Some Changes Made 10. 16. 62
       ABC
    SUPP. :
    Tales of the Unexpected   ep   2. 9. 77 NBC
    The Rockford Files   ep   1. 6. 78 NBC
    Devil Dog: The Hound of Hell   tf   10. 31. 78 CBS
    Greatest Heroes of the Bible   sr nar/ep   The Story of Samson
       and Delilah 11. 19. 78 NBC
    Greatest Heroes of the Bible   sr ret nar   5. 8. 79 NBC
    Young Maverick   ep   1. 9. 80 CBS
    Power   tf   1. 14. 80, 1. 5. 80 NBC
    Greatest Heroes of the Bible   nar ep   Daniel and King Nebuch-
       adnezzar 7. 26. 81 NBC
    Greatest Heroes of the Bible   nar ep   The Story of Esther
       7. 26. 81 NBC
    Greatest Heroes of the Bible   nar ep   Abraham's Sacrifice
       8. 15. 81 NBC

JOURDAN, LOUIS
    SUPP. :
    Man in the Iron Mask   tf   1. 17. 77 NBC
    Great Performances   ep   Dracula (sr)   3. 1. 78 PBS
    The French-Atlantic Affair   ms   11. 15. 79, 11. 16. 79, 11. 18. 79
       ABC
    Charlie's Angels   ep   Nips and Tucks 3. 5. 80 ABC
    Aloha Paradise   ep   2. 25. 81 ABC

JOYCE, ELAINE
  SUPP. :
  The Feather and Father Gang ep   6. 18. 77 ABC
  Quincy, M. E.   ep   9. 16. 77 NBC
  James at 15   ep   12. 22. 77 NBC
  The Love Boat   ep   The Nubile Nurse 2. 25. 78 ABC
  Charlie's Angels   ep   Angel on the Run 5. 3. 78 ABC
  Project UFO   ep   5. 27. 78 NBC
  A Guide for the Married Woman   tf   10. 13. 78 ABC
  CHiPs   ep   10. 21. 78 NBC
  Sword of Justice   ep   10. 28. 78 NBC
  The Love Boat   ep   Gopher's Opportunity 1. 20. 79 ABC
  Sweepstakes   ep   1. 26. 79 NBC
  Delta House   ep   3. 17. 79 ABC
  Alone at Last   pt   6. 24. 80 NBC
  The Ugily Family   pt   7. 26. 80 ABC
  Fantasy Island   ep   12. 6. 80 ABC
  The Incredible Hulk   ep   4. 17. 81 CBS
  Mr. Merlin   sr   10. 7. 81 CBS
  The Love Boat   ep   He's My Brother 12. 5. 81 ABC
  Hart to Hart   ep   'Tis the Season to Be Murdered 12. 22. 81
    ABC

JUMP, GORDON*
  Green Acres   ep   3. 19. 69 CBS
  The Partridge Family   ep   9. 25. 70, 11. 12. 71 ABC
  The New Dick Van Dyke Show   ep   1. 22. 72 CBS
  The Partridge Family   ep   3. 3. 72 ABC
  The Mary Tyler Moore Show   ep   12. 23. 72 CBS
  The Partridge Family   ep   12. 29. 72 ABC
  A Touch of Grace   ep   3. 17. 73 ABC
  The Partridge Family   ep   The Strike-Out King 10. 6. 73 ABC
  The Partridge Family   ep   Art for Mom's Sake 1. 12. 74 ABC
  Chase   ep   1. 23. 74 NBC
  Paul Sand in Friends and Lovers   ep   11. 9. 74 CBS
  Harry O   ep   Lester II 9. 25. 75 ABC
  The ABC Afterschool Special   ep   Fawn Story   sp   10. 22. 75 ABC
  The Bionic Woman   ep   Welcome Home, Jaime 1. 21. 76 ABC
  Alice   ep   10. 13. 76 CBS
  Archie   pt   12. 19. 76 ABC
  The Black Sheep Squadron   ep   3. 8. 77 NBC
  The Hardy Boys/Nancy Drew Mysteries   ep   6. 5. 77 ABC
  Good Times   ep   10. 19. 77 CBS
  Soap   ep   12. 13. 77 ABC
  Ruby and Oswald   tf   2. 8. 78 CBS
  WKRP in Cincinnati   sr   9. 18. 78 CBS
  WKRP in Cincinnati   sr ret   9. 17. 79 CBS
  Goldie and the Boxer   tf   12. 30. 79 NBC
  The Love Boat   ep   4. 19. 80 ABC
  WKRP in Cincinnati   sr ret   11. 1. 80 CBS
  Project Peacock   ep   The Big Stuffed Dog   sp   2. 8. 81 NBC
  Midnight Offerings   tf   2. 27. 81 ABC
  WKRP in Cincinnati   sr ret   10. 7. 81 CBS

-K-

KAHAN, JUDY*
    Doc   sr 9.13.75 CBS
    All's Fair   sr 9.20.76 CBS
    Free Country   sr 6.24.78 ABC
    Mary   sr 9.24.78 CBS
    Love, Natalie   pt 7.11.80 NBC

KAPLAN, GABE
    SUPP.:
    Welcome Back, Kotter   sr ret 9.15.77 ABC
    Welcome Back, Kotter   sr ret 11.11.78 ABC
    Lewis and Clark   sr 10.29.81 NBC

KAPLAN, MARVIN
    SUPP.:
    Alice   sr 10.2.77 CBS
    Alice   sr ret 9.24.78 CBS
    Alice   sr ret 9.23.79 CBS
    Alice   sr ret 11.2.80 CBS
    Alice   sr ret 10.4.81 CBS

KASZNAR, KURT
    A&C:
    Adventures in Paradise   ep   The Black Pearl 10.12.59 ABC
    SUPP.:
    Young Dan'l Boone   ep 10.10.77 CBS
    Suddenly Love   tf 12.4.78 NBC

KATT, WILLIAM*
    Police Story   ep 9.27.74 NBC
    The Greatest American Hero   sr 3.18.81 ABC
    The Greatest American Hero   sr ret 10.28.81 ABC

KAVNER, JULIE
    SUPP.:
    Rhoda   sr ret 10.2.77 CBS
    Lou Grant   ep 11.29.77 CBS
    Rhoda   sr ret 9.23.78 CBS
    No Other Love   tf 3.24.79 CBS
    Revenge of the Stepford Wives   tf 10.12.80 NBC
    Taxi   ep 11.26.80 ABC

KAYE, DANNY
    SUPP.:
    Skokie   tf 11.17.81 CBS

KAZAN, LAINIE
    A&C:
    Police Surgeon   ep 3.16.75 NN
    SUPP.:
    Columbo   ep   Make Me a Perfect Murder 2.25.78 NBC

Greatest Heroes of the Bible ep Abraham's Sacrifice 8. 15. 81 NBC

KEACH, STACY
  A&C:
  The Deputy ep The Return of Simon Fry 2. 13. 60 NBC
  SUPP. :
  Delvecchio ep 1. 2. 77 CBS
  Jesus of Nazareth 4. 3. 77, 4. 10. 77 NBC
  Project UFO ep 4. 9. 78 NBC
  A Rumor of War tf 9. 24. 80, 9. 25. 80 CBS

KEEL, HOWARD
  SUPP. :
  Dallas sr 2. 20. 81 CBS
  Dallas sr ret 10. 9. 81 CBS

KEITH, BRIAN
  A&C:
  Insight ep 9. 22. 74 NN
  The Quest tf 5. 13. 76 NBC
  SUPP. :
  In the Matter of Karen Ann Quinlan tf 9. 26. 77 NBC
  The Hallmark Hall of Fame ep The Court Martial of George
    Armstrong Custer sp 12. 1. 77 NBC
  How the West Was Won ep 2. 19. 78 ABC
  Centennial ms ep The Storm 1. 14. 79 NBC
  Centennial ms ep The Crime 1. 21. 79 NBC
  Centennial ms ep The Winds of Fortune 1. 28. 79 NBC
  The Chisholms ms ep 4. 19. 79 CBS
  The Seekers ms 12. 3. 79, 12. 4. 79 NN
  Power tf 1. 14. 80, 1. 15. 80 NBC
  Moviola: The Silent Lovers tf 5. 20. 80 NBC

KELLERMAN, SALLY
  SUPP. :
  Great Performances ep Verna: USO Girl 1. 25. 78 PBS
  Centennial ms ep Only the Banks Live Forever 10. 1. 78 NBC
  Centennial ms ep The Yellow Apron 10. 8. 78 NBC
  Centennial ms ep The Wagon and the Elephant 10. 28. 78 NBC
  Centennial ms ep For As Long As the Water Flows 11. 4. 78
    NBC

KELLY, JACK
  A&C:
  Kraft Mystery Theatre ep Shadow of a Man 6. 19. 63 NBC
  SUPP. :
  The Bionic Woman ep Claws 1. 5. 77 ABC
  Quincy, M. E. ep 2. 18. 77 NBC
  The Rockford Files ep 9. 16. 77 NBC
  The Hardy Boys sr 11. 5. 78 ABC
  Vega$ ep 4. 25. 78 ABC
  The New Maverick tf 9. 3. 78 ABC
  B. J. and the Bear ep Detective Finger, I Presume 5. 2. 81
    NBC

KELLY, ROZ*
    Starsky and Hutch   ep   10. 15. 75 ABC
    Happy Days   ep   Fonzie Finds Romance 9. 21. 76, 9. 28. 76 ABC
    Starsky and Hutch   ep   The Las Vegas Strangler 9. 25. 76 ABC
    Blansky's Beauties   ep   2. 12. 77 ABC
    Curse of the Black Widow   tf   9. 16. 77 ABC
    Starsky and Hutch   ep   9. 24. 77 ABC
    Kojak   ep   May the Horse Be with You 2. 25. 78 CBS
    Baretta   ep   5. 18. 78 ABC
    The Love Boat   ep   The Minister and the Stripper 11. 17. 78 ABC
    Sword of Justice   ep   12. 17. 78 NBC
    Amateur Night at the Dixie Bar and Grill   tf   1. 8. 79 NBC
    The Dukes of Hazzard   ep   3. 9. 79, 3. 16. 79 CBS
    The Love Boat   ep   11. 10. 79 ABC
    Charlie's Angels   ep   Angels on Skates 11. 21. 79 ABC
    Charlie's Angels   ep   Toni's Boys (a. k. a. The Male Angel
      Affair) 4. 2. 80 ABC
    Murder Can Hurt You!   tf   5. 21. 80 ABC
    Fantasy Island   ep   11. 22. 80 ABC
    Nero Wolfe   ep   5. 5. 81 NBC

KELSEY, LINDA*
    Wide World of Mystery   ep   The Picture of Dorian Gray
      4. 23. 73, 4. 24. 73 ABC
    Emergency   ep   3. 30. 74 NBC
    The Mary Tyler Moore Show   ep   10. 26. 74 CBS
    The Rockford Files   ep   11. 15. 74 NBC
    Barnaby Jones   ep   Dark Homecoming 11. 19. 74 CBS
    Harry O   ep   10. 23. 75 ABC
    Starsky and Hutch   ep   1. 7. 76 ABC
    Eleanor and Franklin   tf   1. 11. 76, 1. 12. 76 ABC
    Doc   ep   1. 31. 76 CBS
    Bert D'Angelo/Superstar   ep   3. 27. 76 ABC
    Captains and the Kings   ms ep   10. 14. 76 NBC
    Most Wanted   ep   10. 23. 76 ABC
    Barnaby Jones   ep   Voice in the Night 12. 2. 76 CBS
    Tales of the Unexpected   ep   2. 9. 77 NBC
    Quincy, M. E.   ep   2. 11. 77 NBC
    Eleanor and Franklin: The White House Years   tf   3. 13. 77 ABC
    Something for Joey   tf   4. 6. 77 CBS
    The Streets of San Francisco   ep   5. 19. 77 ABC
    Lou Grant   sr   10. 18. 77 CBS
    Having Babies   tf   3. 21. 78 ABC
    Lou Grant   sr ret   9. 18. 78 CBS
    Lou Grant   sr ret   9. 17. 79 CBS
    Lou Grant   sr ret   9. 22. 80 CBS
    A Perfect Match   tf   10. 5. 80 CBS
    Lou Grant   sr ret   11. 2. 81 CBS

KENNEDY, GEORGE
    A& C:
    Riverboat   ep   River Champion 10. 10. 60 NBC
    The Islanders   ep   Hostage Island 11. 6. 60 ABC

The Virginian   ep   A Gallows for Sam Horn **12. 2. 64** NBC
The Virginian   ep   Nobility of Kings **11. 10. 65** NBC
SUPP. :
Backstairs at the White House   ms ep   **2. 5. 79** NBC
Never Say Never   pt   **7. 11. 79** CBS
The Archer: Fugitive from the Empire   tf   **4. 12. 81** NBC

KENNEDY, JAYNE*
   Banacek   ep   Rocket to Oblivion **2. 12. 74** NBC
   Cover Girls   tf   **5. 18. 77** NBC
   Police Story   ep   Pressure Point **9. 27. 77** NBC
   The New Adventures of Wonder Woman   ep   Knockout **10. 14. 77**
      CBS
   Trapper John, M. D.   ep   **10. 7. 79** CBS
   The Mysterious Island of Beautiful Women   tf   **12. 1. 79** CBS
   Speak Up America   sr hos   **8. 1. 80** NBC
   The Love Boat   ep   **5. 2. 81** ABC
   Mitchell and Woods   pt   **12. 18. 81** NBC

KENNEDY, MIMI*
   Stockard Channing in Just Friends   sr   **3. 4. 77** CBS
   Getting Married   tf   **5. 17. 78** CBS
   Family   ep   **3. 22. 79**, **5. 10. 79** ABC
   Thin Ice   tf   **2. 17. 81** CBS
   The Two of Us   sr   **4. 6. 81** CBS
   The Two of Us   sr ret   **10. 12. 81** CBS

KERR, DEBORAH
   SUPP. :
   I'd Rather Be Dead   sp hos-nar   **5. 14. 79** NN

KERWIN, LANCE
   A& C:
   Reflections on Murder   tf   **11. 24. 74** ABC
   SUPP. :
   The Death of Richie   tf   **1. 10. 77** NBC
   The New, Original Wonder Woman   ep   The Bushwackers
      1. 29. 77 ABC
   The Bionic Woman   ep   **2. 23. 77** ABC
   The ABC Afterschool Special   ep   The Amazing Awareness of
      Duffy Moon   sp   **3. 23. 77** ABC
   James at 15   tf   **9. 15. 77** NBC
   Young Joe: The Forgotten Kennedy   tf   **9. 18. 77** ABC
   James at 15   sr   **10. 27. 77** NBC
   Salem's Lot   tf   **11. 17. 79**, **11. 24. 79** CBS
   James at 16   sr   **2. 9. 78** NBC
   Family   ep   **11. 23. 78** ABC
   The Boy Who Drank Too Much   tf   **2. 6. 80** CBS
   CBS Library   ep   Flight of the Wild Wolf   sp   **3. 4. 80** CBS
   Hagen   ep   **3. 8. 80** CBS
   Children of Divorce   tf   **11. 24. 80** NBC
   Side Show   tf   **6. 5. 81** NBC
   Advice to the Lovelorn   tf   **11. 30. 81** NBC

KILEY, RICHARD
   A&C:
   The Defenders ep Yankee Go Home 5.2.64 CBS
   Columbo ep 5.5.74 NBC
   SUPP.:
   The Andros Targets ep 3.7.77, 3.14.77 CBS
   Stranger in the Empty Chair sp 3.27.77 NN
   Angel on My Shoulder tf 5.11.80 ABC
   Golden Gate tf 9.25.81 ABC

KIRKLAND, SALLY*
   Hawaii Five-O ep Murder Is a Taxing Affair 10.16.73 CBS
   The Kansas City Massacre tf 9.19.75 ABC
   Bronk ep 10.26.75 CBS
   Baretta ep 1.7.76 ABC
   Griffin and Phoenix tf 2.27.76 ABC
   Shaughnessey pt 9.6.76 NBC
   Captains and the Kings ms ep 11.4.76 NBC
   Kojak ep 11.14.76 CBS
   Stonestreet: Who Killed the Centerfold Model? tf 1.16.77
     NBC
   Starsky and Hutch ep 10.10.78 ABC
   Visions ep Ladies in Waiting 1.8.79 PBS
   Charlie's Angels ep Caged Angels 10.17.79 ABC
   BAD Cats ep 2.8.80 ABC
   Willow B: Women in Prison pt 6.29.80 ABC
   The Georgia Peaches tf 11.8.80 CBS
   Charlie's Angels ep Taxi Angels 2.7.81 ABC

KITT, EARTHA
   SUPP.:
   Police Woman ep 1.11.78 NBC
   To Kill a Cop tf 4.10.78, 4.11.78 NBC

KLUGMAN, JACK
   A&C:
   The Defenders ep Quality of Mercy 9.16.61 CBS
   Naked City ep Stop the Parade! A Baby Is Crying! 3.20.63
     ABC
   SUPP.:
   Quincy, M.E. sr ret 9.16.77 NBC
   Quincy, M.E. sr ret 9.21.78 NBC
   Quincy, M.E. sr ret 9.20.79 NBC
   Quincy, M.E. sr ret 11.12.80 NBC
   Quincy, M.E. sr ret 10.28.81 NBC

KNIGHT, SHIRLEY
   A&C:
   Medical Center ep 11.1.74 CBS
   Return to Earth tf 5.14.76 ABC
   SUPP.:
   The Defection of Simas Kudirka tf 1.23.78 CBS
   Champions: A Love Story tf 1.13.79 CBS
   Playing for Time tf 9.30.80 CBS

KNIGHT, TED*
  The Lieutenant ep Tour of Duty 11. 23. 63 NBC
  The Outer Limits ep The Invisible Army 10. 31. 64 ABC
  The Virginian ep Throw a Long Rope 5. 19. 65 NBC
  Run for Your Life ep The Cold, Cold War of Paul Bryan
    9. 13. 65 NBC
  The Wild Wild West ep The Night of the Kraken 11. 1. 68 CBS
  The Mary Tyler Moore Show sr 9. 19. 70 CBS
  The Mary Tyler Moore Show sr ret 9. 18. 71 CBS
  The Mary Tyler Moore Show sr ret 9. 16. 72 CBS
  Of Thee I Sing sp 10. 24. 72 CBS
  The Mary Tyler Moore Show sr ret 9. 15. 73 CBS
  The Mary Tyler Moore Show sr ret 9. 14. 74 CBS
  The Mary Tyler Moore Show sr ret 9. 13. 75 CBS
  The Mary Tyler Moore Show sr ret 9. 25. 76 CBS
  The Ted Knight Show sr 4. 8. 78 CBS
  Too Close for Comfort sr 11. 11. 80 ABC
  Too Close for Comfort sr ret 10. 13. 81 ABC

KNOTTS, DON
  SUPP. :
  Fantasy Island ep 4. 1. 78 ABC
  Fantasy Island ep 2. 17. 79 ABC
  Piper's Pets pt 5. 31. 79 NBC
  Three's Company sr 9. 25. 79 ABC
  The Love Boat ep 10. 20. 79 ABC
  The Love Boat ep Haven't I Seen You? 4. 5. 80 ABC
  Three's Company sr ret 10. 28. 80 ABC
  Three's Company sr ret 10. 6. 81 ABC

KOPELL, BERNIE
  A&C:
  Ben Casey ep What to Her Is Plato? 10. 18. 65 ABC
  The Mary Tyler Moore Show ep 2. 22. 75 CBS
  Spencer's Pilots ep 10. 1. 76 CBS
  SUPP. :
  The Love Boat II tf 1. 21. 77 ABC
  Code R ep 3. 11. 77 CBS
  The New Love Boat (a. k. a. Love Boat III) tf 5. 5. 77 ABC
  The Love Boat sr 9. 24. 77 ABC
  Fantasy Island ep 4. 1. 78 ABC
  Wild About Harry pt 5. 26. 78 NBC
  The Love Boat sr ret 9. 16. 78 ABC
  A Guide for the Married Woman tf 10. 13. 78 ABC
  Greatest Heroes of the Bible ep Joseph and His Brothers
    11. 22. 78 NBC
  Flying High ep 12. 8. 78 CBS
  Sweepstakes ep 2. 23. 79 ABC
  Supertrain ep 4. 7. 79 NBC
  The Love Boat sr ret 9. 15. 79 ABC
  The Love Boat sr ret 10. 25. 80 ABC
  The Love Boat sr ret 10. 10. 81 ABC
  Hart to Hart ep 11. 3. 81 ABC

KURTZ, SWOOSIE*
Kojak   ep   12.5.76 CBS
Mary   sr   9.24.78 CBS
Great Performances   ep   Ah, Wilderness 1.24.79 PBS
Walking Through the Fire   tf   5.15.79 CBS
Great Performances   ep   Uncommon Women and Others 6.20.79
    PBS
Marriage Is Alive and Well   tf   1.25.80 NBC
The Mating Season   tf   12.30.80 CBS
Love, Sidney   sr   10.28.81 NBC

KURTZMAN, KATY*
Mulligan's Stew   tf   6.20.77 NBC
The Awakening Land   ms   2.19.78, 2.20.78, 2.21.78 NBC
When Everyday Was the 4th of July   tf   3.12.78 NBC
Hunters of the Reef   tf   5.20.78 NBC
The New Adventures of Heidi   tf   12.13.78 CBS
Long Journey Back   tf   12.15.78 CBS
Kaz   ep   12.17.78 CBS
The World of Disney   ep   Donovan's Kid 1.14.79, 1.21.79 NBC
How the West Was Won   ep   3.12.79 ABC
The Love Boat   ep   5.5.79 ABC
Julie Farr, M.D.   ep   6.12.79 ABC
Sex and the Single Parent   tf   9.19.79 CBS
Diary of a Teenage Hitchhiker   tf   9.21.79 ABC
Hawaii Five-O   ep   11.8.79 CBS
Trapper John, M.D.   ep   12.30.79 CBS
Dynasty   sr   1.12.81 ABC
Long Journey Back   tf   3.6.81 ABC

KWAN, NANCY
SUPP.:
Fantasy Island   ep   11.18.78 ABC

-L-

LADD, CHERYL (a.k.a. Cheryl Jean Stoppelmoor)*
Josie and the Pussycats   sr vo   9.12.70 CBS
Josie and the Pussycats in Outer Space   sr vo   9.9.72 CBS
Search   sr   9.13.72 NBC
Ironside   ep   A Game of Showdown 3.22.73 NBC
Satan's School for Girls   tf   9.19.73 ABC
The Partridge Family   ep   Double Trouble 10.20.73 ABC
The Streets of San Francisco   ep   Blockade 1.24.74 ABC
Happy Days   ep   11.12.74 ABC
Switch   ep   12.2.75 CBS
Switch   ep   12.28.76 CBS
Police Woman   ep   3.8.77 NBC
Code R   ep   6.3.77 CBS

Charlie's Angels   sr   9. 14. 77 ABC
The San Pedro Beach Bums   ep   9. 19. 77 ABC
Charlie's Angels   sr ret   9. 13. 78 ABC
Don Kirshner's Rock Concert   ep   9. 23. 78 NN
Charlie's Angels   sr ret   9. 12. 79 ABC
When She Was Bad   tf   11. 25. 79 ABC
Looking Back, Souveniers   sp   5. 19. 80 ABC
Charlie's Angels   sr ret   11. 30. 80 ABC
Charlie's Angels   sr ret   6. 3. 81 ABC

LADD, DIANE*
    Shane   ep   The Distant Bell 9. 10. 66 ABC
    Ironside   ep   Robert Phillips vs. the Man 10. 10. 68 NBC
    The Devil's Daughter   tf   1. 9. 73 ABC
    Movin' On   ep   11. 4. 75 NBC
    Addie and the King of Hearts   sp   1. 25. 76 CBS
    City of Angels   ep   2. 3. 76, 2. 10. 76, 2. 17. 76 NBC
    Police Story   ep   11. 9. 77 NBC
    Black Beauty   ms   1. 31. 78, 2. 1. 78, 2. 2. 78, 2. 3. 78, 2. 4. 78
        NBC
    Thaddeus Rose and Eddie   tf   2. 24. 78 CBS
    Willa   tf   3. 17. 79 CBS
    The Love Boat   ep   The Captain's Ne'er Do-Well Brother
        2. 2. 80 ABC
    Alice   sr   3. 2. 80 CBS
    Guyana Tragedy: The Story of Jim Jones   tf   4. 15. 80 CBS
    Alice   sr ret   11. 2. 80 CBS

LAMAS, FERNANDO
    A&C:
    Combat   ep   Breakout 12. 14. 65 ABC
    SUPP. :
    Quincy, M. E.   ep   1. 2. 77 NBC
    Charlie's Angels   ep   1. 5. 77 ABC
    The Love Boat   ep   1. 21. 78 ABC
    How the West Was Won   ep   4. 23. 79 ABC
    The Dream Merchants   ms   5. 12. 80, 5. 19. 80 NN

LAMAS, LORENZO*
    Whatever Happened to Dobie Gillis?   pt   5. 10. 77 CBS
    Shipshape   pt   8. 1. 78 CBS
    Dear Detective   ep   4. 11. 79 CBS
    California Fever   sr   9. 25. 79 CBS
    Detour to Terror   tf   2. 22. 80 NBC
    Secrets of Midland Heights   sr   12. 6. 80 CBS
    The Love Boat   ep   Matchmaker, Matchmaker Times Two
        11. 29. 80 ABC
    Falcon Crest   sr   12. 4. 81 CBS

LAMOUR, DOROTHY
    SUPP. :
    The Love Boat   ep   12. 20. 80 ABC

LAMPERT, ZOHRA
  SUPP.:
  Hunter ep 4.8.77, 4.22.77 CBS
  Mixed Nuts pt 5.12.77 ABC
  Switch ep 10.14.77, 11.4.77 CBS
  Quincy, M.E. ep 1.27.78 NBC
  Black Beauty ms 1.31.78, 2.1.78, 2.2.78, 2.3.78, 2.4.78
    NBC
  Kojak ep The Halls of Terror 2.18.78 CBS
  Hawaii Five-O ep 10.26.78 CBS
  Lady of the House tf 11.14.78 CBS
  The Suicide's Wife tf 11.7.79 CBS
  The Girl, the Gold Watch and Everything pt 6.13.80 NN
  Secrets of Midland Heights ep 1.3.81 CBS
  The Girl, the Gold Watch and Dynamite pt 5.21.81 NN

LANCASTER, BURT
  SUPP.:
  The Unknown War sr nar 10.7.78 NN

LANCHESTER, ELSA
  SUPP.:
  Where's Poppa? pt 7.17.79 ABC

LANDAU, MARTIN
  A&C:
  Johnny Staccato ep Murder for Credit 9.17.59 NBC
  Tate ep Tiger 8.3.60 NBC
  Shirley Temple Theatre ep The House of Seven Gables 12.11.60
    NBC
  Adventures in Paradise ep Mr. Flotsam 1.23.61 ABC
  Checkmate ep Hot Wind in a Cold Town 6.10.61 CBS
  SUPP.:
  The Death of Ocean View Park tf 10.19.79 ABC
  The Harlem Globetrotters on Gilligan's Island tf 5.15.81 NBC

LANDERS, AUDREY*
  Room 222 ep 3.9.73 ABC
  Marcus Welby, M.D. ep The Light at the Threshold 10.9.73
    ABC
  Emergency ep Computer Error 12.22.73 NBC
  Archie pt 12.19.76 ABC
  The Love Boat ep 10.15.77 ABC
  Police Woman ep 12.6.77 NBC
  Happy Days ep 12.6.77 ABC
  Goober and the Truckers' Paradise pt 5.17.78 CBS
  The Waverly Wonders ep 10.6.78 NBC
  Battlestar Galactica ep 11.19.78 ABC
  Charlie's Angels ep Teen Angels 2.28.79 ABC
  Highcliffe Manor sr 4.12.79 NBC
  The Runaways tf 5.29.79 CBS
  B.J. and the Bear ep 10.27.79 NBC
  Fantasy Island ep 11.10.79 ABC

B. J. and the Bear   ep   12. 1. 79 NBC
Young Maverick   ep   12. 12. 79 CBS
Dallas   sr   1. 16. 81 CBS
Aloha Paradise   ep   4. 15. 81 ABC
White & Reno   pt   5. 31. 81 NBC
Dallas   sr ret   10. 9. 81 CBS
Fantasy Island   ep   Ziegfeld Girls 10. 17. 81 ABC

LANDERS, JUDY*
Daughters   pt   7. 20. 77 NBC
What Really Happened to the Class of '65?   ep   Class Dreamers
    12. 22. 77 NBC
Charlie's Angels   ep   Angels on the Run 2. 22. 78 ABC
Vega$ tf   4. 25. 78 ABC
The Courage and the Passion   tf   5. 27. 78 NBC
Vega$ sr   9. 20. 78 ABC
The Love Boat   ep   Oh, My Aching Brother 9. 30. 78 ABC
The Users   tf   10. 1. 78 ABC
Gossip   pt   6. 10. 79 NBC
The Love Boat   ep   12. 1. 79 ABC
Goldie and the Boxer   tf   12. 30. 79 NBC
Fantasy Island   ep   2. 9. 80 ABC
Buck Rogers in the 25th Century   ep   2. 21. 80 NBC
B. J. and the Bear   sr   1. 13. 81 NBC
White & Reno   pt   5. 31. 81 NBC
Fantasy Island   ep   The Magician 10. 24. 81 ABC

LANDESBERG, STEVE
SUPP. :
Fish   ep   4. 2. 77 ABC
Barney Miller   sr ret   9. 15. 77 ABC
Barney Miller   sr ret   9. 14. 78 ABC
Barney Miller   sr ret   9. 13. 79 ABC
Barney Miller   sr ret   10. 30. 80 ABC
Barney Miller   sr ret   10. 29. 81 ABC

LANDON, MICHAEL
SUPP. :
Little House on the Prairie   sr ret   9. 12. 77 NBC
Little House on the Prairie   sr ret   9. 11. 78 NBC
Little House on the Prairie   sr ret   9. 17. 79 NBC
Little House on the Prairie   sr ret   9. 22. 80 NBC
The Hanna-Barbera Arena Show   sp hos   6. 25. 81 NBC
Little House on the Prairie   sr ret   10. 5. 81 NBC

LANE, ABBE
SUPP. :
Vega$ ep   2. 7. 79 ABC

LANGDON, SUE ANE*
Bachelor Father   sr   1959-61 NBC
Bonanza   ep   The Many Faces of Gideon Flinch 11. 5. 61 NBC
The Man from U. N. C. L. E.   ep   The Skark Affair 10. 13. 64 NBC

Bonanza   ep   Hound Dog 3. 21. 65 NBC
The Wild Wild West   ep   The Night of the Steel Assassin 1. 7. 66
   CBS
Ironside   ep   The Challenge 2. 8. 68 NBC
The Name of the Game   ep   Give Till It Hurts 10. 31. 69 NBC
Arnie   sr   9. 19. 70 CBS
Arnie   sr ret   9. 13. 71 CBS
Love, American Style   ep   12. 17. 71 ABC
The Victim   tf   11. 14. 72 NBC
Honeymoon Suite   pt   3. 12. 73 ABC
Here We Go Again   ep   3. 17. 73 ABC
Wrinkles, Birthdays and Other Fables   sp   10. 29. 73 PBS
Police Story   ep   Collision Course 11. 20. 73 NBC
Banacek   ep   Vanishing Chalice 1. 15. 74 NBC
Grandpa Goes to Washington   sr   9. 7. 78 NBC
When the Whistle Blows   sr   3. 14. 80 ABC
The Love Boat   ep   12. 13. 80 ABC

LANGE, HOPE
   SUPP. :
   The Love Boat II   tf   1. 21. 77 ABC
   The Love Boat   ep   10. 14. 78 ABC
   Like Normal People   tf   4. 13. 79 ABC
   The Day Christ Died   tf   3. 26. 80 CBS
   Beulah Land   ms   10. 7. 80, 10. 8. 80, 10. 9. 80 NBC
   Pleasure Palace   tf   10. 22. 80 CBS

LANSING, ROBERT
   A&C:
   Moment of Fear   ep   Cage of Air 9. 9. 60 NBC
   Bonanza   ep   Cut-Throat Junction 3. 18. 61 NBC
   Insight   ep   3. 23. 75 NN
   SUPP. :
   The Deadly Triangle   tf   5. 19. 77 NBC
   S*H*E   tf   2. 23. 80 CBS
   Life on the Mississippi   tf   11. 24. 80 PBS

LASSER, LOUISE
   SUPP. :
   Just You and Me   tf   5. 22. 78 NBC
   Taxi   ep   12. 3. 80 ABC
   Making a Living   sr   10. 24. 81 ABC
   For Ladies Only   tf   11. 9. 81 NBC

LATHAM, LOUISE*
   The Doctors and the Nurses   ep   Night of the Witch 2. 2. 65 CBS
   Family Affair   ep   9. 12. 66 CBS
   Bonanza   ep   A Real Nice, Friendly Little Town 11. 27. 66 NBC
   The Outsider   ep   10. 9. 68 NBC
   Gunsmoke   ep   12. 9. 68 CBS
   Gunsmoke   ep   The Commandant 2. 3. 69 CBS
   Judd, for the Defense   ep   Between the Dark and the Daylight
      2. 7. 69 ABC

The FBI   ep   2.16.69 ABC
The Name of the Game   ep   The King of Denmark 2.20.70 NBC
The Name of the Game   ep   LA 2017 1.15.71 NBC
The Priest Killer   tf   9.14.71 NBC
McCloud   ep   Encounter with Aries 9.22.71 NBC
Sweet, Sweet Rachel   tf   10.2.71 ABC
The Harness   tf   11.12.71 NBC
Medical Center   ep   Suspected 11.17.71 CBS
The Sixth Sense   ep   3.18.72 ABC
The Streets of San Francisco   ep   11.25.72 ABC
Hec Ramsey   ep   2.18.73 NBC
Dying Room Only   tf   9.18.73 CBS
Hawaii Five-O   ep   10.3.73 CBS
Kojak   ep   Requiem for a Cop 11.28.73 CBS
G.E. Theatre   ep   Tell Me Where It Hurts   sp   3.12.74 ABC
Gunsmoke   ep   3.18.74 CBS
Wide World of Mystery   ep   The Book of Murder 3.19.74 ABC
Winter Kill   tf   4.15.74 ABC
Rhoda   ep   10.7.74 CBS
Medical Center   ep   11.18.74 CBS
Lucas Tanner   ep   12.4.74 NBC
Shell Game   tf   5.9.75 CBS
The Six Million Dollar Man   ep   12.14.75 ABC
Sara   sr   2.13.76 CBS
McNaughton's Daughter   tf   3.4.76 NBC
The Oath   pt   8.24.76 ABC
Stonestreet: Who Killed the Centerfold Model?   tf   1.16.77
   NBC
In the Matter of Karen Ann Quinlan   tf   9.26.77 NBC
Visions   ep   All I Could See from Where I Stood 11.20.77 PBS
The Waltons   ep   12.8.77 CBS
The Awakening Land   ms   2.19.78, 2.20.78, 2.21.78 NBC
Amateur Night at the Dixie Bar and Grill   tf   1.8.79 NBC
Thin Ice   tf   2.17.81 CBS

LAUREN, TAMMY*
   Who's Watching the Kids?   sr   9.22.78 NBC
   Fantasy Island   ep   12.16.78 ABC
   Angie   sr   2.8.79 ABC
   Out of the Blue   sr   9.9.79 ABC
   Quincy, M.E.   ep   The Deadly Arena 9.10.80 NBC
   CHiPs   ep   The Great 5K Race and Boulder Wrap Party 12.7.80
      NBC
   Here's Boomer   ep   Boomer and Miss 21st Century 12.7.80
      NBC
   Nuts and Bolts   pt   8.24.81 ABC

LAURIE, PIPER
   SUPP.:
   In the Matter of Karen Ann Quinlan   tf   9.26.77 NBC
   Rainbow   tf   11.6.78 NBC
   Skag   sr   1.6.80 NBC
   The Bunker   tf   1.27.81 CBS

LAVIN, LINDA
  A&C:
  The Morning After   tf   2. 13. 74 ABC
  SUPP. :
  Alice   sr ret   10. 2. 77 CBS
  Family   ep   10. 25. 77 ABC
  Alice   sr ret   9. 24. 78 CBS
  Like Mom, Like Me   tf   10. 22. 78 CBS
  Kaz   ep   4. 4. 79 CBS
  The Mary Tyler Moore Hour   ep   4. 29. 79 CBS
  Alice   sr ret   9. 23. 79 CBS
  The $5. 20 an Hour Dream   tf   1. 26. 80 CBS
  Alice   sr ret   11. 2. 80 CBS
  Linda in Wonderland   sp   11. 27. 80 CBS
  Alice   sr ret   10. 4. 81 CBS
  A Matter of Life and Death   tf   1. 13. 81 CBS

LAWFORD, PETER
  SUPP. :
  Fantasy Island   tf   1. 14. 77 ABC
  Hawaii Five-O   ep   3. 30. 78 CBS
  Fantasy Island   ep   1. 22. 79 ABC
  The Love Boat   ep   Murder on the High Seas 3. 17. 79 ABC
  Supertrain   ep   4. 14. 79 NBC
  The Mysterious Island of Beautiful Women   tf   12. 1. 79 CBS
  Fantasy Island   ep   12. 20. 80 ABC

LAWRENCE, CAROL
  A&C:
  Cambat   ep   The Furlough 12. 27. 66 ABC
  Marcus Welby, M. D.   ep   The Light At the Threshold 10. 9. 73
    ABC
  SUPP. :
  Three on a Date   tf   2. 17. 78 ABC
  Stranger in Our House   tf   10. 31. 78 NBC
  Greatest Heroes of the Bible   ep   Solomon and Bathsheba
    11. 21. 78, 11. 22. 78 NBC
  Kaz   ep   1. 14. 79 CBS
  The Love Boat   ep   9. 29. 79 ABC
  The CBS Afternoon Playhouse   ep   The House That Half-Jack
    Built   sp   1. 3. 80 CBS
  Mr. and Mrs. Dracula   pt   9. 5. 80 ABC
  The Girl, the Gold Watch and Dynamite   pt   5. 21. 81 NN
  Jacqueline Susann's Valley of the Dolls 1981   tf   10. 19. 81,
    10. 20. 81 CBS
  The Love Boat   ep   10. 31. 81 ABC

LEACHMAN, CLORIS
  A&C:
  Thriller   ep   Girl with a Secret 11. 15. 60 NBC
  SUPP. :
  It Happened One Christmas   tf   12. 11. 77 ABC
  Long Journey Back   tf   12. 15. 78 NBC

Backstairs at the White House   ms ep   1. 29. 79,   2. 5. 79 NBC
Willa   tf   3. 17. 79 CBS
Mrs. R's Daughter   tf   9. 19. 79 NBC
S. O. S. Titanic   tf   9. 23. 79 ABC
NBC Live Theatre   ep   The Oldest Living Graduate   sp   4. 7. 80
     NBC
The Acorn People   tf   3. 2. 81 NBC
Long Journey Back   tf   3. 6. 81 ABC
Advice to the Lovelorn   tf   11. 30. 81 NBC

LEARNED, MICHAEL
     A& C:
     Insight   ep   8. 15. 76 NN
     SUPP. :
     The Waltons   sr ret   9. 15. 77 CBS
     Little Mo   tf   9. 5. 78 NBC
     The Waltons   sr ret   9. 21. 78 CBS
     The Waltons   sr ret   9. 20. 79 CBS
     Nurse   tf   4. 9. 80 CBS
     Off the Minnesota Strip   tf   5. 5. 80 ABC
     Insight   ep   9. 28. 80 NN
     A Christmas Without Snow   tf   12. 9. 80 CBS
     Nurse   sr   4. 2. 81 CBS
     Nurse   sr ret   11. 11. 81 CBS

LEARY, BRIANNE*
     CHiPs   sr   9. 16. 78 NBC
     The Paper Chase   ep   A Case of Detente 4. 17. 79 CBS
     Buck Rogers in the 25th Century   ep   Planet of the Slave Girls
          9. 27. 79 NBC
     The Dream Merchants   ms   5. 12. 80,   5. 19. 80 NN
     Turnover Smith   pt   6. 8. 80 ABC
     Pen 'n' Inc.   pt   8. 15. 81 CBS
     The Fall Guy   ep   The Human Torch 12. 9. 81 ABC

LEE, CHRISTOPHER
     SUPP. :
     Mysteries of the Unknown: The Occult   sp   9. 7. 77 NN
     How the West Was Won   ep   1. 12. 78,   2. 12. 78 ABC
     The Pirate   tf   11. 21. 78,   11. 22. 78 CBS
     Captain America II   pt   11. 23. 79,   11. 24. 79 CBS
     Once Upon a Spy   tf   9. 19. 80 ABC
     Charlie's Angels   ep   From Street Models to Hawaiian Angels
          11. 30. 80 ABC
     Tales of the Haunted   pt hos   7. 12-16. 81 NN
     Goliath Awaits   ms   11. 17. 81,   11. 23. 81 NN

LEE, MICHELE*
     Night Gallery   ep   Since Aunt Ada Came to Stay 9. 29. 71 NBC
     Love, American Style   ep   10. 1. 71,   12. 31. 71 ABC
     Marcus Welby, M. D.   ep   Basic Moment 1. 4. 72 ABC
     Alias Smith and Jones   ep   Which Way to the O. K. Corral?
          2. 10. 72 ABC

Alias Smith and Jones ep Don't Get Mad, Get Even 2. 17. 72
   ABC
Alias Smith and Jones ep 3. 2. 72 ABC
Singles pt 3. 17. 72 CBS
Love, American Style ep 10. 13. 72 ABC
Of Thee I Sing sp 10. 24. 72 CBS
Love, American Style ep 2. 2. 73 ABC
The Michele Lee Show pt 4. 5. 74 CBS
Only with Married Men tf 11. 4. 74 ABC
Dark Victory tf 2. 5. 76 ABC
Over and Out pt 8. 11. 76 NBC
The Love Boat ep 10. 22. 77, 1. 21. 78 ABC
Having Babies tf 3. 28. 78 ABC
Fantasy Island ep 4. 29. 78 ABC
The Love Boat ep 5. 6. 78 ABC
Bud and Lou tf 11. 15. 78 NBC
Fantasy Island ep 12. 7. 79 ABC
Knots Landing sr 12. 27. 79 CBS
Knots Landing sr ret 11. 20. 80 CBS
Knots Landing sr ret 11. 12. 81 CBS

LEIBMAN, RON
   SUPP. :
   The Outside Man pt 4. 8. 77 CBS
   A Question of Guilt tf 2. 21. 78 CBS
   Kaz sr 9. 10. 78 CBS
   Rivkin: Bounty Hunter tf 5. 20. 81 CBS

LEIGH, JANET
   SUPP. :
   Murder at the World Series tf 3. 20. 77 ABC
   Telethon tf 11. 6. 77 ABC
   The Love Boat ep 11. 11. 78 ABC
   Fantasy Island ep 3. 3. 79 ABC
   Mirror, Mirror tf 10. 10. 79 NBC
   The Love Boat ep Locked Away 11. 11. 79 ABC
   Tales of the Unexpected ep I Like It Here in Wilmington
      11. 14. 81 NN

LEMBECK, HARVEY
   A& C:
   Dan Raven ep Buy a Nightmare 1. 6. 61 NBC
   Route 66 ep Blues for the Left Foot 3. 9. 62 CBS
   Chico and the Man ep 2. 25. 76 NBC
   SUPP. :
   Raid on Entebbe tf 1. 9. 77 NBC
   CHiPs ep 1. 19. 78 NBC
   All in the Family ep 11. 5. 78 CBS
   240-Robert ep 10. 15. 79 ABC
   The Love Boat ep 10. 25. 80 ABC

LEMBECK, MICHAEL*
   Gidget Grows Up tf 12. 30. 69 ABC

The Partridge Family   ep   2. 5. 71 ABC
Make Room for Granddaddy   ep   2. 25. 71 ABC
Haunts of the Very Rich   tf   9. 20. 72 ABC
Love, American Style   ep   3. 2. 73 ABC
Blood Sport   tf   12. 5. 73 ABC
Room 222   ep   Cry Uncle 1. 11. 74 ABC
Happy Days   ep   2. 11. 75 ABC
What Really Happened to the Class of '65?   ep   1. 26. 78 NBC
Having Babies III   tf   3. 3. 78 ABC
The Love Boat   ep   Class Reunion 2. 3. 79 ABC
One Day at a Time   sr   10. 21. 79 CBS

LENZ, KAY
   A&C:
   The Weekend Nun   tf   12. 20. 72 ABC
   Owen Marshall, Counselor at Law   ep   3. 14. 73 ABC
   The Streets of San Francisco   ep   Harem 10. 25. 73 ABC
   Petrocelli   ep   12. 17. 75 NBC
   SUPP.:
   Rich Man, Poor Man   ms ep   3. 1. 76, 3. 8. 76, 3. 15. 76 ABC
   Rich Man, Poor Man, Book II   sr   9. 21. 76 ABC
   The Initiation of Sarah   tf   2. 6. 78 ABC
   How the West Was Won   ep   4. 30. 78, 5. 7. 78, 5. 14. 78, 5. 21. 78
      ABC
   The Seeding of Sarah Burns   tf   4. 7. 79 CBS
   Sanctuary of Fear   tf   4. 23. 79 NBC
   Escape   tf   2. 20. 80 CBS
   The Hustler of Muscle Beach   tf   5. 16. 80 ABC

LENZ, RICK (a. k. a. Richard Lenz)
   A&C:
   Owen Marshall, Counselor at Law   ep   N Is For Nightmare
      10. 17. 73 ABC
   Owen Marshall, Counselor at Law   ep   4. 6. 74 ABC
   Hollywood Television Theatre   ep   The Ladies of the Corridor
      4. 10. 75 PBS
   This Is the Life   ep   11. 23. 75 NN
   SUPP.:
   McMillan   ep   1. 2. 77 NBC
   Dynasty   ep   3. 2. 81 ABC
   Palmerstown   ep   5. 19. 81 CBS
   Advice to the Lovelorn   tf   11. 30. 81 NBC

LESLIE, BETHEL
   A&C:
   Riverboat   ep   The Faithless 11. 25. 59 NBC
   Johnny Staccato   ep   The Wild Seed 3. 24. 60 NBC
   The Man from Blackhawk   ep   The Lady in Yellow 6. 17. 60
      ABC
   Adventures in Paradise   ep   Nightmare in the Sun 6. 19. 61 ABC
   Frontier Circus   ep   The Depths of Fear 10. 5. 61 CBS
   Bonanza   ep   The Jacknife 2. 18. 62 NBC

SUPP. :
The White Shadow   ep   11. 27. 78 CBS
The Gift of Love   tf   12. 8. 78 ABC

LINDEN, HAL
SUPP. :
Barney Miller   sr ret   9. 15. 77 ABC
Barney Miller   sr ret   9. 14. 78 ABC
The Mary Tyler Moore Hour   ep   4. 22. 79 CBS
Barney Miller   sr ret   9. 13. 79 ABC
Hal Linden's Big Apple   sp   6. 1. 80 ABC
Father Figure   tf   10. 26. 80 CBS
Barney Miller   sr ret   10. 30. 80 ABC
Barney Miller   sr ret   10. 29. 81 ABC

LINDFORS, VIVECA
A& C:
Five Fingers   ep   Temple of the Swinging Doll 11. 28. 59 NBC
The Nurses   ep   Escape Route 10. 10. 63 CBS
Tenth Level   sp   8. 26. 76 CBS
SUPP. :
A Question of Guilt   tf   2. 21. 78 CBS
Marilyn: The Untold Story   tf   9. 28. 80 ABC
Playing for Time   tf   9. 30. 80 CBS
Mom, the Wolfman and Me   tf   10. 20. 80 NN
The Best Little Girl in the World   tf   5. 11. 81 ABC
For Ladies Only   tf   11. 9. 81 NBC

LINVILLE, LARRY
SUPP. :
Calling Dr. Storm, M. D.   pt   8. 25. 77 NBC
Grandpa Goes to Washington   sr   9. 7. 78 NBC
Barnaby Jones   ep   10. 12. 78 CBS
Supertrain   ep   2. 14. 79 NBC
CHiPs   ep   Chips Goes Roller Disco 9. 22. 79 NBC
The Love Boat   ep   11. 10. 79 ABC
Lou Grant   ep   11. 17. 80 CBS
The Love Boat   ep   April the Ninny 1. 17. 81 ABC
The Love Boat   ep   Return of the Ninny 2. 14. 81 ABC
Fantasy Island   ep   2. 28. 81 ABC
Checking In   sr   4. 9. 81 CBS
The Girl, the Gold Watch and Dynamite   pt   5. 21. 81 NN
Aloha Paradise   ep   3. 11. 81 ABC

LIPTON, PEGGY
SUPP. :
Return of the Mod Squad   tf   5. 18. 79 ABC

LITTLE, CLEAVON
SUPP. :
Supertrain   ep   4. 28. 79 NBC
Uptown Saturday Night   pt   6. 28. 79 NBC
The Love Boat   ep   1. 26. 80 ABC

Fantasy Island ep 5. 2. 81 ABC
Don't Look Back tf 5. 31. 81 ABC

LOCKHART, ANNE*
  Honeymoon Suite pt 7. 26. 72 ABC
  The Sixth Sense ep 9. 30. 72 ABC
  The Hallmark Hall of Fame ep Lisa, Bright and Dark sp
    11. 28. 73 NBC
  Sierra ep 9. 19. 74 NBC
  Get Christie Love! ep 11. 20. 74 ABC
  Happy Days ep 11. 19. 75 NBC
  Barnaby Jones ep 9. 15. 77 CBS
  The Hardy Boys/Nancy Drew Mysteries ep 10. 16. 77 ABC
  Emergency ep 1. 7. 78 NBC
  The Hardy Boys ep 10. 1. 78, 10. 8. 78 ABC
  Project UFO ep 10. 29. 78 NBC
  The Hardy Boys ep 10. 29. 78 ABC
  Battlestar Galactica sr 11. 26. 78 ABC
  B. J. and the Bear ep 10. 20. 79 NBC
  CHiPs ep 10. 27. 79 NBC
  B. J. and the Bear ep 12. 1. 79 NBC
  The Incredible Hulk ep 12. 21. 79 CBS
  Buck Rogers in the 25th Century ep 2. 14. 80 NBC
  Hagen ep 3. 29. 80 CBS

LOCKHART, JUNE
  SUPP. :
  Curse of the Black Widow tf 9. 16. 77 ABC
  Loose Change ms 2. 26. 78, 2. 27. 78, 2. 28. 78 NBC
  The ABC Afterschool Special ep Dinky Hocker sp 11. 15. 78
    ABC
  The Gift of Love tf 12. 8. 78 ABC
  Quincy, M. E. ep 2. 22. 79 NBC
  Greatest Heroes of the Bible ep Jacob's Challenge 3. 18. 79
    NBC
  Walking Through the Fire tf 5. 15. 79 CBS
  Magnum, P. I. ep 2. 12. 81 CBS
  The Greatest American Hero ep Here's Looking at You, Kid
    4. 1. 81 ABC
  Darkroom ep Uncle George 12. 4. 81 ABC

LOCKWOOD, GARY
  A& C:
  The Blue Knight ep 9. 22. 76 CBS
  SUPP. :
  Police Story ep 2. 22. 77 NBC
  Hunter ep 3. 18. 77 CBS
  The Bionic Woman ep 3. 23. 77 ABC
  Starsky and Hutch ep 1. 14. 78 ABC
  The Ghost on Flight 401 tf 2. 19. 78 NBC
  The Incredible Journey of Dr. Meg Laurel tf 1. 2. 79 CBS
  Barnaby Jones ep Man on Fire 9. 20. 79 CBS
  Hawaii Five-O ep 1. 1. 80 CBS

Top of the Hill   ms   2. 6. 80, 2. 7. 80 NN
Trapper John, M. D.   ep   2. 10. 80 CBS
Vega$ ep   11. 19. 80 ABC
Charlie's Angels   ep   Angels of the Deep 12. 7. 80 ABC
The Girl, the Gold Watch and Dynamite   pt   5. 21. 81 NN

LOGGIA, ROBERT
   SUPP. :
   Raid on Entebbe   tf   1. 9. 77 NBC
   Switch   ep   1. 16. 77 CBS
   Police Woman   ep   2. 1. 77 NBC
   The Bionic Woman   ep   2. 23. 77 ABC
   The People vs. Inez Garcia   sp   5. 25. 77 NN
   The Rockford Files   ep   9. 16. 77 NBC
   The Hardy Boys   ep   10. 29. 78 ABC
   Starsky and Hutch   ep   11. 28. 78 ABC
   Sword of Justice   ep   12. 31. 78 NBC
   Vega$ ep   1. 17. 79 ABC
   Hawaii Five-O   ep   3. 1. 79 CBS
   No Other Love   tf   3. 24. 79 CBS
   Kaz   ep   4. 4. 79 CBS
   Vega$ ep   10. 17. 79, 3. 5. 80 ABC
   Charlie's Angels   ep   The Male Angel Affair (a. k. a. Toni's
      Boys) 4. 2. 80 ABC
   Magnum, P. I.   ep   12. 11. 80 CBS
   Enos   ep   2. 18. 81 CBS

LONGAKER, RACHEL*
   The Waltons   sr   11. 18. 76 CBS
   Little House on the Prairie   ep   1. 24. 77 NBC
   The ABC Afterschool Special   ep   My Mom's Having a Baby
      sp   2. 16. 77 ABC
   The San Pedro Beach Bums   ep   10. 17. 77 ABC
   The Waltons   sr ret   11. 17. 77 CBS
   The Waltons   sr ret   10. 26. 78 CBS
   The Waltons   sr ret   10. 11. 79 CBS
   The ABC Weekend Special   ep   The Girl with E. S. P. 10. 20. 79
      ABC
   The ABC Afterschool Special   ep   Where Do Teenagers Come
      From? 3. 5. 80 ABC
   The ABC Afterschool Special   ep   My Mother Was Never a Kid
      3. 18. 81 ABC

LORD, JACK
   A&C:
   Stagecoach West   ep   The Butcher 3. 28. 61 ABC
   Dr. Kildare   ep   A Willing Suspension of Disbelief 1. 9. 64 NBC
   Combat   ep   The Linesman 10. 5. 65 ABC
   SUPP. :
   Hawaii Five-O   sr ret   9. 15. 77 CBS
   Hawaii Five-O   sr ret   9. 28. 78 CBS
   Hawaii Five-O   sr ret   9. 79 CBS
   M Station: Hawaii   tf   6. 10. 80 CBS
   Hawaii Five-O   sr ret   10. 80 CBS

LORD, MARJORIE
SUPP.:
The Nancy Drew Mysteries ep Mystery of the Fallen Angels
4. 17. 77 ABC
Fantasy Island ep 2. 18. 78 ABC
The Pirate tf 11. 21. 78, 11. 22. 78 CBS

LOREN, SOPHIA*
The Hallmark Hall of Fame ep Brief Encounter sp 11. 12. 74
NBC
Sophia Loren: Her Own Story tf 10. 26. 80 NBC

LOUISE, TINA
SUPP.:
SST--Death Flight tf 2. 25. 77 ABC
Dallas ep 4. 16. 78 CBS
The Love Boat ep Second Time Around 1. 13. 79 ABC
Dallas ep 2. 2. 79 CBS
CHiPs ep Chips Goes Roller Disco 9. 22. 79 NBC
Friendships, Secrets and Lies tf 12. 3. 79 NBC
Fantasy Island ep Elizabeth 1. 12. 80 ABC
The Day the Women Got Even tf 12. 4. 80 NBC
CHiPs ep The Great 5K Race and Boulder Wrap Party 12. 7. 80
NBC
Advice to the Lovelorn tf 11. 30. 81 NBC

LOY, MYRNA
SUPP.:
It Happened at Lakewood Manor tf 12. 2. 77 ABC
Summer Solstice sp 12. 30. 81 ABC

LUCKINBILL, LAURENCE
SUPP.:
Columbo ep Make Me a Perfect Murder 2. 25. 78 NBC
Barnaby Jones ep Echo of a Distant Battle 1. 11. 79 CBS
Ike ms 5. 3. 79, 5. 4. 79, 5. 6. 79 ABC
Great Performances ep The Five-Forty-Eight 11. 7. 79 PBS
Return of the Saint ep The Roman Touch 6. 27. 80 CBS
The Mating Season tf 12. 30. 80 CBS
Momma the Detective pt 1. 9. 81 NBC

LUKE, KEYE
SUPP.:
Vega$ ep 1. 31. 79 ABC
How the West Was Won ep 4. 16. 79 ABC
Brothers pt 7. 30. 80 CBS
Charlie's Angels ep Island Angels 12. 14. 80 ABC
Fly Away Home tf 9. 18. 81 ABC
Unit 4 pt 9. 29. 81 CBS
Bret Maverick ep The Yellow Rose 12. 22. 81 NBC

LUNA, BARBARA
A&C:
Side by Side pt 7. 27. 76 CBS

Brenda Starr   tf   5. 8. 76 ABC
SUPP. :
Switch   ep   2. 27. 77, 1. 9. 78 CBS
Project UFO   ep   Mass Sighting 2. 26. 78 NBC
Police Story   ep   The Broken Badge 3. 19. 78 NBC
The Amazing Spider-Man   ep   5. 3. 78 CBS
Hawaii Five-O   ep   10. 4. 79 CBS
Fantasy Island   ep   3. 5. 80 ABC
Buck Rogers in the 25th Century   ep   1. 15. 81 NBC
Freebie and the Bean   ep   1. 24. 81 CBS
Charlie's Angels   ep   6. 3. 81 ABC

LUPINO, IDA
   A&C:
   Insight   ep   3. 2. 74 NN
   SUPP. :
   Charlie's Angels   ep   3. 9. 77 ABC

LYNLEY, CAROL
   SUPP. :
   The Rockford Files   ep   1. 14. 77 NBC
   Kojak   ep   2. 22. 77 CBS
   Having Babies II   tf   10. 28. 77 ABC
   Fantasy Island   ep   Lady of the Evening 2. 25. 78 ABC
   Hawaii Five-O   ep   3. 9. 78 CBS
   The Cops and Robin   tf   3. 28. 78 NBC
   Richie Brockelman, Private Eye   ep   3. 31. 78 NBC
   The Beasts on the Street   tf   5. 18. 78 NBC
   Sword of Justice   ep   10. 19. 78 NBC
   Fantasy Island   ep   12. 2. 78 ABC
   The Love Boat   ep   2. 10. 79 ABC
   Fantasy Island   ep   The Dancer 11. 17. 79 ABC
   Fantasy Island   ep   The Power 5. 10. 80 ABC
   Willow B: Women in Prison   pt   6. 29. 80 ABC
   Fantasy Island   ep   10. 25. 80 ABC
   Charlie's Angels   ep   Island Angels 12. 14. 80 ABC
   Fantasy Island   ep   5. 16. 81 ABC
   Fantasy Island   ep   Cyrano 10. 24. 81 ABC
   Hart to Hart   ep   11. 3. 81 ABC
   Tales of the Unexpected   ep   The Gift of Beauty 11. 21. 81 NN
   Judgement Day   pt   12. 6. 81 NBC

LYON, SUE
   SUPP. :
   Don't Push, I'll Charge When I'm Ready   tf   12. 18. 77 NBC
   Police Story   ep   River of Promises 1. 14. 78 NBC
   Fantasy Island   ep   4. 29. 78 ABC

-M-

McARDLE, ANDREA*
    Welcome Back, Kotter   ep   2. 3. 77 ABC
    Rainbow   tf   11. 6. 78 NBC

MacARTHUR, JAMES
    SUPP. :
    Fantasy Island   ep   3. 18. 78 ABC
    Hawaii Five-O   sr ret   9. 28. 78 CBS
    Time Express   ep   4. 26. 79 CBS
    The Love Boat   ep   Next Door Wife 12. 8. 79 ABC
    The Love Boat   ep   5. 30. 80 ABC
    The Night the Bridge Fell Down   tf   10. 21. 80 NBC
    Alcatraz: The Whole Shocking Story   tf   11. 5. 80, 11. 6. 80 NBC
    Fantasy Island   ep   1. 24. 81 ABC
    Vega$ ep   2. 25. 81 ABC
    Walking Tall   ep   3. 31. 81 NBC

McCAMBRIDGE, MERCEDES
    A&C:
    Who Is the Black Dahlia?   tf   3. 1. 75 NBC
    SUPP. :
    Charlie's Angels   ep   Angels in the Springtime 10. 11. 78 ABC
    The Sacketts   tf   5. 15. 79, 5. 16. 79 NBC
    Hagen   ep   4. 24. 80 CBS
    Magnum, P. I.   ep   Don't Say Goodbye 3. 26. 81 CBS

McCANN, CHUCK
    A&C:
    The Girl Most Likely To ...   tf   11. 6. 73 ABC
    How to Break Up a Happy Divorce   tf   10. 6. 76 NBC
    SUPP. :
    Starsky and Hutch   ep   3. 19. 77 ABC
    All That Glitters   sr   Spring 1977 NN
    Sex and the Married Woman   tf   9. 13. 77 NBC
    Switch   ep   10. 21. 77 CBS
    The Rockford Files   ep   11. 4. 77 NBC
    Fantasy Island   ep   2. 10. 79 ABC
    A New Kind of Family   sr   9. 30. 79 ABC
    If Things Were Different   tf   1. 16. 80 CBS
    Concrete Cowboys   ep   2. 28. 81 CBS
    One Day at a Time   ep   Out of Bounds 3. 8. 81 CBS
    Here's Boomer   ep   Looking Good 11. 1. 81 NBC
    CHiPs   ep   Fast Money 12. 6. 81 NBC
    One Day at a Time   ep   12. 20. 81 CBS

McCARTHY, KEVIN
    A&C:
    Great Ghost Tales   ep   Lucy 7. 13. 61 NBC
    The Defenders   ep   The Hour Before Doomsday 2. 9. 63 CBS
    Fay   ep   9. 4. 75 NBC
    SUPP. :
    Exo-Man   tf   6. 17. 77 NBC

Mary Jane Harper Cried Last Night tf   10. 5. 77 CBS
Flamingo Road tf   5. 12. 80 NBC
Portrait of an Escort tf   10. 8. 80 CBS
Flamingo Road sr   1. 6. 81 NBC
Flamingo Road sr ret   11. 3. 81 NBC

McCLANHAN, RUE
SUPP. :
Maude sr ret   9. 12. 77 CBS
Having Babies III tf   3. 3. 78 ABC
Sergeant Matlovich vs. the U. S. Air Force tf   8. 21. 78 NBC
Grandpa Goes to Washington ep   9. 7. 78 NBC
Apple Pie sr   9. 23. 78 ABC
Rainbow tf   11. 6. 78 NBC
The Love Boat ep The Last Hundred Bucks 12. 9. 78 ABC
Grandpa Goes to Washington ep   1. 9. 79 NBC
Sweepstakes ep   2. 9. 79 NBC
Supertrain ep   5. 5. 79 NBC
Fantasy Island ep   5. 12. 79 ABC
Insight ep   5. 27. 79 NN
Mother and Me, M. D.   pt   6. 14. 79 NBC
Topper tf   11. 9. 79 ABC
Lou Grant ep   3. 17. 80 CBS
Here's Boomer ep Private Eye 5. 16. 80 NBC
The Great American Traffic Jam tf   10. 2. 80 NBC
The Son-in-Law pt   10. 26. 80 NBC
The Love Boat ep   11. 1. 80 ABC
Word of Honor tf   1. 6. 81 CBS
Gimme a Break ep   11. 12. 81 NBC
Darkroom ep Daisies 12. 25. 81 ABC

McCLURE, DOUG
SUPP. :
Roots ms ep   1. 29. 77, 1. 30. 77 ABC
SST--Death Flight tf   2. 25. 77 ABC
Wild and Wooly tf   2. 20. 78 ABC
The Rebels ms ep   5. 21. 79 NN
Nightside tf   6. 8. 80 ABC

McCORMACK, PATRICIA (previously listed as Patty McCormack)
A& C:
Emergency ep   5. 19. 73 NBC
Marcus Welby, M. D.   ep   10. 5. 75 ABC
SUPP. :
The Love Boat ep   11. 25. 78 ABC
The Ropers sr   3. 13. 79 ABC
Emergency ep   6. 26. 79, 7. 3. 79 NBC
The Ropers sr ret   9. 15. 79 ABC
Fantasy Island ep   12. 8. 79 ABC

McCORMICK, MAUREEN*
The Brady Bunch sr   9. 26. 69 ABC
The Brady Bunch sr ret   9. 25. 70 ABC

The Brady Bunch   sr ret   9. 17. 71 ABC
The Brady Kids   sr vo   9. 9. 72 ABC
The Brady Bunch   sr ret   9. 25. 72 ABC
Marcus Welby, M. D.   ep   2. 27. 73 ABC
The Brady Bunch   sr ret   9. 14. 73 ABC
Happy Days   ep   2. 11. 75 ABC
Harry O   ep   Street Games 3. 13. 75 ABC
Joe Forrester   ep   9. 23. 75 NBC
The Streets of San Francisco   ep   11. 4. 76 ABC
Gibbsville   ep   12. 16. 76 NBC
The Brady Bunch Hour   sr   1. 23. 77 ABC
Delvecchio   ep   1. 30. 77 CBS
The Love Boat   ep   First Time Out 10. 29. 77 ABC
The Hardy Boys/Nancy Drew Mysteries   ep   11. 20. 77 ABC
Fantasy Island   ep   3. 11. 78, 10. 14. 78 ABC
Vega$ ep   11. 15. 78 ABC
When, Jenny? When?   sp   1. 23. 79 NN
Lou Grant   ep   Sweep 2. 5. 79 CBS
Fantasy Island   ep   2. 10. 79 ABC
Vacation in Hell   tf   5. 21. 79 ABC
Runaways   tf   7. 10. 79 NBC
Fantasy Island   ep   2. 2. 80 ABC
The Love Boat   ep   3. 1. 80 ABC
Fantasy Island   ep   1. 10. 81 ABC
The Love Boat   ep   First Voyage, Last Voyage 1. 17. 81 ABC
The Brady Girls Get Married   sr   2. 6. 81 NBC
The Brady Brides   sr   3. 6. 81 NBC
The Brady Girls Get Married   tf   10. 27. 81 NBC

McDOWALL, RODDY
   SUPP. :
   Fantastic Journey   sr   2. 17. 77 NBC
   The Rhinemann Exchange   ms   3. 10. 77, 3. 17. 77, 3. 24. 77 NBC
   The Feather and Father Gang   ep   6. 25. 77 ABC
   The New Adventures of Wonder Woman   ep   The Man Who Made
      Volcanoes 11. 18. 77 CBS
   The New Adventures of Wonder Woman   ep   The Fine Art of
      Crime 10. 13. 78 CBS
   The Immigrants   ms   11. 20. 78, 11. 21. 78 NN
   Thief of Baghdad   tf   11. 23. 78 NBC
   Supertrain   ep   4. 28. 79 NBC
   Fantasy Island   ep   5. 12. 79 ABC
   Hart to Hart   pt   8. 25. 79 ABC
   A Man Called Sloane   ep   The Seduction Squad 9. 22. 79 NBC
   Trapper John, M. D.   ep   9. 23. 79 CBS
   Buck Rogers in the 25th Century   ep   Planet of the Slave Girls
      9. 27. 79 NBC
   Mork and Mindy   ep   10. 7. 79 ABC
   Fantasy Island   ep   10. 20. 79 ABC
   The Love Boat   ep   1. 27. 79 ABC
   The Martian Chronicles   ms ep   1. 27. 80 NBC
   The Memory of Eva Ryker   tf   5. 7. 80 CBS
   Return of the King   tf vo   5. 11. 80 ABC

Fantasy Island   ep   10. 25. 80 ABC
Here's Boomer   ep   Boomer and Miss 21st Century 12. 7. 80
    NBC
The Million Dollar Face   tf   3. 12. 81 NBC
Fantasy Island   ep   The Devil and Mr. Roarke 10. 17. 81 ABC
The Golden Age of Television   ep   No Time for Sergeants
    hos   11. 29. 81 NN
Judgement Day   pt   12. 6. 81 NBC

McEACHIN, JAMES
    A&C:
    The Judge and Jake Wyler   tf   12. 2. 72 NBC
    The Alpha Caper   tf   10. 6. 73 ABC
    SUPP. :
    Kingston Confidential   ep   4. 6. 77 NBC
    Emergency   ep   5. 28. 77 NBC
    The Feather and Father Gang   ep   6. 25. 77 ABC
    Westside Medical   ep   6. 30. 77 ABC
    The Six Million Dollar Man   ep   Killer Wind 10. 16. 77 ABC
    Grandpa Goes to Washington   ep   9. 7. 78 NBC
    The Eddie Capra Mysteries   ep   12. 8. 78 NBC
    Quincy, M. E.   ep   1. 11. 79 NBC
    This Man Stands Alone   tf   5. 30. 79 NBC
    Insight   ep   6. 17. 79 NN
    The White Shadow   ep   2. 19. 80 CBS

McGAVIN, DARREN
    SUPP. :
    The Users   tf   10. 1. 78 ABC
    Fantasy Island   ep   11. 4. 78 ABC
    The World of Disney   ep   Donovan's Kid 1. 7. 79, 1. 14. 79 NBC
    Ike   ms   5. 3. 79, 5. 4. 79, 5. 6. 79 ABC
    Not Until Today   pt   6. 27. 79 NBC
    Love for Rent   tf   11. 11. 79 ABC
    Waikiki   tf   4. 21. 80 ABC
    The Love Boat   ep   11. 1. 80 ABC
    The Martian Chronicles   ms ep   12. 7. 80 NBC
    Nero Wolfe   ep   Gambit 4. 3. 81 NBC
    Magnum, P. I.   ep   11. 26. 81 CBS

McGOOHAN, PATRICK
    SUPP. :
    Man in the Iron Mask   tf   1. 17. 77 NBC
    Rafferty   sr   9. 5. 77 CBS

McGUIRE, BIFF
    SUPP. :
    Hawaii Five-O   ep   3. 31. 77 CBS
    Visions   ep   All I Could See from Where I Stood 11. 20. 77 PBS
    The World of Disney   ep   Child of Glass 5. 14. 78 NBC
    Family   ep   5. 16. 78 ABC
    Grandpa Goes to Washington   ep   9. 19. 78 NBC
    Barnaby Jones   ep   11. 16. 78 CBS
    The Paper Chase   ep   Scavenger Hunt 4. 24. 79 CBS

McGUIRE, DOROTHY
   SUPP. :
   Little Women   tf   10. 2. 78, 10. 3. 78 NBC
   The Incredible Journey of Dr. Meg Laurel   tf   1. 2. 79 CBS
   Little Women   sr   2. 8. 79 NBC

MACHT, STEPHEN*
   Kojak   ep   2. 15. 76 CBS
   Serpico   ep   10. 1. 76 NBC
   Amelia Earhart   tf   10. 25. 76 NBC
   Kojak   ep   12. 12. 76 CBS
   The Six Million Dollar Man   ep   1. 2. 77 ABC
   Raid on Entebbe   tf   1. 9. 77 NBC
   Quincy, M. E.   2. 11. 77 NBC
   Kingston Confidential   ep   4. 6. 77 NBC
   Big Hawaii   ep   10. 12. 77 NBC
   Ring of Passion   tf   2. 4. 78 NBC
   Loose Change   ms   2. 26. 78, 2. 27. 78, 2. 28. 78 NBC
   Hunters of the Reef   tf   5. 20. 78 NBC
   The Immigrants   ms   11. 20. 78, 11. 21. 78 NN
   Enola Gay   tf   11. 23. 80 NBC
   The American Dream   sr   4. 26. 81 ABC
   Killjoy   tf   10. 22. 81 CBS

McINTIRE, JOHN
   A&C:
   The Untouchables   ep   A Seat on the Fence 11. 24. 60 ABC
   The New Daughters of Joshua Cabe   tf   5. 29. 76 ABC
   SUPP. :
   Aspen   ms   11. 5. 77, 11. 6. 77, 11. 7. 77 NBC
   The Love Boat   ep   12. 2. 78 ABC
   The Jordan Chance   tf   12. 12. 78 CBS
   Charlie's Angels   ep   Angels on Vacation 1. 10. 79 ABC
   Fantasy Island   ep   1. 27. 79 ABC
   Dallas   ep   3. 16. 79 CBS
   Mrs. R's Daughter   tf   9. 19. 79 NBC
   Shirley   sr   10. 26. 79 NBC
   Young Maverick   ep   12. 26. 79 CBS
   The Incredible Hulk   ep   2. 29. 80 CBS
   The American Dream   sr   4. 26. 81 ABC
   Goliath Awaits   ms   11. 17. 81, 11. 23. 81 NN
   NBC Live Theatre   ep   All the Way Home   sp   12. 21. 81 NBC

McKEON, NANCY*
   Return to Fantasy Island   tf   1. 20. 78 ABC
   A Question of Love   tf   11. 26. 78 ABC
   The Love Boat   ep   11. 17. 79 ABC
   The ABC Weekend Special   ep   The Puppy's Amazing Rescue
      vo   1. 26. 80 ABC
   The ABC Weekend Special   ep   The Trouble with Miss Switch
      vo   2. 16. 80 ABC
   Stone   sr   3. 3. 80 ABC
   The ABC Weekend Special   ep   Scruffy   vo   10. 11. 80 ABC

The Facts of Life   sr   11. 19. 80 NBC
ABC Theatre for Young Americans   ep   Please Don't Hit Me,
  Mom 9. 20. 81 ABC
The Facts of Life   sr ret   10. 28. 81 NBC

MacLACHLAN, JANET
  A&C:
  Barney Miller   ep   10. 28. 76 ABC
  Baretta   ep   12. 1. 76 ABC
  SUPP. :
  The New, Original Wonder Woman   ep   Judgement from Outer
    Space 1. 15. 77, 1. 17. 77 ABC
  Most Wanted   ep   2. 5. 77 ABC
  Rafferty   ep   10. 3. 77 CBS
  Roll of Thunder, Hear My Cry   ms   6. 2. 78, 6. 3. 78, 6. 4. 78
    ABC
  Good Times   ep   10. 7. 78 CBS
  Friends   sr   3. 25. 79 ABC
  Insight   ep   5. 20. 79 NN
  Archie Bunker's Place   ep   11. 16. 80 CBS
  The ABC Weekend Special   ep   Zack and the Magic Factory
    1. 10. 81 ABC
  She's in the Army Now   tf   5. 20. 81 ABC

MacLEOD, GAVIN*
  Mr. Lucky   ep   11. 7. 59, 4. 9. 60 CBS
  McHale's Navy   sr   10. 11. 62 ABC
  McHale's Navy   sr ret   9. 7. 63 ABC
  McHale's Navy   sr ret   9. 64 ABC
  The Man from U. N. C. L. E.   ep   The Hong Kong Shilling Affair
    3. 15. 65 NBC
  McHale's Navy   sr ret   9. 65 ABC
  The Rat Patrol   ep   The Fatal Chase Raid 10. 31. 66 ABC
  The Big Valley   ep   Brother Love 2. 20. 67 ABC
  Ironside   ep   Return of the Hero 4. 4. 68 NBC
  The Big Valley   ep   Presumed Dead 10. 7. 68 ABC
  Hawaii Five-O   ep   The Box 1. 29. 69 CBS
  The Big Valley   ep   Alias Nellie Handley 2. 24. 69 ABC
  Hogan's Heroes   ep   3. 1. 69 CBS
  Judd, for the Defense   ep   Visitation 3. 21. 69 ABC
  It Takes a Thief   ep   3. 25. 69 ABC
  The Name of the Game   ep   Jenny Wilde Is Drowning 3. 27. 70
    NBC
  The Mary Tyler Moore Show   sr   9. 19. 70 CBS
  The Intruders   tf   11. 10. 70 NBC
  The Mary Tyler Moore Show   sr ret   9. 18. 71 CBS
  The Mary Tyler Moore Show   sr ret   9. 16. 72 CBS
  Honeymoon Suite   pt   1. 30. 73 ABC
  The Mary Tyler Moore Show   sr ret   9. 15. 73 CBS
  Love, American Style   ep   Love and the Image Makers 1. 11. 74
    ABC
  The Mary Tyler Moore Show   sr ret   9. 14. 74 CBS
  Rhoda   ep   Rhoda's Wedding 10. 28. 74 CBS

The Mary Tyler Moore Show   sr ret   9. 13. 75 CBS
The Mary Tyler Moore Show   sr ret   9. 25. 76 CBS
The New Love Boat (a. k. a. The Love Boat III)   tf   5. 5. 77 ABC
Ransom for Alice   tf   6. 2. 77 NBC
The Love Boat   sr   9. 24. 77 ABC
The Love Boat   sr ret   9. 16. 78 ABC
Charlie's Angels   ep   Love Boat Angels 9. 12. 79 ABC
The Love Boat   sr ret   9. 15. 79 ABC
Murder Can Hurt You!   tf   5. 21. 80 ABC
Scruples   ms   2. 25. 80, 2. 26. 80, 2. 28. 80 CBS
The Love Boat   sr ret   10. 25. 80 ABC
The Love Boat   sr ret   10. 10. 81 ABC

McNAIR, BARBARA
    SUPP. :
    Police Woman   ep   2. 8. 78 NBC
    Vega$ ep   10. 25. 78, 11. 1. 78 ABC

McNALLY, STEPHEN
    SUPP. :
    Police Story   ep   2. 1. 77 NBC
    Starsky and Hutch   ep   2. 12. 77 ABC
    Police Woman   ep   3. 8. 78 NBC
    Fantasy Island   ep   2. 9. 80 ABC
    Charlie's Angels   ep   Avenging Angel 9. 26. 79 ABC

MACNEE, PATRICK (previously listed as Patrick Mcnee)
    A&C:
    The Twilight Zone   ep   Judgement Night 12. 4. 59 CBS
    The Virginian   ep   A King's Ransom 2. 25. 70 NBC
    SUPP. :
    Dead of Night   tf ep   No Such Thing As a Vampire 3. 29. 77
        NBC
    Evening in Byzantium   ms   8. 14. 78, 8. 15. 78 NN
    The New Avengers   sr   9. 15. 78 CBS
    The Hardy Boys   ep   10. 15. 78 ABC
    Sweepstakes   ep   2. 9. 79 NBC
    The Billion Dollar Threat   tf   4. 15. 79 ABC
    Vega$ ep   1. 21. 81 ABC
    Comedy of Horrors   pt   9. 1. 81 CBS
    House Calls   ep   Uncle Digby 11. 16. 81 CBS

McNICHOL, KRISTY*
    Apple's Way   sr   2. 10. 74 CBS
    The ABC Afterschool Special   ep   Fawn Story   sp   10. 22. 75
        ABC
    Starsky and Hutch   ep   The Hostage 1. 7. 76 ABC
    Family   sr   3. 9. 76 ABC
    The Bionic Woman   ep   The Ghosthunter 5. 26. 76 ABC
    Family   sr ret   9. 28. 76 ABC
    Starsky and Hutch   ep   Little Girl Lost 12. 25. 76 ABC
    The Love Boat II   tf   1. 21. 77 ABC
    Family   sr ret   9. 13. 77 ABC

The Love Boat   ep   Graham and Kelly 10. 8. 77 ABC
The ABC Afterschool Special   ep   The Pinballs   sp   10. 26. 77
    ABC
Starsky and Hutch   ep   The Trap 2. 1. 78 ABC
Family   sr ret   9. 21. 78 ABC
Like Mom, Like Me   tf   10. 22. 78 CBS
Summer of My German Soldier   tf   10. 30. 78 NBC
My Old Man   tf   12. 7. 79 CBS
Family   sr ret   12. 24. 79 ABC
Family   sr ret   6. 4. 80 ABC
Blinded by the Light 12. 16. 80 CBS

McQUEEN, BUTTERFLY
    SUPP. :
    The ABC Afterschool Special   ep   The Seven Wishes of a Rich
        Kid   sp   5. 9. 79 ABC

McQUEEN, STEVE
    A&C:
    The Dick Powell Theatre   ep hos   Thunder in a Forgotten Town
        3. 5. 63 NBC

McWILLIAMS, CAROLINE*
    Quincy, M. E.   ep   5. 6. 77 NBC
    The Andros Targets   ep   5. 16. 77 CBS
    The Incredible Hulk   ep   3. 17. 78 CBS
    Richie Brockelman, Private Eye   ep   4. 7. 78 NBC
    The Many Loves of Arthur   pt   5. 23. 78 NBC
    What's Up Doc?   pt   5. 27. 78 ABC
    Project UFO   ep   Sighting 4015: The Underwater Incident
        9. 21. 78 NBC
    Sweepstakes   ep   3. 16. 79 NBC
    Benson   sr   9. 13. 79 ABC
    The Death of Ocean View Park   tf   10. 19. 79 ABC
    The Aliens Are Coming   tf   3. 2. 80 NBC
    Rage!   tf   9. 25. 80 NBC
    Benson   sr ret   10. 31. 80 ABC
    Benson   ep   11. 6. 81, 11. 13. 81, 11. 27. 81 ABC

MACY, BILL
    SUPP. :
    Maude   sr ret   9. 12. 77 CBS
    Hanging In   sr   8. 8. 79 CBS

MADISON, GUY
    SUPP. :
    Fantasy Island   ep   3. 17. 79 ABC

MAHARIS, GEORGE
    A&C:
    The Snoop Sisters   ep   The Devil Made Me Do It 3. 5. 74 NBC
    Bert D'Angelo/Superstar   ep   6. 26. 76 ABC

SUPP. :
SST--Death Flight   tf   2. 25. 77 ABC
Kojak   ep   3. 8. 77 CBS
Police Story   ep   3. 22. 77 NBC
The Feather and Father Gang   ep   4. 4. 77 ABC
Switch   ep   10. 21. 77 CBS
Return to Fantasy Island   tf   1. 20. 78 ABC
Crash   tf   10. 29. 78 ABC
Fantasy Island   ep   1. 13. 79, 2. 2. 80, 12. 6. 80 ABC
Fantasy Island   ep   Volcano 11. 21. 81 ABC

MAHONEY, JOCK
   SUPP. :
   B. J. and the Bear   ep   1. 13. 81, 1. 20. 81, 1. 27. 81 NBC

MAJORS, LEE
   SUPP. :
   The Six Million Dollar Man   sr ret   9. 11. 77 ABC
   Just a Little Inconvenience   tf   10. 2. 77 NBC
   High Noon, Part II: The Return of Will Kane   tf   11. 15. 80
      CBS
   The Fall Guy   sr   10. 28. 81 ABC

MALDEN, KARL
   SUPP. :
   Captains Courageous   tf   12. 4. 77 ABC
   Skag   sr   1. 6. 80 NBC
   Word of Honor   tf   1. 6. 81 CBS
   Miracle on Ice   tf   3. 1. 81 ABC

MALONE, DOROTHY
   A& C:
   Route 66   ep   Fly Away Home 2. 10. 61, 2. 17. 61 CBS
   The FBI   ep   Break In 12. 23. 73 ABC
   Rich Man, Poor Man   ms ep   3. 8. 76, 3. 15. 76 ABC
   City of Angels   ep   2. 10. 76 NBC
   SUPP. :
   Little Ladies of the Night   tf   1. 16. 77 ABC
   Murder in Peyton Place   tf   10. 3. 77 NBC
   The Hardy Boys/Nancy Drew Mysteries   ep   1. 22. 78, 4. 30. 78
      ABC
   Vega$ ep   10. 18. 78 ABC
   Katie: Portrait of a Centerfold   tf   10. 23. 78 NBC
   Greatest Heroes of the Bible   ep   The Story of Abraham 5. 22. 79
      NBC
   The Littlest Hobo   ep   10. 18. 80 NN

MALONE, NANCY*
   Naked City   sr   10. 60 ABC
   77 Sunset Strip   ep   Deposit with Caution 11. 29. 63 ABC
   Kraft Suspense Theatre   ep   A Cause of Anger 3. 19. 64 NBC
   The Outer Limits   ep   Fun and Games 3. 30. 64 ABC

The Twilight Zone   ep   Stopover in a Quiet Town 4. 24. 64 CBS
Kraft Suspense Theatre   ep   Streetcar, Do You Read Me?
    2. 25. 65 NBC
The Long Hot Summer   sr   9. 16. 65 ABC
Bonanza   ep   The Unseen Wound 1. 29. 67 NBC
The Outsider   tf   11. 21. 67 NBC
Ironside   ep   Officer Bobby 3. 14. 68 NBC
The Big Valley   ep   The Secret 1. 27. 69 ABC
Hawaii Five-O   ep   2. 19. 69, 2. 26. 69 CBS
San Francisco International   tf   9. 29. 70 NBC
McCloud   ep   The Concrete Corral 9. 30. 70 NBC
Dan August   ep   The Titan 1. 6. 71 ABC
The Partridge Family   ep   2. 12. 71 ABC
Man in the Middle   pt   4. 14. 72 CBS
Owen Marshall, Counselor at Law   ep   Sigh No More, Lady
    12. 21. 72 ABC
Set This Town on Fire   tf   1. 8. 73 NBC
The Girls of Huntington House   tf   2. 14. 73 ABC
Rx for the Defense   pt   4. 15. 73 ABC
The FBI   ep   10. 7. 73 ABC
Owen Marshall, Counselor at Law   ep   Child of Yesterday
    11. 28. 73 ABC
Ironside   ep   The Double-Edged Corner 12. 6. 73 NBC
Skyway to Death   tf   1. 19. 74 ABC
A Tree Grows in Brooklyn   tf   3. 27. 74 NBC
Lucas Tanner   ep   5. 8. 74 NBC
The Rockford Files   ep   The Dark and Bloody Ground 9. 20. 74
    NBC
Lucas Tanner   ep   10. 23. 74 NBC
Switch   ep   8. 6. 78 CBS
Like Mom, Like Me   tf   10. 22. 78 CBS
Family   ep   3. 8. 79 ABC
Lou Grant   ep   Strike 2. 16. 81 CBS
The Killing of Randy Malone   tf   3. 11. 81 CBS

MANDAN, ROBERT*
    Mission: Impossible   ep   10. 16. 71 CBS
    Mannix   ep   12. 15. 71 CBS
    Cannon   ep   To Kill a Guinea Pig 2. 1. 72 CBS
    Longstreet   ep   2. 17. 72 ABC
    Mission: Impossible   ep   Break 9. 16. 72 CBS
    Ghost Story   ep   The Summer Show 10. 13. 72 NBC
    Cannon   ep   11. 1. 72 CBS
    The New Adventures of Perry Mason   ep   The Case of the
        Horoscope Homicide 9. 23. 73 CBS
    All in the Family   ep   12. 8. 73 CBS
    Love Story   ep   Time for Love 1. 2. 74 NBC
    Cannon   ep   11. 6. 74 CBS
    Panic on the 5:22   tf   11. 20. 74 ABC
    Maude   ep   12. 2. 74 CBS
    Insight   ep   2. 2. 75 NN
    Barnaby Jones   ep   Counterfall 2. 4. 75 CBS
    Caribe   sr   2. 17. 75 ABC

Petrocelli   ep   3. 2. 75 NBC
Kojak   ep   Secret Snow, Deadly Snow 10. 12. 75 CBS
Maude   ep   12. 1. 75 CBS
One Day at a Time   ep   1. 6. 76 CBS
Doc   ep   1. 17. 76 CBS
Sara   ep   2. 20. 76 CBS
Kingston: The Power Play   tf   9. 15. 76 NBC
The Tony Randall Show   ep   9. 23. 76 ABC
Phyllis   ep   1. 3. 77 CBS
Barnaby Jones   ep   3. 24. 77 CBS
Kingston Confidential   ep   7. 6. 77 NBC
Soap   sr   9. 13. 77 ABC
Barnaby Jones   ep   12. 15. 77 CBS
The Love Boat   ep   Taking Sides 2. 18. 78 ABC
Soap   sr ret   9. 14. 78 ABC
Vega$ ep   10. 18. 78 ABC
You Can't Take It with You   sp   5. 16. 79 CBS
Soap   sr ret   9. 13. 79 ABC
The Love Boat   ep   12. 7. 79 ABC
Soap   sr ret   10. 29. 80 ABC
Fantasy Island   ep   11. 1. 80 ABC
CHiPs   ep   12. 7. 80 NBC
Greatest Heroes of the Bible   ep   The Story of Esther 7. 26. 81
    NBC
Return of the Rebels   tf   10. 17. 81 CBS
Mr. Merlin   ep   10. 28. 81 CBS
Today's FBI   ep   Charleston Chase 11. 8. 81 ABC

MARCHAND, NANCY
    A&C:
    The Defenders   ep   Hollow Triumph 6. 20. 64 CBS
    Theatre in America   ep   A Touch of the Poet 4. 24. 74 PBS
    After the Fall   sp   12. 10. 74 NBC
    The Hallmark Hall of Fame   ep   Valley Forge 12. 3. 75 NBC
    The Adams Chronicles   sr   1. 20. 76 PBS
    SUPP. :
    Lou Grant   sr   9. 20. 77 CBS
    American Short Story   ep   Soldier's Home 8. 11. 78 PBS
    Lou Grant   sr ret   9. 18. 78 CBS
    Some Kind of Miracle   tf   1. 3. 79 CBS
    Willa   tf   3. 17. 79 CBS
    Lou Grant   sr ret   9. 17. 79 CBS
    Once upon a Family   tf   1. 22. 80 CBS
    Lou Grant   sr ret   9. 22. 80 CBS
    Killjoy   tf   10. 22. 81 CBS
    Lou Grant   sr ret   11. 2. 81 CBS

MARCOVICCI, ANDREA*
    Cry Rape!   tf   11. 27. 73 CBS
    Smile Jenny, You're Dead   tf   2. 3. 74 ABC
    Medical Center   ep   9. 23. 74 CBS
    Paul Sand in Friends and Lovers   ep   10. 12. 74 CBS
    Kojak   ep   12. 1. 74 CBS

Mannix   ep   3. 2. 75,   3. 9. 75 CBS
Baretta   ep   10. 13. 76 ABC
Mystery of the Week   ep   Nurse Will Make It Better 8. 3. 77
    ABC
Kojak   ep   Once More from Birdland 10. 30. 77 CBS
Hollywood Television Theatre   ep   The Ascent of Mt. Fuji
    1. 7. 78 PBS
Some Kind of Miracle   tf   1. 3. 79 CBS
Vacation in Hell   tf   5. 21. 79 ABC
Hill Street Blues   ep   2. 7. 81,   2. 14. 81,   2. 21. 81,   2. 28. 81 NBC
Magnum, P. I.   ep   Don't Say Goodbye 3. 26. 81 CBS
Taxi   ep   11. 5. 81 ABC
The Incredible Hulk   ep   11. 13. 81 CBS
Trapper John, M. D.   ep   Cooperative Care 11. 15. 81 CBS
Magnum, P. I.   ep   12. 17. 81 CBS

MARGOLIN, JANET
    A& C:
    The Defenders   ep   Old Lady Ironsides 12. 21. 63 CBS
    Police Story   ep   12. 19. 75 NBC
    Lanigan's Rabbi   tf   6. 17. 76 NBC
    SUPP. :
    Murder in Peyton Place   tf   10. 3. 77 NBC
    Sharon: Portrait of a Mistress   tf   10. 31. 77 NBC
    Starsky and Hutch   ep   1. 19. 77,   11. 26. 77 ABC
    The Eddie Capra Mysteries   ep   Who Killed Charles Pendragon?
        9. 8. 78 NBC
    The Plutonium Incident   tf   3. 11. 80 CBS

MARGOLIN, STUART
    A& C:
    The Virginian   ep   Jed 1. 20. 68 NBC
    The Rockford Files   ep   9. 19. 75,   12. 19. 75 NBC
    Lanigan's Rabbi   tf   6. 17. 76 NBC
    SUPP. :
    The Rockford Files   sr   9. 16. 77 NBC
    The Rockford Files   sr ret   9. 22. 78 NBC
    The Rockford Files   sr ret   9. 28. 79 NBC
    Bret Maverick   sr   12. 1. 81 NBC

MARKHAM, MONTE
    SUPP. :
    Relentless   tf   9. 14. 77 CBS
    Police Woman   ep   11. 1. 77 NBC
    Lucan   ep   1. 9. 78 ABC
    What Really Happened to the Class of '65?   ep   3. 2. 78 NBC
    Trapper John, M. D.   10. 21. 79 CBS
    A Man Called Sloane   ep   10. 27. 79 NBC
    Hawaii Five-O   ep   1. 1. 80 CBS
    Eight Is Enough   ep   3. 26. 80 ABC
    The Love Boat   ep   12. 13. 80 ABC
    Fantasy Island   ep   12. 20. 80 ABC
    Disney's Wonderful World   ep   The Ghosts of Buxley Hall
        12. 21. 80 NBC

Dallas   sr   2. 6. 81 CBS
The Littlest Hobo   ep   2. 14. 81 NN
Hart to Hart   ep   11. 10. 81 ABC
The Fall Guy   ep   License to Kill 11. 18. 81 ABC

MARS, KENNETH (a. k. a. Ken Mars)
   A&C:
   Good Heavens   ep   6. 26. 76 ABC
   Full House   pt   8. 2. 76 NBC
   Family   ep   11. 16. 76, 11. 23. 76 ABC
   SUPP. :
   Baa Baa Black Sheep   ep   2. 1. 77 NBC
   Police Woman   ep   3. 1. 77 NBC
   Columbo   ep   5. 22. 77 NBC
   Project UFO   ep   3. 26. 78 NBC
   The Fighting Nightingales   pt   11. 6. 78 CBS
   Insight   ep   2. 11. 79 NN
   Supertrain   ep   2. 21. 79 NBC
   Sweepstakes   ep   3. 16. 79 NBC
   You Can't Take It with You   sp   5. 16. 79 CBS
   Before and After   tf   10. 5. 79 ABC
   Barnaby Jones   ep   Killin' Cousin 4. 3. 80 CBS
   Hart to Hart   ep   12. 9. 80 ABC

MARSH, JEAN*
   Jane Eyre   tf   3. 24. 71 CBS
   The Persuaders!   ep   2. 16. 72 ABC
   Upstairs/Downstairs   sr   1974-77 PBS
   The International Animation Festival   sr hos   4. 7. 75 PBS
   Hawaii Five-O   ep   11. 23. 78 CBS
   Momma the Detective   pt   1. 9. 81 NBC
   Trapper John, M. D.   ep   1. 18. 81 CBS
   Goliath Awaits   ms   11. 17. 81, 11. 23. 81 NN

MARSHALL, E. G.
   SUPP. :
   The Lazarus Syndrome   ep   9. 4. 79 ABC
   Vampire   tf   10. 7. 79 ABC
   Disaster on the Coastliner   tf   10. 28. 79 ABC
   The Phoenix   tf   4. 26. 81 ABC

MARSHALL, PENNY
   A&C:
   The Feminist and the Fuzz   tf   1. 26. 71 ABC
   Evil Roy Slade   tf   2. 18. 72 NBC
   The Mary Tyler Moore Show   ep   1. 24. 76 CBS
   SUPP. :
   Laverne and Shirley   sr ret   9. 20. 77 ABC
   Laverne and Shirley   sr ret   9. 5. 78 ABC
   Mork and Mindy   ep   9. 14. 78 ABC
   More Than Friends   tf   10. 20. 78 ABC
   Laverne and Shirley   sr ret   9. 13. 79 ABC
   Laverne and Shirley   sr ret   11. 18. 80 ABC

Laverne and Shirley   sr   (animated)   vo   10. 10. 81 ABC
Laverne and Shirley   sr ret   10. 13. 81 ABC

MARTIN, DEAN
  SUPP. :
  Charlie's Angels   ep   Angels in Vegas 9. 13. 78 ABC
  Vega$ ep   9. 26. 79 ABC

MARTIN, DICK
  SUPP. :
  The Love Boat   ep   12. 1. 79 ABC
  Here's Boomer   ep   10. 25. 81 NBC
  All American Ultra Quiz   pt   11. 10. 81, 11. 17. 81 NBC

MARTIN, MARY
  SUPP. :
  Valentine   tf   12. 7. 79 ABC

MARTIN, PAMELA SUE*
  The Girls of Huntington House   tf   2. 14. 73 ABC
  The Gun and the Pulpit   tf   4. 3. 74 ABC
  The Quest   ep   10. 27. 76 NBC
  The Hardy Boys/Nancy Drew Mysteries   sr   2. 6. 77 ABC
  The Hardy Boys/Nancy Drew Mysteries   sr ret   9. 11. 77 ABC
  Human Feelings   tf   10. 16. 78 NBC
  This Is the Life   ep   4. 13. 80 NN
  Fantasy Island   ep   12. 6. 80 ABC
  The Love Boat   ep   12. 13. 80 ABC
  Dynasty   sr   1. 12. 81 ABC
  Dynasty   sr ret   11. 4. 81 ABC

MARTIN, ROSS*
  Philco Television Playhouse   ep   10. 3. 48 NBC
  Studio One   ep   11. 17. 48 CBS
  Lights Out   various ep   7. 19. 49 through 9. 29. 52 NBC
  Treasury Men in Action   ep   9. 11. 50, 12. 4. 50 ABC
  Treasury Men in Action   ep   4. 5. 51 NBC
  Search for Tomorrow   sr   9. 3. 51 CBS
  Concerning Miss Marlowe   sr   7. 5. 54 CBS
  Treasury Men in Action   ep   9. 30. 55 NBC
  Philco Television Playhouse   ep   10. 2. 55 NBC
  Studio One   ep   9. 16. 57 CBS
  Walt Disney Presents   ep   Texas John Slaughter 1958-59 Season ABC
  The Court of Last Resort   ep   The Philip Huston Case 1. 31. 58
    NBC
  Peter Gunn   ep   9. 22. 58 NBC
  Gunsmoke   ep   11. 8. 58 CBS
  Bat Masterson   ep   The Treasure of Worry Hill 12. 3. 58 NBC
  Alcoa Presents (a. k. a. One Step Beyond)   ep   Echo 6. 2. 59 ABC
  Mr. Lucky   sr   10. 24. 59 CBS
  The Twilight Zone   ep   The Four of Us Are Dying 1. 1. 60 CBS
  Peter Gunn   ep   10. 3. 60 ABC
  Laramie   ep   A Sound of Bells 12. 27. 60 NBC

Michael Shayne, Private Detective   ep   Murder Is a Fine Art
   3. 17. 61 NBC
Peter Gunn   ep   9. 21. 61 ABC
The 87th Precinct   ep   Occupation: Citizen 10. 30. 61 NBC
Dr. Kildare   ep   Second Chance 12. 7. 61 NBC
The Twilight Zone   ep   Deathship 2. 27. 63 CBS
Dr. Kildare   ep   To Each His Own Prison 5. 23. 63 NBC
Bonanza   ep   Little Man--Ten Feet Tall 5. 26. 63 NBC
Wagon Train   ep   The Sam Pulaski Story 11. 4. 63 ABC
Vacation Playhouse   ep   I and Claudie 7. 6. 64 CBS
The Wild Wild West   sr   9. 17. 65 CBS
The Wild Wild West   sr ret   9. 16. 66 CBS
The Wild Wild West   sr ret   9. 8. 67 CBS
The Wild Wild West   sr ret   9. 27. 68 CBS
The Immortal   ep   White Elephants Don't Grow on Trees 10. 1. 70
   ABC
Love, American Style   ep   Love and the Nutsy Girl 1. 29. 71
   ABC
The Sheriff   tf   3. 30. 71 ABC
Owen Marshall, Counselor at Law   ep   Make No Mistake
   10. 14. 71 ABC
Columbo   ep   Suitable for Framing 11. 17. 71 NBC
Night Gallery   ep   Camera Obscura 12. 8. 71 NBC
Sealab 2020   sr vo   9. 9. 72 NBC
The ABC Afterschool Special   ep   The Last of the Curlews
   sp vo   10. 4. 72 ABC
The Crooked Hearts   tf   11. 8. 72 NBC
The FBI   ep   The Wizard 11. 12. 72 ABC
Night Gallery   ep   The Other Way Out 11. 19. 72 NBC
The Bold Ones: The Doctors   ep   A Purge of Madness 12. 5. 72
   NBC
Columbo   ep   Requiem for a Falling Star 1. 27. 73 NBC
Butch Cassidy and the Sundance Kids   sr vo   9. 8. 73 NBC
Dying Room Only   tf   9. 18. 73 ABC
Tenafly   ep   Joyride to Nowhere 10. 10. 73 NBC
Ironside   ep   Mind for Murder 11. 15. 73 NBC
McCloud   ep   The Solid Gold Swingers 12. 2. 73 NBC
Skyway to Death   tf   1. 19. 74 ABC
Barnaby Jones   ep   Friends Till Death 2. 17. 74 CBS
The Invisible Man   ep   The Fine Art of Diplomacy 9. 15. 75 NBC
Ellery Queen   ep   10. 16. 75 NBC
The Gemini Man   ep   Minotaur 9. 30. 76 NBC
Sanford and Son   ep   California Crude 10. 8. 76 NBC
Yesterday's Child   tf   2. 3. 77 NBC
Baretta   ep   Not on Our Block 2. 9. 77 ABC
Blansky's Beauties   ep   3. 19. 77 ABC
The New Super Friends Hour   sr vo   9. 10. 77 ABC
Charlie's Angels   ep   Unidentified Flying Angels 11. 2. 77 ABC
Hawaii Five-O   ep   1. 28. 78 CBS
The New Adventures of Wonder Woman   ep   Irac Is Missing
   2. 17. 78 CBS
Wild and Wooly   tf   2. 20. 78 ABC
Quark   ep   All the Emperor's Quasi-Norms 3. 24. 78, 3. 31. 78 NBC

The All New Popeye Hour   sr vo   9. 9. 78 CBS
The Godzilla Power Hour   sr vo   9. 9. 78 NBC
The American Girls   ep   The Cancelled Czech 9. 23. 78 CBS
The Three Robonic Stooges   sr vo   9. 28. 78 CBS
Vega$ ep   10. 11. 78 ABC
Flying High   ep   North by Northeast 10. 13. 78 CBS
Hawaii Five-O   ep   Number One with a Bullet 1. 4. 79, 1. 11. 79
    CBS
The World of Disney   ep   Donovan's Kid 1. 14. 79 NBC
Hawaii Five-O   ep   Stringer 2. 22. 79 CBS
The Wild Wild West Revisited   tf   5. 9. 79 CBS
Return of the Mod Squad   tf   5. 18. 79 ABC
The Return of Charlie Chan (a. k. a. Happiness Is a Warm Clue)
    7. 17. 79 ABC
Hawaii Five-O   ep   A Lion in the Street 10. 4. 79 CBS
Hawaii Five-O   ep   Good Help Is Hard to Find 11. 1. 79 CBS
Famous Classic Tales   ep   Gulliver's Travels   vo   11. 18. 79
    CBS
The Seekers   ms   12. 3. 79, 12. 4. 79 NN
Fantasy Island   ep   The Winetasters 1. 22. 79 ABC
The Love Boat   ep   We Three 1. 12. 80 ABC
More Wild Wild West   tf   10. 7. 80, 10. 8. 80 CBS
Fantasy Island   ep   Instant Millionaire 10. 25. 80 ABC
Mork and Mindy   ep   1. 15. 81 ABC
Greatest Heroes of the Bible   ep   Abraham's Sacrifice 8. 15. 81
    NBC

MARVIN, LEE
   SUPP. :
   Our Time in Hell   nar sp   7. 29. 78 NN

MASAK, RON
   SUPP. :
   Police Story   ep   2. 22. 77 NBC
   In the Glitter Palace   tf   2. 27. 77 NBC
   Police Story   ep   No Margin for Error 4. 30. 77 NBC
   The Feather and Father Gang   ep   6. 18. 77 ABC
   The Rockford Files   ep   12. 9. 77 NBC
   Alice   ep   1. 8. 78 CBS
   Quincy, M. E.   ep   The Trick of Death 9. 22. 78 NBC
   The New Adventures of Wonder Woman   ep   Skateboard Whiz
       11. 24. 78 CBS
   Pleasure Cove   tf   1. 3. 79 NBC
   Police Story   ep   Confessions of a Lady Cop 4. 28. 80 NBC
   The Further Adventures of Wally Brown   pt   8. 21. 80 NBC
   Magnum, P. I.   ep   Skin Deep 1. 15. 81 CBS
   Quincy, M. E.   ep   Sugar and Spice 4. 1. 81 NBC
   Jessica Novak   ep   11. 5. 81 CBS
   Private Benjamin   ep   Undercover Judy 12. 7. 81 CBS

MASON, JAMES
   A& C:
   Omnibus   ep   Napoleon's Letters 2. 8. 53 CBS

Autobiography of a Princess   sp   8. 25. 76 NN
SUPP. :
Jesus of Nazareth   ms   4. 3. 77, 4. 10. 77 NBC
Legend of the Black Hand   ms ep   8. 31. 78 ABC
Salem's Lot   tf   11. 17. 79, 11. 24. 79 CBS

MASON, MARLYN* [sic]
  The Greatest Show on Earth   ep   Leaves in the Wind 11. 26. 63
    ABC
  Bonanza   ep   A Bullet for the Bride 2. 16. 64 NBC
  Kentucky Jones   ep   9. 19. 64 NBC
  The Man from U. N. C. L. E.   ep   The Fiddlesticks Affair
    1. 18. 65 NBC
  Bonanza   ep   Ponderosa Birdman 2. 7. 65 NBC
  Ben Casey   ep   War of Nerves 9. 13. 65 ABC
  The Big Valley   ep   The Fallen Hawk 3. 2. 66 ABC
  The Big Valley   ep   Lady Killer 10. 16. 67 ABC
  The Man from U. N. C. L. E.   ep   The Deadly Quest Affair
    10. 30. 67 NBC
  The FBI   ep   3. 30. 69 ABC
  Love, American Style   ep   Love and the Living Doll 10. 6. 69
    ABC
  Love, American Style   ep   10. 30. 70 ABC
  Harpy   tf   3. 12. 71 CBS
  Escape   tf   4. 6. 71 ABC
  Longstreet   sr   9. 16. 71 ABC
  Ironside   ep   Class of '57 11. 16. 71 NBC
  Banacek   ep   Let's Hear It for a Living Legend 9. 13. 72 NBC
  Banyon   ep   9. 15. 72 NBC
  The FBI   ep   The Fatal Showdown 10. 1. 72 ABC
  That Certain Summer   tf   11. 1. 72 AB C
  The Bold Ones: The Doctors   ep   A Quality of Fear 11. 14. 72
    NBC
  Mission: Impossible   ep   Crack-up 12. 9. 72 CBS
  The Mod Squad   ep   1. 18. 73 ABC
  Medical Center   ep   1. 31. 73 CBS
  Love, American Style   ep   Love and the Burglar 2. 16. 73 ABC
  The Magician   ep   10. 2. 73 NBC
  Love, American Style   ep   Love and the Man of the Year
    11. 23. 73 ABC
  Outrage!   tf   11. 28. 73 ABC
  The Odd Couple   ep   12. 22. 73 ABC
  Lucas Tanner   ep   9. 18. 74 NBC
  Attack on Terror: The FBI vs. the Ku Klux Klan   tf   2. 20. 75,
    2. 21. 75 CBS
  Matt Helm   ep   11. 1. 75 ABC
  Joe Forrester   ep   11. 18. 75, 1. 13. 76 NBC
  Marcus Welby, M. D.   ep   1. 20. 76, 1. 27. 76 ABC
  The Streets of San Francisco   ep   2. 3. 77 ABC
  Tales of the Unexpected   ep   2. 9. 77 NBC
  Most Wanted   ep   3. 14. 77 ABC
  Handle with Care   pt   5. 9. 77 CBS

Barnaby Jones   ep   11. 3. 77 CBS
Last of the Good Guys   tf   3. 7. 78 CBS
Great Performances   ep   The Good Doctor 11. 8. 78 PBS
Project UFO   ep   11. 30. 78 NBC
The New Adventures of Heidi   tf   12. 13. 78 NBC
Spider-Man   ep   12. 30. 78 ABC
The New Adventures of Wonder Woman   ep   The Richest Man
   in the World 2. 19. 79 CBS
Barnaby Jones   ep   3. 15. 79 CBS
Vega$ ep   5. 2. 79 ABC
Skag   ep   1. 17. 80 NBC
House Calls   ep   Bombing Out 2. 2. 81 CBS
Two the Hard Way   pt   8. 11. 81 CBS

MATHERS, JERRY
  SUPP. :
  Flying High   ep   9. 29. 78 CBS
  The Girl, the Gold Watch and Dynamite   pt   5. 21. 81 NN

MATTHAU, WALTER
  SUPP. :
  Hollywood Television Theatre   ep   Actor 2. 21. 78 PBS
  Insight   ep   12. 23. 78 NN
  The Stingiest Man in Town   sp vo   12. 23. 78 NBC

MAYO, VIRGINIA
  SUPP. :
  Lanigan's Rabbi   ep   3. 20. 77 NBC

MEADOWS, AUDREY
  A& C:
  The Eleventh Hour   ep   Does My Mother Have to Know?
    3. 25. 64,   4. 1. 64 NBC
  SUPP. :
  The Honeymooners' Christmas Special   sp   11. 28. 77 ABC
  The Honeymooners' Valentine Special   sp   2. 13. 78 ABC
  The Love Boat   ep   Taking Sides 2. 18. 78 ABC
  The Love Boat   ep   5. 13. 78 ABC
  Starsky and Hutch   ep   11. 14. 78 ABC
  The Honeymooners' Christmas Special   sp   12. 10. 78 ABC
  The Love Boat   ep   3. 1. 80 ABC

MEADOWS, JAYNE
  SUPP. :
  Switch   ep   2. 20. 77 CBS
  Sex and the Married Woman   tf   9. 13. 77 NBC
  The Hallmark Hall of Fame   ep   Have I Got a Christmas for
    You   sp   12. 16. 77 NBC
  Fantasy Island   ep   1. 22. 79 ABC
  The Paper Chase   ep   2. 6. 79 CBS
  Project UFO   ep   7. 5. 79 NBC
  Hawaii Five-O   ep   10. 25. 79 CBS
  Fantasy Island   ep   12. 8. 79 ABC

Ten Speed and Brown Shoe   ep   1. 27. 80 ABC
Trapper John, M. D.   ep   2. 10. 80 CBS
The Love Boat   ep   3. 15. 80 ABC
Aloha Paradise   ep   2. 25. 81 ABC
Enos   ep   4. 8. 81 CBS
Rise and Shine   pt   8. 25. 81 CBS
Fantasy Island   ep   A Night in a Harem 11. 14. 81 ABC

MEARA, ANNE
   A& C:
   This Better Be It   pt   8. 10. 76 CBS
   SUPP. :
   Time Express   ep   4. 26. 79 CBS
   The Love Boat   ep   5. 5. 79 ABC
   Archie Bunker's Place   sr   11. 4. 79 CBS
   Archie Bunker's Place   sr ret   11. 2. 80 CBS
   Archie Bunker's Place   sr ret   10. 4. 81 CBS
   The Love Boat   ep   Love, Honor and Obey 11. 28. 81 ABC

MEEKER, RALPH
   A& C:
   Escape   ep   3. 11. 73 NBC
   Evil Touch   ep   6. 22. 74 NN
   Barbary Coast   ep   9. 29. 75 ABC
   SUPP. :
   Police Woman   ep   12. 6. 77 NBC
   The Eddie Capra Mysteries   ep   12. 22. 78 NBC

MENZIES, HEATHER*
   Dragnet   ep   12. 5. 68, 4. 3. 69 NBC
   Love, American Style   ep   12. 31. 71 ABC
   Man in the Middle   pt   4. 14. 72 CBS
   The Bob Newhart Show   ep   2. 3. 73 CBS
   S. W. A. T.   ep   4. 21. 75 ABC
   James Dean   tf   2. 19. 76 NBC
   The Keegans   tf   5. 3. 76 CBS
   Barnaby Jones   ep   12. 30. 76 CBS
   The Six Million Dollar Man   ep   Fires of Hell 1. 30. 77 ABC
   Tail Gunner Joe   tf   2. 6. 77 NBC
   Logan's Run   sr   9. 16. 77 CBS
   The Love Boat   ep   10. 7. 78 ABC
   The Love Boat   ep   El Kid 12. 9. 78 ABC
   Captain America   tf   1. 19. 79 CBS
   Vega$ ep   2. 28. 79, 1. 2. 80, 4. 22. 81 ABC

MERCER, MARIAN*
   The Sandy Duncan Show   sr   9. 17. 72 CBS
   A Touch of Grace   sr   1. 20. 73 ABC
   Love, American Style   ep   Love and the Itchy Condition 1. 4. 74
      ABC
   Police Woman   ep   11. 1. 74 NBC
   Theatre in America   ep   The Seagull 2. 1. 75 PBS
   Mary Hartman, Mary Hartman   sr   10. 4. 76 NN

King of the Road   pt   5. 10. 78 CBS
Kaz   ep   12. 17. 78 CBS
The Cracker Factory   tf   3. 16. 79 ABC
It's a Living   sr   10. 30. 80 ABC
Benson   ep   2. 27. 81 ABC
It's a Living   sr ret   7. 21. 81 ABC
Making a Living   sr   10. 24. 81 ABC

MEREDITH, BURGESS
   A&C:
   Our American Heritage   ep   The Practical Dreamer 11. 22. 59
      NBC
   SUPP. :
   Johnny, We Hardly Knew Ye   tf   1. 27. 77 NBC
   Tail Gunner Joe   tf   2. 6. 77 NBC
   SST--Death Flight   tf   2. 25. 77 ABC
   The Hallmark Hall of Fame   ep   The Last Hurrah 11. 16. 77
      NBC
   The Return of Captain Nemo   sr   3. 15. 78 CBS
   Kate Bliss and the Ticker Tape Kid   tf   5. 26. 78 ABC
   Those Amazing Animals   sr hos   8. 31. 80 ABC
   Mr. Griffin and Me   sp   1. 11. 81 NN
   Man, Myths and Titans   sp hos-nar   6. 7. 81 NN

MERIWETHER, LEE*
   The Man from U. N. C. L. E.   ep   The Mad, Mad Tea Party
      Affair 2. 1. 65 NBC
   The FBI   ep   11. 10. 68 ABC
   Star Trek   ep   That Which Survives 1. 24. 69 NBC
   Mission: Impossible   ep   3. 2. 69, 3. 9. 69 CBS
   Land of the Giants   ep   3. 23. 69 ABC
   Mission: Impossible   ep   10. 5. 69 CBS
   The New Andy Griffith Show   sr   1. 8. 71 CBS
   The FBI   ep   11. 21. 71 ABC
   Arnie   ep   1. 15. 72 CBS
   Longstreet   ep   2. 24. 72 ABC
   The Doris Day Show   ep   1. 22. 73 CBS
   Barnaby Jones   sr   1. 28. 73 CBS
   Barnaby Jones   sr ret   9. 16. 73 CBS
   Barnaby Jones   sr ret   9. 10. 74 CBS
   Barnaby Jones   sr ret   9. 19. 75 CBS
   Barnaby Jones   sr ret   9. 23. 76 CBS
   Barnaby Jones   sr ret   9. 15. 77 CBS
   Having Babies II   tf   10. 28. 77 ABC
   Cruise into Terror   tf   2. 3. 78 ABC
   True Grit   tf   5. 19. 78 ABC
   Barnaby Jones   sr ret   9. 21. 78 CBS
   Time Express   ep   5. 3. 79 CBS
   Barnaby Jones   sr ret   9. 20. 79 CBS
   CHiPs   ep   Chips Goes Roller Disco 9. 22. 79 NBC
   Mirror, Mirror   tf   10. 10. 79 NBC
   Tourist   pt   7. 17. 80 NN
   CHiPs   ep   12. 7. 80 NBC
   The Love Boat   ep   Clothes Make the Girl 2. 28. 81 ABC

MERMAN, ETHEL
    SUPP.:
    You're Gonna Love It Here   pt   6.1.77 CBS
    The Love Boat   ep   Third Wheel 5.12.79 ABC
    The Love Boat   ep   2.9.80, 10.10.81 ABC

MERRILL, DINA
    A&C:
    Checkmate   ep   A Very Rough Sketch 1.24.62 CBS
    SUPP.:
    The Hardy Boys/Nancy Drew Mysteries   ep   A Haunting We
        Will Go 4.3.77 ABC
    Roots: The Next Generations   ms ep   2.22.79 ABC
    The Tenth Month   tf   9.16.79 CBS
    The Love Boat   ep   11.10.79 ABC

MERRILL, GARY
    SUPP.:
    The World of Darkness   pt   4.17.77 CBS
    The Littlest Hobo   ep   3.21.81 NN

METRANO, ART
    SUPP.:
    Loves Me, Loves Me Not   sr   3.20.77 CBS
    The New Adventures of Wonder Woman   ep   Skateboard Whiz
        11.24.78 CBS
    Today's FBI   ep   Charleston Chase 11.8.81 ABC

METTEY, LYNNETTE*
    Ironside   ep   The Professionals 9.28.71 NBC
    Heat of Anger   tf   3.3.72 CBS
    Amanda Fallon   pt   3.5.72 NBC
    Cannon   ep   11.29.72 CBS
    M*A*S*H   ep   Sometimes You Hear the Bullet 1.28.73 CBS
    M*A*S*H   ep   Sticky Wicket 3.14.73 CBS
    M*A*S*H   ep   Ceasefire 3.18.73 CBS
    Kojak   ep   Knockover 11.14.73 CBS
    Love Story   ep   The Soft Kind Brush 11.21.73 NBC
    M*A*S*H   ep   Carry On, Hawkeye 11.24.73 CBS
    Hawaii Five-O   ep   The Banzai Pipeline 1.1.74 CBS
    Hawaii Five-O   ep   There's One Born Every Minute 1.8.74
        CBS
    Banacek   ep   Now You See Me--Now You Don't 3.12.74 NBC
    M*A*S*H   ep   The General Flipped at Dawn 9.10.74 CBS
    The Rockford Files   ep   In Pursuit of Carol Thorne 11.8.74
        NBC
    Movin' On   ep   2.13.75 NBC
    Harry O   ep   Lester 2.20.75 ABC
    M*A*S*H   ep   Some 38th Parallels 1.20.76 CBS
    The Streets of San Francisco   ep   2.19.76 ABC
    Quincy, M.E.   sr   10.3.76 NBC
    The Moneychangers   ms   12.4.76   12.5.76, 12.12.76 NBC
    Barnaby Jones   ep   The Marathon Murders 2.17.77 CBS

The Six Million Dollar Man   ep   11. 27. 77 ABC
Starting Fresh   pt   6. 27. 79 NBC
The Runaways   ep   8. 7. 79, 8. 14. 79 NBC
Barnaby Jones   ep   11. 29. 79 CBS
Lobo   ep   Lobo and the Pirates 4. 21. 81 NBC
Fitz and Bones   sr   10. 24. 81 NBC

MICHAELSEN KARI*
CHiPs   ep   3. 8. 81 NBC
Gimme a Break   sr   10. 29. 81 NBC

MICHAELSEN, MELISSA*
Orphan Train   tf   12. 22. 79 CBS
Goldie and the Boxer   tf   12. 30. 79 NBC
Me and Maxx   sr   3. 22. 80 NBC
Goldie and the Boxer Go to Hollywood   tf   2. 19. 81 NBC
Broken Promise   tf   5. 5. 81 CBS

MILES, VERA
A&C:
Frontier Circus   ep   Lippizan 10. 19. 61 CBS
Ellery Queen   tf   3. 23. 75 NBC
Rich Man, Poor Man   ms   2. 2. 76, 2. 9. 76, 2. 16. 76, 2. 23. 76,
   3. 1. 76, 3. 8. 76 ABC
SUPP. :
Barnaby Jones   ep   The Reincarnation 11. 17. 77 CBS
Fire   tf   5. 8. 77 NBC
How the West Was Won   ep   2. 26. 78, 3. 5. 78, 3. 12. 78 ABC
Fantasy Island   ep   3. 25. 78 ABC
Operation: Runaway   ep   5. 11. 78 NBC
And I Alone Survived   tf   11. 27. 78 NBC
Roughnecks   ms   7. 15. 80, 7. 16. 80 NN
Magnum, P. I.   ep   11. 26. 81 CBS

MILLAND, RAY
A&C:
Route 66   ep   Two Strangers and an Old Enemy 9. 27. 63 CBS
Ellery Queen   tf   3. 23. 75 NBC
SUPP. :
Seventh Avenue   ms   2. 10. 77, 2. 17. 77, 2. 24. 77 NBC
The Hardy Boys/Nancy Drew Mysteries   ep   2. 12. 78 ABC
Cruise into Terror   tf   2. 3. 78 ABC
Testimony of Two Men   ms   5. 1. 78, 5. 2. 78, 5. 3. 78 NN
Battlestar Galactica   ep   Saga of a Star World 9. 17. 78 ABC
Fantasy Island   ep   11. 4. 78 ABC
The Love Boat   ep   9. 15. 79 ABC
The Darker Side of Terror   tf   4. 3. 79 CBS
Charlie's Angels   ep   Angels in Love 4. 30. 80, 5. 2. 80 ABC
The Dream Merchants   ms   5. 12. 80, 5. 19. 80 NN
Our Family Business   tf   9. 20. 81 ABC

MILLER, DENISE*
Fish   sr   2. 5. 77 ABC

Fish   sr ret   5. 4. 78 ABC
Makin' It   sr   2. 1. 79 ABC
Sooner Or Later   tf   3. 25. 79 NBC
Every Stray Dog and Kid   pt   9. 21. 81 NBC
Archie Bunker's Place   sr   10. 4. 81 CBS

MILLER, DENNY*
   Gilligan's Island   ep   Jungle Man Early 1965 CBS
   Mona McCluskey   sr   9. 16. 65 NBC
   The High Chaparral   ep   A Way of Justice 12. 13. 68 NBC
   Hawaii Five-O   ep   1. 1. 69 CBS
   Vanished   tf   3. 8. 71, 3. 9. 71 NBC
   Gunsmoke   ep   11. 8. 71 CBS
   Dusty's Trail   ep   John L. Callahan 12. 7. 73 NN
   The Six Million Dollar Man   ep   The Pal-Mir Escort 10. 4. 74
      ABC
   Emergency   ep   10. 12. 74 NBC
   Nick and Nora   pt   3. 4. 75 ABC
   The Six Million Dollar Man   ep   10. 26. 75 ABC
   Cannon   ep   11. 5. 75 CBS
   Bronk   ep   1. 4. 76 CBS
   Alice   ep   9. 29. 76 CBS
   Quincy, M. E.   ep   Go Fight City Hall to Death 10. 3. 76 NBC
   Keeper of the Wild   pt   1. 77 NN
   The New Adventures of Wonder Woman   ep   The Pied Piper
      10. 21. 77 CBS
   The Rockford Files   ep   Forced Retirement 12. 9. 77 NBC
   Dr. Scorpion   tf   2. 24. 78 ABC
   Charlie's Angels   ep   Circus of Terror 3. 29. 78 ABC
   Battlestar Galactica   ep   The Gun on the Ice Planet 10. 22. 78,
      10. 29. 78 ABC
   The Incredible Hulk   ep   11. 10. 78 CBS
   Charlie's Angels   ep   Angels on Vacation 1. 10. 79 ABC
   The Runaways   ep   6. 20. 79 NBC
   Vega$ ep   9. 19. 79 ABC
   Young Maverick   ep   11. 28. 79 CBS
   Ten Speed and Brown Shoe   ep   2. 10. 80 ABC
   Beyond Westworld   ep   3. 12. 80 CBS
   Vega$ ep   1. 28. 81 ABC
   Charlie's Angels   ep   Stuntwomen Angels 2. 28. 81 ABC
   Lobo   ep   5. 5. 81 NBC

MILLS, DONNA
   A&C:
   Haunts of the Very Rich   tf   9. 20. 72 ABC
   Rolling   Man 10. 4. 72 ABC
   Night of Terror   tf   10. 10. 72 ABC
   Police Story   ep   9. 9. 75 NBC
   Barnaby Jones   ep   12. 18. 75 CBS
   SUPP. :
   Fire   tf   5. 8. 77 NBC
   Woman on the Run   pt   9. 7. 77 CBS
   Curse of the Black Widow   tf   9. 16. 77 ABC

The Hunted Lady   tf   11. 28. 77 NBC
The Oregon Trail   ep   11. 30. 77 NBC
The Love Boat   ep   12. 10. 77 ABC
Superdome   tf   1. 9. 78 ABC
Doctors' Private Lives   tf   3. 20. 78 ABC
The Love Boat   ep   9. 16. 78 ABC
Hanging by a Thread   tf   5. 8. 79, 5. 9. 79 NBC
Fantasy Island   ep   10. 20. 79 ABC
Young Maverick   ep   12. 26. 79 CBS
Waikiki   tf   4. 21. 80 ABC
Knots Landing   sr   11. 20. 80 CBS
Knots Landing   sr ret   11. 12. 81 CBS

MILLS, HAYLEY*
The Love Boat   ep   2. 17. 79, 2. 9. 80 ABC
The Flame Trees of Thika   ms   1. 3. 82 PBS

MILLS, JOHN
SUPP. :
Dr. Strange   tf   9. 6. 78 CBS
The Love Boat   ep   2. 17. 79 ABC
Tales of the Unexpected   ep   3. 8. 80 NN

MILLS, JULIET
SUPP. :
Alexander: The Other Side of Dawn   tf   5. 16. 77 NBC
The New Adventures of Wonder Woman   ep   The Queen and the
    Thief 10. 28. 77 CBS
The Love Boat   ep   1. 21. 78 ABC
Police Woman   ep   2. 8. 78 NBC
Fantasy Island   ep   2. 18. 78 ABC
Switch   ep   7. 2. 78 CBS
The Love Boat   ep   11. 4. 78, 2. 17. 79 ABC
The Cracker Factory   tf   3. 16. 79 ABC
Fantasy Island   ep   5. 6. 79 ABC
Hart to Hart   ep   2. 5. 80 ABC
Fantasy Island   ep   11. 8. 80 ABC
The Love Boat   ep   Phantom Bride 11. 14. 81 ABC

MILNER, MARTIN
A&C:
DuPont Show of the Week   ep   More, More, More, More,
    More 5. 31. 64 NBC
Insight   ep   5. 25. 75 NN
SUPP. :
SST--Death Flight   tf   2. 25. 77 ABC
Police Story   ep   11. 9. 77 NBC
Black Beauty   ms   1. 31. 78, 2. 2. 78, 2. 3. 78, 2. 4. 78 NBC
Little Mo   tf   9. 5. 78 NBC
Crisis in Mid-Air   tf   2. 13. 79 CBS
The Last Convertible   ms ep   9. 25. 79 NBC
The Seekers   ms   12. 3. 79, 12. 4. 79 NN
Charlie's Angels   ep   Island Angels 12. 14. 80 ABC

Fantasy Island   ep   Show Me a Hero 10.10.81 ABC
The Ordeal of Bill Carney   tf   12.23.81 CBS

MIMIEUX, YVETTE
    SUPP.:
    Snow Beast   tf   4.28.77 NBC
    Ransom for Alice   tf   6.2.77 NBC
    Devil Dog: The Hound of Hell   tf   10.31.78 CBS
    Outside Chance   tf   12.2.78 CBS
    Disaster on the Coastliner   tf   10.28.79 ABC

MITCHELL, CAMERON
    A&C:
    Bonanza   ep   House Divided 1.16.60 NBC
    The Quest   tf   5.13.76 NBC
    SUPP.:
    The Hostage Heart   tf   9.9.77 CBS
    Police Story   ep   11.9.77 NBC
    Lucan   ep   1.2.78 ABC
    How the West Was Won   ep   1.12.78 ABC
    Return to Fantasy Island   tf   1.20.78 ABC
    Black Beauty   ms   1.31.78, 2.2.78, 2.3.78, 2.4.78 NBC
    How the West Was Won 2.19.78 ABC
    Testimony of Two Men   ms   5.1.78, 5.2.78, 5.3.78 NN
    The Bastard/Kent Family Chronicles   ms   5.22.78, 5.23.78 NN
    Project UFO   ep   10.5.78 NBC
    Sword of Justice   ep   10.21.78 NBC
    Greatest Heroes of the Bible   ep   The Story of Joshua 11.20.78
        NBC
    Hawaii Five-O   ep   3.15.79 CBS
    Hanging by a Thread   tf   5.8.79, 5.9.79 NBC
    Charlie's Angels   ep   Avenging Angel 9.26.79 ABC
    Fantasy Island   ep   10.20.79 ABC
    Ohms   tf   1.2.80 CBS
    Wild Times   ms   1.24.80, 1.31.80 NN
    BAD Cats   ep   2.1.80 ABC
    Vega$ ep   4.30.80 ABC
    Turnover Smith   tf   6.8.80 ABC
    Charlie's Angels   ep   From Street Models to Hawaiian Angels
        11.30.80 ABC
    The Incredible Hulk   ep   12.26.80 CBS

MITCHLLL [sic], SCOEY (previously listed as Scoey Mitchell)
    A&C:
    Doc   ep   6.5.76 CBS
    SUPP.:
    Baretta   ep   5.4.77 ABC
    Cindy   tf   3.24.78 ABC
    Baretta   ep   5.18.78 ABC
    Lou Grant   ep   4.2.79 CBS
    Stockard Channing in Just Friends   ep   4.22.79 CBS
    A New Kind of Family   ep   12.15.79 ABC
    Fog   pt   5.23.81 CBS

MITCHUM, ROBERT
    SUPP. :
    Night Kill   tf   12. 18. 80 NBC

MOBLEY, MARY ANN*
    The Man from U. N. C. L. E.   ep   The Moonglow Affair 2. 25. 66
       NBC
    Mission: Impossible   ep   Odd Man Out 10. 8. 66, 10. 15. 66 CBS
    Istanbul Express   tf   10. 22. 68 NBC
    Ironside   ep   The Tormentor 3. 27. 69 NBC
    Love, American Style   ep   10. 29. 71 ABC
    Search   ep   9. 27. 72 NBC
    The Partridge Family   ep   1. 26. 73 ABC
    Love, American Style   ep   Love and the 7-Year Wait 9. 28. 73
       ABC
    The New Adventures of Perry Mason   ep   The Case of the
       Telltale Drunk 10. 14. 73 CBS
    Police Story   ep   3. 12. 74 NBC
    The Girl on the Late, Late Show   tf   4. 1. 74 NBC
    Born Free   ep   11. 18. 74 NBC
    Fantastic Journey   ep   2. 10. 77 NBC
    The Love Boat   ep   Ship of Ghouls 10. 28. 78 ABC
    Fantasy Island   ep   11. 4. 78, 5. 6. 79 ABC
    Vega$ ep   1. 9. 80 ABC
    Disney's Wonderful World   ep   The Secret of Lost Valley
       4. 27. 80 NBC
    Fantasy Island   ep   11. 8. 80, 1. 24. 81 ABC
    The Love Boat   ep   2. 21. 81 ABC

MONTALBAN, RICARDO
    A& C:
    Checkmate   ep   Hot Wind in a Cold Town 6. 10. 61 CBS
    Combat   ep   Gadjo 1. 17. 67 ABC
    McNaughton's Daughter   tf   3. 4. 76 NBC
    SUPP. :
    Fantasy Island   tf   1. 14. 77 ABC
    Police Story   ep   2. 15. 77 NBC
    Captains Courageous   tf   12. 4. 77 ABC
    How the West Was Won   ep   1. 12. 78 ABC
    Return to Fantasy Island   tf   1. 20. 78 ABC
    Fantasy Island   sr   1. 28. 78 ABC
    How the West Was Won   ep   2. 19. 78 ABC
    Fantasy Island   sr ret   9. 16. 78 ABC
    Fantasy Island   sr ret   9. 7. 79 ABC
    Fantasy Island   sr ret   10. 25. 80 ABC
    Fantasy Island   sr ret   10. 10. 81 ABC

MONTGOMERY, BELINDA J. *
    Ritual of Evil   tf   2. 3. 70 NBC
    The D. A. : Conspiracy to Kill   tf   1. 11. 71 NBC
    Alias Smith and Jones   ep   The Day They Hanged Kid Curry
       9. 16. 71 ABC
    The FBI   ep   Recurring Nightmare 9. 19. 71 ABC

Lock, Stock and Barrel   tf   9. 24. 71 NBC
Marcus Welby, M. D.   ep   Men Who Care 10. 19. 71 ABC
Owen Marshall, Counselor at Law   ep   Men Who Care 10. 21. 71
    ABC
The Bravos   tf   1. 9. 72 NBC
The Sixth Sense   ep   I Am Not Part of the Human World
    1. 15. 72 ABC
Women in Chains   tf   1. 25. 72 ABC
The FBI   ep   Desperate Runner 9. 17. 72 ABC
Assignment: Vienna   ep   9. 28. 72 ABC
Cannon   ep   10. 11. 72 CBS
The Rookies   ep   A Deadly Velocity 11. 27. 72 ABC
The Devil's Daughter   tf   1. 9. 73 ABC
The Streets of San Francisco   ep   A Collection of Eagles
    2. 1. 73 ABC
The Crime Club   tf   3. 6. 73 CBS
Medical Center   ep   The Guilty 9. 10. 73 CBS
Barnaby Jones   ep   Blind Terror 9. 16. 73 CBS
Letters from Three Lovers   tf   10. 3. 73 ABC
The New Land   ep   10. 12. 74 ABC
Petrocelli   ep   10. 23. 74 NBC
Movin' On   ep   11. 21. 74 NBC
Police Story   ep   2. 11. 75 NBC
The Streets of San Francisco   ep   2. 20. 75 ABC
Medical Center   ep   11. 24. 75 CBS
City of Angels   ep   3. 2. 76 NBC
The Man from Atlantis   tf   3. 4. 77 NBC
Nashville 99   ep   4. 1. 77 CBS
The Man from Atlantis   sp ep   5. 7. 77, 5. 17. 77 NBC
The Man from Atlantis   sp ep   The Disappearances 6. 20. 77 NBC
Most Wanted   ep   8. 20. 77 ABC
The Hostage Heart   tf   9. 9. 77 CBS
The Man from Atlantis   sr   9. 22. 77 NBC
Quincy, M. E.   ep   Accomplice to Murder 2. 3. 78 NBC
Lou Grant   ep   3. 6. 78 CBS
Julie Farr, M. D.   ep   4. 11. 78 ABC
Sword of Justice   ep   Dead Birds Don't Sing 10. 7. 78 NBC
Murder in Music City   tf   1. 16. 79 NBC
Marciano   tf   10. 21. 79 ABC
Eischied   ep   12. 14. 79 NBC
Fantasy Island   ep   2. 2. 80 ABC
Turnover Smith   tf   6. 8. 80 ABC
Trouble in High Timber Country   tf   6. 27. 80 ABC
Trapper John, M. D.   ep   Girl Under Glass 11. 23. 80 CBS
The Concrete Cowboys   ep   Eldorado 1. 7. 81, 1. 14. 81 CBS
Lobo   ep   3. 3. 81 NBC
The Love Boat   ep   Lost and Found 5. 9. 81 ABC

MONTGOMERY, ELIZABETH
    A&C:
    Johnny Staccato   ep   Tempted 11. 19. 59 NBC
    SUPP. :
    The Awakening Land   ms   2. 19. 78, 2. 20. 78, 2. 21. 78 NBC

A Killing Affair   tf   9. 21. 77 CBS
Jennifer: A Woman's Story   tf   3. 5. 79 NBC
Act of Violence   tf   11. 10. 79 CBS
Belle Starr   tf   4. 2. 80 CBS
When the Circus Came to Town   tf   1. 20. 81 CBS

MOODY, RON
    SUPP. :
    The Word   ms   11. 12. 78, 11. 13. 78, 11. 14. 78, 11. 15. 78 CBS
    Tales of the Unexpected   ep   6. 14. 80 NN
    Nobody's Perfect   sr   6. 26. 80 ABC
    Dial "M" for Murder   tf   4. 9. 81 NBC
    Hart to Hart   ep   Getting Aweigh with Murder 4. 14. 81 ABC
    The Strike Force   ep   The Hollow Man 12. 25. 81 ABC

MOORE, MARY TYLER
    A& C:
    Bachelor Father   ep   1958 CBS
    Steve Canyon   ep   1958 NBC
    Phyllis   ep   9. 27. 76 CBS
    SUPP. :
    Mary   sr   9. 24. 78 CBS
    First You Cry   tf   11. 8. 78 CBS
    The Mary Tyler Moore Hour   sr   3. 4. 79 CBS

MOORE, TERRY
    A& C:
    The Rebel   ep   The Executioners 6. 18. 61 ABC
    SUPP. :
    The Love Boat   ep   Matchmaker, Matchmaker Times Two
        11. 29. 80 ABC

MORAN, ERIN
    A& C:
    The FBI   ep   3. 1. 70, 2. 1. 73 ABC
    SUPP. :
    Happy Days   sr ret   9. 13. 77 ABC
    Happy Days   sr ret   9. 12. 78 ABC
    Greatest Heroes of the Bible   ep   The Story of the Tower of
        Babel 5. 15. 79 NBC
    Happy Days   sr ret   9. 11. 79 ABC
    The Love Boat   ep   11. 1. 80 ABC
    Happy Days   sr ret   11. 11. 80 ABC
    Happy Days   sr ret   10. 6. 81 ABC
    Twirl   tf   10. 25. 81 NBC

MORENO, RITA
    A& C:
    Bourbon Street Beat   ep   Suitable for Framing 5. 16. 60 ABC
    SUPP. :
    Lanigan's Rabbi   ep   1. 30. 77 NBC
    Westside Medical   ep   3. 24. 77 ABC
    The Rita Moreno Show   pt   5. 2. 78 CBS

Rockford Files   ep   9. 29. 78 NBC
Anatomy of a Seduction   tf   5. 8. 79 CBS
Evita Peron   tf   2. 23. 81, 2. 24. 81 NBC
Trapper John, M. D.   ep   Days of Wine and Leo 3. 15. 81 CBS

MORGAN, DENNIS
   SUPP. :
   The Love Boat   ep   3. 1. 80 ABC

MORGAN, HARRY
   SUPP. :
   McLaren's Riders   pt   5. 17. 77 CBS
   Exo-Man   tf   6. 18. 77 NBC
   The Magnificent Magnet of Santa Mesa 6. 19. 77 NBC
   M*A*S*H   sr ret   9. 20. 77 CBS
   The Love Boat   ep   A Friendly Little Game 2. 18. 78 ABC
   Maneaters Are Loose!   tf   5. 3. 78 CBS
   Murder at the Mardi Gras   tf   5. 10. 78 NBC
   The Bastard/Kent Family Chronicles   ms   5. 22. 78, 5. 23. 78
      NN
   Kate Bliss and the Ticker Tape Kid   tf   5. 26. 78 ABC
   M*A*S*H   sr ret   9. 18. 78 CBS
   Backstairs at the White House   ms ep   2. 12. 79, 2. 19. 79 NBC
   Roots: The Next Generations   ms ep   2. 19. 79 ABC
   The Wild Wild West Revisited   tf   5. 9. 79 CBS
   You Can't Take It with You   sp   5. 16. 79 CBS
   M*A*S*H   sr ret   9. 17. 79 CBS
   Better Late Than Never   tf   10. 17. 79 NBC
   Roughnecks   ms   7. 15. 80, 7. 16. 80 NN
   Scout's Honor   tf   9. 30. 80 NBC
   More Wild Wild West   tf   10. 7. 80, 10. 8. 80 CBS
   M*A*S*H   sr ret   11. 17. 80 CBS
   Rivkin: Bounty Hunter   tf   5. 20. 81 CBS
   The Love Boat   ep   The Professor's Wife 10. 10. 81 ABC
   M*A*S*H   sr ret   10. 26. 81 CBS

MORITA, PAT
   A&C:
   Evil Roy Slade   tf   2. 18. 72 NBC
   Sanford and Son   ep   3. 12. 76 NBC
   SUPP. :
   The Love Boat   ep   The Painters 12. 24. 77 ABC
   The Man from Atlantis   ep   4. 25. 78 NBC
   The Love Boat   ep   Pacific Princess Overtures 5. 20. 78 ABC
   Human Feelings   tf   10. 16. 78 NBC
   Young Guy Christian   pt   5. 24. 79 ABC
   For the Love of It   tf   9. 26. 80 ABC
   Aloha Paradise   ep   4. 22. 81 ABC
   Lobo   ep   4. 28. 81 NBC
   Crash Island   pt   4. 11. 81 NBC

MORLEY, ROBERT
   SUPP. :
   Tales of the Unexpected   ep   The Party 11. 28. 81 NN

MORRIS, GREG
　　A&C:
　　The Twilight Zone   ep   The Seventh Is Made Up of Phantoms
　　　　12. 6. 63 CBS
　　SUPP. :
　　The ABC Short Story Special   ep   Valentine's Second Chance
　　　　1. 29. 77 ABC
　　The New Adventures of Wonder Woman   ep   Light-Fingered
　　　　Lady 1. 16. 78 CBS
　　Flight to Holocaust   tf   3. 27. 77 NBC
　　Vega$ tf   4. 25. 78 ABC
　　Fantasy Island   ep   10. 7. 78 ABC
　　The Eddie Capra Mysteries   ep   11. 10. 78 NBC
　　The Love Boat   ep   11. 11. 78 ABC
　　Quincy, M. E.   ep   12. 7. 78 NBC
　　Crisis in Mid-Air   tf   2. 13. 79 CBS
　　Roots: The Next Generations   ms ep   2. 18. 79 ABC
　　Vega$ sr   9. 19. 79 ABC
　　The Love Boat   ep   Till Death Do Us Part 11. 11. 79 ABC
　　Vega$ sr ret   11. 5. 80 ABC

MORROW, VIC*
　　Bonanza   ep   The Avenger 3. 19. 60 NBC
　　Bonanza   ep   The Tin Badge 12. 17. 61 NBC
　　Combat   sr   10. 2. 62 (through 8. 29. 67) ABC
　　Travis Logan, D. A.   tf   3. 11. 71 CBS
　　Hawaii Five-O   ep   Two Doves and Mr. Heron 10. 12. 71 CBS
　　River of Mystery   tf   10. 1. 71 NBC
　　Mannix   ep   Days Beyond Recall 10. 20. 71 CBS
　　Sarge   ep   A Push Over the Edge 10. 26. 71 NBC
　　McCloud   ep   A Little Plot at Tranquil Valley 1. 12. 72 NBC
　　Truman Capote's The Glass House   tf   2. 4. 72 CBS
　　Ironside   ep   Five Days in the Death of Sgt. Brown 9. 14. 72
　　　　NBC
　　The Bold Ones: The Doctors   ep   9. 19. 72 NBC
　　Mission: Impossible   ep   Two Thousand 9. 23. 72 CBS
　　The Weekend Nun   tf   12. 20. 72 ABC
　　The FBI   ep   1. 28. 73 ABC
　　The Police Story   tf   3. 20. 73 NBC
　　Tom Sawyer   sp   3. 23. 73 CBS
　　Love Story   ep   The Cardboard House 10. 31. 73 NBC
　　The Streets of San Francisco   ep   The 24-Karat Plague 11. 8. 73
　　　　ABC
　　Nightmare   tf   1. 8. 74 CBS
　　Police Story   ep   Countdown 1. 15. 74, 1. 22. 74 NBC
　　Evil Touch   ep   2. 10. 74 NN
　　The California Kid   tf   9. 25. 74 ABC
　　Death Stalk   tf   1. 21. 75 NBC
　　The Night That Panicked America   tf   10. 31. 75 ABC
　　Bronk   ep   The Vigilante 3. 28. 76 CBS
　　Roots   ms ep   1. 24. 77 ABC
　　Hunter   ep   4. 8. 77, 4. 22. 77 CBS
　　The Man with the Power   tf   5. 24. 77 NBC

The Hostage Heart   tf   9.9.77 CBS
Curse of the Black Widow   tf   9.16.77 ABC
Wild and Wooly   tf   2.20.78 ABC
Charlie's Angels   ep   Angels in Vegas 9.13.78 ABC
Stone   pt   8.26.79 ABC
The Last Convertible   ms ep   9.25.79 NBC
Paris   ep   9.29.79 CBS
The Seekers   ms   12.3.79, 12.4.79 NN
BAD Cats   sr   1.4.80 ABC
Charlie's Angels   ep   From Street Models to Hawaiian Angels
   11.30.80 ABC
Greatest Heroes of the Bible   ep   Daniel and King Nebuchadnez-
   zar 7.26.81 NBC

MORSE, ROBERT
   SUPP. :
   Fantasy Island   ep   11.25.78 ABC
   The Stingiest Man in Town   sp vo   12.23.78 NBC
   Jack Frost   sp vo   12.13.79 NBC

MULDAUR, DIANA
   A&C:
   The Doctors and the Nurses   ep   A Couple of Dozen Tiny Pills
      1.19.65 CBS
   The Virginian   ep   The Masquerade 10.18.67 NBC
   McCloud   ep   The Park Avenue Rustlers 12.24.72 NBC
   Insight   ep   9.11.75 NN
   The Tony Randall Show   ep   12.9.76 ABC
   SUPP. :
   The Tony Randall Show   ep   1.6.77 ABC
   Police Woman   ep   2.22.77 NBC
   Hunter   ep   2.25.77 CBS
   The Streets of San Francisco   ep   5.5.77 ABC
   Pine Canyon Is Burning   tf   5.18.77 NBC
   The Deadly Triangle   tf   5.19.77 NBC
   Police Story   ep   Pressure Point 9.27.77 NBC
   Rosetti and Ryan   ep   11.3.77 NBC
   Lucan   ep   1.9.78 ABC
   Black Beauty   ms   1.31.78, 2.1.78, 2.2.78, 2.3.78, 2.4.78
      NBC
   Carter Country   ep   2.23.78 ABC
   Maneaters Are Loose!   tf   5.3.78 CBS
   To Kill a Cop   tf   4.10.78, 4.11.78 NBC
   Insight   ep   5.14.78 NN
   The Word   ms   11.12.78, 11.13.78, 11.14.78, 11.15.78 CBS
   Fantasy Island   ep   1.27.79 ABC
   Sweepstakes   ep   2.2.79 NBC
   The Love Boat   ep   2.10.79 ABC
   Hizzoner   sr   5.17.79 NBC
   Police Story   ep   A Cry for Justice 5.23.79 NBC
   The Incredible Hulk   ep   9.30.79 CBS
   The Miracle Worker   tf   10.14.79 NBC
   B.J. and the Bear   ep   2.2.80 NBC

The Return of Frank Cannon   tf   11. 1. 80 CBS
Fitz and Bones   sr   10. 24. 81 NBC
The Incredible Hulk   ep   11. 6. 81 CBS
Quincy, M. E.   ep   Slow Boat to Madness 11. 11. 81,   11. 18. 81
   NBC

MULGREW, KATE*
   Ryan's Hope   sr   7. 7. 75 ABC
   Mystery of the Week   ep   Alien Lover 3. 29. 78 ABC
   The Word   ms   11. 12. 78,   11. 13. 78,   11. 14. 78,   11. 15. 78 CBS
   Dallas   ep   11. 26. 78 CBS
   Mrs. Columbo   sr   2. 26. 79 NBC
   Kate Loves a Mystery   sr   10. 18. 79 NBC
   A Time for Miracles   tf   12. 21. 80 ABC
   The Manions of America   ms   9. 30. 81,   10. 1. 81,   10. 2. 81 ABC

MULHARE, EDWARD
   SUPP. :
   Most Wanted   ep   4. 25. 77 ABC
   Battlestar Galactica   ep   3. 18. 79 ABC
   Hart to Hart   ep   12. 11. 79 ABC

MULLAVEY, GREG
   SUPP. :
   Forever Fernwood   sr   9. 77 NN
   Wilder and Wilder   pt   8. 26. 78 CBS
   Sweepstakes   ep   1. 26. 79 NBC
   This Is the Life   ep   10. 7. 79 NN
   Centennial   ep   The Longhorns 12. 3. 78 NBC
   Insight   ep   7. 13. 80 NN
   Children of Divorce   tf   11. 24. 80 NBC
   Number 96   sr   12. 10. 80 NBC
   Enos   ep   Now You See Him, Now You Don't 3. 4. 81 CBS
   Crash Island   pt   4. 11. 81 NBC
   B. J. and the Bear   ep   Detective Finger, I Presume 5. 2. 81
      NBC
   Trapper John, M. D.   ep   C. O. D. 10. 11. 81 CBS
   Today's FBI   ep   Charleston Chase 11. 8. 81 ABC

MURPHY, BEN
   A& C:
   The Gemini Man   tf   5. 10. 76 NBC
   SUPP. :
   Fantasy Island   ep   2. 10. 79 ABC
   The Love Boat   ep   2. 10. 79 ABC
   Sweepstakes   ep   3. 30. 79 NBC
   The Chisholms   ms   3. 29. 79,   4. 5. 79,   4. 12. 79,   4. 19. 79 CBS
   The Chisholms   sr   1. 19. 80 CBS
   The Secret War of Jackie's Girls   tf   11. 29. 80 NBC
   Unit 4   pt   9. 29. 81 CBS

MURRAY, DON
   SUPP. :
   How the West Was Won   ep   2. 6. 77,   2. 7. 77,   2. 13. 77 ABC

Rainbow   tf   11. 6. 78 NBC
Crisis in Mid-Air   tf   2. 13. 79 CBS
Knots Landing   sr   12. 27. 79 CBS
If Things Were Different   tf   1. 16. 80 CBS
Fugitive Family   tf   10. 1. 80 CBS
Knots Landing   sr ret   11. 20. 80 CBS
Return of the Rebels   tf   10. 17. 81 CBS
Knots Landing   ep   11. 12. 81, 11. 19. 81, 11. 26. 81 CBS

MURRAY, JAN
   SUPP. :
   The Harvey Korman Show   ep   8. 3. 78 ABC
   The Dream Merchants   ms   5. 12. 80, 5. 19. 80 NN

MUSANTE, TONY
   SUPP. :
   Nowhere to Hide   tf   6. 5. 77 NBC
   Legend of the Black Hand   ms ep   8. 24. 78 ABC
   My Husband Is Missing   tf   12. 5. 78 NBC
   Breaking Up Is Hard to Do   tf   9. 5. 79, 9. 7. 79 ABC

-N-

NABORS, JIM
   SUPP. :
   The Love Boat   ep   10. 22. 77 ABC
   Aloha Paradise   ep   2. 25. 81 ABC
   The Love Boat   ep   11. 21. 81 ABC

NAMATH, JOE
   SUPP. :
   The Waverly Wonders   sr   9. 22. 78 NBC
   Marriage Is Alive and Well   tf   1. 25. 80 NBC
   Fantasy Island   ep   5. 2. 81 ABC
   The Love Boat   ep   Then There Were Two 5. 9. 81 ABC

NATWICK, MILDRED
   SUPP. :
   Hawaii Five-O   ep   3. 30. 78, 1. 25. 79 CBS
   Little Women   sr   2. 8. 79 NBC
   You Can't Take It with You   sp   5. 16. 79 CBS
   The Love Boat   ep   5. 3. 80 ABC
   Alice   ep   11. 23. 80 CBS
   Trapper John, M. D.   ep   Is There a Doctor in the Big House?
      11. 29. 81 CBS

NAUD, MELINDA*
   Baa Baa Black Sheep   ep   3. 1. 77 NBC
   Operation Petticoat   tf   9. 4. 77 ABC
   Operation Petticoat   sr   9. 17. 77 ABC

Fantasy Island   ep   5.6.78 ABC
The New Operation Petticoat   sr   9.18.78 ABC
Fantasy Island   ep   Charlie's Cherubs 12.9.78 ABC
Flying High   ep   12.22.78 CBS
Amateur Night at the Dixie Bar and Grill   tf   1.8.79 NBC
The Love Boat   ep   The Switch 1.20.79 ABC
The New Operation Petticoat   sr ret   6.1.79 ABC
Detective School   sr   9.15.79 ABC
Young Maverick   ep   1.16.80 CBS
Night Side   tf   6.8.80 ABC
Today's FBI   ep   Fugitive 11.29.81 ABC

NEAL, PATRICIA
    SUPP.:
    Tail Gunner Joe   tf   2.6.77 NBC
    A Love Affair: The Eleanor and Lou Gehrig Story   tf   1.15.78
        NBC
    The Bastard/Kent Family Chronicles   ms   5.22.78, 5.23.78
        NBC
    The Hallmark Hall of Fame   ep   All Quiet on the Western
        Front   sp   11.14.79 CBS

NELSON, BARRY
    A&C:
    Ring Once for Death   tf   4.22.74 ABC
    SUPP.:
    There's Always Room   pt   4.24.77 CBS
    Mason   pt   7.4.77 ABC
    Washington: Behind Closed Doors   ms   9.6-11.77 ABC
    Kaz   ep   10.1.78 CBS
    Greatest Heroes of the Bible   ep   The Story of Joseph and His
        Brothers   11.22.78 NBC
    Salvage 1   ep   3.19.79 ABC
    The Love Boat   ep   Grandmother's Day 5.12.79 ABC
    Nero Wolfe   ep   4.28.81 NBC
    Here's Boomer   ep   The Prince and Boomer 10.18.81 NBC
    Fitz and Bones   ep   To Kill a Ghost 11.7.81 NBC
    Dallas   ep   12.11.81 CBS

NELSON, DAVID
    SUPP.:
    The Love Boat   ep   Double Wedding 12.16.78 ABC

NELSON, ED*
    The Twilight Zone   ep   Valley of Shadow 1.17.63 CBS
    Dr. Kildare   ep   The Pack Rat and the Prima Donna 11.28.63
        NBC
    The Outer Limits   ep   Nightmare 12.2.63 ABC
    Peyton Place   sr   9.15.64 (through 6.2.69) ABC
    Perry Mason   ep   The Case of the Missing Button 9.24.64 CBS
    The Silent Force   sr   1.11.71 ABC
    The Man and the City   ep   A Very Special Girl 10.6.71 ABC
    Marcus Welby, M.D.   ep   Men Who Care 10.19.71 ABC

Owen Marshall, Counselor at Law   ep   Men Who Care 10. 21. 71
   ABC
The FBI   ep   11. 21. 71 ABC
Cannon   ep   12. 7. 71 CBS
Medical Center   ep   The Nowhere Child 12. 15. 71 CBS
O'Hara: United States Treasury   ep   1. 7. 72 CBS
Night Gallery   ep   Little Girl Lost 3. 1. 72 NBC
The Sixth Sense   ep   Coffin, Coffin in the Sky 9. 23. 72 ABC
Alias Smith and Jones   ep   10. 28. 72 ABC
The FBI   ep   The Engineer 10. 29. 72 ABC
Owen Marshall, Counselor al Law   ep   Who Saw Him Die?
   11. 2. 72 ABC
Search   ep   2. 7. 73 NBC
Escape   ep   2. 11. 73 NBC
The Mod Squad   ep   3. 1. 73 ABC
Mission: Impossible   ep   3. 2. 73 CBS
The Streets of San Francisco   ep   3. 15. 73 ABC
Runaway!   tf   9. 29. 73 ABC
Linda   tf   11. 3. 73 ABC
The FBI   ep   Fatal Reunion 11. 4. 73 ABC
Barnaby Jones   ep   Venus--As in Flytrap 1. 6. 74 CBS
Police Surgeon   ep   House Guest 2. 8. 74 NN
Medical Center   ep   Dark Warning 2. 11. 74 CBS
Houston, We've Got a Problem   tf   3. 2. 74 ABC
Clinic on 18th Street   pt   3. 13. 74 NBC
Police Woman   ep   12. 20. 74 NBC
The Missing Are Deadly   tf   1. 8. 75 ABC
Medical Center   ep   2. 10. 75 CBS
Police Surgeon   ep   2. 23. 75 NN
The Bionic Woman   ep   10. 6. 76 ABC
Most Wanted   ep   11. 27. 76 ABC
Gibbsville   ep   12. 9. 76 NBC
McMillan   ep   1. 30. 77 NBC
The Rockford Files   ep   9. 23. 77 NBC
Murder in Peyton Place   tf   10. 3. 77 NBC
Logan's Run   ep   11. 14. 77 CBS
Superdome   tf   1. 9. 78 ABC
The Rockford Files   ep   3. 3. 78 NBC
Doctors' Private Lives   tf   3. 20. 78 ABC
Leave Yesterday Behind   tf   5. 14. 78 ABC
Dallas   ep   10. 14. 78 CBS
Crash   tf   10. 29. 78 ABC
David Cassidy--Man Undercover   ep   12. 21. 78 NBC
Doctors' Private Lives   sr   4. 5. 79 ABC
Salvage 1   ep   4. 16. 79 ABC
Anatomy of a Seduction   tf   5. 8. 79 CBS
The Rockford Files   ep   10. 12. 79 NBC
Barnaby Jones   ep   Homecoming for a Dead Man 11. 8. 79 CBS
Charlie's Angels   ep   2. 20. 80 ABC
Hagen   ep   4. 5. 80 CBS
The Girl, the Gold Watch and Everything   pt   6. 13. 80 NN
Lou Grant   ep   10. 27. 80 CBS
The Return of Frank Cannon   tf   11. 1. 80 CBS

Trapper John, M. D.   ep   Call Me Irresponsible 1. 25. 81 CBS
Vega$ ep   3. 18. 81 ABC
Walking Tall   ep   3. 31. 81 NBC
Born to Be Sold   tf   11. 2. 81 NBC
Quincy, M. E.   ep   Slow Boat to Madness 11. 11. 81,   11. 18. 81
    NBC
CHiPs   ep   Bomb Run 11. 15. 81 NBC

NELSON, HARRIET
    SUPP. :
    The Love Boat   ep   11. 10. 77 ABC
    Fantasy Island   ep   The Over-the-Hill Caper 4. 15. 78 ABC
    Death Car on the Freeway   tf   9. 25. 79 CBS
    A Christmas for Boomer   pt   12. 6. 79 NBC
    Aloha Paradise   ep   4. 1. 81 ABC

NELSON, RICK
    SUPP. :
    Tales of the Unexpected   ep   3. 9. 77 NBC
    The Hardy Boys/Nancy Drew Mysteries   ep   The Flaming
        Torch Mystery 3. 27. 77 ABC
    Three on a Date   tf   2. 17. 78 ABC
    The CBS Library   ep   A Tale of Four Wishes   sp   11. 8. 81 CBS

NESBITT, CATHLEEN
    SUPP. :
    Great Performances   ep   Abide with Me 12. 7. 77 PBS
    Night Cries   tf   1. 29. 78 ABC

NETTLETON, LOIS
    A&C:
    Great Ghost Tales   ep   Arculario 8. 17. 61 NBC
    This Is the Life   ep   Remember Annie 5. 11. 75 NN
    SUPP. :
    The Streets of San Francisco   ep   4. 28. 77 ABC
    All That Glitters   sr   1977 NN
    The Eddie Capra Mysteries   ep   Who Killed Charles Pendragon?
        9. 8. 78 NBC
    Centennial   ms ep   The Storm 1. 14. 79 NBC
    Centennial   ep   The Crime 1. 21. 79 NBC
    Centennial   ep   The Winds of Fortune 1. 28. 79 NBC
    The Love Boat   ep   Captain Papa 3. 29. 80 ABC
    Tourist   pt   7. 17. 80 NN

NEVINS, CLAUDETTE*
    Headmaster   sr   9. 18. 70 CBS
    The FBI   ep   The Engineer 10. 29. 72 ABC
    Police Story   ep   Requiem for An Informer 10. 9. 73 NBC
    Barnaby Jones   ep   Murder-Go-Round 11. 12. 74 CBS
    Petrocelli   ep   11. 13. 74 NBC
    Archer   ep   The Arsonist 2. 6. 75 NBC
    Harry O   ep   Reflections 11. 20. 75 ABC
    Barnaby Jones   ep   Mystery Cycle 11. 21. 75 CBS
    The Mary Tyler Moore Show   ep   Ted and the Kid 3. 6. 76 CBS

Rich Man, Poor Man   ep   9. 2. 76 ABC
The Possessed   tf   5. 1. 77 NBC
Lou Grant   ep   10. 11. 77 CBS
The Rockford Files   ep   Trouble in Chapter 17 9. 23. 77 NBC
Rafferty   ep   11. 7. 77 CBS
The Fitzpatricks   ep   11. 8. 77 CBS
The Rockford Files   ep   3. 3. 78 NBC
Husband's Wives and Lovers   sr   3. 10. 78 CBS
Switch   ep   8. 20. 78 CBS
More Than Friends   tf   10. 20. 78 ABC
Barnaby Jones   ep   Memory of a Nightmare 12. 14. 78 CBS
Three's Company   ep   1. 16. 79 ABC
Married: The First Year   sr   2. 28. 79 CBS
Mrs. Columbo   ep   3. 22. 79 NBC
Barnaby Jones   ep   Run to Death 1. 3. 80 CBS
Knots Landing   ep   2. 14. 80 CBS
Family   ep   6. 4. 80 ABC
Hart to Hart   ep   A Couple of Harts 10. 13. 81 ABC
Jacqueline Bouvier Kennedy   tf   10. 14. 81 ABC
CHiPs   ep   Concours d'Elegance 12. 13. 81 NBC

NEWLAND, JOHN
  SUPP. :
  The Next Step Beyond   pt hos   1. 5. 78 NN
  The Next Step Beyond   sr hos   9. 9. 78 NN

NEWMAN, PAUL
  SUPP. :
  Angel Death   sp nar   10. 29. 79 NN

NICHOLAS, DENISE (previously listed as Denise Nichols)
  SUPP. :
  Baby I'm Back   pt   10. 22. 77 CBS
  Baby I'm Back   sr   1. 30. 78 CBS
  Ring of Passion   tf   2. 4. 78 NBC
  The Paper Chase   ep   A Matter of Anger 2. 13. 79 CBS
  The Love Boat   ep   1. 19. 80 ABC
  The Secrets of Midland Heights   ep   1. 10. 81 CBS
  Project Peacock   ep   The Big Stuffed Dog   sp   2. 8. 81 NBC
  Aloha Paradise   ep   4. 29. 81 ABC
  The Sophisticated Gents   tf   9. 29. 81, 9. 30. 81, 10. 1. 81 NBC

NIELSEN, LESLIE
  A&C:
  The Nurses   ep   The Warrior 6. 18. 64 CBS
  Bonanza   ep   The Unseen Wound 1. 29. 67 NBC
  Evil Touch   ep   12. 23. 73 NN
  Kung Fu   ep   2. 15. 75, 2. 22. 75, 3. 1. 75, 3. 8. 75 ABC
  The World of Disney   ep nar   The Outlaw Cats of Colossal
     Cave 9. 28. 75 NBC
  SUPP. :
  The Love Boat   ep   12. 3. 77 ABC
  Lucan   ep   12. 26. 77 ABC

What Really Happened to the Class of '65?   ep   2. 16. 78 NBC
The Love Boat   ep   A Selfless Love 2. 25. 78 ABC
Fantasy Island   ep   3. 25. 78 ABC
Little Mo   tf   9. 5. 78 NBC
Fantasy Island   ep   1. 13. 79 ABC
Backstairs at the White House   ms ep   1. 29. 79, 2. 5. 79, 2. 12. 79
    NBC
Vega$ ep   3. 7. 79 ABC
The Love Boat   ep   3. 10. 79 ABC
Ohms   tf   1. 2. 80 CBS
Fantasy Island   ep   1. 26. 80 ABC
The Night the Bridge Fell Down   tf   10. 21. 80 NBC
Aloha Paradise   ep   4. 15. 81 ABC

NIMOY, LEONARD
    A&C:
    The Tall Man   ep   A Gun Is for Killing 1. 14. 61 NBC
    The Twilight Zone   ep   A Quality of Mercy 12. 29. 61 CBS
    The Eleventh Hour   ep   The Color of Sunset 4. 22. 64 NBC
    The Virginian   ep   The Showdown 4. 14. 65 NBC
    The Alfa Caper   tf   10. 6. 73 ABC
    The Missing Are Deadly   tf   1. 8. 75 ABC
    SUPP. :
    In Search Of ...   sr hos-nar   9. 22. 76 NN
    In Search Of ...   sr ret hos-nar   9. 5. 77 NN
    In Search Of ...   sr ret hos-nar   9. 78 NN
    In Search Of ...   sr ret hos-nar   9. 79 NN
    Seizure: The Story of Kathy Morris   tf   1. 9. 80 CBS
    In Search Of ...   sr ret hos-nar   9. 80 NN
    In Search Of ...   sr ret hos-nar   9. 81 NN

NIVEN, DAVID
    SUPP. :
    A Man Called Intrepid   ms   5. 20. 79, 5. 21. 79, 5. 22. 79 NBC

NOBLE, TRISHA*
    The Courtship of Eddie's Father   ep   1. 5. 72 ABC
    Arnie   ep   1. 15. 72 CBS
    One of Our Own   tf   5. 5. 75 NBC
    Executive Suite   ep   9. 20. 76 CBS
    The Rhinemann Exchange   ms   3. 10. 77, 3. 17. 77, 3. 24. 77 NBC
    McMillan   ep   4. 24. 77 NBC
    James at 16   ep   2. 9. 78 NBC
    Testimony of Two Men   ms   5. 1. 78, 5. 2. 78, 5. 3. 78 NN
    The Courage and the Passion   tf   5. 27. 78 NBC
    Fantasy Island   ep   11. 18. 78 ABC
    The Rockford Files   ep   3. 3. 79 NBC
    Mrs. Columbo   ep   3. 22. 79 NBC
    The Wild Wild West Revisited   tf   5. 9. 79 CBS
    Eischied   ep   11. 9. 79 NBC
    Buck Rogers in the 25th Century   ep   12. 27. 79 NBC
    Willow B: Women in Prison   pt   6. 29. 80 ABC
    The Love Boat   ep   11. 7. 81 ABC
    Strike Force   sr   11. 13. 81 ABC

NOLAN, JEANETTE*

    You Are There   ep   The Final Performance of Sarah Bernhardt
       5. 8. 55 CBS
    Hotel de Paree   sr   10. 2. 59 CBS
    Wagon Train   ep   The Janet Hale Story   5. 31. 61 NBC
    The Twilight Zone   ep   The Hunt 1. 26. 62 CBS
    The Twilight Zone   ep   Jess-Bell 2. 14. 63 CBS
    Wagon Train   ep   Charlie Wooster--Outlaw 2. 20. 63 ABC
    The Richard Boone Show   ep   9. 24. 63 NBC
    Slattery's People   ep   Question: What Is Honor ... What Is
       Death?   11. 23. 64 CBS
    Wagon Train   ep   The Chottsie Gubenheimer Story 1. 10. 65 ABC
    The Fugitive   ep   Ill Wind 3. 8. 66 ABC
    Bonanza   ep   Old Charlie 11. 6. 66 NBC
    The Virginian   sr   1967-68 NBC
    Ironside   ep   All in a Day's Work 2. 15. 68 NBC
    The Mothers-in-Law   ep   9. 15. 68, 1. 26. 69 NBC
    Hawaii Five-O   ep   2. 5. 69 CBS
    The Name of the Game   ep   The Other Kind of Spy 4. 10. 70
       NBC
    Alias Smith and Jones   tf   1. 5. 71 ABC
    Longstreet   tf   2. 23. 71 ABC
    The FBI   ep   The Lost Job 9. 26. 71 ABC
    Love, American Style   ep   11. 12. 71 ABC
    Gunsmoke   ep   P. S. Murry [sic] Christmas 12. 27. 71 CBS
    Gunsmoke   ep   One for the Road 1. 24. 72 CBS
    Medical Center   ep   2. 2. 72 CBS
    Cade's County   ep   The Inferno 2. 27. 72 CBS
    Say Goodbye, Maggie Cole   tf   9. 27. 72 CBS
    Medical Center   ep   1. 17. 73 CBS
    Hec Ramsey   ep   2. 18. 73 NBC
    Hijack!   tf   9. 26. 73 ABC
    Mannix   ep   Desert Run 10. 21. 73 CBS
    Hawkins   ep   Blood Feud 12. 4. 73 CBS
    The Streets of San Francisco   ep   The Runaways 12. 6. 73 ABC
    Gunsmoke   ep   Dirty Sally 12. 31. 73, 1. 7. 74 CBS
    Dirty Sally   sr   1. 11. 74 CBS
    Movin' On   ep   12. 26. 74 NBC
    Harry O   ep   Last Heir 1. 9. 75 ABC
    Babe   tf   10. 23. 75 CBS
    Police Woman   ep   Don't Feed the Pigeons 12. 2. 75 NBC
    The World of Disney   ep   The Sky's the Limit 12. 6. 75 NBC
    Law and Order   tf   5. 6. 76 NBC
    The New Daughters of Joshua Cabe   tf   5. 29. 76 ABC
    Hollywood Television Theatre   ep   The Ascent of Mt. Fuji
       1. 7. 78 PBS
    The Awakening Land   ms   2. 19. 78, 2. 20. 78, 2. 21. 78 NBC
    Columbo   ep   The Conspirators 5. 13. 78 NBC
    Lassie: The New Beginning   pt   9. 17. 78 ABC
    The Waltons   ep   9. 28. 78 CBS
    The Love Boat   ep   12. 2. 78 ABC
    Grandpa Goes to Washington   ep   12. 12. 78 NBC
    Charlie's Angels   ep   Angels on Vacation 1. 10. 79 ABC

When the West Was Fun   sp   6.5.79 ABC
Better Late Than Never   tf   10.17.79 NBC
The Misadventures of Sheriff Lobo   ep   12.11.79 NBC
Fantasy Island   ep   12.15.79 ABC
Hart to Hart   ep   1.15.80 ABC
Shirley   ep   1.25.80 NBC
The Incredible Hulk   ep   2.29.80 CBS
Here's Boomer   ep   5.2.80 NBC
The Hustler of Muscle Beach   tf   5.16.80 ABC
Trapper John, M.D.   ep   Cooperative Care 11.15.81 CBS
Goliath Awaits   ms   11.17.81, 11.23.81 NN
NBC Live Theatre   ep   All the Way Home   sp   12.21.81 NBC

NOLAN, KATHLEEN (previously listed as Kathy Nolan)
    A&C:
This Is the Life   ep   10.12.74 NN
    SUPP.:
The Rockford Files   ep   2.25.77 NBC
The Love Boat   ep   First Voyage, Last Voyage 1.17.78 ABC
Testimony of Two Men   ms   5.1.78, 5.2.78, 5.3.78 NN
The Immigrants   ms   11.20.78, 11.21.78 NN
Charlie's Angels   ep   2.7.79 ABC
Jacqueline Susann's Valley of the Dolls 1981   tf   1.19.81,
    1.20.81 CBS
Quincy, M.E.   ep   Sugar and Spice 4.1.81 NBC
The Incredible Hulk   ep   10.9.81 CBS

NOLAN, LLOYD
    SUPP.:
McMillan   ep   3.20.77 NBC
Flight to Holocaust   tf   3.27.77 NBC
Fire   tf   5.8.77 NBC
Police Woman   ep   12.14.77 NBC
Quincy, M.E.   ep   A Test for Living 10.19.78 NBC
The Hardy Boys   ep   10.22.78 ABC
Sweepstakes   ep   2.2.79 NBC
Valentine   tf   12.7.79 ABC

NORTH, JAY
    SUPP.:
Scout's Honor   tf   9.30.80 NBC

NORTH, SHEREE
    A&C:
Ben Casey   ep   For This Relief, Much Thanks 9.9.63 ABC
The Streets of San Francisco   ep   Going Home 10.11.73 ABC
Shadow in the Street   tf   1.28.75 NBC
    SUPP.:
Switch   ep   2.27.77 CBS
Future Cop   ep   4.22.77 ABC
Westside Medical   ep   8.11.77, 8.18.77 ABC
The Night They Took Miss Beautiful   tf   10.24.77 NBC

The Hallmark Hall of Fame ep Have I Got a Christmas for You sp 12.16.77 NBC
Fantasy Island ep 2.11.78 ABC
A Real American Hero tf 12.9.78 CBS
Amateur Night at the Dixie Bar and Grill tf 1.8.79 NBC
Women in White tf 2.8.79 ABC
The Nightingales tf 5.19.79 NBC
Portrait of a Stripper tf 10.2.79 CBS
A Christmas for Boomer pt 12.6.79 NBC
Marilyn: The Untold Story tf 9.28.80 ABC
I'm a Big Girl Now sr 10.31.80 ABC

NOVACK, SHELLY
A&C:
The Virginian ep The Stranger 4.9.69 NBC
The Virginian ep A Time of Terror 2.11.70 NBC
Circle of Fear ep Dark Vengeance 1.12.73 NBC
Kung Fu ep The Soul Is the Warrior 2.8.73 ABC
Delphi Bureau ep 3.31.73 ABC
Bridget Loves Bernie ep 6.30.73 CBS
Barnaby Jones ep 12.18.75 CBS
Switch ep 12.23.75 CBS
Police Story ep Officer Dooly 3.5.76 NBC
SUPP.:
Police Story ep 3.22.77 NBC
The Hardy Boys/Nancy Drew Mysteries ep 4.27.77 ABC
The Love Boat ep Centerfold 9.24.77 ABC
Quincy, M.E. ep 11.18.77 NBC

NUYEN, FRANCE
SUPP.:
Hawaii Five-O ep 1.20.77 CBS
Code Name: Diamond Head tf 5.3.77 NBC
Charlie's Angels ep Angels in Paradise 9.14.77 ABC
Return to Fantasy Island tf 1.20.78 ABC
Death Moon tf 5.31.78 CBS
Fantasy Island ep 11.11.78, 3.8.80, 11.22.80 ABC
Trapper John, M.D. ep The Pagoda Curse 1.25.81 CBS

-O-

OAKES, RANDI*
Twin Detectives tf 5.1.76 ABC
Rosetti and Ryan sr 9.22.77 NBC
Telethon tf 11.6.77 ABC
Switch ep 1.16.78 CBS
CHiPs ep 12.16.78 NBC
B.J. and the Bear ep 2.10.79 NBC

Doctors' Private Lives   ep   4. 19. 79 ABC
CHiPs   sr   9. 22. 79 NBC
Barnaby Jones   ep   1. 17. 80 CBS
CHiPs   sr ret   9. 21. 80 NBC
Fantasy Island   ep   5. 23. 81 ABC
CHiPs   sr ret   10. 4. 81 NBC
The Love Boat   ep   10. 31. 81 ABC

OAKLAND, SIMON*
The Twilight Zone   ep   The Rip Van Winkle Caper 4. 21. 61
   CBS
The Twilight Zone   ep   The 30-Fathom Grave 1. 10. 63 CBS
Bonanza   ep   The Thunder Man 5. 5. 63 NBC
Combat   ep   The Long Way Home 10. 8. 63, 10. 15. 63 ABC
The Outer Limits   ep   Joy Ride 3. 2. 64 ABC
The Doctors and the Nurses   ep   16 Hours to Chicago 2. 9. 65
   CBS
Slattery's People   ep   How Do You Catch a Cool Bird of Para-
   dise? 2. 12. 65 CBS
Daniel Boone   ep   The Mound Builders 9. 30. 65 NBC
Rawhide   ep   Incident at Boot Hill 9. 14. 65 CBS
Mission: Impossible   ep   The Frame 1. 21. 67 CBS
Daniel Boone   ep   Bitter Mission 3. 30. 67 NBC
Bonanza   ep   Justice Deferred 12. 17. 67 NBC
The Wild Wild West   ep   The Night of the Fugitives 11. 8. 68
   CBS
The Name of the Game   ep   The Revolutionary 12. 27. 68 NBC
The Big Valley   ep   The Secret 1. 27. 69 ABC
Bonanza   ep   The Clarion 2. 9. 69 NBC
The FBI   ep   The Maze 2. 9. 69 ABC
Daniel Boone   ep   Bickford's Bridge 2. 20. 69 NBC
Ironside   ep   Puzzlelock 3. 13. 69 NBC
Hawaii Five-O   ep   Strangers in Our Own Land 4. 10. 69 CBS
The Name of the Game   ep   Little Bear Died Running 11. 6. 70
   NBC
The Man and the City   ep   Reprisal 10. 13. 71 ABC
The Cable Car Murder   tf   11. 19. 71 ABC
The Night Stalker   tf   11. 11. 72 ABC
The Night Strangler   tf   1. 16. 73 ABC
Ironside   ep   Love Me in December 2. 1. 73 NBC
Hawaii Five-O   ep   2. 27. 73 CBS
Young Dr. Kildare   ep   3. 2. 73 NN
Toma   tf   3. 21. 73 ABC
The New Adventures of Perry Mason   ep   9. 30. 73 CBS
Toma   sr   10. 14. 73 ABC
The Starlost   ep   11. 1. 73 NN
The Night Stalker   sr   9. 13. 74 ABC
Hawaii Five-O   ep   11. 21. 75 CBS
Ellery Queen   ep   12. 11. 75 NBC
Marcus Welby, M. D.   ep   1. 13. 76 ABC
Baa Baa Black Sheep   sr   9. 21. 76 NBC
Gibbsville   ep   12. 16. 76 NBC

Kojak   ep   Dead Again 12. 19. 76 CBS
The Feather and Father Gang   ep   3. 27. 77 ABC
The Rockford Files   ep   Sticks and Stones May Break Your
    Bones But Waterbury Will Bury You 1. 14. 77 NBC
Young Joe, The Forgotten Kennedy   tf   9. 18. 77 ABC
The Black Sheep Squadron   sr   12. 14. 77 NBC
The Hardy Boys/Nancy Drew Mysteries   ep   1. 1. 78 ABC
Quincy, M. E.   ep   Passing 1. 27. 78 NBC
The Rockford Files   ep   The House on Willis Avenue 2. 24. 78
    NBC
Switch   ep   7. 9. 78 CBS
Evening in Byzantium   ms   8. 14. 78, 8. 15. 78 NN
David Cassidy--Man Undercover   sr   11. 2. 78 NBC
Quincy, M. E.   ep   Speed Trap 10. 12. 78 NBC
CHiPs   ep   11. 10. 79 NBC
The Rockford Files   ep   11. 16. 79, 12. 14. 79 NBC
Charlie's Angels   ep   Angel's Child 1. 9. 80 ABC
The Rockford Files   ep   The Goodhues 3. 27. 80 NBC
Vega$ ep   3. 25. 81 ABC

OATES, WARREN
    A& C:
    The Twilight Zone   ep   The Purple Testament 2. 12. 60 CBS
    Wrangler   ep   Affair at the Trading Post 8. 18. 60 NBC
    Thriller   ep   Knock Three-One-Two 12. 13. 60 NBC
    Stagecoach West   ep   The Renegades 6. 20. 61 ABC
    The Virginian   ep   One Spring Like Long Ago 3. 2. 66 NBC
    SUPP. :
    The African Queen   pt   3. 18. 77 CBS
    Black Beauty   ms   1. 31. 78, 2. 1. 78, 2. 2. 78, 2. 3. 78, 2. 4. 78
        NBC
    Police Story   ep   Day of Terror, Night of Fear 3. 4. 78 NBC
    True Grit   tf   5. 19. 78 ABC
    And Baby Makes Six   tf   10. 22. 79 NBC
    My Old Man   tf   12. 7. 79 CBS
    Tales of the Unexpected   ep   2. 16. 80 NN
    Baby Comes Home   tf   10. 16. 80 CBS
    East of Eden   ms   2. 8. 81, 2. 9. 81, 2. 11. 81 ABC

O'BRIAN, HUGH
    A& C:
    Charlie's Angels   ep   11. 24. 76 ABC
    SUPP. :
    Police Story   ep   1. 11. 77 NBC
    Benny and Barney: Las Vegas Undercover   tf   1. 19. 77 NBC
    Murder at the World Series   tf   3. 20. 77 ABC
    Cruise into Terror   tf   2. 3. 78 ABC
    Greatest Heroes of the Bible   ep   The Story of David and
        Goliath 11. 19. 78 NBC
    Fantasy Island   ep   1. 22. 79 ABC
    The Seekers   ms   12. 3. 79, 12. 4. 79 NN
    Fantasy Island   ep   1. 26. 80, 12. 20. 80 ABC

O'BRIEN, MARGARET
    SUPP.:
    Testimony of Two Men   ms   5.1.78, 5.2.78, 5.3.78 NN

O'BRIEN, PAT
    SUPP.:
    Scout's Honor   tf   9.30.80 NBC
    WKRP in Cincinnati   ep   Jennifer and the Will 12.2.81 CBS

O'CONNOR, CARROLL
    SUPP.:
    All in the Family   sr ret   10.2.77 CBS
    The Hallmark Hall of Fame   ep   The Last Hurrah 11.16.77 NBC
    All in the Family   sr ret   9.24.78 CBS
    Archie Bunker's Place   sr   9.23.79 CBS
    Archie Bunker's Place   sr ret   11.2.80 CBS
    Archie Bunker's Place   sr ret   10.4.81 CBS

O'CONNOR DONALD
    SUPP.:
    Hunter   ep   3.18.77 CBS
    Lucy Moves to NBC   ep   The Music Mart   pt   2.8.80 NBC
    The Love Boat   ep   Seal of Approval 1.10.81 ABC

O'CONNOR, GLYNNIS*
    Senior Year   tf   3.22.74 CBS
    Sons and Daughters   sr   9.12.74 CBS
    All Together Now   tf   2.5.75 ABC
    Someone I Touched   tf   2.26.75 ABC
    The Rookies   ep   3.3.75 ABC
    Harry O   ep   1.8.76 ABC
    The Boy in the Plastic Bubble   tf   11.12.76 ABC
    Rosetti and Ryan   ep   11.10.77 NBC
    Black Beauty   ms   1.31.78, 2.1.78, 2.2.78, 2.3.78, 2.4.78
      NBC
    Little Mo   tf   9.5.78 NBC
    Insight   ep   11.12.78 NN
    The Chisholms   ms ep   3.29.79 CBS
    My Kidnapper, My Love   tf   12.8.80 NBC

O'CONNOR, TIM*
    The Twilight Zone   ep   On Thursday We Leave for Home
      5.2.63 CBS
    The Defenders   ep   The Captive 10.12.63 CBS
    The Outer Limits   ep   Moonstone 3.9.64 ABC
    Peyton Place   sr   9.15.64 ABC
    The Outer Limits   ep   The Soldier 9.19.64 ABC
    The Fugitive   ep   The Cage 11.24.64 ABC
    The FBI   ep   2.16.69 ABC
    The Name of the Game   ep   Brass Ring 1.9.70 NBC
    The House on Greenapple Road   tf   1.11.70 ABC
    Daniel Boone   ep   Israel and Love 5.7.70 NBC
    The Young Lawyers   ep   We May Be Better Strangers 10.26.70 ABC

Mannix   ep   Round Trip to Nowhere 1. 2. 71 CBS
Hawaii Five-O   ep   10,000 Diamonds and a Heart 1. 6. 71 CBS
Incident in San Francisco   tf   2. 28. 71 CBS
Cannon   ep   Scream of Silence 10. 12. 71 CBS
The Failing of Raymond   tf   11. 27. 71 ABC
The FBI   ep   1. 2. 72 ABC
Hawaii Five-O   ep   1. 18. 72 CBS
The Bold Ones: The Lawyers   ep   1. 30. 72 NBC
Owen Marshall, Counselor at Law   ep   2. 10. 72 ABC
Medical Center   ep   9. 13. 72 CBS
Banyon   ep   9. 22. 72 NBC
Gunsmoke   ep   10. 2. 72 CBS
Medical Center   ep   10. 4. 72 CBS
Visions   tf   10. 10. 72 CBS
Cannon   ep   1. 17. 73 CBS
The Streets of San Francisco   ep   2. 22. 73 ABC
The FBI   ep   2. 25. 73 ABC
The Stranger   tf   2. 26. 73 NBC
Search   ep   2. 28. 73 NBC
Rx for the Defense   pt   4. 15. 73 ABC
Cannon   ep   He Who Digs a Grave 9. 12. 73 CBS
Barnaby Jones   ep   Death Leap 9. 23. 73 CBS
Chase   ep   Foul Up 9. 25. 73 NBC
The FBI   ep   The Killing Truth 12. 9. 73 ABC
Banacek   ep   Horse of a Slightly Different Color 1. 22. 74 NBC
Manhunter   ep   2. 26. 74 CBS
Winter Kill   tf   4. 15. 74 ABC
Police Story   ep   9. 17. 74 NBC
Medical Center   ep   10. 21. 74 CBS
Nakia   ep   11. 2. 74 ABC
Insight   ep   11. 3. 74 NN
Get Christie Love!   ep   11. 13. 74 ABC
The Rockford Files   ep   The Dexter Crisis 11. 15. 74 NBC
Police Story   ep   11. 19. 74 NBC
M*A*S*H   ep   1. 21. 75 CBS
The Streets of San Francisco   ep   1. 23. 75 ABC
All in the Family   ep   2. 22. 75 CBS
Ellery Queen   ep   3. 23. 75 NBC
They Only Come Out at Night   tf   4. 29. 75 NBC
Barnaby Jones   ep   10. 24. 75 CBS
Police Story   ep   11. 21. 75 NBC
Matt Helm   ep   12. 13. 75 ABC
Cannon   ep   1. 7. 76 CBS
Maude   ep   1. 26. 76, 2. 2. 76 CBS
State Fair   pt   5. 14. 76 CBS
Columbo   ep   11. 28. 76 NBC
The New, Original Wonder Woman   ep   Judgement from Outer
    Space 1. 15. 77, 1. 17. 77 ABC
The Streets of San Francisco   ep   1. 20. 77 ABC
Tales of the Unexpected   ep   2. 2. 77 NBC
Tail Gunner Joe   tf   2. 6. 77 NBC
Barnaby Jones   ep   3. 3. 77 CBS
The Man with the Power   tf   5. 24. 77 NBC

The Feather and Father Gang   ep   7. 2. 77 ABC
Murder in Peyton Place   tf   10. 3. 77 NBC
Phyllis   ep   10. 27. 77 CBS
Lou Grant   ep   12. 13. 77 CBS
Police Woman   ep   Flip of a Coin 3. 23. 78 NBC
Wheels   ms   5. 7. 78, 5. 8. 78, 5. 9. 78, 5. 14. 78, 5. 15. 78 NBC
Insight   ep   8. 13. 78 NN
The New Adventures of Wonder Woman   ep   The Starships Are
     Coming 2. 2. 79 CBS
Kaz   ep   2. 7. 79 CBS
Buck Rogers in the 25th Century   pt   9. 20. 79 NBC
Buck Rogers in the 25th Century   sr   9. 27. 79 NBC
Barnaby Jones   ep   9. 27. 79 CBS
The Golden Gate Murders   tf   10. 3. 79 CBS
Trapper John, M. D.   ep   12. 7. 80, 4. 12. 81 CBS
Vega$ ep   6. 3. 81 ABC

O'HARA, JENNY*
Brink's The Great Robbery   tf   3. 26. 76 NBC
Return of the World's Greatest Detective   tf   6. 16. 76 NBC
Charlie's Angels   ep   9. 22. 76 ABC
Barnaby Jones   ep   11. 11. 76 CBS
Police Story   ep   12. 14. 76, 12. 21. 76 NBC
Westside Medical   ep   4. 7. 77 ABC
Good Against Evil   tf   5. 22. 77 NBC
Tales of the Unexpected   ep   8. 17. 77 NBC
Kojak   ep   10. 16. 77 CBS
The Hunted Lady   tf   11. 28. 77 NBC
Barnaby Jones   ep   The Devil's Handmaiden 12. 1. 77 CBS
Black Beauty   ms   1. 31. 78, 2. 1. 78, 2. 2. 78, 2. 3. 78, 2. 4. 78
     NBC
A Fire in the Sky   tf   11. 26. 78 NBC
CHiPs   ep   1. 27. 79 NBC
Highcliffe Manor   sr   4. 12. 79 NBC
The Facts of Life   sr   8. 24. 79 NBC
Letters from Frank   tf   11. 22. 79 CBS
Family   ep   6. 18. 80 ABC
Blinded by the Light   tf   12. 16. 80 CBS
CHiPs   ep   New Guy in Town 3. 15. 81 NBC
Simon and Simon   ep   Trapadoors 12. 8. 81 CBS
McClain's Law   ep   Let the Victims Beware 12. 11. 81 NBC

O'HERLIHY, DAN
A& C:
Kraft Mystery Theatre   ep   Port of Revenge 9. 13. 61 NBC
SUPP. :
Good Against Evil   tf   5. 22. 77 NBC
The Bionic Woman   ep   African Connection 10. 29. 77 NBC
Deadly Game   tf   12. 3. 77 NBC
Charlie's Angels   ep   Angels in the Rough 1. 18. 78 ABC
Battlestar Galactica   ep   The Gun on the Ice Planet 10. 22. 78,
     10. 29. 78 ABC
A Man Called Sloane   sr   9. 22. 79 NBC

Barnaby Jones   ep   9. 27. 79 CBS
Hunter's Moon   pt   12. 1. 79 CBS
Mark Twain's Beneath the Laughter   sp   12. 10. 79 PBS
The Hardy Boys/Nancy Drew Mysteries   ep   Will the Real Santa
   Claus ... 12. 18. 77 ABC
Death Ray 2000   tf   3. 5. 81 NBC

OLIVER, SUSAN
   A&C:
   Route 66   ep   Welcome to Amity 6. 9. 61 CBS
   The Magician   ep   11. 6. 73 NBC
   Police Surgeon   ep   5. 17. 75 NN
   SUPP. :
   The Love Boat   ep   1. 24. 81 ABC

OLIVIER, SIR LAURENCE
   SUPP. :
   Jesus of Nazareth   ms   4. 3. 77, 4. 10. 77 NBC
   Come Back Little Sheba   tf   12. 31. 77 NBC
   Great Performances   ep   The Collection 10. 25. 78 PBS

O'LOUGHLIN, GERALD S. *
   For the People   ep   To Prosecute All Crimes 1. 31. 65 CBS
   The Green Hornet   ep   The Hornet and the Fly 3. 24. 67 ABC
   Lassiter   pt   7. 8. 68 CBS
   Mannix   ep   10. 5. 68 CBS
   Hawaii Five-O   ep   The Box 1. 29. 69 CBS
   Hawaii Five-O   ep   3. 12. 69 CBS
   Ironside   ep   Not with a Whimper but a Bang 4. 10. 69 NBC
   Medical Center   ep   Emergency in Ward E 10. 8. 69 CBS
   The D. A. :   Murder One   tf   12. 8. 69 NBC
   The Bold Ones: The Senator   ep   9. 13. 70 NBC
   The Storefront Lawyers   sr   9. 16. 70 CBS
   Hawaii Five-O   ep   And a Time to Die 9. 16. 70 CBS
   Mission: Impossible   ep   10. 16. 71 CBS
   Sarge   ep   11. 16. 71 NBC
   Owen Marshall, Counselor at Law   ep   11. 18. 71 ABC
   Nichols   ep   12. 28. 71 NBC
   Cade's County   ep   Slay Ride 1. 30. 72, 2. 6. 72 CBS
   The FBI   ep   The Set-Up 2. 13. 72 ABC
   Cannon   ep   A Flight of Hawks 2. 22. 72 CBS
   Room 222   ep   The Quitter 2. 25. 72 ABC
   The Rookies   sr   9. 11. 72 ABC
   The Rookies   sr ret   9. 10. 73 ABC
   The Rookies   sr ret   9. 74 ABC
   The Rookies   sr ret   9. 9. 75 ABC
   Murder at the World Series   tf   3. 20. 77 ABC
   Something for Joey   tf   4. 6. 77 CBS
   Quincy, M. E.   ep   Holding Pattern 11. 4. 77 NBC
   A Love Affair: The Eleanor and Lou Gehrig Story   tf   1. 15. 78
      NBC
   Wheels   ms   5. 7. 78, 5. 8. 78, 5. 9. 78, 5. 14. 78, 5. 15. 78 NBC
   Sparrow   pt   8. 11. 78 CBS

The Eddie Capra Mysteries   ep   Who Killed Charles Pendragon?
   9. 8. 78 NBC
Crash   tf   10. 29. 78 ABC
Women in White   tf   2. 8. 79 ABC
Roots: The Next Generations   ms ep   2. 21. 79 ABC
Blind Ambition   ms   5. 20. 79,   5. 21. 79,   5. 22. 79,   5. 23. 79 CBS
Detour to Terror   tf   2. 22. 80 NBC
Wilson's Reward   sp   6. 20. 80 NN
A Matter of Life and Death   tf   1. 13. 81 CBS
Charlie's Angels   ep   Stuntwomen Angels 2. 28. 81 ABC
Fitz and Bones   ep   To Kill a Ghost 11. 7. 81 NBC
Jessica Novak   ep   11. 19. 81 CBS
McClain's Law   ep   11. 20. 81 NBC

OLSON, NANCY
   SUPP. :
   Barnaby Jones   ep   1. 20. 77 CBS

O'NEAL, PATRICK
   A& C:
   Twin Detectives   tf   5. 1. 76 ABC
   SUPP. :
   The Deadliest Season   tf   3. 16. 77 CBS
   Sharon: Portrait of a Mistress   tf   10. 31. 77 NBC
   The Hallmark Hall of Fame   ep   The Last Hurrah   sp   11. 16. 77
      NBC
   Columbo   ep   Make Me a Perfect Murder 2. 25. 78 NBC
   To Kill a Cop   tf   4. 10. 78, 4. 11. 78 NBC
   Calloway's Climb   sp   8. 28. 78 NN
   Kaz   sr   9. 10. 78 CBS
   Like Mom, Like Me   tf   10. 22. 78 CBS
   Make Me an Offer   tf   1. 11. 80 ABC

OPATOSHU, DAVID
   A& C:
   Five Fingers   ep   Station Break 10. 3. 59 NBC
   DuPont Show of the Week   ep   The Triumph of Gerald Q. West
      6. 9. 63 NBC
   The Invisible Man   ep   12. 15. 75 NBC
   SUPP. :
   The Bionic Woman   ep   Doomsday Is Tomorrow 1. 19. 77, 1. 26. 77
      ABC
   Raid on Entebbe   tf   1. 9. 77 NBC
   The Hardy Boys/Nancy Drew Mysteries   ep   3. 6. 77 ABC
   We've Got Each Other   ep   12. 31. 77 CBS
   Little House on the Prairie   ep   3. 13. 78 NBC
   Ziegfeld: The Man and His Women 5. 21. 78 NBC
   Fantasy Island   ep   10. 14. 78 ABC
   Greatest Heroes of the Bible   ep   The Story of Abraham 5. 22. 79
      NBC
   Trapper John, M. D.   ep   2. 24. 80 CBS
   Buck Rogers in the 25th Century   ep   1. 15. 81 NBC
   Masada   ms   4. 5. 81, 4. 6. 81, 4. 7. 81, 4. 8. 81 ABC

OSMOND, MARIE*
    The Gift of Love   tf   12.8.78 ABC
    Marie   pt   12.1.79 ABC
    Marie   sr   12.12.80 NBC

O'SULLIVAN, MAUREEN
    SUPP.:
    Mandy's Grandmother   sp   4.4.80 NN

O'TOOLE, ANNETTE*
    The Partridge Family   ep   2.26.71 ABC
    Hawaii Five-O   ep   10.19.71 CBS
    Search   ep   1.24.73 NBC
    The Rookies   ep   Frozen Smoke 10.1.73 ABC
    The Girl Most Likely To ...   tf   11.6.73 ABC
    The Rookies   ep   Lots of Trees and a Running Stream 12.3.73
        ABC
    Police Woman   ep   Shoefly 12.20.74 NBC
    S.W.A.T.   ep   2.24.75 ABC
    Petrocelli   ep   11.5.75 NBC
    The Entertainer   tf   3.10.76 NBC
    Serpico   ep   10.8.76 NBC
    Barnaby Jones   ep   11.18.76 CBS
    The Tony Randall Show   ep   2.3.77 ABC
    The War Between the Tates   tf   6.13.77 NBC
    What Really Happened to the Class of '65?   ep   Everybody's
        Girl 12.8.77 NBC
    Visions   ep   Ladies in Waiting 1.8.79 PBS
    One on One   tf   10.30.79 CBS
    Love for Rent   tf   11.11.79 ABC
    Stand by Your Man   tf   3.31.81 CBS

O'TOOLE, PETER
    SUPP.:
    Masada   ms   4.5.81, 4.6.81, 4.7.81, 4.8.81 ABC

-P-

PAGE, GERALDINE
    A&C:
    The Nurses   ep   For the Mice and Rabbits 2.27.64 CBS
    Kojak   ep   11.21.76 CBS
    SUPP.:
    Something for Joey   tf   4.6.77 CBS

PAIGE, JANIS
    A&C:
    John O'Hara's Gibbsville   tf   4.12.75 NBC
    Police Story   ep   12.5.75 NBC

Lanigan's Rabbi   tf   6. 17. 76   NBC
All's Fair   ep   9. 27. 76, 11. 8. 76   CBS
SUPP. :
The Betty White Show   ep   9. 19. 77   CBS
Eight Is Enough   ep   11. 30. 77   ABC
Fantasy Island   ep   9. 30. 78   ABC
Hawaii Five-O   ep   10. 19. 78   CBS
The Love Boat   ep   Parents Know Best 2. 25. 78   ABC
Alice   ep   2. 26. 78   CBS
Charlie's Angels   ep   Angels Ahoy 11. 8. 78   ABC
Eight Is Enough   ep   11. 7. 79, 4. 2. 80   ABC
Valentine Magic on Love Island   tf   2. 15. 80   NBC
Angel on My Shoulder   tf   5. 11. 80   ABC
Fantasy Island   ep   1. 10. 81   ABC
Happy Days   ep   5. 19. 81   ABC
Bret Maverick   ep   The Lazy Ace 12. 1. 81   NBC
Flamingo Road   ep   The Powers That Be 12. 15. 81   NBC
Lewis and Clark   ep   12. 19. 81   NBC

PALANCE, JACK
SUPP. :
Buck Rogers in the 25th Century   ep   Planet of the Slave Girls
    9. 27. 79   NBC
Last Ride of the Dalton Gang   tf   11. 20. 79   NBC
The Furry Ape   tf   4. 18. 80   ABC
The Golden Moment: An Olympic Love Story   tf   5. 25. 80,
    5. 26. 80   NBC
Ripley's Believe It or Not   pt hos   5. 3. 81   ABC
Tales of the Haunted   ep   Evil Stalks This House   pt   7. 12-16. 81
    NN
Evil Stalks This House   tf   (reedited from above pilot) 8. 12. 81
    NN
Ripley's Believe It or Not   second pt hos   11. 6. 81   ABC

PALMER, BETSY
SUPP. :
CHiPs   ep   12. 7. 80   NBC
Number 96   sr   12. 10. 80   NBC

PARKER, ELEANOR
SUPP. :
Fantasy Island   tf   1. 14. 77   ABC
Hawaii Five-O   ep   1. 12. 78   CBS
The Bastard/Kent Family Chronicles   ms   5. 22. 78, 5. 23. 78   NN
Fantasy Island   ep   3. 17. 79   ABC
The Love Boat   ep   9. 15. 79   ABC
She's Dressed to Kill   tf   12. 10. 79   NBC
Once Upon a Spy   tf   9. 19. 80   ABC
Madame X   tf   3. 16. 81   NBC

PARKER, LARA*
Dark Shadows   sr   6. 27. 66 (through 4. 2. 71) ABC
N. Y. P. D.   ep   The Love Hustle 12. 31. 68 ABC

Medical Center   ep   The Guilty 9.10.73 CBS
My Darling Daughters' Anniversary   tf   11.6.73 ABC
Kojak   ep   Dark Sunday 12.12.73 CBS
Owen Marshall, Counselor at Law   ep   Etude for a Kidnapper
    1.2.74 ABC
The Chadwick Family   tf   4.17.74 ABC
The Six Million Dollar Man   ep   The Deadly Replay 11.22.74
    ABC
Police Woman   ep   Sidewinder 1.17.75 NBC
The Rockford Files   ep   Sleight of Hand 1.17.75 NBC
The Night Stalker   ep   1.24.75 ABC
Insight   ep   2.2.75 NN
Adventures of the Queen   tf   2.14.75 CBS
Mobile One   ep   9.12.75 ABC
Switch   ep   3.2.76 CBS
City of Angels   ep   3.16.76 NBC
Stranded   pt   5.26.76 CBS
Kojak   ep   Out of the Shadows 10.17.76 CBS
Switch   ep   1.23.77 CBS
Washington: Behind Closed Doors   ms   9.6-11.77 ABC
The Incredible Hulk   tf   11.4.77 CBS
Switch   ep   12.12.77 CBS
Hawaii Five-O   ep   1.2.78 CBS
Baretta   ep   2.23.78 ABC
Quincy, M.E.   ep   Double Death 3.3.78 NBC
Sword of Justice   ep   7.10.79 NBC
The Lazarus Syndrome   ep   9.4.79 ABC
The Solitary Man   tf   10.9.79 CBS
Hawaii Five-O   ep   3.22.80 CBS
Hagen   ep   4.5.80 CBS
Galactica 1980   ep   4.20.80 ABC
Desperate Voyage   tf   11.29.80 CBS
Jessica Novak   ep   Man on the Street 11.26.81 CBS

PARKINS, BARBARA
    A&C:
    The Untouchables   ep   The Lily Dallas Story 3.16.61 ABC
    SUPP.:
    Young Joe, the Forgotten Kennedy   tf   9.18.77 ABC
    Testimony of Two Men   ms   5.1.78, 5.2.78, 5.3.78 NN
    Ziegfeld: The Man and His Women   tf   5.21.78 NBC
    The Critical List   tf   9.11.78, 9.12.78 NBC
    Vega$ ep   11.5.80 ABC
    Fantasy Island   ep   11.22.80 ABC
    The Manions of America   ms   9.30.81, 10.1.81, 10.2.81 ABC

PARKS, MICHAEL
    A&C:
    The Detectives   ep   The Frightened One 1.6.61 ABC
    Straightaway   ep   Pledge a Nightmare 12.1.61 ABC
    Bus Stop   ep   The Opposite Virtues 2.19.62 ABC
    SUPP.:
    Murder at the World Series   tf   3.20.77 ABC

Escape from Bogen County   tf   10. 7. 77 CBS
Police Woman   ep   3. 8. 78 NBC
Hunters of the Reef   tf   5. 20. 78 NBC
Flying High   ep   10. 6. 78 CBS
Rainbow   tf   11. 6. 78 NBC
Night Cries   tf   12. 9. 78 ABC
Fast Friends   tf   3. 19. 79 NBC
Fantasy Island   ep   5. 5. 79 ABC
Shirley   ep   12. 7. 79 ABC
Reward   tf   5. 23. 80 ABC
Dial "M" for Murder   tf   4. 9. 81 NBC

PARSONS, ESTELLE
   SUPP. :
   Backstairs at the White House   ms ep   2. 12. 79, 2. 19. 79 ABC
   Great Performances   ep   Guests of the Nation 2. 9. 81 PBS
   The Gentleman Bandit   tf   5. 6. 81 CBS

PATTERSON, LORNA*
   Beane's of Boston   pt   5. 30. 79 CBS
   The Lovebirds   pt   7. 18. 79 CBS
   Working Stiffs   ep   10. 13. 79 CBS
   Goodtime Girls   sr   1. 22. 80 ABC
   Angie   ep   1. 14. 80 ABC
   Private Benjamin   sr   4. 6. 81 CBS
   Sidney Shorr   tf   10. 5. 81 NBC
   Private Benjamin   sr ret   10. 12. 81 CBS

PATTERSON, NEVA
   A&C:
   The Paul Lynde Show   ep   PS I Loathe You 1. 17. 73 ABC
   Barnaby Jones   ep   12. 18. 75 CBS
   Theatre in America   ep   Eccentricities of a Nightingale 6. 16. 76
      PBS
   SUPP. :
   Visions   ep   Prison Game 1. 13. 77 PBS
   Logan's Run   ep   11. 7. 77 CBS
   Rosetti and Ryan   ep   11. 10. 77 NBC
   Barnaby Jones   ep   12. 15. 77 CBS
   Nowhere to Run   tf   1. 16. 78 NBC
   Quincy, M. E.   ep   1. 27. 78 NBC
   What's Up Doc?   pt   5. 27. 78 ABC
   The Waltons   ep   1. 18. 79 CBS
   Hawaii Five-O   ep   1. 8. 80 CBS
   Joe Dancer   tf   1. 29. 81 NBC
   The Two of Us   ep   4. 20. 81 CBS

PAVAN, MARISA
   SUPP. :
   McMillan   ep   1. 30. 77 NBC
   Switch   ep   9. 23. 77 CBS
   Hawaii Five-O   ep   12. 29. 77 CBS

PEAKER, E. J.
  A&C:
  Police Woman   ep   11. 29. 74 NBC
  Most Wanted   ep   11. 6. 76 ABC
  The Streets of San Francisco   ep   12. 23. 76 ABC
  SUPP. :
  Quincy, M. E.   ep   5. 6. 77 NBC
  The New Adventures of Wonder Woman   ep   Screaming Javelin
    1. 20. 78 CBS
  Charlie's Angels   ep   Winning Is for Losers 10. 18. 78 ABC
  The Greatest American Hero   ep   4. 15. 81 ABC

PEPPARD, GEORGE
  SUPP. :
  Crisis in Mid-Air   tf   2. 13. 79 CBS
  Torn Between Two Lovers   tf   5. 2. 79 CBS
  CHiPs   ep   Chips Goes Roller Disco 9. 22. 79 NBC

PERRINE, VALERIE
  SUPP. :
  Ziegfeld: The Man and His Women   tf   5. 21. 78 NBC

PERSOFF, NEHEMIAH*
  Shirley Temple's Storybook   ep   Ali Baba and the 40 Thieves
    11. 12. 58 NBC
  The Untouchables   ep   The Empty Chair 10. 15. 59 ABC
  Mr. Lucky   ep   10. 24. 59 CBS
  The Twilight Zone   ep   Judgement Night 12. 4. 59 CBS
  Alfred Hitchcock Presents   ep   The Cure 1. 24. 60 CBS
  The Untouchables   ep   Head of Fire, Feet of Clay 4. 21. 60 ABC
  Wagon Train   ep   The Tiburcio Mendez Story 3. 22. 61 ABC
  The Wild Wild West   ep   The Night of the Inferno 9. 17. 65 CBS
  The Big Valley   ep   Legend of a General 9. 16. 66, 9. 23. 66 ABC
  Mission: Impossible   ep   Odds on Evil 10. 22. 66 CBS
  The Dangerous Days of Kiowa Jones   tf   12. 25. 66 ABC
  The Wild Wild West   ep   The Night of the Deadly Blossom
    3. 17. 67 CBS
  The Wild Wild West   ep   The Night of the Underground Terror
    1. 19. 68 CBS
  Walt Disney's World   ep   The Treasure of San Bosco Reef
    11. 24. 68 NBC
  Escape to Mindanao   tf   12. 7. 68 NBC
  The Name of the Game   ep   Revolutionary 12. 27. 68 NBC
  Gunsmoke   ep   The Commandant 2. 3. 69 CBS
  Mission: Impossible   ep   The Vault 4. 6. 69 CBS
  It Takes a Thief   ep   The Great Chess Gambit 4. 15. 69 ABC
  Cutter's Trail   tf   2. 10. 70 CBS
  Dan August   ep   The Color of Fury 10. 28. 70 ABC
  The Chicago Teddy Bears   ep   10. 22. 71 CBS
  Lt. Schuster's Wife   tf   10. 11. 72 ABC
  The Mod Squad   ep   11. 2. 72 ABC
  Adam-12   ep   11. 22. 72 NBC

Cool Million   ep   11. 22. 72 NBC
Mannix   ep   A Puzzle for One 11. 26. 72 CBS
The Streets of San Francisco   ep   12. 23. 72 ABC
Marcus Welby, M. D.   ep   Who Are You, Arthur Kolinski?
    1. 16. 73 ABC
Search   ep   1. 24. 73 NBC
Hawaii Five-O   ep   Will the Real Mr. Winkler Please Die
    2. 6. 73 CBS
McCloud   ep   The Million Dollar Roundup 2. 4. 73 NBC
Hawaii Five-O   ep   9. 25. 73 CBS
Police Surgeon   ep   Kiss and Kill 11. 16. 73 NN
Love, American Style   ep   Love and the Generation Gap 12. 7. 73
    ABC
McMillan and Wife   ep   Man Without a Face 1. 6. 74 NBC
Gunsmoke   ep   Like Old Times 1. 21. 74 CBS
Police Story   ep   The Hunters 2. 26. 74 NBC
The Sex Symbol   tf   9. 17. 74 ABC
The Stranger Within   tf   10. 1. 74 ABC
The Missiles of October   tf   12. 18. 74 ABC
Hawaii Five-O   ep   2. 25. 75 CBS
Gunsmoke   ep   3. 17. 75 CBS
Marcus Welby, M. D.   ep   9. 9. 75 ABC
The Invisible Man   ep   10. 6. 75 NBC
The Hallmark Hall of Fame   ep   Eric 11. 10. 75 NBC
Columbo   ep   Now You See Him 2. 29. 76 NBC
McNaughton's Daughter   ep   4. 7. 76 NBC
Baretta   ep   Soldier in the Jungle 9. 29. 76 ABC
Francis Gary Powers: The True Story of the U-2 Spy Incident
    tf   9. 29. 76 NBC
The Six Million Dollar Man   ep   Death Probe 1. 9. 77, 1. 16. 77
    ABC
Hawaii Five-O   ep   2. 3. 77 CBS
Rich Man, Poor Man, Book II   ep   3. 1. 77 ABC
Hunter   ep   3. 11. 77 CBS
Quincy, M. E.   ep   A Blow to the Head, a Blow to the Heart
    9. 23. 77 NBC
Police Woman   ep   12. 21. 77 NBC
Little House on the Prairie   ep   2. 20. 78 NBC
The Bionic Woman   ep   Out of Body 3. 4. 78 NBC
Richie Brockelman, Private Eye   ep   3. 24. 78 NBC
High Hopes   sr   4. 17. 78 NN
Killing Stone   tf   5. 2. 78 NBC
Ziegfeld: The Man and His Women   tf   5. 21. 78 NBC
The Word   ms ep   11. 14. 78 CBS
Vega$ ep   11. 1. 78 ABC
The Hardy Boys   ep   11. 19. 78, 11. 26. 78 ABC
Greatest Heroes of the Bible   ep   The Story of Daniel in the
    Lion's Den 11. 22. 78 NBC
Fantasy Island   ep   12. 29. 78 ABC
Hawaii Five-O   ep   12. 28. 78, 1. 4. 79 CBS
Supertrain   ep   2. 21. 79 NBC
Battlestar Galactica   ep   3. 18. 79 ABC
The Rebels   ms ep   5. 21. 79 NN
Police Story   ep   A Cry for Justice 5. 23. 79 NBC

The French-Atlantic Affair   ms   11. 15. 79, 11. 16. 79, 11. 18. 79
   ABC
The 13th Day: The Story of Esther   pt   11. 18. 79 ABC
Fantasy Island   ep   2. 2. 80 ABC
The Henderson Monster   tf   5. 27. 80 CBS
Turnover Smith   tf   6. 8. 80 ABC

PESCOW, DONNA*
   Human Feelings   tf   10. 16. 78 NBC
   Rainbow   tf   11. 6. 78 NBC
   Angie   sr   2. 8. 79 ABC
   The Love Boat   ep   2. 10. 79 ABC
   Angie   sr ret   9. 11. 79 ABC
   Advice to the Lovelorn   tf   11. 30. 81 NBC

PETERS, BERNADETTE
   SUPP. :
   The Islander   tf   9. 16. 78 NBC
   The Martian Chronicles   ms ep   1. 29. 80 NBC

PETERS, BROCK
   SUPP. :
   Seventh Avenue   ms   2. 10. 77, 2. 17. 77, 2. 24. 77 NBC
   SST--Death Flight   tf   2. 25. 77 ABC
   Black Beauty   ms   1. 31. 78, 2. 1-4. 78 NBC
   The Bionic Woman   ep   Which One Is Jaime? 2. 25. 78 NBC
   Quincy, M. E.   ep   10. 26. 78 NBC
   Mark Twain's America   ep   Abe Lincoln: Freedom Fighter
     sp   1. 30. 79 NBC
   Roots: The Next Generations   ms ep   2. 22. 79 ABC

PETTET, JOANNA
   SUPP. :
   Winner Take All   pt   4. 1. 77 CBS
   Tales of the Unexpected   ep   8. 17. 77 NBC
   Sex and the Married Woman   tf   9. 13. 77 NBC
   The Love Boat   ep   Next Door Wife 12. 8. 79 ABC
   Fantasy Island   ep   3. 1. 80 ABC
   Charlie's Angels   ep   Nips and Tucks 3. 5. 80 ABC
   Cry of the Innocent   tf   6. 19. 80 ABC
   Tales of the Unexpected   ep   10. 18. 80 NN
   The Return of Frank Cannon   tf   11. 1. 80 CBS
   The Love Boat   ep   I Love You Too, Smith 3. 7. 81 ABC
   Tales of the Unexpected   ep   A Glowing Future 3. 21. 81 NN
   Aloha Paradise   ep   3. 25. 81 ABC

PEYSER, PENNY*
   Rich Man, Poor Man, Book II   sr   9. 21. 76 ABC
   Switch   ep   3. 13. 77 CBS
   The Hardy Boys/Nancy Drew Mysteries   ep   4. 10. 77 ABC
   The Quinns   tf   7. 17. 77 ABC
   The Tony Randall Show   sr   9. 24. 77 CBS
   Having Babies   tf   3. 14. 78 ABC

B. J. and the Bear tf 10. 4. 78 NBC
Barnaby Jones ep Stages of Fear 11. 23. 78 CBS
The Girls in the Office tf 2. 2. 79 ABC
Sweepstakes ep 2. 16. 79 NBC
Wild Times ms 1. 24. 80, 1. 31. 80 NN
The White Shadow ep 12. 23. 80 CBS
National Lampoon's Two Reelers pt 8. 28. 81 NBC
The Incredible Hulk ep 10. 9. 81 CBS

PFLUG, JO ANN
  SUPP. :
  Quincy, M. E. ep 2. 4. 77 NBC
  Operation Petticoat sr 9. 18. 78 ABC
  Quincy, M. E. ep The Trick of Death 9. 28. 78 NBC
  The Love Boat ep The Man Who Loved Women 9. 30. 78 ABC
  Quincy, M. E. 1. 18. 79 NBC
  The Dukes of Hazzard ep 4. 20. 79 CBS
  Operation Petticoat sr ret 6. 1. 79 ABC
  Vega$ ep 9. 19. 79 ABC
  The Love Boat ep 11. 3. 79 ABC
  Charlie's Angels ep Angels on Campus 11. 28. 79 ABC
  Fantasy Island ep 3. 1. 80 ABC
  The Love Boat ep 11. 8. 80 ABC
  The Day the Women Got Even tf 12. 4. 80 NBC
  Nuts & Bolts pt 8. 24. 81 ABC
  The Fall Guy sr 10. 28. 81 ABC

PHILLIPS, MACKENZIE
  SUPP. :
  One Day at a Time sr ret 9. 20. 77 CBS
  One Day at a Time sr ret 9. 18. 78 CBS
  The Love Boat ep 10. 14. 78 ABC
  Fast Friends tf 3. 19. 79 NBC
  The Incredible Hulk ep 9. 21. 79 CBS
  Moviola: The Silent Lovers tf 5. 20. 80 NBC
  One Day at a Time ep Julie's Return 11. 8. 81, 11. 15. 81 CBS

PICKENS, SLIM
  A&C:
  Riverboat ep River Champion 10. 10. 60 NBC
  Americans ep The Invaders 3. 27. 61 NBC
  The Virginian ep Run Quiet 11. 13. 63 NBC
  SUPP. :
  The ABC Weekend Special ep The Winged Colt 9. 10. 77,
    9. 17. 77, 9. 24. 77 ABC
  How the West Was Won ep 3. 26. 78, 4. 9. 78, 4. 30. 78, 5. 7. 78
    ABC
  The Busters pt 5. 28. 78 CBS
  Vega$ ep 10. 25. 78 ABC
  The Sacketts tf 5. 16. 79 NBC
  When the West Was Fun sp 6. 5. 79 ABC
  B. J. and the Bear sr 9. 29. 79 NBC
  Undercover with the KKK tf 10. 23. 79 NBC

The Love Boat   ep   Sis and the Slicker 1. 19. 80 ABC
Swan Song   tf   2. 8. 80 ABC
Jake's Way   pt   6. 28. 80 CBS
Best of the West   ep   9. 17. 81 ABC

PICON, MOLLY
  SUPP. :
Vega$ ep   10. 11. 78 ABC
The Facts of Life   ep   From Russia with Love 12. 16. 81 NBC

PLATO, DANA*
  Beyond the Bermuda Triangle   tf   11. 6. 75 NBC
  Diff'rent Strokes   sr   11. 3. 78 NBC
  Diff'rent Strokes   sr ret   9. 21. 79 NBC
  CHiPs   ep   Chips Goes Roller Disco 9. 22. 79 NBC
  CHiPs   ep   The Case of the   Vanishing Nurse 3. 23. 80 NBC
  Family   ep   6. 25. 80 ABC
  Diff'rent Strokes   sr ret   11. 12. 80 NBC
  The ABC Afterschool Special   ep   Schoolboy Father   sp   10. 15. 80
    ABC
  Diff'rent Strokes   sr ret   10. 29. 81 NBC

PLEASENCE, DONALD
  A& C:
Danger Man   ep   Position of Trust 7. 5. 61 CBS
Danger Man   ep   Find and Return 8. 23. 61 CBS
  SUPP. :
Jesus of Nazareth   ms   4. 3. 77, 4. 10. 77 NBC
Goldenrod   tf   6. 1. 77 CBS
The New Adventures of Wonder Woman   ep   1. 27. 78 CBS
The Deadly Secret of Harvest Home   tf   1. 23. 78, 1. 24. 78
  NBC
The Defection of Simas Kudirka   tf   1. 23. 78 CBS
The Bastard/Kent Family Chronicles   ms   5. 22. 78, 5. 23. 78 NN
Centennial   ms ep   The Wagon and the Elephant 10. 29. 78   NBC
Mrs. Columbo   ep   3. 1. 79 NBC
Gold of the Amazon Women   tf   3. 6. 79 NBC
Better Late Than Never   tf   10. 17. 79 NBC
The Hallmark Hall of Fame   ep   All Quiet on the Western Front
  sp   11. 14. 79 CBS
The French-Atlantic Affair   ms   11. 15. 79, 11. 16. 79, 11. 18. 79
  ABC

PLESHETTE, SUZANNE
  SUPP. :
The Bob Newhart Show   sr ret   9. 24. 77 CBS
Kate Bliss and the Ticker Tape Kid   tf   5. 26. 78 ABC
Flesh and Blood   tf   10. 14. 79, 10. 16. 79 CBS
If Things Were Different   tf   1. 16. 80 CBS
The Star Maker   tf   5. 11. 81, 5. 12. 81 NBC

PLUMB, EVE*
  The Big Valley   ep   Brother Love 2. 20. 67 ABC

The Big Valley   ep   Explosion 11. 27. 67 ABC
Family Affair   ep   11. 11. 68 CBS
The Brady Bunch   sr   9. 26. 69 ABC
The House on Greenapple Road   tf   1. 11. 70 ABC
The Brady Bunch   sr ret   9. 25. 70 ABC
The Brady Bunch   sr ret   9. 17. 71 ABC
The Brady Kids   sr vo   9. 9. 72 ABC
The Brady Bunch   sr ret   9. 25. 72 ABC
Here's Lucy   ep   11. 20. 72 CBS
The Brady Bunch   sr ret   9. 14. 73 ABC
Dawn: Portrait of a Teenage Runaway   tf   9. 27. 76 ABC
Alexander: The Other Side of Dawn   tf   5. 16. 77 NBC
The New Adventures of Wonder Woman   ep   The Pied Piper
     10. 21. 77 CBS
Telethon   tf   11. 6. 77 ABC
The Love Boat   ep   Gopher the Rebel 5. 20. 78 ABC
Little Women   tf   10. 2. 78, 10. 3. 78 NBC
Secrets of Three Hungry Wives   tf   10. 9. 78 NBC
Greatest Heroes of the Bible   ep   The Story of Noah 11. 19. 78,
     11. 20. 78 NBC
Fantasy Island   ep   1. 13. 79 ABC
Little Women   sr   2. 8. 79 NBC
Fantasy Island   ep   9. 7. 79 ABC
The Love Boat   ep   Honeymoon Pressure 3. 29. 80 ABC
The Night the Bridge Fell Down   tf   10. 21. 80 NBC
Fantasy Island   ep   1. 17. 81 ABC
The Brady Girls Get Married   sr   2. 6. 81 NBC
The Brady Brides   sr   3. 6. 81 NBC
The Brady Girls Get Married   tf   10. 27. 81 NBC

PLUMMER, CHRISTOPHER
     SUPP. :
     Jesus of Nazareth   ms   4. 3. 77, 4. 10. 77 NBC
     Desperate Voyage   tf   11. 29. 80 CBS
     The Shadow Box   tf   12. 28. 80 ABC
     When the Circus Came to Town   tf   1. 20. 81 CBS

PORTER, DON
     A&C:
     The Mod Squad   ep   2. 8. 73 ABC
     The Norliss Tapes   tf   2. 21. 73 NBC
     Hawaii Five-O   ep   Tricks Are Not Treats 10. 16. 73 CBS
     Tenafly   ep   The Cash and Carry Caper 10. 31. 73 NBC
     The ABC Afterschool Playbreak   ep   Mother of the Bride
          1. 9. 74 ABC
     The FBI   ep   3. 24. 74 ABC
     Ellery Queen   ep   11. 13. 75 NBC
     SUPP. :
     The Bionic Woman   ep   Deadly Ringer 2. 2. 77, 2. 9. 77 ABC
     Three's Company   ep   12. 6. 77 ABC
     Switch   ep   12. 19. 77 CBS
     Christmas Miracle in Caulfield U. S. A.   tf   12. 26. 77 NBC
     The President's Mistress   tf   2. 10. 78 CBS

The Love Boat   ep   Gopher the Rebel 5. 20. 78 ABC
What's Up Doc?   pt   5. 27. 78 ABC
The Paper Chase   ep   The Man Who Would Be King 9. 26. 78
    CBS
Frankie and Annette: The Second Time Around   pt   11. 18. 78
    NBC
Sword of Justice   ep   12. 17. 78 NBC
Insight   ep   1. 21. 79 NN
Battles: The Murder That Wouldn't Die   tf   3. 9. 80 NBC
Dallas   ep   2. 15. 80 CBS
The Last Song   tf   10. 23. 80 CBS
Fantasy Island   ep   2. 28. 81 ABC
Jessica Novak   ep   A Mirrorful of Gamblers 12. 3. 81 CBS

PORTER, NYREE DAWN
    SUPP. :
    The Martian Chronicles   ms ep   1. 29. 80 NBC

POSTON, TOM
    SUPP. :
    All's Fair   ep   3. 7. 77 CBS
    The Magnificent Magnet of Santa Mesa   tf   6. 19. 77 NBC
    We've Got Each Other   sr   10. 1. 77 CBS
    The Love Boat   ep   A Fine Romance 12. 24. 77 ABC
    Sweepstakes   ep   2. 2. 79 NBC
    CHiPs   ep   2. 24. 79 NBC
    Beane's of Boston   pt   5. 30. 79 CBS
    Mork and Mindy   sr   9. 16. 79 ABC
    Good Time Harry   ep   8. 16. 80 NBC
    Mork and Mindy   sr ret   11. 13. 80 ABC
    The Girl, the Gold Watch and Dynamite   pt   5. 21. 81 NN

POWELL, JANE
    SUPP. :
    Fantasy Island   ep   2. 4. 78, 2. 14. 81 ABC
    The Love Boat   ep   Maid for Each Other 5. 9. 81 ABC

POWERS, MALA
    SUPP. :
    Charlie's Angels   ep   Antique Angels 5. 10. 78 ABC

POWERS, STEFANIE (listed incorrectly as Stephanie Powers in
    Supp. I)
    A& C:
    Shoot-Out in a One-Dog Town   tf   1. 9. 74 ABC
    Police Surgeon   ep   2. 9. 75 NN
    Return to Earth   tf   5. 14. 76 ABC
    SUPP. :
    The Feather and Father Gang   sr   3. 7. 77 ABC
    McMillan   ep   3. 20. 77 NBC
    Washington: Behind Closed Doors   ms   9. 6-11. 77 ABC
    Nowhere to Run   tf   1. 16. 78 NBC
    A Death in Canaan   tf   3. 1. 78 CBS

Hart to Hart   pt   8. 25. 79 ABC
Hart to Hart   sr   9. 22. 79 ABC
Hart to Hart   sr ret   11. 11. 80 ABC
Hart to Hart   sr ret   10. 6. 81 ABC

PRANGE, LAURIE*
The Man and the City   ep   A Very Special Girl 10. 6. 71 ABC
My Three Sons   ep   2. 17. 72 CBS
The Partridge Family   ep   2. 26. 71 ABC
The Waltons   ep   The Fire 1. 11. 73 CBS
Gunsmoke   ep   The Lost 9. 13. 71 CBS
Kung Fu   ep   The Hoots 12. 13. 73 ABC
Chopper One   ep   1. 24. 74 ABC
Trapped Beneath the Sea   tf   10. 22. 74 ABC
Hollywood Television Theatre   ep   The Lady's Not for Burning
    11. 18. 74 PBS
Insight   ep   1. 12. 75 NN
Manhunter   ep   2. 5. 75 CBS
Hawaii Five-O   ep   1. 27. 77 CBS
Switch   ep   2. 13. 77 CBS
Baa Baa Black Sheep   ep   3. 1. 77 NBC
Barnaby Jones   ep   5. 12. 77 CBS
Ransom for Alice   tf   6. 2. 77 NBC
The Incredible Hulk   sp ep   Death in the Family 11. 28. 77 CBS
Barnaby Jones   ep   12. 15. 77 CBS
What Really Happened to the Class of '65?   ep   1. 12. 78 NBC
The Love Boat   ep   Parents Know Best 2. 25. 78 ABC
Testimony of Two Men   ms   5. 1. 78, 5. 2. 78, 5. 3. 78 NN
Insight   ep   7. 16. 78 NN
How the West Was Won   ep   3. 19. 79 ABC
The Incredible Hulk   ep   11. 7. 80 CBS

PRENTISS, PAULA
SUPP. :
Having Babies II   tf   10. 28. 77 ABC
Friendships, Secrets and Lies   tf   12. 3. 79 NBC
Top of the Hill   ms   2. 6. 80, 2. 7. 80 NN

PRESSMAN, LAWRENCE*
The Governor and J. J.   ep   10. 28. 70 CBS
Cannon   tf   3. 26. 71 CBS
The Mary Tyler Moore Show   ep   The Six and a Half Year Itch
    11. 27. 71 CBS
Hollywood Television Theatre   ep   Young Marrieds At Play
    12. 9. 71 PBS
Owen Marshall, Counselor at Law   ep   Burden of Proof 12. 2. 71
    ABC
McMillan and Wife   ep   Till Death Do Us Part 2. 16. 72 NBC
Owen Marshall, Counselor at Law   ep   Who Saw Him Die?
    11. 2. 72 ABC
Marcus Welby, M. D.   ep   Please Don't Send Flowers 11. 14. 72
    ABC
The Snoop Sisters   ep   12. 18. 72 NBC

The Marcus-Nelson Murders   tf   3. 8. 73 CBS
The Delphi Bureau   ep   3. 24. 73 ABC
The Nancy Dussault Show   pt   5. 8. 73 CBS
Marcus Welby, M. D.   ep   Blood Kin 10. 2. 73 ABC
Griff   ep   All the Lonely People   10. 13. 73 ABC
Hawaii Five-O   ep   Why Wait Till Uncle Kevin Dies? 10. 30. 73
  CBS
Owen Marshall, Counselor at Law   ep   The Prowler 12. 12. 73
  ABC
6 RMS RIV VU   sp   3. 17. 74 CBS
Winter Kill   tf   4. 15. 74 ABC
Barnaby Jones   ep   Dead Man's Run 9. 17. 74 CBS
Paper Moon   ep   10. 17. 74 ABC
The Bob Newhart Show   ep   11. 2. 74 CBS
Harry O   ep   Silent Kill 2. 6. 75 ABC
The First 36 Hours of Dr. Durant   tf   5. 13. 75 ABC
McMillan and Wife   ep   Requiem for a Bride 10. 26. 75 NBC
Cannon   ep   1. 7. 76 CBS
Rich Man, Poor Man   ms   2. 1-23. 76, 3. 1-15. 76 ABC
Barnaby Jones   ep   11. 11. 76 CBS
Switch   ep   12. 14. 76 CBS
Police Woman   ep   12. 21. 76 NBC
The Man from Atlantis   ep   3. 4. 77 NBC
Lanigan's Rabbi   ep   4. 24. 77 NBC
The Streets of San Francisco   ep   5. 12. 77 ABC
Mulligan's Stew   tf   6. 20. 77 NBC
The Trial of Lee Harvey Oswald   tf   9. 30. 77, 10. 1. 77 ABC
Mulligan's Stew   sr   10. 25. 77 NBC
The Gathering   tf   12. 4. 77 ABC
Like Mom, Like Me   tf   10. 22. 78 CBS
Blind Ambition   ms   5. 20-23. 79 CBS
Insight   ep   6. 3. 79 NN
Love and Learn   pt   8. 1. 79 NBC
The Gathering, Part II   tf   12. 17. 79 NBC
Ladies' Man   sr   10. 27. 80 CBS
One Day at a Time   ep   11. 9. 80 CBS
Darkroom   ep   Stay Tuned, We'll Be Right Back 11. 27. 81 ABC

PRESTON, ROBERT
  SUPP. :
  American Short Story   ep   The Man That Corrupted Hadleyburg
    3. 17. 80 PBS
  The Chisholms   ms   3. 29. 79, 4. 5. 79, 4. 12. 79, 4. 19. 79 CBS
  The Chisholms   sr   1. 19. 80 CBS

PRICE, VINCENT
  SUPP. :
  The Bionic Woman   ep   Black Magic 10. 8. 77 NBC
  The Love Boat   ep   Ship of Ghouls 10. 28. 78 ABC
  Time Express   sr   4. 26. 79 CBS
  CBS Library   ep   Once Upon a Midnight Dreary   hos   10. 21. 79
    CBS
  Mystery   sr hos   1. 6. 81 PBS

PRINCE, WILLIAM
SUPP. :
Johnny, We Hardly Knew Ye   tf   1. 27. 77 NBC
The Rhinemann Exchange   ms   3. 10. 77, 3. 17. 77, 3. 24. 77 NBC
Best of Families   sr   10. 27. 77 PBS
Aspen   ms ep   11. 6. 77 NBC
The American Girls   sr   9. 23. 78 CBS
Quincy, M. E.   ep   2. 1. 79 NBC
The Paper Chase   ep   A Matter of Anger 2. 13. 79 CBS
The Jericho Mile   tf   3. 18. 79 ABC
Dear Detective   ep   4. 11. 79 CBS
American Short Story   ep   The Greatest Man in the World
   2. 11. 80 PBS
ABC Theatre   ep   A Time for Miracles   sp   12. 21. 80 ABC
Quincy, M. E.   ep   3. 4. 81 NBC
City of Fear   tf   7. 26. 81 ABC
Dynasty   ep   12. 23. 81 ABC

PRINCIPAL, VICTORIA*
Love, American Style   ep   2. 2. 73, 3. 2. 73 ABC
Love Story   ep   When the Girls Come Out to Play 12. 5. 73 NBC
Banacek   ep   Fly Me--If You Can Find Me 2. 19. 74 NBC
Last Hours Before Morning   tf   4. 19. 75 NBC
Fantasy Island   tf   1. 14. 77 ABC
The Rockford Files   ep   1. 14. 77 NBC
The Night They Took Miss Beautiful   tf   10. 24. 77 NBC
Dallas   sr   4. 2. 78 CBS
Dallas   sr ret   9. 23. 78 CBS
Hawaii Five-O   ep   4. 5. 79 CBS
Dallas   sr ret   9. 21. 79 CBS
Pleasure Palace   tf   10. 22. 80 CBS
Dallas   sr ret   11. 7. 80 CBS
Greatest Heroes of the Bible   ep   The Story of Esther 7. 26. 81
   NBC
Dallas   sr ret   10. 9. 81 CBS

PRINE, ANDREW
A& C:
Dr. Kildare   ep   A Game for Three 10. 24. 63 NBC
The Virginian   ep   The Strange Quest of Claire Bingham
   4. 5. 67 NBC
Barnaby Jones   ep   Day of the Viper 10. 7. 73 CBS
Police Surgeon   ep   6. 2. 74 NN
The Gemini Man   ep   9. 23. 76 NBC
SUPP. :
Quincy, M. E.   ep   1. 2. 77 NBC
Tail Gunner Joe   tf   2. 6. 77 NBC
Hunter   ep   3. 11. 77 CBS
The Bionic Woman   ep   Rodeo 10. 15. 77 NBC
Last of the Mohicans   tf   11. 23. 77 NBC
Christmas Miracle in Caulfield, U. S. A.   tf   12. 26. 77 NBC
Hawaii Five-O   ep   4. 27. 78 CBS
W. E. B.   sr   9. 13. 78 NBC

Donner Pass: The Road to Survival tf 10. 24. 78 CBS
Mind Over Murder tf 10. 23. 79 CBS
Mark Twain's America ep Abe Lincoln: Freedom Fighter
    sp 10. 30. 79 NBC
One Day at a Time ep 3. 30. 80 CBS
M Station: Hawaii tf 6. 10. 80 CBS
The Littlest Hobo ep 2. 28. 81 NN
Callie and Son tf 10. 13. 81 CBS
A Small Killing tf 11. 24. 81 CBS

PROWSE, JULIET
   SUPP. :
   The Love Boat ep Doc's "Ex" Change 12. 15. 79 ABC

PURCELL, LEE*
   Bonanza ep The Weary Willies 9. 27. 70 NBC
   Medical Center ep 11. 1. 72 CBS
   Cannon ep He Who Digs a Grave 9. 12. 73 CBS
   Hijack! tf 9. 26. 73 ABC
   The Rockford Files ep 11. 15. 74 NBC
   Cannon ep 4. 2. 75 CBS
   The Waltons ep 10. 23. 75 CBS
   Cannon ep 11. 26. 75 CBS
   Barnaby Jones ep 12. 4. 75 CBS
   Hawaii Five-O ep 1. 29. 76 CBS
   Jigsaw John ep 2. 9. 76 NBC
   The Streets of San Francisco ep 1. 6. 77 ABC
   The Amazing Howard Hughes tf 4. 13. 77, 4. 14. 77 CBS
   Barnaby Jones ep 10. 20. 77 CBS
   Stranger in Our House tf 10. 31. 78 NBC
   Murder in Music City tf 1. 16. 79 NBC
   My Wife Next Door pt 9. 11. 80 CBS
   The Secret War of Jackie's Girls tf 11. 29. 80 NBC
   The Girl, the Gold Watch and Dynamite pt 5. 21. 81 NN
   Killing at Hell's Gate tf 10. 31. 81 CBS

PURL, LINDA*
   Happy Days ep 9. 17. 74 ABC
   Lucas Tanner ep 10. 2. 74 NBC
   Bad Ronald tf 10. 23. 74 ABC
   Sons and Daughters sr 10. 23. 74 CBS
   The Waltons ep The Spoilers 10. 31. 74 CBS
   Hawaii Five-O ep The Hostage 3. 11. 75 CBS
   Medical Center ep 10. 20. 75 CBS
   Medical Story ep Us Against the World 12. 4. 75 NBC
   The Oregon Trail tf 1. 10. 76 NBC
   State Fair pt 5. 14. 76 CBS
   Having Babies tf 10. 17. 76 ABC
   Eleanor and Franklin tf 1. 11. 76, 1. 12. 76 ABC
   The Young Pioneers tf 3. 1. 76 ABC
   The Young Pioneers Christmas tf 12. 17. 76 ABC
   Serpico ep 1. 7. 77 NBC
   Little Ladies of the Night tf 1. 16. 77 ABC

The Waltons   ep   2.17.77 CBS
Black Market Baby   tf   10.7.77 ABC
What Really Happened to the Class of '65?   ep   1.19.78 NBC
The Young Pioneers   sr   4.2.78 ABC
Testimony of Two Men   ms   5.1.78, 5.2.78, 5.3.78 NN
Last Cry for Help   tf   1.19.79 ABC
Women at West Point   tf   2.27.79 CBS
Like Normal People   tf   4.13.79 ABC
The Flame Is Love   tf   10.15.79 NBC
The Night the City Screamed   tf   12.14.80 ABC
The Manions of America   ms   9.30.81, 10.1.81, 10.2.81 ABC
The Adventures of Nellie Bly   tf   6.11.81 NBC

-Q-

QUINN, ANTHONY
   SUPP.:
   Ten Who Dared   sr nar   1.3.77 NN
   Jesus of Nazareth   ms   4.3.77, 4.10.77 NBC

-R-

RAE, CHARLOTTE
   A&C:
   Temperature's Rising   ep   5.1.73 ABC
   McMillan and Wife   ep   Blues for Sally M   5.13.73 NBC
   All's Fair   ep   12.20.76 CBS
   SUPP.:
   C.P.O. Sharkey   ep   3.24.78 NBC
   Family   ep   10.19.78 ABC
   Diff'rent Strokes   sr   11.3.78 NBC
   The Triangle Factory Fire   tf   1.30.79 NBC
   Beane's of Boston   pt   5.30.79 CBS
   The Facts of Life   sr   8.24.79 NBC
   Diff'rent Strokes   sr ret   9.21.79 NBC
   The Facts of Life   sr ret   3.12.80 NBC
   The Facts of Life   sr ret   11.19.80 NBC
   The Facts of Life   sr ret   10.28.81 NBC

RAFFIN, DEBORAH*
   Nightmare in Badham County   tf   11.5.76 ABC
   Ski Lift to Death   tf   3.3.78 CBS
   How to Pick Up Girls   tf   11.3.78 ABC
   Willa   tf   3.17.79 CBS
   The Last Convertible   ms   9.24.79, 9.25.79, 9.26.79 NBC

Mind over Murder   tf   10. 23. 79 CBS
Haywire   tf   5. 14. 80 CBS
For the Love of It   tf   9. 26. 80 ABC
Foul Play   sr   1. 26. 81 ABC
Foul Play   sr ret   8. 16. 81 ABC
Killing at Hell's Gate   tf   10. 31. 81 CBS

RAINES, CRISTINA*
Sunshine   tf   11. 9. 73 NBC
Movin' On   ep   12. 5. 74 NBC
Doctors' Hospital   ep   9. 10. 75 NBC
The Family Holvak   ep   10. 5. 75, 10. 12. 75 NBC
Kojak   ep   Letters of Death 11. 13. 77 CBS
Loose Change   ms   2. 26. 78, 2. 27. 78, 2. 28. 78 NBC
Centennial   ms ep   For As Long As the Water Flows 11. 4. 78
   NBC
Centennial   ms ep   The Massacre 11. 11. 78 NBC
Centennial   ms ep   The Longhorns 12. 3. 78 NBC
Centennial   ms ep   The Shepherds 12. 10. 78 NBC
Centennial   ms ep   The Storm 1. 14. 79 NBC
Centennial   ms ep   The Crime 1. 21. 79 NBC
The Child Stealer   tf   3. 9. 79 ABC
The Tenth Month   tf   9. 16. 79 CBS
Flamingo Road   tf   5. 12. 80 NBC
Flamingo Road   sr   1. 6. 81 NBC
Flamingo Road   sr ret   11. 3. 81 NBC

RAMBO, DACK
SUPP. :
Tabitha   ep   11. 12. 77 ABC
Fantasy Island   ep   2. 11. 78 ABC
Sword of Justice   sr   10. 7. 78 NBC

RANDALL, TONY
SUPP. :
The Tony Randall Show   sr ret   9. 24. 77 CBS
Kate Bliss and the Ticker Tape Kid   tf   5. 26. 78 ABC
Sidney Shorr   tf   10. 5. 81 NBC
Love, Sidney   sr   10. 28. 81 NBC

RAYE, MARTHA
SUPP. :
The Love Boat   ep   My Sister Irene 1. 13. 79 ABC
Alice   ep   2. 5. 79, 11. 11. 79 CBS
Skinflint   sp   12. 18. 79 NBC
Alice   ep   2. 3. 80 CBS
The Gossip Columnist   pt   3. 22. 80 NN
Alice   ep   Henry's Better Half 12. 21. 80 CBS
The Love Boat   ep   Zeke and Zack 12. 5. 81 ABC

REDGRAVE, LYNN*
Centennial   ms ep   The Storm 1. 14. 79 NBC
Centennial   ms ep   The Crime 1. 21. 79 NBC

Centennial ms ep The Winds of Fortune 1. 28. 79 NBC
Centennial ms ep The Winds of Death 2. 3. 79 NBC
Sooner or Later tf 3. 25. 79 NBC
Beggarman, Thief tf 11. 26. 79, 11. 27. 79 NBC
House Calls sr 12. 17. 79 CBS
Gauguin the Savage tf 5. 29. 80 CBS
The Seduction of Miss Leona tf 8. 26. 80 CBS
House Calls sr ret 11. 17. 80 CBS
House Calls sr ret 11. 2. 81 CBS

REDGRAVE, VANESSA*
Playing for Time tf 9. 30. 80 CBS

REED, DONNA
    SUPP. :
    The Best Place to Be tf 5. 27. 79 NBC

REED, ROBERT
    A& C:
    Mannix ep Little Girl Lost 10. 7. 73 CBS
    Rich Man, Poor Man ms ep 2. 1. 76, 2. 9. 76, 2. 16. 76, 3. 8. 76
        ABC
    Lanigan's Rabbi tf 6. 17. 76 NBC
    SUPP. :
    The Love Boat tf 1. 21. 77 ABC
    Roots ms ep 1. 25. 77, 1. 26. 77, 1. 27. 77 ABC
    SST--Death Flight tf 2. 25. 77 ABC
    Barnaby Jones ep 9. 15. 77 CBS
    The Love Boat ep Ex Plus Y 10. 8. 77 ABC
    The Hunted Lady tf 11. 28. 77 NBC
    Lucan ep 3. 27. 78 ABC
    Operation: Runaway sr 4. 27. 78 NBC
    The Love Boat ep 10. 21. 78 ABC
    Bud and Lou tf 11. 15. 78 NBC
    Vega$ ep 11. 15. 78 ABC
    Thou Shalt Not Commit Adultery tf 11. 1. 78 NBC
    Fantasy Island ep 12. 16. 78 ABC
    Hawaii Five-O ep 1. 18. 79 CBS
    The Paper Chase ep 2. 27. 79 CBS
    Love's Savage Fury tf 5. 20. 79 ABC
    Vega$ ep 9. 26. 79 ABC
    Hawaii Five-O ep 10. 18. 79 CBS
    The Seekers ms 12. 3. 79, 12. 4. 79 NN
    Galactica 1980 sr 1. 27. 80 ABC
    Scruples ms 2. 25. 80, 2. 26. 80, 2. 28. 80 CBS
    Nurse tf 4. 9. 80 CBS
    Charlie's Angels ep Angels in Love 4. 30. 80, 5. 7. 80 ABC
    Casino tf 8. 1. 80 ABC
    The Brady Girls Get Married sr 2. 6. 81 NBC
    Nurse sr 4. 2. 81 CBS
    The Brady Girls Get Married tf 10. 27. 81 NBC
    Death of a Centerfold: The Dorothy Stratton Story tf 11. 1. 81
        NBC
    Nurse sr ret 11. 11. 81 CBS

REINER, ROB
  SUPP.:
  All in the Family   sr ret   10. 2. 77 CBS
  Free Country   sr   6. 24. 78 ABC
  More Than Friends   tf   10. 20. 78 ABC
  Archie Bunker's Place   ep   11. 18. 79 CBS

REMICK, LEE
  SUPP.:
  ABC Theatre   ep   Breaking Up   sp   1. 2. 78 ABC
  Wheels   ms   5. 7. 78,   5. 8. 78,   5. 9. 78,   5. 14. 78,   5. 15. 78 NBC
  Torn Between Two Lovers   tf   5. 2. 79 CBS
  Ike   ms   5. 3. 79,   5. 4. 79,   5. 6. 79 ABC
  The Women's Room   tf   9. 14. 80 ABC
  Haywire   tf   5. 14. 80 CBS
  The Ambassadors   sp   6. 13. 81 PBS

REY, ALEJANDRO
  SUPP.:
  The Love Boat   ep   The Duel 3. 14. 81 ABC

REYNOLDS, DEBBIE
  SUPP.:
  The Love Boat   ep   11. 1. 80 ABC
  Aloha Paradise   sr   2. 25. 81 ABC

RHOADES, BARBARA
  A&C:
  The Partridge Family   ep   11. 6. 70 ABC
  Love, American Style   ep   2. 19. 71 ABC
  Night Gallery   ep   Something in the Woodwork 1. 14. 73 NBC
  The Odd Couple   ep   11. 21. 74 ABC
  Punch and Jody   tf   11. 26. 74 NBC
  The Night Stalker   ep   1. 17. 75 ABC
  Manhunter   ep   1. 29. 75 CBS
  Petrocelli   ep   1. 29. 75 NBC
  Bronk   ep   11. 16. 75 ABC
  Columbo   ep   12. 17. 75 NBC
  Starsky and Hutch   ep   12. 17. 75 ABC
  Twin Detectives   tf   5. 1. 76 ABC
  The Bureau   pt   7. 26. 76 NBC
  The Blue Knight   sr   10. 13. 76 CBS
  SUPP.:
  Busting Loose   sr   1. 17. 77 CBS
  Quark   ep   3. 3. 78 NBC
  The Love Boat   ep   5. 6. 78 ABC
  The Eddie Capra Mysteries   ep   Who Killed Lloyd Wesley
     Jordan? 9. 29. 78 NBC
  Rhoda   ep   12. 2. 78 CBS
  Supertrain   ep   2. 14. 79 NBC
  Hanging In   sr   8. 8. 79 CBS
  Sex and the Single Parent   tf   9. 19. 79 CBS
  Stone   sr   3. 10. 80 ABC

The Day the Women Got Even   tf   12. 4. 80 NBC
Side Show   tf   6. 5. 81 NBC

RHUE, MADLYN
A& C:
The Rebel   ep   12. 6. 59 ABC
Bourbon Street Beat   ep   Portrait of Lenore 12. 29. 59 ABC
Laramie   ep   The Pass 12. 29. 59 NBC
Hotel de Paree   ep   Sundance Goes to Kill 1. 22. 60 CBS
The Alaskans   ep   Disaster at Gold Hill 3. 20. 60 ABC
The Untouchables   ep   Head of Fire, Feet of Clay 4. 21. 60 ABC
Bourbon Street Beat   ep   Last Exit 5. 2. 60 ABC
The Outlaws   ep   Ballad for a Bad Man 10. 6. 60 NBC
The Roaring 20s   ep   Burnett's Woman 10. 15. 60 ABC
Checkmate   ep   Target: Tycoon 11. 5. 60 CBS
The Untouchables   ep   The Tommy Karpeles Story 12. 29. 60 ABC
Stagecoach West   ep   Fort Wyatt Crossing 4. 4. 61 ABC
Adventures in Paradise   ep   The Assassins 11. 26. 61 ABC
Medical Story   ep   9. 4. 75 NBC
Manhunter   tf   4. 3. 76 NBC
SUPP. :
Switch   ep   3. 13. 77 CBS
We've Got Each Other   ep   11. 19. 77 CBS
The Tony Randall Show   ep   2. 18. 78 CBS
Charlie's Angels   ep   Angels on the Street 11. 7. 79 ABC
Hart to Hart   ep   11. 13. 79 ABC
Goldie and the   Boxer   tf   12. 30. 79 NBC
Quincy, M. E.   ep   2. 14. 80 NBC

RICH, ADAM*
The Six Million Dollar Man   ep   A Bionic Christmas Card
      12. 12. 76 ABC
Eight Is Enough   sr   3. 15. 77 ABC
Eight Is Enough   sr ret   8. 10. 77 ABC
Eight Is Enough   sr ret   9. 6. 78 ABC
Eight Is Enough   sr ret   9. 5. 79 ABC
The Love Boat   ep   9. 21. 79 ABC
CHiPs   ep   Chips Goes Roller Disco 9. 22. 79 NBC
Code Red   sr   11. 1. 81 ABC

RICHARDS, KIM*
Nanny and the Professor   sr   1. 21. 70 ABC
Nanny and the Professor   sr ret   9. 13. 71 ABC
Here We Go Again   sr   1. 20. 73 ABC
The World of Disney   ep   The Whiz Kid and the Mystery at
      Riverton 1. 6. 74 NBC
Temperature's Rising   ep   1. 8. 74 ABC
The World of Disney   ep   Hog Wild 1. 20. 74, 1. 27. 74 NBC
Police Story   ep   The Wyatt Earp Syndrome 3. 5. 74 NBC
The ABC Superstar Movie   ep   Nanny and the Professor   vo
      4. 6. 74 ABC
Little House on the Prairie   ep   10. 30. 74 ABC
The Streets of San Francisco   ep   2. 13. 75 ABC

Sara   ep   3. 12. 76 CBS
Family   ep   Monday Is Forever 3. 16. 76 ABC
The Rockford Files   ep   10. 8. 76 NBC
Police Woman   ep   12. 21. 76   NBC
Raid on Entebbe   tf   1. 9. 77 NBC
The ABC Afterschool Special   ep   The Horrible Honcho's   sp
    3. 9. 77 ABC
James at 15   tf   9. 15. 77 NBC
James at 15   sr   10. 27. 77 NBC
James at 16   sr   2. 9. 78 NBC
Project UFO   ep   10. 12. 78 NBC
Devil Dog: The Hound of Hell   tf   10. 31. 78 CBS
Hello, Larry   sr   1. 26. 79 NBC
Diff'rent Strokes   ep   3. 30. 79 NBC
Hizzoner   ep   5. 17. 79 NBC
Diff'rent Strokes   ep   9. 28. 79 NBC
Hello, Larry   sr ret   10. 12. 79 NBC
Why Us?   pt   8. 21. 81 NBC

RICHARDSON, (SIR) RALPH
    SUPP. :
    The Man in the Iron Mask   tf   1. 17. 77 NBC
    Jesus of Nazareth   ms   4. 3. 77,   4. 10. 77 NBC

RICHMAN, PETER MARK
    A&C:
    The Twilight Zone   ep   The Fear 5. 29. 64 CBS
    The Nurses   ep   Horns of Plenty 10. 31. 63 CBS
    Medical Story   ep   9. 18. 75 NBC
    SUPP. :
    Dog and Cat   ep   5. 14. 77 ABC
    Quincy, M. E.   ep   10. 14. 77 NBC
    Three's Company   ep   2. 28. 78 ABC
    The Islander   tf   9. 16. 78 CBS
    Dallas   ep   10. 7. 78 CBS
    Greatest Heroes of the Bible   ep   The Story of Moses in Egypt
        11. 20. 78 NBC
    Vega$ ep   11. 22. 78 ABC
    The New Adventures of Wonder Woman   ep   Gault's Brain
        12. 29. 78 CBS
    Starsky and Hutch   ep   2. 6. 79 ABC
    Blind Ambition   ms   5. 20-23. 79 CBS
    Greatest Heroes of the Bible   ep   The Story of Abraham
        5. 22. 79 NBC
    Charlie's Angels   ep   Cruising Angels 12. 12. 79 ABC
    240-Robert   ep   12. 13. 79 ABC
    B. J. and the Bear   ep   2. 9. 80 NBC
    Vega$ ep   Ladies in Blue 3. 19. 80 ABC
    Galactica 1980   ep   4. 20. 80 ABC
    Dynasty   sr   1. 12. 81 ABC
    Lobo   ep   1. 20. 81 NBC
    Dynasty   sr ret   11. 4. 81 ABC
    The Incredible Hulk   ep   11. 13. 81 CBS

RICKLES, DON
   SUPP. :
   C. P. O. Sharkey   sr ret   10. 21. 77 NBC
   For the Love of It   tf   9. 26. 80 ABC

RIGBY, CATHY*
   The Six Million Dollar Man   ep   2. 15. 76 ABC
   The Great Wallendos   tf   2. 2. 78 NBC
   The Hardy Boys/Nancy Drew Mysteries   ep   Arson and Old
      Lace 4. 1. 78 ABC
   CHiPs   ep   Karate 3. 8. 81 NBC

RIGG, DIANA
   SUPP. :
   Queen of Hearts: Eva Peron   sp nar   12. 16. 79 NN

RITTER, JOHN*
   Hawaii Five-O   ep   Two Doves and Mr. Heron 10. 12. 72 CBS
   Evil Roy Slade   tf   2. 18. 72 NBC
   The Waltons   ep   10. 26. 72, 1. 25. 73, 11. 29. 73, 1. 9. 75, 1. 30. 75,
      2. 27. 75, 9. 11. 75, 1. 22. 76, 10. 14. 76, 10. 21. 76, 11. 4. 76,
      12. 23. 76 CBS
   Medical Center   ep   1. 17. 73 CBS
   Bachelor at Law   pt   6. 5. 73 CBS
   M*A*S*H   ep   12. 8. 73 CBS
   Movin' On 1. 16. 75 NBC
   Mannix   ep   4. 13. 75 CBS
   Petrocelli   ep   10. 8. 75 NBC
   Barnaby Jones   ep   The Price of Terror 10. 10. 75 CBS
   The Streets of San Francisco   ep   10. 23. 75 ABC
   The Mary Tyler Moore Show   ep   Ted's Wedding 11. 8. 75 CBS
   The Rookies   ep   11. 25. 75 ABC
   Starsky and Hutch   ep   1. 7. 76 ABC
   Doc   ep   1. 10. 76 CBS
   Rhoda   ep   1. 12. 76 CBS
   Phyllis   ep   9. 20. 76 CBS
   Hawaii Five-O   ep   2. 3. 77 CBS
   Three's Company   sr   3. 15. 77 ABC
   Loves Me, Loves Me Not   ep   3. 23. 77 CBS
   Three's Company   sr ret   9. 13. 77 ABC
   The Love Boat   ep   10. 1. 77 ABC
   Leave Yesterday Behind   tf   5. 14. 78 ABC
   Three's Company   sr ret   9. 12. 78 ABC
   Three's Company   sr ret   9. 11. 79 ABC
   The Ropers   ep   9. 15. 79 ABC
   The Comeback Kid   tf   4. 11. 80 ABC
   Three's Company   sr ret   10. 28. 80 ABC
   Three's Company   sr ret   10. 6. 81 ABC

ROBARDS, JASON
   SUPP. :
   Washington: Behind Closed Doors   ms   9. 6-11. 77 ABC
   A Christmas to Remember   tf   12. 20. 78 CBS

Haywire   tf   5. 14. 80 CBS
The Silken Tent   sp   4. 29. 81 PBS

ROBERTS, PERNELL*
Bonanza   sr   9. 12. 59 NBC
The Big Valley   ep   Cage of Eagles 4. 24. 67 ABC
The Wild Wild West   ep   The Night of the Firebird 9. 15. 67 CBS
Mission: Impossible   ep   Operation ... Heart 10. 22. 67 CBS
Ironside   ep   To Kill a Cop 1. 25. 68 NBC
Mission: Impossible   ep   The Mercenaries 10. 27. 68 CBS
The Name of the Game   ep   Chains of Command 10. 17. 69 NBC
The Silent Gun   tf   12. 16. 69 ABC
San Francisco International   tf   9. 29. 70 NBC
The Bold Ones: The Doctors   ep   1. 3. 71 NBC
The Name of the Game   ep   Beware of the Watchdog 3. 5. 71
    NBC
Marcus Welby, M. D.   ep   The Tender Comrade 9. 14. 71 ABC
Night Gallery   ep   The Tune in Dan's Cafe 1. 5. 72 NBC
Alias Smith and Jones   ep   1. 6. 72 ABC
The Bravos   tf   1. 9. 72 NBC
The Adventures of Nick Carter   tf   2. 20. 72 ABC
Jigsaw   ep   9. 21. 72 ABC
Owen Marshall, Counselor at Law   ep   The Trouble with Ralph
    10. 19. 72 ABC
The Sixth Sense   ep   11. 11. 72 ABC
Banacek   ep   11. 15. 72 NBC
Marcus Welby, M. D.   ep   2. 27. 73 ABC
Mission: Impossible   ep   Imitation 3. 30. 73 CBS
Mannix   ep   Little Girl Lost 10. 7. 73 CBS
Hawkins   ep   Candidate for Murder 3. 5. 74 CBS
Police Story   ep   3. 19. 74 NBC
The Odd Couple   ep   10. 17. 74 ABC
Nakia   ep   11. 30. 74 ABC
Police Story   ep   2. 4. 75 NBC
Dead Man on the Run   tf   4. 2. 75 ABC
Medical Story   ep   9. 25. 75 NBC
The Deadly Tower   tf   10. 18. 75 NBC
Ellery Queen   ep   10. 23. 75 NBC
The Lives of Jenny Dolan   tf   10. 27. 75 NBC
Cannon   ep   1. 14. 76 CBS
The Six Million Dollar Man   ep   Hocus Pocus 1. 18. 76 ABC
Jigsaw John   ep   3. 22. 76 NBC
Barnaby Jones   ep   Testament of Power 1. 20. 77 CBS
Switch   ep   1. 30. 77 CBS
Baretta   ep   The Reunion 2. 2. 77 ABC
Quincy, M. E.   ep   Visitors in Paradise 2. 18. 77 NBC
Most Wanted   ep   3. 14. 77 ABC
Police Woman   ep   3. 22. 77 NBC
The Streets of San Francisco   ep   5. 12. 77   ABC
The Feather and Father Gang   ep   5. 21. 77 ABC
Charlie Cobb: Nice Night for a Hanging   tf   6. 9. 77 NBC
Westside Medical   ep   6. 30. 77 ABC
The Man from Atlantis   ep   11. 8. 77 NBC

The Rockford Files   ep   The House on Willis Avenue 2. 24. 78
    NBC
Mystery of the Week   ep   Alien Lover 3. 29. 78 ABC
The Hardy Boys/Nancy Drew Mysteries   ep   Arson and Old
    Lace 4. 1. 78 ABC
The Hardy Boys   ep   10. 15. 78 ABC
Quincy, M. E.   ep   Death by Good Intention 10. 26. 78 NBC
Centennial   ms ep   For As Long As the Water Flows 11. 4. 78
    NBC
Vega$ ep   11. 8. 78 ABC
Centennial   ms ep   The Massacre 11. 11. 78 NB C
The Immigrants   ms   11. 20. 78, 11. 21. 78 NN
The Paper Chase   ep   A Case of Detente 4. 17. 79 CBS
Night Rider   tf   5. 11. 79 ABC
Hot Rod   tf   5. 25. 79 ABC
Trapper John, M. D.   sr   9. 23. 79 CBS
Vega$ ep   11. 5. 80 ABC
The Love Boat   ep   11. 15. 80 ABC
High Noon, Part II: The Return of Will Kane   tf   11. 15. 80
    CBS
Trapper John, M. D.   sr ret   11. 23. 80 CBS
Trapper John, M. D.   sr ret   10. 4. 81 CBS
Incident at Crestridge   tf   12. 29. 81 CBS

ROBERTS, TANYA*
    Pleasure Cove   tf   1. 3. 79 NBC
    Greatest Heroes of the Bible   ep   Jacob's Challenge 3. 18. 79
        NBC
    Vega$ ep   Ladies in Blue 3. 19. 80 ABC
    Waikiki   tf   4. 21. 80 ABC
    Charlie's Angels   sr   11. 30. 80 ABC
    Charlie's Angels   sr ret   6. 3. 81 ABC

ROBERTS, TONY
    SUPP. :
    McMillan   ep   1. 23. 77 NBC
    Rosetti and Ryan: Men Who Love Women   tf   5. 19. 77 NBC
    Rosetti and Ryan   sr   9. 22. 77 NBC
    The Love Boat   ep   Julie Falls Hard 12. 16. 78 ABC
    The Girls in the Office   tf   2. 2. 79 ABC
    The Love Boat   ep   9. 15. 79 ABC
    If Things Were Different   tf   1. 16. 80 CBS

ROBERTSON, CLIFF
    SUPP. :
    Washington: Behind Closed Doors   ms   9. 6-11. 77 ABC
    Overboard   tf   9. 25. 78 NBC
    The Last Ride of the Dalton Gang   tf   11. 20. 79 NBC
    Fantasy Island   ep   9. 14. 79 ABC

ROBERTSON, DALE
    SUPP. :
    The Love Boat   ep   11. 8. 80 ABC
    Dynasty   sr   1. 12. 81 ABC

ROCCO, ALEX
  SUPP. :
  Starsky and Hutch   ep   2. 26. 77 ABC
  Barnaby Jones   ep   3. 3. 77 CBS
  Dog and Cat   ep   4. 9. 77 ABC
  Baretta   ep   5. 4. 77 ABC
  79 Park Avenue   ms   10. 16. 77, 10. 17. 77, 10. 18. 77 NBC
  Starsky and Hutch   ep   11. 19. 77, 11. 26. 77 ABC
  The Grass Is Always Greener Over the Septic Tank   tf   10. 25. 78
    CBS
  A Question of Guilt   tf   2. 21. 78 CBS
  Riker   ep   Crime School 4. 4. 81 CBS

ROCHE, EUGENE*
  Higher and Higher, Attorneys at Law   pt   9. 9. 68 CBS
  Crawlspace   tf   2. 11. 72 ABC
  Ironside   ep   10. 12. 72 NBC
  The Corner Bar   sr   8. 3. 73 ABC
  Egan   pt   9. 18. 73 ABC
  The Magician   ep   2. 25. 74 NBC
  Winter Kill   tf   4. 15. 74 ABC
  Hawaii Five-O   ep   1. 21. 75 CBS
  The Last Survivors   tf   3. 3. 75 NBC
  The Crime Club   tf   4. 3. 75 CBS
  The Law   tf   4. 16. 75 NBC
  Ellery Queen   ep   9. 25. 75 NBC
  Kojak   ep   11. 2. 75 CBS
  Bronk   ep   11. 9. 75 CBS
  The Art of Crime   tf   12. 3. 75 NBC
  Phyllis   ep   1. 5. 76 CBS
  Harry O   ep   3. 4. 76 ABC
  Mallory: Circumstantial Evidence   tf   2. 8. 76 NBC
  People Like Us   pt   4. 19. 76 NBC
  Local 306   pt   8. 23. 76 NBC
  The Streets of San Francisco   ep   10. 28. 76 ABC
  All in the Family   ep   11. 6. 76 CBS
  Barnaby Jones   ep   12. 16. 76 CBS
  All in the Family   ep   12. 25. 76 CBS
  Starsky and Hutch   ep   1. 22. 77 ABC
  Police Woman   ep   2. 22. 77 NBC
  Tales of the Unexpected   ep   2. 23. 77 NBC
  Starsky and Hutch   ep   4. 2. 77 ABC
  The Possessed   tf   5. 1. 77 NBC
  Corey: For the People   tf   6. 12. 77 NBC
  Lou Grant   ep   10. 4. 77 CBS
  Quincy, M. E.   ep   11. 11. 77   NBC
  The Winds of Kitty Hawk   tf   12. 17. 78 NBC
  What Really Happened to the Class of '65?   ep   Class Dreamers
    12. 22. 77 NBC
  Ghost on Flight 401   tf   2. 19. 78 NBC
  The New Maverick   tf   9. 3. 78 ABC
  Soap   sr   9. 14. 78 ABC
  Kaz   ep   9. 24. 78 CBS
  All in the Family   ep   11. 5. 78 CBS

Vega$ ep   12. 6. 78 ABC
The Child Stealer   tf   3. 9. 79 ABC
Hart to Hart   pt   8. 25. 79 ABC
Love for Rent   tf   11. 11. 79 ABC
Insight   ep   7. 13. 80 NN
Good Time Harry   sr   7. 26. 80 NBC
Rape and Marriage: The Ridout Case   tf   10. 30. 80 CBS
Alone at Last   pt   11. 3. 80 NBC
Miracle on Ice   tf   3. 1. 81 ABC
Two the Hard Way   pt   8. 11. 81 CBS
Darkroom   ep   A Quiet Funeral 12. 18. 81 ABC

ROCKWELL, ROBERT
   SUPP. :
   Diff'rent Strokes   ep   12. 3. 80 NBC
   Benson   ep   2. 20. 81 ABC
   Flamingo Road   ep   11. 10. 81 NBC

RODRIGUES, PERCY
   SUPP. :
   Lucan   ep   1. 9. 78 ABC
   Ring of Passion   tf   2. 4. 78 NBC
   James at 16   ep   6. 22. 78 NBC
   The Duke   ep   4. 5. 79 NBC
   The Night Rider   tf   5. 11. 79 ABC
   Barnaby Jones   ep   1. 10. 80 CBS
   Sanford   sr   3. 15. 80 NBC
   Angel Dusted   tf   2. 16. 81 NBC
   The Fall Guy   ep   10. 28. 81 ABC

ROGERS, GINGER
   SUPP. :
   The Love Boat   ep   11. 10. 79 ABC

ROGERS, WAYNE*
   Stagecoach West   sr   10. 4. 60 ABC
   The FBI   ep   The Tormentors 4. 10. 66 ABC
   Combat   ep   The Gun 9. 13. 66 ABC
   The FBI   ep   The Extortionist 4. 16. 67 ABC
   The FBI   ep   The Legend of Jim Riva 12. 31. 67 ABC
   The FBI   ep   The 9th Man 3. 24. 68 ABC
   The Big Valley   ep   The Jonah 11. 11. 68 ABC
   The FBI   ep   Deadfall 3. 1. 70 ABC
   The FBI   ep   The Traitor 9. 27. 70 ABC
   Cannon   ep   Call Unicorn 9. 28. 71 CBS
   The FBI   ep   Superstition Rock 11. 28. 71 ABC
   M*A*S*H   sr   9. 17. 72 CBS
   Barnaby Jones   ep   9. 30. 73 CBS
   Attack on Terror: The FBI vs. the Ku Klux Klan   tf   2. 20. 75,
      2. 21. 75 CBS
   City of Angels   sr   2. 3. 76 NBC
   Having Babies II   tf   10. 28. 77 ABC
   It Happened One Christmas   tf   12. 11. 77 ABC

Thou Shalt Not Commit Adultry   tf   11.1.78 NBC
The Sacketts   tf   5.15.79, 5.16.79 NBC
House Calls   sr   12.17.79 CBS
Top of the Hill   ms   2.6.80, 2.7.80 NN
House Calls   sr ret   11.7.80 CBS
House Calls   sr ret   11.2.81 CBS

ROLAND, GILBERT
   SUPP.:
   Hart to Hart   ep   2.26.80 ABC

ROLLE, ESTHER*
   Maude   sr   9.12.72 CBS
   Maude   sr ret   9.11.73 CBS
   Good Times   sr   2.8.74 CBS
   Good Times   sr ret   9.10.74 CBS
   Good Times   sr ret   9.9.75 CBS
   Good Times   sr ret   9.22.76 CBS
   Good Times   sr ret   9.21.77 CBS
   Good Times   sr ret   9.16.78 CBS
   Summer of My German Soldier   tf   10.30.78 NBC
   Good Times   sr ret   5.23.79 CBS
   The Incredible Hulk   ep   11.9.79 CBS
   Momma the Detective   pt   1.19.81 NBC
   South by Northwest   sp   6.18.81, 6.25.81 PBS
   Darkroom   ep   Needlepoint 12.11.81 ABC

ROMAN, RUTH
   SUPP.:
   Police Woman   ep   1.25.77 NBC
   Fantasy Island   ep   My Fair Pharaoh 5.10.80 ABC
   Willow B: Women in Prison   pt   6.29.80 ABC

ROMERO, CESAR
   SUPP.:
   Don't Push, I'll Charge When I'm Ready   tf   12.18.77 NBC
   Vega$ ep   11.22.78 ABC
   Fantasy Island   ep   2.17.79 ABC
   Charlie's Angels   ep   Dancin' Angels 2.6.80 ABC

ROONEY, MICKEY
   A&C:
   Frontier Circus   ep   Calamity Circus 3.8.62 CBS
   Year Without a Santa Claus   sp vo   12.10.74 ABC
   SUPP.:
   A Year at the Top   ep   8.5.77 CBS
   World of Disney   ep   Donovan's Kid 1.14.79, 1.21.79 NBC
   My Kidnapper, My Love   tf   12.8.80 NBC
   CBS Library: Misunderstood Monsters   ep   Creole   nar sp
      4.7.81 CBS
   Bill   tf   12.22.81 CBS
   Senior Trip   tf   12.30.81 CBS

ROSS, KATHERINE
  A&C:
  Sam Benedict ep A Split Week in San Quentin 9. 22. 62 NBC
  SUPP. :
  Legend of the Black Hand ms ep 8. 31. 78 ABC
  Murder by Natural Causes tf 2. 17. 79 CBS
  Rodeo Girl tf 9. 17. 80 CBS
  Murder in Texas tf 5. 3. 81, 5. 4. 81 NBC

ROSS, MARION*
  The Outer Limits ep The Special One 4. 6. 64 ABC
  Bob Hope Theatre ep Holloway's Daughters 5. 11. 66 NBC
  Ironside ep Barbara Who 2. 29. 68 NBC
  Any Second Now tf 2. 11. 69 NBC
  Mannix ep Return to Summer Grove 10. 11. 69 CBS
  The Psychiatrist: God Bless the Children tf 2. 14. 70 NBC
  Ironside ep 9. 21. 71 NBC
  Hawaii Five-O ep 10. 26. 71 CBS
  Sarge ep A Push over the Edge 10. 26. 71 NBC
  Longstreet ep 11. 11. 71 ABC
  Love, American Style ep Love and the Happy Days 2. 25. 72
    ABC
  Marcus Welby, M. D. ep 10. 17. 72 ABC
  The Weekend Nun tf 12. 20. 72 ABC
  Mannix ep 3. 4. 73 CBS
  Escape ep 3. 25. 73 NBC
  Emergency ep Inheritance Tax 11. 17. 73 NBC
  Happy Days sr 1. 15. 74 ABC
  Happy Days sr ret 9. 74 ABC
  Petrocelli ep 2. 26. 75 NBC
  Happy Days sr ret 9. 9. 75 ABC
  Petrocelli ep 3. 3. 76 NBC
  Happy Days sr ret 9. 21. 76 ABC
  Happy Days sr ret 9. 15. 77 ABC
  The Love Boat ep 2. 4. 78 ABC
  Happy Days sr ret 9. 78 ABC
  Pearl ms ep 11. 17. 78, 11. 19. 78 ABC
  The Survival of Dana tf 5. 29. 79 CBS
  Happy Days sr ret 9. 11. 79 ABC
  The ABC Afterschool Special ep Which Mother Is Mine? sp
    9. 26. 79 ABC
  The Love Boat ep 1. 19. 80 ABC
  Happy Days sr ret 11. 11. 80 ABC
  Skyward tf 11. 20. 80 NBC
  Who Loves Amy Tonight? sp 3. 28. 81 NN
  True Life Stories ep Family Reunion pt 9. 13. 81 ABC
  Happy Days sr ret 10. 6. 81 ABC
  The Love Boat ep Gladys and Agnes 11. 28. 81 ABC

ROUNDTREE, RICHARD
  SUPP. :
  Roots ms ep 1. 28. 77 ABC
  The Love Boat ep The Affair 1. 19. 80 ABC
  CHiPs ep Shark on the Freeway 2. 22. 81 NBC

ROWLANDS, GENA
SUPP.:
Strangers: The Story of a Mother and Daughter   tf   5.13.79
    CBS

RUBINSTEIN, JOHN
SUPP.:
Corey: For the People   tf   6.12.77 NBC
Stop the Presses   pt   7.15.77 CBS
Lou Grant   ep   9.27.77 CBS
Hawaii Five-O   ep   10.13.77 CBS
What Really Happened to the Class of '65?   ep   The Girl Nobody
    Knew 12.29.77 NBC
The New Adventures of Wonder Woman   ep   The Deadly Toys
    12.30.77 CBS
The Love Boat   ep   1.7.78 ABC
Family   ep   2.7.78, 2.21.78 ABC
The Streets of San Francisco   ep   3.3.77 ABC
Happily Ever After   tf   9.5.78 CBS
Family   ep   10.4.77, 10.12.78 ABC
Gift of the Magi   tf   12.21.78 NBC
Fantasy Island   ep   1.27.79 ABC
The Love Boat   ep   Class Reunion 2.3.79 ABC
Vega$ ep   2.7.79 ABC
The French-Atlantic Affair   ms   11.15.79, 11.16.79, 11.18.79
    ABC
She's Dressed to Kill   tf   12.10.79 NBC
Make Me an Offer   tf   1.11.80 ABC
Moviola: The Silent Lovers   tf   5.20.80 NBC
Killjoy   tf   10.22.81 CBS
Skokie   tf   11.17.81 CBS

RULE, JANICE
SUPP.:
The Word   ms   11.12.78, 11.13.78, 11.14.78, 11.15.78 CBS

RUSH, BARBARA
SUPP.:
The ABC Weekend Special   ep   Portrait of Grandpa Doc 11.5.77
    ABC
Fantasy Island   ep   11.25.78 ABC
The Eddie Capra Mysteries   ep   12.15.78 NBC
The Love Boat   ep   The Now Marriage 1.13.79 ABC
Death Car on the Freeway   tf   9.25.79 CBS
The Love Boat   ep   Eleanor's Return 11.24.79 ABC
The Seekers   ms   12.3.79, 12.4.79 NN
Flamingo Road   tf   5.12.80 NBC
Flamingo Road   sr   1.6.81 NBC
Flamingo Road   sr ret   11.3.81 NBC

RUSSELL, JOHN
SUPP.:
Jason of Star Command   sr   9.15.79 CBS

RUSSELL, KURT*
   The Travels of Jaimie McPheeters   sr   9.15.63 ABC
   The Fugitive   ep   Nemesis 10.13.64 ABC
   The Man from U.N.C.L.E.   ep   The Finny Foot Affair 12.2.64
      NBC
   Gilligan's Island   ep   Fall 1964 CBS
   Daniel Boone   ep   The First Stone 1.28.65 NBC
   Daniel Boone   ep   The Price of Friendship 2.18.65 NBC
   The Virginian   ep   The Brothers 9.15.65 NBC
   The FBI   ep   The Tormentors 4.10.66 ABC
   The Fugitive   ep   In a Plain Paper Wrapper 4.19.66 ABC
   Daniel Boone   ep   The Young Ones 2.23.67 NBC
   Walt Disney's World   ep   The Secret of Boyne Castle 2.9.69
      NBC
   Daniel Boone   ep   Bickford's Bridge 2.20.69 NBC
   Daniel Boone   ep   Target Boone 11.20.69 NBC
   Love Story   ep   Beginner's Luck 11.28.73 NBC
   Police Story   ep   Country Boy 2.19.74 NBC
   Gunsmoke   ep   Trail of Bloodshed 3.4.74 CBS
   Hec Ramsey   ep   Scar Tissue 3.10.74 NBC
   The New Land   sr   9.14.74 ABC
   Harry O   ep   Double Jeopardy 2.13.75 ABC
   Search for the Gods   tf   3.9.75 ABC
   The Deadly Tower   tf   10.18.75 NBC
   Police Story   ep   11.21.75 NBC
   The Quest   tf   5.13.76 NBC
   The Quest   sr   9.29.76 NBC
   Hawaii Five-O   ep   11.17.77 CBS
   Christmas Miracle in Caulfield, U.S.A.   tf   12.26.77 NBC
   Elvis   tf   2.11.79 NBC
   Amber Waves   tf   3.9.80 ABC

RYAN, MITCHELL*
   Dark Shadows   sr   6.27.66 ABC
   Cannon   ep   Fool's Gold 10.19.71 CBS
   O'Hara, United States Treasury   ep   12.10.71 CBS
   Chase   sr   9.11.73 NBC
   Manhunter   ep   The Man Who Thought He Was Dillinger 9.18.74
      CBS
   Cannon   ep   1.22.75 CBS
   Barnaby Jones   ep   2.4.75 CBS
   Baretta   ep   12.17.75 ABC
   The Entertainer   tf   3.10.76 NBC
   Escape from Bogen County   tf   10.7.77 CBS
   Peter Lundy and the Medicine Hat Stallion   tf   11.6.77 NBC
   Christmas Miracle in Caulfield, U.S.A.   tf   12.26.77 NBC
   Having Babies III   tf   3.3.78 ABC
   Having Babies   sr   3.7.78 ABC
   Julie Farr, M.D.   sr   4.11.78 ABC
   Sergeant Matlovich vs. The U.S. Air Force   tf   8.21.78 NBC
   Family   ep   12.7.78 ABC
   Grandpa Goes to Washington   ep   12.26.78 NBC
   Julie Farr, M.D.   sr ret   6.12.79 ABC
   Flesh and Blood   tf   10.14.79, 10.16.79 CBS

Chisholms   sr   1. 19. 80 CBS
Angel City   tf   11. 12. 80 CBS
The Choice   tf   2. 10. 81 CBS
Joe Dancer: The Monkey Mission   tf   3. 23. 81 NBC
The Five of Me   tf   5. 12. 81 CBS
Death of a Centerfold: The Dorothy Stratton Story   tf   11. 1. 81
    NBC
Of Mice and Men   tf   11. 29. 81 NBC

-S-

SAINT, EVA MARIE
    SUPP. :
    A Christmas to Remember   tf   12. 20. 78 NBC
    When Hell Was in Session   tf   10. 8. 79 NBC
    The Curse of King Tut's Tomb   tf   5. 8. 80, 5. 9. 80 NBC
    The Best Little Girl in the World   tf   5. 11. 81 ABC
    The Golden Age of Television   ep hos   Marty 8. 27. 81 NN
    Splendor in the Grass   tf   10. 26. 81 NBC

ST. JACQUES, RAYMOND
    SUPP. :
    Roots   ms   1. 23-30. 77 ABC
    Secrets of Three Hungry Wives   tf   10. 9. 78 NBC
    B. J. and the Bear   ep   11. 10. 79 NBC

SAINT JAMES, SUSAN
    SUPP. :
    Night Cries   tf   1. 29. 78 ABC
    Desperate Women   tf   10. 25. 78 NBC
    The Girls in the Office   tf   2. 2. 79 ABC
    Sex and the Single Parent   tf   9. 19. 79 CBS
    S. O. S. Titanic   tf   9. 23. 79 ABC

ST. JOHN, JILL
    A&C:
    Brenda Starr   tf   5. 8. 76 ABC
    SUPP. :
    Telethon   tf   11. 6. 77 ABC
    The Love Boat   ep   Cyrano de Bricker 3. 17. 79 ABC
    Hart to Hart   pt   8. 25. 79 ABC
    The Love Boat   ep   The Spider Serenade 12. 8. 79 ABC
    Vega$ ep   11. 19. 80 ABC
    The Love Boat   ep   1. 31. 81 ABC
    Fantasy Island   ep   5. 23. 81 ABC

SALMI, ALBERT
    SUPP. :
    Baretta   ep   2. 16. 77 ABC

Police Story ep 3. 22. 77 NBC
Future Cop ep 3. 25. 77 ABC
McNamara's Band pt 5. 14. 77 ABC
79 Park Avenue ms 10. 16. 77, 10. 17. 77, 10. 18. 77 NBC
McNamara's Band pt (second) 12. 5. 77 ABC
James at 16 ep 2. 9. 78 NBC
Greatest Heroes of the Bible ep The Story of Joseph and His
    Brothers 11. 22. 78 NBC
B. J. and the Bear ep 2. 24. 79 NBC
Undercover with the KKK tf 10. 23. 79 NBC
The Great Cash Giveaway Getaway tf 4. 21. 80 NBC
The Yeagers ep 6. 8. 80 ABC

SANDERS, BEVERLY
    A& C:
    Rhoda ep 10. 6. 75 CBS
    SUPP. :
    Rhoda ep 3. 6. 77 CBS
    C. P. O. Sharkey ep 1. 27. 78 NBC
    Barney Miller ep 9. 14. 78 ABC
    Hart to Hart ep 1. 15. 80 ABC
    One Day at a Time ep Out of Bounds 3. 8. 81 CBS

SANDY, GARY*
    Starsky and Hutch ep 11. 27. 76 ABC
    Barnaby Jones ep Renegade's Child 12. 23. 76 CBS
    All That Glitters sr Fall 1977 NN
    CHiPs ep 3. 9. 78 NBC
    WKRP in Cincinnati sr 9. 18. 78 CBS
    WKRP in Cincinnati sr ret 9. 17. 79 CBS
    WKRP in Cincinnati sr ret 11. 1. 80 CBS
    WKRP in Cincinnati sr ret 10. 7. 81 CBS

SANFORD, ISABEL
    SUPP. :
    The Jeffersons sr ret 9. 24. 77 CBS
    The Jeffersons sr ret 9. 78 CBS
    The Jeffersons sr ret 9. 79 CBS
    The Jeffersons sr ret 10. 80 CBS
    The Love Boat ep Tell Her She's Great 11. 29. 80 ABC
    The Jeffersons sr ret 10. 4. 81 CBS

SARRAZIN, MICHAEL
    SUPP. :
    Beulah Land ms 10. 7. 80, 10. 8. 80, 10. 9. 80 NBC

SAVALAS, TELLY
    A& C:
    Great Mysteries ep The Cat and the Canary 9. 27. 60 NBC
    SUPP. :
    Kojak sr ret 10. 2. 77 CBS
    Windows, Doors and Keyholes sp 5. 16. 78 NBC
    The French-Atlantic Affair ms 11. 15. 79, 11. 16. 79, 11. 18. 79
        ABC

Alice   ep   4. 13. 80 CBS
Alcatraz: The Whole Shocking Story   tf   11. 5. 80, 11. 6. 80 NBC
Hellinger's Law   tf   3. 10. 81 CBS
Tales of the Unexpected   ep   Completely Foolproof 12. 5. 81 NN

SAXON, JOHN
   A& C:
   Bonanza   ep   My Friend, My Enemy 1. 12. 69 NBC
   SUPP. :
   Raid on Entebbe   tf   1. 9. 77 NBC
   Most Wanted   ep   3. 7. 77 ABC
   Quincy, M. E.   ep   5. 6. 77 NBC
   79 Park Avenue   ms   10. 16. 77, 10. 17. 77, 10. 18. 77 NBC
   The Immigrants   ms   11. 20. 78, 11. 21. 78 NN
   Greatest Heroes of the Bible   ep   The Story of Solomon and
      Bathsheba 11. 21. 78, 11. 22. 78 NBC
   Hawaii Five-O   ep   2. 8. 79 CBS
   Fantasy Island   ep   2. 17. 79, 12. 1. 79 ABC
   Vega$ ep   11. 5. 80 ABC
   Fantasy Island   ep   2. 21. 81 ABC
   Golden Gate   tf   9. 25. 81 ABC
   Fantasy Island   ep   Cyrano 10. 24. 81 ABC

SCHALLERT, WILLIAM*
   The George Burns and Gracie Allen Show   various ep   1954-
      1955 CBS
   Screen Directors Playhouse   ep   Apples on the Lilac Tree
      7. 25. 56 NBC
   Perry Mason   ep   The Case of the Sulky Girl 10. 19. 57 CBS
   The Loretta Young Theatre   ep   Understanding Heart 11. 10. 57
      NBC
   Gunsmoke   ep   12. 57 CBS
   The Loretta Young Theatre   ep   Second Rate Citizen 4. 27. 58
      NBC
   The Texan   ep   The Troubled Town 10. 13. 58 CBS
   Father Knows Best   ep   11. 17. 58 CBS
   Alcoa Presents   ep   Epilogue 2. 24. 59 ABC
   Maverick   ep   The Strange Journey of Jenny Hill 3. 29. 59 ABC
   The Rifleman   ep   The Mind Reader 6. 30. 59 ABC
   Wanted: Dead or Alive   ep   Fall 1959 CBS
   Dobie Gillis   sr   9. 29. 59 CBS
   Philip Marlowe   ep   The Mogul 12. 1. 59 ABC
   Philip Marlowe   ep   Gem of a Murder 2. 9. 60 ABC
   Philip Marlowe   ep   Murder by the Book 3. 1. 60 ABC
   The Lawman   ep   Reunion in Laramie 3. 13. 60 ABC
   77 Sunset Strip   ep   Legend of the Crystal Dart 4. 15. 60 ABC
   Wagon Train   ep   Trial for Murder 4. 27. 60, 5. 4. 60 NBC
   The Twilight Zone   ep   Mr. Bevis 6. 3. 60 CBS
   Dobie Gillis   sr ret   9. 27. 60 CBS
   Bat Masterson   ep   The Lady Plays Her Hand 12. 29. 60 NBC
   GE Theatre   ep   The Legend That Walks Like a Man 2. 12. 61
      CBS
   Alcoa Presents   ep   Tidal Wave 2. 14. 61 ABC

Checkmate ep The Paper Killer 3. 25. 61 CBS
The Rifleman ep Short Rope for a Tall Man 3. 28. 61 ABC
Perry Mason ep The Case of the Misguided Missile 5. 6. 61
   CBS
The Rebel ep Mission--Varina 5. 14. 61 CBS
Thriller ep The Grim Reaper 6. 13. 61 NBC
Dobie Gillis sr ret 10. 10. 61 CBS
The 87th Precinct ep Empty Hours 11. 20. 61 NBC
Surfside Six ep A Matter of Seconds 11. 27. 61 ABC
Thriller ep Dialogues with Death 12. 4. 61 NBC
Follow the Sun ep Mele Kalikimaka to You 12. 24. 61 ABC
Alfred Hitchcock Presents ep Bad Actor 1. 9. 62 NBC
Have Gun--Will Travel ep 1. 13. 62 CBS
Bonanza ep Look at the Stars 3. 18. 62 NBC
Perry Mason ep The Case of the Melancholy Marksman
   3. 24. 62 CBS
Hennessey ep 8. 27. 62 CBS
Dobie Gillis sr ret Fall 1962 CBS
The Tales of Wells Fargo ep 9. 1. 62 NBC
Stoney Burke ep Five by Eight 12. 10. 62 ABC
Sam Benedict ep Sugar and Spice and Everything 2. 2. 63 NBC
Have Gun--Will Travel ep 3. 30. 63 CBS
The Lucy Show ep 3. 63, 4. 15. 63 CBS
Empire ep Breakout 4. 16. 63 NBC
Alcoa Premiere ep The Town That Died 4. 25. 63 ABC
Rawhide ep 5. 3. 63 CBS
Gunsmoke ep Daddy Went Away 5. 11. 63 CBS
Hazel ep 7. 18. 63 NBC
The Patty Duke Show sr 9. 18. 63 ABC
The Patty Duke Show sr ret 9. 16. 64 ABC
The Patty Duke Show sr ret 9. 17. 65 ABC
Combat ep Headcount 11. 1. 66 ABC
The Virginian ep Deadeye Dick 11. 9. 66 NBC
Pistols 'n' Petticoats ep 1. 28. 67 CBS
The Rat Patrol ep The Bring 'Em Back Alive Raid 3. 13. 67
   ABC
Mission: Impossible ep 3. 18. 67 CBS
Get Smart ep 4. 15. 67 NBC
The Wild Wild West ep The Night of the Bubbling Death
   9. 18. 67 CBS
Ironside ep The Taker 10. 12. 67 NBC
Judd, for the Defense ep To Kill a Madman 11. 24. 67 ABC
Star Trek ep The Trouble with Tribbles 12. 29. 67 NBC
The Guns of Will Sonnett ep 1. 26. 68 ABC
Here Come the Brides ep 10. 16. 68 ABC
The Wild Wild West ep The Night of the Gruesome Games
   10. 25. 68 CBS
Get Smart ep 11. 2. 68 NBC
CBS Playhouse ep Saturday Adoption sp 12. 4. 68 CBS
The Wild Wild West ep The Night of the Winged Terror
   1. 17. 69, 1. 24. 69 CBS
Hawaii Five-O ep 2. 19. 69, 2. 26. 69 CBS
The Mod Squad ep Keep the Faith, Baby 3. 25. 69 ABC

Gunsmoke   ep   8. 25. 69 CBS
Here Come the Brides   ep   9. 26. 69 ABC
The FBI   ep   9. 28. 69 ABC
The Debbie Reynolds Show   ep   9. 30. 69 NBC
Bewitched   ep   10. 9. 69 ABC
That Girl   ep   11. 6. 69 ABC
Room 222   ep   11. 19. 69 ABC
Land of the Giants   ep   11. 23. 69 ABC
Get Smart   ep   2. 6. 70 NBC
Gunsmoke   ep   Albert 2. 9. 70 CBS
Two Boys   pt   7. 6. 70 NBC
Marcus Welby, M. D.   ep   A Very Special Sailfish 9. 22. 70 ABC
Bracken's World   ep   10. 16. 70 NBC
Hawaii Five-O   ep   12. 16. 70 CBS
The Partridge Family   ep   1. 1. 71 ABC
Escape   tf   4. 16. 71 ABC
The Man and the City   ep   A Hundred Black Pages 9. 22. 71
    ABC
The Man and the City   ep   Disaster on Turner Street 10. 20. 71
    ABC
Funny Face   ep   11. 6. 71 CBS
The Man and the City   ep   Pipe Me a Loving Tune 12. 8. 71
    ABC
Owen Marshall, Counselor at Law   ep   Voice from a Nightmare
    12. 16. 71 ABC
The D. A.   ep   12. 24. 71 NBC
Man on a String   tf   2. 18. 72 CBS
The FBI   ep   Dark Journey 3. 12. 72 ABC
Owen Marshall, Counselor at Law   ep   9. 28. 72 CBS
The Delphi Bureau   ep   11. 16. 72 ABC
Banacek   ep   The Two Million Clams of Cap'n Jack 2. 7. 73 NBC
Love, American Style   ep   2. 16. 73 ABC
Kung Fu   ep   The Praying Mantis Kills 3. 22. 73 ABC
Partners in Crime   tf   3. 24. 73 NBC
Ironside   ep   Confessions of a Lady of the Night 9. 13. 73 NBC
Gunsmoke   ep   Matt's Love Story 9. 24. 73 CBS
Hijack!   tf   9. 26. 73 ABC
Love Story   ep   Beginner's Luck 12. 28. 73 NBC
Love, American   ep   Love and Carmen Lopez 12. 28. 73 ABC
The Six Million Dollar Man   ep   Eyewitness to Murder 3. 8. 74
    ABC
Remember When   tf   3. 23. 74 NBC
Barnaby Jones   ep   Dead Man's Run 9. 17. 74 CBS
Manhunter   ep   10. 2. 74 CBS
Death Sentence   tf   10. 2. 74 ABC
Police Story   ep   2. 11. 75 NBC
Promise Him Anything   tf   5. 14. 75 ABC
Ellery Queen   ep   1. 4. 76 NBC
The Bionic Woman   ep   Claws 2. 25. 76 ABC
Little House on the Prairie   ep   3. 11. 76 NBC
Bert D'Angelo/Superstar   ep   3. 20. 76 ABC
Dawn: Portrait of a Teenage Runaway   tf   9. 22. 76 NBC
Switch   ep   10. 12. 76 CBS

All's Fair   ep   10. 18. 76 CBS
Tail Gunner Joe   tf   2. 6. 77 NBC
The Nancy Drew Mysteries   sr   2. 6. 77 ABC
The Nancy Drew Mysteries   sr ret   12. 18. 77 ABC
Little Women   tf   10. 2. 78, 10. 9. 78 NBC
Apple Pie   ep   10. 8. 78 ABC
Grandpa Goes to Washington   ep   12. 5. 78 NBC
The Challenge   sp   1. 18. 79 NBC
Legends of the Superheroes: A Roast   sp   1. 25. 79 NBC
Little Women   sr   2. 8. 79 NBC
Ike   ms ep   5. 3. 79 ABC
Blind Ambition   ms ep   5. 19. 79, 5. 23. 79 CBS
Lou Grant   ep   9. 24. 79 CBS
Archie Bunker's Place   ep   9. 30. 79 CBS
Little House on the Prairie   ep   10. 22. 79 NBC
Peege   sp   12. 28. 79 CBS
The Waltons   ep   2. 14. 80 CBS
Insight   ep   6. 29. 80 NN
The Misadventures of Sheriff Lobo   ep   3. 4. 80 NBC
The Waltons   ep   2. 26. 81, 5. 14. 81 CBS

SCHELL, MARIA
   SUPP. :
Christmas Lilies of the Field   tf   10. 16. 79 NBC

SCHUCK, JOHN (previously listed as John Shuck)
   SUPP. :
Roots   ms   1. 23-30. 77 ABC
Holmes and Yoyo   sp ep   8. 1. 77, 8. 8. 77 ABC
The Love Boat   ep   1. 21. 78 ABC
Fantasy Island   ep   2. 4. 78 ABC
Having Babies   ep   3. 14. 78 ABC
Windows, Doors and Keyholes   sp   5. 16. 78 NBC
Greatest Heroes of the Bible   ep   The Story of Samson and
   Delilah 11. 19. 78 NBC
Turnabout   sr   1. 26. 79 NBC
The Halloween That Almost Wasn't   sp   10. 28. 79 ABC
Fantasy Island   ep   1. 19. 80 ABC

SCOTT, BRENDA
   A& C:
The Virginian   ep   Dark Destiny 4. 29. 64 NBC
Insight   ep   6. 2. 74 NN
   SUPP. :
Quincy, M. E.   ep   9. 30. 77, 10. 14. 77 NBC

SCOTT, DEBRALEE (previously listed as Debra Lee Scott)
   SUPP. :
Forever Fernwood   sr   9. 77 NN
The Love Boat   ep   A Very Special Girl 2. 11. 78 ABC
Welcome Back, Kotter   ep   5. 11. 78 ABC
Death Moon   tf   5. 31. 78 CBS
Angie   sr   2. 8. 79 ABC

Angie   sr ret   9. 11. 79   ABC
Living in Paradise   pt   2. 1. 81   NBC

SCOTT, MARTHA
   A&C:
   Route 66   ep   Welcome to Amity 6. 9. 61   CBS
   Thursday's Game   tf   4. 14. 74   ABC
   Police Woman   ep   9. 27. 74   NBC
   The Abduction of St. Anne   tf   1. 21. 75   ABC
   The Bionic Woman   ep   1. 14. 76   ABC
   SUPP. :
   The Word   ms   11. 12. 78, 11. 13. 78, 11. 14. 78, 11. 15. 78   CBS
   Dallas   ep   1. 14. 79   CBS
   Charleston   tf   1. 15. 79   NBC
   Married: The First Year   ep   2. 28. 79   CBS
   Dallas   ep   10. 5. 79   CBS
   The Love Boat   ep   10. 13. 79   ABC
   Beulah Land   ms   10. 7. 80, 10. 8. 80, 10. 9. 80   NBC
   Father Figure   tf   10. 26. 80   CBS
   The Secrets of Midland Heights   sr   12. 6. 80   CBS

SELLECCA, CONNIE*
   The Bermuda Depths   tf   1. 27. 78   ABC
   Flying High   tf   8. 28. 78   CBS
   Flying High   sr   9. 29. 78   CBS
   Captain America II   pt   11. 23. 79, 11. 24. 79   CBS
   She's Dressed to Kill   tf   12. 10. 79   NBC
   Beyond Westworld   sr   3. 12. 80   CBS
   The Greatest American Hero   sr   3. 18. 81   ABC
   The Greatest American Hero   sr ret   10. 28. 81   ABC

SELLECK, TOM*
   The Movie Murderer   tf   2. 2. 70   NBC
   Sarge   ep   The Combatants 11. 30. 71   NBC
   Owen Marshall, Counselor at Law   ep   12. 5. 73   ABC
   Lucas Tanner   ep   1. 8. 75   NBC
   Returning Home   tf   4. 29. 75   ABC
   Most Wanted   tf   3. 21. 76   ABC
   Charlie's Angels   ep   10. 27. 76   ABC
   Bunco   pt   1. 13. 77   NBC
   Superdome   tf   1. 9. 78   ABC
   The Gypsy Warriors   pt   5. 12. 78   CBS
   The Rockford Files   ep   10. 20. 78   NBC
   Grandpa Goes to Washington   ep   12. 26. 78   NBC
   Boston and Kilbride   pt   3. 3. 79   CBS
   The Sacketts   tf   5. 15. 79, 5. 16. 79   NBC
   Concrete Cowboys   tf   10. 17. 79   CBS
   The Rockford Files   ep   11. 16. 79   NBC
   Magnum, P. I.   sr   12. 11. 80   CBS
   Magnum, P. I.   sr ret   10. 8. 81   CBS

SELLERS, PETER*
   Carol for Another Christmas   sp   12. 28. 64   ABC
   It Takes a Thief   ep   Who'll Bid Two Million Dollars? 10. 2. 69 ABC

SEYMOUR, JANE*
    Our Mutual Friend   sr   4.9.73 PBS
    Benny and Barney: Las Vegas Undercover   tf   1.19.77 NBC
    Seventh Avenue   ms   2.10.77, 2.17.77, 2.24.77 NBC
    Killer on Board   tf   10.10.77 NBC
    The Four Fathers   tf   1.1.78 NBC
    The Awakening Land   ms   2.19.78, 2.20.78, 2.21.78 NBC
    Love's Dark Ride   tf   4.2.78 NBC
    Battlestar Galactica   ep   Saga of a Star World 9.17.78 ABC
    The Dallas Cowboys Cheerleaders   tf   1.14.79 ABC
    East of Eden   ms   2.8.81, 2.9.81, 2.11.81 ABC

SHATNER, WILLIAM
    A&C:
    The Doctors and the Nurses   ep   Act of Violence 2.23.65 CBS
    SUPP.:
    The Oregon Trail   ep   11.30.77 NBC
    How the West Was Won   ep   3.5.78, 3.12.78 ABC
    Testimony of Two Men   ms   5.1.78, 5.2.78, 5.3.78 NN
    The Bastard/Kent Family Chronicles   ms   5.22.78, 5.23.78 NN
    Little Women   ms   10.2.78, 10.3.78 NBC
    Crash   tf   10.29.78 ABC
    Disaster on the Coastliner   tf   10.29.78 ABC
    The Babysitter   tf   11.28.80 ABC
    This Was America   sr hos-nar   4.25.81 NN

SHAVER, HELEN*
    Police Surgeon   ep   1.26.75, 2.1.75 NN
    Lovey: A Circle of Children, Part II   tf   12.13.78 CBS
    United States   sr   3.11.80 NBC
    Jessica Novak   sr   11.5.81 CBS

SHEEN, MARTIN
    A&C:
    The Nurses   ep   The Suspect 9.29.64, 10.6.64 CBS
    Insight   ep   10.5.75 NN
    SUPP.:
    Blind Ambition   ms   5.20-23.79 CBS
    Insight   ep   5.20.79, 7.7.80 NN

SHERMAN, BOBBY
    SUPP.:
    Flying High   ep   11.17.78 CBS
    The Gossip Columnist   pt   3.21.80 NN
    Fantasy Island   ep   1.3.81   ABC
    Lobo   ep   The Cowboy Connection 3.31.81 NBC

SHIELDS, BROOKE*
    The Prince of Central Park   tf   6.17.77 CBS
    Men Who Rate a 10   sp hos   10.7.80 NBC

SHIGETA, JAMES
    SUPP.:
    The Hardy Boys/Nancy Drew Mysteries   ep   4.24.77 ABC

Fantasy Island   ep   2.24.79 ABC
Enola Gay   tf   11.23.80 NBC

SHOOP, PAMELA SUSAN*
The FBI   ep   The Corruptor 2.27.72 ABC
The Rookies   ep   The Bear That Didn't Get Up 10.23.72 ABC
Mannix   ep   10.29.72 CBS
The Mod Squad   ep   11.23.72 ABC
Switch   ep   2.17.76 CBS
The Gemini Man   ep   10.7.76 NBC
Keeper of the Wild   pt   1.77 NN
Code R   ep   4.15.77 CBS
79 Park Avenue   ms   10.16.77, 10.17.77, 10.18.77 NBC
Kaz   ep   12.3.78 CBS
The Dallas Cowboys Cheerleaders   tf   1.14.79 ABC
CHiPs   ep   12.15.79 NBC
B.J. and the Bear   ep   12.15.79 NBC
Hawaii Five-O   ep   1.1.80 CBS
Vega$ ep   1.2.80 ABC
Magnum, P.I.   ep   12.11.80 CBS
B.J. and the Bear   ep   1.27.81 NBC
The Fall Guy   ep   The Meek Shall Inherit Rhonda 11.4.81 ABC
Fitz and Bones   ep   To Kill a Ghost 11.7.81 NBC
Fantasy Island   ep   The Lagoon 11.28.81 ABC
Mitchell and Woods   pt   12.18.81 NBC

SHORE, DINAH
SUPP.:
Death Car on the Freeway   tf   9.25.79 CBS
240-Robert   ep   11.26.79 ABC

SIDNEY, SYLVIA
SUPP.:
Raid on Entebbe   tf   1.9.77 NBC
Snowbeast   tf   4.28.77 NBC
Eight Is Enough   ep   11.9.77 ABC
Siege   tf   4.26.78 CBS
WKRP in Cincinnati   ep   9.18.78 CBS
Kaz   ep   12.3.78 CBS
Supertrain   ep   3.14.79 NBC
California Fever   ep   10.9.79 CBS
The Gossip Columnist   pt   3.21.80 NN
The Shadow Box   tf   12.28.80 ABC
The Love Boat   ep   Momma and Me 3.7.81 ABC
A Small Killing   tf   11.24.81 CBS

SIERRA, GREGORY
SUPP.:
Police Story   ep   1.25.77 NBC
The Night They Took Miss Beautiful   tf   10.24.77 NBC
Police Story   ep   River of Promises 1.14.78 NBC
A.E.S. Hudson Street   sr   3.23.78 ABC
Evening in Byzantium   ms   8.14.78, 8.15.78 NN
The Night the Bridge Fell Down   tf   10.21.80 NBC

300 Miles for Stephanie   tf   11. 2. 81 NBC
Hart to Hart   ep   A Couple of Harts 10. 13. 81 ABC
The Greatest American Hero   ep   Hog Wild 11. 25. 81 ABC

SILVA, HENRY
   A& C:
   Route 66   ep   Squeeze Play 5. 14. 62 CBS
   SUPP. :
   Quark   ep   2. 24. 78 NBC
   Buck Rogers in the 25th Century   pt   9. 20. 79 NBC

SILVERS, PHIL
   SUPP. :
   The New Love Boat (a. k. a. Love Boat III)   tf   5. 5. 77 ABC
   Charlie's Angels   ep   Angels on Ice 9. 21. 77 ABC
   The Night They Took Miss Beautiful   tf   10. 24. 77 NBC
   The Love Boat   ep   11. 26. 77 ABC
   Fantasy Island   ep   12. 2. 78 ABC
   Goldie and the Boxer   tf   12. 30. 79 NBC
   Happy Days   ep   Just a Piccolo 11. 24. 81 ABC

SIMMONS, JEAN
   SUPP. :
   The Dain Curse   ms   5. 22. 78, 5. 23. 78, 5. 24. 78 CBS
   Beggarman, Thief   tf   11. 26. 79, 11. 27. 79 NBC
   The Home Front   pt   10. 9. 80 CBS
   Golden Gate   tf   9. 25. 81 ABC
   Jacqueline Susann's Valley of the Dolls 1981   tf   10. 19. 81,
      10. 20. 81 CBS
   A Small Killing   tf   11. 24. 81 CBS

SIMPSON, O. J. *
   Cade's County   ep   3. 19. 72 CBS
   Owen Marshall, Counselor at Law   ep   3. 7. 73 ABC
   Here's Lucy   ep   9. 17. 73 CBS
   Roots   ms   1. 23-30. 77 ABC
   A Killing Affair   tf   9. 21. 77 CBS
   Goldie and the Boxer   tf   12. 30. 79 NBC
   Detour to Terror   tf   2. 22. 80 NBC
   Goldie and the Boxer Go to Hollywood   tf   2. 19. 81 NBC

SINATRA, FRANK
   SUPP. :
   Contract on Cherry Street   tf   11. 19. 77 NBC
   Most Joyful Mystery   sp   12. 24. 81 NN

SINATRA, FRANK, JR.
   SUPP. :
   The Love Boat   ep   10. 27. 79 ABC
   Police Story   ep   Confessions of a Lady Cop 4. 28. 80 NBC
   Tales of the Unexpected   ep   I Like It Here in Wilmington
      11. 14. 81 NN

SMITH, JACLYN*

The Partridge Family ep When Mother Gets Married 10.23.70 ABC
Probe ep 2.12.72 NBC
McCloud ep 1.7.73 NBC
McCloud ep The Man with the Golden Hat 1.12.75 NBC
Switch ep 3.10.75, 9.16.75, 9.23.75, 10.21.75 CBS
The Rookies ep 12.16.75 ABC
Charlie's Angels tf 3.21.76 ABC
Charlie's Angels sr 9.22.76 ABC
Charlie's Angels sr ret 9.14.77 ABC
The San Pedro Beach Bums ep 9.19.77 ABC
The Love Boat ep 10.1.77 ABC
Escape from Bogen County tf 10.7.77 CBS
The Hardy Boys/Nancy Drew Mysteries ep 10.9.77 ABC
Charlie's Angels sr ret 9.13.78 ABC
The Users tf 10.1.78 ABC
Charlie's Angels sr ret 9.12.79 ABC
Charlie's Angels sr ret 11.30.80 ABC
Nightkill tf 12.18.80 NBC
Charlie's Angels sr ret 6.3.81 ABC
Jacqueline Bouvier Kennedy tf 10.14.81 ABC

SMITH, SHELLEY*

The Associates sr 9.23.79 ABC
Mirror, Mirror tf 10.10.79 NBC
Hart to Hart ep 2.5.80 ABC
Swan Song tf 2.8.80 ABC
Ten Speed and Brown Shoe ep 3.23.80 ABC
The Associates sr ret 3.27.80 ABC
The Stockard Channing Show ep 6.7.80 CBS
The Love Boat ep 10.25.80 ABC
The Night the City Screamed tf 12.14.80 ABC
This House Possessed tf 2.6.81 ABC
Fantasy Island ep 2.14.81 ABC
The Phoenix tf 4.26.81 ABC
Scruples tf 5.22.81 ABC

SMOTHERS, DICK
SUPP.:
Tales of the Unexpected ep Youth from Vienna 10.10.81 NN
Fitz and Bones sr 10.24.81 NBC

SMOTHERS, TOM
SUPP.:
The Love Boat ep 12.13.80 ABC
Fitz and Bones sr 10.24.81 NBC

SNODGRASS, CARRIE
SUPP.:
Love's Dark Ride tf 4.2.78 NBC
Fast Friends tf 3.19.79 NBC
The Solitary Man tf 10.9.79 CBS

SOMERS, SUZANNE*
  Lassie ep 1. 31. 65 CBS
  Sky Heist tf 5. 26. 75 NBC
  Starsky and Hutch ep Savage Saturday 9. 10. 75 ABC
  One Day at a Time ep Waitress Job 3. 2. 76 CBS
  Starsky and Hutch ep Vampire 10. 30. 76 ABC
  Three's Company sr 3. 15. 77 ABC
  Three's Company sr ret 9. 13. 77 ABC
  The Love Boat ep One If by Land 9. 24. 77 ABC
  Starsky and Hutch ep Murder Ward 10. 8. 77 ABC
  The Six Million Dollar Man ep 11. 20. 77 ABC
  It Happened at Lakewood Manor tf 12. 2. 77 ABC
  Happily Ever After tf 9. 5. 78 CBS
  Three's Company sr ret 9. 12. 78 ABC
  Zuma Beach tf 9. 27. 78 NBC
  Three's Company sr ret 9. 11. 79 ABC
  The Ropers ep 9. 15. 79 ABC
  Three's Company sr ret 10. 28. 80 ABC

SOMMARS, JULIE*
  Bonanza ep The Roper 4. 5. 64 NBC
  The Man from U. N. C. L. E. ep The Foxes and the Hounds
    Affair 10. 8. 65 NBC
  The Fugitive ep Stranger in the Mirror 12. 7. 65 ABC
  The Fugitive ep The Blessings of Liberty 12. 20. 66 ABC
  The Man from U. N. C. L. E. ep The When in Rome Affair
    3. 17. 67 NBC
  The FBI ep The Daughter 1. 24. 68 ABC
  Get Smart ep 9. 14. 68 NBC
  The Felony Squad ep 10. 11. 68 ABC
  The Name of the Game ep Nightmare 10. 18. 68 NBC
  Judd, for the Defense ep Transplant 12. 27. 68 ABC
  The FBI ep A Life in the Balance 1. 9. 69 ABC
  Lancer ep The Measure of a Man 4. 8. 69 CBS
  The Governor and J. J. sr 9. 23. 69 CBS
  The Governor and J. J. sr ret 9. 23. 70 CBS
  The Search pt 5. 24. 71 CBS
  Five Desperate Women tf 9. 28. 71 ABC
  The Harness tf 11. 12. 71 NBC
  McCloud ep 11. 24. 71 NBC
  How to Steal an Airplane tf 12. 10. 71 NBC
  Owen Marshall, Counselor at Law ep 9. 21. 72 ABC
  Wide World of Mystery ep I'm the Girl He Wants to Kill
    3. 18. 74 ABC
  Harry O ep Gertrude 9. 12. 74 ABC
  The Rockford Files ep The Kirkoff Case 9. 13. 74 NBC
  McCloud ep The 42nd Street Cavalry 11. 17. 74 NBC
  Barnaby Jones ep Dark Homecoming 11. 19. 74 CBS
  Switch ep 9. 9. 75 CBS
  Ellery Queen ep 10. 30. 75 NBC
  My Wife Next Door pt 12. 31. 75 NBC
  Bronk ep 1. 18. 76 CBS
  Jigsaw John ep 4. 5. 76 NBC
  McMillan ep Coffee, Tea or Cyanide 1. 30. 77 NBC

Fantasy Island ep 12. 16. 78 ABC
Centennial ms ep The Winds of Fortune 2. 3. 79 NBC
Sex and the Single Parent tf 9. 19. 79 CBS
Barnaby Jones ep Design for Madness 10. 18. 79 CBS
Fantasy Island ep 5. 10. 80 ABC

SOMMER, ELKE
  SUPP. :
  Top of the Hill ms 2. 6. 80, 2. 7. 80 NN
  The Love Boat ep 5. 2. 81 ABC
  Fantasy Island ep Druids 11. 14. 81 ABC

SONDERGAARD, GALE
  SUPP. :
  Visions ep Pleasantville 11. 6. 77 PBS
  The Fall Guy ep The Human Torch 12. 9. 81 ABC

SOREL, LOUISE*
  Dr. Kildare ep Marriage of Convenience 2. 11. 65 NBC
  The Fugitive ep The Survivors 3. 2. 65 ABC
  Bonanza ep The Strange One 11. 14. 65 NBC
  Hawk ep 9. 15. 66 ABC
  Daniel Boone ep Beaumarchais 10. 12. 67 NBC
  The Rat Patrol ep The Fatal Reunion Raid 1. 15. 68 ABC
  The Name of the Game ep The White Birch 11. 29. 68 NBC
  Star Trek ep Requiem for Methuselah 2. 14. 69 NBC
  The Survivors sr 9. 22. 69 ABC
  River of Mystery tf 10. 1. 71 NBC
  Medical Center ep The Pawn 12. 1. 71 CBS
  Night Gallery ep Pickman's Model 12. 1. 71 NBC
  The Don Rickles Show sr 1. 14. 72 CBS
  Banacek ep 10. 11. 72 NBC
  Search ep 10. 11. 72 NBC
  Medical Center ep The Outcast 11. 15. 72 CBS
  The FBI ep 11. 26. 72 ABC
  Every Man Needs One tf 12. 13. 72 ABC
  The President's Plane Is Missing tf 10. 23. 73 ABC
  Ironside ep Mind for Murder 11. 15. 73 NBC
  Hawaii Five-O ep Try to Die on Time 12. 4. 73 CBS
  Get Christie Love tf 1. 22. 74 ABC
  Kojak ep Before the Devil Knows 2. 27. 74 CBS
  The Healers tf 5. 22. 74 NBC
  The Mark of Zorro tf 10. 29. 74 ABC
  Insight ep 11. 17. 74 NN
  One of Our Own tf 5. 5. 75 NBC
  Medical Center ep 9. 8. 75 CBS
  Medical Center ep 9. 8. 75 CBS
  The Barbary Coast ep 10. 31. 75 ABC
  Widow tf 1. 22. 76 CBS
  Perilous Voyage tf 7. 29. 76 CBS
  Kojak ep Kojak's Days 2. 1. 77, 2. 8. 77 CBS
  Rosetti and Ryan ep 10. 13. 77 NBC
  When Everyday Was the Fourth of July tf 3. 12. 78 NBC

The Eddie Capra Mysteries   ep   12. 22. 78 NBC
Cliffhangers: The Curse of Dracula   sr   2. 27. 79 NBC
The Return of Charlie Chan   tf   7. 17. 79 ABC
Charlie's Angels   ep   Caged Angel 10. 17. 79 ABC
One in a Million   ep   2. 9. 80, 3. 15. 80 ABC
Ladies' Man   sr   10. 27. 80 CBS

SOTHERN, ANN
  SUPP. :
  Insight   ep   11. 19. 78 NN

SOUL, DAVID
  SUPP. :
  Little Ladies of the Night   tf   1. 16. 77 ABC
  Starsky and Hutch   sr ret   9. 17. 77 ABC
  Starsky and Hutch   sr ret   9. 12. 78 ABC
  Salem's Lot   tf   11. 17. 79, 11. 24. 79 CBS
  Swan Song   tf   2. 8. 80 ABC
  Rage!   tf   9. 25. 80 NBC
  Homeward Bound   tf   11. 19. 80 CBS
  The Manions of America   ms   9. 30. 81, 10. 1. 81, 10. 2. 81 ABC

SPACEK, SISSY*
  Love, American Style   ep   1. 19. 73 ABC
  The Girls of Huntington House   tf   2. 14. 73 ABC
  The Waltons   ep   The Townie 3. 8. 73 CBS
  The Waltons   ep   The Odyssey 9. 20. 73 CBS
  The Rookies   ep   Sound of Silence 12. 17. 73 ABC
  The Migrants   tf   2. 3. 74 CBS
  Katherine   tf   10. 5. 75 ABC
  Great Performances   ep   Verna: USO Girl 1. 25. 78 PBS

SPANG, LAURETTE*
  Short Walk to Daylight   tf   10. 24. 72 ABC
  Emergency   ep   12. 2. 72 NBC
  Alias Smith and Jones   ep   1. 13. 73 ABC
  Emergency   ep   2. 29. 73 NBC
  Marcus Welby, M. D.   ep   The Panic Path 9. 11. 73 ABC
  Chase   ep   Foul Up 9. 25. 73 NBC
  Runaway!   tf   9. 29. 73 ABC
  Adam-12   ep   Venice Division 10. 10. 73 NBC
  The Streets of San Francisco   ep   Harem 10. 25. 73 ABC
  Maneater   tf   12. 8. 73 ABC
  Owen Marshall, Counselor at Law   ep   Second Victim 12. 19. 73
    ABC
  The Six Million Dollar Man   ep   1. 25. 74 ABC
  Happy Days   ep   3. 12. 74 ABC
  Sarah T. --Portrait of a Teenage Alcoholic   tf   2. 11. 75 NBC
  Sunshine   tf   4. 3. 75 NBC
  The Love Boat   ep   9. 18. 76 ABC
  The Gemini Man   ep   10. 28. 76 NBC
  Charlie's Angels   ep   12. 8. 76 ABC
  The Love Boat   ep   A Very Special Girl 2. 11. 78 ABC

Lou Grant   ep   2. 27. 78 CBS
The Man from Atlantis   ep   5. 2. 78 NBC
Colorado C. I.   pt   5. 26. 78 CBS
McNamara's Band   pt   6. 10. 78 ABC
Battlestar Galactica   sr   9. 17. 78 ABC
Project UFO   ep   Sighting 4015: The Underwater Incident
     9. 21. 78 NBC
B. J. and the Bear   ep   9. 29. 79, 10. 6. 79 NBC
Barnaby Jones   ep   The Final Victim 3. 6. 80 CBS
Tourist   pt   7. 17. 80 NN
The Love Boat   ep   Split Personality 2. 14. 81 ABC
Fantasy Island   ep   3. 7. 81 ABC
The Dukes of Hazzard   ep   10. 6. 81 CBS

SPIELBERG, DAVID*
The Bold Ones: The Lawyers   ep   11. 14. 71, 1. 30. 72 NBC
The Bold Ones: The Doctors   ep   9. 26. 72 NBC
Ironside   ep   Down Two Roads 10. 12. 72 NBC
Banacek   ep   11. 15. 72 NBC
Owen Marshall, Counselor at Law   ep   A Piece of God 12. 14. 72
     ABC
Banacek   ep   1. 24. 73 NBC
Jigsaw   ep   2. 24. 73 ABC
Madigan   ep   2. 28. 73 NBC
Toma   tf   3. 21. 73 ABC
Bob & Carol & Ted & Alice   sr   9. 26. 73 ABC
Judgement: The Trial of Ethel and Julius Rosenberg   tf   1. 28. 74
     ABC
The Rockford Files   ep   Charlie Harris at Large 2. 14. 75 NBC
McMillan and Wife   ep   Love, Honor and Swindle 2. 16. 75 NBC
The Rockford Files   ep   Just by Accident 2. 28. 75 NBC
The Bob Crane Show   ep   3. 13. 75 NBC
The Barbary Coast   ep   9. 22. 75 ABC
Kate McShane   ep   9. 24. 75 CBS
The Lindburgh Kidnapping Case   tf   2. 26. 76 NBC
Visions   ep   Two Brothers 10. 24. 76 PBS
Police Story   ep   3. 8. 77 NBC
Westside Medical   ep   4. 7. 77 ABC
The 3,000-Mile Chase   tf   6. 16. 77 NBC
Kingston Confidential   ep   6. 22. 77 NBC
In the Matter of Karen Ann Quinlan   tf   9. 26. 77 NBC
Quincy, M. E.   ep   A Dead Man's Truth 9. 30. 77 NBC
King   ms   2. 12. 78, 2. 13. 78, 2. 14. 78 NBC
Richie Brockelman, Private Eye   ep   3. 17. 78 NBC
Wheels   ms   5. 7. 78, 5. 8. 78, 5. 9. 78, 5. 14. 78, 5. 15. 78 NBC
Sergeant Matlovich vs. the U. S. Air Force   tf   8. 21. 78 NBC
The American Girls   sr   9. 23. 78 CBS
One Day at a Time   ep   1. 17. 79 CBS
Kaz   ep   2. 7. 79 CBS
From Here to Eternity   ms   2. 14. 79, 2. 21. 79, 2. 28. 79 NBC
Operating Room   pt   10. 4. 79 NBC
Trapper John, M. D.   ep   1. 27. 80 CBS
From Here to Eternity   sr   3. 10. 80 NBC

The Henderson Monster tf 5.27.80 CBS
From Here to Eternity sr ret 8.3.80 NBC
Act of Love tf 9.24.80 NBC
Lou Grant et 9.29.80 CBS
CHiPs ep Wheels of Justice 12.21.80 NBC
Lou Grant ep 3.23.81 CBS
Hart to Hart ep Operation Murder 5.12.81 ABC
Here's Boomer ep Boomer and the Musket Cove Treasure
    10.4.81 NBC
Jessica Novak sr 11.5.81 CBS

STACK, ROBERT
    SUPP.:
    The Love Boat ep 11.22.80 ABC
    Strike Force sr 11.13.81 ABC

STACY, JAMES
    SUPP.:
    Just a Little Inconvenience tf 10.2.77 NBC
    My Kidnapper, My Love tf 12.8.80 NBC

STALLONE, SYLVESTER*
    Police Story ep 9.16.75 NBC
    Kojak ep 9.21.75 CBS

STANWYCK, BARBARA
    SUPP.:
    Charlie's Angels ep The Male Angel Affair (a.k.a. Toni's
    Boys) 4.2.80 ABC

STAPLETON, JEAN
    SUPP.:
    Tail Gunner Joe tf 2.6.77 NBC
    All in the Family sr ret 10.2.77 CBS
    All in the Family sr ret 9.24.78 CBS
    You Can't Take It with You sp 5.16.79 CBS
    Archie Bunker's Place ep 9.30.79, 11.18.79 CBS
    The Hallmark Hall of Fame ep Aunt Mary sp 12.5.79 CBS
    Archie Bunker's Place ep 12.9.79 CBS
    Angel Dusted tf 2.16.81 NBC

STAPLETON, MAUREEN
    SUPP.:
    There's Always Room pt 4.24.77 CBS
    The Gathering tf 12.4.77 ABC
    Letters from Frank tf 11.22.79 CBS
    The Gathering, Part II tf 12.17.79 NBC

STEIGER, ROD
    SUPP.:
    Jesus of Nazareth ms 4.3.77, 4.10.77 NBC

STEPHENS, JAMES*
    True Grit tf 5.19.78 ABC

The Paper Chase sr 9.9.78 CBS
Eischied ep Only the Pretty Girls Die 9.21.79, 9.28.79 NBC
The Lazarus Syndrome ep 10.16.79 ABC
The Death of Ocean View Park tf 10.19.79 ABC
Tourist pt 7.17.80 NN

STEPHENS, LARAINE
  A&C:
  Surfside Six ep Squeeze Play 5.14.62 ABC
  Barnaby Jones ep 9.10.74 CBS
  Police Story ep 1.21.75, 1.28.75 NBC
  Police Woman ep 1.24.75 NBC
  The Quest ep 11.10.76 NBC
  SUPP.:
  Police Woman ep 1.18.77 NBC
  Policy Story ep 11.9.77 NBC
  The Next Step Beyond pt 1.5.78 NN
  Police Woman ep 1.11.78 NBC
  Hawaii Five-O ep 4.27.78 CBS
  The Courage and the Passion tf 5.27.78 NBC
  Crash tf 10.29.78 ABC
  The Dallas Cowboys Cheerleaders tf 1.14.79 ABC
  Fantasy Island ep 2.10.79 ABC
  Doctors' Private Lives ep 4.5.79 ABC
  Vega$ ep 9.19.79 ABC
  Eischied ep Only the Pretty Girls Die 9.21.79, 9.28.79 NBC
  Dallas Cowboys Cheerleaders II tf 1.13.80 ABC
  Power tf 1.14.80, 1.15.80 NBC
  The Love Boat ep 12.20.80 ABC
  Fantasy Island ep 3.7.81 ABC
  Scruples tf 5.22.81 ABC

STERLING, JAN
  SUPP.:
  Little House on the Prairie ep 4.18.77 NBC
  Backstairs at the White House ms ep 2.12.79 NBC
  My Kidnapper, My Love tf 12.8.80 NBC
  The Incredible Hulk ep 4.3.81 CBS

STERLING, ROBERT
  SUPP.:
  Beggarman, Thief tf 11.26.79, 11.27.79 NBC

STERLING, TISHA
  SUPP.:
  McMillan ep 1.30.77 NBC
  In the Glitter Palace tf 2.27.77 NBC
  Charlie's Angels ep Angels on the Line 2.14.81 ABC

STEVENS, ANDREW*
  Adam-12 ep Northeast Division 12.5.73 NBC
  The Last Survivors tf 3.4.75 NBC
  Police Story ep 11.21.75 NBC
  The Oregon Trail tf 1.10.76 NBC

Secrets   tf   **2. 20. 77** ABC
Westside Medical   ep   7. 7. 77 ABC
The Oregon Trail   sr   9. 21. 77 NBC
Once an Eagle   ms   **12. 16. 76, 12. 23. 76, 12. 30. 76, 1. 6. 77,**
   1. 13. 77 NBC
The Bastard/Kent Family Chronicles   ms   **5. 22. 78, 5. 23. 78**
   NN
Women at West Point   tf   **2. 27. 79** CBS
The Rebels   ms   5. 14. 79, 5. 21. 79 NN
Topper   tf   11. 9. 79 ABC
Beggarman, Thief   tf   **11. 26. 79, 11. 27. 79** NBC
Miracle on Ice   tf   3. 1. 81 ABC
Code Red   tf   9. 20. 81 ABC
Code Red   sr   11. 1. 81 ABC

STEVENS, CONNIE
  A& C:
  Sugarfoot   ep   The Wild Bunch 9. 29. 59 ABC
  SUPP. :
  The Love Boat   ep   10. 7. 78 ABC
  Fantasy Island   ep   11. 18. 78 ABC
  The Love Boat   ep   Isosceles Triangle 12. 9. 78 ABC
  Love's Savage Fury   tf   5. 20. 79 ABC
  The Love Boat   ep   The Perfect Match 2. 2. 80 ABC
  Scruples   ms   **2. 25. 80, 2. 26. 80, 2. 28. 80** CBS
  Murder Can Hurt You!   tf   5. 21. 80 ABC
  The Love Boat   ep   11. 15. 80 ABC
  Aloha Paradise   ep   2. 25. 81 ABC
  Side Show   tf   6. 5. 81 NBC
  Harry's Battles   pt   6. 8. 81 ABC
  Fantasy Island   ep   Show Me a Hero 10. 10. 81 ABC

STEVENS, CRAIG
  SUPP. :
  The Tony Randall Show   ep   1. 6. 77 ABC
  The Love Boat II   tf   1. 21. 77 ABC
  The Cabot Connection   pt   5. 10. 77 CBS
  Starsky and Hutch   ep   9. 17. 77 ABC
  Quincy, M. E.   ep   10. 28. 77 NBC
  The Hardy Boys/Nancy Drew Mysteries   ep   11. 13. 77 ABC
  Police Woman   ep   3. 15. 78 NBC
  Project UFO   ep   5. 7. 78 NBC
  Secrets of Three Hungry Wives   tf   10. 9. 78 NBC
  The Incredible Hulk   ep   10. 13. 78 CBS
  The Hardy Boys   ep   11. 5. 78 ABC
  David Cassidy--Man Undercover   ep   11. 9. 78 NBC
  Fantasy Island   ep   3. 17. 79 ABC
  The Love Boat   ep   5. 5. 79 ABC
  The Home Front   pt   10. 9. 80 CBS
  Dallas   ep   4. 3. 81, 4. 10. 81 CBS
  Fantasy Island   ep   Lillian Russell 11. 28. 81 ABC

STEVENS, STELLA
    SUPP. :
    The New Love Boat (a. k. a. Love Boat III) tf 5. 5. 77 ABC
    Charlie Cobb: Nice Night for a Hanging tf 6. 9. 77 NBC
    Murder in Peyton Place tf 10. 3. 77 NBC
    The Night They Took Miss Beautiful tf 10. 24. 77 NBC
    The Oregon Trail ep 10. 26. 77 NBC
    Cruise into Terror tf 2. 3. 78 ABC
    The Eddie Capra Mysteries ep Who Killed Charles Pendragon?
        9. 8. 78 NBC
    The Jordan Chance tf 12. 12. 78 CBS
    Hart to Hart pt 8. 25. 79 ABC
    The French-Atlantic Affair ms 11. 15. 79, 11. 16. 79, 11. 18. 79
        ABC
    Friendships, Secrets and Lies tf 12. 3. 79 NBC
    Make Me an Offer tf 1. 11. 80 ABC
    Flamingo Road tf 5. 12. 80 NBC
    Children of Divorce tf 11. 24. 80 NBC
    Flamingo Road sr 1. 6. 81 NBC
    Twirl tf 10. 25. 81 NBC
    Flamingo Road sr ret 11. 3. 81 NBC

STEVENSON, McLEAN*
    That Girl ep 2. 6. 69 ABC
    The Doris Day Show sr 9. 22. 69 CBS
    The Doris Day Show sr ret 9. 14. 70 CBS
    My Wives Jane pt 8. 1. 71 CBS
    The Doris Day Show sr ret 9. 13. 71 CBS
    Love, American Style ep Love and the Penal Code 9. 17. 71
        ABC
    M*A*S*H sr 9. 17. 72 CBS
    Shirts/Skins tf 10. 9. 73 ABC
    The McLean Stevenson Show sr 12. 1. 76 NBC
    In the Beginning sr 9. 20. 78 CBS
    Hello, Larry sr 1. 26. 79 NBC
    Diff'rent Strokes ep 3. 30. 79, 9. 28. 79 NBC
    Hello, Larry sr ret 10. 12. 79 NBC
    The Love Boat ep 5. 2. 81 ABC

STEWART, JAMES
    SUPP. :
    Mr. Krueger's Christmas sp 12. 30. 80 NN

STEWART, MEL
    A& C:
    Julia ep 4. 15. 69 NBC
    Salt and Pepe pt 4. 18. 75 CBS
    SUPP. :
    Tabitha pt 5. 7. 77 ABC
    The Hallmark Hall of Fame ep The Last Hurrah sp 11. 16. 77
        NBC
    Tabitha sr 11. 19. 77 ABC

Ring of Passion   tf   2. 4. 78 NBC
Good Ol' Boys   pt   6. 7. 79 NBC
Marriage Is Alive and Well   tf   1. 25. 80 NBC
The Love Boat   ep   Tell Her She's Great 11. 29. 80 ABC
Little House on the Prairie   ep   12. 6. 81 NBC

STEWART, TRISH*
The Rookies   ep   9. 23. 74 ABC
Barnaby Jones   ep   11. 28. 75 CBS
Time Travelers   tf   3. 19. 76 ABC
Barnaby Jones   ep   1. 27. 77 CBS
The Streets of San Francisco   ep   2. 3. 77 ABC
Most Wanted   ep   3. 7. 77   ABC
Project UFO   ep   10. 12. 78 NBC
Salvage 1   tf   1. 20. 79 ABC
Salvage 1   sr   1. 29. 79 ABC
Barnaby Jones   ep   3. 29. 79 CBS
Barnaby Jones   ep   Temptation 4. 19. 79 CBS
Breaking Up Is Hard to Do   tf   9. 5. 79, 9. 7. 79 ABC
Salvage 1   sr ret   11. 4. 79 ABC
Trapper John, M. D.   ep   3. 9. 80 CBS
The Love Boat   ep   12. 4. 81 ABC

STIERS, DAVID OGDEN*
Charlie's Angels   tf   3. 21. 76 ABC
Cousins   pt   8. 10. 76 ABC
Doc   sr   9. 25. 76 CBS
The Mary Tyler Moore Show   ep   12. 25. 76, 1. 8. 77 CBS
A Circle of Children   tf   3. 10. 77 CBS
The Tony Randall Show   ep   3. 10. 77 ABC
A Love Affair: The Eleanor and Lou Gehrig Story   tf   1. 15. 78
    NBC
Sergeant Matlovich vs. the U. S. Air Force   tf   8. 21. 78 NBC
M*A*S*H   sr   9. 18. 78 CBS
The Paper Chase   ep   12. 19. 78 CBS
Sweepstakes   ep   2. 16. 79 NBC
Breaking Up Is Hard to Do   tf   9. 5. 79 ABC
M*A*S*H   sr ret   9. 17. 79 CBS
NBC Theatre   ep   The Oldest Living Graduate   sp   4. 7. 80
    NBC
Father Damien: The Leper Priest   tf   10. 27. 80 NBC
M*A*S*H   sr ret   11. 17. 80 CBS
M*A*S*H   sr ret   10. 26. 81 CBS

STOCKWELL, DEAN
SUPP. :
Tales of the Unexpected   ep   8. 24. 77 NBC
A Killing Affair   tf   9. 21. 77 CBS
Greatest Heroes of the Bible   ep   The Story of Daniel in the
    Lion's Den 11. 22. 78 NBC
Born to Be Sold   tf   11. 2. 81 NBC

STOCKWELL, GUY
  SUPP. :
  Lanigan's Rabbi   ep   3. 20. 77 NBC
  Quincy, M. E.   ep   12. 2. 77, 12. 9. 77 NBC
  The Hardy Boys/Nancy Drew Mysteries   ep   1. 8. 78 ABC
  Fantasy Island   ep   2. 11. 78 ABC
  Faith for Today   ep   6. 4. 78 NN
  The Eddie Capra Mysteries   ep   12. 8. 78 NBC
  How the West Was Won   ep   1. 2. 79 ABC
  CHiPs   ep   1. 20. 79 NBC

STONE, CHRISTOPHER (a. k. a. Chris Stone)*
  The Outcasts   ep   10. 7. 68 ABC
  The Interns   sr   9. 18. 70 CBS
  Mission: Impossible   ep   10. 16. 71 CBS
  Marcus Welby, M. D.   ep   11. 23. 71 ABC
  Cade's County   ep   1. 23. 72 CBS
  The FBI   ep   Holiday with Terror 12. 3. 72 ABC
  The Streets of San Francisco   ep   The Year of the Locusts
    12. 9. 72 ABC
  Wheeler and Murdoch   pt   5. 9. 73 ABC
  Barnaby Jones   ep   Blind Terror 9. 16. 73 CBS
  The Magician   ep   Nightmare in Steel 12. 18. 73 NBC
  Cannon   ep   Where's Jennifer? 1. 23. 74 CBS
  Chopper One   ep   3. 3. 74 ABC
  Barnaby Jones   ep   Odd Man Loses 10. 8. 74 CBS
  Manhunter   ep   11. 13. 74 CBS
  The Streets of San Francisco   ep   11. 21. 74 ABC
  Police Story   ep   2. 4. 75 NBC
  Hollywood Television Theatre   ep   The Ladies of the Corridor
    4. 21. 75 PBS
  Three for the Road   ep   9. 14. 75 CBS
  Police Woman   ep   9. 19. 75 NBC
  Medical Story   ep   10. 16. 75 NBC
  The Streets of San Francisco   ep   1. 8. 76 ABC
  Barnaby Jones   ep   2. 5. 76 CBS
  Police Story   ep   3. 12. 76 NBC
  Spencer's Pilots   pt   4. 9. 76 CBS
  The Bionic Woman   ep   Fly Jaime 5. 5. 76 ABC
  Spencer's Pilots   sr   9. 17. 76 CBS
  Hunter   ep   3. 4. 77 CBS
  Kingston Confidential   ep   6. 15. 77 NBC
  Logan's Run   ep   11. 7. 77 CBS
  Mulligan's Stew   ep   12. 13. 77 NBC
  The New Adventures of Wonder Woman   ep   Light-Fingered
    Lady 1. 6. 78 CBS
  The Bionic Woman   ep   1. 14. 78, 1. 21. 78, 2. 11. 78, 5. 13. 78
    NBC
  Barnaby Jones   ep   1. 19. 78 CBS
  Black Beauty   ms   1. 31. 78, 2. 1. 78, 2. 2. 78, 2. 3. 78, 2. 4. 78
    NBC
  The American Girls   ep   10. 14. 78 CBS

David Cassidy--Man Undercover   ep   12. 7. 78 NBC
Fantasy Island   ep   3. 3. 79 ABC
Julie Farr, M. D.   ep   6. 12. 79 ABC
CHiPs   ep   10. 13. 79 NBC
Eischied   ep   12. 14. 79 NBC
Buck Rogers in the 25th Century   ep   1. 3. 80 NBC
The Misadventures of Sheriff Lobo   ep   5. 13. 80 NBC
Secrets of Midland Heights   ep   1. 10. 81 CBS
Dallas   ep   4. 3. 81 CBS

STORM, GALE
  SUPP. :
  The Love Boat   ep   11. 3. 79 ABC

STRAIGHT, BEATRICE
  A& C:
  The Hallmark Hall of Fame   ep   The Borrowers   sp   12. 14. 73
    NBC
  Beacon Hill   sr   8. 25. 76 CBS
  SUPP. :
  The Andros Targets   ep   3. 7. 77 CBS
  The World of Darkness   pt   4. 17. 77 CBS
  The New Adventures of Wonder Woman   ep   The Return of
    Wonder Woman 9. 16. 77 CBS
  Killer on Board   tf   10. 10. 77 NBC
  The Dain Curse   ms   5. 22. 78, 5. 23. 78, 5. 24. 78 CBS

STRASBERG, SUSAN
  SUPP. :
  SST--Death Flight   tf   2. 25. 77 ABC
  The Immigrants   ms   2. 20. 78, 2. 21. 78 NN
  Beggarman, Thief   tf   11. 26. 79, 11. 27. 79 NBC
  Sweepstakes   ep   3. 2. 79 NBC

STRASSMAN, MARCIA*
  Wednesday Night Out   pt   4. 24. 72 NBC
  Marcus Welby, M. D.   ep   The Latch-Key Child 2. 19. 74 ABC
  Journey from Darkness   tf   2. 25. 75 NBC
  Welcome Back, Kotter   sr   9. 9. 75 ABC
  Brenda Starr   tf   5. 8. 76 ABC
  Welcome Back, Kotter   sr ret   9. 23. 76 ABC
  The Love Boat II   tf   1. 21. 77 ABC
  Welcome Back, Kotter   sr ret   9. 15. 77 ABC
  The Love Boat   ep   2. 4. 78 ABC
  Fantasy Island   ep   3. 18. 78 ABC
  Welcome Back, Kotter   sr ret   11. 11. 78 ABC
  The Nightingales   pt   5. 19. 79 NBC
  The Rockford Files   ep   10. 19. 79 NBC
  Once upon a Family   tf   1. 22. 80 CBS
  Brave New World   tf   3. 7. 80 NBC
  Good Time Harry   sr   7. 26. 80 NBC

STREEP, MERYL*
  The Deadliest Season   tf   3. 16. 77 CBS

Holocaust   ms   4. 16-19. 78 NBC
Great Performances   ep   Uncommon Women and Others 6. 20. 79
   PBS
Kiss Me Petruchio   sp   1. 10. 81 NN

STRICKLAND   GAIL*
   The Mary Tyler Moore Show   ep   12. 15. 73 CBS
   Barnaby Jones   ep   2. 17. 74 CBS
   Hawaii Five-O   ep   Killer at Sea 2. 19. 74 CBS
   Police Story   ep   Country Boy 2. 19. 74 NBC
   Hawaii Five-O   ep   11. 12. 74 CBS
   Harry O   ep   2. 6. 75 ABC
   The Rookies   ep   12. 9. 75 ABC
   The Bob Newhart Show   ep   1. 24. 76 CBS
   The Gathering   tf   12. 4. 77 ABC
   A Love Affair: The Eleanor and Lou Gehrig Story   tf   1. 15. 78
      NBC
   The President's Mistress   tf   2. 10. 78 CBS
   Lou Grant   ep   2. 13. 78 CBS
   Ski Lift to Death   tf   3. 3. 78 CBS
   One on One   tf   10. 30. 79 CBS
   Letters from Frank   tf   11. 22. 79 CBS
   The Gathering, Part II   tf   12. 17. 79 NBC
   A Matter of Life and Death   tf   1. 13. 81 CBS
   Walking Tall   ep   Deadly Impact 3. 24. 81 NBC
   Darkroom   ep   The Siege of 31 August 12. 11. 81 ABC

STRUTHERS, SALLY
   SUPP. :
   All in the Family   sr ret   10. 2. 77 CBS
   Intimate Strangers   tf   11. 11. 77 ABC
   My Husband Is Missing   tf   12. 5. 78 NBC
   And Your Name Is Jonah   tf   1. 28. 79 CBS
   Archie Bunker's Place   ep   11. 18. 79 CBS
   A Gun in the House   tf   2. 11. 81 CBS

SULLIVAN, BARRY
   A& C:
   Insight   ep   5. 25. 75 NN
   The Bionic Woman   ep   1. 12. 76 ABC
   SUPP. :
   Rich Man, Poor Man, Book II   ep   2. 8. 77 ABC
   Quincy, M. E.   ep   2. 25. 77 NBC
   The Bastard/ Kent Family Chronicles   ms   5. 22. 78, 5. 23. 78 NN
   Fantasy Island   ep   10. 14. 78 ABC
   The Immigrants   ms   11. 20. 78, 11. 21. 78 NN
   Lucan   ep   11. 27. 78 ABC
   Backstairs at the White House   ms ep   2. 5. 79 NBC
   Charlie's Angels   ep   Love Boat Angels 9. 12. 79 ABC
   The Love Boat   ep   9. 22. 79 ABC
   Disney's Wonderful World   ep   The Secret of Lost Valley
      4. 27. 80 NBC
   Casino   tf   8. 1. 80 ABC
   Judgement Day   pt   12. 6. 81 NBC

SULLIVAN, SUSAN*
 Actor's Company ep Macbeth sp 3.11.69 NN
 No Place to Run tf 9.19.72 ABC
 Medical Center ep 9.29.75 CBS
 McMillan and Wife 10.26.75 NBC
 Petrocelli ep 12.24.75 NBC
 Kojak ep 3.7.76 CBS
 City of Angels ep 3.16.76 NBC
 Bell, Book and Candle pt 9.8.76 NBC
 Rich Man, Poor Man, Book II sr 9.21.76 ABC
 Barnaby Jones ep Deadline for Dying 10.14.76 CBS
 The City tf 1.12.77 NBC
 Kojak ep 1.18.77 CBS
 Roger and Harry tf 5.2.77 ABC
 Dog and Cat ep 5.14.77 ABC
 The Magnificent Magnet of Santa Mesa tf 6.19.77 NBC
 Having Babies II tf 10.28.77 ABC
 The Incredible Hulk tf 11.4.77 CBS
 Barnaby Jones ep 1.26.78 CBS
 Deadman's Curve tf 2.3.78 CBS
 Having Babies III tf 3.3.78 ABC
 Having Babies sr 3.7.78 ABC
 Julie Farr, M.D. sr 4.11.78 ABC
 The Comedy Company tf 7.21.78 CBS
 The New Maverick tf 9.3.78 ABC
 Julie Farr, M.D. sr ret 6.12.79 ABC
 Breaking Up Is Hard to Do tf 9.5.79, 9.7.79 ABC
 The Love Boat ep 11.29.79 ABC
 Taxi ep 1.22.80 ABC
 The Ordeal of Dr. Mudd tf 3.25.80 CBS
 City in Fear tf 3.30.80 ABC
 It's a Living sr 10.30.80 ABC
 Marriage Is Alive and Well tf 12.25.80 NBC
 It's a Living sr ret 7.21.81 ABC
 Fantasy Island ep The Perfect Husband 11.21.81 ABC
 Falcon Crest sr 12.4.81 CBS

SUSMAN, TODD
 SUPP. :
 Off the Wall pt 5.7.77 NBC
 Getting There pt 2.12.80 CBS
 Ethel Is an Elephant pt 6.18.80 CBS
 Number 96 sr 12.10.80 NBC

SWANSON, GLORIA
 SUPP. :
 Men Who Rate a 10 sp hos 10.7.80 NBC

SWEET, DOLPH*
 For the People ep To Prosecute All Crimes 1.31.65 CBS
 N.Y.P.D. ep Walk the Long Pier 12.10.68 ABC
 The Migrants tf 2.3.74 CBS
 The Stranger Who Looks Like Me tf 3.6.74 ABC

Billy: Portrait of a Street Kid   tf   9. 12. 77 NBC
A Killing Affair   tf   9. 21. 77 CBS
King   ms   2. 11-14. 78 NBC
What Really Happened to the Class of '65?   ep   5. 25. 78 NBC
Death Moon   tf   5. 31. 78 CBS
Sparrow   pt   8. 11. 78 CBS
Taxi   ep   10. 17. 78 ABC
Little House on the Prairie   ep   12. 18. 78 NBC
Kaz   ep   1. 24. 79 CBS
Mrs. Columbo   ep   3. 1. 79 NBC
Rendezvous Hotel   tf   7. 11. 79 CBS
Flesh and Blood   tf   10. 14. 79, 10. 16. 79 CBS
Marciano   tf   10. 21. 79 ABC
The Hallmark Hall of Fame   ep   Aunt Mary 12. 5. 79 CBS
When the Whistle Blows   sr   3. 14. 80 ABC
Hagen   ep   3. 15. 80 CBS
The Hallmark Hall of Fame   ep   Gideon's Trumpet 4. 30. 80
     CBS
Enos   ep   Guts and Green Strike Again 11. 26. 80 CBS
Hart to Hart   ep   Murder in Paradise 1. 31. 81 ABC
The Acorn People   tf   3. 2. 81 NBC
Hill Street Blues   ep   Gator Bait 3. 7. 81 NBC
The Two Lives of Carol Litner   tf   10. 14. 81 CBS
Gimme a Break   sr   10. 29. 81 NBC

SWENSON, INGA
   SUPP. :
   Testimony of Two Men   ms   5. 1. 78, 5. 2. 78, 5. 3. 78 NN
   Ziegfeld: The Man and His Women   tf   5. 21. 78 NBC
   Grandpa Goes to Washington   ep   12. 12. 78 NBC
   Benson   sr   9. 13. 79 ABC
   Benson   sr ret   10. 31. 80 ABC
   Benson   sr ret   11. 6. 81 ABC

SWIT, LORETTA
   SUPP. :
   The Hostage Heart   tf   9. 9. 77 CBS
   M*A*S*H   sr ret   9. 20. 77   CBS
   The Love Boat   ep   Ex Plus Y 10. 8. 77 ABC
   M*A*S*H   sr ret   9. 18. 78 CBS
   The Love Boat   ep   11. 4. 78 ABC
   Supertrain   ep   2. 28. 79 NBC
   M*A*S*H   sr ret   9. 17. 79 CBS
   Mirror, Mirror   tf   10. 10. 79 NBC
   Friendships, Secrets and Lies   tf   12. 3. 79 NBC
   Valentine   tf   12. 7. 79 ABC
   The Love Tapes   tf   5. 9. 80 ABC
   M*A*S*H   sr ret   11. 17. 80 CBS
   Cagney and Lacey   tf   10. 8. 81 CBS
   M*A*S*H   sr ret   10. 26. 81 CBS

SWOFFORD, KEN
   A&C:
   Gunsmoke   ep   Waste 9. 27. 71 CBS

World of Disney   ep   The Boy and the Bronco Buster 3. 25. 73
NBC
Police Story   ep   1. 21. 75 NBC
The Rockford Files   ep   2. 7. 75 NBC
Switch   ep   9. 16. 75, 9. 30. 75, 12. 16. 75 CBS
SUPP. :
Rich Man, Poor Man   ms ep   1. 11. 77 ABC
The Six Million Dollar Man   ep   1. 30. 77 ABC
Hunter   ep   3. 18. 77 CBS
Young Joe, the Forgotten Kennedy   tf   9. 18. 77 ABC
The Oregon Trail   sr   9. 21. 77 NBC
Police Story   ep   11. 9. 77 NBC
The Rockford Files   ep   12. 16. 77 NBC
The Six Million Dollar Man   ep   Return of Deathprobe 1. 22. 78,
    1. 29. 78 ABC
Crisis in Sun Valley   tf   3. 29. 78 NBC
To Kill a Cop   tf   4. 10. 78, 4. 11. 78 NBC
The Eddie Capra Mysteries   sr   9. 8. 78 NBC
David Cassidy--Man Undercover   ep   1. 18. 79 NBC
Battlestar Galactica   ep   3. 18. 79 ABC
David Cassidy--Man Undercover   ep   7. 5. 79 NBC
California Fever   ep   10. 2. 79 CBS
The Lazarus Syndrome   ep   10. 16. 79 ABC
The Rockford Files   ep   11. 23. 79 NBC
Paris   ep   1. 15. 80 CBS
Disney's Wonderful World   ep   Sultan and the Rock Star 4. 20. 80
NBC
All God's Children   tf   4. 28. 80 ABC
Walking Tall   ep   3. 24. 81 NBC
Riker   ep   3. 28. 81 CBS

SWOPE, TRACY BROOKS*
Conflicts   ep   Me 11. 29. 73 PBS
The Partridge Family   ep   Queen for a Minute 2. 2. 74 ABC
Revenge for a Rape   tf   11. 19. 76 ABC
Serpico   ep   1. 14. 77 NBC
The Love Boat II   tf   1. 21. 77 ABC
Dog and Cat   ep   3. 19. 77 ABC
Starsky and Hutch   ep   I Love You, Rosey Malone 10. 1. 77 ABC
Black Market Baby   tf   10. 7. 77 ABC
Crisis in Sun Valley   tf   3. 29. 78 NBC
Charlie's Angels   ep   12. 6. 78 ABC
The Ultimate Imposter   tf   5. 12. 79 CBS
The Last Convertible   ms   9. 24. 79, 9. 25. 79, 9. 26. 79 NBC
The Secret War of Jackie's Girls   tf   11. 29. 80 NBC

-T-

TABORI, KRISTOFFER
   A&C:
   The Streets of San Francisco   ep   11.18.75 ABC
   SUPP.:
   Seventh Avenue   ms ep   2.10.77 NBC
   What Really Happened to the Class of '65?   ep   12.15.77 NBC
   Black Beauty   ms   1.31.78, 2.1.78, 2.2.78, 2.3.78, 2.4.78
      NBC
   The Rockford Files   ep   10.19.79 NBC
   Trapper John, M.D.   ep   12.9.79 CBS
   American Short Story   ep   Rappaccini's Daughter 2.25.80 PBS
   Brave New World   tf   3.7.80 NBC
   Between the Lines   pt   7.7.80 ABC
   The Chicago Story   tf   3.15.81 NBC

TACKER, FRANCINE*
   The Paper Chase   sr   9.19.78 CBS
   The Associates   ep   10.28.79 ABC
   Dallas   ep   1.18.80 CBS
   Goodtime Girls   sr   1.22.80 ABC

TALBOT, NITA
   A&C:
   Bourbon Street Beat   ep   Mrs. Viner Vanishes 11.30.59 ABC
   Bourbon Street Beat   ep   If a Body 4.18.60 ABC
   Dante's Inferno   ep   Dante Rides Again 1.30.61 NBC
   Follow the Sun   ep   Rage for Justice 9.17.61 ABC
   Honeymoon Suite   pt   11.20.73 ABC
   Insight   ep   8.22.76 NN
   SUPP.:
   Sex and the Married Woman   tf   9.13.77 NBC
   Soap   sr   9.13.77 ABC
   CHiPs   ep   2.23.78 NBC
   Insight   ep   7.16.78 NN
   Supertrain   ep   2.7.79 NBC
   Hawaii Five-O   ep   2.8.79 CBS
   Charlie's Angels   ep   Angels on Campus 11.28.79 ABC
   Lou Grant   ep   12.3.79, 12.10.79 CBS
   Fantasy Island   ep   The Winetasters 12.22.79 ABC
   Trapper John, M.D.   ep   3.9.80 CBS
   Turnover Smith   tf   6.8.80 ABC
   Nobody's Perfect   ep   7.31.80 ABC

TANDY, JESSICA
   SUPP.:
   The Many Faces of Love   sp   3.7.79 PBS

TAYBACK, VIC*
   Rawhide   ep   The Gray Rock Hotel 5.21.65 CBS

Star Trek   ep   A Piece of the Action 1. 12. 68 NBC
Mission: Impossible   ep   The Mercenaries 10. 27. 68 CBS
The Good Guys   ep   1. 29. 69 CBS
The Outsider   ep   Handle with Care 3. 5. 69 NBC
Land of the Giants   ep   10. 5. 69 ABC
Bonanza   ep   Caution: Easter Bunny Crossing 3. 29. 70 NBC
The Mary Tyler Moore Show   ep   Second Story Story 1. 23. 71
    CBS
The Courtship of Eddie's Father   ep   12. 8. 71 ABC
Mannix   ep   Catspaw 12. 8. 71 CBS
Arnie   ep   1. 1. 72 CBS
McCloud   ep   Give My Regards to Broadway 2. 23. 72 NBC
Longstreet   ep   3. 2. 72 ABC
The Bold Ones: The Doctors   ep   9. 26. 72 NBC
The Rookies   ep   The Commitment 10. 2. 72 ABC
Gunsmoke   ep   10. 23. 72 CBS
The Streets of San Francisco   ep   10. 28. 72 ABC
The Mod Squad   ep   11. 30. 72 ABC
Emergency   ep   1. 27. 73 NBC
The Partridge Family   ep   3. 2. 73 ABC
Emergency   ep   3. 3. 73 NBC
Partners in Crime   tf   3. 24. 73 NBC
The Ted Bessell Show   pt   5. 8. 73 CBS
Cops   pt   6. 5. 73 CBS
Griff   sr   9. 29. 73 ABC
The Alpha Caper   tf   10. 6. 73 ABC
Cannon   ep   The Limping Man 11. 14. 73 CBS
M*A*S*H   ep   The Incubator 12. 1. 73 CBS
All in the Family   ep   1. 26. 74 CBS
The Rookies   ep   Take Over 12. 30. 74 ABC
Hawaii Five-O   ep   1. 7. 75 CBS
Barney Miller   ep   2. 27. 75 ABC
On the Rocks   ep   10. 16. 75 ABC
Switch   ep   11. 4. 75 CBS
Dark Victory   ep   2. 5. 76 ABC
Bronk   ep   3. 21. 76 CBS
Family   ep   4. 13. 76 CBS
Alice   pt   8. 31. 76 CBS
Alice   sr   9. 29. 76 CBS
McCloud   ep   10. 24. 76 NBC
The Blue Knight   ep   12. 8. 76 CBS
Little Ladies of the Night   tf   1. 16. 77 ABC
Alice   sr ret   10. 2. 77 CBS
Hawaii Five-O   ep   3. 9. 78 CBS
James at 16   ep   3. 9. 78 NBC
Getting Married   tf   5. 17. 78 CBS
Vega$ ep   9. 20. 78 ABC
Alice   sr ret   9. 24. 78 CBS
The Eddie Capra Mysteries   ep   11. 3. 78 NBC
Sweepstakes   ep   2. 16. 79 NBC
Supertrain   ep   4. 7. 79 NBC
Time Express   ep   5. 10. 79 CBS
CHiPs   ep   Chips Goes Roller Disco 9. 22. 79 NBC

Alice   sr ret   9. 23. 79 CBS
The Love Boat   ep   11. 3. 79 ABC
Fantasy Island   ep   12. 8. 79 ABC
Moviola: This Year's Blonde   tf   5. 18. 80 NBC
Rage!   tf   9. 25. 80 NBC
The Great American Traffic Jam   tf   10. 2. 80 NBC
Alice   sr ret   11. 2. 80 CBS
The Love Boat   ep   10. 25. 80 ABC
CHiPs   ep   12. 7. 80 NBC
Flo   ep   3. 14. 81 CBS
Alice   sr ret   10. 4. 81 CBS
Ron Howard's Through the Magic Pyramid   tf   12. 6. 81, 12. 13. 81,
    NBC

TAYLOR, ELIZABETH
    SUPP. :
    The Hallmark Hall of Fame   ep   Return Engagement   sp
        11. 17. 78 NBC
    General Hospital   ep   11. 10. 81, 11. 12. 81, 11. 16. 81, 11. 17. 81,
        11. 19. 81 ABC

TAYLOR, ROD
    SUPP. :
    The Oregon Trail   sr   9. 21. 77 NBC
    Tales of the Unexpected   ep   2. 23. 80 NN
    Cry of the Innocent   tf   6. 19. 80 NBC
    Hellinger's Law   tf   3. 10. 81 CBS
    Jacqueline Bouvier Kennedy   tf   10. 14. 81 ABC

TEWES, LAUREN*
    Charlie's Angels   ep   Angels in Chains 10. 20. 76 ABC
    The ABC Short Story Special   ep   The Haunted Trailer 3. 26. 77
        ABC
    The New Love Boat (a. k. a. Love Boat III)   tf   5. 5. 77 ABC
    The Love Boat   sr   9. 24. 77 ABC
    Fantasy Island   ep   2. 18. 78 ABC
    The Love Boat   sr ret   9. 16. 78 ABC
    Vega$ ep   10. 25. 78 ABC
    The Dallas Cowboys Cheerleaders   tf   1. 14. 79 ABC
    Charlie's Angels   ep   Love Boat Angels 9. 12. 79 ABC
    The Love Boat   sr ret   9. 15. 79 ABC
    The Love Boat   sr ret   10. 25. 80 ABC
    The Love Boat   sr ret   10. 10. 81 ABC

THINNES, ROY
    SUPP. :
    Tales of the Unexpected   ep   2. 2. 77 NBC
    Secrets   tf   2. 20. 77 ABC
    Code Name: Diamond Head   tf   5. 3. 77 NBC
    Battlestar Galactica   ep   The Gun on the Ice Planet 10. 22. 78,
        10. 29. 78 ABC
    From Here to Eternity   ms   2. 14. 79, 2. 21. 79, 2. 28. 79 NBC
    Supertrain   ep   2. 28. 79 NBC

Return of the Mod Squad   tf   5. 18. 79 ABC
Stone   pt   8. 26. 79 ABC
From Here to Eternity   sr   3. 10. 80 NBC
From Here to Eternity   sr ret   8. 3. 80 NBC
Freedom   tf   5. 18. 81 ABC
Scruples   tf   5. 22. 81 ABC
Sizzle   tf   11. 29. 81 ABC

THOMAS, DANNY
   SUPP. :
   Happy Days   ep   1. 3. 78 ABC
   Three on a Date   tf   2. 17. 78 ABC
   Kojak   ep   3. 18. 78 CBS
   I'm a Big Girl Now   sr   10. 31. 80 ABC

THOMAS, MARLO
   SUPP. :
   It Happened One Christmas   tf   12. 11. 77 ABC
   The Body Human: Facts for Girls   sp hos   10. 7. 80 CBS

THOMAS, RICHARD
   A&C:
   Way Out   ep   The Croaker 5. 12. 61 CBS
   Great Ghost Tales   ep   Shredni Washtar 8. 24. 61 NBC
   SUPP. :
   The Waltons   sr ret   9. 15. 77 CBS
   Getting Married   tf   5. 17. 78 CBS
   Roots: The Next Generations   ms ep   2. 18. 79 ABC
   No Other Love   tf   3. 24. 79 CBS
   The Hallmark Hall of Fame   ep   All Quiet on the Western
      Front   sp   11. 14. 79 CBS
   To Find My Son   tf   10. 6. 80 CBS
   Berlin Tunnel 21   tf   3. 25. 81 CBS

THOMPSON, HILARY* (a. k. a. Hilarie Thompson)
   I Dream of Jeannie   ep   12. 30. 68 NBC
   The Outcasts   ep   The Town That Wouldn't 3. 31. 69 ABC
   The Young Rebels   sr   9. 20. 70 ABC
   Matt Lincoln   ep   1. 7. 71 ABC
   Love, American Style   ep   11. 12. 71 ABC
   The Odd Couple   ep   3. 10. 72 ABC
   Here We Go Again   ep   3. 24. 73 ABC
   Manhunter   tf   2. 26. 74 CBS
   Hec Ramsey   ep   Scar Tissue 3. 10. 74 NBC
   Manhunter   sr   9. 11. 74 CBS
   Harry O   ep   Forty Reasons to Kill 12. 5. 74, 12. 12. 74 ABC
   Barnaby Jones   ep   1. 15. 76 CBS
   Risko   pt   5. 9. 76 CBS
   Archie   pt   12. 19. 76 ABC
   Quincy, M. E.   ep   Visitors in Paradise 2. 18. 77 NBC
   McLaren's Riders   pt   5. 17. 77 CBS
   Cruise into Terror   tf   2. 3. 78 ABC
   Fantasy Island   ep   4. 29. 78 ABC

Operation Petticoat   sr   9. 18. 78 ABC
Barnaby Jones   ep   10. 26. 78 CBS
Charlie's Angels   ep   Counterfeit Angels 1. 24. 79 ABC
Starsky and Hutch   ep   3. 11. 79 ABC
Barnaby Jones   ep   The Final Victim 3. 6. 80 CBS
Camp Grizzly   pt   6. 30. 80 ABC
Number 96   sr   12. 10. 80 NBC

THOMPSON, MARSHALL
   SUPP. :
The Eddie Capra Mysteries   ep   10. 20. 78 NBC

THORSON, LINDA*
   The Avengers   sr   1. 10. 68 ABC
   The Avengers   sr ret   9. 23. 68 ABC
   The Return of the Saint   ep   The Roman Touch 6. 27. 80 CBS
   McClain's Law   ep   Portrait of a Playmate 12. 18. 81 NBC

TIERNEY, GENE
   SUPP. :
Scruples   ms   2. 25. 80, 2. 26. 80, 2. 28. 80 CBS

TILTON, CHARLENE*
   Happy Days   ep   11. 16. 76 ABC
   Dallas   sr   4. 2. 78 CBS
   Dallas   sr ret   9. 23. 78 CBS
   Knots Landing   ep   1. 31. 80 CBS
   Dallas   sr ret   9. 21. 79 CBS
   Diary of a Teenage Hitchhiker   tf   9. 21. 79 ABC
   Dallas   sr ret   11. 7. 80 CBS
   The Love Boat   ep   11. 1. 80 ABC
   Fantasy Island   ep   11. 8. 80 ABC
   Dallas   sr ret   10. 9. 81 CBS

TOBIN, MICHELE*
   The Fitzpatricks   sr   9. 5. 77 CBS
   James at 16   ep   3. 9. 78 NBC
   Grandpa Goes to Washington   sr   9. 7. 78 NBC
   The Love Boat   ep   Second String Mom 5. 12. 79 ABC
   California Fever   sr   9. 25. 79 CBS
   The Boy Who Drank Too Much   tf   2. 6. 80 CBS

TORN, RIP
   SUPP. :
Betrayed   tf   11. 13. 78 NBC
Steel Cowboy   tf   12. 6. 78 NBC
Sophia Loren: Her Own Story   tf   10. 26. 80 NBC

TRAVANTI, DANIEL J. *
   Call to Danger   pt   7. 1. 68 CBS
   Lancer   ep   12. 31. 68 CBS
   The Mod Squad   ep   3. 18. 69 ABC
   The Love War   tf   3. 10. 70 ABC

Mannix   ep   Murder Times Three 12. 1. 71 CBS
Cannon   ep   1. 4. 72 CBS
The Man and the City   ep   1. 5. 72 ABC
Mission: Impossible   ep   1. 15. 72 CBS
The FBI   ep   10. 8. 72 ABC
Barnaby Jones   ep   9. 30. 73 CBS
Gunsmoke   ep   Like Old Times 1. 21. 74 CBS
The FBI   ep   4. 14. 74 ABC
Kojak   ep   A Souvenir from Atlantic City 11. 10. 74 CBS
Gunsmoke   ep   12. 16. 74 CBS
Barnaby Jones   ep   9. 26. 75 CBS
Phyllis   ep   10. 27. 75 CBS
Kojak   ep   A Grave Too Soon 2. 1. 76 CBS
Barnaby Jones   ep   10. 21. 76 CBS
Family   ep   3. 29. 77 ABC
Hart to Hart   ep   11. 13. 79 ABC
Knots Landing   ep   2. 21. 80 CBS
Hill Street Blues   sr   1. 15. 81 NBC
Hill Street Blues   sr ret   10. 29. 81 NBC

TRAVOLTA, ELLEN*
Cover Girls   tf   5. 18. 77 NBC
Welcome Back, Kotter   ep   10. 13. 77 ABC
What's Happening!   ep   10. 20. 77 ABC
Intimate Strangers   tf   11. 11. 79 ABC
The President's Mistress   tf   2. 10. 78 CBS
CHiPs   ep   2. 16. 78 NBC
Wheels   ms   5. 7. 78, 5. 8. 78, 5. 9. 78 NBC
The Courage and the Passion   tf   5. 22. 78 NBC
Are You in the House Alone?   tf   9. 20. 78 CBS
The Love Boat   ep   Rocky 9. 23. 78 ABC
Diff'rent Strokes   ep   11. 10. 78 NBC
Welcome Back, Kotter   ep   11. 25. 78 ABC
Eight Is Enough   ep   11. 29. 78 ABC
Makin' It   sr   2. 1. 79 ABC
Marie   pt   12. 1. 79 ABC
Number 96   sr   12. 10. 80 NBC
Happy Days   ep   2. 24. 81 ABC
Happy Days   ep   Not with My Mother You Don't 10. 13. 81 ABC

TRAVOLTA, JOHN
SUPP. :
Welcome Back, Kotter   sr ret   9. 15. 77 ABC
Welcome Back, Kotter   sr ret   9. 11. 78 ABC

TUCKER, FORREST
A&C:
Whispering Smith   ep   The Trademark 8. 14. 61 NBC
SUPP. :
The Incredible Rocky Mountain Race   tf   12. 17. 77 NBC
Black Beauty   ms   1. 31. 78, 2. 1. 78, 2. 2. 78, 2. 3. 78   2. 4. 78
   NBC
Police Woman   ep   3. 8. 78 NBC

A Real American Hero tf **12. 9. 78** CBS
Fantasy Island ep **2. 10. 79** ABC
The Rebels ms **5. 14. 79, 5. 21. 79** NN
Pottsville pt **8. 6. 80** CBS
Fantasy Island ep Slam Dunk **10. 10. 81** ABC

TUCKER, TANYA*
Amateur Night at the Dixie Bar and Grill tf **1. 8. 79** NBC
The Rebels ms **5. 14. 79, 5. 21. 79** NN
The Georgia Peaches tf **11. 8. 80** CBS
The Love Boat ep Deductible Divorce **10. 17. 81** ABC

TYRRELL, SUSAN
SUPP. :
Open All Night sr **11. 28. 81** ABC

TYSON, CICELY
SUPP. :
Roots ms ep **1. 23. 77** ABC
Wilma tf **12. 19. 77** NBC
King ms **2. 12. 78, 2. 13. 78, 2. 14. 78** NBC
A Woman Called Moses tf **12. 11. 78, 12. 12. 78** NBC
The Body Human: Becoming a Woman sp hos **10. 27. 81** CBS
The Marva Collins Story tf **12. 1. 81** CBS

-U-

UGGAMS, LESLIE
SUPP. :
Roots ms ep **1. 27. 77, 1. 28. 77** ABC
Backstairs at the White House ms **1. 29. 79, 2. 5. 79, 2. 12. 79,
    2. 19. 79** NBC
The Love Boat ep **2. 21. 81** ABC
The Love Boat ep Two Grapes on the Vine **10. 17. 81** ABC
Sizzle tf **11. 29. 81** ABC

ULLMANN, LIV*
Scenes from a Marriage sr **3. 9. 77** PBS
Great Performances ep The Human Voice **11. 28. 79** PBS

URICH, ROBERT*
The FBI ep Desperate Runner **9. 17. 72** ABC
Kung Fu ep Blood Brother **1. 18. 73** ABC
Owen Marshall, Counselor at Law ep **3. 14. 73** ABC
Bob & Carol & Ted & Alice sr **9. 26. 73** ABC
Marcus Welby, M. D. ep Death Is Only a Side Effect **12. 18. 73**
    ABC
S. W. A. T. sr **2. 24. 75** ABC
Gunsmoke ep **3. 17. 75** CBS

Killdozer tf **2. 2. 74** ABC
Nakia ep 10. 26. 74 ABC
The Specialists tf 1. 6. 75 NBC
Bunco pt 1. 13. 77 NBC
Tabitha pt 5. 7. 77 ABC
Tabitha sr 9. 10. 77 ABC
Tabitha sr ret 11. 26. 77 ABC
The Love Boat ep 12. 3. 77 ABC
The Love Boat ep Taking Sides 2. 18. 78 ABC
Vega$ tf 4. 25. 78 ABC
Leave Yesterday Behind tf 5. 14. 78 ABC
Charlie's Angels ep Angels in Vegas 9. 13. 78 ABC
Vega$ sr 9. 20. 78 ABC
The Love Boat ep 10. 7. 78 ABC
The Love Boat ep El Kid 12. 9. 78 ABC
Vega$ sr ret 9. 19. 79 ABC
When She Was Bad tf 11. 25. 79 ABC
Vega$ sr ret 11. 5. 80 ABC
Fighting Back tf **12. 7. 80** ABC
Killing at Hell's Gate tf 10. 31. 81 CBS

USTINOV, PETER
    SUPP. :
    Jesus of Nazareth ms 4. 3. 77, 4. 10. 77 NBC
    The Thief of Baghdad tf 11. 23. 78 NBC
    Omni: The New Frontier sr hos 9. 15. 81 NN
    Dr. Snuggles sr vo 9. 27. 81 NN

-V-

VACCARO, BRENDA
    A& C:
    The Defenders ep Hollow Triumph 6. 20. 64 CBS
    SUPP. :
    Dear Detective sr 3. 28. 79 CBS
    The Pride of Jesse Hallam tf 3. 3. 81 CBS
    The Star Maker tf 5. 11. 81, 5. 12. 81 NBC
    A Long Way Home tf 12. 6. 81 ABC

VALENTINE, KAREN
    SUPP. :
    McMillan ep 1. 2. 77 NBC
    Murder at the World Series tf 3. 20. 77 ABC
    Starsky and Hutch ep 9. 24. 77 ABC
    Return to Fantasy Island tf 1. 20. 78 ABC
    The Love Boat ep 1. 21. 78 ABC
    Go West Young Girl tf 4. 27. 78 ABC
    America 2100 pt 7. 24. 79 ABC
    Eischied ep Only the Pretty Girls Die 9. 21. 79, 9. 28. 79 NBC

VALLEE, RUDY
  SUPP. :
  CHiPs   ep   1. 20. 79 NBC

VAN ARK, JOAN*
  Bonanza   ep   Sweet Annie Laurie 1. 5. 69 NBC
  The FBI   ep   The Maze 2. 9. 69 ABC
  The Guns of Will Sonnett   ep   The Man Who Killed Jim Sonnett
    3. 21. 69 ABC
  Matt Lincoln   ep   10. 29. 70 ABC
  The FBI   ep   The Deadly Gift 10. 3. 71 ABC
  The Bold Ones: The Doctors   ep   11. 7. 71 NBC
  The Odd Couple   ep   3. 3. 72 ABC
  Love, American Style   ep   Love and The Proposal 1972 ABC
  Temperature's Rising   sr   9. 12. 72 ABC
  Night Gallery   ep   The Ring with the Red Velvet Ropes 11. 5. 72
    NBC
  The Judge and Jake Wyler   tf   12. 2. 72 NBC
  M*A*S*H   ep   Radar's Report 9. 29. 73 CBS
  Cannon   ep   Duel in the Desert 1. 16. 74 CBS
  The Girl with Something Extra   ep   A Zicorn in the Rough
    2. 1. 74 NBC
  The ABC Afterschool Special   ep   Cyrano vo sp   3. 6. 74 ABC
  Big Rose   tf   3. 26. 74 CBS
  Mannix   ep   The Girl in the Polka Dot Dress 9. 16. 73 CBS
  The FBI   ep   4. 7. 74 ABC
  Barnaby Jones   ep   The Challenge 9. 24. 74 CBS
  Ironside   ep   Trial of Terror 10. 3. 74 NBC
  The Rockford Files   ep   Find Me If You Can 11. 1. 74 NBC
  Cannon   ep   11. 20. 74 CBS
  Shell Game   tf   5. 9. 75 CBS
  Rhoda   ep   9. 15. 75 CBS
  The Barbary Coast   ep   10. 6. 75 ABC
  Medical Center   ep   11. 3. 75 CBS
  The Rockford Files   ep   Resurrection in Black and White
    11. 7. 75 NBC
  Medical Story   ep   12. 11. 75 NBC
  Petrocelli   ep   2. 4. 76 NBC
  Joe Forrester   ep   3. 1. 76 NBC
  The Six Million Dollar Man   ep   The Bionic Boy 11. 7. 76 ABC
  The Rockford Files   ep   There's One in Every Port 1. 7. 77 NBC
  The Last Dinosaur   tf   2. 11. 77 ABC
  Kojak   ep   Lady in the Squadroom 3. 18. 77 CBS
  McMillan   ep   Have You Heard About Vanessa? 4. 24. 77 NBC
  We've Got Each Other   sr   10. 1. 77 CBS
  Quincy, M. E.   ep   2. 17. 78 NBC
  Having Babies   ep   3. 14. 78 ABC
  Quark   ep   3. 24. 78, 3. 31. 78 NBC
  Testimony of Two Men   ms   5. 1. 78, 5. 2. 78, 5. 3. 78 NN
  Tarzan and the Super 7   sr vo   9. 9. 78 CBS
  Dallas   ep   9. 23. 78 CBS
  Dallas   ep   9. 30. 78 CBS
  The New Adventures of Wonder Woman   ep   Time Bomb 11. 10. 78
    CBS

Vega$ ep   1. 31. 79 ABC
Spider-Woman   sr vo   9. 22. 79 ABC
Dallas   ep   10. 12. 79 CBS
The Love Boat   ep   10. 27. 79 ABC
Dallas   ep   12. 20. 79 CBS
Knots Landing   sr   12. 27. 79 CBS
The Heathcliff and Dingbat Show   sr vo   10. 4. 80 ABC
Thundarr the Barbarian   so vo   10. 4. 80 ABC
Knots Landing   sr ret   11. 20. 80 CBS
The Love Boat   ep   She Stole His Heart 12. 6. 80 ABC
Dallas   ep   1. 23. 81 CBS
Red Flag: The Ultimate Game   tf   10. 3. 81 CBS
The Love Boat   ep   Jewels and Jim 10. 24. 81 ABC
Knots Landing   sr ret   11. 12. 81 CBS

VAN CLEEF, LEE
   A&C:
   Law of the Plainsman   ep   Clear Title 12. 17. 59 NBC
   Stagecoach West   ep   Never Walk Alone 4. 18. 61 ABC
   Laramie   ep   Killer's Odds 4. 25. 61 NBC
   The Twilight Zone   ep   The Grave 10. 27. 61 CBS
   SUPP. :
   Nowhere to Hide   tf   6. 5. 77 NBC

VAN DOREN, MAMIE
   SUPP. :
   Fantasy Island   ep   2. 10. 79 ABC

VAN DUSEN, GRANVILLE*
   Dr. Max   tf   4. 4. 74 CBS
   Harry O   ep   Coinage of the Realm 10. 10. 74 ABC
   The Waltons   ep   11. 14. 74 CBS
   Someone I Touched   tf   2. 26. 75 ABC
   Baretta   ep   This Ain't My Bag 4. 30. 75 ABC
   Switch   ep   9. 30. 75 CBS
   The Night That Panicked America   tf   10. 31. 75 ABC
   Harry O   ep   Past Imperfect 1. 22. 76 ABC
   James A. Michener's Dynasty   tf   3. 13. 76 NBC
   The Bionic Woman   ep   Biofeedback 1. 12. 77 ABC
   The World of Darkness   pt   4. 17. 77 CBS
   The War Between the Tates   tf   6. 13. 77 NBC
   Barnaby Jones   ep   10. 13. 77 CBS
   Kojak   ep   Tears for All Who Loved Her 11. 20. 77 CBS
   ABC Theatre   ep   Breaking Up   sp   1. 2. 78 ABC
   The World Beyond   pt   1. 27. 78 CBS
   Dr. Scorpion   tf   2. 24. 78 ABC
   Love's Dark Ride   tf   4. 2. 78 NBC
   Escapade   pt   5. 19. 78 CBS
   Barnaby Jones   ep   Memory of a Nightmare 12. 14. 78 CBS
   Quincy, M. E.   A Question of Death 1. 4. 79 NBC
   Kaz   ep   3. 21. 79 CBS
   Transplant   tf   4. 17. 79 CBS
   Greatest Heroes of the Bible   ep   The Story of the Ten Com-
      mandments 5. 8. 79 NBC

Quincy, M. E.   ep   Mode of Death 11. 1. 79 NBC
CHiPs   ep   11. 17. 79 NBC
High Midnight   tf   11. 27. 79 CBS
Paris   ep   1. 1. 80 CBS
Stone   ep   1. 14. 80 ABC
My Wife Next Door   pt   9. 11. 80 CBS
Soap   sr   11. 12. 80 ABC
The Wild and the Free   tf   11. 26. 80 CBS
Madame X   tf   3. 16. 81 NBC

VAN DYKE, DICK
SUPP. :
Supertrain   ep   2. 14. 79 NBC
The Mary Tyler Moore Hour   ep   3. 25. 79 CBS
Harry's Battles   pt   6. 8. 81 ABC
True Life Stories   ep   If I Were a Rich Man   pt   9. 13. 81 ABC
Project Peacock   ep   How to Eat Like a Kid   sp   9. 22. 81 NBC

VAN DYKE, JERRY*
My Mother the Car   sr   9. 14. 65 NBC
Accidental Family   sr   9. 15. 67 NBC
Headmaster   sr   9. 18. 70 CBS
Love, American Style   ep   11. 12. 71 ABC
The Mary Tyler Moore Show   ep   11. 4. 72 CBS
The New Dick Van Dyke Show   ep   3. 18. 73 CBS
The Mary Tyler Moore Show   ep   10. 27. 73 CBS
The ABC Afterschool Special   ep   The Amazing Awareness of
    Duffy Moon   sp   3. 23. 77 ABC
Fantasy Island   ep   2. 25. 78 ABC
13 Queens Blvd.   sr   3. 20. 79 ABC
House Calls   ep   The Dead Beat 12. 29. 80 CBS
Fantasy Island   ep   3. 7. 81 ABC

VAN VALKENBURGH, DEBORAH*
Too Close for Comfort   sr   11. 11. 80 ABC
Too Close for Comfort   sr ret   10. 13. 81 ABC

VAUGHN, ROBERT
A&C:
Law of the Plainsman   ep   The Innocent 12. 10. 59 NBC
The Asphalt Jungle   ep   The Scott Machine 6. 25. 61 ABC
Follow the Sun   ep   A Rage for Justice 9. 17. 61 ABC
Columbo   ep   5. 2. 76 NBC
SUPP. :
Washington: Behind Closed Doors   ms   9. 6-11. 77 ABC
The Feather and Father Gang   ep   6. 11. 77 ABC
The Eddie Capra Mysteries   ep   Who Killed Charles Pendragon?
    9. 8. 78 NBC
The Islander   tf   9. 16. 78 CBS
Greatest Heroes of the Bible   ep   The Story of Daniel in the
    Lion's Den 11. 22. 78 NBC
Hawaii Five-O   ep   1. 25. 79 CBS
Backstairs at the White House   ms ep   1. 29. 79 NBC
Centennial   ms ep   The Scream of Eagles 2. 4. 79 NBC

The Rebels   ms   5. 14. 79, 5. 21. 79 NN
Mirror, Mirror   tf   10. 10. 79 NBC
The Franken Project   tf   1. 13. 80 NBC
The Gossip Columnist   pt   3. 21. 80 NN
City in Fear   tf   3. 30. 80 ABC
Trapper John, M. D.   ep   Girl Under Glass 11. 23. 80 CBS
The Love Boat   ep   5. 2. 81 ABC

VIGODA, ABE*
The Devil's Daughter   tf   1. 9. 73 ABC
The Rookies   ep   2. 18. 74 ABC
Kojak   ep   2. 20. 74 CBS
Toma   tf   3. 21. 73 ABC
The Story of Pretty Boy Floyd   tf   5. 7. 74 ABC
Hawaii Five-O   ep   10. 29. 74 CBS
Kojak   ep   11. 3. 74 CBS
Barney Miller   sr   1. 22. 75 ABC
Barney Miller   sr ret   9. 11. 75 ABC
Barney Miller   sr ret   9. 23. 76 ABC
Having Babies   tf   10. 17. 76 ABC
The Bionic Woman   ep   11. 10. 76 ABC
Fish   sr   2. 5. 77 ABC
The Comedy Company   tf   7. 21. 78 CBS
Vega$ ep   9. 20. 78 ABC
The Rockford Files   ep   9. 29. 78 NBC
The Bionic Woman   ep   Black Magic 10. 8. 77 NBC
How to Pick Up Girls   tf   11. 3. 78 ABC
The Love Boat   ep   Home, Sweet Home 1. 20. 79 ABC
Sweepstakes   ep   1. 26. 79 NBC
Supertrain   ep   4. 14. 79 NBC
Eight Is Enough   ep   5. 2. 79 ABC
Fantasy Island   ep   9. 14. 79 ABC
Death Car on the Freeway   tf   9. 25. 79 CBS
Project Peacock   ep   The Big Stuffed Dog   sp   2. 8. 81 NBC
The Littlest Hobo   ep   2. 21. 81 NN
Harper Valley   ep   Stellascam 12. 12. 81 NBC

VINCENT, JAN-MICHAEL
A& C:
Survivors   sr   8. 29. 69 ABC
Deliver Us from Evil   tf   9. 11. 73 ABC

-W-

WAGGONER, LYLE*
Marcus Welby, M. D.   ep   2. 27. 73 ABC
Letters from Three Lovers   tf   10. 3. 73 ABC
The New, Original Wonder Woman   pt   11. 7. 75 ABC
Maude   ep   1. 5. 76 CBS

The New, Original Wonder Woman   sr   4. 21. 76 ABC
The Love Boat 1. 21. 77 ABC
The New Adventures of Wonder Woman   sr   9. 16. 77 CBS
The San Pedro Beach Bums   ep   12. 12. 77 ABC
The New Adventures of Wonder Woman   sr ret   9. 22. 78 CBS
Flying High   ep   11. 17. 78 CBS
The Love Boat   ep   The Second Time Around 1. 13. 79 ABC
Supertrain   ep   4. 14. 79 NBC
Time Express   ep   5. 3. 79 CBS
The Love Boat   ep   10. 6. 79 ABC
The Gossip Columnist   pt   3. 21. 80 NN
The Ugily Family   pt   7. 26. 80 ABC
The Great American Traffic Jam   tf   10. 2. 80 NBC
Happy Days   ep   11. 25. 80 ABC
Fantasy Island   ep   11. 29. 80 ABC
Charlie's Angels   ep   Island Angels 12. 14. 80 ABC
Bulba   pt   8. 3. 81 ABC
Two the Hard Way   pt   8. 11. 81 CBS
Fantasy Island   ep   11. 21. 81 ABC

WAGNER, LINDSAY
  A& C:
  The Six Million Dollar Man   ep   10. 31. 76 ABC
  SUPP. :
  The Bionic Woman   sr ret   9. 10. 77 NBC
  Windows, Doors and Keyholes   sp   5. 16. 78 NBC
  The Incredible Journey of Dr. Meg Laurel   tf   1. 2. 79 CBS
  The Two Worlds of Jennie Logan   tf   10. 31. 79 CBS
  Scruples   ms   2. 25. 80, 2. 26. 80, 2. 28. 80 CBS
  Callie and Son   tf   10. 13. 81 CBS

WAGNER, ROBERT
  SUPP. :
  Switch   sr ret   9. 23. 77 CBS
  The Hardy Boys/Nancy Drew Mysteries   ep   10. 9. 77 ABC
  The Critical List   tf   9. 11. 78, 9. 12. 78 NBC
  Pearl   ms   11. 16. 78, 11. 17. 78, 11. 19. 78 ABC
  Hart to Hart   pt   8. 25. 79 ABC
  Hart to Hart   sr   9. 22. 79 ABC
  Hart to Hart   sr ret   11. 11. 80 ABC
  Hart to Hart   sr ret   10. 6. 81 ABC

WALDEN, ROBERT*
  Bobby Jo and the Big Apple Good Time Band   pt   3. 31. 72 CBS
  The Bold Ones: The Doctors   ep   10. 10. 72 NBC
  The Ted Bessell Show   pt   5. 8. 73 CBS
  The Rookies   ep   Margin for Error 9. 17. 73 ABC
  Columbo   ep   Any Old Port in a Storm 10. 7. 73 NBC
  Shirts/Skins   tf   10. 9. 73 ABC
  The Rookies   ep   Timelock 3. 4. 74 ABC
  Larry   tf   4. 23. 74 CBS
  Bachelors 4   ep   Jerry pt   5. 16. 74 CBS
  Medical Center   ep   9. 23. 74 CBS

The Streets of San Francisco ep 10. 24. 74 ABC
The Great Ice Ripoff tf 11. 6. 74 ABC
Panic on the 5:22 tf 11. 20. 74 ABC
The Rookies ep S. W. A. T. 2. 17. 75 ABC
Kate McShane ep 9. 17. 75 CBS
The Kansas City Massacre tf 9. 19. 75 ABC
Medical Center ep 9. 22. 75 CBS
The Streets of San Francisco ep 11. 6. 75 ABC
Medical Center ep 12. 1. 75 CBS
Doctors' Hospital ep 1. 14. 76 NBC
The Rockford Files ep The Oracle Wore a Cashmere Suit
    10. 1. 76 NBC
Starsky and Hutch ep Murder on the High Seas 10. 21. 76 ABC
Police Woman ep 11. 9. 76 NBC
Police Story ep 1. 11. 77 NBC
The Streets of San Francisco ep 2. 10. 77 ABC
The Hostage Heart tf 9. 9. 77 CBS
Lou Grant sr 9. 20. 77 CBS
Lou Grant sr ret 9. 18. 78 CBS
Centennial ms ep Only the Banks Live Forever 10. 1. 78 NBC
Lou Grant sr ret 9. 17. 79 CBS
The Mysterious Island of Beautiful Women tf 12. 1. 79 CBS
Lou Grant sr ret 9. 22. 80 CBS
Enola Gay tf 11. 23. 80 NBC
CHiPs ep 12. 7. 80 NBC
The Love Boat ep Two Grapes on the Vine 10. 17. 81 ABC
Lou Grant sr ret 11. 2. 81 CBS

WALKER, CLINT
    SUPP. :
    Snow Beast tf 4. 28. 77 NBC
    Centennial ms ep Only the Banks Live Forever 10. 1. 78 NBC

WALKER, JIMMIE (previously listed as Jimmy Walker, Jr.)
    SUPP. :
    Good Times sr ret 9. 21. 77 CBS
    The Love Boat ep One If by Land 9. 24. 77 ABC
    Telethon tf 11. 6. 77 ABC
    Good Times sr ret 9. 16. 78 CBS
    The Greatest Thing That Almost Happened tf 10. 26. 78 CBS
    Good Times sr ret 5. 23. 79 CBS
    The Love Boat ep Till Death Do Us Part 11. 11. 79 ABC
    BAD Cats sr 1. 4. 80 ABC
    Murder Can Hurt You! tf 5. 21. 80 ABC
    The Love Boat ep 11. 15. 80 ABC

WALKER, NANCY
    A& C:
    The Partridge Family ep 1. 5. 73 ABC
    The Mary Tyler Moore Show ep 9. 29. 73 CBS
    Police Story ep 3. 12. 74 NBC
    Thursday's Game tf 4. 14. 74 ABC
    SUPP. :
    Rhoda sr ret 10. 2. 77 CBS

Fantasy Island   ep   4. 1. 78 ABC
Rhoda   sr ret   9. 23. 78 CBS
Human Feelings   tf   10. 16. 78 NBC
The Love Boat   ep   Home, Sweet Home 1. 20. 79 ABC
The Mary Tyler Moore Hour   ep   5. 6. 79 CBS
The Love Boat   ep   The Trigamist 1. 17. 81 ABC

WALKER, ROBERT, JR.
   SUPP. :
   Quincy, M. E.   ep   11. 18. 77 NBC
   The Six Million Dollar Man   ep   2. 20. 78, 2. 28. 78 ABC
   The Eddie Capra Mysteries   ep   Who Killed Charles Pendragon?
      9. 8. 78 NBC
   The Next Step Beyond   ep   11. 18. 78 NN

WALLACH, ELI
   SUPP. :
   Seventh Avenue   ms ep   2. 10. 77 NBC
   The Pirate   tf   11. 21. 78, 11. 22. 78 CBS
   Fugitive Family   tf   10. 1. 80 CBS
   The Pride of Jesse Hallam   tf   3. 3. 81 CBS
   Skokie   tf   11. 17. 81 CBS

WALSTON, RAY
   SUPP. :
   Danny and the Mermaid   pt   5. 17. 78 CBS
   Starsky and Hutch   ep   1. 16. 79 ABC
   Cliffhangers   ep   Stop Susan Williams   sr   2. 27. 79 NBC
   Little House on the Prairie   ep   11. 12. 79 NBC
   Buck Rogers in the 25th Century   ep   11. 22. 79 NBC
   Code Red   ep   The Land of Make Believe 11. 29. 81 ABC
   Trapper John, M. D.   ep   12. 20. 81 CBS

WALTER, JESSICA
   A& C:
   The Doctors and the Nurses   ep   Act of Violence 2. 23. 65 CBS
   They Call It Murder   tf   12. 17. 71 NBC
   SUPP. :
   Visions   ep   Prison Game 1. 13. 77 PBS
   Black Market Baby   tf   10. 7. 77 ABC
   What Really Happened to the Class of '65?   ep   The Girl No-
      body Knew 12. 29. 77 NBC
   Wild and Wooly   tf   2. 20. 78 ABC
   Wheels   ms   5. 7. 78, 5. 8. 78, 5. 9. 78, 5. 14. 78, 5. 15. 78 NBC
   The Love Boat   ep   5. 13. 78 ABC
   Dr. Strange   tf   9. 6. 78 CBS
   Secrets of Three Hungry Wives   tf   10. 9. 78 NBC
   Quincy, M. E.   ep   11. 2. 78 NBC
   Trapper John, M. D.   ep   9. 23. 79, 10. 21. 79, 12. 9. 79, 3. 23. 80,
      2. 22. 81 CBS
   Vampire   tf   10. 7. 79 ABC
   She's Dressed to Kill   tf   12. 10. 79 CBS
   The Love Boat   ep   Doc's "Ex" Change 12. 15. 79 ABC
   The Love Boat   ep   Doc's Dismissal 1. 3. 81 ABC

Aloha Paradise   ep   4. 1. 81 ABC
Scruples   tf   5. 22. 81 ABC
The Love Boat   ep   11. 21. 81 ABC

WARREN, JENNIFER*
After the Fall   tf   12. 10. 74 NBC
Kojak   ep   A Question of Answers 9. 14. 75 CBS
Banjo Hackett   tf   5. 3. 76 NBC
Shark Kill   tf   5. 20. 76 CBS
Serpico   ep   10. 29. 76 NBC
Kojak   ep   Tears for All Who Loved Her 11. 20. 77 CBS
The Fitzpatricks   ep   12. 6. 77 CBS
First You Cry   tf   11. 8. 78 CBS
Steel Cowboy   tf   12. 6. 78 NBC
Champions: A Love Story   tf   1. 13. 79 CBS
Butterflies   pt   8. 1. 79 NBC
Angel City   tf   11. 12. 80 CBS
The Choice   tf   2. 10. 81 CBS
The Intruder Within   tf   2. 20. 81 ABC
Freedom   tf   5. 18. 81 ABC

WARREN, LESLEY ANN (a. k. a. Lesley Warren)*
Cinderella   sp   2. 26. 66 CBS
The Mod Squad   ep   3. 11. 69 ABC
Seven in Darkness   tf   9. 23. 69 ABC
Mission: Impossible   sr   9. 19. 70 CBS
Love, Hate Love   tf   2. 9. 71 ABC
Cat Ballou   pt   9. 5. 71 NBC
Assignment: Munich   tf   4. 30. 72 ABC
The Daughters of Joshua Cabe   tf   9. 13. 72 ABC
Night Gallery   ep   Death on a Barge 3. 4. 73 NBC
The Letters   tf   3. 6. 73 ABC
Wide World Special   ep   It's a Bird, It's A Plane, It's Super-
    man   sp   2. 21. 75 ABC
S. W. A. T.   ep   9. 13. 75 ABC
Doctors' Hospital   ep   9. 24. 75 NBC
Harry O   ep   APB Harry Orwell 11. 6. 75 ABC
The Legend of Valentino   tf   11. 23. 75 ABC
Jigsaw John   ep   2. 16. 76 NBC
79 Park Avenue   ms   10. 16. 77, 10. 17. 77, 10. 18. 77 NBC
Betrayed   tf   11. 13. 78 NBC
Pearl   ms   11. 16. 78, 11. 17. 78, 11. 19. 78 ABC
Portrait of a Stripper   tf   10. 2. 79 CBS
Beulah Land   ms   10. 7. 80, 10. 8. 80, 10. 9. 80 NBC

WATSON, MILLS*
Gunsmoke   ep   12. 9. 68 CBS
The High Chaparral   ep   A Way of Justice 12. 13. 68 NBC
Gunsmoke   ep   4. 14. 69 CBS
Bonanza   ep   Anatomy of a Lynching 10. 12. 69 NBC
Lock, Stock and Barrel   tf   9. 24. 71 NBC
Bonanza   ep   11. 28. 71 NBC

Longstreet   ep   There Was a Crooked Man **12. 9. 71** ABC
Heat of Anger   tf   **3. 3. 72** CBS
Alias Smith and Jones   ep   The Clementine Incident **10. 7. 72**
   ABC
Cool Million   ep   **11. 22. 72** NBC
Gunsmoke   ep   **1. 1. 73** CBS
Ironside   ep   Ollinger's Last Case **1. 4. 73** NBC
The World of Disney   ep   The Mystery in Dracula's Castle
   1. 7. 73 NBC
The Mod Squad   ep   **2. 22. 73** ABC
The Crime Club   tf   **3. 6. 73** CBS
Doc Elliot   ep   And All Ye Need to Know **10. 10. 73** ABC
M*A*S*H   ep   Dear Dad--Three **11. 10. 73** CBS
Emergency   ep   Understanding **12. 15. 73** NBC
Gunsmoke   ep   Family of Killers **1. 14. 74** CBS
Dirty Sally   ep   **2. 1. 74** CBS
The Migrants   tf   **2. 3. 74** CBS
Shaft   ep   The Murder Machine **2. 19. 74** CBS
Police Story   ep   The Hunters **2. 26. 74** NBC
The Story of Pretty Boy Floyd   tf   **5. 7. 74** ABC
The Rockford Files   ep   Exit Prentiss Carr **10. 4. 74** NBC
Amy Prentiss   ep   Baptism of Fire **12. 1. 74** NBC
McCloud   ep   The Man with the Golden Hat **1. 12. 75** NBC
Adventures of the Queen   tf   **2. 14. 75** CBS
Attack on Terror: The FBI vs. the Ku Klux Klan   tf   **2. 20. 75,**
   2. 21. 75 CBS
The Rockford Files   ep   Roundabout **3. 7. 75** NBC
Dead Man on the Run   tf   **4. 2. 75** ABC
The Kansas City Massacre   tf   **9. 19. 75** ABC
Harry O   ep   Group Terror **11. 13. 75** ABC
The Invasion of Johnson County   tf   **7. 31. 76** NBC
Captains and the Kings   ms ep   **11. 4. 76, 11. 11. 76** NBC
The Quest   ep   **10. 27. 76** NBC
Baa Baa Black Sheep   ep   **2. 8. 77** NBC
The Streets of San Francisco   ep   **2. 10. 77** ABC
Ransom for Alice   tf   **6. 2. 77** NBC
The Oregon Trail   ep   **10. 26. 77** NBC
Barnaby Jones   ep   **11. 10. 77** CBS
CHiPs   ep   **1. 12. 78** NBC
The Rockford Files   ep   The Gang at Don's Drive-In **1. 13. 78**
   NBC
Project UFO   ep   Mass Sighting **2. 26. 78** NBC
Police Story   ep   **3. 4. 75** NBC
How the West Was Won   ep   **5. 21. 78** ABC
B. J. and the Bear   tf   **10. 4. 78** NBC
The Hardy Boys   ep   **10. 8. 78** ABC
The Rockford Files   ep   **12. 29. 78** NBC
CHiPs   ep   **1. 6. 79** NBC
The Rockford Files   ep   The Deuce **1. 25. 79** NBC
B. J. and the Bear   sr   **2. 10. 79** NBC
Supertrain   ep   **3. 14. 79** NBC
Sword of Justice   ep   **7. 11. 79** NBC
The Misadventures of Sheriff Lobo   sr   **9. 18. 79** NBC

Lobo   sr   12.30.80 NBC
Harper Valley   sr   10.29.81 NBC

WAYNE, DAVID
  A&C:
The Brian Keith Show   ep   11.23.73 NBC
Gunsmoke   ep   3.3.75 CBS
Adams of Eagle Lake   pt   8.30.75 ABC
Once an Eagle   ms   12.9.76, 12.16.76 NBC
  SUPP.:
In the Glitter Palace   tf   2.27.77 NBC
The Hardy Boys/Nancy Drew Mysteries   ep   5.1.77 ABC
Hunter   ep   5.27.77 CBS
Big Hawaii   ep   11.16.77 NBC
Switch   ep   12.5.77 CBS
Black Beauty   ms   1.31.78, 2.1.78, 2.2.78, 2.3.78, 2.4.78
   NBC
Family   ep   2.21.78 ABC
Loose Change   ms   2.26.78, 2.27.78, 2.28.78 NBC
Dallas   sr   4.2.78 CBS
Murder at the Mardi Gras   tf   5.10.78 NBC
Lassie: The New Beginning   pt   9.17.78, 9.24.78 ABC
The Girls in the Office   tf   2.2.79 ABC
House Calls   sr   12.17.79 CBS
House Calls   sr ret   11.17.80 CBS
House Calls   sr ret   11.2.81 CBS

WAYNE, JOHN
  SUPP.:
The General Electric All-Star Anniversary   sp hos   9.29.78
   ABC

WAYNE, PATRICK*
The Rounders   sr   9.13.66 ABC
The FBI   ep   12.29.68 ABC
Sole Survivor   tf   1.9.70 ABC
Movin' On   pt   7.24.72 NBC
McCloud   ep   2.24.74 NBC
Police Story   ep   10.8.74 NBC
Police Woman   ep   10.25.74 NBC
Yesterday's Child   tf   2.3.77 NBC
Flight to Holocaust   tf   3.27.77 NBC
The Hallmark Hall of Fame   ep   The Last Hurrah   sp   11.16.77
   NBC
Three on a Date   tf   2.17.78 ABC
Shirley   sr   10.26.79 NBC
The Love Boat   ep   10.27.79 ABC
Charlie's Angels   ep   Waikiki Angels 1.4.81 ABC
Fantasy Island   ep   5.9.81 ABC

WEAVER, DENNIS
  SUPP.:
Intimate Strangers   tf   11.11.77 ABC

The Islander tf 9. 16. 78 CBS
Pearl ms 11. 16. 78, 11. 17. 78, 11. 19. 78 ABC
Centennial ms ep The Longhorns 12. 3. 78 NBC
Ishi: The Last of His Tribe tf 12. 20. 78 NBC
Centennial ms ep The Winds of Fortune 12. 8. 79 NBC
The Ordeal of Patty Hearst tf 3. 4. 79 ABC
Police Story ep A Cry for Justice 5. 23. 79 NBC
Stone pt 8. 26. 79 ABC
Stone sr 1. 14. 80 ABC
Amber Waves tf 3. 9. 80 ABC
The Ordeal of Dr. Mudd tf 3. 25. 80 CBS
The Day the Loving Stopped tf 10. 16. 81 ABC

WEAVER, FRITZ
  SUPP. :
  American Short Story ep The Jolly Corner 5. 3. 77 PBS
  The New Adventures of Wonder Woman ep The Return of
    Wonder Woman 9. 16. 77 CBS
  Captains Courageous tf 12. 4. 77 ABC
  Holocaust ms 4. 16-19. 78 NBC
  Hawaii Five-O ep 3. 15. 79 CBS
  Children of Divorce tf 11. 24. 80 NBC
  Magnum, P. I. ep 12. 11. 80 CBS
  Nightkill tf 12. 18. 80 NBC
  Momma the Detective pt 1. 9. 81 NBC
  Quincy, M. E. ep To Kill in Plain Sight 3. 4. 81 NBC
  Tales of the Unexpected ep Wet Saturday 10. 31. 81 NN

WEBBER, ROBERT
  A&C:
  Hawkins on Murder tf 3. 13. 73 CBS
  Griff ep 9. 29. 73 ABC
  Double Indemnity tf 10. 13. 73 ABC
  The Magician ep Lady in a Trap 11. 27. 73 NBC
  Kojak ep The Computer 12. 5. 73 CBS
  Murder or Mercy tf 4. 10. 74 ABC
  The Streets of San Francisco ep 12. 12. 74 ABC
  McCloud ep 1. 12. 75 NBC
  The Rockford Files ep 10. 10. 75 NBC
  Barnaby Jones ep 10. 10. 75 CBS
  S. W. A. T. ep 11. 1. 75 ABC
  McCoy ep 1. 25. 76 NBC
  SUPP. :
  Quincy, M. E. ep 5. 13. 77 NBC
  79 Park Avenue ms 10. 16. 77, 10. 17. 77, 10. 18. 77 NBC
  Barnaby Jones ep 1. 26. 78 CBS
  The World of Disney ep The Young Runaways 5. 22. 78 NBC
  Kaz ep 11. 5. 78 CBS
  The Rockford Files ep 3. 3. 79 NBC
  G. E. Theatre ep The Streets of L. A. sp 11. 13. 79 CBS
  The Two Lives of Carol Litner tf 10. 14. 81 CBS
  Darkroom ep Closed Circuit 11. 27. 81 ABC
  Judgement Day pt 12. 6. 81 NBC

WELCH, RAQUEL
  SUPP. :
  Mork and Mindy   ep   11. 18. 79 ABC

WELD, TUESDAY
  A&C:
  Route 66   ep   Love Is a Skinny Kid 4. 6. 62 CBS
  SUPP. :
  A Question of Guilt   tf   2. 21. 78 CBS
  Mother and Daughter: The Loving War   tf   1. 25. 80 ABC
  Madame X   tf   3. 16. 81 NBC

WELLES, ORSON
  SUPP. :
  It Happened One Christmas   tf   12. 11. 77 ABC
  Mysterious Castles of Clay   sp nar   3. 18. 78 NBC
  A Woman Called Moses   tf nar   12. 11. 78, 12. 12. 78 NBC
  Shogun   ms nar   9. 15-20. 80 ABC
  Greatest Adventure   sp nar   3. 8. 81 PBS

WENDELL, HOWARD*
  NBC Presents   ep   Ring Once for Central 1. 24. 49 NBC
  Cavalcade of America   ep   Slater's Dream 5. 13. 53 ABC
  The Loretta Young Show   ep   Something Always Happens
    5. 23. 54 NBC
  Cavalcade of America   ep   Decision for Justice 2. 15. 55 ABC
  Fireside Theatre   ep   It's Easy to Get Ahead 3. 29. 55 NBC
  You Are There   ep   The Emancipation Proclamation 4. 17. 55
    CBS
  You Are There   ep   Dewey's Victory at Manila 5. 15. 55 CBS
  Front Row Center   ep   Dinner at Eight 6. 1. 55 CBS
  Front Row Center   ep   Ah, Wilderness 6. 15. 55 CBS
  You Are There   ep   The Chicago Fire 12. 11. 55 CBS
  You Are There   ep   Washington Crosses the Delaware 12. 25. 55
    CBS
  Telephone Time   ep   The Key 7. 15. 56 CBS
  Telephone Time   ep   Hatfield, the Rainmaker 10. 28. 56 CBS
  The Adventures of Jim Bowie   ep   The Lottery 1. 57 ABC
  Lux Video Theater   ep   Just Across the Street 1. 10. 57 NBC
  Playhouse 90   ep   The Hostess with the Mostess 3. 21. 57 CBS
  Meet McGraw   ep   Border City 7. 23. 57 NBC
  The Millionaire   ep   The Story of Matt Kirby 9. 18. 57 CBS
  Perry Mason   ep   The Case of the Sulky Girl 10. 19. 57 CBS
  The Schlitz Playhouse of Stars   ep   Bitter Parting 10. 25. 57 CBS
  Matinee Theatre   ep   The Man Without a Country 2. 6. 58 NBC
  No Warning   ep   The Amnesiac 5. 25. 58 NBC
  M Squad   ep   The System 5. 58 NBC
  The Donna Reed Show   ep   9. 24. 58 ABC
  Playhouse 90   ep   The Wings of the Dove 1. 8. 59 CBS
  Zorro   ep   The Gay Caballero 1. 22. 59 ABC
  The George Burns Show   ep   The Orchid Room 3. 17. 59 NBC
  The Restless Gun   ep   One on the House 10. 59 NBC
  The Ann Sothern Show   ep   The Ugly Bonnet 1959 CBS

The General Electric Theater   ep   Goodbye, My Love 10.16.60
    CBS
Bonanza   ep   House Divided 1960 NBC
Alcoa Premiere   ep   Mr. Easy 2.13.62 ABC
Voyage to the Bottom of the Sea   ep   Cradle of the Deep 1966
    ABC
Adam 12   ep   1972 NBC

WEST, ADAM
    SUPP.:
    Police Woman   ep   11.1.77 NBC
    Tarzan and the Super 7   sr vo   9.9.78 CBS
    The American Girls   sr   9.30.78 CBS
    Vega$ ep   2.28.79 ABC
    The Challenge of the Superheroes   sp   1.18.79 NBC
    Tarzan and the Super 7   sr ret   9.15.79 CBS
    Big Shamus, Little Shamus   ep   10.13.79 CBS
    For the Love of It   tf   9.26.80 ABC
    Fantasy Island   ep   10.25.80 ABC

WHELAN, JILL*
    Fantasy Island   ep   9.23.78 ABC
    Friends   sr   3.25.79 ABC
    Fantasy Island   ep   5.13.79 ABC
    The Love Boat   sr   11.3.79 ABC
    The Love Boat   sr ret   10.25.80 ABC
    The Love Boat   sr ret   10.10.81 ABC

WHELCHEL, LISA*
    Family   ep   9.28.78 ABC
    The World of Disney   ep   Shadow of Fear 1.28.79 NBC
    The Facts of Life   sr   8.24.79 NBC
    The Facts of Life   sr ret   3.12.80 NBC
    The Facts of Life   sr ret   11.19.80 NBC
    Skyward   tf   11.20.80 NBC
    Diff'rent Strokes   ep   2.25.81 NBC
    Twirl   tf   10.25.81 NBC
    The Facts of Life   sr ret   10.28.81 NBC

WHITE, BETTY
    SUPP.:
    The Betty White Show   sr   9.12.77 CBS
    With This Ring   tf   5.5.78 ABC
    Snavely   pt   6.24.78 ABC
    The Best Place to Be   tf   5.27.79 NBC
    Before and After   tf   10.5.79 ABC
    The Love Boat   ep   11.22.80 ABC
    Stephanie   pt   9.8.81 ABC
    The Love Boat   ep   Aunt Sylvia 10.17.81 ABC

WHITMAN, STUART
    SUPP.:
    Quincy, M.E.   ep   1.2.77 NBC

Most Wanted   ep   2. 19. 77 ABC
The Hardy Boys/Nancy Drew Mysteries   ep   10. 16. 77 ABC
Fantasy Island   ep   3. 25. 78 ABC
Go West Young Girl   tf   4. 27. 78 ABC
A House in the Woods   sp   9. 10. 78 NN
The Pirate   tf   11. 21. 78,   11. 22. 78 CBS
Fantasy Island   ep   12. 2. 78 ABC
The Last Convertible   ms ep   9. 25. 79 NBC
The Seekers   ms   12. 3. 79,   12. 4. 79 NN
Condominium   ms   11. 20. 80,   11. 24. 80 NN
Fantasy Island   ep   2. 21. 81,   10. 31. 81 ABC

WHITMORE, JAMES
    SUPP. :
    The Word   ms   11. 12. 78,   11. 13. 78,   11. 14. 78,   11. 15. 78 CBS
    John Wayne: An American Legend   sp nar   9. 5. 79 NN
    American Short Story   ep   The Golden Honeymoon 2. 4. 80 PBS
    Rage!   tf   9. 25. 80 NBC
    The White Shadow   ep   10. 16. 80 ABC

WIDMARK, RICHARD
    SUPP. :
    Mr. Horn   tf   2. 1. 79 CBS
    All God's Children   tf   4. 28. 80 ABC
    A Whale for the Killing   tf   2. 1. 81 ABC

WILCOX, LARRY*
    Lassie   sr   10. 7. 71 NN
    Mr. and Mrs. Bo Jo Jones   tf   11. 16. 71 ABC
    The Man and the City   ep   11. 17. 71 ABC
    The Great American Beauty Contest   tf   2. 13. 73 ABC
    Police Story   ep   The Big Walk 12. 4. 73 NBC
    The Streets of San Francisco   ep   The Runaways 12. 6. 73 ABC
    Death Stalk   tf   1. 21. 75 NBC
    Sky Heist   tf   5. 26. 75 NBC
    The World of Disney   ep   Twister, Bull from the Sky 1. 4. 76
        NBC
    Relentless   tf   9. 14. 77 CBS
    CHiPs   sr   9. 15. 77 NBC
    The World of Disney   ep   Trail of Danger 3. 12. 78,   3. 19. 78
        NBC
    CHiPs   sr ret   9. 16. 78 NBC
    The Last Ride of the Dalton Gang   tf   11. 20. 79 NBC
    The Love Boat   ep   5. 3. 80 ABC
    The Love Tapes   tf   5. 9. 80 ABC
    CHiPs   sr ret   9. 21. 80 NBC
    CHiPs   sr ret   10. 4. 81 NBC

WILDE, CORNELL
    SUPP. :
    Fantasy Island   ep   12. 9. 78 ABC

WILKES, DONNA*
    The Courage and the Passion   tf   5. 27. 78 NBC

The Incredible Hulk   ep   11.3.78 CBS
Hello, Larry   sr   1.26.79 NBC
Diff'rent Strokes   ep   3.30.79 NBC
Runaways   tf   6.26.79 NBC
Born to Be Sold   tf   11.2.81 NBC
House Calls   ep   11.23.81 CBS

WILLIAMS, ANSON*
   Love, American Style   ep   Love and the Happy Days 2.25.72
      ABC
   The Paul Lynde Show   sr   9.13.72 ABC
   Marcus Welby, M.D.   ep   The Panic Path 9.11.73 ABC
   The Hallmark Hall of Fame   ep   Lisa, Bright and Dark   sp
      11.28.73 NBC
   Happy Days   sr   1.15.74 ABC
   Happy Days   sr ret   9.10.74 ABC
   Happy Days   sr ret   9.9.75 ABC
   Happy Days   sr ret   9.21.76 ABC
   Happy Days   sr ret   9.13.77 ABC
   The Love Boat   ep   A Fine Romance 12.24.77 ABC
   Happy Days   sr ret   9.12.78 ABC
   Greatest Heroes of the Bible   ep   The Story of the Ten Com-
      mandments 5.8.79 NBC
   Happy Days   sr ret   9.11.79 ABC
   Happy Days   sr ret   11.11.80 ABC
   Happy Days   sr ret   10.6.81 ABC

WILLIAMS, CARA
   SUPP.:
   Visions   ep   Prison Game 1.13.77 PBS

WILLIAMS, CINDY
   A&C:
   Barefoot in the Park   ep   10.29.70 ABC
   Police Story   ep   Requiem for an Informer 10.9.73 NBC
   The Last Detail   pt   6.20.76 ABC
   SUPP.:
   Laverne and Shirley   sr ret   9.20.77 ABC
   Laverne and Shirley   sr ret   9.5.78 ABC
   Suddenly Love   tf   12.4.78 NBC
   Insight   ep   5.6.79 NN
   Laverne and Shirley   sr ret   9.13.79 ABC
   CHiPs   ep   Chips Goes Roller Disco 9.22.79 NBC
   Laverne and Shirley   sr ret   11.18.80 ABC
   CHiPs   ep   12.7.80 NBC
   Laverne and Shirley   sr (animated) vo   10.10.81 ABC
   Laverne and Shirley   sr ret   10.13.81 ABC

WILLIAMS, CLARENCE, III
   SUPP.:
   Return of the Mod Squad   tf   5.18.79 ABC
   The Littlest Hobo   ep   1.5.80 NN

WILLIAMS, HAL*
   Sanford and Son   ep   We Were Robbed 2. 18. 72 NBC
   Kung Fu   ep   The Well 9. 27. 73 ABC
   The Waltons   sr   10. 11. 73 CBS
   The Magician   ep   The Man Who Lost Himself 12. 11. 73 NBC
   Cannon   ep   Photo Finish 1. 2. 74 CBS
   Cannon   ep   Bobby Loved Me 2. 27. 74 CBS
   Police Woman   ep   Anatomy of Two Ropes 10. 11. 74 NBC
   Harry O   ep   Eye Witness 10. 17. 74 ABC
   Good Times   ep   1. 7. 75 CBS
   Harry O   ep   Sound of Trumpets 1. 30. 75 ABC
   Gunsmoke   ep   2. 4. 75 CBS
   Harry O   ep   Double Jeopardy 2. 13. 75 ABC
   Caribe   ep   4. 7. 75 ABC
   Kung Fu   ep   4. 26. 75 ABC
   On the Rocks   sr   9. 11. 75 ABC
   Quincy, M. E.   ep   The Hot Dog Murder 4. 22. 77 NBC
   Off the Wall   sr   5. 7. 77 NBC
   The Waltons   ep   1. 26. 78, 2. 9. 78 CBS
   Good Times   ep   10. 21. 78 CBS
   Thou Shalt Not Commit Adultery   tf   11. 1. 78 NBC
   Roots: The Next Generations   ms ep   2. 20. 79 ABC
   The White Shadow   ep   10. 8. 79 CBS
   Knots Landing   ep   3. 20. 80 CBS
   The Waltons   ep   11. 20. 80 CBS
   Private Benjamin   sr   4. 6. 81 CBS
   Don't Look Back   tf   5. 31. 81 ABC
   Private Benjamin   sr ret   10. 12. 81 CBS

WILLIAMS, PAUL*
   Baretta   ep   9. 10. 75 ABC
   Flight to Holocaust   tf   3. 27. 77 NBC
   The Hardy Boys/Nancy Drew Mysteries   ep   9. 11. 77, 9. 18. 77
      ABC
   Police Woman   ep   12. 28. 77 NBC
   The Love Boat   ep   5. 6. 78 ABC
   Hawaii Five-O   ep   2. 22. 79 CBS
   The Wild Wild West Revisited   tf   5. 9. 79 CBS
   The Mary Tyler Moore Hour   ep   6. 10. 79 CBS
   The Paul Williams Show   pt   6. 27. 79 NBC
   Fantasy Island   ep   11. 15. 80 ABC
   B. J. and the Bear   ep   Blonde in a Gilded Cage 3. 3. 81 NBC
   Fantasy Island   ep   A Night in a Harem 11. 14. 81 ABC

WILLIAMS, ROBIN*
   Happy Days   ep   2. 28. 78 ABC
   Mork and Mindy   sr   9. 14. 78 ABC
   Happy Days   ep   3. 6. 79 ABC
   Out of the Blue   ep   9. 9. 79 ABC
   Mork and Mindy   sr ret   9. 16. 79 ABC
   Mork and Mindy   sr ret   11. 13. 80 ABC
   Mork and Mindy   sr ret   10. 8. 81 ABC

WILLS, CHILL
    SUPP. :
    The Hallmark Hall of Fame   ep   Stubby Pringle's Christmas
        sp 12. 17. 78 NBC

WILSON, FLIP
    SUPP. :
    The Cheap Detective   pt 6. 3. 80 NBC
    The Love Boat   ep   Isaac, the Marriage Counselor 10. 24. 81
        ABC

WINDOM, WILLIAM
    A& C:
    The Detectives   ep   Tobey's Place 9. 29. 61 ABC
    Surfside Six   ep   Affairs at Hotel Delight 11. 6. 61 ABC
    The Gallant Men   ep   10. 5. 62 ABC
    Empire   ep   Hidden Asset 3. 26. 63 NBC
    Insight   ep   1. 18. 74 NN
    The Girl with Something Extra   ep   1. 18. 74 NBC
    Doctors' Hospital   ep   12. 17. 75 NBC
    Doc   ep   10. 2. 76 CBS
    SUPP. :
    McMillan   ep   1. 23. 77 NBC
    Seventh Avenue   ms   2. 10. 77, 2. 17. 77, 2. 24. 77 NBC
    Hunter   ep   3. 4. 77 CBS
    Police Woman   ep   3. 8. 77 NBC
    Quincy, M. E.   ep   4. 15. 77 NBC
    Quincy, M. E.   ep   4. 22. 77 NBC
    Family   ep   5. 3. 77 ABC
    The Oregon Trail   sr   9. 21. 77 NBC
    The Bionic Woman   ep   10. 8. 77 NBC
    Kojak   ep   10. 30. 77 CBS
    Hunters of the Reef   tf   5. 20. 78 NBC
    W. E. B.   ep   9. 28. 78 NBC
    Kojak   ep   Once More from Birdland 10. 30. 77 CBS
    Brothers and Sisters   sr   1. 21. 79 NBC
    Blind Ambition   ms   5. 20. 79, 5. 21. 79, 5. 22. 79, 5. 23. 79 CBS
    Insight   ep   7. 22. 79 NN
    The Love Boat   ep   11. 10. 79 ABC
    Trapper John, M. D.   ep   12. 2. 79 CBS
    Landon, Landon and Landon   pt   6. 14. 80 CBS
    Dallas   ep   12. 5. 80, 12. 12. 80 CBS
    Walking Tall   ep   The Protectors of the People 1. 24. 81 NBC
    The Incredible Hulk   ep   2. 20. 81 CBS
    Side Show   tf   6. 5. 81 NBC
    100 Years of Golden Hits   hos sp   7. 19. 81 NBC
    Quick and Quiet   pt   8. 18. 81 CBS
    Flamingo Road   ep   The Stranger 12. 8. 81 NBC

WINDSOR, MARIE
    A& C:
    The Line-Up   ep   Prince of Penman 1. 16. 60 CBS

Bourbon Street Beat   ep   Ten Percent Blues **2. 8. 60** ABC
Bourbon Street Beat   ep   Teresa **7. 4. 60** ABC
Whispering Smith   ep   The Trademark **8. 14. 61** NBC
Hawaii Five-O   ep   **12. 16. 70** CBS
Insight   ep   **10. 22. 73** NN
Mannix   ep   **2. 10. 74** CBS
This Is the Life   ep   **3. 9. 75** NN
SUPP. :
Project UFO   ep   **10. 20. 78** NBC
Fantasy Island   ep   **1. 13. 79** ABC
Detective School   ep   **9. 29. 79** ABC
Charlie's Angels   ep   Angels at the Altar **10. 3. 79** ABC
Lou Grant   ep   **12. 17. 79** CBS
The Incredible Hulk   ep   **1. 25. 80** CBS
Lou Grant   ep   Libel **12. 8. 80** CBS

WINGER, DEBRA*
The New, Original Wonder Woman   ep   The Feminum Mystique
   11. 6. 76, 11. 8. 76 ABC
The New, Original Wonder Woman   ep   Wonder Woman in
   Hollywood **2. 16. 77** ABC
Special Olympics   tf   **2. 22. 78** CBS
Police Woman   ep   **3. 1. 78** NBC
James at 16   ep   **6. 15. 78** NBC

WINKLER, HENRY
SUPP. :
Happy Days   sr ret   **9. 13. 77** ABC
Happy Days   sr ret   **9. 12. 78** ABC
Mork and Mindy   ep   **9. 14. 78** ABC
Happy Days   sr ret   **9. 11. 79** ABC
An American Christmas Carol   tf   **12. 16. 79** ABC
Fonz and the Happy Days Gang   sr vo   **11. 8. 80** ABC
Happy Days   sr ret   **11. 11. 80** ABC
Happy Days   sr ret   **10. 6. 81** ABC

WINNINGHAM, MARE*
Special Olympics   tf   **2. 22. 78** CBS
Family   ep   **3. 8. 79** ABC
The Young Pioneers   sr   **4. 2. 78**   ABC
Operation: Runaway   ep   **5. 18. 78** NBC
Starsky and Hutch   ep   **2. 6. 79** ABC
Steeltown   pt   **5. 19. 79** CBS
The Death of Ocean View Park   tf   **10. 19. 79** ABC
Amber Waves   tf   **3. 9. 80** ABC
Off the Minnesota Strip   tf   **5. 5. 80** ABC
The Women's Room   tf   **9. 14. 80** ABC
Freedom   tf   **5. 18. 81** ABC
A Few Days in Weasel Creek   tf   **10. 21. 81** CBS

WINTERS, JONATHAN
SUPP. :
Take One   pt   **5. 1. 80** NBC

More Wild Wild West   tf   10.7.80, 10.8.80 CBS
Aloha Paradise   ep   3.11.81 ABC
Mork and Mindy   sr   10.29.81 ABC

WINTERS, ROLAND
    SUPP.:
    The Dain Curse   ms   5.22.78, 5.23.78, 5.24.78 CBS
    You Can't Go Home Again   tf   4.25.79 CBS

WINTERS, SHELLEY
    A&C:
    Big Rose   tf   6.25.74 CBS
    SUPP.:
    Kojak   ep   The Captain's Brother's Wife 2.4.78 CBS
    The Initiation of Sarah   tf   2.6.78 ABC
    Elvis   tf   2.11.79 ABC
    The French-Atlantic Affair   ms   11.15.79, 11.16.79, 11.18.79
        ABC
    Vega$ ep   11.28.79 ABC

WINWOOD, ESTELLE
    SUPP.:
    Quincy, M.E.   ep   1.10.80 NBC

WITHERS, JANE
    SUPP.:
    The Love Boat   ep   4.19.80 ABC
    The ABC Weekend Special   ep   Zack and the Magic Factory
        1.10.81 ABC

WOOD, LANA*
    The Long Hot Summer   sr   9.16.65 ABC
    Peyton Place   sr   1966-67 ABC
    The Wild Wild West   ep   The Night of the Firebird 9.15.67
        CBS
    Bonanza   ep   The Gentle Ones 10.29.67 NBC
    My Friend Tony   ep   The Lost Hours 2.2.69 NBC
    The Wild Wild West   ep   The Night of the Plague 4.4.69 CBS
    Black Water Gold   tf   1.6.70 ABC
    The Over-the-Hill Gang Rides Again   tf   11.17.70 ABC
    O'Hara, U.S. Treasury: Operation Cobra   tf   4.2.71 CBS
    The World of Disney   ep   Justin Morgan Had a Horse 2.6.72
        NBC
    Mission: Impossible   ep   The Deal 9.30.72 CBS
    QB VII   tf   4.29.74, 4.30.74 ABC
    Who Is the Black Dahlia?   tf   3.1.75 NBC
    Starsky and Hutch   ep   Running 2.25.76 ABC
    Baretta   ep   Shoes 10.27.76 ABC
    Nightmare in Badham County   tf   11.5.76 ABC
    Little Ladies of the Night   tf   1.16.77 ABC
    Police Story   ep   3.8.77 NBC
    Corey: For the People   tf   6.12.77 NBC
    A Question of Guilt   tf   2.21.78 CBS

The Next Step Beyond   ep   **12.2.**78 NN
David Cassidy--Man Undercover   ep   1.18.79 NBC
Starsky and Hutch   ep   90 Pounds of Trouble **2.6.**79 ABC
David Cassidy--Man Undercover   ep   7.5.79 NBC
Captain America   pt   **11.23.**79, **11.24.**79 CBS
Nero Wolfe   ep   **2.13.**81 NBC

WOOD, NATALIE
    A&C:
    Heidi   sp   <u>10.1.</u>55 NBC
    Bracken's World   ep   11.4.<u>69</u> NBC
    SUPP.:
    Switch   ep   6.25.78 CBS
    From Here to Eternity   ms   2.14.79, 2.21.79, 2.28.79 NBC
    The Cracker Factory   tf   3.16.79 ABC
    Hart to Hart   pt   8.25.79 ABC
    The Memory of Eva Ryker   tf   5.7.80 CBS

WOODWARD, JOANNE
    SUPP.:
    Come Back, Little Sheba   tf   **12.31.**77 NBC
    See How She Runs   tf   2.1.78 CBS
    A Christmas to Remember   tf   **12.20.**78 CBS
    Angel Death   sp nar   10.29.79 NN
    G.E. Theatre   ep   The Streets of L.A.   sp   11.13.79 CBS
    The Shadow Box   tf   **12.28.**80 ABC
    Crisis at Central High   tf   2.4.81 CBS

WORLEY, JO ANNE
    SUPP.:
    Hawaii Five-O   ep   3.3.77 CBS
    The Love Boat   ep   11.4.78 ABC
    Gift of the Magi   tf   **12.21.**78 NBC
    CHiPs   ep   Chips Goes Roller Disco 9.22.79 NBC
    The Love Boat   ep   **12.1.**79 ABC
    Ron Howard's Through the Magic Pyramid   tf   **12.6.**81, **12.13.**81
      NBC

WRAY, FAY
    SUPP.:
    The Hallmark Hall of Fame   ep   Gideon's Trumpet   sp   4.30.80
      CBS

WRIGHT, TERESA
    SUPP.:
    Grandpa Goes to Washington   ep   10.31.78 NBC
    American Short Story   ep   The Golden Honeymoon 1.2.80 PBS

WYATT, JANE
    A&C:
    Insight   ep   7.29.73 NN
    SUPP.:
    The Father Knows Best Reunion   sp   5.15.77 NBC

Father Knows Best: Home for Christmas   sp   **12.18.77** NBC
Superdome   tf   **1.9.78** ABC
A Love Affair: The Eleanor and Lou Gehrig Story   tf   **1.15.78**
   NBC
Fantasy Island   ep   **5.6.78** ABC
The Nativity   tf   **12.17.78** ABC
The Love Boat   ep   **10.20.79** ABC
Quincy, M.E.   ep   **2.28.80** NBC
The Love Boat   ep   Reunion 4.5.80 ABC

WYMAN, JANE
   A&C:
   The Bold Ones   ep   **5.4.73** NBC
   Insight   ep   **7.14.74** NN
   SUPP.:
   The Incredible Journey of Dr. Meg Laurel   tf   **1.2.79** CBS
   The Love Boat   ep   **3.1.80** ABC
   Charlie's Angels   ep   From Street Models to Hawaiian Angels
      11.30.80 ABC
   Falcon Crest   sr   **12.4.81** CBS

WYNN, KEENAN
   A&C:
   Checkmate   ep   Slight Touch of Venom 6.17.61 CBS
   The Quest   tf   **5.13.76** NBC
   Jerimiah of Jacob's Neck   pt   **8.13.76** CBS
   SUPP.:
   Sex and the Married Woman   tf   **9.13.77** NBC
   Police Woman   ep   **3.30.78** NBC
   The Bionic Woman   ep   Rancho Outcast 5.6.78 NBC
   The Bastard/Kent Family Chronicles   ms   **5.22.78**, **5.23.78**
      NN
   Coach   tf   **3.6.79** CBS
   The Billion Dollar Threat   tf   **4.15.79** ABC
   Dallas   sr   **10.5.79** CBS
   Mom, the Wolfman and Me   tf   **12.20.80** NN
   Joe Dancer: The Monkey Mission   tf   **3.23.81** NBC
   Palmerstown   ep   Scandal 3.24.81 CBS
   Fantasy Island   ep   Mr. Nobody 11.7.81 ABC

WYNTER, DANA
   A&C:
   Cannon   ep   **4.2.76** CBS
   SUPP.:
   W.E.B.   ep   **9.28.78** NBC
   The Love Boat   ep   Murder on the High Seas 3.17.79 ABC
   The Rockford Files   ep   **10.12.79** NBC
   M Station: Hawaii   tf   **6.10.80** CBS
   Ten Speed and Brown Shoe   ep   **6.27.80** ABC
   Hart to Hart   ep   **1.20.81** ABC
   Aloha Paradise   ep   **2.25.81** ABC

-Y-

YATES, CASSIE*
  Barnaby Jones   ep   Wipeout 3. 4. 76 CBS
  The Bionic Woman   ep   Bionic Beauty 3. 17. 76 ABC
  Rich Man, Poor Man, Book II   sr   9. 21. 76 ABC
  The Streets of San Francisco   ep   11. 11. 76 ABC
  Delvecchio   ep   12. 12. 76 CBS
  Barnaby Jones   ep   Circle of Treachery 2. 24. 77 CBS
  Barnaby Jones   ep   Runaway to Terror 5. 5. 77 CBS
  Having Babies II   tf   10. 28. 77 ABC
  Rosetti and Ryan   ep   11. 3. 77 NBC
  Baretta   ep   12. 21. 77 ABC
  Quincy, M. E.   ep   Speed Trap 10. 12. 78 NBC
  Sword of Justice   ep   10. 21. 78 NBC
  Who'll Save Our Children?   tf   12. 16. 78 CBS
  B. J. and the Bear   ep   3. 24. 79 NBC
  The Seeding of Sarah Burns   tf   4. 7. 79 CBS
  Vega$ ep   10. 3. 79 ABC
  Quincy, M. E.   ep   10. 11. 79 NBC
  Barnaby Jones   ep   A Short, Happy Life 3. 1. 79 CBS
  Ten Speed and Brown Shoe   ep   3. 2. 80 ABC
  Nobody's Perfect   sr   6. 26. 80 ABC
  Father Figure   tf   10. 26. 80 CBS
  Mark, I Love You   tf   12. 10. 80 CBS
  Vega$ ep   12. 10. 80 ABC
  Norma Rae   pt ep   A Matter of the Heart 11. 21. 81 NBC
  Of Mice and Men   tf   11. 29. 81 NBC

YORK, MICHAEL
  SUPP. :
  Jesus of Nazareth   ms   4. 3. 77, 4. 10. 77 NBC
  A Man Called Intrepid   ms   5. 20. 79, 5. 21. 79, 5. 22. 79 NBC
  CBS Library: Misunderstood Monsters   ep   Beauty and the
     Beast   vo sp   4. 7. 81 CBS

YORK, SUSANNAH
  SUPP. :
  The Golden Gate Murders   tf   10. 3. 79 CBS

YOUNG, ALAN
  SUPP. :
  The Love Boat   ep   The Minister and The Stripper 11. 17. 78
     ABC
  The ABC Weekend Special   ep   Scruffy   nar   10. 11. 80 ABC

YOUNG, GIG
  SUPP. :
  Spectre   tf   5. 21. 77 NBC

YOUNG, ROBERT
  SUPP. :
  The Father Knows Best Reunion   sp   5. 15. 77 NBC

Father Knows Best: Home for Christmas   sp   12. 18. 77 NBC
Little Women   tf   10. 2. 78, 10. 3. 78 NBC
Little Women   sr   2. 8. 79 NBC

YOUNGFELLOW, BARRIE*
    The Streets of San Francisco   ep   Betrayed 9. 20. 73 ABC
    The Bay City Amusement Company   pt   7. 28. 77 NBC
    Carter Country   ep   1. 12. 78 ABC
    Annie Flynn   pt   1. 21. 78 CBS
    AES Hudson Street   ep   4. 20. 78 ABC
    Barney Miller   ep   9. 14. 78 ABC
    The Eddie Capra Mysteries   ep   11. 3. 78 NBC
    Breaking Up Is Hard to Do   tf   9. 5. 79   9. 7. 79 ABC
    Vampire   tf   10. 7. 79 ABC
    Paris   ep   10. 20. 79 CBS
    Trapper John, M. D.   ep   3. 2. 80 CBS
    Moviola: The Scarlett O'Hara War   tf   5. 19. 80 NBC
    Good Time Harry   ep   7. 26. 80 NBC
    The Single Life   pt   8. 21. 80 NBC
    It's a Living   sr   10. 30. 80 ABC
    It's a Living   sr ret   7. 21. 81 ABC
    Making a Living   sr   10. 24. 81 ABC

-Z-

ZERBE, ANTHONY
    A& C:
    Route 66   ep   Two Strangers and an Old Enemy 9. 27. 63 CBS
    SUPP. :
    How the West Was Won   sr   2. 6. 77 ABC
    In the Glitter Palace   tf   2. 27. 77 NBC
    The Rockford Files   ep   1. 13. 78 NBC
    The World of Disney   ep   Child of Glass 5. 14. 78 NBC
    Centennial   ms ep   1. 14. 79, 1. 21. 79, 1. 28. 79 NBC
    Attica   tf   3. 2. 80 ABC

ZIMBALIST, EFREM, JR.
    A& C:
    Hawaiian Eye   ep   Three Tickets to Lani 11. 25. 59 ABC
    Hawaiian Eye   ep   Blackmail in Satin 2. 28. 62 ABC
    SUPP. :
    A Family Upside Down   tf   4. 9. 78 NBC
    Wild About Harry   pt   5. 26. 78 NBC
    The Day God Died   sp   11. 5. 78 NN
    Terror Out of the Sky   tf   12. 26. 78 CBS
    The Best Place to Be   tf   5. 27. 79 NBC
    Family of Winners   sp   12. 11. 79 NN
    The Gathering, Part II   tf   12. 17. 79 NBC
    Scruples   ms ep   2. 25. 80, 2. 26. 80 CBS

ZIMBALIST, STEPHANIE*
    Yesterday's Child tf 2. 3. 77 NBC
    Lucan ep 9. 12. 77 ABC
    In the Matter of Karen Ann Quinlan tf 9. 26. 77 NBC
    The Gathering tf 12. 4. 77 ABC
    Forever tf 1. 6. 78 CBS
    The Love Boat ep 1. 21. 78 ABC
    Wild About Harry pt 5. 26. 78 NBC
    Centennial ms ep 10. 29. 78 NBC
    Long Journey Back tf 12. 15. 78 ABC
    The Triangle Factory Fire tf 1. 30. 79 NBC
    Family ep 3. 15. 79 ABC
    The Best Place to Be tf 5. 27. 79 NBC
    The Golden Moment: An Olympic Love Story tf 5. 25. 80,
       5. 26. 80 NBC
    The Baby Sitter tf 11. 28. 80 ABC
    Elvis and the Beauty Queen tf 3. 1. 81 NBC

ABOUT THE AUTHORS

JAMES ROBERT PARISH, Los Angeles-based director of marketing for a large direct marketing firm, was born in Cambridge, Massachusetts. He attended the University of Pennsylvania and graduated as a Phi Beta Kappa with an honors degree in English. He is a graduate of the University of Pennsylvania Law School and a member of the New York Bar. As president of Entertainment Copyright Research Co., Inc. he headed a major research facility for the media industries. Later he was a film interviewer for show business trade papers. He is the author of many books, including The Fox Girls, The RKO Gals, The Tough Guys, The Jeanette MacDonald Story, The Elvis Presley Scrapbook, and The Hollywood Beauties. Among those he has co-written are The MGM Stock Company, The Debonairs, Liza!, The Great Spy Pictures, Hollywood on Hollywood, Hollywood Character Actors, The Hollywood Reliables, The Funsters, The Best of MGM, and Film Directors Guide: The U.S.

VINCENT TERRACE, a free-lance writer based in New York City, is a graduate of the New York Institute of Technology and possesses a B.A. in Fine Arts. He is the author of The Complete Encyclopedia of Television Programs: 1947-1979, Radio's Golden Years: 1930-1960, and Television: 1970-1980. He has contributed to The Television Book and The American Academic Encyclopedia, among others. Mr. Terrace has also compiled media information for The Great Gangster Pictures, The Great Science Fiction Pictures, The Great Spy Pictures, and The Great Western Pictures.